D1605896

THE PURSUIT
OF HIGH CULTURE

JOHN ELLA AND CHAMBER MUSIC
IN VICTORIAN LONDON

Music in Britain, 1600–1900

ISSN 1752-1904

Series Editors:
RACHEL COWGILL & PETER HOLMAN
(Leeds University Centre for English Music)

This series provides a forum for the best new work in this area; it takes a deliberately inclusive approach, covering immigrants and emigrants as well as native musicians. Contributions on all aspects of seventeenth-, eighteenth- and nineteenth-century British music studies are welcomed, particularly those placing music in its social and historical contexts, and addressing Britain's musical links with Europe and the rest of the globe.

Proposals or queries should be sent in the first instance to Dr Rachel Cowgill, Professor Peter Holman or Boydell & Brewer at the addresses shown below. All submissions will receive prompt and informed consideration.

Dr Rachel Cowgill, School of Music, University of Leeds, Leeds, LS2 9JT
email: r.e.cowgill@leeds.ac.uk

Professor Peter Holman, School of Music, University of Leeds, Leeds, LS2 9JT
email: p.k.holman@leeds.ac.uk

Boydell & Brewer, PO Box 9, Woodbridge, Suffolk, IP12 3DF
email: editorial@boydell.co.uk

ALREADY PUBLISHED

Lectures on Musical Life
William Sterndale Bennett
edited by Nicholas Temperley, with Yunchung Yang

John Stainer: A Life in Music
Jeremy Dibble

THE PURSUIT
OF HIGH CULTURE

JOHN ELLA AND CHAMBER MUSIC
IN VICTORIAN LONDON

Christina Bashford

THE BOYDELL PRESS

First published 2007
The Boydell Press, Woodbridge

ISBN 978-1-84383-298-0

The Boydell Press is an imprint of Boydell & Brewer Ltd
PO Box 9, Woodbridge, Suffolk IP12 3DF, UK
and of Boydell & Brewer Inc.
668 Mt Hope Avenue, Rochester, NY 14620, USA
website: www.boydellandbrewer.com

A catalogue record of this publication is available
from the British Library

This publication is printed on acid-free paper

Designed and typeset in Adobe Minion Pro by
David Roberts, Pershore, Worcestershire

Printed in Great Britain by
Antony Rowe Ltd, Chippenham, Wiltshire

For my friends

Contents

List of Illustrations

Acknowledgements

T<small>HIS</small> book sprang from my love of chamber music and my curiosity about the (oddly neglected) history of the musical culture of the city in which I lived in the mid-1980s: London. It would have never come into existence but for the encouragement, at crucial stages of its necessarily long gestation, of three people: John Ravell, who kindly gave me access to John Ella's private papers many years ago and rejoiced in the idea that I would one day write this monograph; Cyril Ehrlich, the historian who was a constant source of inspiration and guidance until his death in 2004, and who helped me plan the book; and my husband, John Wagstaff, who contributed professionally as bibliographer, translator and reader, and also provided invaluable domestic and emotional support at home. In addition, I received significant financial assistance from the Arts and Humanities Research Board (UK), Oxford Brookes University, the University of Illinois at Urbana-Champaign, and the Otto Kinkeldey Publication Endowment Fund of the American Musicological Society, and I record my gratitude to them.

Over several years I also benefited from discussion of themes in this book with colleagues in my field. Leanne Langley, Simon McVeigh, John Lowerson and other members of the 'Music in Britain: a Social History' seminar at the Institute of Historical Research in London responded to my ideas, made helpful suggestions, shared findings and stimulated research in myriad ways. Understanding of performance concerns was heightened by fruitful conversations with Clive Brown and Nick Roberts, and by reconstructions of Musical Union concerts in which students in the Pavão Quartet and members of the Leeds University Centre for Historical Performance, among others, participated. Many other scholars gave me specific information and guidance, or patiently answered tiny queries, and to them I am equally indebted. They include Allan Atlas; Alan Bartley; Robert Beale; George Biddlecombe; Stuart Campbell; Maribeth Clark; Dorothy DeVal; Jeremy Dibble; Gabriella Dideriksen; Katharine Ellis; Therese Ellsworth; Lewis Foreman; Peter Franklin; Trevor Herbert; Sarah Hibberd; Steven Kendall; Richard Macnutt; Philip Olleson; Fiona Palmer; Ann Royle; Stewart Spencer; E. Bradley Strauchen-Scherer; and Phyllis Weliver. Cassie Watson gave helpful perspectives on the question of John Ella's medical conditions; and for insights into Ella's family history, a special debt of gratitude goes to Raymond E. O. Ella (historical writer and former genealogist) of the Yorkshire branch of the Ella family.

Meanwhile, coal-face research was facilitated by the many archivists, librarians and others who helped me locate and inspect source materials in their institutions, or answered queries by email. In this regard I wish to acknowledge the practical help of Peter Horton and Paul Collen (Royal College of Music), Andrew McCrea and the late Robin Langley (Royal College of Organists), the late Betty Matthews (Royal Society of Musicians), Janet Snowman, Ruth Darton and Bridget Palmer (Royal Academy of Music), Peter Ward Jones (Bodleian Library, Oxford), Nicholas Bell (British Library), Graham Muncy (Surrey Performing Arts Library), Stephen Roe (Sotheby's), Dominique Hausfater (Paris Conservatoire), Marcus Risdell (Garrick Club), Siobhán Summerfield (Victoria and Albert Museum), Siobhán Ladyman (Cramers), Barry Sterndale Bennett, Jennifer Thorp and John Denison.

The book's preparation was facilitated by the meticulous research assistance of Hannah Chan (USA), who helped considerably with the preparation of the appendices, Joanne Dibley, Rachel Milestone and Michelle Brachet (UK). Melania Bucciarelli kindly provided translations of material in Italian, and Steve Ferre prepared the music examples. Over several years I appreciated those university colleagues who took an interest in the project: they include Dai Griffiths, Paul Dibley, Nicholas Temperley and William Kinderman. I also remain grateful to the 'Music in Britain, 1600–1900' series editors, Rachel Cowgill and Peter Holman, and to Caroline Palmer, Bruce Phillips, David Roberts and the editorial staff at Boydell & Brewer, for coaxing the book towards publication. Finally, I wish to express deep gratitude to David Wright for his many stimulating and sensitive suggestions about the text. I have done my best to eradicate errors and inconsistencies in the pages that follow; those that remain are, of course, my responsibility.

February 2007

List of Abbreviations

ℰ General

b.	born
d.	died
esp.	especially
n.	note
sup.	supplement

ℰ Special Collections, Libraries and Archives

BL	British Library, London
CWA	City of Westminster Archives, London
EllaC	John Ella Collection, Bodleian Library, Oxford
LRO	Leicester Record Office
NA	National Archives, Kew
NAS	National Archives of Scotland
PRO	Public Record Office, National Archives, Kew
RAMa	Royal Academy of Music, London, Archives
RAMm	Royal Acadeny of Music, London, McCann Collection
RCMa	Royal College of Music, London, Archives
RCMl	Royal College of Music, London, Library
RCMp	Royal College of Music, London, Centre for Performance History
UBCsc	University of British Columbia, Vancouver, Special Collections and University Archives

ℰ Journals and Newspapers frequently cited

19CM	*19th-century Music*
CJ	*The Court Journal*
DN	*The Daily News*
DT	*The Daily Telegraph*
ILN	*The Illustrated London News*
JRMA	*Journal of the Royal Musical Association*
MC	*The Morning Chronicle*
MH	*The Morning Herald*
MMR	*The Monthly Musical Record*

MP	*The Morning Post*
MR	*The Musical Record*
MS	*The Musical Standard*
MT	*The Musical Times*
MW	*The Musical World*
M&L	*Music & Letters*
RMU	*Record of the Musical Union*
RMWE	*Record of the Musical Winter Evenings*
ST	*The Sunday Times*

❧ Other works frequently cited

BashfordPCC Christina Bashford. 'Public Chamber-Music Concerts in London, 1835–50: Aspects of History, Repertory and Reception'. PhD, University of London, 1996.

CCSCM *Cobbett's Cyclopedic Survey of Chamber Music.* Comp. and ed. Walter Willson Cobbett. 2 vols. Oxford and London: Oxford University Press, 1929–30.

DavisonFM Henry Davison, comp. *From Mendelssohn to Wagner: Being the Memoirs of J. W. Davison, Forty Years Music Critic of 'The Times'.* London: William Reeves, 1912.

DiehlMM Alice M. Diehl. *Musical Memories.* London: Richard Bentley & Son, 1897.

DNB *Dictionary of National Biography.* Ed. Leslie Stephen and Sidney Lee. 66 vols. London: Smith, Elder, 1885–1901.

EhrlichFP Cyril Ehrlich. *First Philharmonic: a History of the Royal Philharmonic Society.* Oxford: Clarendon Press, 1995.

EhrlichMP Cyril Ehrlich. *The Music Profession in Britain since the Eighteenth Century: a Social History.* Oxford: Clarendon Press, 1985.

EllaMS1 John Ella. *Musical Sketches, Abroad and at Home.* London: Ridgway, 1869.

EllaMS2 John Ella. *Musical Sketches, Abroad and at Home.* 2nd edition. London: Ridgway, 1869 [*recte* 1872].

EllaMS3 John Ella. *Musical Sketches, Abroad and at Home.* 3rd edition. Rev. and ed. John Belcher. London: William Reeves, 1878.

FauquetS Joël-Marie Fauquet. *Les sociétés de musique de chambre à Paris de la Restauration à 1870.* Paris: Aux Amateurs de Livres, 1986.

FétisB *Biographie universelle des musicians.* Ed. F.-J. Fétis. 2nd edition. 8 vols. Paris: Firmin Didot, 1866–8.

FétisBS	*Biographie universelle des musicians.* Supplement. Ed. Arthur Pougin. 2 vols. Paris: Firmin Didot, 1878–80.
GanzMM	Wilhelm Ganz. *Memories of a Musician: Reminiscences of Seventy Years of Musical Life.* London: John Murray, 1913.
GGMVC	*George Grove, Music and Victorian Culture.* Ed. Michael Musgrave. Basingstoke: Palgrave Macmillan, 2003.
Grove3	*Grove's Dictionary of Music and Musicians.* 3rd edition. Ed. H. C. Colles. 5 vols. London: Macmillan, 1927–8.
Grove5	*Grove's Dictionary of Music and Musicians.* 5th edition. Ed. Eric Blom. 9 vols. London: Macmillan, 1954.
HanslickA	Eduard Hanslick. 'Briefe aus London [1862]', *Aus dem Concertsaal: Kritiken und Schilderungen aus den letzten 20 Jahren des Wiener Musiklebens, nebst einem Anhang: Musikalische Reisebriefe aus England, Frankreich und der Schweiz.* Vienna: Wilhelm Braumüller, 1870, pp. 487–517.
HaweisJE	H. R. Haweis. *John Ella: a Sketch from Life.* Pamphlet, London, 1885. [First published in *Truth* (1 Nov 1883), pp. 620–2.]
MBC	*Music and British Culture, 1785–1914: Essays in Honour of Cyril Ehrlich.* Ed. Christina Bashford and Leanne Langley. Oxford: Oxford University Press, 2000.
McVeighA	Simon McVeigh. '"An Audience for High-Class Music": Concert Promoters and Entrepreneurs in Late-Nineteenth-Century London', *The Musician as Entrepreneur, 1700–1914: Managers, Charlatans, and Idealists.* Ed. William Weber. Bloomington and Indianapolis: Indiana University Press, 2004, pp. 162–82.
McVeighCL	Simon McVeigh. *Concert Life in London from Mozart to Haydn.* Cambridge: Cambridge University Press, 1993.
NBMS	*Nineteenth-Century British Music Studies.* Ed. Bennett Zon *et al.* 3 vols. Aldershot: Ashgate, 1993–2003.
NGDM1	*The New Grove Dictionary of Music and Musicians.* Ed. Stanley Sadie. 20 vols. London: Macmillan, 1980.
NGDM2	*The New Grove Dictionary of Music and Musicians.* 2nd edition. Ed. Stanley Sadie. 29 vols. London: Macmillan, 2001.
ODNB	*Oxford Dictionary of National Biography: From the Earliest Times to the Year 2000.* Ed. H. C. G. Matthew and Brian Harrison. 60 vols. Oxford: Oxford University Press, 2004.
RohrCBM	Deborah Rohr. *The Careers of British Musicians, 1750–1850: a Profession of Artisans.* Cambridge: Cambridge University Press, 2001.
WangerméeF	*François-Joseph Fétis: Correspondance.* Comp. and ed. Robert Wangermée. Sprimont: Editions Mardaga, 2006.

1 John Ella in 1851. Lithograph by Charles Baugniet,
published in the *Record of the Musical Union* (1858).
© British Library Board. All Rights Reserved (P.P.1945.1).

The Case for Ella

EMINENT in his own day, neglected by posterity: that has been the lot of John Ella, a man who by the middle decades of the nineteenth century had risen from provincial, artisan-class obscurity to become a figure of power and influence in London musical life and high society, a successful concert manager and entrepreneur, and a relentless and successful proselytizer for the highest of musical art. He was important as an organizer and 'enabler' (the behind-the-scenes fixer who made things happen) rather than as a performer or composer, the traditional subjects for music biography. And, paradoxically for a nation cursed with the label 'Das Land ohne Musik', he operated in times when music mattered to people to a degree that can barely be overstated today, and in London, the city that claimed the largest concentration of public music-making and musicians than any other in Britain or Europe. His Musical Union (1845–81), a concert society devoted to the promotion of chamber music in general, and the heartland of Haydn, Mozart and Beethoven string quartets in particular, was his most celebrated achievement: a quasi-temple for the contemplation of high culture, through what was deemed the best in Western classical music.[1] It brought many of the finest instrumentalists in Europe before a well-heeled audience of serious-minded metropolitan music-lovers, and it endured for more than three and a half decades, combining a lustre of excellence and solemnity with an economic buoyancy that many a Victorian concert-organizer must have envied. In spite of this, the unusual tale of Ella, shaper of musical taste and culture, and of his celebrated concert institution, has never been told in depth, less still has the Musical Union's history been adequately attempted. For Ella is a largely unknown figure, and to some he will seem an obscure subject for a biography.

---

[1] High culture, and John Ella's pursuit of it, is defined in this book as those products of the arts, philosophy and science that have been held in greatest esteem by society and deemed to require sophisticated (i.e. cultured) understanding. Although historically the province of social élites, high culture was in Victorian times becoming increasingly accessible to all who aspired to appreciate it. In particular, definitions of classical (i.e. art) music, as that which appeals to 'developed' taste and is distinct from popular or folk music, were being laid down during the nineteenth century. The tightly constructed instrumental genres of symphony, sonata and string quartet were generally considered to aspire to such yardsticks, and hierarchies of genres and individual works were emerging.

Admittedly, we have been slow to recognize the importance of the role of the enabler or fixer in sustaining musical activity in nineteenth-century Britain.[2] In part this has been tied to a more general failure to appreciate what it was that made the music and musicians of Britain so different from what was to be found in the rest of Europe: notably, Britain's lack of established musical infrastructures and its commercially driven concert life. During Ella's lifetime, most of central Europe (France, Germany, Austro-Hungary, Italy) boasted well-resourced educational institutions for composers and performers, with national opera houses as further training grounds, and it provided meaningful patronage or financial subsidy for musical performances, whether through courts, aristocrats, men of wealth, church, national governments or municipalities. Britain, in sharp contrast, offered relatively modest and unsystematic training opportunities and an open, unrestricted market-place. It also provided sustained employment only through its church music structures, a slight and underwhelming royal music, and its military (this last being a notable oasis of good musical standards, and a source from which skilled wind and brass players often sprang). Meanwhile, and for much of the nineteenth century, concert-giving in Britain happened off its own bat, and mainly because of the nous of individuals, usually the musicians themselves, which meant the job of enabling was crucial to public performance taking place at all. For the first three-quarters of the century at least, only a handful of the ever-swelling number of concert series achieved any permanence beyond two or three seasons. In such conditions, a shrewd and effective organizer like Ella could make an important mark, creating a robust concert-giving enterprise that married artistic excellence with financial success. Even so, Ella was operating during times of change, when older, eighteenth-century practices of giving concerts before what might be described as 'patronage networks' (audiences formed from a small slice of society that musicians serviced in other ways) were giving way to more impersonal and overtly business-driven modes of operation. How he responded to the flux is a significant part of his story.

Among other reasons enablers have escaped scholarly scrutiny is surely the suspicion that such behind-the-scenes people are of little intrinsic interest for a history of music. How can the man who made music happen be as important as those who 'made' the music itself, whether as composers or performers? So the thinking has traditionally gone, even in Ella's lifetime – a period, after all, when the idea of the composer as creative artist crystallized. (And in Ella's case, the fact that he abandoned his run-of-the-mill existence as a practical musician for

---

[2] The term 'enabler', as I use it in relation to Ella, was usefully coined by Cyril Ehrlich in his discussion of Francesco Berger, secretary of the Philharmonic Society of London, in *EhrlichFP*, 138.

fixing, organizing and – ultimately – taste-shaping adds a further stigma: that of the 'failed player'.) On a practical note, too, there are severe difficulties in writing about enablers, because often their activities have vanished from the historical record. For many of them we can only extrapolate how effective they were. But where relevant sources survive (and for Ella they do), it is possible to see what a difference a good organizer could make within Britain's precarious, market-driven musical culture.[3] Indeed, Ella emerges through this enquiry as someone able to make things happen smoothly and successfully in every respect – artistic, logistic and financial; and as someone who learned fast how to attend to detail, to minimize risks, to monitor activities, to adapt quickly and inventively to changing situations, and to exploit opportunities as they arose. What is more, he did it with a good dose of economic caution and a burning conviction for 'serious' music.

Another concept that is crucial to understanding Ella's role in nineteenth-century British musical life is bound up in the term 'sacralization' – the processes by which particular musical works became the focus of deep, quasi-religious veneration as autonomous art objects. The nineteenth century was the period when art music became established as a serious, central part of European bourgeois public life, offering a special, aesthetic experience increasingly within the reach of anyone who aspired to appreciate it (and thousands did).[4] Across national borders and well into the twentieth century, the works of certain European composers – most notably Beethoven and later Wagner – became the focus for intense reverence and inspiration in cultural life at large, with music, of all the arts so treated,

---

3 *EhrlichFP*, 132–57.

4 On the sacralization of high culture in nineteenth-century Europe, see T. C. W. Blanning, 'The Commercialization and Sacralization of European Culture in the Nineteenth Century', *The Oxford Illustrated History of Modern Europe*, ed. T. C. W. Blanning (Oxford: Oxford University Press, 1996), 120–47. The concept is explored in its American context by Lawrence W. Levine in his *Highbrow/Lowbrow: the Emergence of Cultural Hierarchy in America* (Cambridge, MA: Harvard University Press, 1988), 83–168. See also Ralph P. Locke, 'Music Lovers, Patrons and the "Sacralization" of Culture in America', *19CM*, 17 (1993), 149–73.

   Focused work on sacralization's processes (including the emergence of a central canon of 'great', mostly Austro-Germanic, music, and the ritualistic playing out of ideologies in the concert hall), its principal proponents and causes, has also emerged: see, for instance, William Weber, *The Rise of Musical Classics in Eighteenth-Century England: a Study in Canon, Ritual and Ideology* (Oxford: Clarendon Press, 1992); Katharine Ellis, *Music Criticism in Nineteenth-Century France: La revue et gazette musicale de Paris, 1834–80* (Cambridge: Cambridge University Press, 1995); and Rachel Cowgill, 'The London Apollonicon Recitals, 1817–32: a Case Study in Bach, Mozart, and Haydn Reception', *JRMA*, 123 (1998), 190–228.

seeming to hold a particular aura.[5] Some of this was due to music's very nature, for as historian T. C. W. Blanning points out, however many galleries and museums were built to house and sanctify the fine arts, they simply could not match the ultimate, truly communal, transcendent – or 'sacral' – experience that music offered its audience in the form of public performance, whereby the musician was able to 'appeal to a large number of people through their emotions simultaneously and collectively'.[6] Blanning, making use of the ideas of Jürgen Habermas and talking in pan-European terms, attributes much of the rise of sacralized culture to the decline of older forms of patronage for the arts and the emergence of the public sphere in the eighteenth century and to incipient commercialization in the nineteenth, which together bred a tension between sacralization and art as consumerism.[7] In his view, as culture became 'democratized' and available to mass markets, the sacral was increasingly polarized against the popular and vulgar, especially as the latter was evidently almost always driven by commercial concerns.[8]

The lack in Britain of the sort of art-music patronage and infrastructures typical of other European cultures, especially the Germanic states, made musical life more directly relatable to the vicissitudes of market forces. In this context, an investigation of Ella's Musical Union is highly revealing. For, as we shall see, Ella was careful to balance high culture's growing dependence on commercial viability with an insistence on the special condition of the work of art and its sacralized status.[9] He tirelessly sought to establish the instrumental chamber repertoire, especially Beethoven's, presenting it as the acme of musical achievement. And he went to great lengths to explain that repertoire's aesthetic significance and the reasons for insisting on its veneration. But this he did within the boundaries of the marketplace, in the sense that the Musical Union had to be financially self-supporting. So although one case-study will not a full history make, an examination of Ella's

---

[5] Blanning, 'Commercialization', 135–6: 'So powerful was Beethoven's influence that it lasted into the following century, reaching its apotheosis in 1902 when the artists of the Vienna Secession decided to transform their entire building into a temple to receive the statue of Beethoven by the Leipzig sculptor Max Klinger'; see also ibid., p. 139. Beethoven's posthumous impact on subsequent generations of musicians has long been acknowledged.

[6] Blanning, 'Commercialization', 136.

[7] Blanning, 'Commercialization', *passim*. For more on his view of the eighteenth-century background, see his *The Culture of Power and the Power of Culture: Old Regime Europe, 1660–1789* (Oxford: Oxford University Press, 2002).

[8] See Blanning, 'Commercialization', esp. 120, 126, 133–5. These themes often run counter to one another in modern discussions of London concert life (see *McVeighA*, 162).

[9] This idea is touched on in *McVeighA*, 170.

proselytizing for high art among a particular tranche of society on the one hand, and his deft exploitation of the market-place on the other, may help us begin to understand more of the processes of cultural formation in London.

ELLA died in 1888, and it took some two generations before his importance began to be even partially recognized. Most of the existing biographical accounts of Ella date from the first half of the twentieth century, a period when reactions against the Victorians and condescension towards nineteenth-century British music were at a height. They are primarily documentary and anecdotal. After the obituaries there were short entries in the standard dictionaries (the *Dictionary of National Biography*; the several editions of Grove's *Dictionary of Music and Musicians*, and in Walter Willson Cobbett's quirky chamber music encyclopedia), minor coverage in Percy Scholes's compilation of journalistic vignettes from the *Musical Times* (1947) and then, in 1953, a first attempt to draw a proper outline of Ella's career in an article in *Music & Letters* by music-lover and amateur scholar John Ravell. Significantly but unsurprisingly, given the British *Zeitgeist*, Ravell's article was heavily abridged, Richard Capell (*M&L*'s editor) publishing it without the footnotes that had been supplied, and expressing not a little scepticism that 'the interest of the subject warrant[s] this length' [*c*.5,000 words].[10]

The next two decades revealed a little more interest in the broad arena of Victorian music, with Ella and the Musical Union popping up in surveys by Robert Elkin (*The Old Concert Rooms of London*, 1955) and Percy Young (*The Concert Tradition*, 1965), and in the first attempt at a social history of English music by E. D. Mackerness (1964). Yet these books largely repeated existing observations and documents, while occasionally using Ella's published memoirs as source material. Later still, William Weber's *Music and the Middle Class* (1975; 2/2003) swept the Musical Union into a broad comparative social history of European audiences, also on the basis of a few primary documents. What all generalist work lacked was an in-depth history of the Musical Union or a critical biography of Ella on which to build – but it was a topic that would barely have counted as *echt* musicology or have been of interest to mainstream historians thirty or forty years ago. Curiosity about contexts for music performance and reception – today swelling remarkably – was the province of the few, and until relatively recently music in nineteenth-century Britain was considered a marginal area of study. I remember the eyebrows that were raised, then politely lowered, when I announced Victorian chamber-music concerts as my intended research topic in the mid-1980s. In an essentially composer-/work-led musicology, the apparent 'problem' that hardly any British composers were known for their chamber music would have been reason enough

---

[10] Letter from Capell to Ravell (dated 10 January 1952) in my possession.

not to proceed with contextual work. However, as the pioneering scholar of nineteenth-century British music Nicholas Temperley had already shown, many composers did write chamber music, even if little of it was published, and only a few manuscripts appear to have survived.[11] Moreover there was a perception that Britain lacked a substantial tradition of domestic quartet playing – a contention that awaits full testing, but which would have suggested there was little to investigate in terms of social contexts. (Ian Woodfield's recent study of music-making in Anglo-Indian eighteenth-century society demonstrates that such claims may well be unfounded,[12] and the present book makes a small contribution to that debate.) And yet – and here is the rub – European chamber music constituted a large portion of what actually got played in public at the time, with the average middle-class Londoner in the 1860s having, for reasons of economics (chamber music was much cheaper to put on than orchestral music), far more opportunities to hear a Beethoven violin sonata than a Beethoven symphony – and more often than not taking them.

Nowadays, in the wake of a substantial wave of fresh scholarship on the function and meaning of music in nineteenth-century Britain, some of it taking strong bearings from social and economic history, there ought to be little need to defend the subject of this book – in his role as the instigator of London's primary chamber-music society – to the wider world. That said, even in mainstream musicology, the performance and consumption of chamber music in nineteenth-century Europe has been for a long time a curiously neglected area of study, its richness and depths unplumbed until recently. Narratives of nineteenth-century music history typically concentrate on the strong, virile image of the virtuoso performer (Paganini, Liszt) or charismatic conductor (Wagner, Von Bülow) that is seemingly at odds with the essentially democratic, private communion of players at the heart of chamber-music making. Perhaps the diagnosis that Romantic musical idioms were diametrically opposed to the quintessence of quartet writing lurks on in the subconscious, preventing forays into performance contexts. The image of chamber music, especially string quartets, as the province of aficionados, amateur practitioners and connoisseurs can prove problematic too, particularly outside musicology, where the stereotype is reinforced by the still undeniable association of chamber music with high seriousness – most spectacularly in Beethoven's quartets. As the genre widely considered the highest of high musical art, chamber music can, from the perspective of the early twenty-first century, seem uncomfortable to

[11] Nicholas Temperley, 'Instrumental Music in England, 1800–1850' (PhD, University of Cambridge, 1959).

[12] Ian Woodfield, *Music of the Raj: a Social and Economic History of Music in Late Eighteenth-Century Anglo-Indian Society* (Oxford: Oxford University Press, 2000).

people who feel uneasy with notions of élitism.[13] But the Victorians had no such hang-ups: the pursuit of high culture and the acceptance of authority were values that went to the core of society, proclaimed most famously by Matthew Arnold (*Culture and Anarchy*, 1869). And that is why the history of chamber music in Britain, through the career and activities of John Ella, is so rewarding to explore – a pertinent demonstration of what the novelist L. P. Hartley described as the foreignness of the past.[14]

❧ *Sources and problems*

H ISTORIANS and biographers need sources, and with Ella there are materials in abundance, including matters of both public and private record. All require careful selection and judicious interpretation. Most notable of the primary materials is the John Ella Collection (in the Bodleian Library, Oxford), a cache of diaries, letters, photographs, notebooks and scrapbooks that enables a unique view of his doings and changing fortunes, from rank-and-file orchestral fiddler to powerful organizer and taste-shaper. For years the collection sat in a cast-iron trunk, biding its time in the home of a descendent of one of Ella's cousins, until John Ravell tracked it down, used it as the basis for his *Music & Letters* essay, and eventually ensured its survival as a private archive. It was at his house in London that I first glimpsed the materials in 1989 and was permitted to consult them. In late 1995, recognizing my desire and intention to pursue extended research, he kindly put the collection at my disposal in Oxford.

At the collection's heart are Ella's pocket diaries, spanning 1823 to 1887, which he kept zealously for much of his life. Containing only a few gaps in coverage, mostly early on (a handful of diaries are skimpy in their content, especially those for 1823–31; diaries for 1827–8, 1832–4, 1837, 1883 and 1888 do not survive), they offer valuable insights into the changing patterns and rhythms of Ella's professional and social life. That is perhaps their greatest strength, since Ella was no great diarist. It is true that he was, throughout his career, a fluent scribbler (writing for the *Athenaeum*, *Court Journal*, *Orchestra* and *Morning Post*), but he used his diary more as an appointment book and log of activities than as a literary journal or vehicle for extended private testimony. Personal thoughts on much of the life that was being played out – including many significant happenings – are frustratingly

---

[13] There have been several discussions of the perceived 'problem' of classical music in modern culture, e.g. Julian Johnson, *Who Needs Classical Music?: Cultural Choice and Musical Value* (Oxford: Oxford University Press, 2002).

[14] The famous quotation bears repetition: 'The past is a foreign country; they do things differently there' (*The Go-Between*, 1953).

absent. Still, his comings and goings, social encounters, railway journeys and so on are all there in all their valuable ordinariness, with signal events conveniently flagged. And if tedious to read as journals, they nevertheless glint with period detail and yield evidence of private musical culture that is rarely found in historical sources. Besides, there were spells in the diarizing, most notably in the 1830s and 60s, when Ella went beyond his norms, and recorded a vivid, vibrant commentary on the music he played and heard, and the people he met, not just in London but in Paris, Vienna, Prague, Florence and Pest, perhaps in the knowledge that he would use it later as the basis for some journalism. There were also a handful of moments when he confided his hopes, frustrations and despair; and many entries used remnants of shorthand – a version adapted from Samuel Taylor's system of 1786 – often for speed, occasionally for privacy. With perseverance and a cipher to hand, much of the code can be cracked. These are riches indeed. A selection of such telling remarks and useful information has naturally found its way into this biographical narrative.

In the later years of his life Ella began to see his diaries as a source for income generation and a niche in the annals of posterity, and in the 1870s he sought advice and possible collaboration on the project from a friend, the clergyman and writer on music Hugh Haweis. Publication never materialized, yet it is evident, from the layers of inks and nature of alterations in Ella's hand, that he annotated, pruned and corrected entries (even excised pages?) with an eye to excerpts from the diaries being committed to print, something that has to be borne in mind when using the archive today. Similar processes seem to have affected Ella's scrapbooks, which bear further scars of much mind-changing about what should be inserted or retained. There was also an expectation that the entire collection would be inspected critically after his death: his executors (John Belcher the architect, and the banker Thomas Phillips) were instructed to 'examine' his 'private correspondence[,] diaries and memorandum books' and to destroy or sell them as they saw fit.[15] He would not have been the first to try to massage his posthumous reputation.

Whether the selection of personal materials that survives in the Ella Collection was made by his executors and for what reasons; whether most of the filtering was done by Ella before his death; or whether the shape of the collection is the result of other, more serendipitous causes, I cannot judge, but evidently only a portion of what once existed has lasted. Among the practical uses Ella found for his diary was the industrious recording of letters sent and received, an activity that reached a peak during the years of the Musical Union, and suggesting a correspondence of tens, if not hundreds, of thousands of items. Yet of that mountain of letters, only

---

[15] John Ella's will, dated 23 September 1880, proved 6 November 1888 (Principal Probate Registry, London).

about 300 survive in the Ella Collection and are a somewhat haphazard selection, mostly dating from his later years. Clearly the majority was destroyed, either by Ella (he frequently noted that he had read and destroyed correspondence) or his executors. In addition, Ella saw some letters as having potential importance for the historical record, and he retained a few from star Musical Union artists, invariably correspondence that reflected well on his relationship with the performers. He preserved such items alongside photographs and other memorabilia.

Other documents seem to have survived by chance. Some have disappeared altogether. These include materials relating to the administration of the Musical Union. Many institutional records, such as addresses of subscribers, subscription ledgers, neatly presented formal accounts, and so on – the sort of business documentation that is so firmly and conveniently in place for the Philharmonic Society, and which must have once existed, even allowing for Ella's autocratic ways of working – are simply not there, although there are a couple of personal account books, covering the 1850s and 60s, that are a gold-mine of information. More often than not, facts and figures on the business side of the Musical Union have to be pieced together from diverse parts of the archive. Further gaps in the sources include material relating to the early years of Ella's life and to his private worlds. Although its absence has proved frustrating, there are ways forward, however imperfect. For short stretches of this study, historically informed conjecture and reconstruction of norms (always labelled as such) play an important part. In Chapter 2, for example, knowledge of artisan-class life and education in Leicester helps us imagine what Ella's youth might have been like. To compound the general difficulties, contradictions between the source materials abound; I indicate in footnotes how I have reconciled significant discrepancies.

In spite of these caveats about unevenness, inconsistency and possible distortion, the Ella Collection remained a vital source for this monograph. At the same time, other primary materials offered complementary information and importantly different perspectives on the man and his activities. They include manuscript correspondence between Ella and his patrons and associates, housed in a range of research libraries; published memoirs and manuscript sources connected with a host of his contemporaries; the annual *Record of the Musical Union* (1845–81), a compilation of the season's printed concert programmes, written by Ella and supplemented by news, gossip and features on a wide range of musical issues; his volume of reminiscences, mostly culled from the *Record of the Musical Union* and entitled *Musical Sketches, Abroad and at Home* (1869; 3/1878); and other miscellaneous journalism by him and others. Published information is by no means unproblematic to interpret, and chief among the problems of handling Ella's published material is the puffery and exaggeration he (like so many Victorians) indulged in, in respect of his own achievements. Nearly all openly authored sources of the period were prone to anything from euphemistic restraint to 'spin', from suppression of information to rose-tinted nostalgia. Meanwhile, in the press, where anonymity supposedly shielded a critic's identity, partisanship flourished (Ella's included), a feature that can be revealing of local professional politics. Indeed, opinion was often divided on Ella's entrepreneurial initiatives, making journalism a lively constituent of the source material. Both general newspapers and specialist music periodicals are drawn on in this study, although the sheer volume of available material, as well as issues of bias, has demanded informed and representative selection. I have also, for purposes of broad contextualization and an understanding of the interplay of continuity and change in musical culture across the period, been able to draw on the *Concert Life in 19th-Century London Database*.[16]

ᵴ Biographical and historical approaches

THIS book is a study of Ella's life, work and times. It combines a biography of Ella with a history of the Musical Union, including its players, repertoire and audiences, and sets them against the backdrop of gradually shifting contexts for concerts, chamber music and cultural life in Victorian London. Themes of enabling, sacralization, social networks and upward mobility loom large. Since this is the first full-length biography of its subject, the chapter framework is deliberately chronological, in the hope of establishing the sequence of Ella's career, and delivering a sense of the competing influences on the man, the complexities of his motivations, the messiness of his daily life, and the gradual sense of change within and around it. It was a long life: 1802–88, the story beginning in Leicester during the Napoleonic wars and ending in the relentlessly growing capital of the 1870s and 80s – a span of time when concert life, among other things, altered considerably. No attempt is made to document Ella's story year by year. In a biography of a creative artist, a composer particularly, there might be good reasons for wanting to document happenings in painstaking, chronological detail, since all sorts and sequences of events, social relationships and so on, might have a bearing on artistic decisions and directions. But with a figure like Ella, that level of close narration is not just unnecessary but actually undesirable. Although, at a few junctures in his life-story, events unfold in a closely documented, sequential way, elsewhere the narrative prefers a synthesized, synoptic view of the changing rhythms and patterns of Ella's social and professional life over a decade or more.

Biography may seem an unusual framework in which to position a history of a concert institution. But here the material dictates the shape, since the Musical Union's leadership and management was solely in Ella's hands for thirty-six of its

---

[16] Research project in conjunction with Rachel Cowgill and Simon McVeigh.

thirty-seven years. 'The Musical Union is John Ella, and John Ella is the Musical Union, and without him it would be nothing', wrote a music critic on Ella's retirement in 1880, unwittingly prophesying the society's rapid demise under another concert manager in 1881, and summing up perfectly the inseparability of the two subjects.[17] In the post-1845 chapters of the book, the narrative necessarily shifts back and forth between sections shadowing Ella's changing fortunes and his negotiation of public and private spheres, to ones examining the Musical Union, its repertoire and audiences over time. In fact, Ella was engaged in a range of additional activities (running an amateur opera club, giving lectures on music, and so on), most of them over a significant period of years; their histories too are entwined with his biography. At the same time, a few elements of Ella's personal life and family situation have been included, where relevant, to create a meaningful context for his quest for social advancement and to explain the typically Victorian tensions that developed between Ella's public and private domains.

The problems of how to integrate life and 'works' or, in Ella's case, 'achievements' are familiar to all biographers. In many chapters the reader is invited to make several journeys through a specified time span, exploring it through deliberately juxtaposed topics and perspectives. For example, in a chapter that covers eleven years from 1858 to 1868 the period is visited four times: the first section concerns the Musical Union as it became embedded into St James's Hall and as Ella responded to competition from other series; in the second, Ella's newly founded institution, the Musical Union Institute, which provided him not only with a 'shop front' and permanent base, but also a lobbying post for addressing issues of national music education and government support for music more generally, is unravelled; in the third, the narrative switches dramatically to Ella's personal world; in the fourth, the function and significance of his trips abroad, of which there were several in the 1860s, are discussed. It should be obvious that in real life none of these events existed for Ella in such a self-contained manner, and there is necessary interweaving between sections, as well as a few overlaps of chronology between chapters.

Inevitably, the events Ella organized, the musicians who played in them, and the subscribers who supported them are best understood when related to the broader historical situation – social, geographical, musical, intellectual and so on. Indeed, Ella's importance is so singularly bound up with the milieux in which he worked that without such a contextualization his life story would amount to a pretty dry and meaningless repository of facts. At the most basic level, then, this book attempts to incorporate a sense of London's changing demography and urbanization, and its cultural-cum-concert life. Between his first days in the capital

---

[17] *MMR*, 10 (1880), 115.

in the early 1820s and his twilight years of the 1880s, Ella saw London expand in terms of both population and conurbation, to become a gargantuan settlement: the 'primate city', vastly larger than any other in Britain, indeed Europe, and the trading and financial centre of the world.[18] In 1821 it had some 1.3 million residents, living within the area we now think of largely as the West End and City; if necessary it could be traversed on foot. By 1881 the population had become a vast 4.7 million, the majority of whom inhabited the newly created, sprawling suburbs; the only way they might ever comprehend the city's geography was through the innovations of rail travel.[19] Residential estates were laid down and grand buildings erected, including the rebuilt Houses of Parliament, Paxton's Crystal Palace in Hyde Park (later removed to Sydenham), the rival Alexandra Palace in Muswell Hill, the South Kensington museums, the Royal Albert Hall and several railway termini.

In step with population growth came an increase in the supply of – and demand for – cultural activities, especially music, as time for leisure pursuits rose and the number and types of people able to afford them swelled dramatically. So whereas in Ella's youth the face of London music was a seasonal splurge of opera and concerts, mostly on specific weekdays between March and July in the small area of the West End and servicing the aristocracy and high society, by his old age it had become an almost year-round, over-stuffed bazaar of musical events, accessible to men and women from all walks of life (both those able to pay for their ticket and those attending the free Sunday concerts 'for the people'), in suburbs and centre alike. The concert repertoire had grown too, embracing the music of Rossini, Mendelssohn, Schumann, Schubert, Berlioz and eventually Wagner, to whose Festspielhaus in Bayreuth Ella journeyed in 1876. More broadly, mindsets and value systems regarding music and culture were shifting, as were attitudes towards social hierarchies, gender, education, travel and communications. These were times of change indeed, and they envelop much of the narrative; a few chapter sections focus on contexts.

The book's range of secondary references draws on established work in mainstream urban and social-economic history and the relatively new, socially oriented strand of music history for nineteenth-century Britain. Historical thinking that has guided this study includes: on the music side, Cyril Ehrlich's *The Music Profession in Britain since the Eighteenth Century* and his *First Philharmonic*, the latter important for signalling the crucial role of the enabler and for its methodology for writing concert history; on the cultural history side, T. C. W. Blanning's

---

[18] Roy Porter, *London: a Social History* (London: Penguin Books, 1996), 207.

[19] Figures from *The London Encyclopedia*, ed. Ben Weinreb and Christopher Hibbert (London: Papermac, 1983), 613–14.

writings on the 'sacralizing' of culture in the public spaces (galleries, concert halls) of modern Europe; and for social history, David Cannadine's work on the British aristocracy, and F. M. L. Thompson's *The Rise of Respectable Society*, with its emphasis on social emulation and self-respect as significant Victorian values, and its avoidance of rigid class stereotypes. Underpinning much of the work is the idea that musical activities and values are socially and culturally defined, and the notion, derived from the influential work of the sociologist Pierre Bourdieu, of Ella's chamber concerts functioning both as symbols of social identity and distinction for its audiences, and as 'embodied cultural capital'. What makes all this so pertinent for a Victorian music history is that this was an era when a deep-felt love of music, and a desire to cultivate and appreciate it, were nothing out of the ordinary, and an era when chamber music came to be defined throughout Europe as a repertoire with an intrinsic, aesthetic value that separated it from the more everyday elements of life, and one that challenged the human spirit and intellect. Also germane to the century was an emerging ideology of a hierarchy of composers and compositions, with certain pieces of art music repeatedly judged demonstrably more complicated in their design and more challenging in their expressive palette than others.[20] The desire to explain what made particular pieces of music so great, through an exploration of how a chamber work was constructed, was central to Ella's activities, and it gives this social history of music an important aesthetic dimension.[21]

Perils and pitfalls bedevil any exploration of Ella's long and unusual life and achievements. To those already mentioned could be added the difficulty of writing about performers and performances in the era before recorded sound, or the danger that, in putting the case for the neglected hero, the biographer, through subtle manipulation of language, over-blows the trumpet. Conviction and enthusiasm come easily; one can but proceed with caution and candour. Moreover, one can, by juxtaposing contradictory evidence in the sources – particularly the gap between what Ella might say in print and what he might admit privately to his diary or to friends – tease out some of the inconsistencies in his psyche.

In the book's opening chapters, Ella's formative influences and experiences, his motivations and his achievements are explored with a view to explaining how

---

[20] These questions have been much discussed in recent musicology. See, *inter alia*, Katharine Ellis, 'The Structures of Musical Life', *The Cambridge History of Nineteenth-Century Music*, ed. Jim Samson (Cambridge: Cambridge University Press, 2002), 343–70, at 347–55.

[21] On the case for considering the aesthetic within social-cultural histories of music's sacralization, see Locke, 'Music Lovers'.

he rose from an anonymous and lowly social position to hold a position of cultural authority within wealthy metropolitan society. Amidst all this is an ongoing need to distinguish between the ordinary and the extraordinary in the historical context, in order to understand, for example, how it was that his successful social advancement set him apart from most of the orchestral musicians whose drudgery he had once shared; and why putting on concerts was nothing unusual, but making a healthy profit from them was. From Chapter 3 onwards the book draws out continuities and discontinuities in the Musical Union's social, economic and artistic history while also analysing Ella's skill as a concert promoter and establisher of musical values, and the curious interplay between the two roles in a commercially driven environment. Emphasis is placed on his unique modes of taste-shaping, including his creation of an ethos of sacralized high culture and social-artistic élitism at the Musical Union – what Cobbett described as 'not only the aristocracy of [social] rank but […] the aristocracy of music […] and the aristocracy of executive art'.[22] Issues of audience identity and behaviour are integral to this narrative, which consequently develops broader themes of class, social respectability, gender and taste.

In Chapters 5 and 6 the Musical Union is compared with the Monday and Saturday 'Popular' Concerts, a series of similar eminence and longevity, which shared the same venue for more than twenty years, but which famously – and in contrast to Ella's élite audience – drew what became known as the 'shilling' public and operated on much bigger, business-like lines. Part of the aim here is to illuminate the apparent paradox of the 'aristocratic' Musical Union thriving at a time of wide 'democratization' of art-music concerts in London, and to point up how the emerging changes to concert life impacted on Ella's activities.[23] The book's later chapters also see Ella attempting to expand his influence, trying fresh initiatives, which he glosses with lofty titles, such as the Musical Winter Evenings, the Musical Union Institute and the Società Lirica.

The concluding chapter draws Ella's story to a close, and seeks to understand his achievements, posthumous reputation and significance to music history. It considers the extent to which the Musical Union's metropolitan location and social identity, and/or Ella's skills and limitations, contributed to the institution's success and ultimate demise. It also assesses how influential and typical the Musical Union was in the broader context of British and European musical culture, particularly as regards its social profile and its establishment of listening practices that instilled veneration for the chamber repertoire.

---

[22] 'Musical Union', *CCSCM*.

[23] The phrase 'democratization of music' is used throughout the narrative to refer simply to the opening up of music to the lower social orders.

While the book's title alludes to Ella's lifelong, personal pursuit of high culture, it also signals his actions and agendas in promoting the 'best music' among London audiences, and his unswerving mission to persuade others to pursue high culture with similar commitment and dedication. The use of the term 'Victorian' in the book's subtitle and narrative is intended primarily to evoke a broad time-frame for chamber music concerts during Ella's lifetime (1830s to 1880s), although I have tried to remain alive to the problems inherent in the use of 'Victorian' as a qualitative adjective, which extend far beyond its coupling with 'music' and the derisive stereotypes that have been perpetuated on the back of it. However, many of the multiple meanings and contradictions that historians have identified within the people and the period strongly resonate in Ella and his associates; and I hope this 'Victorian-ness' will ultimately be a source of fascination to readers.

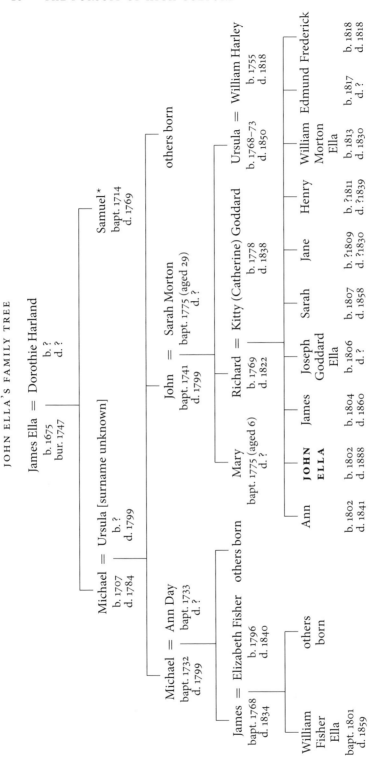

JOHN ELLA'S FAMILY TREE

James Ella = Dorothie Harland
b. 1675   b. ?
bur. 1747   d. ?

Michael = Ursula [surname unknown]
b. 1707   b. ?
d. 1784   d. 1799

Samuel *
bapt. 1714
d. 1769

others born

John = Sarah Morton
bapt. 1741   bapt. 1775 (aged 29)
d. 1799   d. ?

Mary
bapt. 1775 (aged 6)
d. ?

Michael = Ann Day
bapt. 1732   bapt. 1733
d. 1799   d. ?

Ursula = William Harley
b. 1768–73   b. 1755
d. 1850   d. 1818

Richard = Kitty (Catherine) Goddard
b. 1769   b. 1778
d. 1822   d. 1838

James = Elizabeth Fisher   others born
bapt. 1768   b. 1796
d. 1834   d. 1840

others
born

William
Fisher
Ella
bapt. 1801
d. 1859

Ann

JOHN
ELLA

b. 1802   b. 1802
d. 1841   d. 1888

James   Joseph
         Goddard
         Ella

b. 1804   b. 1806
d. 1860   d. ?

Sarah   Jane   Henry

b. 1807   b. ?1809   b. ?1811
d. 1858   d. ?1830   d. ?1839

William   Edmund Frederick
Morton
Ella

b. 1813   b. 1817   b. 1818
d. 1830   d. ?   d. 1818

* For this line of descent, and further details of other family members' birth, baptism, marriage etc., see Raymond E. O. Ella's construction of the Yorkshire branch of the family tree from the seventeenth century (copy in EllaC, MS 159).

CHAPTER 1

From Leicester to London, 1802–29

I<small>N</small> an era when professional musicians – that is, those who earned their living through music – were often born into families of the same, the conditions surrounding the birth and childhood of John Ella seem distinctly unusual. He was born on 19 December 1802 in Leicester, to a confectioner and his wife, Richard and Kitty (Catherine) Ella, and at least initially was intended for his father's trade.[1] How and why, given these circumstances, he came to prosecute music and, later on, to move in high London society; what marks were left on him by the events of his childhood and youth; and why he later chose to suppress some of his family connections, while vaunting others, are among the intriguing questions his life story poses – a story that must therefore start with his family's social background.

❧ *Leicestershire beginnings*

It was [...] at Dolby [sic] Hall that I first heard Beethoven's trios, Haydn's and Mozart's sonatas ❧ *RMU* (1859)

Walked on the Ashby Road – & saw on the Hill, Burleigh Hall, where I once passed some agreeable days, in my youth[,] fiddling with old <u>*Miss*</u> *& Dr. Tate – Trios by Kalkbrenner –*

❧ Ella's diary, 8 November 1853

T<small>HE</small> Ellas had their origins in Yorkshire, in the north of England, right back to Saxon times, but in the eighteenth century part of the family went south, presumably in search of better prospects.[2] John Ella's father, Richard Ella (1769–1822), moved to Loughborough, not far from Leicester, in 1774, while still a

---

[1] Not born at Thirsk, as J. A. Fuller Maitland stated in his entry on John Ella for *DNB* (1889), following the obituary by T. L. Southgate (*MS*, 6 October 1888, p. 213). On this point, see John Ravell, 'John Ella, 1802–1888', *M&L*, 34 (1953), 93–105.

[2] The notable family history has been documented by Raymond E. O. Ella in his *Four Anglian Kings of Northumbria (or Four Yorkshire Anglo-Saxon Crowns)*, 2nd edition (Otley: Northern Line Design, 2002). Yorkshire was part of Northumbria at this period. Raymond E. O. Ella's construction of the Yorkshire branch of the family tree since the seventeenth century (copy in EllaC, MS 159), and other privately communicated information, has provided much background data for this section.

child.[3] Richard was taken there by his mother and father (also a John, and a farmer) at the suggestion of Michael Ella, his father's enterprising brother, who had already settled in the town and was trading as an innkeeper, later establishing a successful business in canal boats – the new and growing means of transporting goods around the country.[4] Richard's father soon found work in the area, and Richard himself learned through apprenticeships his trade as a baker.[5] By 1796 Richard Ella was set up in Leicester, taking on his own apprentices; and by 1800, possibly earlier, he was living and working in the Market Place, in the centre of the town (Fig. 2).[6] His marriage to Kitty, daughter of a local man, Joseph Goddard, probably a carpenter, came in February 1801. Within two years she had given birth to two children, Ann (January 1802) and our John Ella (December 1802); several others followed.[7] Like their ancestors, they were baptized into the Anglican faith,

3 A settlement certificate, finalized 31 January 1774 (LRO, DE 1834/1/10), confirms that the family moved to Loughborough from Kir[k]by Knowle in the North Riding.

4 John Ella senior is described in the settlement certificate as a 'yeoman' (implying someone owning land) and in the apprenticeship records for his son Richard as a 'farmer' (see *Register of the Freemen of Leicester*: ii: *1770–1930*, ed. Henry Hartopp; Leicester: Corporation of the City of Leicester, 1933, p. 466). Further detail on him and other family members is in Appendix V.

   The terms of Michael Ella's will (LRO, PR/T/1799/62/1–2) show how successful he was in enterprise, bequeathing his commercial interests, land and property to his sons, and sharing £2,000 among his daughters. Two generations later, our John Ella would show similar business instincts.

5 Richard Ella began a series of apprenticeships in 1784. In 1796, on completing a seven-year term, he was made a freeman of Leicester. (Hartopp, *1770–1930*, 466 and 76.)

6 Hartopp (*1770–1930*) shows that Richard Ella was training apprentices in Leicester, first in bakery and later in confectionery, from December 1796. The poll book for the 1800 election (he was entitled to vote, courtesy of his freeman's status) lists him as a baker in the Market Place: see *A Copy of the Poll* [...] *Taken in the Borough of Leicester* [...] *1800* (Leicester: Ireland & Son, 1801).

7 According to notes made by John Ella in later life (EllaC, MS 88/vi), there were ten children: six boys and four girls. By 1822 one of the children had died, to judge from the inscription on Richard Ella's gravestone at St Martin's Cathedral, Leicester, which records nine offspring. Baptismal and burial records of St Martin's Church show there were in addition to Ann and John: James (b. 1804), Joseph Goddard (b. 1806), Sarah (b. 1807), William Morton (b. 1813), Edmund (b. 1817) and Frederick (b. 1818), a child who died in infancy – a total of six boys and two girls. The baptism of Henry (b. 1811), a brother who went to India, has not been located; nor has that of a sister, Jane (b. Leicester 1809; d. [place unknown] 1830, according to the *International Genealogical Index*).

2   The Market Place, Leicester, in the eighteenth century. From Mrs T. Fielding Johnson,
Glimpses of Ancient Leicester, in Six Periods (Leicester: Clarke & Satchell, 1906).

John's ceremony taking place on 23 December 1802 in St Martin's Church, Leicester, not far from the Market Place: the family lived in quarters that were attached
to – probably above – the shop.[8]

These were humble beginnings, but as a freeman of the borough Richard Ella
had a certain status within the community and collected rates for the local parish.[9]
Moreover, like many of his social group he seems to have aspired to improve his
family's prosperity and prospects. By 1804 he had risen to become a confectioner,
rather than a mere baker of bread,[10] and a few years later was advertising his fine

[8] The shop was located in the narrow lane, then called the Backside (or Cornwall),
to the south of the Corn Exchange.

[9] See n. 5 above. Richard Ella is listed as one of the overseers of the tax in some of the
extant rate books for St Martin's parish (in which the Market Place was located) at
this period, and seems to have taken his turn at collecting the monies. The books
for October 1809 and May 1810 (LRO, 21D51/2/4 and 21D51/2/6) were his.

[10] Hartopp (*1770–1930*) indicates a shift from apprentices assigned to Richard Ella the
baker (1796, 1797) to Richard Ella the confectioner (1804). In the 1800 poll book he
is listed as a baker. From January 1808 he advertised as a maker and seller of cakes
in the *Leicester Journal*, and in 1815 he was listed as a confectioner trading in the
Market Place in *The Leicester Directory containing a General List of the Merchants,
Tradesmen, Manufacturers, and Principal Inhabitants of Leicester* (Leicester: J. Fowler,
1815).

cakes and other delicacies to the 'Ladies and Gentlemen of Leicester and its vicinity' in the local press.[11] In this artisan-shopkeeper's milieu, on the cusp between the lower-middle and working classes, John Ella and his brothers and sisters grew up, doubtless witnessing commercial practice and the wooing of customers on a daily basis, and learning the importance of deference, respectability and hard work to social advancement. They were never as well off as their upwardly mobile cousins the Harleys in Loughborough (Richard's sister Ursula had married a local brewer, William Harley).[12] Nor could they come anywhere near the affluence and social status of their more distant relatives the Fisher Ellas in the Leicestershire village of Wymeswold. (James Ella, son of the go-ahead Michael Ella, had married into the Fisher family, recent purchasers of an old estate there, and became squire of Wymeswold Manor.)[13] But the Ellas of Leicester, including young John, must have gathered an appreciation of such fine living, albeit at a distance.

Unfortunately, few events of John Ella's childhood and youth are documented in detail, Ella being later concerned to repress information about his modest family origins, and much of what passed in his early years must remain circumstantially argued and imagined. Even so, it seems that the conditions of his Leicester upbringing brought particular benefits of education, training and exposure to music which, had he grown up elsewhere, a boy of his social status might never have encountered. His schooling is a case in point, a clue to the nature of which is provided by one of his friends in old age, the Rev. Hugh Haweis, who in a short biographical account of Ella in the 1880s wrote that Ella had told him that 'when a lad he got a prize for his paintings in water-colours, and distinguished himself in Latin'.[14] Both achievements are corroborated by the survival of a couple of botanical watercolours that he painted at the age of eleven, and by what we know of Ella's facility with language in later life and his propensity for classical references.[15] Given that he was born in an age when compulsory, free primary education for all

[11] *Leicester Journal* (29 December 1815) [advertisement for 'Twelfth Day Cakes'].

[12] An indication of the Harley wealth is signalled in William Harley's will (LRO, PR/T/1818/82), dated 1816, in which he bequeathed £2,000 to his son Edward, and £500 each to his other three children.

[13] James Ella's son, William Fisher Ella (John Ella's second cousin), inherited considerable wealth and land (see James Ella's will; LRO, PR/T/1834/54). He carried the title 'Lord of the Manor', which referred to the ownership of land, including manorialship rights, but did not connote peerage or parliamentary privileges – unlike the aristocrats with whom John Ella would fraternize many years later.

[14] *HaweisJE*, 2.

[15] The pictures, signed by Ella and dated 22 June 1814 and 25 April 1814 respectively, are in EllaC, MSS 75 and 76.

English children had not been contemplated, the fact that Ella received an education at all may seem quite remarkable, the more so that it involved a training in Latin. However, many shopkeepers in the English 'petite bourgeoisie', concerned for their family's future prospects and respectability, looked to schooling for their children as a way of insuring against bad times ahead, and providing opportunities for social betterment.[16] Indeed, skills in foreign language would later set Ella apart from many of his musical contemporaries.

In the early nineteenth century Leicester was a sizeable Midlands town, growing apace. In 1801 its population was nearly 17,000, four times larger than its biggest neighbour in the county, Loughborough; by 1821 it had almost doubled, as people migrated in from the surrounding countryside.[17] Like many urban centres in England's rapidly industrializing economy, it had manufacturing, but this was founded on stockings and still mostly organized as cottage industry in people's homes or in workshops, not in the large factories that were the more typical symbol of urban growth at this period.[18] The town also had its wealthy middle classes and local gentry, along with a social, cultural and intellectual life, much of which was animated by a group of Nonconformists, leaders of the town's industry and commerce.[19] Accordingly, for a town of this size and local importance, there was a range of private schools and academies (some boarding, some day schools – the existence of up to thirty boys' schools has been traced in the first two decades) catering for both those who desired a fashionable education for their sons and, to a lesser extent, daughters (who learned dancing, music, languages, drawing, painting and so on), and those, typically tradesmen, who wanted a more commercial training for young men (English, mathematics, book-keeping, for example).[20]

We do not know which school(s) Ella attended; but we might imagine that Ella's

---

[16] For further discussion, see Geoffrey Crossick, 'The Petite Bourgeoisie in Nine-teenth-Century Britain: the Urban and Liberal Case', *Shopkeepers and Master Artisans in Nineteenth-Century Europe*, ed. Geoffrey Crossick and Heinz-Gerhard Haupt (London: Methuen, 1984), 62–94, at 79–81.

[17] Statistics from Zena Crook and Brian Simon's essay 'Private Schools in Leices-ter and the County, 1780–1840', *Education in Leicestershire, 1540–1940: a Regional Study*, ed. Brian Simon (Leicester: Leicester University Press, 1968), 106.

[18] In the mid-nineteenth century all this would change: factories would appear and other industries (bootmaking, light engineering) emerge; see Colin D. B. Ellis, *History in Leicester, 55BC–AD1976*, 3rd edition (Leicester: Information Bureau, 1976), 104.

[19] For instance the Literary Society and the Adelphi Society, both established by the publisher and radical Richard Phillips, a locally born man who had been educated in London; Crook and Simon, 'Private Schools', 109–10.

[20] Crook and Simon, 'Private Schools', 111–13, 118.

parents found the money to send their boy to an institution such as the private day school in Applegate (established 1807), where subjects were charged for *pro rata* (6d a week for reading; 1s a week for elocution), and 'drawing and Latin' were on the curriculum; or to the Silver Street academy, run by Henry Carrick, which offered practical study for 'those destined for a commercial life'.[21] Equally, it is possible that John attended the locally endowed Free Grammar School, the building of which still stands in the aptly named Free School Lane in the 'old town' district. It so happened that Richard Ella, having served a seven-year apprenticeship to a baker who was a Freeman of Leicester, was himself entitled, according to statutes dating back to the sixteenth century, to be 'made free'. Freeman's status – effectively bringing membership of the local guild of merchants – was conferred on him in 1796 and gave him both the right to trade in the borough and to send his sons to the locally endowed Free Grammar School once they reached the age of seven.[22] Here Ella would have gained a solid grounding in English, Latin, Greek, Writing and 'Accompts' [i.e. accounts] – a strong ability in the latter undoubtedly became one of his hallmarks later in life.[23] Whether Ella took up his place, to be followed by his younger brothers, we do not know, since no registers or records of the school's pupils survive from this period (1809–16), and in any case the school was in serious decline from about 1802, with only a handful of free scholars – out of the several who were eligible – in attendance.[24] But if he did attend, it seems likely that his father would have had to pay something towards the privilege – by 1816 boys 'on the Foundation' were being charged a guinea on admission and a fee of two guineas per annum.[25]

[21] Crook and Simon, 'Private Schools', 113, 111.

[22] *Register of the Freemen of Leicester*: i: *1196–1770*, ed. Henry Hartopp (Leicester: Corporation of the City of Leicester, 1927), p. xx. Sons could be sent to school 'without payment'.

[23] Nicholas Carlisle, *A Concise Description of the Endowed Grammar Schools*: i: *Bedford-Lincoln* (London: Baldwin, Cradock and Joy, 1818), 771. Carlisle notes that a child had to be 'capable of reading correctly a Chapter in the Testament' before being admitted, so Ella would have had to have had some rudimentary schooling.

[24] Brian Simon, 'Local Grammar Schools, 1780–1850', *Education in Leicestershire*, ed. Simon, 130–55, at 137–8. Carlisle's *Concise Description* (p. 774; the survey was compiled in 1817) records that it was 'in the remembrance of many persons now living that this School was filled with the sons of Freemen, to the number of three hundred'. *The Victoria History of the County of Leicester*: iv: *The City of Leicester*, ed. R. A. McKinley (Oxford University Press, for University of London, 1958), 332, states that in 1816 there were just fourteen free scholars and no private boarders. The school closed in 1841.

[25] Carlisle, *Concise Description*, 772. The two guineas were 'in lieu of *Potation money*, as has been usual heretofore'. The school's rules were articulated in 1816.

In 1817, aged fourteen, John Ella began an apprenticeship to his father in the confectionery trade, and around the same time may well have started to earn money as a musician in the locality too.[26] Precisely how he came to acquire his skills as an instrumentalist – seven years later he would claim to be proficient on the violin, cello and piano – is unclear.[27] He possibly received some tuition from a local music teacher, the numbers of whom were increasing in Leicester, as demand for pianos and lessons, for young women in particular, grew.[28] Or, perhaps more likely, he picked up the basic skills much more informally, once provided with an instrument or two: self-teaching was not uncommon.[29] But whatever the source of his elementary learning, it is highly probable that Ella's pursuit of music was subsequently encouraged by the local hosiery manufacturer, avid amateur musician and energizing force in Leicester's musical life William Gardiner (1770–1853), and by the coincidental arrival of a clutch of high-calibre French string players in the town.[30]

Leicester at the turn of the eighteenth century offered a wide array of musical culture and activity, such that could creep into the awareness of a boy like Ella. The town was by no means inconsequential as a county centre for plays, balls and

[26] The date of his apprenticeship to Richard Ella is given in Hartopp, *1770–1930*, 567. In the application for John Ella's membership of the Royal Society of Musicians [RSM], the relief fund established in the early eighteenth century to protect musicians against the misfortunes of ill health and old age, his recommenders (Samuel Lyon, François Cramer and William Knyvett, all senior London musicians) stated – presumably on Ella's authority – that he had 'practised music for a livelihood upwards of seven years'. The application was made in 1824, in time for ballots in August–December, which places his first paid work as a musician in Leicester around 1817. (Archives of the Royal Society of Musicians, London, A322.) Max Wade-Matthews, *Musical Leicester* (Wymeswold: Heart of Albion Press, 1998), 29, implies that Ella was active as a music teacher in Leicester, but cites no evidence in support of the claim; I have been unable to trace any such activity in newspapers or local trade directories.

[27] The statement about his playing the three instruments is in the RSM application.

[28] Information about Leicester piano teachers comes from Wade-Matthews, *Musical Leicester*, 29–30. John's sister Ann is also known to have played the keyboard (Mary Kirby, *"Leaflets from my Life": a Narrative Autobiography*; London: Simpkin, Marshall, 1887, p. 33), so presumably the children had access to a piano. On shopkeepers being prepared to invest in music lessons, see Crossick, 'Petite Bourgeoisie', 81.

[29] *EhrlichMP*, 99.

[30] For a study of Gardiner, see Jonathan Wilshere, *William Gardiner of Leicester, 1770–1853: Hosiery Manufacturer, Musician and Dilettante* (Leicester: Leicester Research Services, 1970). Gardiner's published writings and reminiscences have proved invaluable as sources for historians of Leicester in this period.

concerts, and had its own theatre and fashionable Assembly Rooms. Both were situated in and around the Market Place, scarcely a stone's throw from Richard Ella's shop.[31] Local amateur and imported professional musicians typically came together for festivals and concerts; meanwhile, music was also made by local militia bands and the congregations of the Nonconformist churches, especially the Great Meeting chapel, which was also a 'pivot of the social and intellectual life' enjoyed by many of Leicester's doctors, lawyers and rich hosiers.[32] In fact, in the early nineteenth century much of Leicester's performance activity gathered momentum and a distinctly metropolitan aura. From 1801 to 1815 the theatre company was managed by the Irish actor William Macready, whose son William Charles Macready would become the celebrated tragedian. Macready senior introduced plays, scenery, actors and actresses hotfoot from the capital, and also ran companies in Birmingham, Sheffield, Newcastle and Manchester.[33] Meanwhile, notable singers and instrumentalists tended to stop in the town if touring the provinces, Leicester's convenient position on the English road network being a distinct advantage.[34] The phenomenally gifted opera singer Angelica Catalani, for example, appeared in 1810.[35]

Of particular importance to Ella's story were four French string players, François and Henry Fémy (violinist and cellist), Charles Guynemer and the great Pierre Baillot, a professor at the Paris Conservatoire (both violinists), who visited Leicester between 1814 and 1817, and surely gave Ella a whiff of the consummate skill of French instrumentalists. From at least one of them he eventually took lessons. The first to arrive were the Fémys, who played concertos and chamber music in Leicester Musical Society concerts in 1814; they were followed by Guynemer (1815) and Baillot (1815–16), both of whom led the society's orchestra and displayed their technical skills in concertos. Baillot's visit was a much

---

[31] A descriptive account of musical activity can be found in Wade-Matthews, *Musical Leicester*. For more on Leicester's theatrical life, see Helen Leacroft and Richard Leacroft, *The Theatre in Leicestershire: a History of Entertainment in the County from the 15th Century to the 1960s* (Leicester: Leicestershire Libraries and Information, 1986), 15–25. Ella would have been aware of the theatre's work, since his father's shop was used as an outlet for its ticket sales: as noted in a theatrical advertisement in the *Leicester Chronicle* (13 September 1817). It is possible, too, that John Ella may have played along in the theatre's orchestra around this time.

[32] Crook and Simon, 'Private Schools', 106. Gardiner's father, Thomas (1743–1837), was choirmaster of the Great Meeting (Wade-Matthews, *Musical Leicester*, 7).

[33] Leacroft and Leacroft, *Theatre in Leicestershire*, 17.

[34] Wade-Matthews, *Musical Leicester, passim*.

[35] Leacroft and Leacroft, *Theatre in Leicestershire*, 18.

talked-about event. The *Leicester Journal* critic swooned at his talents, remarking that he 'led the band with an ardour we never before witnessed' and saying of his solo-playing that 'the art with which he illicits [*sic*] the boldest and tenderest tones, from the violin, is [?]entirely new, and his exertion surpasses every thing we have hitherto heard'.[36] Presumably others concurred – Gardiner described the visit as a 'carnival of music' for the town.[37] Ella, in all likelihood, witnessed a good deal of this activity, even if just listening in at rehearsals. Indeed, since Baillot's musical philosophy would, decades later, become something of a touchstone for Ella, we may well conclude that the beginnings of Ella's admiration dated from this time.

How all four Frenchmen came to be in Leicester in quick succession is curious, but largely attributable to social networks and the circumstances of time and place. The Fémys arrived with their father Ambroise, a Martinique merchant and amateur violinist, who was making a business call on Gardiner.[38] After work was done, the father apparently joined his sons, both of whom had been schooled at the Paris Conservatoire, to play Beethoven's 'serenade trio' (presumably op. 8) to Gardiner.[39] Gardiner, whose interest in Beethoven's music was second to none, was enraptured with their playing and musicianship, thereafter almost certainly acting as conduit for the sons' engagements at the Musical Society. The next arrival, Charles Guynemer, had links with Baillot as both pupil and brother-in-law, having married his teacher's sister. He had worked in Paris as a violinist.[40] Recently, according to Gardiner, Guynemer had taken up as a French civil servant, collecting taxes in Belgium, but when the defeat of

---

[36] *Leicester Journal* (5 April 1816).

[37] William Gardiner, *Music and Friends, or Pleasant Recollections of a Dilettante*, 2 vols. (London: Longman, Orme, Brown & Longman, 1838), 507. Gardiner was, it should be said, a fair judge of quality, having experienced professional music-making in London since the 1790s; see Wilshere, *William Gardiner*, 12–13.

[38] Gardiner, *Music and Friends*, 488–90. François Fémy was a pupil of Kreutzer at the Paris Conservatoire (*FétisB*). In 1816 and 1818 he appeared in performances of chamber music at the Philharmonic Society in London, and a symphony of his was performed there in May 1816 (see Myles Birket Foster, *History of the Philharmonic Society of London, 1813–1912* (London: John Lane, The Bodley Head, 1912), p. 26). John Feltham, *The Picture of London, for 1818* (London: Longman, Hurst, Rees, Orme & Brown, [1818]), 276, lists Fémy as an important 'rising' composer of symphonies.

[39] Gardiner, *Music and Friends*, 489.

[40] Evidence of Guynemer's activity as a performer in Paris is slight. *FauquetS*, 44, 271, states that Guynemer had played in the inaugural concert of Baillot's quartet series in December 1814.

Napoleon and capture of Paris by the Allies put an end to this employment he set off for England, with a letter of introduction from the celebrated composer and pianist Muzio Clementi.[41] 'A fortnight had not elapsed before I discovered him to be a most accomplished musician', wrote Gardiner years later, explaining how they had come to play string quartets together.[42] Once again, in all likelihood, Gardiner made the introductions to the Leicester Musical Society. The story of Baillot's arrival in the town is less well documented. Having seen the Bourbon Restoration close the Conservatoire (temporarily, as it turned out) in July 1815, Baillot had set off on a European tour, arriving in England in late 1815 and giving concerts in London and a series of provincial centres, including Leicester (December 1815 and spring 1816).[43] Since the Leicester performances were given alongside Guynemer, and Gardiner makes no mention of his own connections with Baillot, we may reasonably imagine it was the combination of family and professional ties that brought the great violinist to the locality.[44]

Unlike Baillot and the Fémys, whose visits were fleeting, Guynemer stayed on in Leicester until 1817, appearing in local concerts and running with his wife a little school to teach dancing, French and music.[45] In the knowledge of this we might speculate that Ella, who by 1823 could count Guynemer among his London acquaintances, got to know the Frenchman during his time in Leicester, and even that he took some lessons from him and his wife.[46] French was, after all, to become the foreign language in which he had most fluency; and it would have been a golden opportunity to learn how to fiddle properly. Admittedly Ella only ever

---

[41] Gardiner, *Music and Friends*, 506–9.

[42] Gardiner, *Music and Friends*, 507.

[43] The Conservatoire reopened in 1816 as the Ecole Royale de Musique. Baillot's tour took him to Belgium, Holland and on to England; see Charles Guynemer, *Essay on Chamber Classical Music* (London: the author, 1846), 6. Guynemer, *Essay*, 6, says Baillot played at Leicester, Birmingham, Liverpool, Manchester and London. The London concerts were at the Philharmonic Society on 26 February, 13 May and 27 May 1816 (Birket Foster, *History of the Philharmonic*); on these dates he played in chamber music performances, supported in several of them by François Fémy on second violin. By November 1816 Baillot was back in Paris, leading his quartet concerts once again (*FauquetS*, 295–6).

[44] In addition to playing solo concertos, Baillot performed duos with Guynemer. Information from advertisements in *Leicester Journal* (22 December 1815 and 22 March 1816).

[45] As advertised in the *Leicester Journal* (19 January 1816 onwards).

[46] Ella's association with Guynemer is indicated by appointments in his diary for 1823 (EllaC, MS 98). The nature of their interaction at this point is unclear; perhaps Ella took lessons from Guynemer, or simply saw him socially.

allowed it to be known that he had learned with François Fémy, from whom he later took lessons in London (another connection seemingly born in Leicester);[47] but that scarcely rules out the possibility of being also taught by Guynemer. In any case he must have had several opportunities to hear the Frenchman play.

Ella's informal musical education was not just about gaining the technical skills of practical musicianship. An equally important core value, almost certainly laid down in these Leicester years, was his love and appreciation of classical music, in particular his admiration for Beethoven, and here the figure of Gardiner emerges once more. Documentary evidence linking Ella with Gardiner in these first decades of the century is sparse, but the key is Ella's admission that he first heard chamber music by Haydn, Mozart and Beethoven – a repertoire only gradually becoming known in England – at the Leicestershire country house of the Hon. Mrs Bowater, Old Dalby Hall in the Vale of Belvoir.[48] Since her musical parties are known to have been organized by Gardiner, it seems probable it was he who opened Ella's eyes and ears to this other world, the boy perhaps being taken along to play an inner part in a quartet, perhaps simply to scurry about and help with the practical arrangements. Given these circumstances, the fact that Gardiner was a linchpin of Leicester musical life, that he developed a reputation for encouraging and teaching local musicians of talent (quite possibly ushering Ella towards the French violinists), and that a lot of hard, surviving evidence demonstrates that Ella and Gardiner were well acquainted from the 1820s onwards both in London and Leicester, the conclusion that Gardiner was a mentor and formative influence on Ella seems inescapable.[49] What is more, Gardiner's enthusiasm for Viennese chamber music and his championship of Beethoven were, in the early nineteenth century, almost without equal in England. He had been one of Beethoven's first

---

[47] As stated in the preliminary pages to *RMU* (1879). The information appeared during Ella's lifetime in *FétisB*, *HaweisJE*, the first edition of George Grove's *Dictionary*, and later in obituaries.

[48] *RMU* (1859), sup., 22. The connection with Mrs Bowater is documented in Gardiner's *Music and Friends, or Pleasant Recollections of a Dilettante*, supplementary vol. (London: Longman, Brown, Green, & Longmans, 1853), 142–7. We know, too, that Ella played chamber music in at least one other local country house: Burleigh Hall (diary entry, 8 November 1853, quoted at the head of this section).

[49] Gardiner's reputation for fostering young talent is documented in Wade-Matthews, *Musical Leicester*, 95. On Ella's proximity to Gardiner in London, see *Music and Friends* (1838), 688–90, and entries in Ella's diaries for 21 May 1824 and 3 November 1826 (EllaC, MSS 99 and 101). Their encounters in Leicester can also be traced: see diaries, 8 October 1826, 22 October 1830 and 2 December 1839 (EllaC, MSS 101, 103 and 108).

English advocates, in 1794 playing in a performance of the E♭ string trio op. 3 (a manuscript copy of which had been brought to Leicester in the fiddle case of the Abbé Döbler, chaplain to the Elector of Palatine, who was fleeing the wars in Europe).[50] This was three years before the work was published in London, and on his own admission, the composition, 'so different from anything I had ever heard, awakened in me a new sense, a new delight, in the science of sounds'.[51] A quest to obtain more of Beethoven's music, initially from Germany, began, and heralded a lifetime's enthusiasm for the composer and his works. Gardiner adapted the music of Beethoven, along with passages from Haydn and Mozart, in his own oratorio *Judah* (1821), and actually wrote to Beethoven offering him 100 guineas for an overture to the work.[52] By 1817 he owned, and had presumably attempted, eighty-four quartets by Haydn, sixteen by Mozart and twelve by Beethoven.[53] Of course, Gardiner's activities need to be understood as part of the wider and remarkably rapid journey of Beethoven's music to public acceptance and reverence in England during the first three decades of the century. But as yet, in a place like Leicester, such a strong belief in this composer and familiarity with his music would have been unusual; so we must consider that it was through Gardiner that Ella's knowledge of, and devotion to, high serious chamber music, especially Beethoven's, first developed.

[50] Gardiner, *Music and Friends* (1838), 112–14; (1853), 142–4 [year given as 1793]. See also Geoffrey Syer, 'Beethoven and William Gardiner', *MT*, 128 (1987), 256–8: the Abbé played the violin, Gardiner the viola, and Valentine, a local musician, the cello.

[51] Gardiner, *Music and Friends* (1853), 143.

[52] He also adapted the three composers' music in his *Sacred Melodies* (published 1812–38). A useful overview of these and other achievements is in Jonathan Wilshere, 'Gardiner, William', *NGDM2*. It was characteristic of Gardiner that he should travel to Bonn for the unveiling of the Beethoven statue in 1845.

[53] Gardiner, *Music and Friends* (1838), 507–8. See also his retrospective remarks on p. 831: 'Many have been the changes in our party through the last fifty years; still we contrive, once a fortnight, to regale our ears with a quartett of Haydn, Mozart, or Beethoven. My oldest musical friend, Mr. Bankart, I still find by my side, with his violoncello; and, with our excellent leader, Mr. Gill, Mr. Graham, and Mr. Scott, we play the whole of Beethoven, except his posthumous quartetts, which we conceive require the penetration of the angel Gabriel to understand.'

❧ *Moving out*

50th anniversary of my residence in London
◞ Ella's diary, 19 December 1870

ELLA'S apprenticeship to his father was never served out, and by December 1820 – possibly as soon as early summer 1819 – Ella had moved to London and was about to begin patching together a living as a jobbing musician.[54] The change-around is significant, since a critical part of running a small business in the nineteenth century was family labour, and there was surely an expectation that John, as eldest son and apprentice, would inherit and continue Richard Ella's shop and trade. If that were not to happen, then the family would have surely hoped that John would find some other respectable occupation. Following music as a career was unlikely to fit that specification. It was known to be precarious: vulnerable to the fluctuations of the market, the season, and health; and it had connotations of raffishness and immorality, particularly from its connections with the theatre world.[55] One can imagine the warnings issued to the young Ella.

In the 1810s no musician could make a complete living from playing even in London, let alone in a growing centre like Leicester, without diversifying activities. Take Ebenezer Jones, who led the Leamington and Birmingham Quadrille Bands: in 1815 he was also set up in Leicester as piano tuner and teacher of piano, violin and cello.[56] It is possible that Ella had hoped initially to run his musical career in Leicestershire alongside work in the family shop and bake-house as a way of accommodating family wishes while minimizing the financial risk of operating as a musician; or that he had viewed the confectionery apprenticeship

54 Ravell, 'John Ella', 95, reported that Ella had been in London in 1819, staying with François Fémy in Queen Street, Soho, taking violin lessons from him, and even deputizing in an orchestra for him on one occasion (see n. 69 below). I have been unable to locate the source of Ravell's information connecting Ella and Fémy at this period; it was apparently inscribed in a volume of Leclair sonatas which Fémy presented to Ella in 1820, and which Ravell told me he had seen in the collection of Ella's music at the Royal College of Organists in London (later dispersed) while researching his article; the volume is described in 'John Ella'. However, a remark in Ella's diary years later (24 February 1836; EllaC, MS 106) confirms the basic information, Ella recalling the nature of his violin practice 'during my residence with my master Monsr. Femy', though putting no date on the episode.

  In spite of not completing his apprenticeship, John Ella received the freemanship of Leicester on 15 June 1826, on account of being a freeman's son.

55 On negative perceptions of the music profession, see *RohrCBM*, 15–21.

56 Wade-Matthews, *Musical Leicester*, 29–30.

as a fallback, in case his musical aspirations came to nothing. Yet, more likely, youthful ambition grew strong, Ella's French heroes having given the world outside Leicester exotic appeal. And realism was setting in, in the form of an awareness, probably fostered by Gardiner, that if Ella were to make a truly successful life in music it would be in the capital and not in Leicester, where opportunities were limited and where in any case the prospects for prosperity were in question as an economic depression in the hosiery industry set in after the ending of the French wars.[57] London, by comparison, was indisputably the richest centre for musical careers to be played out, in terms of the quality and quantity of activity on the one hand, and the demand and spending power for lessons, instruments, concerts and the like on the other. It had long been the honey-pot to which provincial musicians were drawn in large numbers, in spite of the fact that its market-place operated on a deeply competitive basis, and living costs were not cheap.[58]

Ella would have made his journey to London by coach – a distance of just under 100 miles, covered in about sixteen hours and at quite an expense. In 1801 the fare was 25s for a seat inside, 12s 6d for one outside; the money had presumably been saved up carefully. Left behind to make and sell cakes were his parents and surviving brothers and sisters. James, his closest brother in age, had already taken on an apprenticeship to his father (1818), and would in time become a master confectioner, active in Birmingham.[59] After his father's death (1822) the cake shop would be run first by his mother, Kitty, and later by Ann, John's eldest sister.[60] Another sister, Sarah, later married Joseph Croshaw (1838), also a baker, and stayed in Leicester, ensuring the trade was maintained in the

[57] Gerald T. Rimmington, *Education, Politics and Society in Leicester, 1833–1903* (Hantsport: Lancelot Press, 1978), 10; see also R. H. Evans, 'The Expansion of Leicester in the Nineteenth Century', *The Growth of Leicester*, ed. A. E. Brown (Leicester: Leicester University Press, 1972), 63–77; and for detailed discussion, A. Temple Patterson, *Radical Leicester: a History of Leicester, 1780–1850* (Leicester: University College, 1954), 104–29.

[58] On the difficulties of making a musical living in London, see *McVeighCL*, 199–202.

[59] As indicated by James Ella's death certificate; he died 16 June 1860. For a while in his youth James seems to have lived in London: he is detailed as a confectioner, from London, in the list of voters in *The Poll for Electing Two Burgesses to Represent the Borough of Leicester* [...] *1826* (Leicester: Albert Cockshaw, 1826).

[60] Kitty Ella is listed as a confectioner, trading in the Market Place, in *The Leicester Directory* (Leicester: T. Combe and Son, [1827]), and as taking on apprentices in 1823 and 1831 in Hartopp, *1770–1930*. She died in 1838. Ann Ella is also listed in trade directories (1840, 1841) as a confectioner, but operating from Cheapside, the area on the north-east corner of the Market Place.

extended family. Others, like John, took routes out, one going to India, another to America.[61]

Compared with Leicester, London in 1820 must have seemed another world, with mind-stretching experiences around almost every street corner. Seat of monarchy and government, prosperous centre for banking, shipping and commerce, its West End abuzz during the 'season' with high society and its pleasures, London was the hub of the nation and growing Empire, and of a size and order all of its own in population, geography and activities.[62] Its lack of dependence on one industry, and its multi-layered economy, much of it supporting the lives of the rich, made it like no other British city in the nineteenth century.[63] It was also growing fast. In Ella's lifetime London would change unrecognizably, its population trebling to more than four million, dwarfing the boom cities of the industrial north. What is more, its urban spread would spill out miles in all directions, a haphazard growth led by speculative building and private capital rather than systematic government-controlled planning, and energized by horse-drawn tram companies, railway construction and a sea-change in the relationship between place of work and domicile: what we now call commuting. In this way, areas that were once rural villages – Hampstead in the north, Norwood in the south, Leyton in the east, Chiswick in the west – were sucked into the expanding conurbation, producing a series of discrete neighbourhoods, with distinctive social character and in some cases the dire problems of poverty and poor sanitation that Charles Dickens would highlight in his novels.[64]

But all that was ahead. When Ella arrived there, the capital held much the same physical and social shape that it had during Haydn's visits in the 1790s, with its two distinctive quarters on the north side of the river, the fashionable West End and the commercial City district, and with the enclave of Southwark, characterized

---

[61] His brother Henry had gone to India, but died in 1839 leaving a wife and child, according to entries in John's diary (11 February 1839, and the summary at the end of the year; EllaC, MS 108). Meanwhile Joseph Goddard Ella had set off for America, Ella's address book showing addresses for him in Philadelphia and New York that same year.

[62] 1.3 million people, slightly more than 10 per cent of the population of England and Wales, were living there in 1821: Francis Sheppard, *London, 1808–1870: the Infernal Wen* (London: Secker & Warburg, 1971), p. 84. Leicester numbered just over 30,000 inhabitants.

[63] Roy Porter, *London: a Social History* (Harmondsworth: Penguin Books, 1996), 186–7. The opportunities for employment ranged from 'middle-class jobs in shipping, banking, investment and insurance' that the commercial sector generated, to work in 'retailing, porterage and transport', which supported the wealthy classes.

[64] For further discussion, see Porter, *London*, 205–38.

by its maze of warehouses, on the opposite bank. That said, the urban landscape was altering, most dramatically under the direction of John Nash, whose designs for Regent's Park and for Regent Street, the latter with its spectacular, sweeping Quadrant, brought an Italianate grandeur to the West End. Meantime, gas street-lighting was being introduced in the main residential and commercial areas. Ella, whose first lodgings appear to have been in Queen Street, near Soho Square[65] – an area abutting the fine residences of the West End and famously populated (then) by musicians – cannot fail to have been swept up in the contemporaneity of it all as he explored and learned about his new environment.

Easy access to the heart of the West End was important for any working musician. This area, which had grown up around Parliament and the court, had during the late eighteenth century become strongly associated with high society, wealth and the conspicuous consumption of luxury goods and culture, including music. It was home to the principal theatres and concert rooms, public and private: the King's Theatre in the Haymarket, where Italian opera played; the Hanover Square Rooms, where Haydn's London symphonies had first been heard; the Argyll Rooms, where the recently established Philharmonic Society was to be found; and the grand houses in which private entertainments were held. Within decades, wide social change in the structure of audiences for art music would come about, as the more middling and lower classes gained access to performances in central London; but at the point of Ella's initiation into metropolitan music-making, concerts were still restricted by price and subscription, making them the province of the affluent upper-middle classes and aristocracy. The West End also provided a huge market for music lessons, which all musicians needed to give if they were to survive. Servicing it was a network of music shops and instrument dealers close by: Monzani and Hill (sheet music) in Regent Street, Broadwood (pianos) in Great Pulteney Street, the Forster violin shop in the Strand, and so on. With accommodation in Soho, where he could practise and teach, and from where most essential travelling for rehearsals, performances and purchasing musical supplies could be done on foot, Ella had chosen well, possibly on Gardiner's advice.

But if some aspects of establishing a career as an instrumental musician looked straightforward to Ella, others surely presented hurdles and challenges. To start with, the English musician's work was typically pieced together in a freelance way from diverse sources. Year-round continuous employment was almost unheard of, working conditions often miserable, and the lifestyle vulnerable to changing market conditions, accidents of health and so on. It was deeply competitive too, each person jealously looking after his (still only occasionally her) own interests. The amounts earned by the majority were modest: annual earnings of leading

[65] See n. 54 above.

instrumentalists might reach £300, even £500, but far more musicians accumulated less, say between £100 and £200, placing the average musician on a par with a tradesman or artisan shopkeeper and a little above an artisan labourer.[66] What is more, the notion of a proper music profession – in the sense of 'institutionalized pride of calling and allegiance to idealized codes of practice', not to mention judiciously organized standards of training, a *bona fide* system of formal qualifications, union protection and the like – was still many decades off, as Cyril Ehrlich's seminal history has demonstrated.[67] In such a climate, getting established was difficult – as much about the adroit handling of social relations and the working environment as anything else. Even for the most talented singers and instrumentalists, the teaching of amateurs was a necessary drudge, offset by its ability to provide a remunerative and relatively steady source of income: half a guinea for an hour's tuition was good money.[68] Yet developing a teaching practice took time and required the regular oiling of contacts. Employment as a performer, in concerts or the theatre, could supplement such work (though it would rarely stand alone, even with the greatest players), but in days when agents and 'diary services' were unimagined, there were no easy routes in, and no alternatives for garnering experience and learning repertoire save 'on the job'. In sum, one had to get one's face known by the people who mattered, to seize opportunities as they arose, and thence to secure a reputation as a skilled and reliable pair of hands and ears. Outlays were required too: a smart wardrobe for teaching and performing was a sartorial necessity. And it helped to have someone, typically one's teacher, to make recommendations and even to pass on work experience through the 'deputy system'. In Ella's case this may have happened through François Fémy, with whom he appears to have shared his first London address.[69]

[66] *EhrlichMP*, 49. For a helpful comparison with salaries in a wide range of other social/occupational groups, see *RohrCBM*, 186–7 (table 21).

[67] Quotation from *EhrlichMP*, 31; see *passim* for further discussion.

[68] The importance of teaching to the London musician is explored in Philip Olleson, 'Samuel Wesley and the Music Profession', *MBC*, 23–38, esp. 29–30.

[69] See n. 54 above. It is possible that Ella began an apprenticeship to Fémy. He deputized for him, 'frightened out of my senses', in the violin section of the Philharmonic Society on the occasion when a symphony by Fémy was being tried (information and quotation from Ravell, 'John Ella', p. 95). This probably took place in early 1819 (two trials are noted in the Directors' minutes; BL, RPS/MS/279, ff. 60v–61r and 63v), and may have been the cause of a dispute between the Directors and Fémy, which eventually resulted in his being 'allowed to resume his situation in the Orchestra' (RPS/MS/279, f. 74v; minute for 21 March). Fémy seems to have returned to France by the early 1820s. On apprenticeships for musicians, see *RohrCBM*, 68–71, and *EhrlichMP*, 7–9.

Ella probably recognized that to ensure short-term survival, some other, non-musical employment had best be found. At least, this is the most plausible explanation for his later insistence that, prior to obtaining his first professional engagement as a performer in January 1821 (in the Drury Lane Theatre orchestra), he had been 'quill-driving in an attorney's office'.[70] This was presumably a clerical job for which his Leicester education would have prepared him well, and was probably located in one of the legal districts, perhaps Lincoln's Inn or the Inner or Middle Temple. It would have been a respectable, if not especially well-paid, occupation – more dignified than handling cakes – and would have underpinned the transition to musical employment.[71] Moreover, it was easily embellished years later to produce a more acceptable version of Ella's origins: his entry in François-Joseph Fétis's *Biographie universelle*, the information for which Ella almost certainly supplied, described Ella as having been 'intended for the profession of lawyer, by his parents', and then thwarting their expectations at the age of seventeen [i.e. in 1819] by going into music.[72]

ࣷ *Scraping a living*

Note read from Mr. Ella to Sir G. Smart requesting a Situation in the
Orchestra   ࣷ Philharmonic Society minute, 19 October 1821

AT what point Ella abandoned the quill, we cannot be sure – presumably not until he felt he had enough reliable work in the musical sphere. But within two years he was working wholly as a musician, to judge from his diary for 1823, the earliest such volume to survive.[73] In the meantime, experience and connections were being built up effectively: an opportunity to deputize as a cellist (rather than a violinist) in the Italian Opera orchestra was taken (1821); and a letter to Sir George Smart of the Philharmonic Society, asking for a place in the orchestra

---

[70] *RMU* (1869), 32. The information first surfaced in *MW* (7 August 1845), 373–4, where 'a private letter, addressed to ourselves by an artist who respects Mr. Ella' announced the same, describing Ella, rather grandly, as an 'embryo lawyer' and 'a member of both the learned and *polite* professions, being amateur, lawyer, and artist within the space of three months'.

[71] *RohrCBM*, 186 (table 21), suggests a clerk's annual income was £75.

[72] *FétisBU*. The French reads: 'Destiné à la profession d'avocat dès l'âge de dix-sept ans, par ses parents, il trompa leur attente en se vouant à la musique par amour pour cet art'. Fétis's dictionary has long been considered error-ridden, the Belgian being more concerned with producing a comprehensive monument to music than with the factual disciplines of lexicography.

[73] EllaC, MS 98.

brought forth one engagement there in 1822, and more in 1823.[74] Ella also found employment at one of Smart's concerts in the City of London (1821).[75] Closely identified with the port and commerce, and still at the initial stages of its dramatic transformation from busy trading area into formidable banking and insurance quarter, this London district had developed its own middle-class identity and discrete cultural activities, which, while not as extensive as the music-making in the West End, offered useful supplementary opportunities for getting work and experience.[76] The career breakthrough for Ella, however, occurred in May 1822, when an emergency at the opera house before a performance of Rossini's *Il barbiere di Siviglia* created the need for a last-minute stand-in, Ella recalling several years later that 'Marshall [a violinist] […] having suddenly been seized with a fit, Spagnoletti [the leader] sent for me, to Queen St Soho No 6, desiring me, at the same time, to come to the Orchestra in full-dress.'[77] Ella's wonderment at the opera house on this evening was still vivid: 'King George 4th […] came in Grand State. All the Ladies were in Plumes, & the House, I have never seen since, was worthily attired for Regal Presence.'[78]

How soon Marshall's misfortune was turned permanently to Ella's advantage is not revealed, but Ella considered his entry to the band to date from this moment. By January 1823 he had a position at the back of the first violin section, one he would hold for twenty-five years.[79] The remuneration was modest: rank-and-file players earned considerably less than section leaders and principal wind players (most of whom received 15s per night), and junior members (such as Ella, presumably, in

[74] Ella notes his first engagement at the Opera in a memorandum preserved in one of his scrapbooks (EllaC, MS 81, p. 5). Evidence of his engagements by the Philharmonic in 1821–3 is supplied by the Directors' minute books (BL, RPS/MS/279, ff. 171r and 179v: minutes for 19 October 1821 and 21 February 1822; RPS/MS/280, f. 9r: minute for 1 March 1823), and by the accounts for 1822 and 1823 (RPS/MS/299; entered as an extra player). There is no indication, however, of whether this employment was as violinist or cellist.

[75] A note in *RMU* (1873), 4, indicates this was a City of London Grand Concert, held on 19 December 1821.

[76] For a discussion of City traditions, including some insights into the nature of audiences there, see Rachel Cowgill, '"Wise Men from the East": Mozart's Operas and their Advocates in Early Nineteenth-Century London', *MBC*, 39–64.

[77] Memorandum (dated 1858) in EllaC, MS 81, p. 5.

[78] Ibid.

[79] Ella's position in the orchestra (number seven, out of nine first violins) is given in a list of personnel headed 'Opera Band 1823' in the front of his diary for that year (EllaC, MS 98); the daily entries show he was working at the opera house regularly from January 1823.

these early years) got less again, typically 10s 6d per night; there was no extra pay for rehearsals.[80] Yet securing this work was significant, because, with two evening performances weekly plus daytime band calls for rehearsals between January and July, it virtually guaranteed Ella a constant trickle of money over several months of the year; and because it gave him the opportunity of learning an important repertoire and of frequently hearing the best instrumentalists and singers perform. It also wired him into the principal network of working musicians, which included such leading players as the double bass virtuoso Domenico Dragonetti, the violinists Paolo Spagnoletti and Nicolas Mori, the cellist Robert Lindley and the horn player Giovanni Puzzi, to name just a few. From such a matrix of connections more work could and would flow.

By 1824 Ella had secured further positions in the orchestras of the Philharmonic Society (better paid, but only eight performances a year), and the Antient Concerts (twelve performances); he was also playing in a stream of other performances: the oratorios at Drury Lane, more concerts in the City, the benefits of prominent performers in the West End, and so on.[81] Concerts were almost always

---

[80] Decades later, in *RMU* (1869), 8, Ella claimed to have been drafted into the understaffed (four-strong) viola section by Rossini for a performance of *Zelmira* in 1824, and that whenever Rossini used a small orchestra at the King's Theatre he placed Ella as the principal viola, a position that was relatively well remunerated. On the fees paid to the musicians at the Opera and general conditions of employment, see Rachel Cowgill and Gabriella Dideriksen, 'Opera Orchestras in Georgian and Early Victorian London', *The Opera Orchestra in 18th- and 19th-Century Europe*: i: *The Orchestra in Society*, ed. N. M. Jensen and F. Piperno, Musical Life in Europe, 1600–1900: Circulation, Institutions, Representation (Berlin: Berlin Verlag, forthcoming), 259–321, at 273–6.

[81] As indicated by Ella's diaries for 1823 and 1824 (EllaC, MSS 98 and 99), the Philharmonic Society Directors' minutes and account books (BL, RPS/MS/280 and 299), and the programmes for the Antient Concerts (in Oxford University, Faculty of Music Library). Ella's Philharmonic fee in 1824 was £13 2s 6d for eight concerts (including nine rehearsals), roughly half a guinea for each rehearsal and one guinea per concert, the base rate of pay for its rank and file violinists. By 1826 the amount paid to such players had risen to £19 13s 9d for the same number of band calls (as per the account book: BL, RPS/MS/299). Less is known about Antient Concert remuneration, but in 1826 Ella received £12 12s for the twelve concerts (one guinea each; as noted – in code – in the accounts at the end of his 1826 diary; EllaC, MS 101). A letter from John Weldon, secretary to the Antients' management committee (EllaC, MS 81, p. 65), dated 12 June [no year], shows the committee agreeing to Ella's suggestion for a pay rise – to £1 11s 6d for each concert and rehearsal – on account of his track record in the orchestra and his gentlemanly discourse, thus eventually bringing the fee in line with Philharmonic rates. Bargaining one's corner was part of standard working practice in this 'pre-trade union' culture.

under-rehearsed, as was the British way, and we may assume that Ella developed the sight-reading skills necessary for survival. All this performance work together rendered only about £100 per annum, to judge from Ella's own note of his accounts at the end of 1826.[82] It was as well, then, that teaching opportunities grew alongside, Ella doubtless learning quickly how to court and maintain wealthy amateurs seeking musical skills and guidance, and drawing on his experience of Richard Ella's commercial practices.[83] Lord Saltoun of Abernethy, to whose nieces Ella gave lessons, and who would later become a significant patron, emerged from this environment; their first encounter dated from January 1823.[84]

But for all this busy-ness, the graft was hard, security tenuous and remuneration volatile. Many of the difficulties stemmed from the seasonal pattern of the work, and the fact that the principal opportunities for making money were concentrated in the three months or so from Easter to July that constituted the 'high season'. This was the period when almost all the British nobility and gentry – the 'bon ton' – left their country estates for their London town houses (typically those in the area running between Park Lane and Piccadilly – the focal point for West End rank and fashion) to participate in the dizzying whirl of metropolitan life, music included. In truth, the season proper began somewhat earlier, its commencement coinciding with the opening of Parliament, a moveable feast which fell sometime after Christmas – landed wealth and political power in Britain being intrinsically linked historically. For this reason there were always some families up in town through the early months of the year, and for them, entertainments such as the Opera, with which the élite were traditionally connected, were provided, as were music lessons and private parties. So there were possibilities, albeit limited ones, for musicians to grind out a winter living. But everyone knew the most lucrative weeks for musicians were from Easter until the horse races at Ascot and the rowing regatta at Henley. Once Parliament adjourned and the grouse-shooting began on the 'Glorious Twelfth' of August, the fashion left for the country, and with it most

---

[82] This included £55 from opera work, £20 from the Philharmonic, 12 guineas from the Antient Concerts, 9 guineas from Royal Academy of Music performances, and 8 guineas from miscellaneous concerts: £106 9s in all. Noted in shorthand (using a system where a = 1, b = 2 etc.) in accounts at the back of the 1826 diary (EllaC, MS 101).

[83] Around 1824, when he submitted for membership of the Royal Society of Musicians, his recommenders (all senior London musicians) endorsed the fact that he had 'teaching'. How much, we do not know.

[84] Note to the diary entry for 10 January 1823 (EllaC, MS 98). In a handwritten annotation to a copy of his published RMU obituary of Saltoun, preserved in one of his scrapbooks (EllaC, MS 81, p. 2), Ella dated the meeting as 11 January 1823; a memorandum on the same page further refers to the nieces' lessons.

3 Handwritten list of musicians hired for the Yorkshire Music Festival, 1828. York City
Archives © (Acc.150.47). Ella's name appears in the left-hand column.

opportunities for musicians' employment. Money made in the times of plenty thus usually had to be stored up and eked out during the fallow period.

The cream of London's freelance performers, including the leading orchestral musicians with whom Ella was now working and identifying, fared better in the latter part of the year, securing engagements on the regional festival and concert circuit.[85] Soon Ella gained a place in this milieu, his diary, scrapbook cuttings and published anecdotes placing him at the grand choral festivals at York (1823, 1825), Norwich (1824), Edinburgh (1824) and Hereford (1825), for example, and demonstrating the extent of the musical engagements and social openings that could be had *en route*.[86] Late August to mid-December 1824 saw him journey to Cheltenham, Worcester, Norwich, Leeds, York, Tadcaster, Newcastle, Edinburgh, Carlisle and Manchester, and even spend time in Leicester playing at concerts and visiting family and friends.[87] In the process, more potential patrons were found, one such

[85] For a purview of the provincial circuit, see Fiona M. Palmer's study of Dragonetti's freelance activities, *Domenico Dragonetti in England (1794–1846): the Career of a Double Bass Virtuoso* (Oxford: Clarendon Press, 1997), 206–21.

[86] Diaries for 1823, 1824 and 1825 (EllaC, MSS 98, 99, 100) and press cuttings (EllaC, MS 81, pp. 84 and 85 [re the Yorkshire Festival, 23–6 September 1823]). See also reminiscences in *RMU* (1866), 30 [York, 1823, Norwich, 1824]; (1868), sup., 1 [York, 1823]; (1870), 8 [Edinburgh].

[87] 1824 diary (EllaC, MS 99).

being Francis Maude, barrister and serious music-lover, who had a country house (Hatfield Hall) near Wakefield and with whom Ella became acquainted on one of these journeys.[88] Then it was back to London, as seasonal activities were set in motion again.

Given the precariousness of being a London musician, and Ella's lack of family connections in the music world, it seems remarkable that within a few years of his arrival he was able to survive so well as a working violinist. Still, if Ella got off to a good start he did so because certain elements of managing a musical career came easily to him. A sense of thrift, self-organization and reliable book-keeping were vital skills which many musicians struggled with but never mastered. Not so for Ella, whose commercial experience and instincts stood him in good stead, and whose neatly kept appointments diary and memoranda from this period demonstrate his control over what he did from the outset.[89] In addition, he was ever shrewd. When a row flared up in the Opera orchestra in summer 1828 over the management's attempt to introduce restrictive working practices, Ella was not one of the many musicians who put their names to statements of protest, preferring instead to keep on the right side of the Opera's management and stay in work.[90] Like many musicians, he entered wealthy households to play and teach – situations in which an ability to learn the social graces of the upper classes and to mingle discreetly and appropriately with one's betters were important assets, always helped along by sharp wits, a good ear for accent and syntax, and a modicum of familiarity with how life was conducted there.[91] Again Ella must have been at an advantage, able to recall the *status quo* at Dalby Hall and adapt quickly to new situations.

---

[88] *RMU* (1866), 30. A (manuscript) biographical sketch of Maude by Ella is in one of Ella's scrapbooks (EllaC, MS 81, p. 63).

[89] On thrift and book-keeping, see *EhrlichMP*, 47. From the outset (1823), Ella kept notes of income, expenditure and current balance (albeit in shorthand) in his diary.

[90] The controversy is documented in Cowgill and Dideriksen, 'Opera Orchestras'. An extended pamphlet, *An Explanation of the Differences Existing Between the Manager of the Italian Opera and the Non-Conforming Members of the Late Orchestra*, part of which was signed by sixteen members of the orchestra who had resigned in protest, was published in 1829, probably sometime after 17 January. Ella and Spagnoletti, both initially associated with the dissenters if a newspaper report of January 1829 is to be believed (*Times*, 23 January 1829), had already returned to their positions for the new season and did not sign the *Explanation*, or an earlier letter of protest to the management (dated 16 December, and reprinted in the *Explanation*). In fact, Ella seems to have largely succeeded in keeping himself at a distance from the dispute. I am grateful to Rachel Cowgill for providing me with this reference to Ella's role in the affair, and for sharing additional information.

[91] See *EhrlichMP*, 31–42.

The musical learning curve was steeper; but Ella was young and eager, and he quickly accumulated experience as player and teacher, picked up orchestral protocols and so on. Within a few years he had not only been exposed to a wide range of repertoire almost certainly unknown to him hitherto, but was also finding ways of compensating for gaps in his own education and training. From the pit at the opera house in the mid-1820s he would have learned through frequent repetition operas such as Rossini's *Il barbiere di Siviglia, Tancredi, La donna del lago, Otello, La gazza ladra, Semiramide,* and Mozart's *Don Giovanni* and *Le nozze di Figaro*. He would have had fair exposure to many others, including works now long forgotten by all but hard-bitten enthusiasts for eighteenth- and early nineteenth-century opera – Zingarelli's *Romeo e Giulietta*, Mayr's *Medea in Corinto* and Meyerbeer's *Il crociato in Egitto* (the first of the composer's operas staged in England; 1825) to name but three – and ballet scores a-plenty.[92] Along the way there were chances to hear the best European singers, for example the *prime donne* Angelica Catalani and Giuditta Pasta, the young Maria Malibran (singing Rosina in Rossini's *Barbiere*) and the extraordinary castrato singer, vestige of a former era, Giovanni Battista Velutti.

Between times, playing for the Philharmonic, Ella would have had memorable encounters with the orchestral repertoire: the symphonies of Beethoven (including the momentous Ninth at its première in 1825) plus quite a few of Haydn's and Mozart's; several overtures, including favourites by Cherubini (e.g. *Les deux journées, Anacréon*) and Weber (*Freischütz, Euryanthe*) as well as Beethoven (*Coriolan, Egmont, Fidelio*) and Mozart (*Zauberflöte, Figaro*); and a miscellany of concertos, often the performer's own compositions, which sometimes meant a sparkling display of pianism by Moscheles or Hummel.[93] Some of these works – especially Beethoven's – would endure in concert programmes for decades to come, as the symphonic repertoire took on a newly found historical dimension and canonic gravitas virtually unknown in previous generations. On Antient Concert nights the offering was usually (though not exclusively) sacred music, for the most part vocal, and always eighteenth-century or earlier – such was the deliberate antiquarianism of this particular institution, which also contributed to

92 This cross-section of works has been reconstructed with reference to Ella's diaries and to primary and secondary accounts of the King's Theatre repertoire, namely Earl of Mount Edgcumbe, *Musical Reminiscences, containing an Account of the Italian Opera in England from 1773 to 1834*, 4th edition (London: John Andrews and F. H. Wall, 1834), Jennifer Lee Hall, 'The Re-fashioning of Fashionable Society: Opera-Going and Sociability in Britain, 1821–1861' (PhD, Yale University, 1996), Appendix E, and Theodore Fenner, *Opera in London: Views of the Press, 1785–1830* (Carbondale and Edwardsville: Southern Illinois University Press, 1994), 297–300.

93 The repertoire is helpfully analysed in *EhrlichFP*, Appendix 1.

the developing idea of a corpus of exemplary masterworks.[94] A cross-section of repertoire would include choruses, recitatives, arias and overtures from a wide range of Handel oratorios, especially *Messiah* and *Israel in Egypt*, extracts from Purcell's anthems and theatre music (for instance *The Tempest*, *Dido and Aeneas*), some Handel coronation anthems, a little of Mozart's sacred music, some Corelli concerti grossi, the odd Morley or Wilbye madrigal, plus soundings from composers such as Marcello, Martini, Croft and Arne.

Meanwhile, Ella availed himself of every opportunity to make chamber music, or so it seems from his appointment diaries, which list quartet party after quartet party, sometimes at his lodgings, sometimes at another's, and usually involving fellow rank-and-file players, though occasionally a more prominent performer of the calibre of Mori, Lindley or Spagnoletti.[95] Fiddlers Antonio Oury and William Watts, players with good if modest credentials, were the most regular companions, and as far as we can tell the function of these occasions was usually one of social and musical pleasure – of trying and learning repertoire, perhaps with an eye to getting paid work at the chamber music parties that came up in the houses of wealthy amateurs, and which Ella occasionally participated in. Playing chamber music was almost every string player's cherished leisure pursuit, one that strengthened friendship, professional bonds and status simultaneously. A letter to Ella from the eminent pianist Ignaz Moscheles, dating from this period, sets the tone: 'Sir[,] I shall be happy if you will join us to-morrow evening about 8 o'clock to try Pixis Quintetto [for piano and strings]; we shall be quite entre nous and you will find an instrument here.'[96] Mostly, Ella's diary does not reveal what was played on similar occasions; one imagines a fair amount of Haydn, Mozart and early Beethoven was involved.[97] What is certain, though, is that it helped instil in Ella a familiarity with, and an affinity for, the 'music of friends' that would last a lifetime.

Ella also attempted to extend his musical education, seeking tuition on the piano and double bass on the one hand, and in harmony, counterpoint and composition on the other. He apparently took keyboard lessons with Thomas Haydon, London organist and all-round musician, in 1823; and it was with Haydon that he

---

[94] Arguably the earliest example of canon formation in England. For this thesis, see William Weber, *The Rise of Musical Classics in Eighteenth-Century England: a Study in Canon, Ritual, and Ideology* (Oxford: Clarendon Press, 1992).

[95] *BashfordPCC*, 78–82.

[96] EllaC, MS 81, p. 1.

[97] Only two works are named: a quartet by Romberg in F and two quartets by Onslow (diary, 14 March 1825; EllaC, MS 100).

first encountered Bach's preludes and fugues.[98] But for the remainder of this supplementary tuition Ella turned initially to the brand new Royal Academy of Music,
a talking point in musical circles, which opened its doors in March 1823 with the
intention of producing a new generation of skilled British musicians who could
compete more effectively with those trained abroad.[99] Organized by a group of
aristocrats with musical enthusiasms and patriotic agendas but no experience or
understanding of pedagogy, and using funds raised from public subscription and
student fee income (there was little hope of government subvention), the new school
was, from the outset, doomed to a life of poverty and academic mediocrity, at odds
with its grandiose image and royal patronage.[100] The mostly British-trained teaching staff was generally good rather than universally top-rank, and through most of
the nineteenth century the institution would do little to ameliorate the problems
that flowed from the nation's lack of a high-quality training ground for its musicians. Student numbers were small and entrants young (usually between ten and
fourteen years old – this was long before conservatoires offered a practical alternative to university degrees), their admission governed far more by their ability to
pay the fees than by the identification of real aptitude and potential talent. Few
'achieved much distinction'.[101] In the 1820s, these problems had yet to become fully
evident, although financial issues were already beginning to loom. So, with the
Academy actively advertising for more advanced students ('Persons of very Superior and distinguished Talents') in 1825, and few alternatives available, there was
every reason why Ella should seek tuition there, despite being older than most of the
students.[102]

[98] According to Ravell, 'John Ella', 95. I have been unable to trace the source of this
information.

[99] On the complex agendas behind the foundation of the RAM, see Leanne Langley,
'Sainsbury's *Dictionary*, the Royal Academy of Music, and the Rhetoric of Patriotism', *MBC*, 65–97. For details on the staff, curriculum and other related matters in
the period up to 1850, see *RohrCBM*, 79–85.

[100] The best analysis of the Academy's shortcomings as a training school remains
EhrlichMP, 79–88.

[101] *EhrlichMP*, 79. Ehrlich also points out that between 1823 and 1866, 1,300 students
passed through its doors (approximately thirty per year on average), representing
perhaps only 7 per cent of the national population of working musicians.
    Problems with advanced music education in Britain persisted for decades:
see David Wright, 'The South Kensington Music Schools and the Development
of the British Conservatoire in the Late Nineteenth Century', *JRMA*, 130 (2005),
236–82.

[102] Royal Academy of Music Committee Minute Book no. 1 (in RAMa), p. 158 (minute
dated 29 October 1825). The decision to advertise in the press is noted on p. 154
(minute of 10 October 1825).

Having already offered his 'gratuitous services […] to look over the practice of the Boys', Ella was admitted on 16 November 1825 and placed with the composer and organist Thomas Attwood (a respected teacher and pupil of Mozart), from whom he took lessons in harmony for a short while.[103] Before long, too, Ella was picking up payment for his 'assistance in the [Academy] Orchestra', both on the violin and double bass, and enjoying the designation 'sub-professor', a reflection of unpaid work he was doing with the younger pupils.[104] It may well have been through the Academy that Ella first encountered William Crotch, the institution's first Principal, who was well known as a lecturer at the Royal Institution and other learned societies: in 1825 Ella was turning pages for him at a lecture on Haydn's *Creation*, which Crotch was illustrating from the keyboard.[105] Lowly the task may have been (possibly unpaid too), but doing jobs like this well was part of the self-promotion and building of contacts that an aspiring musician had to undertake.

[103] Ella's offer of his services to the Academy is noted in the Committee Minute Book no. 1, p. 133 (minute dated 12 July 1825). His registration is noted in the Candidates Foundation Register, f. 22 (recommended by Lord Burghersh), also in RAMa, and confirmed by his diary entry for the same day (16 November 1825: EllaC, MS 100). His first lesson with Attwood is also noted (diary, 21 November 1825). How long the lessons continued is not clear. The Foundation Register does not indicate when Ella left, or why; his association with the institution continued until at least 1828.

[104] The Committee Minute Book, p. 174 (minute dated 1 June 1826), indicates that Ella was to receive payment. The orchestral lists in programmes for the Royal Academic Concerts, 1826, also held in RAMa, further indicate that Ella (a violinist) was both sub-professor and student. This accords with Ella's later statement that he had been 'sub-professor, inspector of practice, and student in harmony, under Attwood' at the Academy (*EllaMS1*, 316), and with J. R. Sterndale Bennett's account of his father's first day as a pupil in March 1826: 'John Ella … was giving lessons that day as a sub-professor' (J. R. Sterndale Bennett, *The Life of William Sterndale Bennett* (Cambridge: Cambridge University Press, 1907), p. 15). *EhrlichMP* notes that sub-professors were 'barely trained pupil-teachers who received no payment'[,] and 'were widely employed' (p. 81; citing Frederick Corder, *A History of the Royal Academy of Music from 1822 to 1922* (London: F. Corder, 1922), p. 63: a discussion of the 1840s and 50s). On at least one occasion Ella played double bass, not violin, in the RAM orchestra; see Corder, *History*, 33.

[105] *RMU* (1875), 20 [Ella's reminiscence].

🎵 *New horizons*

*[F]or five francs, in 1827, I received instruction in Paris, such as
I could not obtain, at any price, in London, viz., in counterpoint,
composition, and instrumentation*   ∾ *RMU* (1872), sup.

O NE of the subjects not on the curriculum at the Royal Academy of Music in
its early decades was counterpoint.[106] We may assume that Ella, now versed
in Attwood's harmony, was aware of this lacuna, and alive to the importance of
seizing any opportunity for extending his range of skills and receiving expert tuition. In autumn 1827, in Paris, he commenced a series of lessons in counterpoint,
instrumentation and composition with François-Joseph Fétis, professor of counterpoint at the Conservatoire – an investment in training that would pay dividends
later in his career.[107] How and why Ella came to be in the French capital (he seems
to have stayed until early 1828)[108] is a story in itself, almost certainly linked to his
emerging ability to advance his career in diverse directions. Once more we must
read between the lines of the surviving evidence; and although there may have
been more than one motivating factor, the circumstances were probably linked to
the following episode.

It so happened that the enthusiastic amateur Lord Saltoun had lighted on Ella
as someone suitable to organize private music-making at that nobleman's London
home in Albemarle Street, off Piccadilly.[109] Through this channel Ella became
connected with Saltoun's network of like-minded friends, and by 1826 the musical activities he was supervising for them had crystallized into what Ella termed
'the Saltoun Club',[110] a group of amateur instrumentalists and singers who came
together regularly under Ella's musical direction to perform extracts from (mostly)
European operas specially adapted for domestic forces by Ella, who was able
to draw usefully on his new-found familiarity with the repertoire at the King's
Theatre, and (one imagines) on contacts and resources from this world.

---

[106] *RohrCBM*, 82.

[107] *RMU* (1871), sup., p. i. Fétis was also librarian at the Conservatoire, 1826–31.

[108] This is suggested by the fact that he later produced a medley of operatic numbers,
arranged for chorus and small band, entitled *Souvenir de Paris 1828* (it was played
at a concert organized in 1831). It is further confirmed by remarks by Ella in *MW*
(5 January 1838), 2. The 1828 diary is not extant.

[109] The Saltoun Club's origins are recounted by Ella in 'La Società Lirica. Belgravia,
1870', *RMU* (1870), sup, pp. i–iv.

[110] The term is used in his 1844 diary (EllaC, MS 113; e.g. entries for 13 and 20 May).
Fuller Maitland used the phrase 'Saltoun Club of Instrumentalists' in his *DNB*
article.

The Saltoun amateurs were from the sphere of wealth and fashion that attended the Italian Opera, so this was absolutely their type of music. They were also the sort of people who saw participation in music-making as an important and mean-ingful leisure pursuit. While many frequenters of the King's Theatre may well have used opera-going as little more than a means of demonstrating or gaining social status, of participating in subtle forms of sociability, and of acquiring their 'cultural capital' relatively passively, others of them – including the group around Saltoun – were strongly committed to music *per se* and invested not just time but also effort in its cultivation.[111] Among them were men such as Colonel Sir Henry Torrens (1779–1828), who played the flute; the Scots baronet Sir George Clerk (1787–1867), Member of Parliament with a government position in the Admiralty, who was in the viola section; Hon. General Arthur Upton (1807–83) of the Coldstream Guards, one of the violins; and the musical amateur Philip J. Salomons (1797–1866), one of Dragonetti's pupils and a second cousin of the Jewish banker David Salomons, on the double bass. Their women participated by singing in the chorus, or in the case of Miss Cornewall – probably Anna-Maria Cornewall, spinster sister of Sir George Cornewall, Bt (1774–1835) – playing the piano, these being the socially acceptable modes of music-making for females. A handful of professional orchestral play-ers, some choristers from the opera house, and student singers for solo vocal work, were hired in by Ella to ensure an acceptable performance standard was achieved: Dragonetti, Lindley, Charles Weichsel (violin) and Charles Nicholson (flute) appear in the one surviving band list of the period.[112] Typically, overtures and symphonies were played by the little orchestra before dinner; afterwards a selection of opera numbers was given *tutti*. It was a significant first opportunity for Ella to organize performances and 'fix' calibre players, and it gave him valuable experience for future projects, not to mention a strong taste of what it meant to cross social boundaries. In the meantime, the parties became a frequent, talked-about feature of the Saltoun calendar, lasting until the mid-1840s. In the 1830s William Gardiner recounted hearing 'parts of the new operas cleverly arranged for his lordship's parties by Mr. Ella', and remarked on the cleverness of Ella's mode of deepening amateurs' appreciation, curiously foreshadowing things to come: '[i]t is like reading the play before you go to see it; you enter more into the minutiae of the composition, which is apt to escape you in the representation'.[113] As for the spe-cifics of repertoire, we may assume that much of it was drawn from Italian operas

---

[111] On the social functions of opera-going in this period, see Hall, 'The Re-fashioning of Fashionable Society'.

[112] A conflated list of orchestral players is given in 'La Società Lirica', p. ii.

[113] Gardiner, *Music and Friends* (1838), 692–3. The episode probably dated from the 1830s. Gardiner lists other aristocratic participants.

in current or recent production at the King's Theatre.[114] But as we shall see in the next chapter, some of the items were almost certainly drawn from Continental operas as yet unheard in full in London.

How the Saltoun activities brought about a connection with Paris and a new direction for Ella's education is best explained in Ella's own words. They are from his obituary of Saltoun in 1854:

> If there be one event in my life which has especially influenced my studies, and brought me into contact with the aristocratic musical families of England, it was the unlimited confidence which this nobleman placed in my judgment in the engagement of artists and preparing music for his private amusement. I had *carte blanche* to translate, and adapt for a chamber band (*Otetto*) and chorus, selections from the best German, English, French, and Italian operas. This occupation obliged me frequently to visit the continent to consult scores, which, to the discredit of this nation, are not found in any of our public musical libraries.[115]

From evidence scattered in Ella's later published writings, we know he felt frustrated for much of his life by the lack of a substantial collection of music (in particular scores) in London that could be consulted freely and easily.[116] Admittedly, there were improvements in London library provision during the century, as the article 'Musical Libraries' in the first edition of George Grove's *Dictionary of Music and Musicians* (1879–89) indicates, not least through the amassing of performance material by concert institutions, the Sacred Harmonic Society and the Philharmonic Society in particular.[117] But around the time Ella was arranging Saltoun's parties a well-resourced library did not exist. At the British Museum, where readers' tickets were issued only to scholars and students, and always with considerable palaver, the holdings of music were meagre enough to cause Vincent Novello, the distinguished organist, editor and publisher (father of J. Alfred, who founded

---

[114] According to a report of one such event in *MP* (2 March 1829), selections were typically taken from the operas of Mozart, Rossini and Weber, with excerpts from the ballet *La somnambule* being performed only days after its introduction at the King's Theatre.

[115] *RMU* (1854), 4. A copy of this obituary, annotated by Ella, and other Saltoun memorabilia, are in EllaC, MS 81, p. 2.

[116] As stated in his manifestos, years later, for a Musical Union Library; printed on the back covers of *RMU* for 1849 and 1850.

[117] The *Dictionary* was initially issued in fascicles, like a periodical. The section containing this article first appeared in April 1880; see Leanne Langley, 'Roots of a Tradition: the First *Dictionary of Music and Musicians*', GGMVC, 168–215, esp. table 8.1.

the publishing house), to write to Parliament in 1824, campaigning for improvements.[118] Gifts were the backbone of its collection, and no European music had ever been purchased: 'the works of Bach, Beethoven, Mozart and Rossini were scarcely represented'.[119] Meanwhile, as Ella had doubtless seen for himself, the Royal Academy of Music's collection was effectively a private resource for teaching purposes, and at an embryonic stage in its formation, the collection-building policy (as enshrined in the original rules and regulations of the Academy) based on self-support. Professors were expected to donate any published compositions at the time of publication.[120] Only in 1827 was it deemed necessary to appoint a librarian to take 'charge of the Books'.[121] The Conservatoire in Paris, by comparison, offered public access to a rich store of curated treasures, with which Ella later claimed familiarity ('upwards of twelve thousand volumes!'),[122] and there is little doubt, since this seems to have been the sole European city he visited in the 1820s and 30s, that this was where he did most of his studying and copying of opera scores for Saltoun's parties, perhaps purchasing a few vocal scores of contemporary works about town too.[123]

Whether Saltoun suggested or helped finance at least the first visit (a second followed – again, out of season – in 1829), or whether the initial venture was made on Ella's own initiative, is unknown. The diaries for 1827 and 1828 have not survived, while that for 1829 is kept cursorily as an appointments book. Yet, given

---

[118] Philip John Weimerskirch, *Antonio Panizzi and the British Museum Library*, The 1981 AB Bookman's Yearbook (Clifton, NJ: Bookman's Weekly, 1982), 101. The letter, quoted in full in Alec Hyatt King, 'The Music Room of the British Museum, 1753–1953: its History and Organization', *Proceedings of the Royal Musical Association*, 79 (1952–3), 65–79, argued for the appointment of a music librarian.

[119] Weimerskirch, *Antonio Panizzi*, 101.

[120] W. W. Cazalet, *The History of the Royal Academy of Music, Compiled from Authentic Sources* (London: T. Bosworth, 1854), 346 [article 12].

[121] Committee Minute Book (RAMa), p. 235 (minute for 6 December 1827).

[122] 'Musical Union Library', *RMU* (1849), back cover.

[123] The Conservatoire library's music holding was impressive. In the late 1820s it included older Italian operas, accessioned during the Napoleonic era. Although royal assent for 'legal deposit' of printed music was not granted until 1834, the right was petitioned for as early as 1816 by the then librarian Nicolas Roze, suggesting an active desire to collect new music. See Cathérine Massip, 'La Bibliothèque du Conservatoire (1795–1819): une utopie réalisée?', *Le Conservatoire de Paris, 1795–1995: des Menus-Plaisirs à la Cité de la musique* (Paris: Buchet/Chastel, 1996), 117–31. For this reference I am grateful to Dominique Hausfater, formerly of the Bibliothèque Nationale, where the Conservatoire collection is now housed. Some Paris editions (vocal scores etc.) of early nineteenth-century operas are listed in Ella's catalogue of his private music library, which was built up over his life (EllaC, MS 54).

what we know of Ella's character and drive as they emerge later on, it seems probable that he planned, and invested in, the expedition himself. For it is hard to understand why, if Saltoun did subsidize the trips, Ella never vaunted the gesture as an unusually generous example of aristocratic patronage in Britain, particularly in his obituary of the nobleman. Besides, it is easy to imagine Ella setting out in search of both composition lessons and opera scores, encouraged by information from fellow musicians in London who knew Paris and what it could offer.[124] Alternatively, perhaps he journeyed with the main intention of finding tuition, and chanced upon the resources at the Conservatoire, quickly setting about some transcription for the opera club back home.[125] Or vice versa. It matters little. What is significant is how Ella made the most of the situation: it was to be to his double advantage that Fétis not only taught counterpoint at the Conservatoire but held the post of librarian there too.

ALTHOUGH we can only imagine what Ella's first experience of foreign travel and French culture was like, it surely stretched his horizons in yet more directions, with much striking him as different or 'Other'. The French monarchy had been restored, but Paris was still understood as the birthplace of revolution: bloodshed and the Napoleonic régime were in the urban memory, and the country's entrance controls were strict.[126] Catholicism was widely observed. Social customs, from eating to greeting, were bound to surprise; and even if we

---

[124] One such informant might have been Frenchman N. C. Bochsa, a harp professor and vital administrative force behind the Academy in its early days (see Langley, 'Sainsbury's *Dictionary*'), who knew the Conservatoire well and with whom Ella was acquainted at this period, to judge from his diary for 1826 (9 February and preliminary pages; EllaC, MS 101), which indicates that he spent the evening with Bochsa on the day the latter was suspended from the Academy on grounds of moral scandal (for detail, see Langley, p. 89, n. 80). Later, however, Ella chose to distance himself from the association: see his accounts of Bochsa's appointment and ultimate resignation in *RMU* (1872), sup., p. vi and (1875), 28, and *EllaMS1*, 315–18.

[125] In a serialized account of his Paris visits published later in *CJ* (1836), Ella hinted that his object had been to find lessons, and made no mention of the library work. We should note, however, that it fitted his purposes to place his story's emphasis on studying in Paris.

[126] Britain had only recently repealed its own temporary laws regarding powers to deport suspicious aliens: see Andreas Fahrmeir, *Citizens and Aliens: Foreigners and the Law in Britain and the German States, 1789–1870* (New York and Oxford: Berghahn Books, 2000), 102–3. The legislation, passed in wartime (1793), was nevertheless out of character for Britain, which went on to welcome foreigners throughout the nineteenth century.

assume Ella had a reasonable command of written French, communication in the course of daily life must have been a challenge. As a city, Paris was smaller than London, not only in terms of population (more than 700,000 in 1821, compared with the 1.3 million in the British capital) but also physical size and layout – urban expansion, and the wide and elegant boulevards of Baron Hausmann, were still to come. Nevertheless there was much to explore in the urban geography, whether the narrow streets and alleys in the old city, the landscaped areas laid down in the seventeenth century to mark *La gloire de la France* (the Tuileries gardens and the Palais du Louvre), or the ongoing building in a 'forest glade' of the Arc de Triomphe and surrounding area, one of the more obvious Napoleonic legacies.[127] While as yet there was little evidence of the impact of the Industrial Revolution on the French capital, there were signs of growing commercial life – including covered arcades of shops to protect the fashionable world from the perils of street life, and newly built counting houses. Moreover, more than a decade on from the end of the wars with Britain, Paris appeared to be flourishing culturally; and, as we shall see, it was in this sphere that the biggest and longest-lasting impressions on Ella were to be made. London may have been an eye-opener after Leicester, but this was something else.

Musically, much was happening and standards seemed high. A school for church musicians, the Institut de Musique Religieuse Classique, headed by Alexandre Choron, had opened in 1817. The Conservatoire had been restructured, and Luigi Cherubini was now its director; students were admitted on the basis of their quality, and provided with free tuition. A new house had been built in the Rue Le Peletier (1821) for the national opera company, the Opéra, one of Paris's three main institutions for opera (the others being the Opéra-Comique and the Théâtre-Italien). And concert life was starting to flower: F.-A. Habeneck, for example, was about to found his Société des Concerts du Conservatoire (1828), a series of orchestral performances that would do much to establish Beethoven in France.[128] Of course, all was relative; and there may indeed have been grumbles and dissatisfaction locally with the amount of financial support forthcoming for the arts

---

[127] My description of the social and political backdrop to Paris follows the depiction in Alistair Horne, *Seven Ages of Paris: Portrait of a City* (Basingstoke and Oxford: Pan Macmillan, 2003), 241–52; the phrase 'forest glade' is from p. 244.

[128] The descriptions of musical life here lean on 'Paris, VI: 1789–1870' (by David Charlton *et al.*) and 'Conservatoires, III: 1790–1945' (section by Cynthia M. Gessele) in *NGDM2*, and on Ralph P. Locke, 'Paris: Centre of Intellectual Ferment', *The Early Romantic Era: Between Revolutions: 1789 and 1848*, ed. Alexander Ringer (Basingstoke and London: Macmillan Press, 1990), 32–83. For a history of Habeneck's concerts, see D. Kern Holoman, *The Société des Concerts du Conservatoire, 1828–1967* (Berkeley and Los Angeles: University of California Press, 2004).

from the French government. But to British-born Ella the existence of state money to institutionalize musical activity and training must have seemed nothing short of astonishing, the resultant high standards of performance proof of its efficacy. Meanwhile, his exposure to the city's public performances and private 'salon' culture revealed still more about the quality of music-making, and how the art itself seemed to be regarded and valued by the French.

Ella was not the only London musician in Paris at the time, and on his visit of 1827–8 – possibly also in 1829 – he consorted with two Irishmen, Michael Balfe, who was there pursuing a career as a singer, and George Osborne, who was studying the piano with J. P. Pixis and harmony and counterpoint with Fétis.[129] They were roughly the same age as Ella; as was Oury, who happened to be in Paris for violin lessons and who completed what seems to have been an expatriate gaggle. We know of Oury's presence because a few years later Ella wrote up his French experiences in a serialized column for the *Court Journal*, entitled 'Musical Recollections of a Winter in Paris'.[130] The narrative unfolds in the first person, anonymously, and Ella is introduced as one of the four friends, whose experiences the 'author' shared, the account seemingly conflating the events of 1827, which included his first meeting with Fétis – a 'heavy, scowling-looking personage', the eminent 'editor of *La revue musicale*, and one of the most erudite musicians in Europe'[131] – with those of 1829, when he came across Vincent Novello and his wife.[132] The Novellos had brought their young daughter Clara, already an emerging singer of considerable talent, to audition for a place at Choron's institution. What emerges from this account, and from other snippets that Ella recounted later in life, is a strong sense of what struck him as different from, and typically better than, how things were done in London. One can detect how much he was bowled over by aspects of French musical culture and why he came to admire several of the people he met there.

The number of lessons Ella received from Fétis is not recorded, but the programme of study was probably intensive, since Ella would later remark that Fétis considered a three-month course of practical harmony adequate for 'a youth

---

[129] *RMU* (1871), sup., p. i. Studying abroad was highly desirable (though not cheap to undertake) and some instrumentalists managed to do so; see *RohrCBM*, 71–2.

[130] (23 January 1836), 51; (6 February 1836), 83–4; (20 February 1836), 115–16; (12 March 1836), 165; (2 April 1836), 211. Ella's authorship of the column is confirmed by the preservation of some of the published articles in one of his scrapbooks (EllaC, MS 81, p. 17), and by information in his 1836 diary (EllaC, MS 106): see 8, 9 and 23 January, 15 February, 12 and 14 March. (In one entry – 9 January – Ella describes it as a 'sketch of Paris in 1830', but this seems to have been an error of memory.)

[131] *CJ* (6 February 1836), 84.

[132] *CJ* (20 February 1836), 115.

favorably [*sic*] organized', and daily instruction highly desirable.[133] Moreover, in comparison with London, and even allowing for differences in the cost of living, tuition seemed remarkably cheap.[134] Ella studied privately, not through the Conservatoire (at the time, the institution did not enrol foreigners), but he nonetheless gained a fair awareness of its activities.[135] The curriculum aimed to provide an all-round musical education for students, and Ella explained in the *Court Journal* that he was 'forcibly struck' by the combination of practical ability and theoretical awareness that French-trained musicians demonstrated, there seeming to be none of that division between English professors, so many of whom were deemed 'either […] unimaginative theorists, or […] ignorant practical players'.[136] Besides which, instruction was driven by a national desire to produce young musicians of excellence, and the very best composers and performers were hired to teach them, coming from Germany and Italy where necessary to ensure these goals were met. Ella heard the quality for himself at the Concours du Conservatoire, an annual competition to identify the best student of each instrument on the curriculum, held in public and before a jury. Cherubini, Reicha, Fétis, Boieldieu, Hérold, Catel, Onslow and Rossini, an 'extraordinary *réunion* of men of learning and genius', comprised the panel for the violin contest in 1829, and were notably all-round musicians, not string specialists.[137] The test piece, a Viotti concerto, was played '*à la perfection*' by the twelve candidates; and each pupil was then, to Ella's amazement, 'led in by a professor[;] a book was opened at hazard, and the talent of the candidate soon put to the critical trial, by playing two pages of a composition at sight!', and before an audience.[138] No greater test to distinguish the true musician from the mere mechanical imitator could, Ella ruminated, be invented. He also invoked Fétis's counsel that without an understanding of harmony a student was rarely able to sight-read music fluently, noting with pleasure that the two best

---

[133] *RMU* (1849), 20. *CJ* (23 January 1836, p. 51) maintained that 'Ella had the entire sum for his lessons in counterpoint remitted to him, with a compliment to his industry'.

[134] 4s 2d per lesson, compared with 10s 6d in London: *RMU* (1865), sup., 28.

[135] I am indebted to Dominique Hausfater for this information, and for checking that Ella's name does not appear in Constant Pierre's *Le Conservatoire national de musique et de déclamation: documents historiques et administratifs* (Paris: Imprimerie Nationale, 1900), a listing of all the students, teachers and staff from 1795 to 1900.

[136] *CJ* (12 March 1836), 165.

[137] *CJ* (20 February 1836), 115.

[138] Ibid. Years later Ella remembered the test piece as a Rode concerto: *RMU* (1872), sup., p. vi.

sight-readers were judged prizewinners. Such an exhibition of student skill and training was largely unimaginable at the Royal Academy of Music.[139]

In his articles Ella further suggests that he spent much time listening to student exercises and performances at Choron's academy, and attending the three principal opera houses, thus gaining further exposure to music – some of it new to Ella's ears – and to local styles and standards of singing and playing.[140] We have little indication of what Ella heard, but can make intelligent guesses on the basis of what was in repertoire at the time, and of the works that Ella would champion once returned to England. Significantly, the Opéra and Opéra-Comique would have offered many works that had yet to reach London to any meaningful degree. French grand opera by Auber and Rossini, and *opéras-comiques* by such composers as Boieldieu, Kreutzer and Méhul were the staple of these companies' diets. At the Opéra in particular, adventurous scenery and costuming showed just what could be achieved through seriously handled stagecraft, so germane to French grand opera. We may assume that Ella, with the Saltoun Club's activities in the back of his mind, did his utmost to obtain scores.

Ella marvelled too at the central and lively role that private salons played in sustaining Parisian musical life, and he wrote fluently of his experiences at some of them, including those held by the pianist-composer Frédéric Kalkbrenner, *chez* the music publisher Maurice Schlesinger, at Fétis's house, and at Rossini's.[141] These were excellent occasions to meet and connect with Paris's active and influential musicians, and it was here, to Ella's delight, that he gained introductions to the likes of Georges Onslow, prolific composer of chamber music, the sensational young pianist Camille Moke (later to become Madame Pleyel), Jean-Joseph Vidal, an able violinist, and the cellist Nicolas Baudiot. Very probably the forging of links seemed easier here than in London. There were also opportunities to listen to first-rate performers at close range – Maria Malibran and Adolphe Nourrit were among the singers Ella heard at Kalkbrenner's – and to witness more new 'good' music, especially Austro-German chamber repertoire.[142] The parties at Schlesinger's gave Ella what was surely his first exposure to the extraordinary late quartets of the 'great man' Beethoven, another formative experience.[143] (He may also have attended the celebrated quartet concerts of Pierre Baillot, remembered from his

[139] *CJ* (20 February 1836), 115–16.

[140] *CJ* (23 January 1836), 51. On Italian opera singers, see *CJ* (2 April 1836), 211.

[141] *CJ* (23 January 1836), 51; (6 February 1836), 83–4; (12 March 1836), 165; and (2 April 1836), 211. Paris musical salons had none of the negative aesthetic and domestic connotations that would later attach to the term 'salon music'.

[142] At Kalkbrenner's he heard Onslow's G minor quintet: *CJ* (6 February 1836), 84.

[143] *CJ* (23 January 1836), 51.

Leicester youth: he would later recall the 1827 trip in terms of 'the famed quartet party of Baillot […] the rendezvous of all true disciples of the classical art'.)[144]

For all this, the French salon offered something extra – a forum for informed discussion and serious debate about music and the arts. Evenings at Fétis's were 'conducted with much sound reasoning, philosophical observation, and good temper', his teacher arguing virtuosically for the genius of both Handel and Beethoven.[145] Kalkbrenner's weekly soirées similarly impressed for the selectivity of the assembly, and once more for the sheer unusualness of what they offered. '[C]rowded to excess, as usual in Paris', they drew together 'families of title and men of talent', wrote Ella. 'It was here that I saw verified the truth of those sketches of Parisian society which appear so unlike what we witness in England.'[146] Also dawning on Ella was the realization of just how much the music of Beethoven was revered in these circles. The imprint of these experiences would be seen in his activities and initiatives years later in London.

The teaching and ideas of Fétis would also stay with Ella – not just the Belgian's ways of analysing harmony, understanding counterpoint and appreciating orchestration, but his general outlook on music, namely the value of education, the importance of training musicians well, the role of the national conservatoire, and the desirability of cultivating amateur taste. Like many students who encounter an influential teacher at a formative career stage, Ella developed a special allegiance to Fétis's thinking and strong bonds of loyalty, respect and quasi-kinship to the person.[147] Indeed, it may not be stretching the imagination too far to suggest that Fétis served as his role model. Fétis (like Ella) patched together a successful freelance living from various sources; he had a good deal of influence in Paris (just as Ella eventually would know in London); he was something of a *littéraire* (Ella would soon try his hand at journalism); he possessed a natural bent for books and facts (which Ella would later develop); and he was above all (at least to Ella in the 1820s) the epitome of a serious-minded musician and man of strong opinions.[148]

In the meantime, Ella's emerging awareness of the limitations and weaknesses of the quality of music-making in London was sharpened by Fétis's visit to England in spring 1829, and by the publication of a series of letters that he wrote

---

[144] *EllaMS1*, 284.

[145] *CJ* (12 March 1836), 165.

[146] *CJ* (6 February 1836), 83.

[147] A handful of letters from Ella to Fétis (published in *WangerméeF*) bear witness to Ella's affection for his master. His obituary of Fétis, for *RMU* (1871), sup., p. i, gives further indication of their relationship.

[148] For more on Fétis, see the article by Katharine Ellis in *NGDM2*.

on the state of music there in the *Revue musicale*; Fétis was the journal's editor.[149] Famously picked up, translated and published soon after in the *Harmonicon* (a monthly music journal edited by William Ayrton, a skilful administrator and behind-the-scenes figure in London musical life), the letters were a frank, sometimes bemused and chauvinistic, and often acidic account of what Fétis experienced, all judged against the standards and practices he knew from the Continent.[150] There was scrutiny of the Philharmonic Society orchestra, the culture of the Melodists' Club (a men's glee club), the Royal Academy of Music and its teaching staff, a benefit concert for the Sons of the Clergy at St Paul's Cathedral (at which he sat next to Mendelssohn, also on a first visit to England) and the Italian Opera, and much reflection on the native creative tradition. A few things and people came out well: the provincial music festivals and the mass-singing tradition, the vitality of madrigal composition in the sixteenth century, a few of the professors at the Academy, and Dragonetti's remarkable double bass playing in the Philharmonic orchestra. Fétis also displayed acute curiosity for the goings-on at the Welsh Eisteddfod. But there was much to be lamented and puzzled at, including the lack of counterpoint teaching that had driven Ella to Paris, the difficult 'industrial relations' at the opera house, the absence of (what was to him) good church music (he was confounded by the appeal of Purcell's Te Deum and Jubilate) and of nuanced and disciplined orchestral playing. Most significantly, in terms of the arguments and activities Ella would later carry on, Fétis diagnosed these cultural deficiencies as emanating from Britain's unique social and economic conditions: from the government's unwillingness adequately to support the Royal Academy of Music to train up the best national talent; from the compromises that were inevitable in a system where economic concerns led artistic ones; and from the British aristocracy, whose superficial engagement with music and the arts he believed did a great deal of damage. (We may assume Fétis, arriving from a country whose national conservatoire had been grounded in revolutionary ideals, was well aware of the embedded class system in Britain. These were days before even the Reform Bill of 1832.)

Much has been made of the fact that Ayrton crossed swords with Fétis by publishing gritty ripostes to the Belgian's letters in defence of British music and its

---

[149] The letters appeared in both periodicals in 1829. They are summarized and discussed in Vincent Duckles, 'A French Critic's View on the State of Music in London (1829)', *Modern Musical Scholarship*, ed. Edward Olleson (Stocksfield: Oriel Press, 1980), 223–37. A letter from Fétis to Ella, dated 15 February 1828 [*recte* 1829], indicates that Fétis made contact with Ella during his trip (EllaC, MS 81, p. 3).

[150] Duckles, 'A French Critic's View', 237, gives bibliographic details of the material published in the *Harmonicon*. For a rounded picture of Ayrton's contribution to London musical life, see the article on him by Leanne Langley in *NGDM2*.

institutions.[151] What seems more significant here, especially since Ella was still to return to Paris for more lessons with Fétis and knew of the correspondence, is that these observations by his teacher, allied to his own youthful impressionability and affinity for aspects of French musical life, seem to have taken root in Ella's belief system. In the short term he would speak more through words than actions, and always with discretion. His criticism of the shortcomings of the Royal Academy of Music in the *Court Journal* was done at one remove, so that, coming out of the Concours du Conservatoire in 1829, and reeling at the quality of what they had heard, Ella, Oury and the fictional author are 'tapped on the back by Monsieur T., saying, "Ah! ah! Messieurs, you do not manage these things quite so well at your Academy in London, *avec vos Seigneurs!*" To this we made no reply.'[152] It would be years before Ella had the confidence to speak out bluntly on this issue. Yet it seems he was already seeing the grass as greener on the other side of the Channel, since he had now had many experiences of music there, and was developing an awareness of the contrasting infrastructures that supported the arts in the two cities.

[151] Duckles, 'A French Critic's View'. Ella's memories of Fétis's visit to England appear frequently in *RMU*: see esp. *RMU* (1871), sup., p. i [Fétis obituary] and (1876), 16, sup., 38.

[152] *CJ* (20 February 1836), 115.

CHAPTER 2

Successes, Frustrations, Ambitions, 1828–44

To trace John Ella's life from his mid-twenties into his early forties is to witness a career develop and a young man change: from a junior, pretty anonymous orchestral player into a musician active at the centre of things, with a stake and say in many activities, and ambitions and visions for serious music-making. As the years elapsed Ella consolidated his playing and teaching, and increased his circle of amateur patrons. He added to his portfolio of activities, seeking out new openings and learning how to handle risk. And while gaining professional experience, he developed firm views on the music and performers around him, and on how London's musical institutions were run. For Ella was, as much through force of character as through family background, an ambitious individual, determined to better himself financially and socially and to make some sort of mark in his chosen *métier*. Such aspirations were not unusual among young men of his class and occupation, but what separated Ella from many of his peers were his remarkable ability to sniff out and grasp opportunities, his realistic grasp of commercial matters, and his readiness to avoid or abandon projects that looked incapable of delivering adequate benefits.

Ella's metamorphosis was not just a matter of youthful ambition: the times, which were nothing if not auspicious, played their part. Musical life was expanding, as the number of musicians offering their goods and services in the metropolis increased, along with the size and intensity of 'consumer' demand – much of it driven by a culturally aspirant and increasingly leisured, wealthy middle class – for enjoyable and 'improving' musical wares. This point is well demonstrated by the striking number of London concert institutions, the many 'Mushroom Musical Societies' (Ella's words),[1] that were begun during the 1830s: organizations such as the Società Armonica (1830), the Sacred Harmonic Society (1832), the Choral Harmonists (1833), the Society of British Musicians (1834), and several concert series promoting chamber music (from 1835). There was also considerable growth in the provision of instruments and music lessons, as well as in the publishing and selling of not just music, but words about it too. It is no coincidence that this period saw ever more growth in music journalism, both in general newspapers and the emerging specialist music press. The *Musical World* and *Musical Times*, two long-lived journals founded in 1836 and 1844 and nowadays much used as sources of information and contemporary opinion,

---

[1] Diary, 18 March 1836 (EllaC, MS 106).

are symbolic of the energizing spirit of this era. Riper circumstances for Ella to branch out his activities and sharpen his musical identity could scarcely be imagined.

❧ *Enterprise and advancement*

Mr. Ella's Morning Concert, on Tuesday next, the 19th inst., at 46, Great Marlborough-street, to commence at Two o'Clock. A Selection from Marschner's Grand Romantic Opera, "Der Templer," adapted to the Italian by Mr. Ella, will be sung for the first time in this country by Mad. Stockhausen, Miss Childe, Messrs. Braham, Bennett, and Seguin. Mr. Phillips and other eminent Artists have also promised their kind assistance. Tickets, 10s. 6d. each, to be had of Lonsdale and Mills, 140, New Bond-street.   ∾ MP (16 July 1831)

Most professional musicians in the London market-place understood the importance of exploring diverse ways of making money from their skills and aptitudes. For Ella, whose natural initiative had already taken him some distance, an obvious opening to try was organizing musical performances on a commercial basis. According to his own testimony, his first attempts at concert promotion date from around 1830.[2] They are significant in several respects, but mostly because they taught him quickly how precarious the business of putting on concerts for financial gain could be. Concert promotion was a form of petty entrepreneurship, whereby a speculator launched and managed a project, minimized the economic risk to himself, balanced its income and expenditure, and drew personal profit from the surplus. In the performing arts it was an especially volatile activity. Many musicians dabbled in it, albeit with less innovation and financial investment than we would nowadays understand by the concept.[3] The stakes and takings of most concert enterprises were much smaller than those of the theatres and opera houses; initiatives were often short-lived, and choice of venue more flexible. But many of the same idiosyncrasies of risk

---

[2] The principal evidence for these activities is divided between an account book, labelled 'Concerts Book 1829' (EllaC, MS 82) and programmes, letters and ephemera preserved in one of Ella's scrapbooks (MS 81, pp. 5, 7–9; 12–13; also the material between pp. 14 and 15). Ella also wrote about these attempts at concert promotion years later: see e.g. *RMU* (1850), 33; and 'Music in London – No. 4', *MR* (1857), pp. xiv–xv.

[3] For an insightful discussion of the way in which concert entrepreneurship developed in the nineteenth century, and the ways it differs from concert promotion in modern times, see *McVeighA*.

applied.[4] For live music, like live theatre, required its consumers to come and buy at a predetermined time and place, making it unlike most other artistic 'products' that were offered in the London market-place, such as literature, paintings, sculpture, and even the raw tools for music-making such as scores, parts and instruments, which were on sale continuously and often across several outlets. Concerts, in comparison, were one-off moments of consumption, and potential concert-goers had to be wooed into choosing a specific event, or set of events, over competing attractions and other uses of their leisure time. Programmes, which were characteristically long and varied in their repertoire, were almost never publicly repeated *in toto* (contrast the theatres and, later on, touring by musicians); they were 'once only' opportunities for audiences to hear a particular set of works played and sung by a specific group of performers. Even so, custom had to be fought over, since the supply of events often outstripped demand, and there was always the risk that an audience might be lost at the last through unforeseen circumstances. Most crucially of all, the promoter had to invest considerable time and money to make the event happen at all – rooms had to be hired, advertisements placed, music obtained, and so on; and performers needed (eventually) to be recompensed. How great the inbuilt volatility, how fine the line between potential profit and loss, as many an eighteenth-century concert-giver had discovered to his or her cost.[5]

The tried and tested way to minimize risk and maximize one's chances of success was to sell tickets in advance by offering subscriptions, usually to a series of three or more concerts. Money could thus be accrued up front, facilitating cash flow and allowing for the monitoring of demand, perhaps even adjustment of expenditure, as finance came in. At the same time, the establishment of a concert series, as opposed to one-off events, helped the promoter create presence and what today we might call 'brand identity' during the congested season. Moreover, audience exclusivity was assured, since 'public' subscriptions were purchased only by those with the wherewithal to pay for an entire series. In the most fashionable part of the West End where Ella chose to operate, subscriptions of one guinea or more for three concerts were not unusual. Yet even with all these structures to tap into, success could not be guaranteed. Losses were common, suggesting, as Simon McVeigh has repeatedly argued, that there were myriad ulterior reasons for putting on concerts.[6]

---

[4] For parallels with the theatrical world, see Tracy C. Davis, *The Economics of the British Stage, 1800–1914* (Cambridge: Cambridge University Press, 2000), esp. 166–7.

[5] On the economics of London concert promotion in the eighteenth century, see *McVeighCL*, 167–81.

[6] *McVeighA*, 164–6.

Ella's principal initiatives were two subscription series of *soirées musicales*, the first of which he mounted in February and March 1830 at 28 Edwards Street, Portman Square, an area just north of Oxford Street towards its Hyde Park end. He had taken lodgings at no. 28 around Christmas 1829, probably with an eye on location – the surrounding area was a salubrious one, in easy reach for the *beau monde*, and thus desirable for a working musician.[7] A second series followed in 1831 at the Argyll Rooms, near Regent Circus (Ella now living in Frith Street, off Soho Square). Both featured a small group of performers and a diet of mostly vocal music. A few singers gave excerpts from operas (arias, duets, quartets and so on) accompanied by a tiny chamber band that also performed the odd contrasting instrumental item, as can be seen from a surviving programme (Fig. 4).[8]

Much common sense lay behind Ella's choice of music and musicians. The opera arrangements were his own, many of them surely recycled with due economy from the amateur parties *chez* Saltoun.[9] Moderate numbers of performers, of good if not top-class calibre, and including some débutant singers, kept expenditure down and were selected from his networks; and the need, if not the desirability, for rehearsal was minimized, since several of the performers were probably already familiar with the music from the Saltoun meetings. This was true of Anna Rivière, an Academy student who would later, as Madame Bishop (wife of the composer H. R. Bishop), enjoy an international career; she sang in both initiatives.[10] There was also a good deal of imagination and innovation, not to mention French inspiration, in Ella's repertoire selection, suggesting that even at this early stage in his career he was keen to stretch conventions and audiences. The very act of programming operatic arrangements with chamber band placed something different before the concert-goer, while the selections themselves contained a fair number of novelties, hotfoot from Paris; these Ella sought to champion, surely still enthralled by the music he had witnessed there. So, while his concerts included current or recent repertoire from the London opera house – for instance, excerpts from Rossini's *Zelmira* and *La gazza ladra*, Mozart's *Don Giovanni* or Bellini's *Il pirata* that would make a direct appeal to fashionable taste – there was also, in

[7] The street, parallel to Oxford Street, was the stretch of thoroughfare linking (Lower) Seymour Street with Wigmore Street; later in the century it was renamed Barrett Street.

[8] Programmes for the 1830 and 1831 series (EllaC, MS 81, pp. 8–9 and 13) suggest that Ella played the violin in the band at first, but then turned, from the fourth concert of 1830, solely to directing the music.

[9] 'The whole of the Music is arranged for *Petit Orchestre*, by Mr. ELLA': programme for the second concert, 1830 (EllaC, MS 81, p. 8).

[10] Her participation in the Saltoun Club is documented in 'La Società Lirica. Belgravia, 1870', *RMU* (1870), sup., p. ii.

Mr. ELLA's

SECONDE SOIRÉE MUSICALE,

Under the Patronage of Her Majesty,

FRIDAY, 11*th* MARCH, 1831,

AT THE ARGYLL ROOM.

*SOUVENIR DE PARIS, 1828, Instrumentale e Coro.... *Ella.*

*SINFONIA e DUO, " *Segui, o cara, i passi miei,*" Miss ⎱ *Spohr.*
    WILLIAMS and Mr. BENNETT.................... ⎰

*INTRODUCTION to the First Act of " *Der Templer,*"— ⎫
    Scott's *Ivanhoe (De Bracy and Attendants)*, Mr. BENNETT ⎬ *Marschner.*
    and Coro, " *Ci nascondiamo al Bosco là, fra poco passerà ;*" ⎪
    (*Gilberto,*) Mr. SEGUIN .... ⎭

DUO, " *Bell' Imago,*" Miss MASSON and Mr. SEGUIN ...... *Rossini.*

DUO, "*Claudio! Claudio!*" Messrs. BENNETT and SEGUIN.. *Mercadante.*

*TYROLEAN AIR and VAR. Piano-Forte, M. SCHLESINGER *Hummel.*

*ROMANZA, " *L' ombrosa Notte vien,*" Miss MASSON ...... *Hummel.*

*VAUDEVILLE—Trio and Coro, "*Venite tutti quanti quà, le* ⎱ *Hummel.*
    Nozze a celebrare,*" .... ⎰

ARIA, Miss WILLIAMS .... *Pacini.*

*THE SOLDIER'S GLEE (translated from the German,) ⎱ *Spohr.*
    " *No Song nor Sound to a Soldier's Heart*" .... ⎰

ARIA, " *Languir per una bella,*" Mr. BENNETT............ *Rossini.*

ARI.., " *Il Braccio,*" Miss MASSON...................... *Nicodini.*

FINALE, Miss WILLIAMS, Messrs. BENNETT, GALLI, &c. &c. *Rossini.*

BAND.

Messrs. WATTS, GRIESBACH, GUYNEMERE, WATKINS, SEYMOUR, HOWELL,
    HILL, DORRELL, CARD, ABEL, and LUCAS.

Conducteur, ... Mr. ELLA.

* *These Pieces are performed for the First Time in this Country.*

The Third and last SOIRÉE MUSICALE will take place on FRIDAY, the
    18th Instant, a Subscription to which will admit Three Persons.

Printed by T. Brettell, Rupert Street, Haymarket.

4 Handbill for Ella's second Soirée Musicale, 11 March 1831.

Reproduced by kind permission of the Bodleian Library, Oxford.

almost equal measure, much that was untried in Britain. The most notable of the latter was Rossini's opera *Guillaume Tell*, which had been premièred in Paris in August 1829 but would not be heard at the King's Theatre for another decade.[11] Ella arranged several numbers and introduced them in Italian translation. He also programmed extracts from Auber's *La muette de Portici* (premièred in Paris, 1828),

---

[11] The first performance at Her Majesty's (formerly the King's) Theatre, London was in 1839. It had been staged a few months earlier at Drury Lane; see Gabriella Dideriksen, 'Repertory and Rivalry: Opera at the Second Covent Garden Theatre, 1830 to 1856' (PhD, University of London, 1997), 181.

and instrumental medleys of his own composition, such as his *Souvenir de Siège de Corinthe* and *Souvenir de Paris 1828*. Unusual too was his endorsement, in the 1831 concerts, of numbers from a group of German operas by Marschner (*Der Templer und die Jüdin*), Hummel (*Mathilde de Guise*) and Spohr (*Faust* and *Jessonda*) – all rendered in Italian or English, and mostly as yet unstaged in London and Paris. Exactly where and how Ella had encountered these works is unclear, although the circulation in England of published excerpts and vocal scores, and performances of extracts at London concerts, may well be significant.

Occasionally Ella slipped in a meaty instrumental work: a quartet by Mayseder or Haydn, a piano trio by Beethoven, and so on – the type of music he already held dear. And sometimes a concerto was included: in 1830 the *émigré* pianist Louise Dulcken, sister of the violinist Ferdinand David, played one by Henri Herz.[12] There was evidence too of Ella already wanting to direct listeners' concentration, as well as to inform taste: one handbill notes that the instrumentation of the ballet music and 'Chœur Tyrolien' from *Guillaume Tell* is 'worthy of particular attention', and announces its repetition at the final concert of the series 'with additional Movements; and Remarks illustrative of the Dramatic Situations, as performed in Paris […] inserted in the Programme'.[13] All were signs of things to come.

Recruitment of audiences came about through personal contacts in the eighteenth-century manner, with Ella approaching people in his network of amateurs in advance with entreaties to act as official patrons, to subscribe or to spread the word to others.[14] In the main he used the press, meaning the fashionable papers

---

[12] EllaC, MS 81, p. 8. Ella later claimed that this performance (18 February 1830) was Dulcken's London début (*RMU*, 1850, p. 33). In fact, her début had already occurred: according to *Recent Music and Musicians as described in the Diaries and Correspondence of Ignatz Moscheles*, ed. Charlotte Moscheles (New York: Henry Holt, 1873), 151, she was performing in London in 1829 (confirmed by a concert bill for the Argyll Rooms, 8 July 1829, in RCMp). Puffery of achievements and claiming of 'firsts' were common during the period. I am grateful to Therese Ellsworth for sharing information on Dulcken with me.

[13] Programme for the second soirée (18 February) 1830: EllaC, MS 81, p. 8. The music is from the divertissement in Act 3.

[14] As suggested by the letter to Ella from the Duke of Leinster, dated 20 December 1829, preserved in EllaC, MS 81, p. 7. It reads: 'I received your letter of the 15.th DecR this day, & will with pleasure comply with your request to be amongst the Patrons of your intended "Soirees de Musique Instrumentale["]'. A list of official patrons for the 1830 series was advertised in *MP* (11 February 1830). In addition to Leinster there were Lord Saltoun, Sir George Warrender, Sir Henry Webb, Sir James Langham, Sir George Clerk and Sir George Cornewall (all baronets), major-generals Sir Andrew Barnard and Sir John Campbell, Lieut.-Col. Ellis, Capt. Elliot, Henry Sanford and D. Maude.

such as the *Morning Post* and the *Court Journal*, to communicate information to existing subscribers, rather than to drum up support in the first instance;[15] though new faces were welcomed and he would have doubtless been pleased to see some of the concerts favourably reviewed afterwards.[16] His aim, self-evidently achieved, was to cultivate as many serious-minded patrons as possible from the tight-knit world of rank and fashion. Takers' names, noted in a surviving account book, include: Sir Henry Webb, 7th Bt, Sir Andrew Barnard (distinguished military man, KCB), Sir William Curtis, 2nd Bt (son of the late MP of the same name), Lord and Lady Saltoun themselves, Lord Burghersh, a certain Mr Cohen (a Jew, of Camberwell), the amateur double bass player P. J. Salomons (also Jewish, with City connections), a Mr and Miss Gardiner (perhaps William Gardiner from Leicester) and a Mr and Mrs Tudor.[17] For many in this group, the chance to hear professionals perform some of the operatic arrangements they themselves had attempted at Saltoun's parties, plus the suggestion that the clientele would include others in their social-musical entourage, must have been a strong inducement to attend.

The income from each series totalled about £90.[18] Set against this were several items of expenditure over and above payments to the musicians: advertising and printing, the copying of parts, lighting, hire of seats (or in the case of the Argyll Rooms, the hall), porterage and a 'man to take tickets' were among several operating essentials that needed attention and disbursement.[19] In 1830 expenditure ran at some £150 (half of which went to the musicians, and a goodly portion to the singers, who would have expected to earn more than most of the

---

[15] Advertisements give information about the times of concerts and collection of tickets: e.g. *CJ* (19 February 1831), 128, and *MP* (11 February 1830; 17 and 24 February; 11 March 1831). Details about how to apply for subscriptions is secondary. Payments for placing advertisements in *The Times*, *MP*, *MH* and *CJ* are recorded in the account book, EllaC, MS 82, p.[11].

[16] *CJ* (25 February 1831), 159–60; *MP* (13 and 20 February; 6 and 20 March 1830; 28 February; 14 and 28 March 1831).

[17] EllaC, MS 82, pp.[3, 9–10]. Some of the 1830 subscribers were official patrons; see n. 14 above. On Cohen, see n. 43 below. Some dating errors seem to have occurred in the accounts, probably because the task was done after the fact. Page [1] contains the accounts for an 1829 [not 1830] benefit concert at Mrs Henshaw's; while pp.[3–5] document the 1830 series of soirées, not the 1831 set. Cross-referencing with financial information about the soirées in *MR* (1857), pp. xiv–xv, and the programmes in EllaC, MS 81, pp. 8–9 and 13, has suggested this reading.

[18] EllaC, MS 82, p.[3; series for 1830, erroneously labelled 1831] and pp.[9–10; series for 1831].

[19] See e.g. the itemized expenses for the 1830 and 1831 series: EllaC, MS 82, p.[5, 11].

instrumentalists), creating a loss of c.£57 and a tough lesson in concert promotion.[20] Undaunted, Ella tried again, cutting the number of concerts from four to three in 1831, engaging a few higher-calibre performers and paying their elevated prices. The virtuoso horn player Giovanni Puzzi, a favourite in aristocratic circles, and his wife Giacinta, a soprano at the opera house, were hired for one concert, as was the tenor Alberico Curioni.[21] Curioni was paid ten guineas (five times what the average string player received). It was an intelligent move by Ella to invest in better-known artists to bring in more subscribers, and was in keeping with the glitzier image of the second series, Ella having obtained official 'patronage' from a group of female royals comprising Queen Adelaide (wife of William IV) and the duchesses of Kent and Cumberland (the King's sisters-in-law).[22] Such support was a type of window-dressing, de rigueur for fashionability. Yet even with these modifications, increased numbers of subscribers and concomitant profits were not forthcoming, and Ella had to shoulder a greater loss this time: some £70, which would have made a considerable dent in his annual earnings.[23]

Probably, Ella did not see the deficit so starkly. Concerts were, as already indicated, often loss-leaders, necessary for what they offered by way of advertising a musician's skills to his wider clientele, their benefits gaugeable only in the long term through the financial returns of teaching, other forms of amateur 'patronage' and general social and professional advancement. One imagines Ella sensed that not getting the formula 'right' early on was no reason to give up (he had twice drawn in nearly 100 amateurs), which would explain why in 1832 he was ready for a third attempt, announcing a subscription list for six more *soirées musicales*.[24] But with fewer than twenty subscribers signed up – significantly fewer than he had

[20] £57 8s (EllaC, MS 82, p.[5]). This tallies perfectly with Ella's account of the enterprise in *MR* (1857), p. xiv. Some of the instrumental soloists (e.g. Mme Dulcken) may have given their services free, their generosity being publicized by Ella in his concert programmes.

[21] On Puzzi and the private concert circuit, see Elizabeth Bradley Strauchen, 'Giovanni Puzzi: his Life and Work: a View of Horn Playing and Musical Life in England from 1817 into the Victorian Era (c.1855)' (DPhil, University of Oxford, 2000), 108–14.

[22] A subscription ticket listing all three patronesses survives in EllaC, MS 81, p. 12, as does a communication, dated 21 December 1830, on behalf of the Duchess of Cumberland, granting permission for use of her name as patroness for the series of concerts 'for the performance of dramatic music, and for the encouragement of talented young artists' (EllaC, MS 81, p. 60).

[23] The loss is calculated in the account book (EllaC, MS 82, p.[11]), and corroborated by Ella in *MR* (1857), p. xiv.

[24] As indicated in *RMU* (1850), 33.

achieved previously – Ella decided not to risk any more of his money.[25] He shut down the enterprise, demonstrating a shrewdness of judgement that would stand him in good stead later in his career.

There were, in any case, other avenues to explore. End-of-season benefit concerts – an old formula of miscellaneous repertoire, deliberately showcasing musicians' talents, in which the performer-promoter took the profits, confrères sometimes gave their services free, and pupils and patrons were encouraged to attend – were one such.[26] They were becoming increasingly common in the 1820s as all sorts of hopeful musicians tried their luck.[27] Ella played in dozens of them, gratis: by 1845 he would estimate having given his services 280 times over the past twenty years.[28] Now, beginning in 1829, he also put on a few events for his own benefit, supported by a remarkable smattering of top-rank performers (reflecting his increasing contacts with the best London musicians), in private houses not formal halls, and 'publicly' advertised in the papers to wealthy society.[29] At these concerts Ella wisely put himself forward as adapter of opera

[25] Ibid.

[26] On the eighteenth-century origins of benefits, see *McVeighCL*, 176–81.

[27] On changes in the quantity, significance and profitability of benefit concerts during the early nineteenth century, see Simon McVeigh, 'The Benefit Concert in Nineteenth-Century London: from "Tax on the Nobility" to Monstrous Nuisance', *NBMS*, 1, ed. Bennett Zon (Aldershot: Ashgate, 1999), 242–66. By the 1820s a situation of over-supply was emerging, with most performers making losses on their benefits. Poor musical standards often resulted, and the idea of the benefit took on a sense of 'artistic prostitution' (p. 249). Later in his career Ella took a robust view of benefit concerts (as shown in passages quoted by McVeigh); as early as 1833 he was becoming exercised by the indifferent, often poor, quality of such performances: see his column in the *Athenaeum* (6 July 1833), 443–4.

[28] *RMU* (1845), 23.

[29] Ella's 1829 concert was held at Mrs Henshaw's residence in Wimpole Street on 24 June and advertised in that day's *MH* (also *MP*, 19 June). For it, Ella secured the singers Maria Malibran and Henriette Sontag, among others, plus a small orchestra. Fétis was maestro. From the account book (EllaC, MS 82, pp.[1; concert erroneously labelled as 1830]) it appears that although most artists gave their services free, Ella had to pay Dragonetti. An extant ticket is preserved in one of the scrapbooks (EllaC, MS 81, p. 5). For a review, see *MP* (26 June 1829).

Ella also held a morning concert in 1831 (19 July); an evening event in 1835 (13 July) and another morning concert in 1837 (11 July). For assorted documentation relating to these concerts, see the cuttings in the scrapbook, EllaC, MS 81, between pp. 14 and 15, and the material on p. 15. Adverts and reviews may be found in *MP* (16 and 22 July 1831); *MC* (11 July 1835); *Times* (13 July 1835); *CJ* (18 July 1835), 457; and *MP* (14 July 1835). The account book further suggests a benefit concert in 1830 *chez* Sir George Warrender (EllaC, MS 82, p. 7).

numbers, composer and director, rather than violinist. For however good an ensemble player he might have been, he was not in the technical league of a Mori or a Spagnoletti, and he would have been foolish to attempt concertos and showpieces. Instead, his programmes were largely consistent with the formats of his subscription concerts, and included his arrangements from lesser-known dramatic works: an unusual choice for a benefit, and one perfumed with a seriousness often lacking in the benefit culture. At the concert at Ella's home (now in Newman Street) in July 1835, he put forward his 'express adaptations' used at 'the private performances of Lord Saltoun', winning plaudits for selectivity – of audiences, performers and repertoire – and taste.[30] The opera numbers, sung by a quartet of celebrated singers (among them Luigi Lablache, Antonio Tamburini and Maria Malibran), were complemented by more 'standard' benefit fare: a violin concerto composed and played by De Bériot (Malibran's husband), horn solos from Puzzi, and Ella's own instrumental sextet arranged for piano *à quatre mains* (W. S. Bennett and Edouard Schulz's), violin, viola, cello and double bass. To judge from Ella's financial accounts, some of these concerts produced small profits.[31]

Another of Ella's activities was fixing private concerts – sometimes called 'music parties' – financed by wealthy individuals. In these circumstances, Ella was the impresario – to use a helpful modern definition[32] – responsible for most of the arrangements and none of the financial risk. Firm historical evidence for this sort of pursuit is rare, but materials preserved by Ella give an indication of the nature of one such project. From a letter written to him by Sir George Warrender (a serious-minded music-lover who was already on the directorial board of the Royal Academy of Music), apparently dated in 1830, we learn:

> I think of having five nights for music previous to the Easter vacation [i.e. Holy Week] and while there is no employment for the musical people in the private houses in town – I propose to give the preference in the final instance to the pupils of the R. A. of Music[,] and you may propose to Miss Childe and to Mr Seguin Twenty Guineas each for these five nights – to a second soprano & tenor [?]three Guineas each night they come – to each of the persons engaged for

---

30 *CJ* (18 July 1835), 457.

31 According to EllaC, MS 82, p.[1], the 1829 concert made a profit of £52, though it should be noted that Mrs Henshaw put in a remarkable £20, Lord Saltoun 12 guineas, and another patron 13 guineas. The 1830 and 1831 benefits made small losses (of roughly £7 and £8 apiece), but that of 1835 appears to have made a profit of £26 6s, and that of 1837 rendered £45 (see op. cit., pp.[7, 12, 14, 15]).

32 Davis, *Economics*, 166.

the orchestra one Guineas [*sic*] and ½ – the orchestra will attend rehearsals if
required – [.][33]

And we see that Ella set to work, producing formal programmes of his excerpts
from Italian, French and German operas, arranged for soloists and string band
– presumably to the patron's taste and subject to his broad approval.[34] Whether
Ella, who directed the performances, was paid for his trouble is not revealed. If
not, he must have judged the work worth while for the experience and networking
advantages it brought forward.[35] In any case, Ella's participation in private music-
making took on many guises, of which the formal private concert, fixed by Ella
with paid performers, was at one extreme. At the other was the ubiquitous invitation to dinner, in return for which a musician might afterwards accompany at the
piano some of the amateurs in their impromptu music-making. In between came
a host of scenarios, in many of which the players probably received no remuneration but banked on indirect benefits at other times.

Ella's doings in the shadowy world of private music, as far as can be made out
from his diaries, covered a wide range. To start with, there were Saltoun's amateur
opera parties which continued to blossom under Ella's direction and Saltoun's
generous support until the mid-1840s. They were a significant, seemingly remunerative, component of Ella's activities, and they formed a breeding ground for
other projects as well as the advancement of his career.[36] We have already seen

---

[33] EllaC, ms 81, p. 11.

[34] Six programmes for these concerts are in EllaC, ms 81, pp. 10–12; the first five presumably relate to the events specified in Warrender's letter. Only the sixth programme carries a precise date (7 May 1830), and was probably a separate event; it
used higher-calibre artists (the singers Maria Malibran, Signor Donzelli, and Mme
Stockhausen). Reports of some of these concerts can be found in *MP*: see 16 March,
9 April and 10 May 1830.

[35] Entries in Ella's diary for April and May 1829 (EllaC, ms 102) further suggest he had
organized concerts for Warrender in 1829. Reports in *MP* (15 and 25 April, 6 May
and 2 June 1829) confirm this, indicating that the singers on this occasion were
stars from the opera house, that Giovanni Puzzi was the musical director, and
that the musical arrangements were Ella's own. The vein of activity is further corroborated by Ella's claim, in *EllaMS1*, 167, that 'for several seasons' he had '[admin-
istrative?] direction of concerts at the residence of the late Sir George Warrender'.
Anecdotes relating to the concerts appear also on pp. 24–5. It is Warrender, not
Saltoun [as implied], who is further described as annually expending £1,000 in
private concerts, including events at his country house at Cliefden (near Maidenhead) on p. 38.

[36] The diaries carry several references to meetings at Saltoun's, and to series of
'Amateur Parties', which may well have been one and the same. That Ella both
received some form of payment from him, and paid some of the professional

how he made good use of the amateur contacts forged here, not to mention his musical arrangements, in his concert speculations. He also advertised his opera adaptations and services to amateur singers.[37] With some of the Saltoun Club families, Ella found a forum for his passion for instrumental chamber music and a cradle in which to nurture amateur interest in it. To the Hon. Major Legge's family seat at Blackheath, out to the south-east of London, Ella would regularly go to eat and to play music, often piano trios, with his host (a keen cellist) and family members or friends.[38] Elsewhere he might be found supervising amateurs in trios, quartets or in larger ensemble music, with some meetings possibly even run formally, by subscription.[39] On other occasions he participated in, and probably organized, after-dinner concerts in private houses, involving an invited group of professional players; the repertoire could range from string quartets and instrumental sonatas to opera adaptations. A final variant demands mention too: informal musical gatherings at Ella's house before invited assemblies of patrons, such as the 'Party chez moi' in March 1836, at which the offering (from Tolbecque, Rousselot, Nadaud, Ella and Schulz) was Beethoven's second quartet from op. 59, Thalberg's piano fantasia on *Robert le diable*, and a quintet and piano sextet by Georges Onslow, whose chamber music was much in vogue.[40] There were some sixteen 'visitors', and Ella wrote afterwards that he 'never enjoyed an evening's Music more satisfactorily'.[41] At much of this private music-making it

musicians engaged, is indicated by the entry for 22 August 1836 and the accounts for August 1840 (EllaC, MSS 106 and 109). Subscriptions from amateurs, as indicated in Ella's 1840 diary accounts, may have been collected for these parties.

[37] *MP* (13 February 1836): 'Amateur Vocalists desirous of enjoying the advantage of singing dramatic music, with orchestral accompaniments, at their private residence, may be supplied with Music and receive every instruction and information by Mr. Ella.'

[38] See e.g. the diary entry for 21 January 1839 (EllaC, MS 108), where dinner at Major Legge's is noted, and followed by the remark: 'Played Beethoven's Trio C minor'. Major Legge's brother was the fourth Earl of Dartmouth.

[39] An entry in Ella's diary of 16 April 1838 (EllaC, MS 107), for example, indicates an appointment with three amateurs for 'Trios'. On other occasions we find evidence of Major Legge asking Ella's advice about finding 'a large Amateur Practical Sinfonia Party' to join (diary, 18 January 1839; EllaC, MS 108), and the Barker family asking him 'to fix regular evenings' for music parties at their and friends' houses (24 January 1839). Other diary entries referring to amateurs' subscription events may denote this sort of venture, or simply Ella's ongoing organization of Saltoun Club activities.

[40] Diary, 1 March 1836 (EllaC, MS 106).

[41] Ibid.

is easy to imagine Ella leading the choice of repertoire and driving the practical arrangements.[42]

The private sphere was crucial because it spawned further potential patronage. Frequent invitation to just a handful of houses, such as we know Ella achieved in the mid-late 1830s when he was often to be found at the Legges, the Freelings (almost certainly Clayton Freeling, son of the postal reformer Sir Francis Freeling, Bt, and his wife), the Robins (possibly the house of George Robins, the flamboyant auctioneer), and the Barkers (probably of Cadogan Place), was all it took for him to access a much larger community of music-lovers; and before long the circle was widening at the edges. Wealthy middle-class businessmen – City bankers, Jewish merchants and the like – people who were melding into fashionable society and might well have a strong penchant for music, gradually came into Ella's orbit.[43] He also had his first meaningful contact with royalty through the agency of the Countess of Dartmouth, who introduced him to the Duke of Cambridge (George III's youngest son), an ardent violinist. Within a week Ella was playing quartets with him and Major Legge, under the leadership of the Earl of Falmouth.[44]

Excursions into upper-class worlds were famously fraught with social dangers, and Ella was conscious of minding his Ps and Qs. After a lively discussion at the Freelings' house in 1836 he noted with relief: 'I was gratified to hear that I was not considered too presumptive and positive in my opinion on Dramatic Music, (on March 11th. dinner Party)!'[45] Even more daunting, presumably, were invitations to join the out-of-season house parties at patrons' country estates, which were forthcoming during the 1830s: but he accepted them nonetheless. In autumn 1835 he spent several weeks at Moccas Court in Herefordshire, home of Sir George Cornewall, passing a few days at Tregoyd, seat of Lord Hereford (the families were

---

[42] A letter (EllaC, MS 81, p. 4) from Warrender to Ella, probably dating from c.1839, will serve as an example of Ella's role. It indicates that Warrender had asked Ella to organize a party of the principal Italian singers from the opera house, plus Ella himself, to dine and perform at Warrender's country house near Maidenhead.

[43] E.g., his diary records his meeting, in Cornhill in the City, a banker named B. King, whose 'wife is an amateur singer and a pleasing looking person', and who invited Ella to visit his home in Brussels (5 January 1839; EllaC, MS 108); and dining and playing music at the house of the Jewish Mr Cohen, in Camberwell, south of the river (27 March 1836; EllaC, MS 106). On another occasion he wrote of a night's 'music of the Amateurs […] [with] Ministers & Merchants' (4 February 1836; EllaC, MS 106).

[44] The 1838 diary (EllaC, MS 107) chronicles their meetings from the initial invitation (20 March) to their first chamber-music encounter (25 March), and to a quartet party (2 April) at which the Duke's collection of old Italian instruments was used.

[45] Diary, 30 March 1836 (EllaC, MS 106).

intermarried). Likewise he enjoyed several spells at Chipstead Park in Kent, home of Frederick Perkins, part-owner of a London brewing company.[46] Such visits would be repeated in subsequent years, as would his journey to Saltoun's Scottish highland estate, first made in 1839.[47] The cost of that year's trips – some £37, covering travel (by train, increasingly), new clothes, lodgings *en route*, all totted up at the back of his diary – was presumably considered money well spent.[48]

But as much as Ella picked up the country pursuits of fishing and shooting on these trips, and might later wish it to be thought that he had always been at one with the nobility and gentry, it seems probable that he was invited along in these early years to animate musical entertainments, and was kept apart from the more intimate family activities.[49] Still, he could enjoy the perks of being a house guest; and the experiences were formative and worth while in manifold ways, social and professional. For the 1838 Christmas revels at Chipstead Ella organized and directed music, which included arrangements of opera overtures as well as waltzes and a set of quadrilles of his own composition scored for piano duet, cornet, cello, double bass, triangle and musical glasses. The pieces were played by the family's guests, among them the parliamentarian Henry Broadwood,[50] and a delighted Frederick Perkins decided 'very handsomely' to offer himself as 'proprietor of the music', providing a lithograph of Chipstead Park for publication.[51] Ella, who called the work *Souvenirs de Chipstead* (Fig. 5), was surely proud: being a published composer was a further indication of rising career success.

Ella's self-appointed training in harmony and counterpoint, along with his accumulating experience as an arranger, served him well around this time, and he produced several other compositions and arrangements for private use within

[46] The visits to Moccas and Chipstead are noted in diary entries between August and December 1835 (EllaC, MS 105). Ella's association with Moccas Court is further outlined in a handwritten annotation in one of the scrapbooks, accompanying a letter to Ella from Sir George Cornewall dated 14 March 1831: EllaC, MS 81, p. 63. In it Ella claims that 'Until the death of this amiable lover of music, Sir Geo: Cornwall Bart [i.e. 1835], I never failed to visit Moccas-Court, when in England for any vacation.' His first visit was in the 1820s, probably 1825.

[47] Ella's diary for September and October 1839 (EllaC, MS 108) documents this visit.

[48] Back pages of the 1839 diary (EllaC, MS 108).

[49] Odd remarks in the 1839 diary (EllaC, MS 108) suggest that social distance was maintained between Ella and his hosts during a visit to Saltoun's estate; see for instance his careful noting of the visiting nobility he encountered (4 September and *passim*), and the requirement for him to share a bedroom with two other house guests (17 September).

[50] Diary, entries from 24 to 31 December 1838 (EllaC, MS 107).

[51] Diary, 16 January 1839 (EllaC, MS 108).

5 Title-page of Ella's *Souvenirs de Chipstead* (London: Mills, [1839]).
Reproduced by kind permission of the Bodleian Library, Oxford.

the circles of his patrons. Traces of these missing pieces are littered across Ella's diaries: a minuet and trio for violin and piano noted here, a piece for guitar and violin there, usually for one patron or another, and indicating the hours of industry Ella put into these workaday activities in order to establish himself as an organizer of music for the domestic milieu.[52] Only a few were published; most seem to have perished. Of the former there were, in addition to the Chipstead dances, an arrangement of an Italian canzonetta for voices and accompaniment (1828), a set of quadrilles for piano duet dedicated to the Viscountess Hereford (1830), and a march, written in the year of Victoria's coronation with a dedication to the Duchess of Kent, which went into at least three editions.[53] More than one is imbued with the spirit of the Italian Opera House.

An important part of Ella's portfolio continued to be the provision of instrumental lessons to amateurs, and he seems to have found a further niche as a teacher of harmony – an understanding of which he maintained was essential for all musicians, especially keyboard players. For a while he ran harmony classes for the females in the Legge entourage at Blackheath, and at one point was writing a manual for his pupils.[54] Another role for Ella was as go-between in the sale or purchasing of instruments. He tested and bought pianos on behalf of wealthy amateurs out of town, and on one occasion set off for the provinces with one of

[52] In his diary, 15 May 1836 (EllaC, MS 106), Ella described 'a sketch I had once written "impromptu" for Violin & Piano, a ["]Minuetto & Trio" in which I had a lucky combination of subjects', which won the approval of a German visitor. Staying at Colonel Charles Ellis's country house in November 1839, Ella '[r]ead Col: Ellis's story of "Dolores" in N. P. Journal & wrote musical illustrations, & made pictures of it – for Guitar & Violin &c...' (diary, 13 November 1839; EllaC, MS 108).

[53] *Amo te solo: a Favorite Italian Canzonetta as a Duett, for Two Soprano Voices, or Soprano and Tenore, with an Accompaniment for the Piano Forte or Guitar* (London: F. T. Latour, [1828]); *Quadrilles, as Duets, for two Performers on the Piano Forte* (London: Lonsdale & Mills, [1830]); *Victoria March, for Two Performers on the Piano Forte* (London: R. Mills, [1838]; 3rd edition, Lonsdale [after 1869]). Copies are in EllaC (MSS 78/v [*Quadrilles*] and vi [*Victoria March*, 3rd edition]), and at the BL [*Amo* and *Victoria March*, 1838], where a manuscript version of the march, for solo piano with cello accompaniment, is also preserved (Add. MS 38488 A, ff. 240r–245r).

Louise Dulcken seems to have played a role in securing the dedication for the coronation march: see Ella's diary entry for 25 February 1838 (EllaC, MS 107). She was well connected in royal circles, often styling herself as 'Pianiste to Her Majesty the Queen' [the Duchess of Kent's daughter], and obtaining the duchess's patronage for her own initiatives. I am grateful to Therese Ellsworth for this information.

[54] On the Blackheath classes, see the diary for 24 February and 10 March 1838 (EllaC, MS 107); on the harmony manual, see 15 February 1836 (MS 106).

Wheatstone's concertinas – the latest in musical fashions – 'to sell'.[55] This deliberate diversity is hinted at in an advertisement in the *Morning Post* of 1839: 'Mr. Ella
respectfully informs his Pupils that he is returned to town, to resume his *professional occupations* – Jan. 3. 15, Norton-street'.[56]

As for concert enterprise, that remained in the background after Ella's subscription soirées of 1830–1, Ella having quickly learned about the risk anything bar a
benefit entailed. Even here he probably displayed increased wariness, as the market
started to flood; his benefit at Frederick Perkins's London house in July 1837 was
almost certainly his last attempt at this formula.[57] An invitation to join in 'the
Promenade concert speculation in the Strand' in 1838 – one of several new enterprises promoting orchestral selections to a wide public – was declined,[58] perhaps
because Ella doubted its financial viability or perhaps because it looked 'below the
salt' for someone already identified with élite taste. Perhaps, too, Ella was becoming leery of collective enterprise: a disillusionment with the Philharmonic Society's *modus operandi* had grown over this decade.[59] It would be seven years before
Ella solicited another subscription list, and then it would be for chamber music.
Yet all the while his broader ambitions grew, for however successful, socially and
professionally, he was becoming, he wanted something more. He confided these
thoughts and frustrations to his diary at the end of 1838:

> In a professional point of consideration, I cannot say that I am at all content
> with myself. My Profits have certainly been as good as in any previous year,
> but I have not been able to strike out a new & important track for the gratifi-
> cation of my ambition – My general musical talent, I am convinced, qualifies

55 On piano transactions, see e.g. Ella's diary, 22 July 1839 (EllaC, MS 108), where Ella
    notes receiving acknowledgement that a piano sent to Yorkshire had arrived. The
    concertina transaction and intention to sell it is indicated by his diary entry for
    7 September 1838 (EllaC, MS 107), the day before he left for Gloucester, and by
    information in the company's ledgers for 1838 (Horniman Museum, London,
    Wayne Archive, Wheatstone Sales Ledger C104a, p. 13): 'Mr Ella, Sep 7' [without
    serial number of instrument, or indication of intended purchaser]. I am indebted
    to Allan Atlas for alerting me to this reference, and for fruitful follow-up
    discussion.

56 *MP* (4 January 1839). My italics.

57 Documents relating to this concert are preserved in EllaC, MS 81 (scrapbook),
    between pp. 14 and 15, and on p. 15.

58 Diary, 13 December 1838 (EllaC, MS 107). Various promenade concerts of this
    period are chronicled in Percy Scholes, *The Mirror of Music, 1844–1944: a Century
    of Musical Life in Britain as Reflected in the Pages of the Musical Times* (London:
    Novello, 1947), 192–3.

59 As discussed in the next section of this chapter.

me for the direction of something good if not great – and I yet remain prepared to take advantage of the first opportunity to make use of my <u>means</u>.[60]

❧ Newspapers and diaries

*It is quite amusing to read the different accounts in the Daily
Journals of the Opening of the King's Theatre! The Times says that
"Barret is the best oboe in Europe["]! The Post says that Cooke
cannot well be spared from the Band! The observations about the
Singers are perfectly ridiculous & not worthy of credit!. How very
ignorant all these Newspaper Critics are in Music!*

↜ Ella's diary, 7 March 1836

ONE further strand to Ella's professional activities, entwined with his
orchestral employment, was his work as a journalist, which became
prominent during the 1830s. In writing for the press he found another source of
income, social contacts and potential influence, and was seemingly stimulated to
pen descriptive and critical accounts of his daily life and musical encounters in his
diaries as well. It was an important time for Ella to be exploring his literary inclinations. He was young and sentient, and absorbing new music almost weekly, while
deepening his appreciation of those pieces that were slowly becoming seen as repertoire classics. In London's concert halls there was a stream of instrumental music
by Spohr, Hummel, Mendelssohn and others to discover. At the King's Theatre
Beethoven's *Fidelio* and works by Bellini and Donizetti were among the several
new operas he learned and assessed. Encounters in Paris meanwhile opened his
ears to Berlioz's music and several grand operas by Meyerbeer.

We have it on Ella's own authority that the beginnings of his journalistic work
date from 1828, and accelerated thereafter.[61] 1828 was the year he started writing for the *Morning Post*, probably having provided unsolicited copy in the first
instance.[62] The timing may well have been significant: in early December 1828
Ella's nomination for associate membership of the Philharmonic Society – an

---

[60] Diary for 1838, entry at the year's end (EllaC, MS 107). 'Means' probably refers to
Ella's sense of his skills and talents, though it could also refer to the small inherit-
ance that Ella had received following his mother's death that year.

[61] As noted by Ella on p. 233 of his copy of William Grainge's *The Vale of Mowbray:
a Historical and Topographical Account of Thirsk and its Neighbourhood* (London:
Simpkin, Marshall, 1859), in the possession of John Ravell in the 1990s.

[62] A note from the *MP* editor to Ella (dated 1828 by Ella; in EllaC, MS 29) suggests that
Ella sent in unsolicited copy as 'X.Y.Z.', though whether material was published
with that signature is unclear. The acronym is alluded to by Ella in *RMU* (1874), 16

elected position, open to playing members of the orchestra, for which professional abilities and good character were the chief criteria – was blackballed by six of the fourteen voting directors.[63] It is not known why the six voted thus, but a best guess is that there were sticking points over personality, and that Ella may have been considered by some of the directorate, which included senior figures such as William Ayrton and J. B. Cramer, as overly self-seeking and inappropriately forward for his age and experience. Of course, had Ella achieved his goal he would have found himself on the first rung of a ladder that might eventually have led to a seat at the centre of power in what was intended as the forum for the most serious music-making in the capital: from associate member, to member and then to director. But it was not to be, and his embrace of journalism in the 1830s, which included writing for the *Athenaeum*, 1831–4 (not to mention his sudden interest in concert promotions in 1830–1), may well have been triggered by the dissolution of these hopes.

As a genre of writing, music criticism in its many manifestations (performance reviewing, reflective discussion, historical enquiry, news, opinion and so on) was in its infancy in Britain in the first quarter of the century; but by the 1830s it was starting to proliferate, as the number and types of newspapers and readerships grew and the quantity of musical performances of interest to a wide audience increased.[64] The number of journalists rose accordingly. Some writers, gentlemen amateurs such as Leigh Hunt and Edward Holmes, were genuinely knowledgeable and articulate, and wrote mostly for the monthly and quarterly periodicals at the market's literary end. Many others, especially on the 'newsier' titles, were hacks, sometimes drafted in from theatrical or other arts criticism, often ignorant of music and feeble if not incompetent wordsmiths of it. Remuneration was modest, but provided many journalists with a useful supplement to other earnings.[65] There was certainly a place for a literate and competent musician like Ella in this world.

and (1880), 28. In the former he suggests he wrote 'incognito' for a 'couple of years' before being unmasked.

The obituary of Ella by T. L. Southgate (*MS*, 6 October 1888, pp. 213–15, at 214) claimed that Ella had at one time been a music critic on *MC*. This remains unsubstantiated.

63 General Minute Book (BL, RPS/MS/275), f. 140r: 'Upon a Ballot for Mr. Ella there appearing 8 Ayes and 6 Noes he was rejected' (minute, 8 December 1828).

64 The best overview of English music journalism at this period is Leanne Langley's discussion of Britain (up to 1890) in the entry 'Criticism' in *NGDM2*. She argues that music journalism proliferated and diversified faster than musical culture did.

65 On fees, see Christopher Kent, 'Periodical Critics of Drama, Music, and Art, 1830–1914: a Preliminary List', *Victorian Periodicals Review*, 13 (1980), 31–55; £2 or £3 per

One of the conventions behind much British press writing – especially in the daily and weekly papers, which carried mostly reviews of music and events – was the anonymity of its contributors. Columns were usually unsigned, a feature that makes recovering authors' identities a considerable challenge, and is further complicated by the fact that few newspapers employed one single music critic, writers tending to work for more than one title simultaneously.[66] This means two things for a rounded understanding of Ella's journalistic career: firstly, that any hope of identifying a complete body of Ella's work from the *Post*'s pages will probably long remain unrealized, given that we do not know for sure what Ella wrote on and in which issues his material was published;[67] and secondly, that although he claimed to have written on music for the *Morning Post* between 1828 and 1842, it does not follow that he was behind every review, or even the majority of them.[68] The paper used several music writers, some of whom (Charles Lewis Gruneisen and John Parry) were almost certainly more prominent writers than Ella.[69] Furthermore, partisanship was common and, thanks to the convention of anonymity, can be difficult to expose after the fact. In their own day journalists would have accepted that, despite the mask of secrecy, their associations with particular papers were understood within literary circles, and that some readers could make informed guesses as to who had written what. It is possible that Ella wrote the favourable reviews of his concerts in the 1830s for the *Post*; moreover, he might have expected, as someone known at the editorial office, to see positive coverage from another

week might have been average. No firm indication of Ella's earnings from journalism in the 1830s has been found in the diaries.

[66] Attribution of anonymous music criticism is the subject of Leanne Langley, 'Italian Opera and the English Press, 1836–1856', *Periodica musica*, 6 (1988), 3–10.

[67] With patience and a keen eye to Ella's literary style and hobby-horses, a few tentative attributions have been made; see Christina Bashford, 'The Late Beethoven Quartets and the London Press, 1836–ca.1850', *Musical Quarterly*, 84 (2000), 84–122.

[68] As per Ella's annotation to his copy of Grainge's *Vale of Mowbray*; the information was repeated in John Ravell, 'John Ella, 1802–1888', *M&L*, 34 (1953), 93–105, at 98. Ella appears to have written dispatches for *MP* from Vienna in 1845.

[69] In the late 1820s, for instance, the coverage of London's main musical institutions seems to have come from someone other than Ella, an older writer (identity unknown) with much experience of music in Germany. Equally, Ella's closely kept diaries of the late 1830s, which tend to indicate when his material was published in newspapers, contain little to suggest he was writing regularly for *MP*. He did read the paper, and often noted where he disagreed with the music critic. Set against this, some *MP* reviews of chamber music concerts in the same period appear to have come from Ella's pen. Perhaps Ella concealed his authorship of these even from his diary.

critic on the team.[70] Other literati would surely have understood any partiality about Ella in this newspaper thus.[71]

Much more, however, is known about Ella's work for the *Athenaeum*, the weekly gazette for literature and fine arts that had been founded in 1828. Ella took on the role of principal music critic towards the end of 1831 and held it until 1834, when the job passed to Henry Chorley, with whose trenchant views on music the periodical henceforth became identified.[72] During the journal's early years an office copy was 'marked up' with the names of writers alongside their contributions. Although not all these volumes survive, enough do to clarify the nature and rough extent of Ella's criticism.[73] Put together with internal, corroborative evidence from material published in the *Athenaeum*'s 'Music' column, one gets a picture of Ella regularly criticizing performances at the King's Theatre, the Antient Concerts and the Philharmonic Society from his seat in the orchestra, and of his providing much of the other writing on music, including reviews of publications. Clearly, to Ella and his editor C. W. Dilke there was nothing incongruous about someone publicly criticizing performances in which he had played a part, albeit from the back of the violin section. Avid reader of the newspapers that he soon became, Ella was both bemused and outraged at the ignorance and inaccuracies that many music writers demonstrated in their notices.[74] What he surely felt he could bring

---

[70] Such practices operated in connection with some of the concerts Ella organized. According to Ella (see evidence in *MR*, 1857, p. xv; and Ella's attribution of a *MP* review to Gruneisen in EllaC, MS 81, mounted cuttings preserved between pp. 14 and 15), Gruneisen wrote favourably of events in 1835 and 1837. Ella may well have been the author of *MP* reports on a series of concerts in 1844, as discussed on p.111 below.

[71] See e.g. the partisan review of the Saltoun Club (*MP*, 2 March 1829), which describes Ella as the 'clever musician' who had produced an arrangement of airs from the ballet *La somnambule* entirely from memory shortly after it was first performed at the King's Theatre.

[72] Ella's period on the *Athenaeum* is documented by Leslie A. Marchand, *The Athenaeum: a Mirror of Victorian Culture* (Chapel Hill: University of North Carolina Press, 1941), 184 (n. 57), 222. On Chorley's arrival at the paper and on his personality as critic, see Robert Terrell Bledsoe, *Henry Fothergill Chorley: Victorian Journalist* (Aldershot: Ashgate, 1998), 27–9, 44–6 and *passim*. Ella himself (*RMU*, 1874, p. 16) claimed it was only after his anonymity was compromised on *MP* that he moved to the *Athenaeum*.

[73] The marked copies are in the City University Library, London. Ella's name first appears in December 1831, and features regularly in the files for 1833 and 1834. Music criticism is not attributed in the 1832 copies.

[74] His diary was often the sounding post. 'Criticism in the Post of last night [concert at Exeter Hall] applauds to the skies Willman who was deputised by Lazarus on

to the job was an accurate account of proceedings, a background awareness of music, institutions and performers, and the informed judgement and trained ear of the professional musician.

This is indeed the impression that Ella's identified writing for the *Athenaeum* creates.[75] He had heard enough performances even in just eight years in London to have something to judge new artists and renditions against, and to give his criticisms authority and credibility. He could admire Laure Cinti-Damoreau's singing – her correct intonation, novel ornamentation and tender expression – but suggest she lacked Maria Malibran's power and depth in 'passages of pathos'.[76] He could complain of a lack of expression in Mori's violin playing in Beethoven's op. 29 string quintet at a Philharmonic concert, by comparing him with Baillot, whom he had known 'move an audience to tears' in the same work, presumably remembering either Leicester or Paris.[77] And of Mendelssohn's solo playing in Mozart's D minor piano concerto, he could boldly say: 'in point of taste, feeling, and execution, we never heard [it] surpassed'.[78] His developing sense of what constituted appropriate performance style also began to emerge, and excesses in cadenzas were singled out, even if in the cases of the flautist Nicholson or the great tenor Rubini they were largely excused;[79] and he was ready to chastise the Opera orchestra for overpowering singers.[80] On top of this, Ella was emboldened to expose what he saw as shoddiness within London's musical institutions: to criticize the Philharmonic Society and the Society of English Vocalists for allowing its 'chief actors' to double as managers; to draw attention to the decision by the directors of the ailing Concerts of Antient Music to reduce the salaries of the orchestra and choir; and to censure the manager of the King's Theatre for varying the starting time of performances 'without announcement or intelligible reason'; or for hiring a poor soprano.[81]

For all this, Ella did more than simply remark on the quality of performances and institutions. As a critic he saw his task primarily to write about and judge the

the Clarionet: what foul ignorance the scribblers', ran one entry (8 February 1838; EllaC, MS 107). See also the quotation at the head of this section.

75 This discussion is based around columns in the *Athenaeum* of 1833 that are attributable to Ella on the basis of the annotations in the City University archive and internal evidence.

76 *Athenaeum* (4 May 1833), 283.

77 *Athenaeum* (2 March 1833), 140.

78 *Athenaeum* (18 May 1833), 316.

79 *Athenaeum* (30 March 1833), 204 and (8 June 1833), 364.

80 *Athenaeum* (13 April 1833), 235.

81 *Athenaeum* (12 January 1833), 28; (26 January 1833), 60; and (30 March 1833), 204.

music he heard. He commented on both the new and the familiar, was equally at ease with operatic repertoire and orchestral works, and was keen to explain his assessments with reference to passages he heard or knew. Underpinning almost all his pronouncements was a belief (probably absorbed from Fétis) in the 'science of music' as the arbiter of good composition: a composer's ability to handle harmony, counterpoint and orchestration, and to combine motifs with originality, were the qualities he most frequently lighted on, sometimes with a self-conscious parading of technical language. Symphonies by Spohr, Mendelssohn and especially Beethoven were notable heights of such composition, and pointing up their 'cleverness' was how Ella attempted to communicate appreciation to readers. In the opera house, music had to match the dramatic situation as well as succeeding technically, which meant that Beethoven's *Fidelio* passed Ella's test, while Bellini's *Norma*, in spite of its popular acclaim and the casting of the great soprano Giuditta Pasta in the title role, did not. Ella upheld the former for its unique combination of simplicity (four-part canon), complexity (counterpoint in the accompaniments), expressiveness (the 'deep feeling' of the Prisoners' Chorus) and 'sublime combinations of voices and instruments in the last finale'.[82] *Norma*, on the other hand, he deemed second rate for its inability to move beyond attractive *bel canto* melodies, the composer having 'never yet shown any feeling for the higher order of dramatic music, or any power in combining the effects of principals, chorus and orchestra, in scenes of action', a tendency that was worsened by offensive harmonies (to Ella's ear) and meagre accompaniments.[83] Only Bellini's *Il pirata* seemed to satisfy.[84]

Taken as a whole, this body of critical writing suggests Ella was already developing a sense of musical 'gold standards' and becoming keen to tell his readers what he felt constituted the best repertoire. On one occasion, songs and 'musical pieces' commodified for the drawing room were written off as trash (there was after all a body of 'masterpieces' for the chamber).[85] Indeed, we may conclude

---

[82] *Athenaeum* (13 April 1833), 235.

[83] *Athenaeum* (29 June 1833), 420 and (6 July 1833), 443. Only the final scene won approval. For similar censure of Bellini, see *Athenaeum* (27 July 1833), 500 [on *I Capuleti e i Montecchi*].

French operas did rather better. The music of Auber's *Fra diavolo* was admired for being 'always in keeping with the scene' (*Athenaeum*, 17 December 1831, p. 821). Although Ella admitted he would be wrong to expect the 'counterpoint of a German scholar' (ibid.), he felt the general style and harmonic palate warranted merit. Hérold's *Zampa* was deemed particularly distinguished, especially for its ability to communicate different psychological states simultaneously (*Athenaeum*, 27 April 1833, p. 267).

[84] *Athenaeum* (27 July 1833), 500. Ella deemed it Bellini's best work.

[85] *Athenaeum* (4 May 1833), 283–4.

that Ella's period on the *Athenaeum* constituted an important formative experience. It required him to form opinions on music and articulate them clearly and succinctly. It taught him how to write regularly, with discipline and to deadlines, and it gave him the confidence to speak out on matters he believed in. Most of all, it encouraged him to see himself as one to whom others might turn for information and authoritative elucidation. Doubtless it was intoxicating for a young man to think that more people than he could ever know personally were reading his columns, and possibly taking his views on board.

Why Ella was eventually replaced by Chorley is not obvious, but by January 1836 Chorley was doing the *Athenaeum* job full time, and there is no strong evidence that Ella continued to contribute.[86] There is nothing on record to suggest a sacking or any acrimony on Ella's part towards Dilke. (In later life our man would publicly take umbrage if slighted or passed over, almost as a matter of course.) He may have left of his own volition, deciding that performance reviewing was eating up too many hours when other, more potentially rewarding openings were emerging in the private sphere.[87] Or Dilke may have gently engineered the changeover, given that Chorley was working alongside Ella on the paper during 1834.[88] Whatever the reason, it did not extinguish Ella's literary ambition, though he seems to have been content henceforth to write mainly occasional, though often lengthier, pieces for a range of papers, always more on the side of news and reportage than anything philosophical or discursive. His reminiscences of Paris for the *Court Journal* of 1836 have already been encountered. He went on to produce a series of essays for the *Musical World* describing his follow-up visit of 1836–7, enthusing about the music of Meyerbeer, Berlioz and others; and he may have contributed other pieces to it too.[89] Meanwhile, when more substantial possibilities offered

---

[86] See Bledsoe, *Henry Chorley*, 27–8, 44–5, 69, 71. Bledsoe explains that the precise point of the change-over is unclear; he considers, however, that Chorley wrote most of the reviews from 1835 onwards. Ella's diary for 1836 refers to his writing for *CJ* and *MW*, but not the *Athenaeum*.

[87] It seems unlikely that Ella was paid well for the work. Chorley's salary, as a staff worker on the journal in 1833, was £50 for the first six months, £65 for the second (Marchand, *The Athenaeum*, 183).

[88] Recommendations had been made to Dilke on Chorley's behalf since 1830 (Bledsoe, *Henry Chorley*, 14).

[89] For a full citation of his *MW* essays, see n. 136. Other contributions by Ella may include the review of William Gardiner's *Music and Friends, or Pleasant Recollections of a Dilettante*, 2 vols. (London: Longman, Orme, Brown & Longman, 1838) published in the issue of 4 April 1839, which makes copious and informed reference to the writings of Fétis. Ella's diary, 20 March 1839 (EllaC, MS 108), indicates that he had that day written for *MW*.

themselves, Ella did not pursue them. Probably around 1837 the publisher J. Alfred
Novello, then proprietor of the paper, apparently offered it to him for sale.[90] Ella
refused, he said, on Dilke's advice, presumably deeming the economic risk too
great.[91] Moreover, in 1839 there was talk of his possibly taking over as the journal's
editor, but this too seems to have come to nothing.[92] It would have meant reducing other activities, which might not have seemed palatable. However, Ella was not
above hawking for piecework as a writer-reviewer: finding himself in Gloucester
for the music festival in September 1838, he attempted to offer his services to a local
newspaper.[93]

O N 1 January 1836 Ella turned over a new leaf in his diary-keeping, replacing
his pocket diary, which had served as an appointments book up till then,
with a larger *Daily Remembrancer*, which he now wrote up habitually as a journal.[94]
Like many a would-be diarist he found his commitment flagged periodically, and
by 1840 he had returned to the pocket format, with the consequent loss of close
observation and literary expansiveness. But for a few years he diarized assiduously,
leaving us a set of insights into his professional activities, travels, and even his
mindset, motivations and family affairs, and revealing still more of his views on
music, musicians and the London 'music scene' (Fig. 6). The job of critic predisposed Ella to form and record judgements on music. In the diaries opinions appear
in profusion, and range from his ceaseless admiration for Mozart's *Don Giovanni*,
in spite of having played it almost 100 times, to his derision for 'twaddling' English

[90] J. Ella, 'The "Musical World"', *Orchestra* (3 March 1866), 363–4.

[91] Ibid. The account is consistent with remarks in Ella's diary (23 February 1838; EllaC,
MS 107) to the effect that Dilke thought *MW* would not last. A brief account of
Novello's proprietorship of the journal is given in Victoria L. Cooper, *The House of
Novello: Practice and Policy of a Victorian Music Publisher, 1829–1866* (Aldershot:
Ashgate, 2003), 138–42.

[92] Diary, 8 March 1839 (EllaC, MS 108): 'M^r R: [Robins; one of his patrons] flattered
me in the belief of my ability to express myself sufficiently well to undertake the
Superintendence [*sic*] of the M. W.' There is no follow-up evidence in the diaries
to suggest that Ella took on the role; nor did Ella later flaunt it as an achievement,
which he surely would have done had he held the position. However, a letter
published in *MW* (7 August 1845, p. 374) asserted that Ella had 'at one time' been
the journal's editor.

[93] Diary, 9 and 10 September 1838 (EllaC, MS 107). He also asked (14 September 1838),
unsuccessfully, for a reporter's ticket to 'the Ball'.

[94] Up to 1835 the extant diaries are pocket books. The diary for 1837 is missing,
breaking the narrative.

March—1836.   51

Friday. 25.

Fire Insurances due.—MOON ENTERS FIRST QUARTER.

Saturday 26.

6 A page from Ella's 1836 diary.
Reproduced by kind permission of the Bodleian Library, Oxford.

glees.[95] These views largely underscore, sometimes intensify, his discourse in the
Athenaeum, giving weight to the perception that Ella's tastes in music were crys-
tallizing during these years. Particularly relevant in terms of how Ella's musical
preferences would eventually be expressed are his growing admiration for the
Viennese chamber repertoire and his reactions to works by British composers.

Apart from showing just how much domestic music-making Ella was engaged
in, the daily log vividly communicates both his exhilaration at exploring what
must have seemed like an almost unending repertoire of substantial chamber
works, and his developing veneration for the music of Beethoven. In January 1836
Ella records how he and the pianist Edouard Schulz (with whom he shared digs)
purchased, played and learned many of the Beethoven piano sonatas and violin
sonatas, the first attempt at op. 47 sending them 'to bed full of musical happiness'
on account of the work's 'Grandeur & effect' and precipitating earnest resolutions
from Schulz to play 'one of Beethoven's Sonatas every morning', much to Ella's
approval.[96] Ella's developing credo for good instrumental music and its importance as spiritual nourishment then emerges in the following passage:

> The difference of Fashionable Piano-F. music & really classical is, that the one
> aims at effect with Melody, Ingenuity of Harmony, and violent transitions;
> the other, by superior and more natural treatment of its Melodies in
> Counterpoint. The one takes you by surprise and gives you a momentary
> sensation of pleasure[,] the other excites your admiration & imagination,
> with a permanent source of food for reflection – the one is gulped at one
> repast, the other is but tasted with a desire to taste again, the oftener the
> more relished. The one is top and bottom, & the other a complete structure
> of legitimate material.[97]

Such words help us understand how Ella weighed up works he encountered for a
first time, and why he would despair of musicians – professional as well as amateur
– who could not grasp the beauties and originality of Beethoven's music.[98]

95 On *Don Giovanni*: 'it leaves the other Italian operas at an unmeasurable distance!'
    (diary, 19 May 1838; EllaC, MS 107); on glees, see the diary, 4 January 1836 and the
    'occasional memoranda' at the end of January 1836 (EllaC, MS 106).

96 Quotations from the diary, 5 January 1836 and 'occasional memoranda' following
    the entry for 10 January 1836 (EllaC, MS 106). The entries for the whole month
    show how often they were playing the sonatas; what Ella refers to in the diary as
    op. 57 is clearly the 'Kreutzer' sonata op. 47.

97 'Occasional memoranda' following the entry for 10 January 1836 (EllaC, MS 106).

98 See e.g. the entry for 20 January 1836 (EllaC, MS 106), where a potpourri of opera
    airs by Czerny, arranged for quintet, is dismissed as 'noisy trash' while the first
    movement of Spohr's nonet, also adapted for quintet, disappoints on account of

On British composition, already generally perceived to be at a low ebb, Ella's views were characteristically mixed, with works measured against Continental exemplars and ideals of great composition. After a concert by the Society of British Musicians, a group of composers self-consciously devoted to raising the profile of homespun works, he lamented that most of 'the exhibition of tonight' was not 'very flattering to Native Genius', despairing of the lack of originality in most of the programme. Still, this did not prevent him admiring the workmanship in a piano concerto by Charles Neate, and finding cleverness in a string quartet 'à la Haydn' by T. P. Chipp.[99] On another occasion he would pronounce G. F. Perry's *The Fall of Jerusalem* 'often tediously uninteresting, & seldom original & never […] Sublime in effect', always – one imagines – with the sounds of *Messiah*, which he loved, ringing in his ears.[100] Set against this, he considered Balfe's *Falstaff* a successful mix of good melodies, methodical (if not first-class) scoring and set pieces *alla* Italian opera; Barnett's *Farinelli* was, he felt, beautifully orchestrated.[101] In years to come Ella would become strongly associated with European repertoire to the exclusion of anything British, and would be much reviled by sectors of the British press and subsequent generations of writers because of it. Diatribes against Ella became so pernicious later in the century that it is worth emphasizing at this juncture that the young Ella, who saw himself as a composer of sorts, was willing to acknowledge what he felt was good – as well as bad – among his fellow compatriots' output, and that he appeared reasonably open-minded about native composition, while holding on to Beethoven as the model of perfection.[102]

Ella's diaries also show instrumentalists and singers being weighed up against his perceptions of excellence, and often with greater frankness than might appear in print. He admired the great sopranos (Grisi, Malibran, Pasta, Persiani) and

its 'want of invention and power of producing contrast'. Elsewhere (14 March 1836) Ella would refer to the 'extraordinary stupidity of some musicians not to discern the beauties & originality of Beethoven'; or (30 March 1836) endorse those few 'English amateurs', such as the Freelings, who were able to 'enjoy, at a first hearing, the beauties of Beethoven', in this case a rendition by Schulz and Ella of the 'Kreutzer' sonata.

99 Diary, 4 January 1836 (EllaC, MS 106). The *Musical Library Monthly Supplement* (1836), 44, identifies the work as a 'MS. quintet [*sic*] in E minor, for violins, viola, and violoncello'.

100 Diary, 7 February 1838 (EllaC, MS 107); on his admiration for the 'magnificence' of the choruses in *Messiah*, see diary, 20 December 1839 (EllaC, MS 108).

101 Diary, 19 July 1838 and 28 February 1839 (EllaC, MSS 107 and 108).

102 On Ella's sense of himself as a composer, see the diary, 25 January 1836 (EllaC, MS 106): he was pleased when Bochsa said he had heard good things about Ella's sextet, which had been played at Ella's benefit concert the previous year.

tenors (Tamburini, Rubini and Lablache), though not unequivocally: he could be censorious of Tamburini and Malibran for their inappropriate excesses in caden-zas, of Grisi's acting, and so on.[103] And while he might delight at Ignaz Moscheles's 'masterly' piano-playing, and judge the violinist Ferdinand David 'a great artist', he was alert to and appalled by the declining quality of Mori's fiddling.[104]

The diaries contain further censure of the music societies he played for, criti-cisms often coloured by his experiences in Paris. He was frustrated, for example, by the small string section at the Opera and by the number of errors in the band parts that arose from hiring poor copyists, thus protracting rehearsals, although he admired the fresh standards and disciplines that the recently appointed Ital-ian conductor Michael Costa was bringing to bear.[105] Besides, he keenly regretted the absence of a true and adequately supported national opera house in London: somewhere that would be both a forum for indigenous repertoire and a training ground for British singers.[106]

He felt strongly about the poor performance standards at the Antient Con-certs, to which feeble choirs and amateur conductors contributed.[107] But he was even more exercised by the 'stale' selections of works made by the noblemen directors, who chose music for reasons of antiquarianism and regardless of its aesthetic merit.[108] In his view, the men he dubbed 'the Ancient Bigots' displayed

---

[103] A spread of Ella's comments on singers can be found in the following entries: 14 April 1836 (Grisi and Tamburini); 21 April 1836 (Pasta's and Grisi's acting com-pared); 12 May 1836 (Malibran's embellishments, high notes and vocal quality); 31 May 1836 (Tamburini's embellishments and intonation); 22 May 1838 (Persiani and Rubini); 1 June 1838 (Grisi and Tamburini); and 21 June 1838 (Lablache and Tamburini): EllaC, MSS 106 and 107.

[104] See entries for 11 May 1836 (Moscheles), 5 and 16 April 1838 and 1 April 1839 (Mori) and 16 March 1839 (David): EllaC, MSS 106, 107 and 108. Mori died in June 1839.

[105] On the size of the opera band, see the diary, 17 February 1836 (EllaC MS 106): 'He [Costa] has often told me that he would first cut away two feet off the stage, and add 12 more Violins, 4 [?four] tenors, four Cellos & four Double-Basses!'. On problems with the parts, including Costa's careful correction of them ahead of rehearsals and a comparison with Paris, see the entries for 17 March, 24 and 29 June 1836. As a conductor, Costa was a disciplinarian (and admired by Ella for it) and wrought much change. His style of rehearsing and conducting is discussed in Michael Musgrave, 'Changing Values in Nineteenth-Century Performance: the Work of Michael Costa and August Manns', MBC, 169–91.

[106] Diary, 5 April 1836 (EllaC, MS 106).

[107] Diary, 4 and 18 May 1836 (EllaC, MS 106).

[108] For instance by the Archbishop of York, as per the diary, 7 March 1836 (EllaC, MS 106). Ella deemed Lord Burghersh the only nobleman-director capable of making good selections of repertoire (diary, 9 March 1836).

affectations for understanding art music that were matched only by their subscribers.[109] More to Ella's liking as regards repertoire were the Philharmonic's concerts,
but disillusionment with the society's management was mounting, the appointment of a mediocre British bassoonist over the more talented Paris-trained Fried-
rich Baumann (a Belgian who played in the King's Theatre orchestra) incurring
a particularly lengthy outpouring.[110] In December 1839, with the wounds from
his blackballing doubtless still smarting, and aware that the society was falling
into financial difficulties, Ella diagnosed too much 'Ignorance & Bigotry' in their
Council.[111] When changes to the orchestra's seating arrangements ensued in February 1840 he tendered his resignation, presumably feeling secure enough to stand
the loss of income. It was politely accepted.[112] In the meantime, new initiatives
such as the Melophonic Society and Società Armonica rarely pleased; and older
traditions, such as the choral singing at Westminster Abbey, could disappoint.[113]
No wonder he was privately thinking he was ready to direct 'something good if not
great'.[114]

   That said, not all aspects of London's public musical life were unpalatable to
him. Choral standards at the Sacred Harmonic Society concerts at Exeter Hall
were improving and could draw praise;[115] and he attended several of the newly
flourishing chamber music concerts, a subject we shall return to later. And whatever the artistic merits of the Promenade concerts, Ella understood their importance in providing employment to orchestral musicians during the slack part of
the year.[116] Indeed, his views were usually permeated by an optimistic, typically
Victorian, belief in progress. By the late 1830s he was convinced that many things
about London music should and could be better done, and was starting to see
himself as the person to bring about improvements.

[109] Diary, 9 March 1836 (EllaC, MS 106).

[110] Diary, 20 February 1836 (EllaC, MS 106).

[111] Comments at the end of the 1839 diary (EllaC, MS 108).

[112] Directors' minutes (BL, RPS/MS/281), f. 38v (minute for 16 February 1840). The
    Philharmonic directors accepted with regret that 'he [Ella] should have found dis-
    tinctions [? differences in the treatment of members] in the Orchestra which they
    had never Contemplated'.

[113] On the Melophonic, see the diary, 1 February 1838; on the Società Armonica and
    its audiences, see 30 May 1836 and 11 June 1838; on Westminster Abbey music, see
    13 January 1839 (EllaC, MSS 106, 107 and 108).

[114] See p. 73 above.

[115] Diary, 16 and 30 March 1838, 21 December 1838 and 27 December 1839 (EllaC,
    MSS 107 and 108).

[116] Remarks at the end of the 1839 diary (EllaC, MS 108).

I F all this literary effort produced someone more assured in his opinions, and ambitious for what he might achieve for the musical world, it also brought a dawning awareness of the difference between the written word and the spoken word, and the importance of gentlemanly tact and discretion when 'in society'. On one occasion he rued having been too frank about the weaknesses of Balfe's song 'Despair', to the composer's face:

> I regret much ever being employed to act "critic and reviewer;" it has accustomed me to speak as I was wont to write – i-e candidly and critically – I am conscious of my unpopularity on this score; I must determine on acting a little the Hypocrite and maintain silence.[117]

Ella's growing renown in musical circles, allied to his successful association with high society, was meanwhile making him a controversial figure in some quarters, as a lively episode from autumn 1839 makes clear. Ella was away from London when a heated correspondence in the *Musical World* broke out over the merits of Mozart's music.[118] There were two main factions, one defending the composer's eminence, the other branding the music lightweight and inferior to the works of Rossini, Handel, Beethoven and others. Amidst the fray, one pro-Mozart correspondent who was using an alias drew bad blood from another (writing as 'Indicator'), the latter exposing the former as 'that very conceited and very foolish writer *Un fanatico per la Musica*, otherwise Count Huguenots Ella, the *ciarlatano* of the Philharmonic and Opera orchestras, the intimate ally of the Duke of Cambridge, Captain Blackheath Legge, Lord Saltoun, and Mr. Thalberg Schulz'.[119] In fact, Ella had been incorrectly identified, and since he felt it worth while confiding to his diary that a letter from one F. [i.e. B. Forrester] Scott of Leicester, published in the paper some weeks later, 'settles the matter', we may imagine that follow-up correspondence in his defence made for sweet reading.[120] All the same, there were lessons for Ella in the episode, notably the

[117] Diary, 22 January 1836 (EllaC, MS 106).

[118] *MW* (17 October 1839), 382–5.

[119] *MW* (14 November 1839), 450–1, at 451.

[120] Diary, 12 December 1839 (EllaC, MS 108). The letter, which appeared in *MW* (12 December 1839), 515–16, pointed out that Ella had been in Scotland during the controversy and had given his permission to Scott to write the letter. The journal published an apology on p. 522 of the same issue.

'Scott' was almost certainly the string-playing amateur who was one of William Gardiner's regular quartet partners (as indicated in *Music and Friends*, 1838, p. 831). Scott and Ella were acquainted. Ella's diary indicates he had joined Gardiner's group to play Beethoven quintets during a visit to Leicester in 1836 (entry for 5 September; EllaC, MS 106); Scott is named as one of the participants.

importance of growing a thick skin if he was to continue to develop a public profile.

Like all caricatures, the *Musical World*'s contained a grain of truth. Ella had become known as an enthusiastic promoter of Meyerbeer's *Les Huguenots* and all things French; he was also advancing socially, both through his musical activities and his desire for cultural improvement. (He was reading rapaciously, visiting galleries of fine art, attending lectures and so on.) His visible connections with the aristocracy would have generated hostility from within the British music profession, which had always had a love-hate relationship with the upper classes, who were, historically, the main supporters of music. Musicians sought and needed their patronage, though were typically treated as little more than servants. That is, unless they were from abroad – the aristocracy had always tended to favour Continental music and indulge foreign musicians (who had the further advantage of understanding the rules of courtly etiquette) over native ones, which was a source of professional tension.[121] When, during the nineteenth century, some British musicians such as Ella started to enjoy a less rigid relationship with the wealthier ranks, others who were not thus favoured were antagonized.[122] That was ahead. For the moment, Ella's diary reveals just how eye-opening and alien these worlds were to a shopkeeper's son from Leicester. In 1836 he reeled at the 'splendour of the Staircase, the Gallery, the Beauty and Dresses of the Nobility' at a private concert at the Duke of Sutherland's.[123] At Victoria's Coronation in 1838 (Sir George Smart had hired him for the orchestra) he found the 'spectacle of the Ceremony & the coup d'œil of the Pageant' defied his 'Power of description[.] I would not have missed the sight'.[124]

Notes confided by Ella to his diary in November 1838 about 'Lester [*sic*] & its stupid inhabitants', and his mocking of the naivety and inaccuracies of William Gardiner's public remarks on music, suggest the more familiar Ella became with London high life, the more he distanced himself from his roots, and viewed himself as a cut above his origins.[125] Still, he continued to visit family in Leicester,

[121] These issues are explored in the eighteenth-century context in *McVeighCL*, 187–8, 202–4.

[122] In his *Music of the Raj: a Social and Economic History of Music in Late Eighteenth-Century Anglo-Indian Society* (Oxford: Oxford University Press, 2000), 216–17, Ian Woodfield argues that some signs of change may be seen to emerge in the 1780s and 90s, especially in expatriate society. He points out that there were nevertheless limits to friendships made between musicians and members of high society.

[123] Diary, 13 July 1836 (EllaC, MS 106).

[124] Diary, 28 June 1838 (EllaC, MS 107).

[125] The remark about Leicester is in the diary, 28 November 1838 (EllaC, MS 107). The quality and inappropriateness of Gardiner's publicly espoused ideas are noted in

usually while travelling to provincial festivals, when he would pick up work in Leicester performances as one of London's élite musicians, or seek out the communion of chamber music with the town's most discerning amateurs. On his own admission, ties to his immediate family were not strong, with the exception of his mother and elder sister, Ann.[126] Yet in 1836 he was thinking hard about the benefits of marriage, gazing on happy couples, pondering Schiller on matrimonial happiness, and presumably feeling he could afford the requisite outlay on a household.[127] That there had been at least one realistic candidate for a spouse earlier in the decade is revealed by a letter of 1831 to Ella from Sir George Cornewall, who congratulates him on avoiding the temptation of early marriage:

> [N]o good comes of it at your time of Life & you would be fettered in your actions & deprived of the Power of going to & fro to Paris, or of making your Country Tours, when Music invites. No, avoid the God Hymen for the present at least.[128]

Perhaps Cornewall's influence persisted: in spring 1839 Ella pronounced himself wary of wedlock, seeing unhappy marriages around him and reminding himself that 'Artists should be careful when they marry'.[129] At the year's end he claimed to be at peace with remaining single, hoping he might end his days living with his sister Ann as an 'old Bachelor & Maid' – and content for now, we may imagine, to focus on the professional furrows he wished to plough.[130]

---

the entry for 12 April 1838. The first volumes of Gardiner's *Music and Friends* were published in 1838.

[126] 'The Death of my dear Mother seems to have united the scattered fragments of existing affection between our relations into one more natural feeling!' (remarks at the end of the 1838 diary; EllaC, MS 107). His fondness for Ann is frequently noted in the diaries, likewise his anguish at her final illness and death (1841).

[127] John Tosh, *A Man's Place: Masculinity and the Middle-Class Home in Victorian England* (New Haven and London: Yale University Press, 1999), 108–9, points out that middle-class men were generally urged to leave marriage until they had accumulated enough wealth to set up a complete home. This could mean waiting until their late twenties or thirties.

[128] Scrapbook, EllaC, MS 81, p. 63. Dated 14 March 1831.

[129] Diary, 21 March 1838. Compare Ella's sanguine view of marriage in the entries for 18 January, 4 April and 27 July 1836 with his more cautious remarks on the subject on 21 March and 1 April 1838, and 10 January 1839 (EllaC, MSS 106, 107 and 108).

[130] Remarks at the end of the 1839 diary (EllaC, MS 108).

Yet by 1841 Ann Ella was dead, the fourth in a recent sequence of family bereavements which had begun with his mother's death in 1838 and which threw up a series of small legacies.[131] These windfalls Ella invested with typical acuity. We know this because the tiny pocket diaries he kept from 1840, while rarely rising above a memorandum of appointments, contain week-by-week grids of income and expenditure. They show both the interest drawn from invested sums and, in 1840, the arrival of a 'legacy' of £200 from his maternal grandfather.[132] For this reason, and because not all the amounts coming in were payments for his professional activities, the turnover naturally appears far greater than what Ella was making from his work. However, if we factor out legacies, reimbursements for goods purchased on another's behalf, repayments of small loans to his friends and so on, we can form estimates of Ella's basic income from music: c.£290 in 1840, c.£240 in 1841 – enough to enable Ella to carry on a modest middle-class lifestyle and to pick and choose his work, dropping the orchestral jobs he felt less comfortable with and pursuing additional openings within his private networks. The resignation from the Philharmonic in 1840 was preceded by his withdrawal from the Antient Concerts (1839);[133] he nevertheless continued in the Opera and other bands.

[131] His mother, Kitty, died in 1838; there followed in 1839 the deaths of his brother Henry (in India) and maternal grandfather. Ann died in February 1841. Kitty's personal estate (worth £1,500) was to be divided equally between the seven surviving children. According to the terms of her late husband's will (copy in NA, PROB–11/1664), the family shop and home was to be held in trust for Kitty until her death, following which it was to be sold. We may assume this happened. Ann, who subsequently operated as a confectioner, but in Cheapside on the other side of the Market Place, left all her 'Real and Personal Estates' to John; her will was sworn under £600, suggesting this included her domicile. John Ella would later (1850s) sell a house in Leicester, presumably this one. Copies of both women's wills are in LRO (PR/J/1838/60 and PR/T/1841/51).

[132] Diary for February 1840 (EllaC, MS 109). This ties in with remarks in Ella's 1839 diary (9 February; MS 108) that in his grandfather's will £200 (in code: £B00) was left to 'each of us'. Ella followed it with the comment: 'shabby?', suggesting it was much less than he had expected. He says as much in the end-of-year summary at the back of the diary: 'My Grandfather's legacy to his grandchildren is but a little he intended to have left Mother! It matters not – money does not always purchase happiness'.

[133] His name disappears from the Antients' orchestral lists in 1839; and his diaries cease noting attendance at rehearsals and concerts.

❧ *Continental travel*

> *Rome* [...] *I hope to live to see this ruined City. I shall never be*
> *settled until my ramble thro'* *Italy* *has been achieved –*
>
> ⁓ Ella's diary, 25 February 1839

Ella's appetite for foreign travel, whetted by his first visit to Paris in 1827–8, showed no signs of diminishing in his thirties and forties, when he undertook more tours. This was scarcely to be surprised at, since he stood to gain so much through exposure to music and culture in the major cities of Europe and since the thrill of crossing borders was still strong for a man reared in a slowly industrializing market town in the English Midlands. Musicians had always stood to make such passages in the course of their work more often than most other members of the lower-middle classes, and often did so with success even if their command of foreign language was nebulous, their principal mode of communication being sounds rather than words. Ella, however, was going not primarily to play (though he took his violin and viola; chamber music was a good way to develop friendship bonds) and certainly not to find work, but to meet, listen and learn. Here he benefited from the fact that Continental travel, once largely the province of the aristocracy, was becoming more affordable to the middling orders. It was also getting easier, with improvements in road communications, although it would be some years before Ella would see European travel transformed and journey times slashed with the advent of trains.

Paris was the most obvious centre of attraction, and Ella made another extended visit there during the late autumn and early winter of 1836–7.[134] He also longed to see Italy. He claimed he had intended travelling on there from Paris in 1829, but had been unable to tear himself away from the captivations of the French capital, which included the spell-binding *Guillaume Tell*.[135] How financially viable a journey to Italy would have been at that stage in Ella's career is difficult to judge; but ten years later the urge was strong (as demonstrated by the quotation at the head of this section), and in August 1842 he set off for Rome, returning to London via Paris in early March 1843. His activities and impressions of both trips were confided first to his diary (more sparsely in 1842 than in 1836, but indicative nonetheless); then the most striking memories were expanded in accounts for the British press.[136]

---

[134] It is possible he also visited Paris in 1832–4: diaries are not extant for these years.

[135] *MW* (26 January 1838), 52.

[136] Diary entries for the visit to Paris run from 7 November 1836 till the end of the year (EllaC, MS 106). Ella's expenditure on the trip, entered at the end of the 1836 diary, indicates that he stayed until 28 January 1837; unfortunately the 1837 diary does not

These sources make for colourful travelogues and scene-setting, though their main value is their revelations of what Ella experienced musically and socially, and the ideas he took back to London.

In 1836 the two-and-a-half-day journey to Paris (via Calais and Abbeville) was made by steamer and carriage, the latter 'tediously slow' at times, as Ella was forced to dismount and walk up hills, although comfortable by 1830s standards, since the roads were reasonably well tarmacked.[137] Having taken rooms in a hotel on arrival (9 November), he began his *vie parisienne* with *élan*, taking in the sights and cultural treasures, moving among musicians he already knew, and securing the social introductions and dinner invitations on which his networking, and occasional gossip-mongering, would thrive. Older and more established in the world of London music than he had been on his previous visits, Ella seems to have integrated into Paris life quickly, now having adequate French to converse and comprehend what went on around him, a range of contacts to exploit, and ever more experiences and opinions to share.[138] His social round included existing acquaintances from London and Paris: the celebrated singers Lablache, Tamburini and Rubini, the cellist Scipion Rousselot, one of the string-playing Tilmant brothers, the publisher Maurice Schlesinger, the composers Meyerbeer, Ferdinand Ries and George Osborne, and the conductor Michael Costa to name just some of the musicians most frequently mentioned, and even an English amateur or two. Introductions were also made: to, among others, the venerable Italian opera composer Ferdinando Paer (whom Ella found an amiable raconteur), the conductor at the Opéra F.-A. Habeneck (stern and authoritative), and Heinrich Panofka, then active in Paris as a composer, critic and violinist (a good though not especially powerful player, according to Ella's

survive. The 1842 and 1843 diaries (EllaC, MSS 111 and 112) follow his activities in entries spanning 14 August 1842 to 5 March 1843.

Ella wrote up his musical experiences in Paris in a series of essays, 'Music in Paris in 1837', for the *MW*: (1 December 1837, pp. 184–5; 15 December 1837, pp. 209–11; 29 December 1837, pp. 241–4; 5 January 1838, pp. 2–3; 12 January 1838, pp. 24–6; 26 January 1838, pp. 50–2; 27 June 1838, pp. 144–6; 2 August 1838, pp. 225–7; 9 August 1838, pp. 242–3; 23 August 1838, pp. 270–2). From Italy in 1843 he sent a series of dispatches to *MP*, which appeared as follows: 'Rome, January 23', *MP* (8 February 1843); 'A Theatrical Row in Italy!', *MP* (23 February 1843); 'Florence, Feb. 4', 'Turin, Feb. 9', *MP* (24 February 1843).

[137] Diary, 8 and 9 November 1836 (EllaC, MS 106).

[138] His French must have been reasonably fluent, though after a night at the Gymnase theatre, he noted how much he had to concentrate on the dialogue – 'they speak very fast'. Diary, 22 November 1836 (EllaC, MS 106).

impressions).[139] Notably absent, doubtless to Ella's *chagrin*, were Rossini, who was away in Bologna, and Fétis, now based in Brussels, where he had become director of the Conservatoire.[140]

This matrix of connections was Ella's passport to French salon culture and its music-making. Whether it amounted to dropping in on Osborne and hearing him play a Beethoven piano trio with amateurs, or attending the Tilmant brothers' weekly chamber-music séances, at which the cream of French musicians gathered, the impact was much the same: of a lively, top-quality chamber music culture that outstripped anything on offer in London, particularly in terms of professional string playing, style and ensemble.[141] In his diary Ella noted having heard at the Tilmants' Onslow's newly written quintets (one was probably op. 25) and Beethoven's quartets (including op. 95 and one of the 'late' works), though registered his reactions only cursorily – he knew roughly what to expect, even if he could not fully comprehend the mysteries of late Beethoven.[142] Some time later he recalled the performances in detail in a *Musical World* essay, suggesting strong impressions had been made:

> [T]he quartets at Tilmant's were executed in a way I had been little accustomed to hear – affinity of taste, expression, and style of bowing, congeniality of temperament in the whole of the individuals, a just discrimination in the *abandon* of passages which simultaneously called for its indulgence[;] these, and other rare qualities, were developed in an ensemble perfectly unique.[143]

The gatherings were well attended – Ella counted some sixty 'artists' one evening.[144] But what possibly astonished him most, to the extent that he noted it down, was being assured by a musician from Marseilles that Beethoven's late quartets were played and relished in the southern city.[145] Probably, the contrast with London, where these late works had only just begun to be introduced, and to a mixed reception, could not have seemed greater.

[139] Diary, 18 December 1836 (Paer), 10 December 1836 (Habeneck) and 5 December 1836 (Panofka): EllaC, MS 106.

[140] Rossini's departure, the day Ella arrived, was noted in *MW* (12 January 1838), 24.

[141] Ella's attendance is noted in the diary entries for 25 November (Osborne and Tilmant), 1 and 15 December 1836 (Tilmant): EllaC, MS 106. The trio, in B♭, might have been op. 11, or conceivably op. 97.

[142] Ibid.

[143] *MW* (5 January 1838), 2.

[144] Diary, 1 December 1836 (EllaC, MS 106).

[145] Ibid.

At public performances elsewhere in Paris, other horizons of expectation were being stretched, as Ella encountered music by Berlioz and a new and challenging opera from the more familiar pen of Meyerbeer, whose *Robert le diable* he had heard during its production by a French company at the King's Theatre in 1832.[146] We know that Ella had made Meyerbeer's acquaintance when the composer was in London to supervise the rehearsals, and had warmed to him[147] as well as to *Robert*, which he would later pronounce Meyerbeer's finest work.[148] He had also been intrigued, earlier in 1836, by mixed reports from Paris about the composer's latest creation, *Les Huguenots*: he had enjoyed Fétis's remarks on the work in *Le temps*, and had received enthusiastic accounts from an English witness, the soprano Elizabeth Masson.[149] Moreover, he had intended to obtain the choral parts, presumably with the Saltoun circle in mind.[150] Getting to hear the new opera was thus a high priority for him, a fact nicely encapsulated by Ella's bribing his way up the queue outside the Opéra to ensure admission.[151] The day after this performance he articulated his thoughts: the fourth and fifth acts were 'truly sublime', and there was some ingenious, what he called 'excentric', orchestration; but there were a fair number of oddities, including the stretched vocal range for the principal bass, and the ballet tunes lacked the elegance and originality of those in *Robert*.[152] Still, even at this first hearing Ella had the foresight to realize that the opera needed to be seen several times if full appreciation was to be achieved – a viewpoint possibly

[146] *RMU* (1864), sup., 2. The King's Theatre production, begun 11 June 1832, had been preceded by performances of English adaptations at Drury Lane (as *The Daemon*, 20 February), and Covent Garden (*The Fiend-Father*, 21 February); and by an English parody of the opera at the Adelphi (*Robert le diable, the Devil's Son*, 23 January); as noted in Alfred Loewenberg, *The Annals of Opera, 1597–1940*, 3rd edition (London: John Calder, 1978), col. 736.

[147] *RMU* (1864), sup., 2. In *RMU* (1880), 28, Ella recorded that Meyerbeer, Mendelssohn and Costa had attended a party at Ella's home in May 1832. A letter from Meyerbeer to Ella, preserved in autograph manuscript and printed transcription (the latter dated 3 June 1832 by Ella) in EllaC, MS 79, p. 9, gives further evidence of their cordial social connection.

[148] *RMU* (1864), sup., 3. He attempted to get to see a performance in Paris during his stay in 1836, though found he could not purchase a pit seat due to the opera's immense popularity (diary, 28 November 1836; EllaC, MS 106).

[149] Diary, 16 March and 14 June 1836 (Fétis) and 18 March (Masson): EllaC, MS 106. Fétis's article appeared in the issue of *Le temps* for 5 March. Masson, a pupil of Pasta, claimed she would happily go back to Paris to hear the work a third time.

[150] Diary, 18 March 1836 (EllaC, MS 106).

[151] Diary, 23 November 1836 (EllaC, MS 106).

[152] Diary, 24 November 1836 (EllaC, MS 106).

encouraged by Meyerbeer, who, on learning that Ella had heard it only once, sent him free tickets, enabling six further nights of discovery.[153] Ella's diary shadows his slowly developing understanding of this epic historical opera and his perseverance with it, perhaps because he knew Fétis had already pointed up its merits. After returning to London (January 1837) he produced an extensive synopsis and analysis of the work as part of his series 'Music in Paris in 1837' for the *Musical World*.[154] He attempted to explain how the music articulated the unfolding drama and characterizations, yet admitted his own initial difficulties with the opera and recommended repeated hearings before passing judgement.[155] This particular lesson would stay with him. Even now, there were parts he struggled with, and he wrote freely and critically of them; but his bottom line was that this was an opera which, though lacking the melodic appeal of *Robert*, was so skilfully and theatrically conceived that musicians would and should admire it. It was already, in Ella's own words, widely considered Meyerbeer's *chef-d'œuvre*.[156]

Berlioz's music was more of a challenge, not only because Ella heard two long, programmatic instrumental works, the *Symphonie fantastique* and *Harold en Italie*, once only, but also because it was virgin territory for him.[157] The composer had a good reputation in Paris, and Ella had heard he was one of the rising stars. He knew Berlioz's music criticism and admired it, and thought well of Berlioz

---

[153] As retold in *MW* (27 June 1838), 144, and *RMWE* (1852), 20. There was probably some poetic licence at work here, since the diary (14 December 1836; EllaC, MS 106) suggests that this episode occurred after Ella had heard the work twice, and that this was not the men's first encounter after Ella heard the work. That he attended six performances seems likely, because in addition to 23 November he was present on 7, 14 and 28 December 1836, and probably again in January 1837.

[154] *MW* (27 June 1838), 144–6; (2 August 1838), 225–7; (9 August 1838), 242–3; (23 August 1838), 270–2.

[155] A similar sentiment is expounded by Ella in his diary (14 March 1836; EllaC, MS 106): 'Persons, however well informed in art, should never hastily come to conclusions on the merits of Music by a single hearing, especially when the Composition is not done justice to by the Performers' [in response to a London performance of Beethoven's piano fantasia op. 80, given by Lucy Anderson at the Vocal Concerts].

[156] *MW* (23 August 1838), 272.

[157] He heard the works on 4 December 1836. A handbill for the concert, with programme details, survives in EllaC (MS 9/xxiv). Ella noted the event in his diary (4 December 1836; EllaC, MS 106). Possibly the only experience of Berlioz's music Ella had had thus far was when the Philharmonic Society in London tried out one of the overtures (February 1834; review by Ella in *Athenaeum*, 15 February 1834, p. 130). He deemed the work 'by no means so satisfactory' as one by Andreas Romberg, also played.

for his endorsement of *Les Huguenots*.[158] But he did not know the music. Even though the two 1836 performances (at the Conservatoire, in the same concert) were conducted by the composer, with the accomplished Chrétien Urhan taking the viola solo in *Harold*, Ella found the works difficult to grasp, and while 'much delighted with some parts of Berlioz's descriptive music' and judging the composer a 'perfect master of Instrumentation', he could not accept this was a man of genius.[159] He was nonplussed by the melodic lines, and admitted to his diary that he found some of them 'barberously uncooth [sic]'.[160] In print he was more circumspect, but the basic sentiments remained.[161] Where Berlioz won with Ella was in his matching of the music to the dramatic situation, a précis of which, in the case of the *Symphonie fantastique*, Berlioz had already committed to prose for distribution to concert audiences. If the listeners at the Conservatoire concert were provided with the résumé (and there is every reason to think they were), Ella found no need to comment on it, perhaps because it seemed in the same mould as an opera libretto.[162] Still, the innovation was important and striking, and if he did handle concert literature on this particular evening, Ella surely did not forget it: within ten years he would be introducing programme notes at his own concerts in London.

Meanwhile, there was other new music for Ella to explore in Paris, particularly operas: Adam's *Le postillon de Lonjumeau*, Louise Bertin's *Esmeralda* and Halévy's *La juive* are among the works we know he heard.[163] There were also unknown singers to appraise in the theatre and the salon, from the fresh voices of Emma Albertazzi and Julie Dorus-Gras to the more peculiar sounds of Adolphe Nourrit and Nicolas Levasseur.[164] And diverse experiences beckoned: Jullien's and Musard's promenade concerts, albeit lightweight in repertoire, impressed by the extraordinary discipline of the orchestral players and the size of crowd they drew; and there

---

[158] *MW* (15 December 1837), 210–11.

[159] Diary, 4 December 1836 (EllaC, MS 106).

[160] Ibid.

[161] *MW* (15 December 1837), 210–11.

[162] The modern critical edition (*Hector Berlioz: New Edition of the Complete Works*, vol.16, ed. Nicholas Temperley, p. 167) indicates that a printed programme was almost certainly provided for the 4 December 1836 performance; extant copies are in the Bibliothèque Nationale, Paris (Collection Macnutt). The comments Ella made in his diary for that day (EllaC, MS 106) suggest an awareness of the work's programmatic intent.

[163] Diary, 5 December (Adam), 21 November (Bertin) and 13 November (Halévy) 1836 (EllaC, MS 106).

[164] Diary, 16 and 22 December (Albertazzi) and 28 December (Dorus-Gras, Nourrit and Levasseur) 1836 (EllaC, MS 106). *MW* (26 January 1838), 52. The nasal sounds

was seemingly no end of improved or invented instruments and gadgets to inspect if one wished.[165]

So what did Ella take back to London with him? A sense, as ever, of what seemed better and stronger: the luxuriously large orchestras at the Conservatoire concerts and the Opéra; the administrative and financial brilliance of the Opéra's manager, Louis Véron, in the face of cuts in state subsidy; the warmth with which Meyerbeer's operas were regarded; the government's generous support of Rossini; the quality of French quartet playing; the evident demand for renditions of weighty chamber music, especially Beethoven's; and so on. All these and other commendable aspects of Paris music he explained in the *Musical World* essays. Not that Ella was blindly in love with all things French, or that his critical faculties switched off in this sympathetic environment. He was ready to point out how much the changes wrought by the constitutional monarchy (imposed after July 1830) had adversely affected musicians and cultural life;[166] he also attempted an honest appraisal of the new music he encountered. Still, his preferences for musical life across the Channel were clear. And if the downside of these experiences was that they fed Ella's frustration about the state of affairs in London, the upside was that they made him ponder seriously how things might be changed, sowing ideas that would germinate during the next decade. On a lighter, purely sartorial, note we might consider whether it was in Paris that Ella picked up his propensity for flamboyant dressing which, while not as outré as Henry Chorley's colourful dress sense (also presumably Paris-inspired; he too went frequently), was nevertheless unusual in an Englishman.[167] 'Quite bridegroom-like in his dark-blue frock-coat, light tie, and spotless lavender kid gloves' was how one writer later described Ella.[168] We know he bought clothes and accessories there.[169]

of French vocalization still sounded odd to Ella, who found the bass Levasseur too tremulant and the high tenor Nourrit too gutteral; but Cinti-Damoreau, Cornélie Falcon and Dorus-Gras seemed palatable.

[165] As described in the 1836 diary entries for 10 and 13 November (Jullien), 11 and 17 December (Musard), 18 and 29 November and 2 December (instruments and gadgets): EllaC, MS 106.

[166] *MW* (1 December 1837), 184–5.

[167] Bledsoe, *Henry Chorley*, 10, 302.

[168] *DiehlMM*, 116. She also noted that he was 'careful, if not punctilious, in the matter of dress'.

[169] Accounts at the end of the 1836 diary (EllaC, MS 106) record that he bought a new coat, gloves, cravats and boots. In 1843 he bought boots, gloves and an umbrella (entry for 1 March; EllaC, MS 112).

ITALY was different. At this point in its history it was a loose collection of states with a shared artistic-intellectual culture, not a unified kingdom or republic; and its musical and social practices were emphatically geared around opera.[170] Symphonic traditions, with their orchestras, chamber music and so on, had yet to take root with any strength. Even on its own, the peerless opera and singing culture might have been enough to attract Ella, familiar as he was with Italian *émigré* musicians in Paris and London. But there was also the extraordinary store of Italian art, sculpture and architecture that had for decades been the focus for young Englishmen on the Grand Tour. We may guess that Ella wanted to experience this for himself and felt he could now afford to do so.

The outward-bound journey of 1842 took Ella across Germany to the Alps, through the St Gotthard Pass, and on to a series of Italian towns and cities spanning from Milan in the north to Naples in the south.[171] His destination was Rome, where he spent nearly three months; but he also stopped in Florence (fourteen days) and Naples (just under three weeks).[172] The pocket diary – he had abandoned full journal writing – documents each stage of the travels and outlines daily activities, occasionally registering his rapture on seeing the unimagined beauties of natural scenery and artistic production, sometimes in words, more usually in accumulations of exclamation marks. We see he visited, and often revisited, the major art galleries, museums, churches and cathedrals. We receive, too, the tiniest glimpse of the many riches he absorbed: Titians in Venice, Raphaels in Florence, mosaics of Pompeii at Naples, the Coliseum, the Forum and the Sistine Chapel in Rome. It was a cultural journey in all senses.

Music was never far away, and Ella was eager to find it, opera-going being much cheaper here than in London. He heard a string of works, including Mercadante's *Il giuramento* in Milan and his *Il reggente* in Turin, Meyerbeer's *Roberto il diavolo* in Padua, Donizetti's *Roberto Devereux* in Naples and his *Lucia di Lammermoor* in Rome and Florence, Bellini's *I puritani* in Genoa and

---

[170] On the social history of music in early nineteenth-century Italy, see John Rosselli, *Music and Musicians in Nineteenth-Century Italy* (London: B. T. Batsford, 1991), 13–89.

[171] He set off on 14 August 1842 and arrived in Italy a month later, having spent time exploring the Swiss landscape around Interlaken and Lucerne. (Diary for 1842, EllaC, MS 111.)

[172] He was in Florence between 3 and 17 October 1842, in Naples between 20 October and 8 November 1842, and in Rome from 9 November 1842 to 31 January 1843. The journey home, through Pisa, Genoa, Turin, Lyons and Paris, took just over a month. (Diaries for 1842 and 1843: EllaC, MSS 111 and 112.)

Rome, his *La sonnambula* in Naples and *I Capuleti* in Venice.[173] And he reported on what he heard, including new singers bound for London and stars already known at Her Majesty's Theatre, in dispatches to the *Morning Post*: its readers were bound to be interested.[174] Sacred music (the unique sounds of the choir of the Sistine Chapel, which still employed castrati), military bands, and the odd concert further filled up his diary.[175] There were also opportunities to socialize with musicians he knew. Passing through Bologna he caught up with Rossini; in Florence he saw the tenor Nicola Ivanoff; and in Rome he visited Clara Novello.[176] Finally, we spy him with the English community in Rome, listening to and making chamber music.[177] Their number included the Rev. Goddard, whose quartet parties Ella attended that December, and a Mrs Lockhart (from London), whom Ella later described as the 'modern "De Stael" of Rome [...] Intelligent, <u>handsome</u>, witty, fascinating[,] good vocalist (mezzo-soprano)[,] Declamist [...] & Pianist'.[178] It was for her amateur circle that the ever-versatile Ella composed a bagatelle for piano quintet in three short movements, and was rewarded for his troubles with a diploma that bestowed honorary membership of the Accademia Filarmonica Romana, a grand-sounding society run by a group of local amateur musicians.[179]

[173] As indicated in diary entries for 1842 (EllaC, MS 111): 16 September (*Il giuramento*), 24 September (*I Capuleti*), 27 September (*Roberto diavolo*), 9 October (*Lucia*), 21 October (*Roberto Devereux*), 5 November (*Sonnambula*); and 1843 (EllaC, MS 112): 16 January (*Lucia*), 7 February (*Puritani*), 9 February (*Il reggente*); and by his essays for *MP*.

[174] As detailed in n. 136 above.

[175] As per the 1842 diary entries for 16 September (a concert in Milan, at which he heard an 'extraordinary' violinist); 23 and 30 October (military bands in Naples); 17 and 18 November (Mass at St Peter's in Rome); 22 November (music at the church of St Cecilia, Rome); and 8 December (*a cappella* music in the Sistine Chapel): EllaC, MS 111. His experiences of sacred music in Rome are recorded in his *MP* dispatch (8 February 1843).

[176] Diary, 1 October (Rossini), 9 and 12 October (Ivanoff), 30 December (Clara Novello) 1842: EllaC, MS 111.

[177] Diary entries during December 1842 and January 1843 (EllaC, MSS 111 and 112) give an indication of these activities. On 5 November 1842 he purchased some strings, presumably for the instrument(s) he had with him, so it seems likely he played as well as listened.

[178] Quartet parties *chez* Rev. Goddard are noted in the diary, 7 and 14 December 1842 (EllaC, MS 111); an invitation to Ella from Mrs Lockhart (Rome, 1842) is preserved in one of Ella's scrapbooks, along with his own biographical notes about her (see EllaC, MS 81, p. 66).

[179] The episode is described in Ella's *MR* (1857), p. xv, and in his notes in the scrapbook, EllaC, MS 81, p. 66. The latter refers to his having written the diploma-winning

Badge of fraternity that it was, and not the professional recognition that it sounded like, it was nevertheless stored away by Ella for possible future use.

By 1843 chamber music and opera were well established as Ella's twin passions. Stopping in Paris on his homeward journey he would seek out both.[180] We can only guess how strange the weeks in Italy must have seemed without large amounts of the former. So we should not be surprised that Ella managed to manœuvre himself into what little serious quartet activity was going on there. Nor that he gravitated towards the visiting upper-class English population and its domestic music-making: apparently, an interest in classical instrumental music in Rome during the pre-Unification era was mainly confined to its foreign residents, and Ella's social skills and ambitions travelled well.[181] At the same time, his spell abroad confirmed his growing sense of himself as a discerning judge of music: in his published accounts of the visits 'metropolitan Ella' is becoming 'cosmopolitan Ella'.

His broader cultural ambitions had been well sated. He had seen the acknowledged masterpieces of Italian painting, sculpture and architecture from the Renaissance onwards. And his strategy to advance himself socially had been successful. He could now consider his classical education almost on a par with his aristocratic and gentlemen patrons (far beyond that of most British-born musicians), and might hope to discuss experiences abroad with them. He had not explored Germany and Austria, but would do so in a few years' time. Most importantly, he had learned how another country regarded and revered the high arts: what it did well and not so well in the domain of music; and how it used its fine arts in profusion to decorate its theatres and concert halls as well as its churches.[182] One setting, a Genoese palace, would stay in his memory for its apt positioning of a marble statue to a goddess of silence above the entrance to its music room.[183] Even so, the dearth of classical instrumental music, and the absence – except in enclaves of foreigners – of anything amounting to a serious Italian chamber-music tradition must have given him pause for thought. If Paris made him discontent with

piece expressly for Mrs Lockhart. However, in a reminiscence (*RMU*, 1872, sup., p. v), Ella explained the circumstances differently: the piece had been written at great speed, as part of a 'tilt with some fellow-students to write a concerted piece of music for a chamber concert of amateurs'. On the Accademia Filarmonica, see the article on Rome in *NGDM2* (section written by Bianca Maria Antolini).

[180] He arrived in Paris on 15 February 1843 and left on 3 March, reaching London on 5 March (1843 diary, EllaC, MS 112).

[181] 'Rome', *NGDM2*.

[182] 'Turin, Feb. 9.', *MP* (24 February 1843).

[183] Willert Beale, 'A Morning Call on Mr. Ella', *Liverpool Journal* (18 February 1871); reprinted in the preliminary pages to *EllaMS2*, 13, n. 2. A (rare) copy of this edition is in EllaC (MS 86).

the lot of string quartets and salon culture in London, his experience of chamber music in the Italian states surely indicated that the English situation had latent potential.

❧ *Chamber music*

> *The quintett [sic] concerts, commenced towards the close of the year by Blagrove and others, have opened a quiet musical entertainment that we shall see extend far and wide with immense results for music. [...] Quartett playing, which was always ineffective in the Philharmonic Concert-room, must now be supplied by something else – but that style, now that rivalry is openly in the field (the gauntlet thrown and taken up), will be brought to higher perfection than was ever known in this country.*   ∞ *Atlas* (31 January 1836)

So far, this narrative has alluded to chamber music in London, both in private and public, but has specified little: and it is time for this aspect, which will provide a stronger backdrop to Ella's developing ambitions and ideas, to catch up. We will start with the most striking development of the period: the introduction and relatively rapid take-off of subscription concerts built around the core classical repertoire of string quartets, quintets, piano trios, duo sonatas and hefty solo piano sonatas. Such specialist events, typically deemed 'choice and intellectual',[184] were a reflection both of the growth of the market and of chamber music's developing status as a pinnacle of high musical art, and they represented a new, artistically aspirational strand in London concert-giving. Ella was aware of them, attended them, even played the viola in a few of them (1843–4), and possibly reviewed some of them for the *Morning Post*.[185] At the cutting edge of musical culture in London, these concerts form part of the context out of which Ella's Musical Union came.

Activity began in the 1835–6 season, when some relatively junior musicians including the violinist Henry Blagrove and the cellist Charles Lucas, both budding, serious-minded players on the London orchestral circuit, put on a series of 'Concerti da Camera' in the Hanover Square Rooms, and followed it with another, the 'Quartett Concerts' (in which they were joined by another aspiring violinist, Joseph Dando, who had almost simultaneously established a similar series in the

---

[184] Quotation from the *Athenaeum* (19 March 1836), 211 [describing the Quartett Concerts].

[185] Ella played in Madame Dulcken's Soirées Musicales between November 1843 and January 1844. On reviews he may have written of chamber concerts, see n. 230 below.

City, known already for its zealous, bourgeois music-lovers). These initiatives drew sizeable audiences and stimulated other musicians, especially the older leading players, Mori, Lindley and Dragonetti, to try similar events. A rival series with an equally grand title, the Classical Chamber Concerts, commenced immediately; others followed. By the early 1840s the events had grown in number, especially in the West End, with several series in private houses as well as halls, often spearheaded by pianists (such as Louise Dulcken, William Sterndale Bennett and Ignaz Moscheles), sometimes by orchestral players (the horn player Giovanni Puzzi tried Classical Wind Concerts), and even by institutions (notably the Society of British Musicians). Most were occasional ventures of between three and six concerts; some, like the Quartett Concerts, endured for a few seasons and benefited from a regular group of performers. (The advent of permanent professional quartets was, it should be noted, still decades away.) The lead players usually took the financial risk and shared any profits.[186] What made such concerts so attractive, in comparison with larger, orchestral events, were their economics and logistics: rehearsals were easy to organize and their number could be minimized, since many musicians already knew the repertoire. Even then, profit margins were likely to be small, and upfront subscription remained crucial.

In some regards, London appears to have been following a European trend. Pierre Baillot had begun subscription string quartet soirées in Paris in 1814, and had been followed more recently by an initiative from the Tilmant brothers.[187] Ignaz Schuppanzigh, famous for his association with Beethoven, had established a similar undertaking in Vienna (c.1805) at Prince Razumovsky's palace; Carl Möser had opened up chamber music soirées in Berlin (1813–14).[188] That London had gone so long without a type of concert that was established in the major cities of Europe two decades earlier had been remarked upon, and may well seem odd, given the significant Continental presence in London music-making.[189]

---

[186] An account of these concerts is in *BashfordPCC*, 109–50. A digest of West End events is in Christina Bashford, 'Learning to Listen: Audiences for Chamber Music in Early-Victorian London', *Journal of Victorian Culture*, 4 (1999), 25–51.

[187] For more on these societies, see *FauquetS*, 41–79, 119–22.

[188] On Schuppanzigh's series, see Mary Sue Morrow, *Concert Life in Haydn's Vienna: Aspects of a Developing Social and Musical Institution* (Stuyvesant, NY: Pendragon Press, 1989), 9–10, 404. The Berlin concerts arc noted in Christoph-Hellmut Mahling, 'Berlin: "Music in the Air"', *The Early Romantic Era: Between Revolutions, 1789 and 1848*, ed. Alexander Ringer (Basingstoke and London: Macmillan Press, 1990), 109–40, at 116–17. By 1827 or 1828 these soirées had become permanent institutions.

[189] The absence of chamber music concerts had been noted by the more cosmopolitan music critics; see e.g. *MC* (22 March 1836): 'Till the present season, *soirées* of this

But alternative outlets for chamber music performance in London had long existed. One such was the private sphere, the most natural of milieux for quartets and the like. We have already noted informal activities in connection with Ella, and there was much more to be found, with some events functioning as private concerts. In truth, too, any attempt retrospectively to impose a clear dividing line between private and public chamber concerts is fraught with difficulties. The London chamber concerts of the 1830s were public inasmuch as they were advertised and reviewed in the press and run commercially, but their restrictive social and economic profiles (location, dress code, cost, and so on) were designed to limit their catchments socially, and gave them the air of exclusivity, little different from a private club. Meanwhile, many public concert-givers were at pains to emulate the atmosphere of the private house. And to be fair, even in Vienna the relationship between Schuppanzigh's public and private entertainments seems blurred.[190]

Another outlet for chamber music in London was the public orchestral concert, into which one work, typically a string quartet or quintet, was often slipped. This was true of Philharmonic Society programming, which aspired to a certain seriousness, but the practice actually dates earlier, to the 1780s and 90s, when Haydn and Pleyel quartets, especially works with concertante textures, were frequent choices in broad-based concerts.[191] By the second and third decades of the nineteenth century, the store of chamber repertoire in orchestral performances had stabilized around pieces by Haydn, Mozart and Beethoven (early period) – compositions with a relatively equal distribution of interest between the parts. Also included were a few more contemporary works such as quartets and quintets by Onslow, Spohr and Mayseder, and the tuneful septets by Beethoven and Hummel. Even so, to the real chamber music enthusiast these concerts were little more than tokenism, and did not satisfy an aficionado's needs.[192] A Philharmonic programme

kind, though familiar to the *dilettanti* of Vienna and Paris, were quite unknown here.' Or earlier, in *MP* (26 March 1828): 'We would readily promote, and do earnestly recommend a few Professors to establish a subscription party for the performance of Chamber Music [...] In Vienna, Dresden, and other parts of the Continent, this plan is adopted and succeeds.'

[190] Schuppanzigh's (morning) subscription concerts seem to have developed out of regular performances on Friday mornings at Prince Lichnowsky's and Prince Razumovsky's (Morrow, *Concert Life*, 9–10).

[191] See *BashfordPCC*, 84–107, and Meredith McFarlane and Simon McVeigh, 'The String Quartet in London Concert Life, 1769–1799', *Concert Life in Eighteenth-Century Britain*, ed. Susan Wollenberg and Simon McVeigh (Aldershot: Ashgate, 2004), 161–96.

[192] The point was well made by the *Atlas* (8 November 1835), 709: 'This species of music [chamber music], albeit confined to a very small circle of players, and to a

of 25 February 1833 will illustrate this point. A Beethoven string quintet was the central work in the programme's second half, being preceded by Haydn's 'Clock' Symphony (no. 101) and an aria from a Spohr opera, and followed by a duet from Rossini's *La gazza ladra* and an overture by Vogel.[193] In addition, there was some dispute as to whether string quartets could ever succeed in large public halls, and Ella for one queried publicly the wisdom of performing such repertoire in this milieu.[194]

The arrival of dedicated chamber concerts in London's public musical life after 1835 effectively ended the repertoire's inclusion in orchestral concerts, and by the 1840s the Philharmonic concerts had all but ceased to include chamber music.[195] But while bespoke concerts of chamber music may have been more to the enthusiast's liking, the problem of the performance space remained. As we shall later see, some concert-givers devised practical solutions to make formal halls more intimate, while the shift into private houses had the built-in advantage of verisimilitude through a more casual and comfortable salon-like environment, with sofas and chairs arranged informally, and refreshments on hand.[196] Meantime, although house concerts reduced expenditure (no hall to hire), they constrained the potential size of the audience and any profits. Even with minimized rehearsal costs and relatively easy organization, few speculations made money, as one writer observed:

> The custom of giving *soirées musicales* at their [musicians'] own residence is progressing rapidly. It is generally admitted that these small concerts do

very meagre selection of compositions, always formed one of the grand attractions of the Philharmonic Concert. […] Repetitions without end, both in music and players, are the fault of the miniature performances of the Philharmonic Society, and amateurs year after year are left to exclaim at tasteless selections and good things omitted'. The writer was probably Edward Holmes.

[193] Myles Birket Foster, *History of the Philharmonic Society of London, 1813–1912* (London: John Lane, The Bodley Head, 1912), 120.

[194] *Athenaeum* (8 March 1834), 188: 'we think the piece [J. B. Cramer's piano quintet] is more fitted for the chamber than a concert room' [Ella's authorship confirmed by the files at City University, London]. The view was fairly common: see e.g. the comments on chamber music in Philharmonic concerts in *MP* (16 April 1828): 'We are still of [the] opinion that a Philharmonic Concert is not the place to enjoy a Quartetto' [reviewer almost certainly not Ella].

[195] *EhrlichFP*, 46, notes the changeover but does not explain it in these terms.

[196] For descriptions of the arrangements in public halls, see e.g. *Musical Library Monthly Supplement* (April 1836), 69, and *ST* (3 April 1836); and on house concerts, see *Britannia* (9 December 1843), 775, and *MP* (12 March 1844). For discussion, see Bashford, 'Learning to Listen'.

not pay, but the professors urge that they keep their teaching connection together, and add to their individual fame.[197]

From the outset, the new chamber concerts were strongly associated with serious taste and discerning listeners, some groups of players even daring to attempt Beethoven's late quartets.[198] In addition, a much larger repertoire than had before been available in public programmes was being performed: '[t]he hearer felt [...] he was making some important additions to the stock of his musical notions, which assured him that his time was well employed'.[199] What was played ranged from Haydn's early string quartets opp. 17 and 20 to Mozart's mature string quintets, from Beethoven's horn sonata and cello sonatas to Mendelssohn's string quartets and quintets (newly introduced), and from selections from Bach's '48' preludes and fugues to Beethoven's 'Appassionata', 'Pathétique' and 'Waldstein' sonatas.[200] However, in keeping with how repertoire was normally packaged in London concerts, these hefty instrumental chamber works were interspersed by songs and duets; and the programmes, long by today's standards, were further relieved by the inclusion of ensemble pieces that made less taxing demands on the listener. The following programme of one of Mori and Lindley's concerts of 1837 gives a flavour:

Spohr	Nonet op. 31 for violin, viola, cello, double bass, horn, bassoon, clarinet, flute and oboe
Haydn	Canzonet, 'Despair'
Beethoven	Quartet for two violins, viola and cello op. 18 no. 6
Mozart	Aria, 'Parto' (*La clemenza di Tito*)
Handel	Trio for violin, cello and double bass
	————
Moscheles	Septet op. 88 for piano, violin, viola, clarinet, horn, cello and double bass
Beethoven	Cantata 'Adelaida' op. 46
Winter	Air, 'Sommo Dio' (*Zaira*)
Mendelssohn	Quintet for two violins, two violas and cello op. 18[201]

---

[197] *Britannia* (2 March 1844), 138.

[198] Bashford, 'Late Beethoven Quartets'.

[199] *Atlas* (15 November 1835), 728 [the writer was almost certainly Edward Holmes].

[200] Full repertoire lists are in *BashfordPCC*, Appendix C.

[201] Repertoire details principally from *MP* (14 February 1837).

Beethoven's music dominated all concerts, with most of the middle-period works, and some of the later ones, brought out for a first time. Some, such as the quartets op. 59 no. 1 and op. 74, were among the more frequently performed works, for while such compositions had yet to achieve full 'masterwork' status, Beethoven was already, just ten years after his death, considered a truly canonic figure.[202] Ella, for one, was in seventh heaven at hearing Beethoven at Mori and Lindley's concerts, and wrote about it in his diaries. Everything else in a programme paled in comparison. Op. 59 no. 1 was 'transcendent[al]ly superior to all other Compositions performed[,] and ill prepared us for the enjoyment of anything else'.[203] The alternation of 'simplicity, and intense thought' in the adagio in op. 59 no. 2 was nothing short of wonderful.[204] And Moscheles's performance of the piano part to the op. 97 'Archduke' trio inspired Ella and Schulz to 'get up' more of the sonatas for violin and piano.[205]

The majority of concerts, especially Blagrove's and Mori's series, were aimed at wealthy West End-dwelling amateurs, and the serious music-lovers among them at that. The more socially notable members of audiences were picked out in newspaper reviews, as a way of indicating a concert's prestige, and from these we know that the events attracted several of the aficionados already in Ella's orbit, for example the Duke of Cambridge, Lord Burghersh, General Upton and the Duke and Duchess of Leinster.[206] Musicians also attended, and were customarily admitted for free. Again the eminent were worth reporting: the elderly Thomas Attwood and William Carnaby, both organists and composers, the violinist Franz Cramer, and the younger Cipriani Potter, pianist, composer and recently appointed Principal of the Royal Academy of Music.[207] Non-newsworthy listeners included Ella, who we know received complimentary tickets for Mori and Lindley's concerts and attended several times, noting afterwards the names of amateurs he recognized, as well as his reactions to the music. 'Spoke with Mr Sanford M^r & M^{rs} F[reeling]: Miss M & Miss Doyle – they were all delighted with the [concert]', he wrote in 1836,

[202] *BashfordPCC*, 243.

[203] Diary, 10 February 1836 (EllaC, MS 106).

[204] Diary, 3 March 1836 (EllaC, MS 106).

[205] Diary, 28 January 1836 (EllaC, MS 106).

[206] See e.g. the accounts of a Classical Chamber Concert in *MH* (26 February 1836), and a Quartett Concert in *ST* (11 March 1838). Others named included Sir Andrew Barnard (*MP*, 21 December 1835), the Duke of Newcastle and the Dean of Wells (*MH*, 26 February 1836), Major Stevens and Sir William Curtis (*MP*, 8 February 1839).

[207] *Musical Magazine* (December 1835), 184 [reporting on the Concerti da Camera].

after a performance that included Beethoven's quartet op. 59 no. 1 and the first double quartet of Spohr.[208]

The pioneering concert-givers of the mid-1830s thus did not find it diffi-cult to draw in an adequate-sized chamber music audience, and they attracted people with a serious, practical bent towards domestic music-making. As the *Morning Chronicle* critic, remarking on the audience at the Concerti da Camera, pointed out:

> Concerts of this description are not calculated to become popular. They will not be attended by those whose chief objects of attraction are English ballads or the airs of the last new opera. But this metropolis now contains a large and rapidly increasing body of amateurs, of both sexes, who are conversant with the higher branches of instrumental music, and to whom it must be a source of great pleasure to hear the most exquisite works of the greatest masters. To those who are themselves performers, such concerts as these are full of instruction.[209]

Even allowing for the journalistic ploy of praising the 'quality' of the audience, the modern reader can be in little doubt that the writer had the measure of the situation: that the quick flowering of the chamber concert in London had con-firmed there was latent, specialist demand 'out there'. Indeed, demand was further stimulated by the growing supply of events. And although nothing like the size of the metropolitan audience that might, by the century's end, be gathered every night of the week and all year round, the 1830s audience was significant for its time, and endorses the idea that a taste for chamber music had grown up behind closed doors in the early part of the century. It was a demand that Ella would later draw on.

For all that, the question of who pursued serious chamber music in the domestic sphere at this time is not easily answered. As is well known, music had long been considered a respectable pastime, particularly for women, who typically learned the piano and how to sing – accomplishments that continued to have strong value in the marriage market. Most other (melody) instruments, including strings and woodwinds, in which the body was required to take on unseemly positions, were gendered male and out of bounds to females. Even then, not all instruments were acceptable for gentlemen, leisured males tending to take up only the flute, violin, viola or cello (brass and other winds had coarser social connotations) and pursuing

---

[208] Diary, 10 February 1836 (EllaC, MS 106). Sanford was probably Harry Sanford, the viola player in the Saltoun Club, who worked in the Treasury (*RMU*, 1870, sup., p. ii). The identities of Miss M. and Miss Doyle have not been ascertained.

[209] *MC* (9 November 1835).

music with less application than their female counterparts. Socially, music-making was far less important for men than for women. Boys were frequently discouraged from taking too zealous an interest, and there were no cultural pressures on them to succeed at it, the professional pursuit of music being left to the more middling social orders (another reason for not taking it too seriously): during the eighteenth century the hapless gentleman string-player had become a well-worn stereotype.[210] In well-to-do quarters, too, music-making was deemed emasculating and inappropriate for the down-to-earth British male – cultural anxieties that dogged the development of musical life in Britain for generations.[211]

Yet, despite this, many men *did* learn instruments; some of them achieved a good, even high, standard, and several used chamber music to bond socially with other males and to bring a distinctive cultural meaning into their lives. By the late 1700s the string quartet party had become an established recreation in some respectable circles, offering heartfelt, rational refreshment as well as camaraderie, and was probably far more prevalent than many later commentators believed.[212] Moreover, the private quartet tradition continued into the nineteenth century, albeit with a low 'public' profile. Of course, by the 1830s the technical difficulties of more modern repertoire were acting as a constraint on what could be reasonably attempted by amateurs, and the close, interwoven part-writing, as opposed to clearer, treble-dominated textures, of many works (e.g. later Haydn, Mozart and Beethoven) were a deterrent for many. Still, for however many quartet groups that were 'too easily satisfied with imperfect and slovenly performance',[213] there were some who attained reasonable results, even if by playing fast movements at sedate speeds, or taking other liberties.

---

[210] Woodfield, *Music of the Raj*, 127–30, discusses the prevalence of the ideology about amateur male string playing and the real regret that some men felt at not having studied the violin with more application earlier in life. He also suggests that Lord Chesterfield's celebrated disdain for the English gentleman musician was a view shared more by the aristocracy than by the aspirant upper middle classes.

[211] For general discussion of this issue, see *RohrCBM*, 18–21.

[212] As argued by Meredith L. B. McFarlane, 'The String Quartet in Late Eighteenth-Century England: a Contextual Examination' (DMus, Royal College of Music, 2002), *passim*. The vitality of the quartet tradition amongst English males in India is demonstrated in Woodfield, *Music of the Raj*, 211–13.

[213] *MC* (9 November 1835). Contemporary caricatures of inept amateur string- and quartet-playing, among both Frenchmen and Englishmen, can be found in George Dubourg, *The Violin: Being an Account of that Leading Instrument and its Most Eminent Professors* (London: Henry Colburn, 1836), 207–10. Dubourg mentions the innovatory London quartet concerts and advises amateur quartet players to attend them (p. 220).

The Duke of Cambridge and Earl of Falmouth are prime examples of the more able player. They were among the wealthy amateurs whose music-making Ella supervised or participated in, and would later lend their support to his Musical Union. Ella, we know, had little patience with dilettante noblemen musicians, but he later described Falmouth as 'a most excellent amateur violin player', and Cambridge as leading quartets 'with accuracy and unaffected taste'.[214] They had, we may assume, persevered with their private music lessons and were the antithesis of flamboyant aristocrats: Cambridge was 'as triumphantly ordinary as a royal duke can be', and most unlike his brothers; Falmouth had a double first-class degree from Oxford.[215] Both had a sober taste in music. They owned collections of fine Italian instruments by Amati, Stradivarius and so on, as well as extensive libraries of chamber music.[216] When Ella first played quartets with them in 1838, the repertoire chosen included Haydn's quartets op. 76 no. 3 ('Emperor') and op. 76 no. 5, and Mozart's D major quintet and his D minor quartet (K421, presumably).[217]

Military men were also known for their musical competencies and serious inclinations: within Ella's circle there were Major [later General] Legge (cello), Captain Jekyll (flute), General Upton (violin), Captain Newbury (violin) and a number of others, including many from the 'Guards'.[218] Upton, for example, already a member of the Saltoun Club, became a keen chamber musician, the dilettante composer John Lodge Ellerton later dedicating a piano quartet to him. Military music at the time was not built exclusively around wind and brass instruments; string players had been *bona fide* members of militia bands since the eighteenth century; and

[214] *RMU* (1850), preface; and (1860), 32.

[215] Elizabeth J. Morse, preface to Grace E. Moremen, *Adolphus Frederick, Duke of Cambridge – Steadfast Son of King George III, 1774–1850* (Lewiston, NY: Edwin Mellen Press, 2002), p. xxiv; and Walter Hawken Tregallas, 'Boscawen' [i.e. Earl of Falmouth], *DNB*.

[216] A sense of their collections is given in A. Hyatt King, *Some British Collectors of Music, c.1660–1960* (Cambridge: Cambridge University Press, 1963), 48; detailed information can be obtained from the sale catalogues of Puttick & Simpson (28–9 November 1850 and 26–8 May 1853), who auctioned both collections after the owners' deaths. In 1847 Falmouth had purchased the music library of the late Thomas Alsager, avid chamber-music lover, Ella acting as intermediary in the transaction; see *RMU* (1847), 4.

On Cambridge's instrument collection, see Ella's diary, 2 April 1838 (EllaC, MS 107): 'His R. H. the Duke of Cambridge honored me at 3 with his Company & brought his Fiddles & Viola & Cello'. On Falmouth's instruments, see *RMU* (1860), 32; and (1867), sup., 2.

[217] Diary, 25 March and 2 April 1838 (EllaC, MS 107).

[218] As per the list of Saltoun Club participants given in 'La Società Lirica. Belgravia, 1870', *RMU* (1870), sup., p. ii.

well-born officers such as Legge played recreationally. Musical parties formed a central part of life in garrisons and their adjacent civilian communities, where local amateurs typically mixed with players from the regiment. Quartet gatherings were not unknown, perhaps providing a means for officers to distance themselves socially from the more mundane aspects of military life.[219]

Women rarely participated in serious musical conversations, which were inherently deemed masculine. Typical chamber music for them would have been accompanied sonatas, or piano music *à quatre mains*. The heftier repertoire for larger ensembles by Beethoven and Mendelssohn, even some of the big duo sonatas, required pianists with more experience of ensemble playing than most lady amateurs had.[220] Yet there were some who stood out or crossed boundaries. Ella remembered playing Beethoven's (violin) sonatas with the daughter of Francis Maude, of Wakefield, 'a most excellent pianist', and hearing Viscountess Hereford perform, probably in the piano part of Beethoven's D major trio (op. 70 no. 1).[221] In any case, for all amateur chamber players – male or female, good or bad – the new public concerts were highly instructive, since by hearing the great works performed well by 'able professors' they would have something to aspire to in their own music-making.[222] Meanwhile, what Ella desired most in an amateur was an earnest interest in 'good' music, the Freelings being some of the most discerning listeners in this respect.[223]

[219] On the presence of string players and quartet parties in eighteenth-century militia life, see McFarlane, 'The String Quartet in Late Eighteenth-Century England', 77–8, 108.

[220] Ella, participating in a domestic performance of an arrangement of Onslow's sextet, commented critically afterwards that 'The Lady player is evidently not au fait at playing Concerted Music' (diary, 19 February 1836; EllaC, MS 106). It was for similar reasons, perhaps, that Ella regretted the rarity of getting violin sonatas and piano trios by 'good' composers played (diary, 14 January 1836).

[221] See Ella's notes in respect of a letter from Maude (EllaC, MS 81, p. 63), and his diary entry for 10 January 1836 (EllaC, MS 106). In the latter he recalls hearing the Beethoven trio for the first time, and witnessing Viscountess Hereford play, during his first visit to Moccas Court. Since elsewhere (EllaC, MS 81, p. 63) he would refer to the viscountess as the 'Best Amateur I have ever known', the implication seems to be that she performed the piano part to the Beethoven trio on this occasion. Ella also mused (*RMU*, 1860, p. 30) that he had 'often been agreeably surprised by the superior skill of ladies, presiding at the pianoforte, accompanying the most intricate and varied music'.

[222] *MC* (9 November 1835).

[223] Diary, 30 March 1836 (EllaC, MS 106). The passage reads in full: 'There are few English amateurs who could enjoy, at a first hearing, the beauties of Beethoven, more than M^r & M^rs. F:' ['Kreutzer' sonata]. Contrast this with his remarks (diary,

The impression created may be to the contrary, but Ella was not involved in all networks of amateur chamber-music players and devotees in and around London, although he probably knew of the most vibrant. The private parties of Thomas Massa Alsager, a clothworker's son from Southwark who had become financial writer on *The Times* and an amateur musician of some ability, are a case in point.[224] Alsager was well connected in literary circles, numbering Charles Lamb and Leigh Hunt among his acquaintances, and had a strong affinity for fine music, later becoming an earnest advocate for Beethoven. In the 1830s he regularly invited leading musicians to his Bloomsbury home on Sundays to listen to and play chamber music. Mendelssohn and his father were among the guests on one occasion in 1833, when works by Onslow and Mendelssohn's own string quintet (op. 18) and octet were performed.[225] Ella and Alsager knew of one another, Ella once being asked to fill in on second violin, but they were not closely associated.[226] Professional musicians' homes were further places where chamber music happened and more ambitious repertoire was likely to be heard, although Ella, self-evidently, was involved in only a fraction of them. His friendship circles extended only so far. The composer William Horsley's house in Kensington Gravel Pits, for example, was outside his ambit, though it was often filled with musical visitors, including Mendelssohn and Moscheles.[227]

19 February 1836) that the 'Belle of the Party was the daughter of a General – and exhibited the bad taste of a Fashionable Aristocrat by talking loud when good music was played & going into ectacies [*sic*] with the brille of nonsensical passages of Czerny's on the Piano'.

[224] On Alsager's parties and his championship of Beethoven's quartets, 1829–46, see David B. Levy, 'Thomas Massa Alsager, Esq.: a Beethoven Advocate in London', *19CM*, 9 (1985–6), 119–27. His earlier attraction to Mozart's music is unravelled by Rachel Cowgill in her '"Wise Men from the East": Mozart's Operas and their Advocates in Early Nineteenth-Century London', *MBC*, 39–64.

[225] Sebastian Hensel, *The Mendelssohn Family (1729–1847) from Letters and Journals*, 2nd edition, trans. Carl Klingemann and an American collaborator, 2 vols. (New York: Harper, 1882), i, 297.

[226] The invitation is in an undated letter to Ella (addressed as 'Dear Sir') from Alsager, in one of the scrapbooks (EllaC, MS 81, p. 18). Ella's awareness of Alsager's activities, and the cordial but not familiar nature of their relationship, is indicated by Ella's account of the circumstances leading up to the foundation of the Musical Union in *MR* (1857), p. xv.

[227] Daughter Sophy, an able pianist, described one lengthy, but probably typical, day in 1834, when piano quartets (Mendelssohn and Mozart), violin sonatas (Beethoven and Mozart), a dirge for voices by her father, and a chamber arrangement of a Haydn symphony were played by the Horsleys and some of their guests. See *Mendelssohn and his Friends in Kensington: Letters from Fanny and Sophy Horsley*

W<small>E</small> have already seen how Ella, in the 1830s, hosted and played in informal performances of chamber music with his professional peers (men of medium calibre) before invited amateurs at his own home. Such parties continued into the early 1840s, and in April 1844, roughly a year after his return from Italy, Ella began weekly *réunions* at his latest lodgings in Mortimer Street, to the east of Regent Street at its northern end, seemingly in the same spirit.[228] In reality, though, these events were different. To begin with, Ella mostly did not play, but organized instead. By coincidence, a cluster of eminent Continental musicians were visiting London that season, and Ella, having spotted a golden opportunity, persuaded them to come and perform for the sake of 'good music' and perhaps a few networking opportunities too.[229] Secondly, he invited in larger numbers of listeners than hitherto, among them the distinguished musicians Costa, Dragonetti, Moscheles, Puzzi, J. B. Cramer, and Sigismund Thalberg; amateur music-lovers from Ella's social networks were also in evidence. Thirdly, he manœuvred the events into the public eye. For although the parties were private and free to Ella's guests, he ensured they received lengthy and favourable coverage in the *Morning Post*, almost certainly writing the notices himself and probably with the intention of generating a good-sized audience for the one concert towards the end of the 'run' which he opened to public subscription and from which he stood to make money.[230]

The most striking feature of the performances – fourteen in all – was the calibre of the players and the salon-like atmosphere that Ella emulated. His choice of the French 'réunion' was surely deliberate, and experiences in Paris influential. His frustration with the quality of chamber music performances in London had been confided to his diary more than once. Mori and Lindley might have been the leading orchestral string players, but as chamber musicians they were inexperienced and lacked both nuance and passion.[231]

written 1833–36, ed. Rosamund Brunel Gotch (London: Oxford University Press, 1934), 172–3. The women performers mentioned are Horsley's wife (daughter of the composer J. W. Calcott), Sophy and a certain Harriet Neill. Karl Klingemann was in the audience.

[228] The concerts began on 16 April. A list of dates is in *BashfordPCC*, Appendix F.

[229] A letter from Mendelssohn, accepting Ella's invitation, is transcribed in *MR* (1857), p. xvii.

[230] *MP* (17 and 24 April, 1, 8, 15, 22 and 30 May, 5, 13, 19 and 27 June, 3 and 17 July 1844). The identification of Ella as the author of the reports is hinted at in *RMU* (1865), sup., 9; and esp. (1870), 4: 'After my description of his [Joachim's] playing had appeared in *The Morning Post*, my private reunions were crowded to hear this […] youth.'

[231] Diary, 27 January and 7 April 1836 (EllaC, MS 106).

On other levels their concerts had not worked either, and in February 1836 Ella had written bluntly:

> I find that the performances [of Mori and Lindley] do not improve: the Quartet of Beethoven Op [18 no. 3] was not given as it ought to have been; there was no light and shade. Rousselot [...] also remarked that a <u>Seance</u> of Quartets in Paris consists of three, & insinuated that <u>6</u> Instrumental & <u>4</u> Vocal pieces [were too many]. Saw Duke of Leinster who [?]shared my expressed opinion that a Quartet party is best in the <u>Middle</u> of a room.[232]

Blagrove's ensemble had also disappointed: '[a]s in all the Quartets I have heard in Public[,] there wanted passion in the performance'.[233] Now was Ella's chance to try alternative ways of doing things. Among the visiting performers he engaged in 1844 were three high-calibre Continental violinists: the thirteen-year-old Joseph Joachim (already a captivating player of some maturity), the Paris-trained Prosper Sainton (soon to settle in London) and Heinrich Ernst (a fine technician and interpreter). They were the principal leaders. Playing the cello were Rousselot, the newly arrived sensation Alfredo Piatti, a German named Hausmann, and the young composer Jacques Offenbach, who was having some success as an instrumentalist; there was even a chance to hear Mendelssohn, already a huge star in England, at the piano in his D minor trio. It was a forceful attempt to show what a difference could be made by placing artists with strong techniques and copious experience of chamber playing in the principal roles. Meanwhile, most of the inner parts were taken by London-based musicians, men who could be relied on to do a good job: for instance, Henry Hill (the leading viola player), Charles Goffrie and Guynemer (violins). Ella played the viola or second violin, but only occasionally.[234]

String quartets, quintets and the occasional piano trio or quintet by the classical masters formed the core of Ella's weekly selection, as they did in public chamber concerts; and there was almost always one of the 'splendid productions of the Master Mind', Beethoven.[235] But following French practice, vocal music was absent, and there were no more than three, occasionally four, pieces – that being the limit of anyone's concentration, to Ella's mind. Besides which, the inclusion

---

[232] Diary, 25 February 1836 (EllaC, MS 106). Ella had reservations about long programmes: after a Società Armonica concert later that year he noted: 'The selection of Music was altogether excellent: too much of it, as usual' (diary, 24 March 1836).

[233] Diary, 22 March 1838 (EllaC, MS 107).

[234] There were a number of other occasional participants, both foreign and British; the most notable were Camillo Sivori (violin) and Ignaz Moscheles (piano).

[235] The words are Ella's and from the diary, 28 January 1836 (EllaC, MS 106).

of a lighter showpiece in which one of the star players displayed his technique seemed to owe something to Paris models too, particularly to Baillot's concerts which often ended with such an item.[236] After Joachim's second appearance for Ella, when he led Haydn and Beethoven quartets, the column in the *Post* claimed with satisfaction: 'Nothing, indeed, could exceed the enthusiasm which this *matinie* [*sic*] [received,] reminding us of scenes witnessed only in the cities of France, Italy, and Germany.'[237] Three months later Ella's series was summed up elsewhere as having produced performances 'unparalleled in this country, partly owing to the extraordinary talent of those who have contributed their professional services, and also to the taste and judgment of Mr. Ella in restricting the programmes to music of standard excellence'.[238] The best music and the best players made a striking combination. Other journals said much the same.[239] One surviving letter from an audience member, Lady Duoro, referred to the events as great treats, with 'magnificent music'.[240] The absence of songs in the final, subscription concert (at Saltoun's residence, 9 July 1844) is worth noting, since such programming was rare in public concerts and suggests that Ella felt confident he could find support for an entirely instrumental programme from within his patronage base.[241] The subscription cost one guinea, and Ella claimed, years later, to have shared the proceeds among the artists, who had played at the other *réunions* for free.[242]

Whether these concerts sowed seeds in Ella's mind for future projects, or whether he viewed them as a test-bed for an idea half formed, is unclear. But within months he was making plans for an institutionalized, commercially run chamber music society called the Musical Union that owed much to the 1844 initiative. Later, in print, he would rewrite the history of London chamber music, suggesting there had been little concert activity – with the exception of Mori's and

[236] For Baillot's programmes, see *FauquetS*, 293–331.

[237] *MP* (23 April 1844). This was surely by Ella.

[238] *Maestro* (20 July 1844), 141. The critic was probably Gruneisen.

[239] Concerts were also covered by the *Britannia*, *ST*, *Athenaeum* and *MW*; for a list of reviews, see *BashfordPCC*, Appendix F.

[240] Letter dated 20 May 1844 in the scrapbook, EllaC, MS 79, p. 16.

[241] Examples of public chamber concerts that had already eschewed vocal music include Dando's concerts at the Horn Tavern in the City of London, 1835–8, and H. J. Banister's 1844 Quartet Parties. Ella nevertheless played slightly safe and put together a somewhat lighter programme for the concert: Hummel's septet op. 74, an Onslow quintet, a Haydn quartet, and two instrumental fantasias.

[242] Subscription rate from advertisements in *MP*; see e.g. 4 July 1844. Ella's assessment of the concert is in *MR* (1857), p. xvii. See also *RMU* (1880), 29: 'These […] meetings […] involved me in no expense, and were but little trouble.'

Blagrove's initiatives – in the period before 1845, a picture that was downright inaccurate.[243] He would further interpret his concerts of the 1830s (those featuring his arrangements of opera excerpts) as the legitimate, most significant predecessors of the chamber concert phenomenon, which reached its first maturity in the Musical Union. In this version of events Ella sought to place himself at the centre of the story, and suggested that establishing chamber concerts in London had been his long-term aspiration. He intimated that the idea for the Musical Union had come out of the 1844 matinées, and that it had even been suggested by one of the amateurs.[244] We know that Ella had been harbouring ambitions to do something significant since 1838 at least, that he was pretty disillusioned with many of London's concert institutions and general levels of music appreciation, and that he admired Parisian quartet and salon culture. But in the early 1830s he did not articulate – not, at least, in any form left to posterity – that a chamber music society was his chief ambition, and in all likelihood the idea came upon him gradually. (Paradoxically, Ella's later account of the Musical Union's origins does little justice to his taking advantage of the chamber concert phenomenon of the 1830s to mould his own institution.) That it had taken Ella several years to identify an appropriate project was probably because he was naturally cautious in business and had already learned harsh lessons about concert promotion. Professional collaboration in administration seems to have been out of the question for him. As events and ambitions coalesced during 1844, his ideas finally crystallized. He, unlike us looking in from posterity, had no idea whether his project would work. But the moment seemed good.

---

[243] 'Music in London – No. 4' and 'Music in London – No. 5', *MR* (1857), pp. xiv–xv and xvii–xviii.

[244] Op. cit., p. xv. Discussed in Chapter 3.

CHAPTER 3

Establishing the Musical Union, 1845–8

Ella soon set about launching his new initiative. Perceiving adequate demand for what he wanted to promote, he now planned a subscription society for chamber music concerts of the best possible musical character and the highest seriousness. It was a bold scheme, not without risk, and would keep him busy during the most frenetic months of the musical year, teaching him more about concert promotion. It would also give him a more direct and effective means for shaping audience taste than he could have hoped to achieve through his writing for the press, and eventually it would see him make his finest and most enduring contribution to London music.

❧ Ideas and ideals

In every city on the continent, the musical traveller will invariably find some locality consecrated to the intellectuality of art, where the performance of the most elevated order of instrumental chamber music brings together the practical, theoretical, and literary members of the profession, and the amateurs of cultivated and refined taste, affording the mutual advantages of social intercourse between men of musical genius and education, from the various schools of Europe, with the noble, wealthy, and accomplished virtuosi. Such a desideratum will be accomplished at the "réunions" of the above organized Society of Amateurs. ∽ *RMU* (1845)

A PRINTED prospectus, probably issued around the end of 1844, hinted at the shape of things to come, while referring back to the spirit of Ella's *réunions* the previous season and to the several eminent musicians who had appeared at and attended them.[1] The new society, to be known as the Musical Union, was intended to cultivate 'the highest order of Instrumental Chamber Music' – by implication, the heartland of Haydn, Mozart and Beethoven – 'executed by first-rate Artists'; and to 'promote Social Intercourse between Native and Foreign Practical, Theoretical, and Literary Members of the Profession, and Amateurs of cultivated and refined taste' in seeming emulation of Parisian salon culture.[2] Further gravitas

[1] EllaC, MS 81, between pp. 18 and 19. Musicians named included Mendelssohn, Moscheles, Ernst, Sivori, Piatti, Sainton, Joachim, Rousselot and Dragonetti.

[2] Ibid.

was borrowed from Cicero (Ella chose as a motto Cicero's words 'Honor alit artes' / 'Honour nourishes the arts'), and there was the promise of a published record of activity, along with other trappings of institutionalization including a prominent list of office-holders.

A group of carefully chosen London grandees, the officers were men who combined high social standing with a love of classical music, often quartet playing; seventeen of them had agreed to endorse Ella's project by forming a committee under the chairmanship of the Earl of Falmouth to sanction activities.[3] Above him, at the top of the tree were the Duke of Cambridge as President and the Earl of Westmorland (Lord Burghersh) as Vice-President. All three men and others on the committee – Sir George Clerk, Bt, the Hon. Major Arthur Legge, and, especially, Lord Saltoun – had been known to Ella for fifteen years or so through his initiatives in the private sphere, including the amateur opera club; and doubtless Ella was able to draw on the goodwill that these connections had engendered in order to persuade the men to back his scheme.[4] There were precedents, in that some of the hierarchy had lent their names to other London institutions and were known publicly for such associations: Westmorland was a director of the Concerts of Antient Music and fronted the Royal Academy of Music (Clerk, Falmouth and Sir Andrew Barnard, also chosen by Ella, had been members of its founding subcommittee of management), while Saltoun was a figure-head for the Madrigal Society. Both were prominent in the Melodists' Club.[5] Aware of the trick of asserting quality by association, Ella thus blatantly linked his 'product' with the music-loving nobility and gentry. He also emphasized classical values and the intellectual weight of the endeavour. And in presenting himself as 'Director' of the Musical Union he asserted his recently acquired, serious-sounding affiliation as 'Hon. Mem. of the Phil. Acad. of Rome'.[6]

Naturally, practicalities needed thinking through. The risks involved in promoting concerts in London, as Ella had learned, were high, and the best way forward for any such enterprise in the 1840s was still the subscription system. Concerts of

---

[3] Ibid.

[4] The other members of the proposed committee were: the Viscounts Templetown and Adare, the Hon. Captain Cadogan, Sir Richard Bulkeley Philipps, Bt, General Sir Andrew Barnard, General Sir John Campbell, and Messrs. E. Jekyll, C. Raper, C. [= ?J.] Clerk, S. Shelley, Clayton Freeling, C. Lukin and C. Staniforth (ibid.). By the time of the first concert, the personnel had changed: Jekyll and Raper had been replaced by the Hon. Lawrence Parsons and Frederick Perkins (see *RMU*, 1845, p. 1).

[5] According to *MP* (30 June 1847), the Earl of Westmorland and Lord Saltoun were Vice-Presidents of the Melodists' Club, and the Duke of Cambridge its President.

[6] Prospectus (EllaC, MS 81, between pp. 18 and 19).

string quartets and the like, as we have seen, had the built-in economic advantage of only a few players to pay and rehearse, but Ella nevertheless (and somewhat remarkably) managed to raise committee donations to a 'reserved fund', to insure against losses.[7] The Musical Union was to function as a club, with concerts open to members only; and membership could be gained only by election and payment of a subscription. The rate was set at one guinea for eight concerts, a relatively inexpensive amount when compared with other fashionable West End chamber concerts, at which a guinea for three or four concerts was the norm. Not that that suggested access for *hoi polloi*: the Musical Union's system of recruitment guaranteed an essentially private circle, as a grand announcement of the society in the *Morning Post* in January 1845 made evident.[8] Social superiority was also indicated by the appointment of Cramer, Beale & Co., music sellers and publishers of quality in Regent Street, as treasurers.[9]

Ella planned to hold fortnightly concerts on Tuesday afternoons at the height of the season, from March to June, when high society was 'up in town'. The venue was again to be his residence in Mortimer Street (no. 70), near Cavendish Square, an address abutting an area of wealth and fine living. By definition and practice, afternoon concerts were the province of the leisured classes (nobility, gentry, upper-middle classes), women in particular, and Ella surely envisaged an audience similar to the one he had gathered for his *réunions* the previous year, and overlapping with the constituency of the Saltoun Club. He hoped, nevertheless, to enlarge the clientele (female networks could be useful), and had contingencies for changing the accommodation should this come about.[10] Tickets were not transferable, but the Union's system of recommendation for membership, which brought in families from the network of 'rank and fashion', was designed to extend the audience in a controlled way.[11] Subscribers were expected to be keen music-lovers and have a 'practical knowledge of art'.[12] The concert dates and Tuesday afternoon time were

---

[7] See the 'Report of the Director to the "Committee of the Musical Union"', *RMU* (1845), 2. Ella here suggested that he might use the money to subsidize subscriptions, and hoped that the organization would prove financially viable and remove the need for such a fund in future.

[8] *MP* (1 January 1845). It used the rhetoric quoted at the head of this section.

[9] The company seems to have handled subscription income. No official accounts survive, but Ella kept track of the institution's income and expenditure, informally.

[10] 'Report', *RMU* (1845), 2: 'Should I not be able to afford accommodation to all the members who are expected to attend each meeting, I shall engage, adjoining my own residence, a spacious private music room, in size and shape admirably calculated for the special objects of the society.'

[11] A surviving ticket and template is in EllaC, MS 81, p. 19.

[12] 'Report', *RMU* (1845), 2.

carefully picked, not only to avoid potential clashes with competing metropolitan events (musical or otherwise) or his own regular playing engagements, but also, according to the promotional literature, to buttress the Philharmonic Society's concerts on previous Monday evenings. The Philharmonic drew serious music-lovers with an interest in orchestral repertoire, and Ella claimed to seek through his timing to capitalize on such people being in town, while also hoping to net for the Musical Union a high-calibre Continental artist who had been hired by the Philharmonic.

Six weeks after Ella had reported (on 1 February) to his committee on general progress and arrangements for the season, the institution was up and running, the first concert taking place on 11 March 1845, not *chez* Ella, but in Blagrove's concert rooms, also in Mortimer Street (no. 71), seemingly an indication that subscribers had been found and that Ella's hopes about demand had been met. A string quartet for the first four concerts had been formed from the best locally available players: French violinist Prosper Sainton (leader), Charles Goffrie (violin II), Henry Hill (the finest viola player in town) and the French cellist Scipion Rousselot. All four had participated in Ella's 1844 concerts and on the opening afternoon they performed Haydn's op. 71 no. 1 and Beethoven's rousing Razumovsky op. 59 no. 3. Sainton and Rousselot then joined the lesser-known Edward Roeckel in Hummel's piano trio op. 83, the pianist following up with a short solo of his own composition. Perhaps not glittering as a line-up, it was nevertheless a group of solid performers; as has already been noted, this was almost a half-century before permanent, touring foursomes with distinctive identities, such as the Brodsky or Joachim Quartets, were regularly heard at British concerts, so a strong leader and cellist were important assets. The size of the audience on this auspicious occasion is not known; nor do we have insight into Ella's private reflections on the day, there being little time for diary writing during this particularly busy season. After the first concert he simply noted that 'all went admirably well'.[13] Seven concerts then followed, with a changing roster of London pianists, including Lucy Anderson, Julius Benedict and Wilhelm Kuhe, and, towards the season's end, two distinguished visitors in the strings: Camillo Sivori, known for graceful playing and virtuosity, and the magnificent Henry Vieuxtemps, both of whom appeared as leaders.

In itself, the advent of another set of commercially run, seriously inclined chamber concerts in a West End house was not particularly notable. The last two seasons had seen several initiatives in an established format of long concerts of Austro-German instrumental works (interspersed with vocal numbers), and Ella's

---

[13] Diary, 11 March 1845 (EllaC, MS 114).

musical selection was drawn from much the same store. Music by Beethoven dominated the Union's opening season (a range of the string quartets, including op. 130 – programmed in the last concert of the season – the 'Kreutzer' sonata for violin and piano op. 47, the septet op. 20 and the string quintet op. 29), and was supported by string quartets and quintets by Haydn and Mozart plus a few early Romantic works in predominantly classical moulds (Weber's duet for clarinet and piano op. 48, Mayseder's piano trio op. 52 and Spohr's double quartet no. 3, op. 87). But in almost every other respect, including programming, ethos and conduct, Ella's set-up was distinctive. Most significantly, Ella kept concerts short and concentrated (as with the 1844 *réunions*), comprising just three instrumental works, played complete, and no songs or duets (the valedictory piano solo of the inaugural concert was not repeated, although in later seasons it would reappear). The format was strikingly modern-looking and emphasized Ella's unabashed commitment to a focused repertoire, as well as his seriousness of purpose. No one could be in any doubt that this was about music for music's sake. Nor, if one looked at the institution's literature, that serious, religious-like devotion to music was required from audiences: it was – as every concert programme pointed out – to be a 'locality *consecrated* to the intellectuality of art' [my italics], and its repertoire was frequently characterized as emanating from the 'divine muse'.[14] Subscribers were referred to as 'members', suggesting that they belonged to a special community. Institutional longevity was also an aspiration: the Musical Union was intended to run and run, and this also placed it apart from most other initiatives. Only the Beethoven Quartett Society, set up around the same time by Thomas Alsager for the performance and veneration of Beethoven's string quartets in concerts comprising three works, one from each 'period' of Beethoven's life, approached the Musical Union's character and ideals. It gave its first concert a little over a month after the inauguration of Ella's scheme. It too had grown out of activities in the private sphere (Alsager's 'Queen Square Select Society'); but its membership (fifty names initially) was small in comparison, and it drew a somewhat different audience of professional musicians.[15] Unlike the Musical Union, it lasted only a few seasons. It was floundering by 1849 and dead by 1853.[16]

Ella's definition of chamber music as works for small instrumental ensembles

[14] *RMU* (1845), 1. There are multiple references to the 'divine muse' or 'holy muse' (e.g. in *RMU*, 1845, p. 40).

[15] On the Beethoven society's origins, including the profile of the Queen Square Select Society, see David B. Levy, 'Thomas Massa Alsager, Esq.: a Beethoven Advocate in London', *19CM*, 9 (1985–6), 119–27. Perceived competition from the Beethoven group may have influenced Ella's decision to programme op. 130 at the Musical Union.

[16] For a summary of the society's history, see *BashfordPCC*, 180–97.

with one player per part, and his insistence on its exemplification by the Viennese Classical repertoire, is significant historically because the generic category of
'chamber music' was by no means fixed in England mid-century. Many musicians
allowed for a looser, pluralistic and essentially pre-nineteenth-century understanding of what it entailed, along the lines of 'works for small forces performed
in small spaces, and comprising either vocal or instrumental composition', and
with no exclusion of works on the basis of style (flamboyant virtuosic) or scoring (more than one player per part). That said, things were starting to shift as
part of a wider realignment of musical values. Since the mid-1830s the serious
'classical chamber music' camp among London concert-promoters had been tending towards the instrumental ensemble repertoire from Haydn onwards that Ella
now championed as the most intellectual of musical art – although in practice
most concert-givers admitted a broader range of compositions, including vocal
numbers. In time, others would join Ella's train. The violinist Charles Guynemer,
a figure from Ella's past, laid down similarly austere parameters in his *Essay on
Chamber Classical Music* (London, 1846).[17] For him, the chamber repertoire was
solely instrumental, embracing sonatas (including solo ones – not initially part of
Ella's vision), string trios, quartets and quintets, and various combinations with
piano; it excluded 'ephemeral effusions of fashion' or anything 'intended for the
display of any *peculiarity of execution*', and it upheld the genre as combining genius
with science.[18] Meanwhile, only institutions such as the Beethoven Quartett Society and the Quartett Association (established 1852 and loosely named, since it
extended to trios, quintets and so on) were playing out a similar focus on instrumental music and anticipating an understanding of the chamber genre and repertoire that crystallized decades later.

Defining and programming a corpus of high art music was one thing; getting
audiences to engage with it was another. Ella, sensible of the importance of understanding to true appreciation and the development of taste, made elucidation and
close listening the kernel of the society's mission and identity. To this end he came
up with the innovative idea of writing explanatory programme notes about the
works performed, complete with thematic incipits in music type, and including
them in a printed pamphlet of general news and articles that was distributed to the
audience. We shall examine the style and function of the programme notes in due

---

[17] Guynemer's thinking seems to have been influenced by recent events in London
as well as by his brother-in-law Pierre Baillot. He wrote about both the Musical
Union and Beethoven Quartett Society in his pamphlet. Ella was characteristically
quick to reprint some of Guynemer's remarks in his concert programmes.

[18] Charles Guynemer, *Essay on Chamber Classical Music* (London: the author,
1846), 9.

course; for now the reader may simply observe that the provision of such literary matter helped Ella construct and foster the serious ethos he so strongly desired. The entire season's pamphlets were later bound up and sold as the *Record of the Musical Union* by Cramer, Beale & Co. in a further bid to suggest both gravitas and permanence.

In addition, the institution's image blended this intellectual aspect with strong suggestions of musical sociality and reverence, Ella's choice of name Musical *Union* giving out multiple meanings that were apt for his setting. On one level the name could refer to the coming together of musicians and the powerful social and musical pleasure at the heart of chamber-music playing. On another it could connote the social dimension of quiet, communal listening that Ella encouraged, or the salonesque intellectual intercourse between players and audience that he hoped would develop. Additionally, it could indicate the spiritual joining together of the composers whose music was experienced. On an 1845 ticket the union of music is depicted through design: a lyre-shaped curlicue acts as a frame in which the names of Beethoven, Mozart, Haydn, Weber, Onslow, Mendelssohn, Spohr, Boccherini, Romberg, Hummel and Fesca are entwined, with the canonic Beethoven in the centre.[19] Finally, the name might invoke the quasi-religious communion between players, listeners and composers in the moment of performance. The masthead for the programme-note pamphlets, designed by Sir Joseph Bonomi of the Sir John Soane Museum, depicted the same combination of erudition, sociality and divinity through three classical, allegorical figures: Apollo holding hands with two would-be muses, Melodia and Harmonia (Fig. 7).[20]

In the face of Ella's grand rhetoric and emblems, it is worth pondering the potent mix of factors that fired him. We know he nurtured ambitions to leave a mark on musical life, was convinced of his higher destiny, and was determined to improve his social and economic status. His youthful exposure to the quartet repertoire had drawn him to the cause of chamber music; he had already gained an appreciation of the difficulties of concert-giving; and he was aware of how poorly London's musical culture compared – in quality, if not in quantity – with cities in Europe, particularly Paris. There may have also been a dawning realization that as a performer, however adequate and reliable, he would never be 'top-drawer'. As events came together in the mid-1840s, Ella saw an opening for doing something different with the chamber concert formula, by separating concert promotion from performance (previous initiatives had been run by players), transforming the programme format, and building an institutional edifice around the enterprise that insisted on music's place in high culture. Beneath the surface was the hope

[19] *EllaC*, MS 81, p. 19.

[20] Preliminary pages to *EllaMS2*, 13 (n. 1).

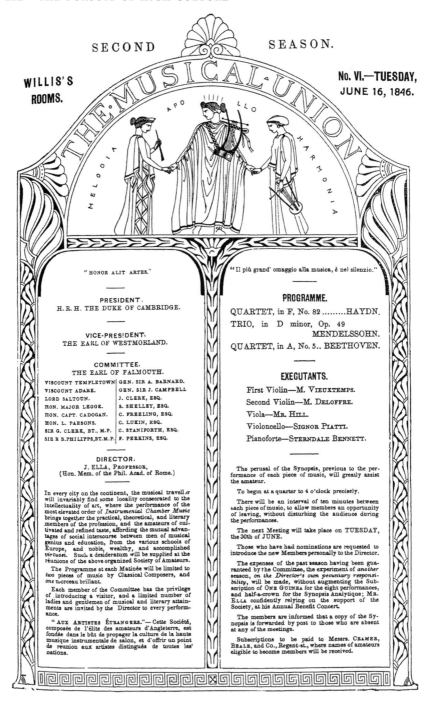

7 Front page of one of the Musical Union concert programmes, showing the institution's distinctive masthead. From the *Record of the Musical Union* (1846); reproduced by kind permission of the Bodleian Library, Oxford.

of creating serious music-making that would compare well with what went on in Europe.

While the Musical Union may have looked on paper like a collectively instigated effort, directed in the old patrician ways of the Concerts of Antient Music with Ella as mere lackey, in fact the inspiration and much of the leadership had come from Ella himself.[21] In the first season, admittedly, the committee met formally and had a modicum of control, having contributed to the 'reserved fund' and holding the power of veto on financial affairs and some influence on artistic matters. In the longer term, however, it did little more than rubber-stamp Ella's activities and reinforce their social prestige.[22] The strengthening of Ella's influence occurred towards the end of the 1845 season. In an earlier address to the committee he had communicated his hopes of building a subscription list that would enable the society eventually to break even without recourse to reserves.[23] But at the series' close, the outlook was apparently troubling, and there was a hastily arranged benefit concert for the Musical Union's 'Director' on 8 July 1845 (tickets 21s. and 10s 6d) in the larger venue of the Concert Room of the Princess's Theatre, which stood to the north-east of Oxford Circus between Oxford Street and Castle Street. The event was open to non-subscribers and featured a more populist mix of chamber music, instrumental solos and songs.

Significantly, changes to the society's financial management had been passed by the committee three days earlier, confirming that the books had not balanced and that the society's *modus operandi* needed adjustment.[24] Evidence in Ella's private financial notebook enhances the picture, indicating that the season's outgoings stood at £300 against an income of *c.*£150 from the membership of 146 – a loss of around £150.[25] The benefit, on the other hand, apparently brought in takings of

[21] That the impetus for the Musical Union came from Ella, rather than his patrons, is strongly suggested by the 'Report', *RMU* (1845), 2. Addressed to the principal patrons, and dated 1 February 1845, it opens: 'It is now three months since I first solicited your patronage'. The wording of a letter to Ella from the Earl of Westmorland, dated 9 December 1844, in EllaC, MS 81, between pp. 20 and 21, also indicates that Ella proposed the establishment of the committee.

[22] The committee's 'hands-off' management was noted or inferred by several contemporary observers: see e.g. *Life and Letters of Sir Charles Hallé being an Autobiography (1819–60) with Correspondence and Diaries*, ed. C. E. Hallé and Marie Hallé (London: Smith, Elder, 1896), 103; and *DiehlMM*, 114.

[23] 'Report', *RMU* (1845), 2.

[24] A programme for the benefit is in EllaC, MS 81, p. 19. The committee's resolution (5 July) appears in the prospectus for the 1846 season, in the same manuscript, p. 20.

[25] Expenditure for 1845 is noted in the account book, EllaC, MS 6, p. 14. The season's membership size (146) and income (£153 6s) is based on information given in op.

£150, an encouraging development and enough to break even overall.[26] Yet, writing in print thirty-five years later, Ella claimed there had been an end-of-season deficit of £80 (not £150) that nearly put an end to the enterprise.[27] So where does the truth lie? Public statements by musicians about money are notoriously unreliable, especially those given at such a distance of time by someone prone to exaggerate. A best guess is that the deficit referred to the financial situation before the benefit took place, but after the 'reserved fund' had been drawn on – a good example of Ella being economical with the truth for the sake of effect.[28] In the years to come, Ella would often downplay the commercial aspect, preferring to emphasize his altruism in the name of art. As one commentator explained: Ella was 'especially anxious to impress his hearers [in conversation] with the fact – or rather, perhaps, idea – that he rather lost by his concerts than otherwise'.[29] Nonetheless, Ella, who had proposed the administrative reforms to the committee, must have sensed he needed more independence for the project to survive. Henceforth, the committee agreed, he should have the 'entire pecuniary responsibility' for managing the society and should be allowed to increase the membership, something he may have argued for all along.[30] The number of subscribers had been capped, perhaps at the committee's behest (to ensure the perception of exclusivity), perhaps due to the capacity of Blagrove's rooms. Meanwhile, estimates for expenditure had apparently been exceeded, Vieuxtemps, for one, costing more than expected.[31]

cit., p. 47. A membership of 195 is listed in *RMU* (1845), but that calculation incorporates people who had applied for membership for the 1846 season.

[26] EllaC, MS 6, pp. 47 and 89. Ella's calculations of income, possibly entered some time after the event, are inconsistently given. The benefit income is noted as £150 in both places in the notebook, but on p. 47 he calculates the figure on the basis of 140 tickets sold at a guinea each, whereas we know (from EllaC, MS 81, p. 19) that Ella advertised tickets at a guinea and half a guinea. How much was spent on the benefit is unknown; but the amount was probably small.

[27] *RMU* (1880), 29. The £80 deficit is also in *HaweisJE*, 2, though *RMU* (1853), 34, suggests a loss of £100. In 'The Honorarium of Artists, 1870', *RMU* (1870), sup., p. vii, Ella refers to the 'failure of the first season in 1845'.

[28] I have found no indication of the size of the 'reserved fund', but this thinking revises my thesis in 'John Ella and the Making of the Musical Union', *MBC*, 200, where I assumed the deficit had been calculated at the end of the entire season.

[29] *DiehlMM*, 118.

[30] EllaC, MS 81, p. 20: '*Resolved* [...] That the Committee accede to the request of Mr. Ella, to add to the Members of this Society, and to have the entire pecuniary responsibility for its management.'

[31] *RMU* (1845), 35. Ella claimed that he had paid double the usual rate (and double the maximum paid by the Philharmonic) for Vieuxtemps, subsidizing the fee himself.

It should come as no surprise that, in an age of growing print journalism and voracious reading publics, the new institution's ideals and fortunes were being closely scrutinized by the musical press. Most coverage was positive, but there was a sprinkling of negative comment, typical of the partisanship and petty-mindedness that characterized much British music journalism in the nineteenth century and thwarted its wider appreciation well into the twentieth. The spears, it has to be said, were almost certainly hastened along by Ella's close control of the 'free list' by which newsmen attended concerts. Only 'gentlemen of musical literary attainments, known to the Committee or Director' (for which read 'journalist friends of Ella') were given admission – a shameless tactic for getting a good press, especially where it mattered (for Ella, this meant the fashionable gazettes and morning papers), but one that virtually guaranteed hostility from other quarters. So while writers such as George Hogarth (Dickens's brother in law) for the *Morning Chronicle* and Charles Gruneisen for the *Morning Post* were invited in and wrote warmly, those who were excluded carped from the sidelines.[32] The principal malcontents were Henry Chorley and J. W. Davison, whose writings and reputations were for decades over-played as sources for understanding music in nineteenth-century Britain, and whose critical legacies may well have shaped views of Ella and the Musical Union long after his death.[33] Both were already known to Ella.[34] Chorley was the first to enter the fray, parodying the institution as the 'Musical Ruin' before it had got off the ground, and thereafter grumbling that the institution had not lived up to its promises, that the subscription was unnecessarily low (the 'gentle' subscribers could easily afford to pay more), and claiming that the performers were not paid.[35] The last point was notably incorrect. His views,

[32] Hogarth wrote about the society in *MC* (12 March 1845) after its inaugural matinée. His authorship of this notice is revealed in *RMU* (1845), 8, in material presumably added for the final printing of the concert pamphlets as the annual record of achievement. The information also appears in the prospectus for the 1846 season, a copy of which is preserved in EllaC, MS 81, between pp. 20 and 21. Gruneisen's authorship of a favourable review of the benefit concert in *MP* is indicated by a handwritten annotation by Ella in the same manuscript, p. 19.

[33] On the over-emphasis on Chorley and Davison, see Leanne Langley, 'Criticism, ii: 3(i): Britain to 1890', *NGDM2*.

[34] Evidence that Ella was already aware of Davison is suggested by Ella's diary, 7 January 1840 and 7 January 1841 (EllaC, MSS 109 and 110). He had known Chorley through the *Athenaeum*.

[35] *Athenaeum* (4 January 1845), 18–19; (1 February 1845), 129; (15 March 1845), 276; (5 April 1845), 338; (19 April 1845), 396; (17 May 1845), 500–1; (21 June 1845), 621. Chorley further complained that Ella's performers had not matched the calibre of player that his prospectus had proposed (5 July 1845, p. 668).

sarcastic and nasty in tone, were given further endorsement in editorials in the *Musical World*, now under the direction of Davison (soon to be appointed music critic on *The Times*), who suggested Ella was motivated largely by egotistical interests.[36] In the brouhaha that ensued, Davison admitted his error about artists' fees and modified his views, though Chorley did not, continuing to assert that artists had been exploited and preferring to claim that the need for the end-of-season benefit had shown the society to be financially unviable in its original form.[37] Perhaps he touched a nerve: the two men would remain on difficult terms for years.

The season over, there were other things to do. By August, Ella was embarked on a further leg of his European tour, this time through Germany and Austria (with several weeks in Vienna), absorbing more foreign experiences that would have a lasting impact on him. These included a chance meeting with Richard Wagner *en route*; a visit to the recently unveiled Beethoven statue in Bonn; and, in Vienna, quartet performances and social interaction at Prince Czartoryski's palace, the purchase of fragments of manuscript music believed to be by Mozart from the collector Aloys Fuchs, encounters with Berlioz and his music, and more.[38] '[R]eluctant to return to my native country' and feeling once again how dimly London music-making compared with yet another Continental city, Ella arrived home early in 1846.[39]

[36] Davison's remarks are in *MW* (13 February 1845), 73–4; (6 March 1845), 110. A warmer tone in *MW* reviews (1 May 1845, p. 208 and 15 May 1845, p. 232) may be the work of Desmond Ryan ('D.R.'), who signed the positive account of the benefit concert in *MW* (17 July 1845), 346.

[37] *MW* (7 August 1845), 373–4. That Davison was the author is confirmed by a handwritten annotation against the text of this review, as republished in the 1846 Musical Union prospectus (EllaC, MS 81, between pp. 20 and 21). For Chorley's complaints, see the *Athenaeum* (5 July 1845), 668.

[38] The trip is documented in his diaries for 1845 and 1846 (EllaC, MSS 114 and 115), through episodes later recounted in *RMU* (including the meeting with Wagner: 1855, sup., p. 33), and in a series of dispatches ('from a correspondent') outlining his impressions of Vienna, plus a piece on Prague, Dresden and Leipzig, which were published in *MP* from 27 November 1845 (see also 4 December 1845; 25 December 1845, 31 December 1845; 7 January 1846, 26 January 1846, 5 February 1846 and 23 February 1846); copies of some of these press cuttings are in EllaC, MS 81, pp. 23–4. In all these essays Ella repeatedly compares and contrasts his observations with the state of music in London.

Ella also obtained autograph manuscripts by Beethoven. These and the Mozart items are preserved as part of Music Loan 79 in the BL.

[39] The quotation is from *MP* (23 February 1846). We do not know when he arrived in London; the noting of London appointments in his diary resumes after a short gap, in late February 1846.

He had already managed to attend to advance advertising for the ensuing Musical Union season.[40]

🎵 *Finding the formula*

It was up-hill work at first, but it had in it the germs of success.
A lesser artist would have been discouraged.   ∽ *HaweisJE*

IN a prospectus for the 1846 concerts, probably issued shortly after his return, Ella announced his intention to double the Union's membership.[41] If achieved, the measure would produce an income of some £300 (double what had been raised from subscriptions in 1845) – probably enough to break even, though it would still take something extra to push the society into profit. Ella began by asking existing subscribers to nominate further (suitable) names, while he and his committee reserved the right to bring personal guests.[42] If it sounded like a good strategy, there must have been a limit to how effective the immediate network could be in achieving the goal, for Ella soon recognized that a wider audience must be sought by different means. By April he was embracing press advertising, with '[a]mateurs, desirous of obtaining nomination from the committee' invited to send in their names and addresses.[43] We cannot know for sure, but armed with this more public campaign Ella probably felt the desired outcome was attainable. By the mid-1840s demand for 'good music' in London was rising, especially among the middle classes (the upper echelons of which were in Ella's purview), and at a rate roughly in step with the much-written-about swelling of the capital's population.[44] Moreover, chamber music had shown itself able to draw audiences of 400

---

[40] An advertisement for the Musical Union, dated 27 January and sent from Berlin, appeared in *MW* (7 February 1846), 66.

[41] EllaC, MS 81, between pp. 20 and 21. The intention is noted in Ella's report to the committee and dated 1 February 1846.

[42] Ibid. The committee could vet the nominations. A scheme for associate members, also the substance of the advertisement in *MW* (7 February 1846), 66, never materialized. The plan was to attract people who were unable to attend the afternoon concerts; they would have been admitted to an evening rehearsal the day before.

[43] *MC* (10 April 1846). On 31 May 1846, an advertisement in the *Observer* indicated vacancies for fifty additional members. In 1845 Ella had made little use of the press, other than to disseminate information to subscribers: see *MH* and *MC* (24 February 1845).

[44] *EhrlichMP*, 59.

or more, notably for Mori and Lindley's Classical Chamber Concerts during the previous decade.[45]

To accommodate the larger clientele Ella would need a more capacious venue than Blagrove's rooms, and for the opening of the 1846 season he returned to the Princess's Theatre's concert rooms. Their suitability, however, was quickly called into question (too echoey a space), and by the second concert another location had been found: Willis's Rooms (formerly named Almack's) in King Street, St James's, at the heart of Piccadilly. Used in the eighteenth century for balls and dancing, the building had since been put over to wider uses, and not just concerts: literary readings, lectures, dinners and public meetings all took place in this building of dignified if ageing gentility. 'Musty and faded grandeur' is one memory of its ambiance.[46] Nonetheless, it turned out to be a reasonable choice, given the absence of a purpose-built recital hall in London at the time. In a more respectable location than the Princess's Theatre, it had a strong aura of 'rank and fashion' and thus might attract more subscribers, and it even had associations with chamber music, Mori and Lindley's (and others') concerts having taken place there.[47] There were teething troubles with the acoustic, but they were quickly addressed. As for the economics, some 275 Musical Union memberships were probably issued for the concerts of 1846.[48] This was not quite enough to meet Ella's stated target, in spite of a rearguard membership drive during June; but the growth was of the right order and would have paid for any increased costs associated with the new venue. A final, populist Director's Matinée, open to 'strangers', with players giving their services free, seems to have sorted out the bottom line.[49]

[45] *MH* (29 January 1836) [estimate of 400]; *ST* (18 February 1838); and *MP* (13 February 1839) [*c*.600].

[46] *DiehlMM*, 115.

[47] According to Robert Elkin, *The Old Concert Rooms of London* (London: Edward Arnold, 1955), 81, the rooms were in use until 1890.

[48] My reading of EllaC, MS 6, p. 47, suggests that 275 people bought subscriptions, bringing in £288 15s. (This compares with 331 members listed in *RMU* for 1846; there is no indication that this included names of visitors and other guests, but practice in *RMU* from 1847 would suggest this was the case.)

[49] The expenditure for the season was put by Ella at £360 (EllaC, MS 6, p. 14); if calculated without the benefit takings, the bottom line is a loss of £70 (half that of the previous year at this stage).

The assumption that the players gave their services for the benefit free comes from a letter from Ella to Fétis, written in the early 1850s, in which he refers to the terms accepted by Marie Pleyel when last in London [1846] – 10 guineas for one matinée, plus playing *gratis* at the benefit. (*WangerméeF*, 439; I have revised Wangermée's dating on the basis of the letter's corroborating evidence concerning the Quartett Association, which flourished 1852–4.)

Yet benefits were not fail-safe ways of raising money; and still more needed to be done to ensure the institution's profitability and survival. Backed by the committee, Ella made further changes for the 1847 season: a confident, arguably overdue, doubling of the subscription rate to two guineas, and the integration of the Director's less austere matinée into the run of eight concerts.[50] The subscription had been set relatively low (as Chorley had gleefully pointed out), and somewhat inexplicably so, given Ella's business instincts. Perhaps he had wanted to ensure value for money: Musical Union concerts were half the length of other chamber concerts, for which a guinea subscription bought entry to three or four events, so in terms of quantity of music 'purchased', they would have worked out at about the same. If so, it was a misplaced premise: the hike in price did not significantly affect audience numbers (the published lists of members fell by only eighteen names in 1847), and it virtually doubled the guaranteed up-front income at a stroke. The 'Director's Matinée' became institutionalized as the seventh of the eight concerts, and members were encouraged to bring non-members (who could pay for one-off admissions) or to transfer their tickets for this particular concert if not attending themselves, so it surely acted as a taster event for new subscribers as well as a money-raising one. Single tickets for the benefit were also available to 'strangers' from one or two chosen music shops. In addition, Ella began advertising half-guinea tickets for the other concerts in the series 'on application to the Director' via those shops, and he later encouraged all subscribers to bring and pay for guests at the door for any concert.[51] Finally, the *Athenaeum* was admitted to the press

Benefit tickets were priced at one guinea for members (best seats) and 10s 6d for visitors (gallery and back seats): see advertisements in *RMU* (1846), 24, and the *Observer* (14 June 1846). The revenue from visitor tickets appears to have been £128 1s (243 tickets), if EllaC, MS 6, p. 89, is to be believed. Meanwhile, information on p. 47 of the same manuscript puts the total benefit income at £258 4s 6d (including ?248 tickets at 10s 6d), suggesting *c*.£130 raised from members buying tickets. This, taken with the subscription income, would indicate that by the end of the season Ella had raised just under £547 and made substantial profits overall. Ella's later public remark (*RMU*, 1880, p. 29) that the second season rendered 'little profit' thus seems disingenuous, unless one (again) discounts the benefit.

[50] 'Resolution of the Committee', *RMU* (1846), 29: Being 'anxious that the Director should be remunerated *out of the funds subscribed for the performances* under his direction', the committee resolved to double the subscription (the price would henceforth include the annual *Record*, which had hitherto been sold, additionally, for 2s 6d), and that one of the eight concerts should be of 'the miscellaneous character of the Concert given by the Director in past seasons'. The 'rules' were restated in the advertisement for the 1847 'Grand Matinée' in *RMU* (1847), 28.

[51] The rules for obtaining single tickets were stated in a committee resolution at the end of the 1846 season (*RMU*, 1846, p. 29), and in press advertisements during

group, Ella presumably deciding it was better to have Chorley grumbling 'inside the tent', rather than outside it, or hoping he might modify his views once he experienced the concerts (to some extent he did). Davison seems to have been allowed in too.[52] Together, these measures represented a successful attempt to increase takings and hook potential subscribers, and they opened up the society to yet more people.

Of course, care was needed lest the club should lose its tag of social and musical exclusivity, and Ella proceeded to balance matters admirably, drawing in more listeners on the one hand while assuring his stalwarts on the other that the institution's cachet was being preserved. New members had to be introduced to the Director on the day.[53] Urging members to suggest still more names at the end of the 1847 season, Ella emphasized the importance of recruiting 'people like us':

> [D]esirable as it is to encrease [*sic*] the list of members, we will studiously
> avoid the risk of destroying the sociality of the meetings; and leave it to our
> friends to explain the precise nature of the performances, so that none may
> be induced, from mistaken impressions, to swell our ranks, with feelings
> alien to the character of the performances.[54]

Prince Albert's arrival as official patron in 1846 probably helped, in that it brought increased prestige and assurances of quality, even though his association with the institution was merely symbolic (no evidence has emerged to indicate he attended Musical Union concerts, despite his celebrated musical interests). The single tickets were advertised as being limited in number too,[55] the Musical Union bridging the worlds of commercial concert-giving and select society, and reminding the modern reader that in the mid-nineteenth century there was no clear dividing line between public and private spheres.

The quality of the music-making was an ongoing, central concern for Ella, though here he had strong ideas of how things should be. From the outset, the cornerstone of his concerts was Beethoven, whose music, easily dominant in the broader repertoire by 1845, was becoming widely understood as the quintessence of musical achievement, standing alongside the poems of Homer, plays

---

1847 (see e.g. *Athenaeum, MC*). During 1848 press advertisements encouraged members to bring paying guests.

[52] At what point Davison was admitted is unclear; but more favourable criticisms appear in *MW* from 1846, suggesting he had gained entry after his change of heart at the end of the 1845 season. Reports crept into *The Times* from 1848.

[53] As stated in concert programmes (*RMU*, 1846 onwards).

[54] *RMU* (1847), 36.

[55] E.g. the advertisement in the *Athenaeum* (22 May 1847), 554.

of Shakespeare, painting of Michelangelo and philosophy of John Stuart Mill as the epitome of serious culture. Beethoven's early- and middle-period string quartets, piano trios and violin sonatas, backed up by what would become Haydn's and Mozart's more celebrated string works (op. 76 and 77 by Haydn, Mozart's op. 10 onwards) – essentially the core classical chamber repertoire that would be explored and upheld not only at the Musical Union but by later generations – formed a substantial proportion of the musical stock for Ella's programmes (see Appendix II), and were hallowed choices. The composers were, in Ella's words, the 'three immortal masters'.[56] Chamber music provided Ella with a remarkably rich and extensive repertoire to draw on, but some works began to be favoured even in the first four seasons. Beethoven's quartets op. 18 nos. 1, 5 and 6, the first and third 'Razumovskys' (op. 59) and the 'Harp' quartet (op. 74), the op. 70 no. 1 and op. 97 ('Archduke') piano trios, the 'Kreutzer' sonata (op. 47), the C major string quintet (op. 29) and the septet (op. 20) were all played more than once, as were a handful of quartets by Haydn (op. 64 no. 5, op. 74 no. 3, op. 76 nos. 4 and 5, and op. 77 no. 1) and Mozart (G major K387, C major 'Dissonance' K465 and D major K575), and the G minor string quintet by Mozart (K516). The only competitor works in terms of 'repertoire share' at this point were Onslow's string quintets opp. 25, 34 and 58 (now largely unknown), Spohr's double quartet no. 3, op. 87, and Mendelssohn's op. 12 string quartet and op. 18 string quintet. Within a few years, other works by Mendelssohn that Ella now tried out (e.g. string quartets op. 44 nos. 1 and 2, and piano trio op. 49) would become central. Schumann's piano quartet op. 47, given in March 1848 with Roeckel at the piano, was the one, not especially successful, foray into Romantic repertoire. In the event, the audience seemed unmoved, in spite of Ella's commendation of 'the beauty of its harmonies, the classical purity of its scoring, and orthodox development of its *motivi*' in the programme note, and further experimentation with Schumann's music was avoided for a while.[57] The piece, along with the other Schumann 'classic', the piano

[56] *RMU* (1848), 2. On the development of Mozart's canonic status in Britain, see Rachel Elizabeth Cowgill, 'Mozart's Music in London, 1764–1829: Aspects of Reception and Canonicity' (PhD, University of London, 2000).

[57] *RMU* (1848), 2. Most press commentators found the work difficult; see the *Athenaeum* (1 April 1848), 344–5; *Atlas* (1 April 1848), 228; *MC* (29 March 1848); and *MW* (1 April 1848). *DN* (30 March 1848) referred to it being 'coldly received', the *Britannia* (1 April 1848, p. 215) to it not meeting with 'the unanimous approval of the connoisseurs'. Only *ILN* (1 April 1848, p. 217) and the *Britannia* – reviews almost certainly written by Ella's friend Gruneisen – made a case for the work, the piece in *ILN* paraphrasing characterizations in Ella's programme notes.

In a clever *volte face* in the programme for the following concert (*RMU*, 1848, p. 6), Ella acknowledged that his experiment with new music had failed and

quintet op. 44, became established in the Musical Union's repertoire only in the 1860s.

The art of programming required sensitivity to musical content as well as to audience taste and education. As we have seen, more than three ensemble works was undesirable to Ella's way of thinking. After attending one of Charles Lucas's concerts in February 1845, only weeks before the Musical Union opened, he had reckoned: '4 Quartets <u>too</u> much'.[58] There was a need for contrast, too, and this Ella often supplied by a work with piano, sometimes a true 'morceau brillant' (for instance Mayseder's piano trio op. 52; 1845), typically sandwiched between the two other pieces. An intention to include in every concert a 'lighter' ensemble composition had been part of the society's principles for the first season of 1845 (Ella's then sole concession to leavening, and possibly following Baillot's Parisian example), though the 'rule' was never consistently applied, and, with the integration of the Director's Matinée into the main concert series, such pieces often found a home elsewhere.[59] Experimentation with programme packages was in any case par for the course, and a process by which Ella learned.

Ella also realized that if audience appreciation of the 'difficult' territory of chamber music was to be developed and maintained, it had to be through performances of the highest standard, both technically and interpretatively. This meant hiring European stars rather than British-trained players (whose competencies, thanks to the nation's lack of the sort of systematic education available in France and Germany, were weak in comparison), and Ella brought in several Continental performers who had been tempted to the capital during the season or were temporarily resident there. Such a policy had its precedents: European musicians had been making fast money in London for at least a century and the musical culture was inherently cosmopolitan. But it was not without problems either, and the sidelining of British players awoke myriad social and nationalistic tensions, as Ella would come to appreciate.

promised it would not be repeated, 'flattering' his audience about their powers of discrimination and taste for more classical composition. Years later, Ella changed his tune, suggesting that ineffective performance had contributed to the work's poor reception on this occasion (*RMU*, 1869, p. 16).

[58] Diary, 19 February 1845 (EllaC, MS 114).

[59] In the 'Report', *RMU* (1845), 2, Ella suggested that the idea (clearly his) prefigured the suggestion by the Earl of Westmorland in a letter of 1 February 1845 to avoid the programming becoming 'too exclusive'. That letter, preserved in EllaC, MS 81, between pp. 20 and 21, is in fact dated 9 December 1844; it may well have been that Ella was deliberately falling in step with Westmorland, even if he was not prepared to admit it publicly. The 'rule' was formally dropped from the society's literature in 1851.

In the shorter term Ella's aim was to strengthen the depth of his performer base, surely encouraged by the good press that star players engendered. He was even willing for them to perform the odd 'showcase' work if they desired.[60] Vieuxtemps, a regular London visitor, continued to be a favoured leader, along with Sainton; but other fine string players joined the roster, namely Bernhard Molique (1848), a sound musician trained in both the French and German styles of violin playing, and the sensational, still young, Joseph Joachim (1847), who had played for Ella in 1844. Joachim's rendition of Beethoven's 'Kreutzer' sonata stimulated general purring in the press, the critic for the *Daily News* suggesting that his interpretation was 'more to our satisfaction than any other performers we have ever heard'.[61] Pianists rotated too and their calibre gradually increased, presumably as opportunities and Ella's growing purse allowed. The great Marie ('Madame') Pleyel played in 1846. Charles Hallé, fleeing revolutionary Paris where opportunities for playing and teaching were collapsing, was the big catch from the flood of refugees in 1848 who were welcomed to (then) asylum-friendly England.[62] The pressmen were unanimous about his performance in Beethoven's 'Archduke' trio – 'profound and poetical' (*Musical World*) – and his instinctive chamber music technique; only the acute ear of *The Atlas*'s critic (possibly Edward Holmes) sensed a need for greater breadth of style in the concert hall.[63] Hallé liked what he heard and saw and, though settling in Manchester soon after, maintained his links with the London circuit and played almost every season for Ella into the 1860s, often giving authoritative readings of Beethoven.

Ella had made it a matter of institutional principle to provide 'an arena for the display of talent from *all* the various schools of Europe' rather than to develop one permanent string quartet party.[64] So there was a balancing act to

---

[60] E.g. Vieuxtemps played one of his *Morceaux de salon*, accompanied by his wife, in 1847; Hallé performed one of his piano solos in 1848.

[61] *DN* (9 June 1847). The writer was probably George Hogarth.

[62] Hallé, *Life and Letters*, 92–3: 'from the day after the Revolution the pupils disappeared, and at the end of a week I could only boast of one (he was an old Englishman), and my friends Alard and Franchomme had none left. The audience at our third concert did not number fifty people, although every place was subscribed for. The outlook was most gloomy.' On the influx of refugee musicians more generally, see *RMU* (1848), 10.

[63] *MW* (20 May 1848), 333; *Atlas* (3 June 1848), 373 [regarding a performance of Beethoven's cello sonata in A major op. 69].

[64] *RMU* (1846), 18. The passage reads in full: 'If economy of expense and trouble were an object, it would be far more convenient to engage one party permanently throughout the season; but this would be considered exclusive, and contrary to the spirit of the society, which professes to afford an arena for the display of talent

be mastered – of ringing the changes among the lead players while developing familiarities of ensemble and repertoire. Henry Hill's regular occupancy of the viola chair surely helped continuities of ensemble playing, and some middle- or lower-string combinations emerged season by season (see Appendix III). The engagement (1846) of the cellist Alfredo Piatti, perhaps remembered by some members from Ella's *réunions*, was significant too. He would become an almost permanent fixture until 1866, offering both stability and panache.

But what did performances sound like? Hard as this is to answer in the era before sound recording, there is reasonable evidence that the style of chamber playing would have incorporated many more freedoms than are commonly heard today, including liberties with tempo (hurried crescendos, slowing diminuendos), note values (arpeggiated keyboard chords; rhythmic freedoms) and pitch (particularly string portamenti), and with vibrato used by the string players as an ornament – not continuously as in modern-day practice.[65] As for ensemble, here the main issue was rehearsal time. Most musicians knew much of the repertoire through playing for pleasure; and for chamber music it was typical in London for pre-concert rehearsal to be held in the performers' time (and at their expense), something that was potentially less of an issue for concerts promoted by players than those, like the Musical Union's, where musicians were hired by a manager.[66] Committed to a product of quality, Ella was careful to explain publicly the Musical Union's procedures. He acknowledged that 'careful and patient rehearsals' were the only way to achieve truly 'satisfactory execution'.[67] But he could insist on very little, because there were limits to what artists would agree to for the terms offered, and real difficulties amid 'their numerous engagements during the bustle and excitement of the London season' of finding 'sufficient hours disengaged to suit all parties'.[68] Often there seems to have been only one rehearsal, a significant weakness in Ella's set-up from the start. Indeed, given Ella's flexible performer-roster, the quest for adequate rehearsal would be a recurrent issue. Engaging star players who knew

from *all* the various schools of Europe, and to produce works of *every* composer of merit.'

[65] See Clive Brown, *Classical and Romantic Performing Practice, 1750–1900* (Oxford: Oxford University Press, 1999), 382–8, 396–9, 574–87, 612–13.

[66] But even in concerts organized by musicians, problems could arise. William Watts, second violinist in the Classical Chamber Concerts, resigned in 1837 over what he considered insufficient remuneration, given the excessive rehearsal time (letter from Watts to Mori; BL, RPS/MS/369, f. 15).

[67] *RMU* (1847), 2.

[68] Ibid.

the repertoire well often alleviated matters, especially when a great interpreter was at the helm.[69] But at other times, ensemble could be unsatisfactory.[70]

The environment for performance and listening was crucial to Ella's vision for chamber music, and during this early phase of the Musical Union's lifespan a range of practices was explored. Ella knew better than most people that the act of putting string quartets and the like into a concert hall the size of Willis's (a shoebox shape of 90 ft, perhaps 100 ft, × 40 ft, and 30 ft high) threw up significant contradictions, since chamber music in general and string quartets in particular had already come to be understood as a genre geared to small spaces and to notions of conversation and inwardness, not to the world of public address and large audiences, regardless of any gestures within the music that pointed to the contrary.[71] The Mozart and Haydn quartets, touchstone of so much Musical Union repertoire, were a case in point. Originally intended for performance in a room (chamber) of limited size, most of this music was designed to be played for its own sake and the enjoyment of its players – perhaps in the presence of a few listeners, though not necessarily so.[72] Ella may have initially hoped that audiences could be kept small enough to

[69] See *MW*'s verdict (22 May 1847, p. 336) on the 'irreproachable' ensemble in quartets led by Vieuxtemps (with Piatti on cello).

[70] *MW* (1 May 1845), 208, noted that Sainton, Goffrie, Hill and Rousselot were 'completely out for sixteen consecutive bars' in the first movement of Haydn's quartet in G minor op. 74/3; while the *Atlas* (1 May 1847, p. 315) felt that a performance of Haydn's op. 76 no. 1 was marred by the players (who included new faces: Joseph Hellmesberger on violin and Hausmann on cello) seeming 'somewhat strange to one another', and the 'unity of style which forms a complete whole' being 'deficient' – also suggesting that Haydn and Mozart quartets needed more rehearsal than they often received. Meanwhile the *Spectator* (4 April 1846; p. 331) ruminated on Benedict's 'complete misunderstanding' of Mozartian style, and his poor execution ('we believe there were amateur ladies in the room who would have done better'), signing off with the warning: 'as he [Ella] undertakes to produce true readings of classical works, he will perceive that rehearsals, subject to animadversion and correction, are sometimes as necessary to artists as to amateurs'.

[71] In an essay on the eighteenth-century string quartet ('Haydn, Mozart and their Contemporaries' in *The Cambridge Companion to the String Quartet*, ed. Robin Stowell, Cambridge: Cambridge University Press, 2003, pp. 185–209), W. Dean Sutcliffe challenges what he calls the 'string quartet lore' that emphasizes the genre's exclusive image based around intimacy and its conversational aspects, and points to several examples of popular or theatrical styles being juxtaposed with more learned, 'higher' music within several of Mozart's and Haydn's works.

[72] An exception here is Haydn's opp. 71 and 74 quartets, which have long been seen to mark a departure into a more 'public' style of music for the concert hall, the works being written specifically for Salomon's concerts in London. See Mary Hunter, 'Haydn's London Piano Trios and his Salomon String Quartets: Private vs. Public?',

preserve a physical sense of private sphere, but increasing listener numbers had emerged as the only way of making the enterprise work financially in the London market-place. While larger audiences sorted out the society's coffers, they necessitated a bigger auditorium than was ideal for chamber music aesthetically.

At the first concerts at Willis's (1846), the acoustic was widely noted as an improvement on that at the Princess's Theatre but still imperfect, there being 'some indistinctness produced by the reverberation of sound'.[73] The problem was caused by a less-than-capacity audience in a hall that seated up to 900, and the effect was probably worse the further one sat from the musicians. Ella's response, first tried at the concert in the Princess's Theatre in July 1845, was imaginative and intensely musical, and it gave the concerts a special aura. Instead of putting the chamber group at one end of the room with the audience in rows facing them, as was usual at most concerts then as now, he placed the players in the centre of the floor, facing inwards on a slightly raised platform, and had the audience spread around them on all sides.[74] This playing 'in the round' meant the distance between the players and listeners, even those in the back rows, was reduced considerably. It also made it possible for the audience to 'connect' with the players, to share vicariously in their musical conversations, and to focus on the essence of the music, in an arrangement that aped the atmosphere of both the house concert and the chapel of devotion. The new arrangement was in use by the end of the 1846 season, and was adapted further in 1847, when Ella elevated the seating so that the players were effectively in the 'centre of an amphitheatre' and sound was dampened more.[75]

Ella was not the first in London to face the problems of a large concert space. As has already been indicated, in the ten years before the foundation of the Musical Union, chamber concert promoters using the same and other public venues

Haydn and his World, ed. Elaine Sisman (Princeton and Chichester: Princeton University Press, 1997), 103–30, at 103–4.

73 *DN* (23 April 1846). See also *MH* (23 April 1846).

74 The use of the raised platform at the Princess's Theatre was noted in *ST* (13 July 1845), and is depicted in the engraving of a Musical Union concert at Willis's Rooms published in *ILN* (27 June 1846, p. 420): see Fig. 8. The accompanying commentary (pp. 419–20) describes the layout in some detail, this coverage suggesting what Ella was doing was highly newsworthy.

75 This description of the new auditorium arrangement is in *MC* (24 March 1847). A notice in *RMU* towards the end of the previous season (see 1846, no. 7, p. 25) indicates that 'additional stuffed seats' were also to have been purchased, following a member's complaint about the quality of the seating. A few years later (1855) Ella experimented further, raising the performers' dais so that those 'seated at the extremity of the room' could better see and hear (*RMU*, 1855, p. 10).

of similar size had been similarly challenged by their accommodation.[76] With critics huffing and puffing about how attenuated the music sounded when performed in a half-filled formal hall, promoters and players had sought various solutions. For the Classical Chamber Concerts Mori and Lindley had erected a partition across the room at Willis's, to make the performance space smaller. Blagrove and Lucas, for their Quartett Concerts, had done the same; but as audiences grew, the men decided to place the quartet alongside one of the long walls of the Hanover Square concert room, and to sit the audience around it in a sort of semicircular arrangement. As a result, 'all were enabled to hear as well as only one fourth could under the usual plan, and such a result could not be priz'd too highly where music so nicely delicate in all its parts was to be listened to and appreciated'.[77] Meanwhile, the pianist Ignaz Moscheles had invented a similar plan for his chamber concerts (also at Hanover Square) and, pre-echoing Ella's arrangements at Willis's, positioned himself and his co-instrumentalists in the centre of the room, in 'a sort of magic circle, with his audience all spread around him'.[78] Ella had witnessed some of these concerts, and may well have been moved to put his own players in the round because of the general approval these intimate layouts were accorded, and because of subsequent moves by other musicians to hold chamber concerts in private houses.[79] It was, in any case, in line with his own thinking. As early as 1836 he had registered private dissatisfaction that chamber players did not sit centrally at concerts.[80] All the same, years later in public he would imply that his choice of layout for the Musical Union was consonant with the example of the quartet concerts he had attended in autumn 1845 at Prince Czartoryski's palace in Vienna – a connection surely intended to impress his subscribers.[81]

With audiences settled, Ella could begin to develop his plans for improving listener appreciation of high-serious music. The project pivoted around three

---

[76] For further discussion, see Chapter 2, p.103.

[77] *MH* (8 February 1839).

[78] *The Times* (31 March 1837) [review of Quartett Concerts].

[79] Ella's diaries indicate he had attended some of the Quartett Concerts in 1840 and 1841. He would surely have known, or read, of Moscheles's experiments.

[80] Diary, 25 February 1836 (EllaC, MS 106); the passage is cited in Chapter 2, p.112, n. 232.

[81] As per the endpaper for *RMU* (1871), where Ella justifies his 'in the round' arrangement. The Czartoryski layout is further described in *EllaMS1*, 206, and in several passages in *RMU* (e.g. 1860, sup., pp. 21–2). Ella's presence at a quartet performance at Czartoryski's, led by Mayseder, is documented in the diary (2 October 1845; EllaC, MS 114).

interlocking ideals: teaching subscribers how to listen effectively to chamber works; enabling them to develop an informed familiarity with, and quasi-devotional respect for, the repertoire; and encouraging them to connect – viscerally, spiritually, intellectually – with the chamber music during performance. There can be little doubt these goals represented a formidable challenge, partly because the chamber repertoire was among the most extensive and demanding that Victorian concert-goers were ever likely to encounter (works from Beethoven onwards, with their lengthy movements of abstract music, were especially tough to grasp). But it was also because Ella was trying to reach this Utopia in the days before gramophone recordings offered the possibility of repeated, concentrated hearings in the privacy of the home.

Ella's analytical programme notes on the ensemble works performed in each concert were the all-important building-block of this strategy, and they broke new ground. At the time, London concert-goers were used to receiving no more than a running order of pieces, and possibly a book of words to the songs to be sung. (That Ella was not the actual inventor of the programme note is barely relevant here; what *is*, is that he was the first to provide audiences regularly with notes.)[82] Intended primarily to signpost the main themes and important aural moments in each movement of music, Ella's notes began with the principal themes quoted in music type and they continued with a short prose synopsis that characterized the music, often with recourse to technical terms. Many of them included a seasoning of biography and compositional history; some summed up the work's expressive essence or transcendental qualities. Unsystematic, idiosyncratic and more than a touch knowing though they may well seem to modern eyes, Ella's notes were nevertheless a significant attempt to enable audiences to engage seriously with chamber music, and to listen closely to it in a musically informed manner. In a culture where knowledge was valued, and where people were both able to read music and prepared to try to fathom that which they could not immediately understand in any prose reading matter, such aims and ideals were not out of place.

To maximize the notes' usefulness, listeners were advised to read them 'previous to the performance of each piece of music' – a ten-minute interval between pieces gave them ample opportunity to do this – so they could recognize the themes and follow the music's development aurally in the concert.[83] Ella also displayed a quotation from his hero Baillot in each and every Musical Union programme, further

---

[82] For an overview of programme note provision in nineteenth-century Britain, see Christina Bashford, 'Not Just "G.": Towards a History of the Programme Note', *GGMVC*, 115–42.

[83] Instructions to do this appear in *RMU* between 1846 and 1851.

emphasizing the influence of French culture on his thinking.[84] Translated, it means: 'It is not enough for the performers to be prepared for what they are going to play, the audience must be prepared for what it is going to hear.' In fact, preparation for and reinforcement of the music before or after the performance were to become a central tenet of Ella's philosophy. By 1851 Ella seems to have taken to sending out programmes ahead of the concert, with the express intention that subscribers prepare in advance – by studying the notes at home, perhaps tracing out themes repeatedly on a piano – rather than trying to read the words during (or immediately before) the performance.[85] And while we cannot know this for sure, some listeners may have gone further in their preparation, especially those who owned scores of the classic chamber works, and, as the decades went by, four-hand piano transcriptions.

Silence in the concert hall was intrinsic to the business of serious, concentrated listening to chamber music and, in turn, to its 'sacralization'. In fact, for Ella, absolute quiet was a pre-condition for performance, and he did his utmost to insist on its sanctity. The aphorism 'il più grand'omaggio alla musica, è nel silenzio' ('the greatest homage to music is in silence') appeared in the printed programmes, beneath the allegorical masthead, from 1846 and quickly became part of the institution's signature, enforcing its image as temple of high musical art. According to Ella, the phrase had been suggested by the statue to the goddess of silence which he had seen recently in Genoa.[86] In addition, Ella repeatedly called for silence during the music, and people were asked not to move in and out of the hall while the music was being performed. Notices to this effect, with strategic use of capital letters and bold type, appeared in the programmes from 1847. There was also, to begin with, the ten-minute interval between pieces which allowed for comings and goings, as well as programme-reading.

That Ella needed to spell out these protocols is an indication that notions of concert etiquette were still evolving during the mid-nineteenth century. While a general quietening down was taking place at serious concerts of art music around

---

[84] 'Il ne suffit pas que l'artiste soit bien préparé pour le public, il faut aussi que le public le soit à ce qu'on va lui faire entendre' (Pierre Baillot, *L'art du violon*; Paris: Au dépôt central de la musique, 1834; reprinted in the original language in every Musical Union programme, 1845–81).

[85] It is unclear when he began doing this. He first notes it in his diary, 7 April 1851 (EllaC, MS 120). Berlioz, a visitor to the Musical Union that same year, drew attention to the practice in a column sent to the *Journal des Débats*, cited in English translation in A. W. Ganz, *Berlioz in London* (London: Quality Press, 1950), 92. This practice became a hallmark of the institution.

[86] As noted in Willert Beale, 'A Morning Call on Mr. Ella', *Liverpool Journal* (18 February 1871); reprinted in the preliminary pages to *EllaMS2*, 13 (n. 2).

this time, and at chamber concerts in particular, it was still relatively rare, even in so-called quiet concerts, for pin-dropping silence to be upheld throughout, and more than common for some whispering or disturbance to compete with the music. Late-comers and early-goers were among the many problems and, with concert audiences growing constantly, educating publics about how to behave and listen was an ongoing process. The shift towards concentrated, silent listening was closely bound up with evolving systems of etiquette, themselves a reflection of new social values. It was also related to changing value-systems for music and art itself, which were producing a new belief in the serious appreciation of music as a worth-while intellectual activity, and a concomitant reverence for the work of musical art which touched on the spiritual.[87]

Some of Ella's disciplines were achieved as much through force of personality as through printed reminders. Extraordinary as it may seem, Ella soon developed a reputation for his gestures of control over those who were his social betters and unused to being told, by the likes of a mere musician, how to behave. Anecdotes are plentiful, and that of Ella's friend Haweis typical. It refers specifically to the Musical Union's early years:

> Any attempt at talking or disturbance was promptly checked by the loud and authoritative "hush" of the Professor [Ella]. […] The late Duke of Cam-bridge, during his presidency of the Musical Union [1845–50], was always present at the *matinées*. "Ah," he once remarked at a musical party where every one was talking; "you should get Ella here; he'd soon stop that."[88]

[87] On the cult of quiet, attentive and musically informed listening at chamber con-certs, see Christina Bashford, 'Learning to Listen: Audiences for Chamber Music in Early-Victorian London', *Journal of Victorian Culture*, 4 (1999), 25–51. On the shift to silence in the concert hall more generally, and an argument that empha-sizes changing social circumstances, new musical styles, emerging bourgeois values and psychological anxieties as conditioning changes in listening patterns, albeit in Paris, see James H. Johnson's provocative *Listening in Paris: a Cultural History* (Berkeley and London: University of California Press, 1995). See also the discussion of absorbed listening as an introspective experience born of Romanti-cism in Peter Gay, *The Bourgeois Experience: Victoria to Freud*: iv: *The Naked Heart* (New York: W. W. Norton, 1995), 11–35. With Ella's notes, and much British music appreciation literature, the principal goal was active, structure-oriented listening; a quasi-narrative encouraged people to follow the linear sequence of thematic and tonal events aurally. Rational activity that this was, it did not preclude emotional or quasi-spiritual enjoyment.

[88] *HaweisJE*, 1. Jennifer L. Hall-Witt ('Representing the Audience in the Age of Reform: Critics and the Elite at the Italian Opera in London', *MBC*, pp. 121–44) argues that (middle-class) music critics in the 1830s and 40s contributed substan-tially to the negative images of the élite, deliberately stylizing aristocratic audiences

Whether absolute silence was consistently achieved is open to dispute. Since Ella had to reiterate the 'rules', one suspects that quiet was hard won. Still, something special was unfolding, and Ella's measures placed the Musical Union in the vanguard of London concert culture. Critics and foreign visitors such as Onslow, who attended a concert in May 1846, remarked on the serious intellectual atmosphere at concerts.[89] There was even an attempt to capture the unusual ambiance in an engraving in the *Illustrated London News* (1846); see Fig. 8. The image depicts an earnest audience reading programme notes and listening carefully, and suggests that this was the gold standard to which all were expected to aspire, even though Ella himself probably considered reading words and listening to sounds as separate activities. The image also carried the revealing detail of small pocket-sized scores: probably an attempt to represent the scores of the core chamber repertoire that were being issued through the London publishers Ewer and Augener in the 1840s and 50s.[90] A further suggestion of how listeners might engage with the music during performance, they reflected the growing reverence for the musical text, their prayer-book size a telling sign in this respect. Ella was quick to reprint the image and accompanying article in the *Record of the Musical Union* for 1846, ensuring dissemination to his own audiences.

In all likelihood Ella had models in mind for the conduct of the institution, some formed from his own experiences, others copied or developed from the organization and ethos of other learned clubs and societies. He later pinpointed Mrs Grote, the celebrated intellectual force in London society, as the person who suggested

at the Italian Opera as poor listeners interested only in the superficial aspects of music, as part of a broader wave of anti-aristocratic feeling in the period following the 1832 Reform Bill. Privately Ella expressed caustic views about the behaviour of high society, noting annoyance at a general's daughter who behaved poorly at a private concert (diary, 19 February 1836; EllaC, MS 106; cited in Chapter 2, p. 110, n.223), though rarely spoke out publicly. His measures for reform were, by definition, practical as opposed to rhetorical.

[89] He was especially struck by seeing women following scores. His letter was published by Ella in *RMU* (1846), 16, and thereafter further disseminated (with commendation) in press reviews, in a good example of how Ella's journalism for the Musical Union helped shape its broader reception. For more on Onslow and Ella, see Baudime Jam, *George Onslow* (Clermont-Ferrand: Editions du Melophile, 2003), 455–7.

[90] The scores, initially published in Mannheim by K. F. Heckel, covered a large slice of the Viennese repertoire (all the Haydn and Beethoven quartets, Mozart's celebrated quartets and quintets, and so on) – effectively the nexus of Ella's programming. They were truly pocket size, smaller than the modern miniature score. For further discussion, see Cecil Hopkinson, 'The Earliest Miniature Scores', *Music Review*, 33 (1972), 138–44, and Bashford, 'Learning to Listen', 39–40.

VIEUXTEMPS.   DELOFFRE.   HILL.   PIATTI.   ELLA.
QUARTET PARTY AT THE MUSICAL UNION.

8 'Quartet Party at the Musical Union'. Engraving published in the *Illustrated London News*, 27 June 1846. Reproduced by kind permission of the Bodleian Library, Oxford. Musicians from left to right: Vieuxtemps, Deloffre, Hill, Piatti. The front row of the audience includes John Ella (fourth from right), the Duke of Cambridge (third from right) and the Earl of Westmorland (extreme right).

setting up the Musical Union, and acknowledged the idea for the programme notes as having come from Clayton Freeling, a committee member (1845–53) and friend of the novelist Anthony Trollope.[91] We have seen that Ella was a frequent and enthusiastic visitor at the Freelings' home; he particularly admired their serious approach to life.[92] He was also known in the Grote household, having made the acquaintance of Mrs Grote and her husband in the 1830s, when he had been struck by the flow of conversation, by George Grote's erudition and powers of argument, and by Mrs Grote's intellect.[93] If Mrs Grote and Clayton Freeling were the source

[91] Mrs Grote's role is noted in *RMU* (1880), 29; Freeling's influence is acknowledged in Ella's obituary of him in *RMU* (1854), 4. Trollope's friendship with Freeling is charted in his *An Autobiography*, 2 vols. (Edinburgh and London: William Blackwood & Sons, 1883).

[92] 'There is much enjoyment under all Circumstances, in the society of kind and Intellectual Persons', he mused in 1845, 'and an evening at M^r. Freelings is always to me an Intellectual treat'. Diary 29 January 1845 (EllaC, MS 114).

[93] Diary, 24 January 1836 (EllaC, MS 106): 'Partie a trois at diner; conversation flowed delightfully [...] I have seldom had so favorable an impression from a short acquaintance as M^r. G. has produced on me. Full of solid reading, and sound reasoning, every expression he utters is 'proof' for ["]point" – Deliberate

of these ideas, they had fallen on fertile soil, listener preparation having already been shown to be something Ella was starting to take seriously in the Saltoun Club and related activities. Moreover, the realization of the plan was Ella's own, albeit strongly mediated by French culture. One clear-cut source of inspiration was Baillot's ideas on the importance of playing to an informed audience, which Ella enshrined in the programme pamphlets. The quotation of musical incipits, too, may have borrowed from Baillot's practices at his quartet concerts in Paris.[94] More specifically, the possibility of providing listeners with words about music may have begun to make sense to Ella when he saw what Berlioz achieved by providing French audiences with a printed programme for performances of the *Symphonie fantastique* in the 1830s. But the most striking derivation of Ella's thinking seems to have been Fétis, whose pioneering *La musique mise à la portée de tout le monde* (1830, 2/1834), published in English translation in 1844 as *Music Explained to the World or, How to Understand Music and Enjoy its Performance*, Ella would later recommend to amateurs.[95] Fétis's text is insightful on the importance of repeated listening for a full understanding of instrumental chamber music, and it hints at the need for 'analysis' while going further than Baillot in prescribing the nature of audience preparation:

> The last step in the musical education of an amateur, who has not made any elaborate study of music, is the instrumental style. Thus there are few persons, strangers to this art, who like to hear quartets, quintets, or other pieces, not designed to shew the skill of a performer. In this kind of music, the end is not distinct, the object is not palpable. To please the ear is certainly one of the essential parts of instrumental as well as of all other music; but it must also excite; it has its peculiar language of expression, which no other language interprets; and, therefore, we must divine this language instead of comprehending it, and this requires practice. I would say [...] we must have patience to hear it without prepossessions, even though it should not

in speaking one plainly perceives that he first thinks: he is amiable withal and even I feel encouragement to tilt with them; altho' by so doing I only feel the more my littleness, yet my earnest call forth [*sic*] his clear and well digested opinions.' The following day (25 January) Ella wrote of Mrs Grote that she was 'evidently a sensible and clever woman, acquainted with all the <u>Liberal</u> Litterati [*sic*] of the day. I do feel proud of enjoying her friendship. There was quite enough said by both M^{r.} & M<u>rs</u> G: to induce me to seek their society for mental enjoyment alone.'

94 *FauquetS*, 291.

95 The translation was published by H. G. Clarke. Ella recommended the text in *EllaMS1*, 99. In 1985 it was issued in facsimile, with an introduction by Bernarr Rainbow, by the Boethius Press.

please; with perseverance, we shall at length enjoy it, and then we may begin
to analyse it; for this kind of music also has its melodies, its rhythm, its
symmetrical quantities, its varieties of form, its effects of harmony, and its
modes of instrumentation. By the application of the processes of dramatic
analysis, we shall acquire notions of it, as well as of every other kind of
music.[96]

Much of this reads like a manifesto for the Musical Union. It also suggests an
attempt by Ella to put his teacher's ideas into practice.

More broadly, Ella's initiative and modus operandi seem to owe a good deal
to the ethos and operation of learned clubs and societies in Britain, the numbers of which had multiplied significantly during the eighteenth century, covering a diversity of interests and propelled by a 'new stress on public and personal
improvement', to quote the historian Peter Clark.[97] There is much in Clark's study
of the organization and membership of these clubs that resonates with what we
know of the Musical Union: copious rules and regulations, especially concerning conduct and admission, a hierarchy of 'officers' and a committee, power in
the hands of men, the publication of a record (or transactions) of the society, the
use of symbolic imagery, and even the provision of a chair on a dais for the presiding officer.[98] The use of a mahogany 'compass-seat elbow-chair with crimson
velvet (and a pedestal)' for the president of the Dilettanti Society comes uncannily
close to later descriptions we have of Ella sitting on a 'gilded seat' or 'a kind of
throne' in the front ring of the audience.[99] Of course, clubs and societies ranged
wide in terms of interest and function; and features of several institutions such as

96 Fétis, *Music Explained*, 294–5. The suggestion behind Baillot's remarks was that
the performer should introduce the pieces to be performed to his listeners, so
that they got a sense of what they were going to hear. By this he seems to have
meant giving the audience the names of the works to be performed, their keys,
nicknames and movement designations (tempi, character etc.) in a programme,
and perhaps some sort of introduction as to the work's notional content, particularly when dealing with music that was new to its public. It is unclear whether he
was advocating a printed programme or spoken commentary. See Pierre Marie
François de Sales Baillot, *The Art of the Violin*, ed. Louise Goldberg (Evanston, IL:
Northwestern University Press, 1991), 463–4.

97 Peter Clark, *British Clubs and Societies, 1580–1800: the Origins of an Associational
World* (Oxford: Clarendon Press, 2000), 470.

98 Clark, *British Clubs*, 194–273.

99 Clark, *British Clubs*, 247. The 'gilded seat' is from the article on the Musical Union
by Walter Willson Cobbett in *CCSCM*. The description of the 'throne' is from
GanzMM, 111. These descriptions probably refer to the 1860s or 70s, after the
Musical Union had moved into more lavish accommodation in St James's Hall.

feast days, drinking and conviviality (notably in meetings that were exclusively for men), or a sense of shared administration, were absent from the Musical Union, which had most in common with learned or scientific societies, boasted a large female contingent, and was run so strongly by one person. Perhaps the Musical Union's serious literary atmosphere had roots in Ella's knowledge of Leicester's Literary and Philosophical Society (William Gardiner was a founder member in 1835), which had admitted women as a way of keeping the institution afloat in its early years.[100]

With the Musical Union's ethos established as uncompromisingly earnest, Ella had to perform clever sleights-of-hand when programming the Director's Matinée, the repertoire mix of which ran against the grain. The following programme (1847) typifies the less austere tone: two movements from Onslow's string quintet op. 25 (led by Sainton); Mozart's quartet in D K575 (led by Joseph Hellmesberger from Vienna); a Lied by Lüders, 'Die beyden Grenadiere', text by Heine, sung by the Bohemian baritone Jan Křtitel Pišek (a much-in-demand concert singer); the andante and finale from Spohr's third double quartet op. 87 (leaders Prosper Sainton and Louis-Michel-Adolphe Deloffre; the latter had become a regular occupant of the second violin's seat); an aria 'La primavera' by a composer named Bieling, sung by one Mlle di Mendi; Hummel's septet op. 74 in D minor for piano, flute, oboe, horn, viola, cello and double bass (the piano part was played by Louise Dulcken and the wind parts by orchestral players Ribas, Barret and Jarret; James Howell, Dragonetti's 'heir apparent', was the double bassist); an aria from Conradin Kreutzer's romantic opera *Das Nachtlager in Granada* ('Die Nacht ist schön'; Pišek, with obbligato violin from Hellmesberger); Beethoven's quartet op. 18 no. 6 led by Joachim; a German Lied (Pišek once more); and to end, a trio concertant for three violins by Joseph Hellmesberger's brother, Georg, and performed by the two of them and Sainton. This pot-pourri of vocal and instrumental music, and the lighter tone of the selection, was definitely a compromise on the vision set out in the society's first prospectus. But Ella was fast becoming a shrewd operator, ready to find pragmatic solutions if it meant the difference between keeping his institution alive or not. In any case the sober spirit of chamber music hovered; Ella slipped in serious repertoire (e.g. Beethoven's op. 18 no. 6, complete) alongside the gobbets of easier listening, and he continued to produce programme notes for these occasions. In them he acknowledged that the offerings were lighter than at other Musical Union concerts (though implicitly superior to run-of-the-mill benefit fare); he argued that excising movements from masterworks was excusable for a gala event; and he stressed the importance

---

[100] Jonathan Wilshere, *William Gardiner of Leicester, 1770–1853: Hosiery Manufacturer, Musician and Dilettante* (Leicester: Leicester Research Services, 1970), 19.

of drawing new listeners into difficult music through its more accessible moments.[101] In effect he was articulating the concept, well known in the early twenty-first century, of popular classics.

❧ *Audiences and networks*

The Musical Union already includes amongst its members the best known practical amateurs of the aristocracy. The time of its meetings is convenient for all parties, enabling them to fulfil their numerous morning and evening engagements, allowing a spare hour in the afternoon for the intellectual enjoyment of the cabinet gems of musical art.   ᵔᵔ *CJ* (4 January 1845)

FROM its inception the Musical Union was termed by the press an institution of the aristocracy. This was partly due to the visibility of the nobility in lists of committee members and subscribers, and among audiences at concerts (the committee sat in the front rows), and partly because Ella constructed an identity for the organization that linked musical, intellectual and social élitism. Taken literally, the 'aristocratic' label was an overstatement in that it ignored the several subscribers from the landed gentry and upper-middle classes who were an accepted part of the capital's fashionable world. 'High society' might have been a more accurate description, but there were good reasons why 'aristocratic' was preferred, and particularly why it persisted, Ella gaining in later life an increasingly unfavourable reputation with some of his press peers for consorting with the 'nobs'. Used loosely, 'aristocratic' nevertheless captured the halo of leisure and wealth, as well as high musical values, that ringed the institution.

Audiences of the past are a notoriously elusive lot, and even with the Musical Union, where audience information survives, an unequivocal delineation of the profile and balance of its constituent social groups, including the extent of aristocratic membership, remains beyond our grasp. To start with, despite subscribers' names being published in the annual *Record*, there is generally not enough corroborative detail – forenames, initials, addresses, occupations and so forth – to identify who was who in every case. Many surnames in Ella's lists are not distinctive enough to enable specific identification; and the pool of possible London-ites is so immense as to render the task impossible. (Doing the same job for a provincial town or city, with smaller communities of permanent inhabitants, might be less problematic.) In addition, the lists of 'members' are typically inflated by the inclusion of those who came occasionally as guests or purchased tickets, and

---

[101] E.g. *RMU* (23 June 1846), 2; (1848), 26.

they do not always distinguish this group from subscribers proper. Meanwhile, the handwritten ledgers of members' names and addresses that must once have existed are not extant.

It follows too that allocating names to broad social groups is a tricky undertaking, even assuming we could define those groups firmly in the first place. A tally of titled names gives only a rough indication of the aristocratic constituency, since it does not include associated family members who did not bear titles (children of baronets), those whose clanship may not be obvious (daughters who married out; aristocrats without titles whose parents did not attend the Union), or those whose titles were conferred and not hereditary (here there are further problems with knights' wives who came without their husbands). Meanwhile, even with known non-aristocrats, it can be hard to disentangle concert-goers belonging to the landed gentry – 'the untitled aristocracy of England' as Burke described them[102] – from those in the upper-middle classes. Who qualified as gentry was and is open to dispute; and the division between the groups is often fuzzy, some landed gentry having positions in the old professions (the clergy and the law for instance), and some men from industry and commerce acquiring land. To compound matters, an unidentified non-titled person could be from a middle class, gentry or aristocratic family.[103]

Despite these caveats and methodological flaws, basic counts of titled names can still usefully indicate background trends of class. We can surmise that Ella's widening of the Musical Union's audience after 1845 did not upset the proportion of aristocracy attending concerts (the seventy-two known members of titled families in the 195-strong list of names published in 1845 had grown to 119 out of 310 by 1848, representing 37 and 38 per cent of the audience respectively), though in the longer term the balance would change.[104] Approximately half of the known aristocrats were from the upper ranks of the British nobility (in descending order, dukes, marquesses, earls, viscounts and barons): people such as the Duke and Duchess of Roxburghe, the Earl of Cawdor, the Viscount Adare (committee member; later to become the third Earl of Dunraven) and the Hon. Lawrence Parsons (also on the committee; the youngest son of the second Earl of Rosse).

[102] In his *Landed Gentry* of 1886. The passage is cited in David Cannadine, *The Decline and Fall of the British Aristocracy* (London: Papermac, 1996), 12.

[103] The difficulties are well articulated in F. M. L. Thompson, *English Landed Society in the Nineteenth Century* (London: Routledge & Kegan Paul, 1963), 22, 109–50, and in J. V. Beckett, *The Aristocracy in England, 1660–1914* (Oxford: Basil Blackwell, 1986), 16–42.

[104] It should be stressed again that these totals almost certainly included one-off guests and visitors. For information on the size of the membership list in *RMU* for 1845, see n. 25 above.

The other half were from minor aristocratic families such as those headed by the baronets Sir George Clerk of Penicuik, Scotland (committee man; 1787–1867; sixth baronet), Sir Charles Lemon of Carclew, West Cornwall (1784–1868; second baronet) and Sir Robert Brownrigg (1817–82; second baronet), whose father had been Governor of Ceylon; many were from families that had been ennobled for only one or two generations. Meanwhile, the influx of new listeners up to 1848 seems not to have disturbed the ratio of known gentry to upper-middle classes.[105]

Of course, class is but one aspect of Ella's concert-goers' identities, and should be allied to information about social status, wealth, gender, domicile, occupation, interests, tastes and so on, if we are to sense what sort of people they were. With this end in view, and the impossibility of a comprehensive study notwithstanding, we can seek out common denominators by focusing on a small cross-section of names that recur in the membership lists – in effect, concert-goers who can be positively identified either through their social status, prominence in Victorian society or connections with Ella (though herein lies a further problem, since focusing on those around Ella risks highlighting people in his immediate network to the exclusion of those who were not, so conclusions need to be tempered accordingly). The discussion that follows aims to characterize the Musical Union audience with this in mind.[106]

It is well known that the British aristocracy and landed gentry was effectively a tight-knit and hierarchical caste of wealth and power, admission to and progression through which could be won by the negotiation of various hurdles and rituals.[107] An intricate web of family relationships, especially those gained through marriages, and strong social networks were the by-product, and has special significance to our story, since it bound many of Ella's audience together while

[105] Some seventeen of the 127 non-titled people listed in *RMU* (1845) can be identified with some certainty in Burke's *A Genealogical and Heraldic Dictionary of the Landed Gentry of Great Britain & Ireland* (London: Henry Colburn, 1846); compare with thirty-seven of the 200 non-titled Musical Union-ites in the *Dictionary* of 1848 – a slight, and probably insignificant, increase in the number of identified gentry from 9 to 12 per cent of the entire membership. In reality the proportion of gentry to middle classes may well have been larger.

[106] Unless otherwise stated, biographical information on individuals in this section has been compiled from standard reference sources including the *DNB*, *ODNB*, Burke's *Landed Gentry* and *Peerage*, and *Who's Who of British Members of Parliament*: i: *1832–1885*, ed. Michael Stenton (Hassocks: Harvester Press, 1976).

[107] Beckett, *Aristocracy*, Chapter 3: 'The Making of the Aristocracy: the Channels of Admission'.

providing the trelliswork on which his own social and professional ambitions could grow. The family of Sir George Cornewall, Bt (1774–1835), to whose London and Herefordshire homes Ella had become a regular visitor and musical *animateur* in the 1830s, was a case in point. Several of Cornewall's sisters had made good marriages. Frances Elizabeth was now the Dowager Viscountess Hereford, and Caroline was Lady Duff Gordon. Both signed up to the Musical Union in 1845, along with Sir George's widow and his unmarried sister Anna-Maria. (A more indirect family link was evident through Mrs Frankland Lewis of Harpton Court, Radnorshire, a subscriber for several years. She was the second wife of Thomas Frankland Lewis, MP, landowner and one-time Poor Law commissioner, soon to be given a baronetcy; his first wife had been Harriet Cornewall, another sister, who had died in 1839.) These Cornewall women were typical: graced with musical aptitude, and schooled in singing and piano-playing by the best of tutors.[108] Ella had connections with all of them. The Viscountess he would later describe as the '[b]est Amateur I have ever known', and would praise her brother, that 'amiable lover of music' and enthusiastic cellist.[109] In London for the season, they took in a range of music from the Italian Opera to the Antient Concerts and the Philharmonic, as well as private gatherings (some of which involved Ella). For all that, the prospect of joining Ella's institution might have given them cause for a little apprehension, the world of quartet playing being an eminently male-gendered domain. If so, the knowledge that others from one's family and extended circle were joining was doubtless reassuring. In turn, the Musical Union might, and undoubtedly did, strengthen bonds of kinship and friendship.

Similar forces were at work among the family and friends of Sir George Clerk, Bt. Ella, who had encountered him in the 1820s at the Hon. General Arthur Upton's music parties and drawn him into the Saltoun Club, now signed up him and his eldest son James to the Musical Union committee.[110] Music was a family passion: Sir George's great-grandfather John, second baronet, had been a proficient amateur composer;[111] Sir George and his children learned to play as a matter of course. Lady Clerk and four of the (twelve) sons and daughters were enrolled

---

[108] Letter of 26 November 1872 to Henrietta Master; reproduced in Nicholas Thompson, 'Moccas Court, Herefordshire – II: the Property of Mr Richard Chester-Master', *Country Life* (25 November 1976), 1554–7, at 1554–5.

[109] Annotations, made in 1863 and 1864, to letters to Ella from Viscountess Hereford and Sir George Cornewall (EllaC, MS 81, p. 63).

[110] Ella noted his first meeting (1824) with Sir George Clerk in a photograph album (EllaC, MS 1, p. 3).

[111] See the preface to Sir John Clerk of Penicuik: *Sonata in G for Violin with Keyboard and Optional Cello Continuo*, ed. David Johnson and Edna Arthur (Edinburgh: David Johnson, 1990).

in the Musical Union from 1845, and some of the younger children attended once they were old enough.[112] It may have even been the case that Lady Clerk (Maria, daughter of Ewan Law of Horsted, Surrey; she had married Sir George in 1810) was the conduit for bringing in extended family members. (Were the five Laws in the membership list of 1845 her relatives?)

Other Musical Union supporters turn out to have been in the Clerks' social circle, as evinced by an amateur watercolour depicting music-making at the family's town house in Park Street in the West End in 1848 (Fig. 9). Several of Sir George's family – his mostly grown-up children James, John, Alexander, Edward, Isabella, Maria and 'Ebby' (probably the youngest daughter: Elizabeth Henriette) – are here shown with Lord Gerald Fitzgerald, second son of the Duke of Leinster (a committee member), Sir Archibald Macdonald, Bt (he and his wife appear in the membership lists from 1846), and the Earl of Falmouth (chair of the com-mittee, also president of the Beethoven Quartett Society, and, as we know, an enthusiastic quartet player). Ella, who continued to foster his connections with this group of people outside the Musical Union's immediate activities, is direct-ing the music and, significantly, is the picture's focal point. Although the painting shows an ensemble of miscellaneous instrumentation, perhaps trying one of Ella's small-band arrangements, the men would have been equally likely to have played string quartets, to judge from evidence uncovered in connection with the Earl of Falmouth and the Duke of Leinster.[113] Some of the musical friendships pre-dated the Musical Union, but Ella's institution was poised to strengthen such circles of private music-making.

In addition to shared social networks, musical interests and abilities, the common characteristics of Musical Union supporters were affluence and status, a home base in London for the 'season' (before suburban spread took hold, this meant a house in the West End, or somewhere in striking distance of it by private carriage) and ample leisure time, often used for a range of intellectual pursuits. Take for example Harriet ('Mrs') Grote, supposed originator of the 'idea' of the Musical Union, who attended off and on for several seasons. Her husband George Grote, of the banking family of Grote, Prescott & Co., combined his wealth and banking position with scholarly endeavours and public responsibility (he was a notable historian of Greece, was closely involved in the setting up of London University, sat as a Whig MP, 1832–41, and was a trustee of the British Museum). The Grotes

---

[112] James, John, Isabella and (probably) Maria Clerk were regular attendees.

[113] See the discussion in Chapter 2, p. 108. That Leinster owned a collection of chamber music is suggested by a bound volume of Cherubini string quartet parts, with a leather label on the front board bearing the words 'Duke of Leinster', in the Surrey Performing Arts Library, Dorking.

9 'A Rehearsal'. Watercolour sketch by Jemima Blackburn (*née* Wedderburn) of music-making, under Ella's direction, at the London house of her uncle, Sir George Clerk, 1848. Reproduced by kind permission of the National Portrait Gallery, London. From left to right: Ebby Clerk, John Ella, Maria Clerk and Isabella Clerk (at piano), Edward Clerk, Alexander Clerk, the Earl of Falmouth (seated), Sir Archibald Macdonald (playing double bass), Lord Gerald Fitzgerald, James Clerk, John Clerk.

divided their time between country houses in the Home Counties and residences in the West End (from 1848 till 1871 they lived in Savile Row, Piccadilly), with Mrs Grote, a formidable intellectual force in London society, becoming known for her conversational powers and literary skills. According to the first *Dictionary of National Biography*, she was an 'accomplished musician' and shared with her husband a love of music, attending concerts and the opera, and airing opinions in her diaries.[114] She cultivated friendships with Mendelssohn and other Continental musicians, and was just the sort of person to whom Ella's enterprise appealed.

Whether loyal concert-goers or (like George Grote) their spouses, the men in and around the Musical Union were mostly London 'somebodies'. Several of the more minor aristocrats and prominent gentry held appointments in Parliament or the Civil Service that provided further networks of contacts. Sir George Clerk was educated at Oxford and practised as an advocate before becoming an MP and

[114] Article by 'G. C. R.'. Mrs Grote's diary included comments on music; see Hall-Witt, 'Representing the Audience', 135, n. 61.

holding a series of government posts including Vice-President of the Board of Trade, 1845–6. The Hon. Henry Fitzroy (son of Baron Southampton, and married into the Rothschild dynasty) was Lord of the Admiralty, 1845–6, and Under Secretary of State for the Home Department, 1852–5; he and his wife appear in the membership lists for 1848. Likewise Edward Horsman, a barrister by profession, was MP for Cockermouth at the time of joining the Musical Union (1845), having already served (1840–1) as Lord of the Treasury; Mrs Frankland Lewis's husband, who, as we have seen, had had a career in politics, was soon to be made a baronet. (Frankland Lewis's son by Harriet Cornewall, George Cornewall Lewis, would also enter politics, eventually becoming Gladstone's Chancellor of the Exchequer.) More modestly and typically, Charles William Packe, from an old family at Prestwold Hall, Leicestershire, was MP for that county and attended Ella's concerts from 1847 along with his wife Mrs Reading Packe; while Miss Bucknall Estcourt (also listed from 1847) could boast that her landowning father Thomas was MP for the University of Oxford. For men, membership of one or more of the Westminster clubs was also *de rigueur*: Horsman belonged to the Reform, as did Wynn Ellis, John Bowes and Ralph Bernal (all subscribers), Packe and Estcourt to the Carlton, and so on.

Other Musical Union men had carved out distinguished careers and a position in society via the military: Major-General John Campbell and Lieut.-General Andrew Barnard (both committee members) had been awarded knighthoods in 1815 for service in Portugal and Spain. The Major Buckley who appears in the lists along with a 'Miss Buckley' – surely his daughter or sister – was probably Edward Pery Buckley of the Coldstream Guards, owner of a country estate in Hampshire, a local magistrate and deputy lieutenant, and an equerry to the Queen. As a member of the landed gentry, he had played a role in regional politics: that virtually went with the territory. Indeed, a number of the women who attended the Musical Union were married to deputy lieutenants and magistrates in the counties of their estates: for instance, Mrs James Carrick Moore of Corswall, Wigtownshire, and Mrs Henry Morgan Clifford of Perristone, Herefordshire. There were surely many more like them, some coming to town for just a few seasons, others being more permanently committed to a lifestyle that annually took in London.

Also laced into the hierarchies were men from the old professions or those whose families had attained wealth and significant status in society through their positions in the banking, manufacturing and merchant sectors. The majority of Musical Union-ites seem to have been from this group: people such as Dr John Elliotson, the distinguished physician and mesmerist and son of a prosperous apothecary and chemist; Rev. and Mrs J. S. Ogle, from Kirkley, Northumberland (with an address in Eaton Square, Belgravia – upcoming area of fashion); and the committee member Frederick Perkins, partner in Barclay, Perkins & Co's brewery in Southwark, with the country estate in Kent that Ella knew so well. Perkins's father (John), a founding partner, had been the manager of Thrale's brewery and, like Samuel Whitbread before him, had become entrenched in high society – the brewing industry being one of the easiest routes to assimilation among the gentry.[115] Then there was Grote the banker, and representatives from the younger, aspiring professions, such as Owen Jones, the architect and son of a furrier who would later design St James's Hall (he and his wife are listed as Musical Union members for 1845; they lived in Argyll Street, behind Piccadilly). And there were the dozens of unidentified, untitled names who were probably linked into the lower ranks of this wealthy world: people from families with less of a public profile, and probably a few *parvenus*.

While some people may have been attracted to the Musical Union for reasons other than the musical experience, it seems likely that most of them, particularly those who attended concerts over several seasons, were driven by a love of serious music and a desire to discover more about it. They were people who were prepared to invest considerable time and effort in learning to play and appreciate music (which for them was an 'embodied' form of cultural capital). Typically, they were ready to pursue other intellectual interests: many of the people identified were signed up to additional forms of mental enrichment, the civilizing importance of culture and learning being the overriding ideology of the time. Several Musical Union men were known for their tendencies towards a range of cerebral pursuits from the scientific to the artistic and literary, and belonged to special-interest societies. Ogle was a member of the Newcastle Literary and Philosophical Society; William Gardiner, also on the Musical Union list for the 1845 season, has already been noted as active in a similar role in Leicester; Perkins was a book collector of note, a member of the Art Union of London, which aimed to improve middle-class taste for fine art, and a Fellow of the Linnean Society; and Jones had a penchant for serious matters (in 1848 Ella witnessed a discussion about the moral guidance and education of young people at Jones's house).[116] Benjamin Bond Cabbell, a barrister, MP and subscriber from 1845, was a well-known art patron and philanthropist; he too was involved in the Art Union. Further up the social tree, some of the baronets took on roles within learned societies: Sir George Clerk was President of the Zoological Society (1862–7), Sir Charles Lemon a founder and President of

---

[115] Beckett, *Aristocracy*, 91. John Perkins's sons Henry and Frederick were both involved in the firm. On its history, see Peter Mathias, *The Brewery Industry in Britain, 1700–1830* (Cambridge: Cambridge University Press, 1959), *passim*. Although Burke's *Landed Gentry* of 1846 and 1848 did not mention Frederick Perkins, he was listed as a member of the local landed gentry in Pigot's 1840 directory for Kent.

[116] Diary, 19 January 1848 (EllaC, MS 117).

the Royal Statistical Society (1834) and President of the Royal Geological Society of Cornwall (1840–50). Both men, like Cabbell, were elected fellows of the Royal Society.

As for the women, evidence for their intellectual leanings is constrained by their having inhabited the private sphere, Mrs Grote standing out as something of an exception in the historical record. But doubtless there were others, since women were a significant presence in the Musical Union even if the society's public hierarchy and power base were unequivocally male. Women made up 48 per cent of the membership list of 1845, 54 per cent in 1848, and their numbers would grow still more over the ensuing decades, challenging the conventional wisdom that the intellectual appreciation of music was too demanding for the female mind. As it happened, the tendency to programme piano ensemble music may well have been an attempt by Ella to attract women, whose musical experience and literacy were embedded in the piano culture.[117] Given, too, that Ella sought to foster conversation between artists and amateurs after concerts, there may have been additional opportunities for women to greet famous performers and to secure their services for private music at their soirées or 'at-homes'.

Absent from the published membership were significant numbers of professional musicians. If they came at all it was as guests, to judge from newspaper accounts of who attended. Berlioz, Verdi and Onslow, the conductor Michael Costa, the pianist Ignaz Moscheles, and local musicians in Ella's entourage (Osborne, Schulz, Charlotte Dolby) were among those recognized by observant critics. In contrast, the Beethoven Quartett Society, to which Ella himself subscribed, was attracting greater numbers of (mostly male) musicians. This is not so surprising, because the Beethoven club was a different animal, with an emphasis on sharing existing reverence for a body of music with other 'apostles', rather than educating, as Ella was, an eager but less-informed flock.

In sum, the Musical Union plugged into a closed world of serious-minded lady and gentlemen amateurs with a keen interest in furthering their musical-intellectual knowledge. Theirs was a world in which everyone knew someone, and a world whose inhabitants made the most of the opportunities – musical, social, intellectual, commercial, even political – that were on offer when 'rank and fashion' descended on the capital. Many of them advertised their status in *Boyle's Fashionable Court and Country Guide, and Town Visiting Directory*, a contemporary

---

[117] This is suggested by the wording of an advertisement tipped into the copy of *RMU* (1848) in Brussels, Bibliothèque Royale. Here, in a puff for Hallé's first appearance, playing Beethoven's 'Archduke' trio, Ella saw fit to 'assure our lady-amateur pianists that they have a treat to come of the most refined and intellectual order'.

social register.[118] Several seem to have been involved with the Saltoun Club, whose activities were sometimes documented in the *Record of the Musical Union*; indeed, the chamber music society may even have been a source of renewal for the opera group.[119] Some of the audience came and went; others continued to attend for many seasons, the Musical Union acting as a focus for social cohesion as well as music appreciation. Such people were united by a shared cerebral interest in high-quality music and a belief in the civilizing power of culture. In turn, the Musical Union stood to legitimize their good taste, continued membership giving them a distinctive marker of cultural identity within their broader social group.

Yet without doubt, the idea of a deeply serious undertaking such as the Musical Union being supported by a close-knit section of high British society jars with the archetypal portrayal of fashionable life as all froth and frivolity, just as it bucks the trend of the aristocracy and gentry being concerned only with hunting, shooting and fishing. Admittedly, the high musical proclivities of Ella's audiences were atypical of the upper-class group as a whole. Far greater numbers of the *beau monde* went to the Italian Opera, and did so as much for the socializing as for the singing.[120] Ella was as aware of the situation as anyone. Years later he would admit in public that '[e]xperience [...] has long proved that a wide difference exists between the frivolous tastes of volatile fashionables and the sterling qualities of the aristocracy devoted to pursuits of mental enjoyment',[121] simultaneously lamenting to himself the shortcomings of the aristocracy as a whole. In one of his scrapbooks he described Sir Velters Cornewall (Sir George's son, and fourth baronet) in these terms: 'Alas! as usual, the son, Sir Velters, inherits none of the

---

[118] William Weber, *Music and the Middle Class: the Social Structure of Concert Life in London, Paris and Vienna* (London: Croom Helm, 1975), 164 (table 15), estimated at least 71 per cent of the Musical Union membership were listed in *Boyle's Guide* for 1848.

[119] *RMU* (1845) contains a series of announcements about Saltoun Club meetings (e.g. pp. 6, 12, 20), which, according to *MP* (14 January 1845), was reorganized around this time to bring in professional players.

[120] Although the nature of the opera audience changed between the 1820s and the 1840s, with the number of noblemen and women regularly attending dipping and the middle-class presence increasing, aristocrats and their families continued to attend occasionally and constituted a significant proportion of the audience. On this, and related social and political issues including the gradual change in the opera house as a central site for socializing among high society, see Jennifer Lee Hall, 'The Re-fashioning of Fashionable Society: Opera-Going and Sociability in Britain, 1821–1861' (PhD, Yale University, 1996), 70–6 and Appendix G.

[121] *EllaMS1*, 168.

Artistic sympathies of his Father – & is yet a Garçon! Magistrate, good, and useful – shoots & rides!'[122] Still, Ella took pride in his achievement of coaxing and publicly demonstrating a strand of aristocratic feeling for high-class music. Improving the taste and musical enthusiasms of the people he saw as the guardians and potential sponsors of a better musical culture in Britain was central to his vision. Writing to Davison around the time of Chorley's attacks of 1845, he argued: 'Of course, every institution supported by the aristocracy must have enemies amongst levellers, republicans and atheists; […]. Now, if we are to ridicule the aristocracy, where must we seek for patronage?'[123]

Among various devices Ella used to promote his institution to the aristocracy was an appeal to national pride. At the outset he suggested to his committee that the Musical Union could 'do much towards rescuing this country from those reflections which musical travellers are doomed to hear in France, Italy, and Germany, on the musical taste of this country', elsewhere remarking *ad nauseam* on the British aristocracy's poor reputation abroad as serious lovers of music, and exploiting not only collective feelings of patriotism but also the enduring, problematic relationship with Britain's European neighbours.[124] In the short term it may have looked as if hopes for improving the musical reputation of high society were bearing fruit, when in 1847 in fashionable Brighton, Ella's violinist-friend Antonio Oury and his wife, the pianist Anna Caroline Oury (*née* de Belleville; she had played Beethoven's 'Archduke' at the Union in 1846), set up a subscription society for instrumental chamber music in imitation of Ella's. Called the Brighton Musical Union, it used Cramer's shop in Brighton as a ticket outlet and attracted some of Ella's audience.[125] With a winter resort season that ran from October to

---

[122] EllaC, MS 81, p. 63. The annotation was made in 1864 in respect of a letter from Sir George Cornewall.

[123] *DavisonFM*, 81. See also the article, contributed by 'G. F. G.' (described as 'an amateur, member of this Society') on 'The Influence of Patronage on Art', in *RMU* (1845), 53–4, which argues that standards of musical appreciation in the middle and lower orders would be improved by increasing the levels of understanding and taste in the aristocracy, and through the processes of emulation.

[124] E.g. 'Report', *RMU* (1845), 2. On the complexities of the national psyche in the decade after Waterloo, and its manifestation within musical culture, see Leanne Langley, 'Sainsbury's *Dictionary*, the Royal Academy of Music, and the Rhetoric of Patriotism', *MBC*, 65–97.

[125] *MW* (6 November 1847), 712, and *ILN* (13 November 1847), 314. Subscriptions cost 10s for a series of three concerts; single admissions were available at 5s (advertisement in the *Brighton Guardian*, 27 October 1847). The *Guardian*, like the *Brighton Gazette* and *Brighton Herald*, carried reviews of most of the concerts. How long the concerts lasted has not been determined, but Oury had been giving quartet concerts in Brighton since at least 1841, events that are traceable in *MW*.

March, and able to capitalize on the stream of wealthy Londoners who hastened there for sea air and entertainments on the new railway (built 1841), the location was well-nigh perfect. Among patrons and subscribers for the first season were the earls of Westmorland, Falmouth, the Hon. Lawrence Parsons, the Hon. General Upton, Hon. Captain Newbury and other key supporters of Ella's organization.[126] Performers associated with the 'London' Union, notably Hill and Piatti, formed the nucleus of the artists engaged, and the club sought, as had Ella initially, to incorporate *morceaux brillants* into its otherwise focused and serious instrumental programmes. How long it lasted is unclear.

THE prevalence of aristocratic families in Ella's Musical Union, so frequently remarked upon by his contemporaries, can be further contextualized by comparing it with the two principal concert-giving bodies in London in the mid-1840s: the Concerts of Antient Music, begun in 1776 and closely identified with the nobility, though losing such support around this time; and the Philharmonic, which had never seriously wooed the aristocracy but which insisted on considerable social control and drew a clientele largely from the professional middle classes.[127] For this we return to those (imperfect) numbers, remembering that both sister-organizations were providing evening concerts not matinées, and thus had a wider public than Ella to draw on.

In his study of London concert life, 1830–48, William Weber calculated that in 1848 there were just forty-one titled Antient Music subscribers (out of 220 subscribers in all) and just twenty-two from noble families at the Philharmonic (out of 439), the same year that Ella had apparently attracted 124 aristocrats (out of a total of 312); he also argued that the Musical Union 'developed a public higher in status than even the Concerts of Antient Music had had in its heyday'.[128] Later on he

---

[126] *MW* (6 November 1847), 712. Names are also given in the *Brighton Gazette* (4 November 1847).

[127] *EhrlichFP*, 15: 'Most of them [Philharmonic subscribers, c.1813] can be loosely categorized as drawn from the professional, as distinct from trading, middle class'. This accords with Weber's analysis in *Music and the Middle Class*, 65, although the general caveat that the names of untitled subscribers may nevertheless conceal strong family ties to the aristocracy and gentry still holds. On the Philharmonic's need to court some members of high society, see *EhrlichFP*, 15–19; see also 40.

[128] Weber, *Music and the Middle Class*, 65, 162–3. Quite when the 'heyday' was is not defined, but the argument implies the 1820s. It states that in 1820, 214 of the 683 Antient subscribers (31 per cent) were titled, compared with 41 out of 220 (18 per cent) in 1848. An 1820s highpoint for the Antient Concerts is reinforced in Weber's later book *The Rise of Musical Classics in Eighteenth-Century England: a Study in Canon, Ritual and Ideology* (Oxford: Clarendon Press, 1992), 159, where he reckons on he

suggested the Musical Union 'grew from its [the Antients'] model both socially and musically'.[129] Although both institutions fostered erudition and attracted listeners from the upper ranks of London society, attempts to elide these two series on the basis of the class structure of audiences, or to see the one as a part replacement for the other, with the Antients conveniently dying off in 1848, need careful handling, because the musical agendas, organizational bases, and social profiles were not identical. Certainly, the Antient Music series was a serious venture, its leaders (a committee of aristocrats) cultivating a repertoire associated with science and the mind; but this had initially been achieved through the repeated, self-conscious and antiquarian promotion of 'old' music (Baroque and earlier – Handel in particular – and typically sacred choral works), and by tapping into eighteenth-century arguments about the merits of the 'antient' or 'old' style ('learned' counterpoint) versus the 'modern' (effectively *galant* or classical music with a greater emphasis on melody and harmony).[130] According to Weber's thesis in his later study, the enterprise became associated in the eighteenth century with high moral values and political purpose through its ritualistic promotion of a canon of old music, and was a way for the aristocracy consciously to assert their moral propriety and justify culturally their established 'hegemony' within British society.[131]

that in 1786, 132 of the subscribers (30 per cent) were from titled families, a similar percentage as regards 1820, but a smaller total.

Of course, although there were 124 titled Musical Union subscribers out of 312 (40 per cent) in 1848, this total remains smaller numerically (if not in terms of percentages) than the Antients' 214 of 1820 or 132 of 1786. (Incidentally, my calculations suggest only 119 Union people out of 310 listed for 1848 came from titled families: 38 per cent aristocracy.)

[129] Weber, *The Rise of Musical Classics*, 20.

[130] However, in the 1820s, with audiences falling, the Antients had admitted sacred music by Mozart, Haydn and Beethoven – what Rachel Cowgill calls a 'paradigmatic shift' in the society's ideology that 'required a relaxation of [the] ideological framework', to embrace newer repertoires. See her 'The London Apollonicon Recitals, 1817–32: a Case Study in Bach, Mozart, and Haydn Reception', *Journal of the Royal Musical Association*, 123 (1998), 190–228, at 223. On related issues, and the role of Mozart's music in healing the Antient/Modern schism, see Cowgill, 'Mozart's Music', 107–40 [includes critique of Weber's thesis].

[131] The persuasiveness of this argument hinges on a couple of factors, including the fact that the Antient Concerts were attended by the royal family in the 1780s, and by people from a range of wealthy classes, in front of whom much ceremonial display by the directors was carried out musically and socially. More broadly, Weber suggests that political motivations and heightened class awareness shaped the ideas of some of the leading figures in the Antient Concerts, particularly the Earl of Sandwich. See Weber, *The Rise of Musical Classics*, 143–67.

The notion of classical chamber music (a repertoire that connoted the intellect) being used in the 1840s to promote similar agendas by later generations from the same social class does have an attractiveness about it, not least because the building of a canonic repertoire and the emergence of associated ideologies and performance rituals are central themes in the Musical Union's history.

But caution is needed because, as we know, the Musical Union's agendas emanated from a jobbing musician – not a group of grandees. Moreover, although there was some overlap between clienteles, by no means the majority of committed supporters of the Antients in the mid-1840s attended Ella's society, and of those that did, only a handful were titled.[132] In fact, almost as few of Ella's noble listeners were signed up with the Philharmonic.[133] Two of the directors of the Antients, the Duke of Cambridge and the Earl of Westmorland, were regulars at the Musical Union, but they were the cream of serious music-lovers anyway, the Duke being equally ready to attend the Philharmonic.[134] In truth, more of Ella's audience subscribed to the Philharmonic than to the Antient Concerts, but neither institution had a majority representation in the Musical Union.[135] Of course, in terms of musical agendas, Ella's initiative had far more in common with the Philharmonic's promotion of the best music through Austro-German instrumental repertoire, and its insistence on Beethoven, than with the Antients' mostly vocal repertoire and self-conscious ideology of antiquarianism, despite their recent forays into broader programming, with choral works by Haydn, Mozart and Beethoven. And while the core classical chamber repertoire was becoming enshrined as canonic at the Musical Union and ageing by the day, we should remember that the rehabilitation of older, Baroque, instrumental chamber music was never one of Ella's aims. Nor was modern music

---

[132] According to my calculations, committed Antient Music supporters (that is subscribers, not occasional purchasers of tickets) constituted between 4 and 8 per cent (between 28 and 54 people) of Ella's listed audiences for 1845–50. Occasional ticket purchasers increase the proportion to 21 per cent. Within these groups, aristocratic names were in the minority. For example in the names listed for the Musical Union season of 1848, only nine titled audience members were known to have subscribed to the Antient Concerts in the previous five seasons (up to another twenty-four may have occasionally bought Antient Concert tickets).

[133] Between thirteen and fifteen of those with titles in the Musical Union lists subscribed to the Philharmonic in 1848.

[134] On Cambridge at the Philharmonic, see *EhrlichFP*, 4, 16.

[135] Philharmonic subscribers appear to have constituted between 12 and 18 per cent (between 76 and 113 people) of Ella's listed audience, 1845–50; see also n. 132 above. It is possible that others in Ella's audience were lapsed Antient Concert attendees, or from families who gave support in earlier decades; more research is needed.

banned from programmes: works by Mendelssohn and later composers had their place.

The Union's overriding ethos remained promoting a body of great instrumental compositions in the name of high art; and most of its followers seem to have been attracted first and foremost by the society's highbrow, intellectual character and its programmes of relatively modern, intimate music. (This is important because these were times when London music was beginning to open up to the 'shilling public', and showmen such as Louis Jullien were drawing massive crowds to 'promenade' extravaganzas in the Surrey Gardens.) Possibly a significant secondary concern for Ella's audiences was to assert publicly their social dominance and difference, given that the concerts were likely to be reported in the press; however, the opportunities at matinées for show and ceremonial were, compared with what happened socially and musically at the Antient Concerts, less apparent.[136] Perhaps more likely, some subscribers may have seen the Musical Union and its secluded afternoon meetings in Piccadilly as a refuge, particularly those who, in the climate of debate about social change that emerged in the years following the 1832 Reform Bill, feared the infiltration of their leisure activities by the lower orders, and who wanted to assert difference through withdrawal, exclusivity and renewed possibilities for building social networks.[137] From this perspective, the Philharmonic, with its evening concerts and more middle-class audience, may have seemed unpalatable to many, making the Musical Union the more appropriate choice.

❧ *Going it alone*

> *Last evening I received your Letter, and sincerely regret your resolve to quit the Orchestra* [...] *As I like to speak of Others as I have found them, I only say, it would give me great pleasure to see you again made one of us, and shake hands with a brother Artist, and Gentleman –*   ∾ Letter to Ella from J. M. Ribas, of the Opera orchestra, 22 August 1848

As examples of concert organization the Philharmonic and the Musical Union were also miles apart. The Philharmonic, working to co-operative ideals, was run by committee and prone to be weighed down by its own invented structures. There were an appointed secretary and treasurer, both musicians

---

[136] See Weber, *The Rise of Musical Classics*, 155.

[137] There may be a parallel here with the vogue for private concerts in the 1780s, which Simon McVeigh (*McVeighCL*, p. 47) interpreted as a quest for exclusivity at a time of rising public entertainments.

by trade, who took on the roles without training and for a meagre stipend.[138] Their function was to carry out 'actions' discussed and passed by the directors at lengthy meetings, rather than to organize, plan and respond on their own initiative to changing circumstances. Compare the autocratic organization of the Musical Union, where Ella made his own decisions, used his committee for authoritative weight and window-dressing, and stood to reap the financial benefits if things worked well. Ella was aware of shortcomings in the Philharmonic's management and may have reacted against it in the shaping of his own institution.

Ella's relationship with the Philharmonic had been complicated. The scars of his earlier blackballing were slow to heal, and he would launch public attacks on the management for several years, including in the *Record of the Musical Union*. Yet he maintained admiration for the society's founding ideals, and even returned to the orchestra in 1846, when his friend, the also-once-ostracized Costa, took over as conductor and began to introduce much-needed discipline.[139] If Ella had once held hopes of joining the inner sanctum of the Philharmonic's directorate with a view to finding power and influence in London music, they had been long since dashed, along with his illusions about its leadership. So perhaps there really was, in Ella's choice of nomenclature for the roles in his own institution, intentional side-swiping at the Philharmonic's arcane distinctions between 'members', 'associate members', 'directors', players and subscribers? At the Musical Union, members and subscribers were one and the same thing, and Ella was the sole director.

Moreover, Ella was demonstrating a nose for business and good commercial sense, which was to keep the Musical Union afloat economically while the Philharmonic sank. Financial information for this first period of the Musical Union's lifespan is pretty sketchy, but figures jotted by Ella in a financial notebook give a sense of how dramatic and swift the financial turnaround after the first season of 1845 had been, and just how good a decision it had been to shift the 'entire pecuniary responsibility' onto himself. At the end of the 1847 series, Musical Union subscriptions had brought in £539 14s, while income from single-ticket sales (available for all concerts in the series) generated a further

---

[138] By the 1830s the treasurer's role had become more independent (*EhrlichFP*, 54).

[139] His re-engagement at the Philharmonic is documented in the Directors' minutes (BL, RPS/MS/281, f. 158v [minute for 22 February 1846]), and in the accounts (RPS/MS/300; payments for 1846–8). According to John Ravell ('John Ella', 96), in 1847 Ella was also appointed to lead the second violins in Costa's orchestra for the newly formed opera company at Covent Garden. The source of the information appears to be a contract, dated 21 August 1846, for work as either a first or second violin at Covent Garden for three seasons, 1847–9 (EllaC, MS 81, p. 69).

£103 8s 6d.[140] Expenditure stood at £400 (of which £210, according to Ella's later public pronouncements, was artists' fees), leaving a balance of almost £250 for Ella.[141] These were significant profits – as much as many 'rank and file' London instrumentalists would have pieced together through playing and teaching, and more than several lesser musicians might have hoped for.[142] Even twenty years later Ella privately estimated his total outgoings for the year at only £320.[143]

By the end of the 1847 season, Ella must have looked back with feelings of vindication at his earlier decision to turn down a clerical job in the Civil Service, offered through his patronage network, probably by George Cornewall Lewis, then Poor Law Commissioner.[144] Although we do not know what the post entailed, it would have certainly given Ella his much-coveted financial security and enhanced social status. Whether it was his natural belief in himself, his determination to etch a career in music, his personal vision and desire to proselytize on behalf of high art, or simply romantic idealism, Ella had declined the career shift, though only after some consideration. There had apparently also been a similar offer to go

---

[140] Subscription numbers and income are indicated in the account book (EllaC, MS 6), p. 47; single-ticket sales are explicated on pp. 89 and 94 (p. 47 gives a slightly lower sum for these; it appears to have been revised upwards later).

[141] Total expenditure is indicated in EllaC, MS 6, p. 14, while the fees to artists are noted in 'The Honorarium of Artists, 1870', *RMU* (1870), sup., p. vii. Profits for 1847 are considerably lower than the £400 calculated in Bashford, 'John Ella', 200. Here I extrapolated from the membership lists in RMU, now known to have included visitor names.

[142] On musicians' incomes, see *EhrlichMP*, 44–50, and *RohrCBM*, 154–64.

[143] EllaC, MS 6, p. 257.

[144] Probably the occasion on which Ella asked Saltoun for the character reference, dated 27 February 1845, that is preserved in EllaC, MS 81, p. 2. Accompanying it is a note, written several years later in Ella's hand, explaining the circumstances of this proposed 'government appointment' and the need for a reference. Ella's memory may have been serving him poorly when he made the annotation, inasmuch as he identified Sir Frankland Lewis, the first Poor Law Commissioner (appointed 1834), as the origin of the job offer; but Sir Frankland had stepped down in 1839. His son George Cornewall Lewis held the position from 1839 to 1847. Internal evidence within the reference confirms a mid-1840s dating.

To date, no evidence has corroborated Davison's suggestion in *MW* (7 August 1845), 374, quoting a similarly worded testimonial by Saltoun, that Ella was a candidate in the elections for the Edinburgh Professor of Music in 1845. If Ella flirted with the idea of making an application, he must have later abandoned it. I am grateful to Stuart Campbell for help on this matter, and to the archivist at the University of Edinburgh for permission to consult the Reid Bequest.

and work for the government in India (also rejected).[145] In January 1848, with what one imagines was some optimism for the future of the Musical Union, Ella moved into new lodgings in Welbeck Street, further west and a little more up-market.[146]

Six months later, however, as the 1848 series drew to a close, there was still much to ponder. Although the Musical Union was once more in profit, the surplus was less spectacular than the previous year, because of a fall-off in subscriptions.[147] On the other hand, what had been demonstrated that season were the all-round benefits to be gained by hiring stellar pianists and leaders, as performance quality and single-ticket revenue increased alike, and this boded well for the future.[148] In August 1848 Ella seems to have felt confident enough of his nascent financial position to resign his post in the Opera orchestra after a row in the band-room, effectively shunning an important and regular source of supplementary income.[149] Quite possibly, too, he shrugged off his subsequent loss of Philharmonic work (from December 1848), being happy to break decisively from the grind of orchestral playing and the connotations of low social status it carried.[150] After all, he was developing an iron belief that he could make the Musical Union prosper.

[145] EllaC, MS 81, p. 2.

[146] Address change noted in his diary for 1848 (5 January; EllaC, MS 117).

[147] Subscriber numbers were down (membership income standing at only £420), rendering profits in the region of £170. Calculated from information in the account book (EllaC, MS 6, pp. 14, 47, 89 and 94).

[148] Charles Hallé's presence, in particular, had increased the revenue from single tickets across the season (see EllaC, MS 6, p. 94). This point is developed in the next chapter.

[149] Ella's account of the Opera dispute – over payments for a benefit performance – is recorded in one of the scrapbooks (EllaC, MS 81, p. 68).

[150] Ella ceases to appear on the payroll in the Philharmonic's accounts (BL, RPS/MS/300) from 1849, the directors' unanimous decision not to reengage him being noted in the minutes of their meeting of 21 December 1848 (RPS/MS/282, f. 28r).

CHAPTER 4

Consolidation and Expansion, 1849–57

In 1849 changes were coming to the fore that were to affect both Ella's concert society and the London music scene. This was not just a matter of the influx of performers seeking temporary asylum from the rash of Continental uprisings (1848) and their aftermaths, significant though this was, inasmuch as it brought more glistening quality and a sharper competitive edge to the musical market-place. Portents of new practices and values were emerging as well. Michael Costa was instituting a new order of orchestral discipline at the Philharmonic and at Covent Garden, where the recently instituted Royal Italian Opera was bedding in; the effects were audible.[1] The Antient Concerts, legacy of a former, patriarchal era, had quietly expired, the last concert taking place in June 1848, while the death of Mendelssohn (November 1847), much of whose classically sculpted music was still relatively new to London, continued to be mourned as a national tragedy.[2] Add to this the extraordinary Jenny Lind, the 'Swedish Nightingale', who had first sung in London during 1847. In summer 1848 she had returned, making big money and once more accompanied by a commercial hype that fore-shadowed things to come.[3] For a moment, too, some of the country's élite and

---

[1] In 1846 Costa took on the conductorship of the Philharmonic, and left the orches-tra of Her Majesty's Theatre. He took several of the opera players, including Ella, with him to establish (1847) a band for the new Royal Italian Opera company at Covent Garden. On Costa's reforms, see Michael Musgrave, 'Changing Values in Nineteenth-Century Performance: the Work of Michael Costa and August Manns', *MBC*, 169–91.

[2] Press coverage of Mendelssohn's death tells much of the story; see Percy Scholes, *The Mirror of Music, 1844–1944: a Century of Musical Life in Britain as Reflected in the Pages of the Musical Times* (London: Novello, 1947), 419–20. Several all-Mendelssohn concerts followed in the months after Mendelssohn's passing: in the sphere of chamber music there was Sterndale Bennett's Performance of Classi-cal Pianoforte Music at Hanover Square Rooms on 15 February 1848, and Willy's Quartet Concert at Erat's Rooms on 23 February 1848. Fundraising for a memorial scholarship to enable a student to study in Leipzig began too, and included a per-formance of *Elijah* at Exeter Hall on 15 December.

[3] George Biddlecombe sums up the commercial exploitation of Lind well: 'Soon the "Jenny Lind" steam engine of the London and Brighton Railway, "Jenny Lind" gloves, statuettes, photographs, prints, decorated boxes, sheet music songs, and, perhaps less flatteringly, an elephant testified to her fame' in his 'The Construction of a Cultural Icon: the Case of Jenny Lind', *NBMS*, 3, ed. Peter Horton and Bennett

probably many a foreign musician had wobbled at the prospect of revolution in Britain, as some 85,000 Chartists prepared to meet at Kennington Common on 10 April 1848. But the expected discontent came to nothing, just as government seems privately to have predicted.[4] Ella, presumably reflecting the views of some of his friends in high places, had written in his diary: '<u>Chartists</u>' meeting – <u>Shops closed</u> – London alarmed at the National Convention Meeting on Kennington Common – visited Tamburini[,] R. St – & quieted their fears [?]for a revolution'.[5]

What the arrival of refugee musicians in 1848 had demonstrated to Ella was just what benefits could be obtained by hiring a distinguished chamber music player. Sales of visitor tickets, an important tool for increasing subscribers in the longer term, leapt with the billing of great players: so whereas the concert involving the relatively undistinguished Edward Roeckel (piano) and Prosper Sainton (leader) had brought in a meagre £4 14s 6d of additional revenue, that featuring Charles Hallé and Sainton had raised £25 14s 6d.[6] And as musicians continued to arrive in London from 'the troubled Continent' in 1849,[7] Ella's eye was keenly trained on incoming players. Moreover, he was able to devote more time to the Musical Union and to furthering his other ambitions, being no longer constrained during the season by orchestral rehearsal schedules.

In fact, during the next nine years Ella's aptitude for making things happen began to blossom as he responded to changing circumstances, seized opportunities, experimented with due caution, and expanded his portfolio and vision when and where it seemed appropriate to do so. The Musical Union's activities became consolidated, profitability shot up, and the institution began to look like a permanent part of the London scene, with a developing reputation for artistic and musical excellence, intellectual gravity and serious audiences. All the while, Ella's own economic circumstances improved; by 1857 he was inching ever upwards in London society, establishing a working life that was outside the norms for British musicians.

Zon (Aldershot: Ashgate, 2003), 45–61, at 45. Lind sang at the fundraising *Elijah* concert in December 1848.

[4] K. Theodore Hoppen, *The Mid-Victorian Generation, 1846–1886* (Oxford: Clarendon Press, 1998), 130.

[5] Diary, 10 April 1848 (EllaC, MS 117).

[6] Account book (EllaC, MS 6), p. 94.

[7] *RMU* (1849), 12. England was known as a sanctuary for refugees: from 1823 to the end of the century it did not expel a single asylum-seeker (contrast today): see Bernard Porter, *The Refugee Question in Mid-Victorian Politics* (Cambridge: Cambridge University Press, 1979), 1.

❧ *Artists from abroad*

There are also in London several Quartet and Chamber Music Societies, of which the most flourishing at the present time is called the Musical Union. It was founded by Mr. Ella, a distinguished English artist, who directs it with a care, an intelligence and a devotion beyond all praise.   ∾ Hector Berlioz, *Journal des Débats* (May 1851); translated from the original French

AMONG the 'phalanx of first-rate violinists'[8] arriving in London in 1849 in search of better prospects were Delphin Alard (from the Paris Conservatoire) and Heinrich Ernst (trained in Vienna), men with fine quartet-playing credentials, albeit from different national traditions of violin technique. Both were hired by Ella to lead at some of the season's matinées, as was the resident *émigré* Sainton.[9] Ernst, the big star who had played at Ella's private parties in 1844, ushered in Mendelssohn's string quartet op. 44 no. 3 and Beethoven's op. 96 violin sonata, works not yet heard on Musical Union afternoons. He also led a performance of Beethoven's op. 130 quartet, arguably the most accessible of the late group, and the one 'late' work that Ella (for all his private admiration of the set) ever admitted to programmes, being both sensitive to the imperative for adequately rehearsed performances if the compositions were to be communicated convincingly, and ever fearful of alienating his audience if too much 'difficult' music were programmed. Joachim meanwhile was claimed for the Director's concert (he led Beethoven's op. 18 no. 1), along with the Italian double bass player Giovanni Bottesini and the mezzo-soprano Mathilde Graumann, who would later, as Mathilde Marchesi, become a celebrated voice teacher. At the keyboard Hallé was in residence for five of the eight concerts, with Henri Mortier de Fontaine (a Beethoven interpreter who had been recommended strongly to Ella and who played at the benefit), Otto Goldschmidt (pupil of Mendelssohn, who turned out to be less of a sure bet) and the trusty Sterndale Bennett, each in place for one other. Between them they

---

[8] *RMU* (1849), 2.

[9] The Continental visitors, particularly Ernst, received enthusiastic press. *MW* (5 May 1849, p. 278) said, 'Alard's *début* in London may be pronounced one of the most successful in musical records', and noted Ernst's playing as 'magnificent', especially in combination with Hallé. Of Ernst, *ILN* (5 May 1849, p. 290) opined: 'The wondrous powers of Ernst were never heard in greater perfection – the poetry of his style, and the impassioned sentiment he infused into the adagios, raised the enthusiasm of the amateurs to the highest pitch', and even Chorley admitted: 'So intense a satisfaction [...] we have derived from no other violinist' (*Athenaeum*, 5 May 1849, p. 466).

performed in a range of piano trios and violin or cello sonatas by Beethoven and Mendelssohn.

After concerts, Ella carefully recorded in a notebook the relationship between single-ticket sales and the presence of star artists, presumably reflecting and acting on the data, though also providing posterity with some estimation of the artists' commercial 'drawing power'. While he took advantage of the arriving talent, Ella tended to book only European players with established reputations, or those, like Alard, who came with personal recommendations. What he wanted was artists with an affinity for the chamber repertoire, not flamboyant performers with little sympathy for, or experience of, ensemble playing or the music of the 'divine muse', as he often described it. In public Ella might protest that his 'limited means do not allow us to increase the number of our meetings, and to let our members hear all [the refugee musicians] who deserve a share of their patronage',[10] but in reality he was probably becoming cautious of risking the Musical Union's growing prestige on an unheard-of performer who lacked solid testimonials. At any rate, he would soon propose a solution for filtering unknown quantities. In the meantime, it seems, poor decisions such as the hiring of the untried Goldschmidt (to play Mendelssohn's op. 66 trio) for the first concert of the 1849 season, which brought in only an extra £9 9s from ticket sales and paled alongside the £43 11s 6d that Hallé raised at the sixth matinée (in Beethoven's trio op. 1 no. 2), were avoided in future.[11] Good takings on the day were becoming the principal goal, Ella now allowing tickets to be sold in more impersonal ways, direct from Cramer's, with no requirement to 'apply to the Director' or any mention of limits on numbers.

With Hallé came significant new repertoire. At his 1848 appearances he had played in three ensemble works – Beethoven's 'Archduke' trio, the cello sonata op. 69 and Mozart's G minor piano quartet – as well as contributing solo piano items (Heller, Weber, and his own composition); but from 1849 he began to be heard in Beethoven's piano sonatas, hitherto neglected at the Musical Union but now admitted to the programme slot that had up till then contained the *'brillant'*, or piano, ensemble work. The 'Appassionata' sonata op. 57 was the first to be given (1849), followed by the 'Waldstein' op. 53 (1850), op. 31 no. 3, op. 26 (1851) and a few others, apparently at Hallé's suggestion; he had successfully introduced some of

---

[10] *RMU* (1849), 12.

[11] EllaC, MS 6, p. 93. Meanwhile, the range of artists at the Director's day 1849, which included Joachim, Bottesini and Mortier de Fontaine, brought in a stunning £75 5s 6d – representing more than 140 extra listeners – substantially more than had been generated the previous year (£45 13s 6d), when Hallé had been the only star. Op. cit., pp. 93–4.

10   Page from Ella's account book for 1853–4, recording ticket sales, concert by concert. Reproduced by kind permission of the Bodleian Library, Oxford.

them in Paris. If Hallé is to be believed, Ella was initially unenthusiastic about programming them – something that seems surprising, given Ella's predilection for Beethoven. Hallé's claim was that Ella had worried the works were too *outré* for his audience and had insisted they had never been performed publicly in London.[12] The latter point was incorrect: they had been given by Moscheles, Bennett and Dulcken among others at concerts in the early 1840s, as Ella surely knew.[13] So perhaps it was Ella's preconception of chamber music as ensemble repertoire that made him nervous about including a solo sonata as one of the three major pieces. Whatever the truth of the matter, Ella put a different spin on matters in his programme pamphlet, here asserting that a sonata's inclusion was a response to 'the desire of many of our members, anxious to hear one of the[se] […] remarkable works executed by Hallé.'[14] Henceforth Beethoven's middle-period sonatas became standard Musical Union fare, later performed by such interpreters as Clara Schumann and Hans von Bülow.

The flow of refugees continued into the 1850s and was augmented by visitors from abroad, including those who hastened to Joseph Paxton's glass construction in Hyde Park in 1851 to see the Great Exhibition of the Industry of All Nations.[15] In the longer term, the number of newly arriving political exiles dropped off, but London's attraction to Continental travellers remained, fuelled by the fact that travel was becoming quicker and cheaper with the growth of railway

---

[12] *Life and Letters of Sir Charles Hallé being an Autobiography (1819–1860) with Correspondence and Diaries*, ed. C. E. Hallé and Marie Hallé (London: Smith, Elder, 1896), 103–4.

[13] *BashfordPCC*, Appendix C, 135–7.

[14] *RMU* (1849), 31. Hallé's memoirs (*Life and Letters*) are somewhat confused on the chronology and details of this episode, but suggest – plausibly enough, given what we know of Ella's savvy and his admiration for Beethoven – that once Ella saw how favourably the works were received, particularly by his female amateurs who began asking for them at their own private concerts, he brooked no opposition, cautioning only that Hallé should choose works that would be readily appreciated.

[15] The difficulties of quantifying foreign visitors to Britain in the nineteenth century have long been acknowledged, on the basis that before 1914 incoming travellers were not required to show passports or to register with the British police. See Jack Simmons, *The Victorian Railway* ([London]: Thames & Hudson, 1991), 294. Andreas Fahrmeir, however, in *Citizens and Aliens: Foreigners and the Law in Britain and the German States, 1789–1870* (New York and Oxford: Berghahn Books, 2000), 102–6, shows that some form of 'alien registration' was in place from the Napoleonic wars until 1852, and provides useful statistics indicating general trends, including a huge leap in the number of foreigners passing through the ports of London, Dover and Folkstone during 1851 (from 8,947 in 1850 to 25,210 in 1851 and back to 7,308 in 1852).

networks.[16] Some visitors arrived seeking to make significant sums of money in this most commercial of cultural environments; they tended to stay only for the high season, returning home shortly afterwards.[17] This was true of Continental musicians, whose sources of income were prone to dry up shortly after midsummer. For all that, working the London season as a performer was no cakewalk: competition was stiff, and not everyone prospered, as Ella himself was keen to point out, and as Wagner learnt on his visit in 1855.[18]

Ella, of all people, stood to benefit from the annual influx, and through the 1850s his star cast regularly featured a mix of *émigrés* and travelling foreigners, the latter usually contracted by letter ahead of their visits. Among the players of quality residing in London, Piatti (who played in sixty-three out of seventy-two Musical Union concerts, 1849–57) and Hallé (thirty-eight concerts) were those most frequently engaged, followed by Ernst (twenty-seven) and Sainton (seventeen). The most celebrated visiting instrumentalists up to 1857 were Joachim (one concert, 1852), Marie Pleyel (likewise), Sivori (eight concerts, 1851–7), Vieuxtemps (fourteen concerts, 1851–4), the double bassist Bottesini (ten concerts, 1849–57; a favourite 'turn' at the Director's Matinée) and Clara Schumann (seven concerts, 1856–7), whose intelligent and imaginative piano playing set new standards. Ella continued to calculate their drawing power objectively in his financial notebook and also recorded odd moments of excitement in his diary, scribbling after one of Clara's concerts: '594 – person [*sic*] present! the fullest room I have ever had.'[19] New faces with robust recommendations and real promise were integrated too, among them the pianist Wilhelmine Clauss (a young Bohemian player who consistently produced good revenue on single tickets), the violinist

[16] On patterns in refugee traffic, 1848–c.1860, and the potency of the 'refugee question' in the 1850s, see Porter, *The Refugee Question*, 1–30. As Porter demonstrates, more than half of the refugees made for London, many settling there. The 1850s were a peak in refugee immigration; towards the end of the decade large numbers left, most of them heading for the USA.

[17] For evocative pictures of such cultural tourism, see Rupert Christiansen, *The Visitors: Culture Shock in Nineteenth-Century Britain* (London: Chatto and Windus, 2000), and for a broader historical interpretation of the trend, see the review by Peter Mandler ('Where Cash was King') in the *Times Literary Supplement* (7 July 2000), 3–4.

[18] Ella's views can be seen in *RMU* (1849), 12; (1853), 6; and (1856), 26. The first of these contains this salutary warning to the majority: 'Many of these foreign artists, like the seekers of gold in the land of California, will return to their native homes grievously disappointed in their expectations'. Wagner's disillusionment over his net profit of 1,000 francs (£40) – 'the hardest money I have ever earned' – is depicted in Christiansen, *The Visitors*, 58.

[19] Diary, 13 May 1856 (EllaC, MS 125).

Ferdinand Laub (who would later gain real eminence as a quartet player in Berlin and Vienna), and Anton Rubinstein, whose pianism was first heard at the Musical Union in 1857, beginning a long and celebrated association with the society.

With so many stellar players on the books, Ella began writing about their artistry in the prefatory remarks to his programme notes, simultaneously reinforcing the image of the Musical Union as *the* institution of quality. In particular, Ella gave a strong steer as to what to expect from them in performance. The following gives a flavour:

> Vieuxtemps will again afford us an opportunity of appreciating his magnificent interpretation of Mendelssohn's Quintet [op. 87], and in his solo will also display the wonderful resources of his instrument in a variety of new and brilliant creations of his own. The pianoforte part of Beethoven's Trio [op. 97] we have never heard more satisfactorily performed than by Hallé, and with such coadjutors as Vieuxtemps and Piatti, we are led to anticipate a masterly rendering of this splendid composition.[20]

Features aimed at puffing star artists, plus 'trails' and listings of the latest (or expected) arrivals from the Continent also abounded in the programme pamphlets, and were intended to whip up expectation, often in advance. Crude though such promotion techniques may seem by modern standards, they nevertheless constituted a new, growing and increasingly legitimate aspect of mid-nineteenth-century commercial practice and were effectively part of the business deal.[21] Ella indicated as much to Fétis when trying to hire Madame Pleyel: 'You know well that I have my PEN to serve her, and by playing at the New Philharmonic and the Union, her name will allways [*sic*] be before the public, which for her will do much to benefit her in America'.[22] Needless to say, writers such as Davison and Chorley, ever ready to arbitrate on journalistic standards, considered such hard-selling inappropriate and vulgar, Chorley recoiling from Ella's modern ways 'after the manner of Barnum'.[23] Objections were made, too, to Ella feeding the audience

[20] *RMU* (1852), 30.

[21] For further discussion, see Marjorie Morgan, 'Puffery Prevails: Etiquette in 19th-Century England', *History Today*, 41 (August 1991), 27–33.

[22] Letter to Fétis, 15 March [?1852] (*WangerméeF*, 439; I have revised Wangermée's dating on the basis of the letter's corroborating evidence concerning the Quartett Association, which flourished 1852–4).

[23] P. T. Barnum, the American showman-manager. From a passage in the *Athenaeum*, reprinted in *MW* (25 July 1857), 468, and *DavisonFM*, 233. The passage refers to Ella as 'a writer of paragraphs and panegyrics […] resolute to provoke attention to himself by the indelicacy of self-praise'.

in advance with an appreciation of the performers' artistry (making the critics' job redundant); and there were suggestions that Ella was simply attracted uncritically to foreign players. Davison cited Ella's advancement of Clara Schumann and Anton Rubinstein as evidence of undiscriminating praise, failing to see either that change was afoot in the world of concert promotion, or that enmeshed in Ella's methods was a desire to help his listeners understand who the best performers were, and why.[24]

What no critic remarked on – probably because horizons of expectation were constrained to know little better – was the stylistic heterogeneity that many of Ella's ensembles must have presented. With combinations of string players trained in Franco-Belgian, German and even Italian techniques, and all the differences of tone production, bow strokes and so on that this entailed, plus little rehearsal time, there can have been little of the cohesive sound and matching articulations that have come to be expected of string quartets in the twentieth century, or that might have been found in centres outside Britain where most string players would have been trained in the same national tradition. As a matter of fact, we can be pretty sure Ella was aware of this aspect, clearly the downside of London's musical cosmopolitanism. He would later, writing about orchestras, observe that '[f]or unity of style, taste and feeling, the result of national schools, we have nothing in London to compare with the first class orchestra of Paris, and, for the same reason, those of Vienna', and remark that '[o]ur cosmopolitan London orchestras', in comparison, contained 'no two of the same style of playing'.[25] But unsurprisingly he kept quiet when it came to his own institution, and, making a virtue out of necessity, played up the pre-eminence of individual performers and celebrated the opportunities the Musical Union offered for international collaboration: it was 'un point de réunion aux artistes distingués de toutes les nations'.[26]

As a medium by which Continental performers could gain access to the lucrative, if shadowy, world of private concerts and music lessons, the Musical Union was, at this point in its history, probably second to none. Not only could private engagements be clinched after performances in the *conversazione*-style atmosphere that Ella encouraged between artists and audience, but Ella prepared the

---

[24] Examples of Davison's remarks are in *MW* (3 May 1856), 284; (17 May 1856), 315; and (23 May 1857), 324–5, 328–9. Contrast his and Chorley's mindsets with the views of the *Atlas* critic in the mid-1850s, almost certainly Edward Holmes, who commended Ella for forming his own, well-judged opinions of unheard artists and then acting upon them by placing those performers in Musical Union concerts (review of 10 June 1854, reprinted in *RMU* (1854), 26–8).

[25] *Orchestra* (February 1876), 202.

[26] As per programmes up to 1854.

way for such link-ups through his printed puffs. Hard evidence for connections between the Musical Union and domestic music-making is difficult to uncover, though Ella's diary gives clues that may reflect broader trends. Entries for 1853, for instance, record a series of private dinner parties at the house of Musical Union-ites Captain and Mrs Kelso, at which Ella joined one 'Capt. Fleming' (seemingly an amateur cellist) to play chamber music with Molique, Vieuxtemps and one of the latter's pupils; works such as Beethoven's quartets op. 18 nos. 1 and 4, and trio in E♭ (probably the string trio op. 3) were thus attempted.[27] How remuneration for the likes of Vieuxtemps worked in these circumstances must remain a matter for speculation, but at the very least the Musical Union was functioning as a cog within London's larger musical wheel, opening up contacts and opportunities for its artists (and this may be why many great musicians agreed to play for fees which, while not penny-pinching, were nonetheless relatively modest).

Full institutional accounts for the 1850s do not survive, but we know that Ella negotiated fees for Musical Union appearances on a case-by-case basis, and that the players with the greatest reputations, skills and artistry commanded most money. In 1853, for example, a first-class leader such as Vieuxtemps received £110 for nine concerts inclusive of rehearsal (c.£12 per concert), a star pianist slightly less (Mlle Clauss seems to have been paid £10 10s for a concert; Hallé's fee worked out at £8 per appearance), while the cellist Piatti got £73 10s for eight perform-ances (just over £9 for each). In comparison with what less prominent players received, these rates were pretty good – the viola player Hill was paid £3 3s per concert, a one-off call for a wind player was £2 2s – and they were mostly better than what was on offer at the Philharmonic for orchestral work, and in some cases for solo appearances.[28] Even with the hidden networking benefits that Ella's

---

[27] See 5, 7 and 12 May 1853 (EllaC, MS 122). The prevalence and dynamics of this type of music-making are indicated in Paula Gillett, 'Ambivalent Friendships: Music-Lovers, Amateurs, and Professional Musicians in the Late Nineteenth Century', *MBC*, 321–40, which discusses activities in London houses in the 1870s and 80s involving such stars as Joachim, Clara Schumann and Pauline Viardot.

[28] Information on fees has been gleaned from Ella's account book (EllaC, MS 6), p. 27. Many of the accounts from this period are noted in shorthand, but those for 1853 are spelt out numerically, and concur with those that are given, for other years, in code. The fees he paid to Clauss are in line with those offered to Mme Pleyel in a letter to Fétis dated 15 March [?1852] (*WangerméeF*, 439).

On the low fees paid for orchestral and most solo work at the Philharmonic around this time, see *EhrlichFP*, 56, 72–3, 84, 102, 104. In 1843 rank and file players got £13, and some £11, for eight concerts and nine rehearsals, leaders got £27, and principal players £17; Sivori was paid £21 for two concerto appearances (£10 10s pro rata), while the pianist Louise Dulcken got 5 guineas for one performance. The orchestral fees rose only a little in subsequent years (*EhrlichFP*, 72–3). In 1856 the

concerts offered, employment volatility remained an issue for all musicians, and it seems that around this time Ella stopped relying on artists' goodwill for the Director's Matinée and started paying them.[29]

Although only a handful of the Continental musicians arriving in London were hired for the Musical Union, many incoming players seem to have tried to solicit engagements.[30] Others were invited to concerts by Ella as special guests, or they requested admission out of curiosity for the society's burgeoning reputation. (It was unlikely, given Ella's Europhilia and instincts for self-promotion, that they would be refused.)[31] 1851 marked a first high point in terms of European interest, with Berlioz, who was in London to act as a juror at the Great Exhibition, writing a celebrated account of Ella's society for the Parisian *Journal des Débats*.[32] Berlioz had attended the Musical Union during his visit to London in 1848; now he returned and lavished admiration in print, highlighting Ella's intelligent leadership and the quality of the music-making to his French readers. He also drew attention to Ella's programme notes, a novelty that surely struck a chord with him, given his own previous attempts to provide audiences with an account of the *Symphonie fantastique*'s literary 'programme'. In general Berlioz considered Ella's method of

Philharmonic offered Clara Schumann only double what Dulcken had been paid, seeing it as the 'amount usually paid by the Society to artists of the highest class' (*EhrlichFP*, 105, n. 43). We should note, however, that the Philharmonic was largely unwilling to respond to 'the rising market price of unique talent' (*EhrlichFP*, 85), and that low fees continued to be paid well into the 1870s.

[29] The accounts for 1853 show that fees paid to artists now included payments for the Director's Matinée: see EllaC, MS 6 (account book), p. 27. Rumours, presumably based on former practice, persisted: in 1857 Ella was moved to state publicly that 'The annual performance of solo, concerted, and vocal music [...] is not, as often reported, one of those entertainments to which artists are importuned to *give* their services without *honorarium*: on the contrary, it is by far the most costly *Matinée* of the series' (*RMU*, 1857, p. 30).

[30] See e.g. the letter from August Müller, dated 4 June 1851 (EllaC, MS 81, p. 47), in which the musician asks to perform a double bass solo in one of Ella's forthcoming concerts, and offers to play for free. His request was unsuccessful. Increasingly, Ella could pick and choose.

[31] According to an advertisement in *MW* (6 April 1850), 219, a 'limited number of resident artists and members of foreign academies' would receive free admission on application to Ella. The *RMU* (1849) membership list contains the uncorroborated claim that during the 1849 season 'four hundred free admissions were given to ladies and gentlemen of artistic, literary, and scientific fame'.

[32] Translated in A. W. Ganz, *Berlioz in London* (London: Quality Press, 1950), 90–4. The piece, on the state of England's musical institutions, also spoke favourably of the Beethoven Quartett Society.

'analysis' good, recognizing that the programme notes appealed 'to the eye as well as the mind, by adding to the critical text musical extracts, the theme of each piece, the most important musical figure or the most striking harmonies or modulations. One could not do more.'[33]

The essay appeared on 24 May. By 17 June Ella had reprinted the full passage in his concert pamphlets.[34] Henceforth the men became firm acquaintances, Ella often calling on Berlioz when visiting Paris. Behind their relationship was a tacit recognition of the professional benefits they could provide for one another. Ella had already begun to act as a low-key ambassador for Berlioz, publishing favourable comment on the man and his music in the Musical Union's programmes; other gestures would follow.[35] For his part, Berlioz was nursing hopes of settling in London permanently, and Ella, like the other English journalists Berlioz consorted with, must have seemed a useful friend. Plaudits and dedications, such as his inscription of *La fuite en Egypte* 'à Mr Ella' in 1852, flowed easily.[36] For all that, Berlioz's remarks about the Musical Union, even allowing for the deliberately rosy glow about England he evoked for readers in France, seem to have been apposite. Berlioz was well attuned to chamber music. He was a respected French critic, and no mean judge of quality; moreover, his comments were in line with wider approbation. In subsequent years, other high-profile European musicians visited the Musical Union – Jenny Lind (1852), Spohr (1853) and Meyerbeer (1855) included. Both Spohr and Meyerbeer were sufficiently impressed by the concerts to write to Ella and tell him so. Ella similarly paraded their comments in the society's

[33] Ganz, *Berlioz*, 92.

[34] *RMU* (1851), 36.

[35] He would later attempt (unsuccessfully) to secure a performance of *La fuite en Egypte*, and reprint the list of Berlioz's complete works from Richault's Paris catalogue in *RMWE* (1852), sup., 41–2, before joining the committee of musicians who raised money to support the publication of *Faust* after the debacle of *Benvenuto Cellini* at Covent Garden in 1853.

[36] This work became the second part of *L'enfance du Christ*. Berlioz dedicated part one to Edward Holmes, and part three to the publisher Frederick Beale. Berlioz had jokingly attributed *La fuite* to the spurious Renaissance composer Pierre Ducré, as he explained to Ella (who had queried the attribution) in a letter of 15 May 1852, which appears in *RMU* (1852), 13–14. Another example of Berlioz's affection for Ella is an engraved portrait (by Baugniet), inscribed to Ella, which he presented to him before leaving for France in summer 1851 (diary, 29 July 1851: EllaC, MS 120). A photograph of the portrait is in EllaC, MS 91.

The Berlioz–Ella relationship is examined in greater depth in Christina Bashford, 'More than Dedication?: Hector Berlioz and John Ella', *The Musical Voyager: Berlioz in Europe*, ed. David Charlton and Katharine Ellis (Frankfurt am Main: Peter Lang, 2007), pp. 3–24.

literature, famous personalities being useful for developing the society's reputation, both at home and abroad.[37]

The international spirit of 1851 further sharpened Ella's promotional activities. Seeing the well-respected French artist Charles Baugniet was in town, Ella commissioned from him a commemorative tableau of eighteen figures – the sixteen principal Musical Union artists of Exhibition Year, plus Ella symbolically holding his *Record* and Baugniet his sketchpad. The lithographed image (Fig. 11) was sold by subscription to members for 10s, and there was even a private reception at Willis's Rooms to launch it.[38] Ella provided much accompanying rhetoric in his programme pamphlets, most of which re-emphasized the Musical Union as a forum for the coming together of national styles, now effectively echoing the Exhibition's stated remit to display and celebrate the 'Industry of All Nations'.[39] As is well known, the Exhibition was supposed simultaneously to demonstrate British prowess in making things, whether objects of industry, design or art.[40] Of course, the nation's musicians, unlike the leading British figures in the plastic arts and the sciences, were deemed to have little claim to pre-eminence, but Ella included Hill (viola player), Bennett (composer and pianist) and himself as representatives of national excellence. And, for once, Ella's ethos of high, foreign quality took second place to the notion of an international union of equals, his complaints about the inferiority of British musical culture to that of Europe falling silent temporarily.[41]

---

[37] On Spohr and Meyerbeer's visits, see *RMU* (1852), 32; (1853), 42; and (1855), 28 and 30. Ella's use of their remarks in puffs can be found in later *RMU*s, beginning in 1859.

[38] As indicated in *RMU* (1851), 53. Ella's diary (EllaC, MS 120) indicates the reception took place on 25 July 1851. For more on the lithograph, see *RMU* (1851), 32, 44, 52. A second image of sixteen figures, entitled 'L'analyse', was made by Baugniet in 1853 (part of the process is charted in Ella's diary entries for 5 July, 6 and 18 August: EllaC, MS 122) and later reproduced for sale to members: *RMU*, 1855 and 1862, preliminary pages. That image included notable players and visitors such as Spohr, Berlioz and Lindpaintner. It is reproduced in *GanzMM*, 110. Baugniet also made lithograph portraits of celebrated artists and visitors which Ella reproduced as frontispieces to *RMU*: Ernst, Molique and Vieuxtemps (1854), Meyerbeer (1855), Fétis (1856), Rubinstein (1857), Ella himself (1858) and Spohr (1859).

[39] *RMU* (1851), 2, 6, 10, 12, 14 and 26.

[40] Roy Porter, *London: a Social History* (London: Penguin Books, 1996), 291.

[41] Earlier examples of these complaints can be found in *RMU* (1845), 42, 58; (1846), 16; (1850), 36.

11 'Artists Engaged during the Seventh Season [of the Musical Union]'. Lithograph by Charles Baugniet, 1851. Copyright of The Royal Academy of Music, London. From left to right: Eckert, Sainton, Vieuxtemps, Ernst (seated), Deloffre, Hill, Laub, Sivori (with violin), Bottesini (with double bass), Pauer, Piatti (with cello), Pilet, Menter, Hallé (at piano), Seligmann, Sterndale Bennett, Ella (with *Record of the Musical Union*), Baugniet.

❧ *Musical Union extended*

MUSICAL WINTER EVENINGS [...] *By establishing these entertainments, we shall increase our store of well-practised works, extend musical patronage, and afford amateurs and artists a neutral territory for amusement and social intercourse at a time of year when neither are satiated with the excess of music given during The Season.*

∾ *RMU* (1852)

B Y the early 1850s the Musical Union began to thrive financially. The process was rather slow at first – there had been a dip in subscriptions in both 1848 and 1849 – but growth gradually won out. Sales of single tickets increased significantly in 1849 (Ella proudly chirped about achieving 'double the number of visitors' that year) and held up thereafter, as Ella increased the number of West End outlets at which admissions could be purchased.[42] Then from 1850 the subscription list

---

[42] Ella claimed the increase in visitor numbers in *RMU* (1849), 28, and the membership list for 1849 ('upwards of four hundred [visitor admissions] were purchased

started to increase: rising from 274 subscribers in 1850 (up seventy on the previous year), to 385 by 1853 and 430 in 1857.[43] As survival looked more certain, Ella began to expand his activities.

The first public intimation that he had 'other projects of a musical nature in view' came in July 1849,[44] and in 1850 he tried out one of them: an additional matinée, held on 11 June, for the trial (try-out) of new compositions and performers, and for the vetting of unknown artists who might perform at Musical Union concerts proper.[45] Glowing from its apparent success (he claimed publicly that 250 members had turned out for it) and from the society's general well-being, Ella set about formalizing similar arrangements for 1851.[46] The resultant 'extra *matinées*' (sometimes called 'private *réunions*') were packaged as a sub-series of concerts and took place at Willis's Rooms on Tuesday afternoons, alternating with the main series; in the first instance they ran only until 1854, though they were revived later in the decade.[47] A discrete subscription list and system of single-ticket sales was balanced by relatively small outlays on fees to the débutant performers.[48] A neat formula, it aimed to bring artistic benefits

during the season'). The assertion is borne out by the figures for ticket sales in EllaC, MS 6 (account book), pp. 93–4: £103 8s 6d in 1847; [£132 16s 6d] in 1848; £250 0s 6d in 1849. Figures for 1851–7, given on pp. 47 and 90–3, show the continued growth and importance of this source of revenue; *RMU* in this period also makes reference to healthy ticket sales. By 1854 tickets could be purchased at Cramer's, at Chappell's, at the concert rooms (through Ollivier) or *chez* Ella in Welbeck Street (*RMU*, 1854, p. 1).

The temporary dip in subscriptions in 1848 and 1849 is suggested by the published list of names in *RMU* (1856), 26, where Ella claims a 20 per cent reduction in numbers in those years. This roughly concurs with the numbers of paid-up subscribers noted in his account book (257 in 1847, down to 200 in 1848 and 1849: MS 6, p. 47).

43 Figures from the account book (EllaC, MS 6), p. 47. Appendix IV gives further information on the changing size of the subscription list.

44 *RMU* (1849), 32.

45 The programme for the 1850 matinée is in EllaC, MS 81, p. 43. Earlier in the season Ella had intimated he would try to set up an additional private concert for the performance of Beethoven's quartet op. 131 (*RMU*, 1850, p. 12). Whether this came off is not clear; it was not part of the 11 June concert.

46 *RMU* (1850), 28.

47 There were four such concerts in 1851, and two in 1852, 1853 and 1854. Anton Rubinstein was introduced at an extra matinée in 1857, participating in his piano trio op. 52.

48 The account book (EllaC, MS 6, p. 19) lists fees paid to Musical Union artists for the 1852 season, and includes small amounts paid to débutants who performed in

at a minimal cost and risk.[49] Concert programmes closely mirrored the Musical Union's and were built around established repertoire favourites by Haydn, Mozart and Beethoven, although there were more showpieces for soloists: understandable, given the concerts' function. Instrumentalists introduced through these concerts included Ernst Pauer, Ferdinand Laub, the cellist Joseph Menter, and the prodigy pianist Master Arthur Napoleon. Sometimes a singer was programmed, a means of talent-scouting for the Director's Matinée; among the new voices were those of Mlle Johannsen (from Denmark), Herr Reichart (Vienna) and Jules Lefort (France). Several of the artists did go on to be hired for Musical Union concerts. Meanwhile, the performance of untried works was never more than a secondary concern: new music, when it happened, tended to be of the solo virtuoso variety. First performances of Schubert's piano fantasia op. 103 (1853) and Johannes Verhulst's now-forgotten quartet in D minor op. 6 (1854) were the exception rather than the rule, and a saxophone fantasia, arranged and played by Henri Wuille, who was grandly announced as 'Soloist in the Private Band of H. M. the King of the Belgians' (1852), was possibly the most exotic offering.[50]

Other of Ella's ideas hatched around 1849–51 were more obviously linked to his proselytizing agendas. The most ambitious was to found a permanent institute around the Musical Union, centred on a building that would house a library and instrument collection as well as facilities for rehearsals, trials, concerts and musical conversation, all in the name of improving the appreciation of serious music within high society. In the pages of his concert pamphlets Ella aimed to soften

the extra concerts; most were paid 'c/c', i.e. £3 3s [a = 1; b = 2; o = 0]. Meanwhile, accounts for 1853 (op. cit., p. 29) suggest the total bill for the two extra concerts or 'receptions' came to £12 ('ab'); in 1854 the figure was £20 ('bo'; p. 28). Information on the subscription and ticket system is in *RMU* (1851), 8–9.

49 The suggestion from *MW* (14 June 1851), 369 (reprinted in *RMU*, 1851, p. 43), was that although the concerts were not profitable, Ella could absorb the losses. Ella's account book confirms that he made a small loss (some £34) on the 1851 sub-series (EllaC, MS 6, p. 92).

50 The contents of the first of the 1851 trial concerts gives a taste of the format: Mozart's G major quartet K387 led by Laub with Menter on cello; a cello solo from Menter of his own composition (*Fantaisie sur un thème russe*); a performance of Mendelssohn's D minor piano trio op. 49 with the pianist Pauer (a third trialist); and Vieuxtemps' *Fantaisie caprice* op. 11 played by Laub. In addition, there were songs sung by Herr Reichart (from the Vienna Opera) – works by Schubert and Jäger – and a 'brilliant solo' on the piano from Pauer. Another untried pianist, Eckert, was the accompanist. In this instance all five musicians passed the test and were hired for official Musical Union concerts, though it would not always happen this way. Some trials included old hands like Vieuxtemps, Piatti and Hallé.

up potential donors (the scheme was to be privately financed), and got as far as outlining plans.[51] But the foundation of two bodies with similar objectives, the Musical Institute of London (November 1851) and the Réunion des Arts (1851), both operating in the West End, seems to have caused him to delay.[52] Ella subscribed to the Réunion des Arts and wrote approvingly of the spirit of its activities, which included concerts and lectures, in his Musical Union columns. He also made the (probably pragmatic) decision to join the Musical Institute's managing council and almost certainly learnt important lessons from the experience. Although the Institute was dissolved in October 1853, Ella waited a few more years before putting his own plans into action.[53]

A third initiative came more quickly to fruition: public evening concerts of chamber music. These were begun in 1852 and in the same vein as the Musical Union meetings, though held during January, February and March, ahead of the busy, deeply competitive 'high' season. Since the mid-1830s the winter months had been the prime time for resident musicians to give chamber concerts, and several series had had reasonable success at this point in the calendar.[54] For while part of fashionable society, particularly its pleasure-seeking ranks or those lacking London-based professional activities, may not have been up in town in the New Year, experience had already shown there were enough music-lovers with serious cultured interests around, including people from the middle classes, to make such

---

[51] The back covers of *RMU* (1849 and 1850) outlined plans for a Musical Union library and institute. These were followed by a series of references to the proposals (*RMU*, 1851, pp. 28, 48, 54, 56; 1852, dedication page, 13; 1853, dedication page, 16). There was also campaigning in *RMWE*, including the suggestion that profits from the (new) evening concerts would be used to realize the scheme (see 1852, p. 1; 1853, p. 22; 1854, p. 28). The first intimation of hopes of founding a library can be traced to *RMU* (1847), 12.

[52] For the aims and modus operandi of the *Réunion des Arts*, see *RMWE* (1853), 15–16 and *MW* (17 May 1851), 315 and (18 November 1854), 763. The violinist Goffrie, who played second violin for Musical Union concerts, 1853–5, was the Réunion's manager; Ella was a member. The club seemingly fizzled out in 1859.

[53] On the Musical Institute, see Alec Hyatt King, 'The Musical Institute of London and its Successors', *MT*, 117 (1976), 221–3; Ella joined its council in 1852. After the Institute's demise, its library was sold by Puttick & Simpson, in December 1853 (see James B. Coover, *Private Music Collections: Catalogs and Cognate Literature*, Warren, MI: Harmonie Park Press, 2001, p. 272).

[54] They included the events put on by the Society of British Musicians, Madame Dulcken, William Sterndale Bennett, Charles Lucas and others in the West End (usually in private rooms), and by Joseph Dando and others in the City. See Christina Bashford, 'Learning to Listen: Audiences for Chamber Music in Early-Victorian London', *Journal of Victorian Culture*, 4 (1999), 25–51, at 31–2.

events viable if not hugely profitable.[55] Evening concerts, after all, could attract professional men and others who would have been unable to attend afternoon performances; and middle-class demand for music was known to be on the increase.

Ella called his new concerts 'Musical Winter Evenings' and, like his 'extra matinées', they operated on similar artistic lines to the Musical Union, promoting the best in chamber music and using some of the same performers (those living in London at this time of year), the same venue (Willis's), programme notes, association with high society (a group of well-born women in the sister organization, headed by the Duchess of Roxburghe, gave their names as official patrons), and so on. The programme pamphlets even shared the classical masthead (which had been redesigned and modernized in Exhibition Year), thus signifying the events as carriers of high culture and trading on the Musical Union's growing reputation for high seriousness and artistic excellence. For the evening concerts, however, Ella had a different, more middle-class audience in view, his admitted aim being to 'enlarge our sphere of action' within the capital.[56] To this end, and aware of competition from other events, he set the subscription at a fairly standard £1 10s for the series of six concerts and opened up single tickets to all comers, undercutting the going rate for several other West End soirées. So while in February 1852 the veteran pianist Charles Neate advertised single tickets for his Quartett and Pianoforte Soirées at the Beethoven Rooms, Queen Ann Street, in conjunction with Sainton, Piatti *et al.*, at 10s 6d, the Musical Winter Evenings charged only 7s for similar fare.[57] Moreover, Ella offered Musical Union members a reduced subscription rate, to encourage their support and generate critical mass. He also made the programming less austere by adding to the selection of ensemble works and piano solos a few short vocal numbers (songs and opera arias sung by relatively inexpensive singers); this was in keeping with what was typically offered at London chamber concerts at this time of year, and doubtless an attempt to appeal to broader taste. Even so, his fundamental idea remained elevating minds by exposing 'the musical amateurs of this vast metropolis' to the best of musical art, and there was much

---

[55] Remarks in *MW* (31 January 1839), 71–2, illustrate the point, though suggest the winter audience was relatively small: 'If the reader [will] only call to mind the character of an audience at a benefit morning concert, late in July, where all the prodigious people go, and compare it with that of one of our serial concerts which begin at this period of the season [i.e. January], and which are often but slenderly attended, he will be struck by the difference; – the one all fashion, noise, astonishment, and *exhaustion* – the other comparatively scanty in its numbers, but attentive, and full of freshness and enjoyment'.

[56] *RMWE* (1852), 2.

[57] Advertisements for Neate's concerts and the Musical Winter Evenings can be found in *MW*.

Beethoven, Mozart, Haydn and Mendelssohn to be had.[58] There were subsidiary agendas too, including the possibility – publicly stated – of investing the concerts' profits in his broader campaign for a Musical Union institute and library; and the more highfalutin' hope of inducing high-calibre European artists to come to London earlier in the season than usual.[59]

The evening concerts, which lasted until 1858 (with a break in 1856), proved an economic challenge. Ella had expected to lose money during the first year, which he did; and he moved quickly thereafter to experiment with arrangements in order to achieve the right 'fit'.[60] In subsequent seasons the number of concerts was reduced or increased, the prices of subscriptions and tickets were cut or raised, more or fewer artists were engaged, and so on, in order to find a way of ensuring the concerts ended up in the black. But whereas such tactics had paid off handsomely for Ella regarding the Musical Union, with the Musical Winter Evening concerts the results were more modest, and, while he avoided losses, he was able ultimately to secure only small profits.[61] That was a fair achievement within the competitive London concert market, but Ella had probably hoped for much more, dropping the concerts completely in 1856 after a poor season during the height of the Crimean War (1855), in which profits had totalled less than £3.[62] While such a slender gain might have been enough for a Neate, for whom concert-giving was a necessary, sometimes loss-leading, part of promoting oneself as an all-round London musician, for Ella, who was trying to make a living primarily through

---

[58] *RMWE* (1852), 2.

[59] *RMWE* (1852), 1. A letter to Fétis of 10 December 1851 (*WangerméeF*, 294; my dating revises Wangermée's on the basis of my inspection of the MS letter, and knowledge of Ella's itinerary for 1851) indicates that Ella initially toyed with the idea of producing programmes with special historical interest and was asking Fétis to recommend repertoire ('quelque chose d'originale ancienne').

[60] In *RMWE* (1852), 1, Ella stated clearly to readers that the 'commencement of a new undertaking is often unpromising', and told Fétis privately that 'I expect to lose money the first year' (*WangerméeF*, 294). At the end of the season he claimed in *RMWE* (1852), 44, to have made a loss, but to be able to offset it by the profits from the Musical Union. This is borne out by the notes in his account book (EllaC, MS 6, p. 16), where a bottom line of –£132 12s 6d is reduced to –£32 12s 6d.

[61] Part of the problem seemed to lie in Ella's decision to include vocal music (presumably a conscious attempt to draw in new audiences), for the cost of hiring singers pushed up the costs considerably. (On this point, see *RMU*, 1851, p. 10.) Ella made vocal numbers a less prominent part of the programming as early as 1853, and dropped them altogether in 1855.

[62] Down to £2 12s in 1855, against £42 6s the previous year: figures extrapolated from the account book (EllaC, MS 6), pp. 35 [income, 1852–5], 25 [expenditure and balance for 1854], and 28 [expenditure for 1855].

'moving and shaking', the returns were presumably not big enough to warrant the time and energy spent.

As far as we can tell, Ella's evening subscribers were split almost fifty–fifty between newcomers and existing Musical Union followers.[63] Understandably, given the time of day the concerts took place, there were more men than normally attended the Musical Union, and almost certainly more of what we would understand as an upper-middle-class presence.[64] Among the new faces drawn to the Musical Winter Evenings were Professor Richard Owen and his wife, one Dr Halley and his wife, and some of the womenfolk of Morton Peto. Owen, the son of a merchant, was an anatomist and physiologist, with a growing reputation and interest in fossils. Dr Halley was probably the Nonconformist divine Robert Halley, son of a nurseryman.[65] Morton Peto, railway contractor and now MP, was the archetypal self-made man; he had begun life as an apprentice builder. Other subscribers came from the aristocracy (for instance Lady Stratheden Campbell); and there were a couple of musicians, the pianist Edouard Schulz (an old friend of Ella's) and Henry Leslie (an amateur – a jeweller by trade – who was beginning to shine as a choral conductor). They were joined by several of the Musical Union faithful, who included some of Ella's stalwarts such as Sir George and Lady Clerk and the Freelings, as well as more recent neophytes, for instance Edmund Grove (brother of George Grove, the man who would later compile the famous *Dictionary of Music*; both were trained as engineers) and Thomas Brassey and his wife. Brassey was a railway contractor and a significant representative of big 'new' money.

Yet for the Musical Winter Evenings to have taken off in the way Ella had hoped – that is, by opening up a new and discrete constituency of music-lovers – the proportion of non-Union members among the evening subscribers would have had to have been much greater – as Ella realized.[66] Equally, the audience

---

[63] Based on the evidence of published lists of subscribers in *RMWE*. With this in mind, Ella's remarks, made a few years later in the programme for a Musical Union Soirée (3 March 1857; published as *RMU*, 1857, p. 2), that 'the majority, much to our surprise, consisted of members of the Musical Union' seem overstated. Still, the general sentiment of the passage in question – that a large enough new audience had not been found – was correct.

[64] According to lists published in Ella's programmes (*RMWE*, 1852, p. 44, *RMU*, 1853 and 1854), supporters of the Winter Evenings numbered 181 in 1853 and 179 in 1854, of which 69 and 67 respectively (nearly 40 per cent) were men. Significantly fewer titled names appear than in the Musical Union lists (19 out of 181 in 1853, or *c.*10 per cent), suggesting a more middle-class constituency.

[65] There was also a London physician of this name who was treating Ella around this time (as per the diary, 5 and 6 December 1853; EllaC, MS 122).

[66] *RMU* (1857), 2.

base would have had to have grown larger than it seemed capable of doing: the subscription list clustered around 165 names. Had Ella been prepared to invest in creating a more distinctive and separate identity for the evening series, over and above giving it an individual name, things might have worked out differently. But what he might have initially felt was a strength – that is, a strong social-musical identification with the sister project – may have turned out to be a weakness. In all this we should remember that Ella did not, at this point in his career, have separate, pre-existing networks in the broad middle classes equivalent to his high-society links that had proved so effective in gathering a core Musical Union audience and then extending it. Successfully locating and building a new audience would have meant opening up performances to more middling Londoners at cheaper prices, and exploiting different strategies in concert promotion.

Meanwhile, the parent concert club was doing well, drawing in more people, including gentry folk and representatives from the professional, upper-middle classes who were eager to 'belong' to the upper social world, and it was delivering substantial profits to Ella. Among Musical Union newcomers combining serious cultural interests with wealth and leisure were: William Tite, the merchant's son who became a celebrated architect and director of the London and Westminster Bank, and his wife; the Oxford-educated John Lodge Ellerton, amateur chamber-music composer who had married the sister of an earl; the wife of the political economist and writer Nassau Senior; and the well-known actress Fanny Kemble, also celebrated for her readings of Shakespeare. Fresh blood was essential, since some of the older supporters, including several committee men such as the Duke of Cambridge, the Earl of Falmouth, Lord Saltoun and Clayton Freeling, passed away in the early 1850s (the Duke of Leinster became President in 1851). Indeed, as the subscription list swelled Ella felt the need to spell out a formal set of rules for members, endorsed by the committee in 1853, at one of the few meetings they are known to have had.[67] Some new members, like Edmund Grove, extended their support to the Musical Winter Evenings, a gesture that was balanced by a few

---

[67] The meeting was held at the Thatched House Tavern, St James's, on 15 April 1853 and chaired by Lord Saltoun. The resolutions, which restated many of the existing rules and practices, were prominently displayed in *RMU* (1853), 12, and from 1854 they were printed on the front page of every programme. There were new provisos, intended to give Ella leverage over his players: that all engagements of artists had to be sanctioned by the committee (whether this happened is doubtful, but it was a useful 'shield' for Ella to hide behind to speed up negotiations, as evinced by Ella's letter to Fétis over the hiring of Mme Pleyel, cited in n. 22); that every artist was required to attend as many rehearsals as possible; and that all artists should be at the concert hall fifteen minutes before the performance began.

A final resolution that the committee should agree to any speculations made on its behalf in the name of a Musical Union institute may suggest some of his patrons

evening-concert subscribers (e.g. the Owens and Sir Charles Eastlake, president of the Royal Society of Arts, and his wife) deciding to take out memberships to the Musical Union. But with the evening events having produced neither outright failure nor resounding success, Ella decided in 1857 to refocus on his core activity and audience, rekindling the winter concerts after a year's gap under the name 'Musical Union Soirées'. By identifying them definitively with the Musical Union, Ella was abandoning all ideas of creating a separate institution for the middling orders, and accepting that his strengths lay in exploiting the distinctive social cachet that the Musical Union had developed. And if he privately convinced himself that middle-class demand for chamber music at this time of year was simply not big enough to realize adequate profits, or that allowing in 'ordinary people' would automatically alienate upper-class patrons, he would be proved wrong a few years later, when the enterprising S. Arthur Chappell launched the Monday Popular Concerts and proceeded to find the right formula, at once musical, social and economic.

None of this should detract from the fact that the rising fortunes of the Musical Union represented a considerable achievement, particularly so because in the 1850s Ella was contending with competition from a new institution with similar agendas for promoting high chamber music, the Quartett Association. Emanating from some of Ella's players (the violinist Sainton, the viola player Hill, and Piatti, prince of cellists), this initiative involved a series of six subscription concerts of instrumental chamber music (in all genres) during the high season, on Wednesday afternoons in Willis's Rooms.[68] It began in 1852. Similarities with the Musical Union were striking, right down to the provision of analytical programme notes (earnestly and excessively written by the composer G. A. Macfarren), short programming (three substantial instrumental ensemble works, followed by instrumental solos, usually showpieces – now a feature of Ella's programmes), royal patronage (Queen Victoria, whose private band Sainton led), and insistence on high performance quality (many of Ella's pianists, including Marie Pleyel and Hallé, played). The significant differences were the Quartett Association's intention to programme unusual music and to use a permanent ensemble of locally available quartet players, as some earlier initiatives had also done (thus avoiding problems of securing adequate rehearsal time that Ella's more *ad hoc* ensembles generated). Repertoire experiments included the occasional programming of works by British composers and the championing of Beethoven's late string quartets. Both were initiatives that Ella generally shied away from, even though the Beethoven Quartett

were urging caution on that front, and it is worth noting that Ella's promotion of plans for an institute ceased for a while.

[68] Subscriptions cost £1 11s 6d for six concerts; tickets were 10s 6d.

Society, which had exposed the whole spectrum of the composer's string quartets, was teetering in 1852 on the brink of extinction, so a gap was opening up. As for the question of ensemble, having a stable performance group ought to have given the Quartett Association players the edge in chamber playing, given that Ella's first violinist usually changed from concert to concert, and earlier efforts, such as Henry Blagrove's, to establish a permanent concert foursome had won wide approval. In the eyes of some, the Quartett Association's arrangement brought a good quality of ensemble,[69] but since the leading at each meeting was divided between the two violinists, Sainton and H. C. Cooper, the difference was probably less pronounced than it might otherwise have been. '[A]t the end of each concert we were always left balancing the merits of the two violinists', the violin enthusiast Hugh Haweis remarked approvingly some years later, suggesting that Sainton's playing was 'full of fire, brilliancy, and delicacy', while Cooper had 'more tone, and a depth and passion'.[70]

These distinctions (they were no more than that) aside, the Quartett Association was clearly aiming to attract the same type of leisured, serious-minded music-lover that Ella cultivated. As such it was a calculated attempt to seize some of his *haut ton* audience, or at least to persuade them to divide their loyalties. That, at least, was how Ella saw it. He referred to Sainton *et al.* privately as his 'ungrateful opponents', and tried to make it a condition of contracting Madame Pleyel, Hallé and Pauer for the Musical Union that they would not perform for the opposition, though it seems unlikely he succeeded.[71] It might not have given Ella much comfort, even if he had realized it at the time, but the fact was that the Musical Union was perceived as a success story, worth emulating. No archives survive to shed light on the Quartett Association's business history, but the institution ran for three seasons only, folding after 1854. According to George Grove, its demise was due to a lack of support.[72] But there must have been other reasons for its

---

[69] *MW* (12 June 1852), 373: 'Every time MM. Sainton, Cooper, Hill, and Piatti meet together, their performance is more highly finished'. *MW* (3 July 1852), 421: '[I]t would be hardly possible to hear a quartet played with a nicer observance of detail, and a more satisfactory *ensemble*, than by [these men].'

[70] H. R. Haweis, *My Musical Life* (London: Longmans, Green, 1912), 24. Robert Elkin, *The Old Concert Rooms of London* (London: Edward Arnold, 1955), 80–1, outlines the Quartett Association–Musical Union rivalry, but states wrongly, given what we know of time of day and cost of its concerts, that the former was 'a brave attempt to spread the charms of chamber music among a wider circle and on a more 'popular' basis' [than the Musical Union].

[71] Letter to Fétis, dated 15 March [?1852] (*WangerméeF*, 439).

[72] George Grove, 'Quartett Association, The', *A Dictionary of Music and Musicians*, ed. George Grove, 4 vols. (London: Macmillan, 1879–89).

extinction, and one suspects that what Sainton's group lacked was someone with Ella's business acumen, which was proving so crucial to sustaining the Musical Union.

❧ *Music and words*

The Analyses which you give of the works executed at your meetings are written with equal science and fine observation; and they contain excellent criticisms. They must powerfully aid such of the audience as are not professional musicians to note instantly the severer beauties of the morceaux, which without that guide would probably have escaped them at a first hearing.

ᔄ Letter from Meyerbeer to Ella, printed in
French in *RMU* (1855); translated in *RMU* (1872)

D URING the 1850s the Musical Union's repertoire coalesced, establishing a musical identity for the institution that would endure till 1881 while also contributing to the broader processes by which hierarchies of musical works developed in Britain.

A bedrock of ensemble chamber works by Haydn, Mozart and Beethoven, most of the works we now think of as 'classics' (such as Haydn's 'Emperor' quartet or Beethoven's 'Spring' sonata), had been put in place in the first few seasons, and they continued to be heard – all part of the journey that ultimately established their special status. But now, other pieces were gradually added to stock. These works – all standard repertoire today – included Beethoven's violin sonatas op. 30 nos. 2 and 3, and op. 96, and the second and third op. 1 piano trios, Haydn's quartets op. 54 nos. 2 and 3, and Mozart's D major string quintet, the clarinet quintet and the two B♭ quartets, K458 'The Hunt' and K589 (one of the cellistic 'Prussians'). Also absorbed in the 1850s were several of the solo piano sonatas of Beethoven (through Hallé). Most striking of all was the amount of Mendelssohn's chamber music, some of which had begun to be heard in the institution's early years. After the composer's death Mendelssohn's music took up a position of dominance in the Union's repertoire that was second only to Beethoven, outstripping both Mozart and Haydn: see Appendix II. Many Mendelssohn works were quickly taken on board and assimilated: his piano trio op. 66, string quintet op. 87, cello sonata op. 45, piano quartet op. 3 no. 3, the last of the op. 44 quartets, the quartet fragments op. 81 (suggested by Ernst) and much of the solo piano music. In tandem, there was a final flowering for Onslow's quartets and quintets – rarely heard past his death-year of 1853. Meanwhile, the instrumental music of the longer-deceased Schubert was mostly still untried, as elsewhere in London concerts.[73] Ella made just two attempts at an introduction: the D minor quartet 'Death and the Maiden', which was led by Joachim in 1852, and the piano duet fantasia op. 103 at an extra concert in 1853. Strikingly, large-scale chamber works by contemporary British composers such as G. A. Macfarren, Sterndale Bennett, W. S. Rockstro or Kate Loder were conspicuous by their absence, even though Ella had programmed one or two in the institution's early years.[74] This was in spite of their adherence to classical models and in the face of considerable bile from the pro-British press lobby: but of course Ella's line-up of increasingly non-British players was unlikely to know or champion such repertoire.[75]

The contours of the Musical Union's repertoire were broadly mirrored in the Musical Winter Evenings, where Beethoven's works were ascendant, followed closely by Mendelssohn's and, in equal second place, Mozart's. The latter's quintets for strings, and the clarinet quintet, were prominent. Whether Ella was seeking to appeal to a new type of audience through a mixture of classicism and lyricism is difficult to determine, since programming decisions were negotiated with artists

[73] Championship of Schubert's music came about in the 1860s and 70s, largely through the efforts of such figures as Charles Hallé, August Manns and George Grove. For an overview, see John Reed, 'Schubert's Reception History in Nine-teenth-Century England', *The Cambridge Companion to Schubert*, ed. Christopher H. Gibbs (Cambridge: Cambridge University Press, 1997), 254–62; on Grove, see Michael Musgrave, 'The Making of a Scholar: Grove's Beethoven, Mendelssohn and Schubert', *GGMVC*, 86–114.

[74] Bennett's piano sextet op. 8 had been played by the composer in the 1845 season; George Osborne had played his third piano trio in 1846.

[75] That much chamber music had been composed by British composers is not to be doubted, though there were considerable problems in the public perception of its quality (see Simon McVeigh, 'The Society of British Musicians (1834–65) and the Campaign for Native Talent', *MBC*, 145–68). Only a small amount was published, and very little of the manuscript remainder, on which we might make critical judgements, survives.

On the patriotic music press, see e.g. the *Dramatic and Musical Review* (16 March 1850), 84: 'It may be questioned, however, whether or not an undue pref-erence is given at the meetings of the Musical Union to foreign artists who have been engaged'. See also the blunter assertion in *The Times* (12 July 1849; Davison) that '[a]t one of the meetings at which Herr Ernst played, that admirable violin-ist, we understand, proposed to introduce a quartet by Macfarren, which Mr. Ella declined to admit. This was an ill compliment [...] to Mr. Macfarren, who, how-ever inferior he may be to the acknowledged great masters of instrumental music, is probably a more original, and certainly a more agreeable composer, than either Mayseder or Onslow'. The *Times* review is pasted into one of Ella's scrapbooks (EllaC, MS 81, p. 35), and against the claim that Ella had refused Ernst's suggestion of the Macfarren work, Ella has annotated 'all very untrue J. E.'

and not simply imposed, as was also the case at the Musical Union.[76] However, he would have seen the sense in allowing works with proven attractiveness, such as Mozart's clarinet quintet or Mendelssohn's string quartet op. 44 no. 2, to be programmed more than once.[77] Certainly the presence for two seasons (1853–4) of stable quartet groupings led by Molique (with Goffrie and Piatti) may have shaped some of the more unusual choices, producing performances of a variety of Spohr's chamber output and, most tellingly, works of Molique's own composition. Likewise, pianists probably drove the appearance of Schubert's two substantial piano trios, op. 99 and 100, as yet unbroached at the Musical Union itself (the first was performed by Pauer, 1855, the other suggested and played by Hallé, 1853), and the attempt at Schumann's piano quintet (Mlle Clauss, 1853).[78]

Ella continued to insist on concentrated programmes in both sets of concerts, spelling out the rationale as follows:

> Three pieces of music, of classical design, are sufficient to satisfy the minds of all who view art through a proper medium, and receive its influence on an impressible nature, and we never depart from this rule without feeling that we have trespassed upon the attention of our intelligent audience.[79]

Although there was elasticity in the choice of repertoire, one aspect quickly crystallized: the inclusion of a work with, or for, piano, initially a piano trio, quartet, quintet or duo sonata, and later a solo sonata. The last of these genres loosened up any unwritten definition of chamber music as group experience; and around the same time the informal Musical Union 'principle', established in 1845, of having one *brillant*-style work in each concert fell away.

Meanwhile, at the Union a formula of three ensemble works followed by instrumental solos was emerging, the piano work frequently centred between string quartets and quintets, effecting contrasts of instrumentation and idiom. A chronological sequence of ensemble works sometimes occurred, but was unusual

---

[76] Fétis had apparently argued for the advantages of involving artists in programming choices; see *RMU* (1861), 5.

[77] In *RMU* (1851), 26, Ella wrote of the ensemble chamber music of Mendelssohn and Mozart. In his view, 'the lovely simplicity of the gentle Mozart' and 'the elaborated combinations of the ardent Mendelssohn' addressed 'the tastes of all persons'.

[78] That Hallé was behind the introduction of these Schubert works is strongly suggested by his autobiography: 'My choice of pieces was then unfettered, and it was a pleasure to me to introduce many works unknown to the audience until then. Among these was Schubert's trio in E flat' (Hallé, *Life and Letters*, 112). The passage continues with an anecdote suggesting Ella had only moderate sympathy with the work.

[79] *RMU* (1851), 22.

and as such could generate comment from Ella.[80] The idea of programme coherence being defined cumulatively, whether through increasing musical weight or historical style, was by no means a standard concept in the Victorian period, and although Ella would sometimes subscribe to it instinctively (preserving heavy-weight Beethoven for the end of a concert), contrast of style or forces seems to have been a far more important element in building programmes. However, most concerts were concluded by those short and often lighter instrumental solos, intended to display the skill and artistry of the star players, whether this amounted to Bottesini or Vieuxtemps playing flashy works of their own composition, or to Hallé taking his leave with considered renderings of piano pieces by Chopin or Mendelssohn. In programming terms, it was the equivalent of rounding off a good, nourishing meal with a few *petits fours* or other sweet delicacies. Since the choices were invariably the artists', associations became evident between certain performers and particular repertoires: Hallé often chose Chopin, Heller or Mendelssohn, while Piatti played his own showpieces for cello. Marie Pleyel picked pieces by Liszt (a friend of hers). At the Musical Winter Evenings there was a similarly light ending, but generally we see even more experimentation in programme design (including the incorporation of glees and part-songs, and variety in the order of items), with distinctive menus emerging each season, presumably as part of Ella's ongoing attempts to ensure the concerts' success by matching repertoire to audience. Sample programmes for both series are given in Appendix 1.

How best to approach and understand the works being performed was something Ella addressed through his programme notes. As the repertoire consolidated, Ella found he had built up a stock of notes on most of the major chamber works.[81] Alongside the analyses came much counsel about how to go about appreciating chamber music and how to cultivate taste in high art, including practical advice on ways of listening, warnings that the processes of comprehension would be slow, and glimpses of the divine rewards that awaited the patient and diligent follower.[82] This was Ella furthering the 'sacralization' of the music, and his methods ranged from tingeing the writing with an appeal to listeners' national pride ('it should be the ambition of every genuine amateur to appreciate that in art which has the power to enrapture the enlightened understanding of German, French, Italian and

---

[80] As in *RMU* (1852), 34: 'The programme comprises three works [Haydn quartet op. 50/4, Beethoven piano sonata op. 57 'Appassionata', Mendelssohn quartet op. 12], illustrative of three remarkable epochs in the progress of chamber music'.

[81] Showpieces were rarely thus treated.

[82] Listeners were advised that new music should not be judged hastily (*RMU*, 1851, p. 2), and that attention should be always directed to the composition not the performer (*RMU*, 1850, p. 6); see also *RMU* (1852), 10; (1854), 14.

English musicians') to insisting on the superiority of music among the arts, and its equation with religion ('[p]armi les arts la musique seul[e] peut être purement religieuse'), leaving the Musical Union as the 'honoured Temple of the Classical Muse' with a 'duty rather to lead than to follow […] taste'.[83] The barbarians were, to Ella's way of thinking, definitely at the gate – for '[a]t all events, we should much prefer to lead the musical mind than pander to the sensual taste of the million, by *vulgarizing*, under the pretence of *popularizing*, art'.[84] Although future generations might consider such material ephemeral, Ella's literature was in fact carefully prepared and proofread (sometimes run past Clayton Freeling, for whose judgement he had much admiration), and also preserved for future contemplation in the *Record of the Musical Union* and *Record of the Musical Winter Evenings*.[85] Each year Ella sent copies to the British Museum library, and sometimes to friends and associates abroad, such as Fétis.[86]

In 1857 Ella launched a companion publication to the *Record of the Musical Union* called, somewhat confusingly, the *Musical Record*. Ella named himself 'Proprietor and Editor' and claimed to use its pages to 'give a faithful report of the proceedings of all organized institutions', though in practice it was a vehicle for promulgating his views on London music.[87] The periodical was issued between April and August, free of charge to members of the Musical Union and others, and it carried news, reports of events, retrospectives of the season, short articles, puffs on his own artists, and commercial advertisements (this last aspect was a new

---

[83] *RMU* (1849), 10; (1850), 33; (1852), 30; and (1854), 42.

[84] *RMU* (1849), 22.

[85] On the need for a second pair of eyes, see *RMU* (1851), 38: 'To guard against even the appearance of partizanship in the pages of our Records (which are entirely of our own concoction, and often too hastily written to satisfy ourselves), we invariably submit the last proof, before publication, to the inspection of a literary gentleman of acknowledged talent, with instructions to erase or modify an expression (*verbum ardens*) which in his judgment is likely to provoke censorious observations.' The identification of Freeling seems likely from the comment in one of Ella's diaries (entry for 7 January 1851; EllaC, MS 120) that he had called on Freeling '& left proof of Circular – approved & sent for print'. Freeling had been, by Ella's own admission in his obituary notice (*RMU*, 1854, p. 4), a great source of encouragement to him in his programme note writing.

[86] The copies now housed in the BL are marked in Ella's hand as destined for the British Museum. Fétis received copies too, writing to Ella in 1856 to obtain missing volumes (see 'Opinions of Foreign Musicians', *RMU*, 1862, preliminary pages). Some of these copies are now archived in the Bibliothèque Royale, Brussels.

[87] Quotation from no. 2 (5 May 1857), p. v. The editorial in no. 1 (21 April 1857), p. i, claimed the journal would be a 'guide to what is best entitled to their [Musical Union members' and foreigners'] attention'.

departure, and an attempt to raise revenue).[88] Presumably the advertising revenue was not forthcoming, as Ella quickly subsumed the periodical's content into supplements to the *Record of the Musical Union* (1858 onwards), though not before he had used it as a soapbox to chafe at monster concerts and other indications of an encroaching vulgarization of public taste.[89]

As a professional wordsmith, Ella displayed fairly average abilities. His literary style is best described as competent and fluent, lacking the flair and incisiveness that singles out his more distinguished contemporaries, such as Edward Holmes. Ella's musical observations in his programme notes were accurate, his musical judgements sound, and he was led as much by the ear in performance as by the eye in score study. Comparisons with other works in his library of aural memories came with remarkable ease. He was well read, and keen to impart others' erudition, be it the insights of Reynolds on fine art or the Russian writer Wilhelm von Lenz on Beethoven.[90] But there was little in Ella's prose that marked him as an original critic, even though his programme 'analyses' were path-breaking and had significant influence on other writers. His programme material was compiled as a job of work, against deadlines and commercial concert pressures. If he was happy to let the notes stand thereafter, stetting them for future concerts and only rarely making changes to content, it was largely because pragmatism was a norm of journalistic necessity.[91]

Ella was most at home when writing notes on classical repertoire. In 'sonata form' first movements he often walks the listener through (what he hears as) the main musical events in sequence, characterizing the principal thematic ideas of the exposition and saying one or two things about their employment and development by the composer, likewise pointing out the nature of a distinctive harmonic shift or formal procedure. There is no attempt at systematic description of the

---

[88] Issues were available on Wednesdays for general circulation (ibid.). In no. 2 (5 May 1857), p. v, Ella claimed a circulation of 2,000 (plus 500 kept back for binding), which, although almost certainly exaggerated, confirms that he was aiming at a readership outside the Musical Union.

[89] Discussed below in connection with Howard Glover; these columns continued a stance already struck in *RMU*: see (1850), 20; (1853), 20, 30; (1856), 2.

[90] Reynolds is mentioned in relation to the Archduke trio: 'Art, in its perfection, is not ostentatious' (*RMU*, 1851, pp. 15–16). Lenz is cited in the note on the piano sonata in D minor op. 29 [i.e. op. 31 no. 2] (*RMU*, 1854, pp. 7–8).

[91] A few notes underwent revision and expansion, e.g. those for Beethoven's quartet op. 74 and piano sonata op. 57. The programme note writer who stands out as someone compelled to revise his analyses continually is George Grove: see Christina Bashford, 'Not Just "G.": Towards a History of the Programme Note', *GGMVC*, 115–42.

musical events, the like of which later programme annotators would delight in. Rather, his is a simple 'tasting' guide.

In general, the more challenging, less familiar works receive lengthier, more in-depth treatment. A Haydn quartet or an early Beethoven piano trio that was familiar to amateur players might be deemed to speak for itself or treated to simple characterization;[92] but middle-period Beethoven or Mendelssohn would require more intellectual engagement and detailed explication. The following passage from an analysis of Beethoven's quartet op. 74 gives a fair example of Ella's style.

The Adagio [1st movement], with a lingering suspense in melancholy phrases of touching expression, interrupted by fitful starts and mysterious silence, leads into the Allegro by a rich sequence of Beethoven's favourite progressions 6-3 cres., with the violoncello reiterating the opening subject. The third and fourth notes in the first bar of this Allegro, and the melodic form of the fourth, are portions of the subject which are most frequently employed and presented with every possible variety of combination – pizzicato, in imitations, and more particular in working up the final grand climax of arpeggio passages for the leading violin. The third and fourth quotations

---

[92] As in the following comment on the first movement of Haydn's quartet op. 76/5: 'The simple structure of this Allegretto, with its theme and variations, calls for little remark. The theme is presented with more interest in the quick coda [...] terminating with a spirited succession of ascending and descending scales together' (*RMU*, 1850, p. 18). Works that were really well known might get no analysis whatsoever. As with Beethoven's piano trio op. 1/2: 'The popularity of this Trio [...] spares us the necessity of giving any analysis' (*RMU*, 1849, p. 22). And op. 1/3: 'We shall spare ourselves the labour of analysing a Trio so well know[n] to amateurs, by merely directing attention to the subjects and harmonies quoted' (*RMU*, 1851, p. 19).

are also prominent and interesting features, and the second subject, led by the viola, generates a succession of agreeable passages in the accompaniment. The descent of detached harmonies with the pizzicato fragment of the subject (No. 3), and the startling chords suddenly intruding upon the sustained dissonant harmony (No. 4), are effects suggestive and surprising, and strikingly characteristic of the genius of Beethoven. The second part of this movement is more impassioned and intensely exciting. After dwelling some time in new harmony (c major), with combinations of nervous and strongly-accented counterpoint for the violin and violoncello, with animated distribution of harmony for the other instruments, this episodical matter gently subsides into delicate imagery, too ethereal for analysis, and best left to tell its own tale. The original subjects are again repeated, and after a delicious repose of sustained harmony, ppp., commences the arpeggio referred to above, with melodic forms in the second violin giving additional interest and greatly contributing to the effect of the climax. A few bars are yet added of simple harmonies, and, with a short crescendo, bring this most romantic and powerfully conceived movement to a satisfactory termination.[93]

Leaving aside the period quaintness of Ella's expression, or the limitations of his analytical understanding by modern standards, one cannot help but be struck by the prevalence of technical terms (a feature that came to characterize English writing for the concert hall), and by the implications this has for the levels of musical understanding in his audiences. Assumptions of harmonic and formal comprehension are everywhere: in terms and phrases such as augmented fifth; 6-3 progression; tonic pedal; first and second subject; or the first and second parts of a sonata allegro. From the early twenty-first-century perspective the existence of such vocabulary in concert literature seems extraordinary – so much so that it would be all too easy to dismiss it as evidence of a culture of hollow connoisseurship. But these were notably different times. Ella's goal was to illuminate, and his audience was generally willing and eager to be enlightened. More specifically, he believed that through the judicious use of music examples and an invitation to readers to study the material further in private, the meaning of technical terms would become evident. If he challenged the understanding of some subscribers, nobody objected, let alone thought it alienating, such was the reverence for cultural authority and emphasis on the learner's role and responsibility in the educational pact.[94]

---

[93] *RMU* (1853), 23. The numbering of the music examples was unusual for Ella.

[94] Initially Ella called his programme notes 'synopses analytiques', later (from 1851) preferring the anglicized 'analytical synopses'. Subsequent note-writers similarly

As a method of comprehending music, Ella's approaches owed much to European theoretical traditions, an aspect further reflected by Ella's private library, which included composition manuals by A. B. Marx, Fétis, Reicha and Albrechtsberger.[95] His understanding of sonata form was largely thematic, so what mattered most was how the composer treated the melodic 'motivi', combined them contrapuntally, or clothed them in unexpected harmonies. When confronted by especially complex passages – notably in Beethoven – and when in all likelihood he was pushing at the limits of his own technical understanding, he might alert the listener to the riches on offer but advocate repeated listening as the key to understanding, thus: '[I]n the more vague parts, omitted in our analysis of this Quartet [op. 59 no. 2], there is nothing that will not become perfectly clear to his [the listener's] comprehension after frequent hearings.'[96] Or he might switch attention to matters of interpretation and performance, and make only general comments about compositional technique, as in this extract: 'The elegance of this

adopted the designations 'analytical notes' or 'historical and analytical notes'. With their emphasis on the term 'analysis', these labels tempted twentieth-century musicologists to approach the material primarily as music analysis, rather than literature for music appreciation or to aid close listening. From this came the inevitable conclusion that as analysis *per se* English programme notes were poor exemplars in comparison with central European traditions of analytical writing, in that they avoided engagement with deeper notions of structure and connectivity between musical ideas, and preferred a linear account of foreground events. The fact that the two writing traditions were functionally different has been largely ignored by musicologists. Thus, the analytical line of argument is taken by Catherine Dale in her discussion of programme notes in 'Towards a Tradition of Music Analysis in Britain in the Nineteenth Century', *NBMS*, 1, ed. Bennett Zon (Aldershot: Ashgate, 1999), 269–302, and is used as the premise for her 'The "Analytical" Content of the Concert Programme Note Re-examined: its Growth and Influence in Nineteenth-Century Britain', *NBMS*, 2, ed. Jeremy Dibble and Bennett Zon (Aldershot: Ashgate, 2002), 199–222.

95 The catalogue (EllaC, MS 54) indicates he owned A. B. Marx's *General Musical Instruction* (4th edition; ? London: Novello, 1854) and *School of Musical Composition* (London: Cocks, 1852), Fétis's *Traité au contrepoint* (Paris, [?1827]) and an English translation of a harmony text, probably Fétis's *Méthode* […] *d'harmonie* (Paris, [?1827]), Reicha's *Traité de mélodie* (Paris, [1814]) and *Course of Musical Composition* (London: Cocks, [1854]; originally published in French, 1826), and Albrechtsberger's *Methods of Harmony, Figured Base, and Composition* (2nd edition; London: Cocks, 1834). Ella's largely thematic understanding of sonata form probably stemmed from his reading of Reicha and Marx. For more on the analytical tradition, see Dale, '"Analytical" Content', and *Music Analysis in the Nineteenth Century*, ed. Ian Bent, 2 vols. (Cambridge: Cambridge University Press, 1994), i, 152–3.

96 *RMU* (1849), 11.

opening melody requires a delicate and tasteful delivery, and the entire movement, abounding with innumerable devices, pleasing subjects, and combinations,
admits of great variety of effects' (the only comment on the first movement of the
'Spring' sonata).[97] This particular gambit is most commonly found in Ella's coverage of finales, and that might lead one to suspect that pressures of time sometimes
took their toll on programme note production.

It seems only fair to point out, too, that while Ella set great store by explaining
the objective elements of music, he did not eschew engaging with works emo-
tionally or suggesting interpretative ways of understanding them, especially when
the music confounded explication by technique alone. In his 'analysis' of the slow
movement of Beethoven's quartet op. 18 no. 1, for example, he draws on an expressive vocabulary and quotes lines by Milton, while admitting that '[a]ll power of
language is inadequate to convey to the mind what Beethoven has here so intensely
expressed'.[98] On another occasion he attempts to describe the sensations excited
by the finale of Mozart's G minor quintet: '[i]t seems, as it were, the plaint of a
dejected and broken spirit wandering in search of her last hope, when a brighter
prospect gradually steals over her senses, and her gladdened heart bounds with
joy!'[99] Elsewhere he could even admit: 'Trop d'analyse détruit le sentiment'.[100]
He would not be the first to struggle with the difficulty of summing up music in
words.

Beneath Ella's explanations of how the music 'worked' were fundamental
value judgements about composers and pieces, most of them in keeping with
wider understanding of music and its hierarchies. These assumptions were struck
in the Musical Union's first decade and remained in place throughout the society's lifetime, becoming the criteria against which Ella measured new repertoire.
Unquestionably, Beethoven was at the peak of the mountain, Ella repeatedly
reinforcing his unique status to listeners. He was the 'great master', 'the greatest
musician that ever lived' and the 'Michael Angelo of modern musical composition',[101] whose unassailability rested on his music's originality and inventiveness
(the qualities Ella believed defined 'genius'), its daring and its profound expressive power – what Ella once defined as the 'philosophical gravity pervading [...]
[his] more serious movements [...] which touch and elevate the better feelings of

---

97 *RMU* (1851), 35.

98 *RMU* (1856), 4.

99 *RMU* (1852), 38.

100 In his analysis of Mendelssohn's quartet op. 44/3 (see *RMU*, 1851, p. 30).

101 These three comments first appeared as analyses in *RMU* (1849), 31 [on op. 57];
(1847), 7 [op. 70/2]; and (1846), 3 [op. 59/2]. They were much disseminated through
reprinted programme notes for later performances.

human nature'.[102] Beneath Beethoven sat Mozart, paradigm of classical perfection and working-out. Ella likened his quartets to 'the temples of ancient Greece', the composer himself to the painter Raphael.[103] One level lower, but still deemed an inventive master-mind, was Haydn, whose technique Ella repeatedly measured against that of the two successors, so that passages in Haydn's quartets were seen inevitably to foreshadow Mozart and, particularly, Beethoven. Indeed, Ella further assessed all other composers' chamber music against the three of them. Using such criteria, Mendelssohn's music succeeded, with Ella able to show links back to Beethoven, Mozart and Haydn, through such characteristics as originality of form, elegance, fine counterpoint, thematic development, and a range of emotion from the pensive and expressive (op. 80 quartet, written on the death of Mendelssohn's sister Fanny) to the delicate and charming (as in so many of the scherzos). When it suited him, Ella was prepared to propose Mendelssohn as another universal genius, and even to endow him with the accolade of being the greatest *performer*-composer ever – a tribute that nevertheless left Beethoven's position as the greatest composer intact, since Mendelssohn could never surpass Beethoven's ultimate supremacy in Ella's mindset, however central his music might become.[104]

Taken together, this quartet of chamber music composers was truly canonic, and Ella's insistence on their supremacy through the Musical Union's literature reinforced the processes of sacralization in the concert hall. Put another way, Ella was determined that these were the men whose music should be most known and honoured by his subscribers. Even so, Ella did not wish to inspire blind reverence: he wanted audiences to appreciate precisely what made the masters so great, and in his programme notes he frequently identified passages of genius and originality in their works. Thus there was no 'nobler specimen of […] science and genius' than the finale to Mozart's quartet K387; the finale to Haydn's op. 77 no. 1 showed 'wonderful power of mind'; there was genius in the harmonic shifts in the minuet of Beethoven's op. 18 no. 5; and 'the very apex of musical sublimity' was the adagio of Mendelssohn's quintet op. 87.[105]

Simultaneously, critical hierarchies within the repertoire emerged, some of them reflected in frequency of performance, others not. For Ella personally, Beethoven's abstruse late quartets were 'marvellous' productions, not to be written off if initially unfathomable, and he promoted them as the zenith of the

---

[102] *RMU* (1856), 3 [on op. 18/1].

[103] *RMU* (1851), 10 [on K387]; and (1849), 14 [on K464].

[104] *RMU* (1852), 18 [on op. 44/3].

[105] Found respectively in *RMU* (1851), 11; (1855), 31; (1852), 7; and (1852) 30.

composer's achievement.[106] He had been a subscriber to the Beethoven Quartett Society in 1845 and had written sympathetic criticism about the late works after their London premières in the 1830s.[107] But, as we know, he was cautious about programming them, for artistic and box-office reasons, and allowed op. 130 alone into the Musical Union. Meanwhile, there was phenomenal music to be found in the middle-period quartets, Ella acknowledging that the three in op. 59 were widely 'considered his *chefs d'œuvre*', particularly idolized by professional musicians, though perhaps privately favouring op. 74.[108] All of these were frequently programmed. The same was true of most other music in the Pantheon, for instance Mozart's quintet in G minor ('perfection in art'), his 'Dissonance' quartet (known for its 'celebrity'), Haydn's op. 76 no. 3 'Emperor' (a 'perfect specimen of genius and learning') and Beethoven's op. 29 quintet – a work that later generations of critics would curiously often pass over, but which Ella considered unmatched by modern composers, and a composition in which Beethoven's 'master-spirit is everywhere evident'.[109] Certain works that, in the course of time, would achieve masterwork status had a low profile for a variety of reasons, some judgemental, some purely practical, some less easily explained. Mozart's C major quintet (the finale of which Ella recognized as an epic piece of part-writing), Schubert's quartet in D minor 'Death and the Maiden' and his two great piano trios (a repertoire that Ella publicly said did not match the 'more experienced writers' but was worth airing if only because it was more 'orthodox in design' than some of the more modern repertoire; privately, though, he considered op. 100 'a poor affair'), and Beethoven's cello sonata op. 102 no. 1 ('considered too rhapsodic and abstruse for public taste') all made rare appearances at the Musical Union.[110] Other pieces, especially much of Schubert's remaining string chamber music and Beethoven's

---

[106] *RMU* (1856), 23 [on op. 130]; the comments were first made in *RMU* (1849), 22.

[107] Ella as Beethoven aficionado and critic is covered in my 'The Late Beethoven Quartets and the London Press, 1836–ca.1850', *Musical Quarterly*, 84 (2000), 84–122.

[108] These views on op. 59 were first stated in *RMU* (1846), 3; and (1847), 11. On op. 74 Ella remarked: 'That it is one of the best, most perfect in order, and r[h]ythmical expression of ideas, simple, elegant, mysterious, and grand, there is no question; and we were not surprised to find it more popular in Vienna, than any composed during the middle period of Beethoven's life'. (*RMU*, 1847, pp. 15–16).

[109] Taken from *RMU* (1852), 38; (1852), 28; (1858), 19; and (1851), 46 respectively. Ella, in his programme note on op. 29 (printed on pp. 47–8), claimed the 'finest and most original portion' of the work was the presto finale, 'said to be descriptive of a storm'.

[110] Ella's remarks on 'Death and the Maiden' and Beethoven's cello sonata are from the programme notes: see *RMU* (1852), 7, and (1860), 31 respectively. The comments on Schubert's op. 100 are in Ella's 1853 diary (EllaC, MS 122, entry for 5 February).

late piano sonatas, remained absent from programmes, while later Romantic masterworks arrived slowly. What we may take from all this is that Ella's notion of
what constituted a canonic chamber work was largely in line with that accrued by
posterity, but that there were moments of surprising dissonance: witness his views
on Schubert, or his assessment of Beethoven's op. 29 and the crowd-pleasing septet
op. 20.

꧁ *Upward mobility*

*Baines represents a house in the Regent's Park, with an emigrative
tendency towards Belgravia – musical daughters – Herr Moscheles,
Benedick [sic], Ella, Osborne, constantly at dinner – sonatas in P
flat (op. 936), composed and dedicated to Miss Euphemia Baines, by
her most obliged, most obedient servant, Ferdinando Blitz.*

~ W. M. Thackeray, *The Newcomes* (1853–5)

W E left Ella's own story, inasmuch as it can be separated from the Musical
Union's, in Welbeck Street in 1848, the year he quit orchestral playing to
concentrate on organizing. New openings were now sought, 1849 proving a year of
transition worth dwelling on. As already noted, the giving of music lessons to leisured amateurs was a vital source of a musician's income, and Ella had always done
varying amounts of it as circumstances dictated. But in 1849 he decided to add a
distinctive twist to what he offered. 'Having retired from an occupation which
has actively employed my time in every species of music in the best orchestras
during the greater part of my life', he wrote in a Musical Union programme at the
start of the season, 'it is my intention to devote my spare hours to the organization
of amateur musical societies, and to that most needed, though most neglected,
branch of musical education in this country – lessons in accompaniment combined with elementary instruction in practical harmony.'[111] The rhetoric of altruism may have masked financial imperatives, but the idea was in keeping with Ella's
broader goals for improving levels of music appreciation, and the networks were in
place. Through its shorthand system, Ella's diary for 1849 shows him giving lessons
to a handful of notables, including several women, most of them probably from
families associated with the Musical Union: Bayley, Marshall, Hardy and Staples.[112]
Whether Ella was actually teaching general musicianship and the art of accompaniment, as opposed to piano technique, we cannot be sure. Also, worthy though
the scheme was, it seems unlikely it took off, because Ella continued to uphold the

[111] *RMU* (1849), 8.

[112] EllaC, MS 118, *passim*.

merits of a general education, claiming in 1850 that '[t]he value of accompaniment lessons is not yet understood' in England, and eventually seems to have ceased this form of lesson-giving altogether.[113]

Ella meanwhile took a renewed interest in animating amateur music-making and fixing private concerts. Both were areas he knew well, although the Saltoun Club's activities lapsed around 1846, presumably as Ella channelled his energies into establishing the Musical Union.[114] By 1849, however, Ella was back, directing rehearsals and concerts in the Park Street town house of Sir George Clerk (summer 1849) in much the same vein as he had for Saltoun, and employing new arrangements of numbers from operas (particularly Meyerbeer's) he especially admired.[115] Some of the performers would have been from the Musical Union circle, if a one-off concert at the Clerks' the previous year, also under Ella's direction, is anything to go by: it assembled a group that included two of the Misses Cornewall, Miss E. Law and Henry Curtis among the singers, and the Earl of Falmouth, Hon. Lawrence Parsons, Sir Archibald Macdonald and Lord Gerald Fitzgerald in the band.[116] Around the same time (1849–50) Ella advanced a second body of choral repertoire, when he became fixer-cum-treasurer for a small group of male singers from revolutionary Hungary in what was a characteristic piece of

[113] *RMU* (1850), 34. The discussion cites a Viennese critic: 'Lessons from a well-educated accompanyist inspire confidence, instill [*sic*] principles of taste and expression, and to a skilful pupil, advanced in the mechanism of the piano, are of the highest importance.' Little evidence of such harmony teaching appears in the diary thereafter.

[114] The primary sources do not agree as to when the demise of the 'Saltoun Club' came about. Ella's obituary of Saltoun (*RMU*, 1854, p. 4) dated it from the time Saltoun went to China to lead troops in the opium war, i.e. 1841–3; but elsewhere he put its extinction at 1846 (*EllaMS3*, p. 439) or 1847 (*RMU*, 1870, p. 4). The *RMU* for 1845 includes several notices of Saltoun Club meetings; and we can safely assume that the meetings continued till at least 1845. (A notice in *MP*, 4 May 1844, indicates that the club celebrated Saltoun's return from China by a *soirée musicale*.)

[115] Documentation for these events (including programme information) is in 'Private Amateur Music', *RMU* (1849), 35, and EllaC, MS 81 (scrapbook), pp. 30–1. Ella's 1849 diary (23 and 29 March; EllaC, MS 118) notes rehearsals. Almost certainly Ella had the Meyerbeer excerpts sung in French – an innovative gesture, since Meyerbeer's operas were typically heard on the London stage in Italian translation. Ella's programmes also included extracts from Rossini (Italian operas as well as *Guillaume Tell*) and Spohr's *Jessonda* (the latter given in English).

[116] Performers in a Soirée Dramatique at 8 Park Street on 17 May 1848 are listed in a document in EllaC, MS 81 (scrapbook), p. 28. A handbill for the performance is also preserved (ibid., p. 29) and the concert written up in *MW* (5 August 1848), 498. A second handbill in Ella's scrapbook (also at p. 29) reveals another performance of operatic selections (venue not given) on 7 June 1848.

opportunism. The men, 'The Hungarian Vocalists', were seeking concert engagements in London, both private and public, with a repertoire of classical part-songs
and vocal quartets (by Mendelssohn, Mozart, Weber and others), along with items
of home-grown flavour. Having given the singers (unusual) exposure at Musical
Union concerts and tested interest, Ella gained openings for them. He organized
their appearance at 'upwards of seventy of the Nobility's Concerts' in London in
1849, according to a flyer for a provincial tour, and had them sing before sizeable
audiences, to judge from a handbill for a concert (July 1849) at Grosvenor House,
one of the great London mansions on Park Lane, at which Ella noted 256 people
present.[117] The Hungarians were in town for just two seasons, so the venture was
short-term for Ella, but the choir caused enough of a stir for Cramer, Beale & Co.
to be persuaded (probably by Ella) to issue an expensive sheet music anthology,
Songs of the Hungarian Vocalists, for voice(s) and piano.[118]

Ella's diary does not reveal what his income for 1849 amounted to, but he
kept track of his personal expenditure, noting everything from outlays on concerts to doctors' bills, from new gloves and boots to household coals. Scraps
in his account book indicate that the Musical Union had produced a profit of
£212 13s, a healthy amount (up on the previous year);[119] but it would have left
no room for complacency: although tickets were selling well, subscriptions had
yet to make the big up-turn described earlier in this chapter, and Ella's new professional activities were still bedding in. Preparing his diary for the new year of
1850, he inscribed a memorandum about prosecuting that core Victorian value,
thrift.[120]

A s it turned out, the 1850s brought good fortune: Ella's new work patterns
consolidated and his economic situation improved, so much so that he soon
scaled back his one-to-one teaching – an unusual and highly significant break
which, along with his cessation of orchestral playing, set him apart from mainstream London musicians, economically and socially. Organizing the Musical
Union and related initiatives occupied the lion's share of his time, and just about
everything else he did – some of it coming and going from year to year as circumstances dictated – was bound up with that same slice of London society, whether

---

[117] EllaC, MS 81, pp. 37 (flyer) and 36 (handbill).

[118] A copy of the music, with an autograph dedication by Ella to the Misses Ewart,
Musical Union members, is in the BL, where its date of issue is tentatively given as
1850. An illustrated title-page is preserved in EllaC, MS 81, pp. 38–9.

[119] Deduced from EllaC, MS 6, pp. 14 and 47.

[120] Note in the 1850 diary (EllaC, MS 119), ahead of the 1 January entry: 'Il faut que je
_____ mes frais! – thrift.–!'

it involved arranging the purchase of a Wheatstone concertina or a Broadwood
piano for a lady amateur, organizing subscriptions to Baugniet's lithograph of
Musical Union artists, or setting up domestic quartet playing between subscribers
and artists. At one point the amateur opera group looked poised to become a more
permanent sideline, Ella presumably recognizing the advantages of exploiting the
choral and orchestral arrangements he had made over twenty years for the Saltoun
Club. By 1851 he had even formalized the venture as 'Mr. Ella's Private Amateur
Union', with weekly rehearsals from January to Easter, and a series of private concerts.[121] But the initiative fell away, presumably as concert promotion jostled for
attention and looked more profitable. It would be resuscitated years later, when
needs were different. For now, the combination of private-sphere activities was
working well for Ella, and benefits were set to flow. In the immediate term they
would swell his purse, but they would also build feeder mechanisms for the Musical Union membership, the growth of which was soon to increase his livelihood
dramatically.

What most characterized Ella's new living was its melding of social and professional activities on a daily basis. Wherever possible he carried on the lifestyle of
a West End gentleman. The diaries of the early 1850s bring it all to life: in any one
month of the high season he would accept several dinner invitations from wealthy
acquaintances, enjoying evenings of fine food, wine and social intercourse, where
tittle-tattle could be exchanged and serious matters discussed, either through
words or music (often he would take along his violin and viola). New contacts
were made, Ella noting down names afterwards in his diary: Thomas Brassey first
appears at a party at one Mr Lloyd's in 1852.[122] Some days he would take tea with,
or make afternoon calls on, his lady patronesses; he would listen to their family
members sing or play; he would arrange and participate in some chamber music,
which remained his abiding passion; he might go to a private view at the Royal
Academy, hear a lecture at the Royal Society of Arts, or take in the latest diorama,
and so on.

At other times he would eat, drink, gossip, even spar, with professional associates. These included Musical Union artists such as Vieuxtemps and Piatti, business
colleagues (like Frederick Beale), and journalistic friends and foes (Gruneisen
was a regular dining partner; and, surprising as this may seem, he shared repasts
and conversation with Davison and Chorley). Musical events were not neglected
either: Ella's theatre habit, in particular, was fed regularly through visits to the

---

[121] A printed prospectus and programmes are in EllaC, MS 81, pp. 52–3; the club and
its performances are further documented in 'Private Amateur Concerts', *RMU*
(1851), 41–3.

[122] Diary, 16 June 1852 (EllaC, MS 121): 'intro: to Mr Brassey'.

Italian Opera (accompanying Berlioz to hear *Guillaume Tell* in April 1852), or play-going at the Lyceum, Haymarket and other venues. Concert attendance persisted too, with Ella naturally and professionally curious about new ventures. He was delighted with the New Philharmonic orchestra – thought Beethoven's Ninth Symphony under Berlioz in 1852 '<u>Magnificent!</u>', and the '1<u>st</u> Violins superb' in a concert that included Mendelssohn's 'Italian' Symphony in 1853, though he found Wagner's *Tannhäuser* overture 'ill played' and 'long, & tedious' in 1854.[123] He was optimistic about the prospects for the Crystal Palace, in Sydenham, where the glass building used for the Great Exhibition had been reassembled. The opening was in June 1854, and Ella wrote warmly of it in the Musical Union programme book.[124] Soon there would be a feast of activities out in south-east London, including what would become the capital's first permanently staffed and properly disciplined orchestra under August Manns, and Ella would become an *habitué* of its concerts.[125]

All this activity was interpolated between Ella's busy work routines. The calls on artists, the trips to the bank with coins, notes and cheques, the visits to Richards the printer or to Cramer's music shop took him out and about a great deal, but he would also spend long spells at home, writing and answering dozens of letters, preparing and checking copy for his concert programmes, addressing envelopes, numbering tickets, counting up and logging takings and so forth. It must have been tedious work, but it was meticulously done. From time to time visitors would call, including hopeful performers to whom Ella would listen and sometimes offer a concert engagement; and Musical Union artists would rehearse in his presence the day before the concert.[126] Out of season, as the frenzy abated, Ella continued to accept invitations to be a late-summer houseguest with many of 'his families' on their rural estates. Scotland, especially the Clerk family's seat at Penicuik near Edinburgh, had been a favourite destination in 1846–8, and he headed north by train again in 1850, 1853 and 1856, joining other London socialites, making yet more acquaintances as he moved from house to house, participating in the

---

[123] Diary, 12 May 1852, 16 March 1853 and 1 May 1854 (EllaC, MSS 121, 122 and 123). On the New Philharmonic, newly formed rival to the Philharmonic Society, see *EhrlichFP*, 97–8.

[124] *RMU* (1854), sup., 37.

[125] On Manns, see Musgrave, 'Changing Values'. Ella's attendance at Crystal Palace concerts is regularly noted in his diary, and not just on Saturdays.

[126] Indications of Ella's presence at rehearsals can be found in many places in the diary: e.g. 4 April and 2 May 1853 (EllaC, MS 122). For examples of listening to hopeful performers, see the diary entries for 13 January 1852 (a pianist named Dupont; EllaC, MS 121) and 22 June 1854 (Mlle Eschborn, a vocalist; EllaC, MS 123).

grouse-shooting, fishing and walking, and overseeing and instigating musical entertainments as needed.[127]

During these years Ella's financial position solidified. By 1853, and in spite of disappointments with the Musical Winter Evenings, the Musical Union's balance sheet was looking extremely healthy: 385 subscriptions realized some £800 in up-front income, which was amplified by the stunning £341 5s that Ella counted in single-ticket sales.[128] Expenditure amounted to c.£344 in general outgoings and just over £366 on artists' fees, and Ella stood to rake off a surplus of more than £440 from the Union alone.[129] That represented twice as much as the society had been delivering four years earlier, and it was additional to what he was receiving from other work. Remarkable, too, was the fact that these healthy earnings had come from the notoriously volatile business of concert promotion. Although this money sustained his improved lifestyle in the short term, Ella was never profligate with his gains, sensing that the good times would not last forever. Victorian society lacked the safety nets of the modern welfare state, and musicians were particularly prone to live out their final years in penury, however flush their careers had once been.[130] Common sense would have indicated that this was the moment to insure against leaner years and the uncertainties of old age.

Enter the stock market and young George William Bryant Kiallmark, son of George Frederick Kiallmark (1804–87), English-born musician and almost exact contemporary of Ella.[131] George Frederick had studied with Kalkbrenner and others in Paris, and was a pianist who worked as a teacher and performer on the London circuit. Ella had known him and his wife since the late 1830s, and had become a frequent visitor at their house. In the 1850s George junior, in his mid-twenties, trying his hand as a musician and soon to be married, was acting as an investment broker for people seeking to purchase stocks and shares, and

---

[127] The Clerks' estate was a principal destination, but Ella visited other family seats too, such as Philorth (Saltoun family), Arndilly (Grants), and others in the north of England.

[128] Account book (EllaC, MS 6), pp. 47 [subscription and single ticket income] and 90 [single-ticket sales].

[129] EllaC, MS 6, p. 27 [expenditure]. The precise amounts were £344 18s 9d and £366 18s.

[130] For more on the possibility of destitution, see *RohrCBM*, 157–63, and *EhrlichMP*, 26–9.

[131] Biographical detail about the Kiallmark family is in James D. Brown and Stephen S. Stratton, *British Musical Biography: a Dictionary of Musical Artists, Authors and Composers, born in Britain and its Colonies* (London: William Reeves, 1897); additional information can be traced through the *International Genealogical Index*. G. W. B Kiallmark was born in 1826, and married on 20 April 1854 (Ella attended).

now moved to assist Ella. There was nothing particularly out of the ordinary in this. In the middle years of the century, as Britain's economy grew, small investors emerged *en masse*, looking to the markets and its middlemen, rather than the mattress, to increase their personal wealth, and musicians joined the throng.[132]

Ella's first shares (to the tune of £387 in 'Eastern Counties' – presumably the railway company) were apparently bought through Kiallmark's brokerage in August 1852, and were followed in 1853 by further investments in a range of sources, again via Kiallmark.[133] Personal recommendation counted for a lot, as did spreading the risk. Ella also sank money into the Devon Mines through Frederick Beale, and invested in two plots of ground in Brockley Hill by way of the Conservative Land Society (formed 1852; Gruneisen was secretary).[134] By August 1853 he had some £660 invested, with returns of about 7 per cent.[135] The following March Ella finally sold property in Leicester, a decision cautiously made but one that raised £1,200 in capital (for Ella, a significant sum), which he deposited at the Union Bank in the short term, investing it only after further reflection and advice.[136] In later years Ella must have been thankful he had resisted any urge to pass this nest-egg through Kiallmark's hands, for in 1860 the latter would emerge as a 'bankrupt' and 'swindler' – Ella's own words.[137] Kiallmark invested Ella's money

---

[132] Adverts to attract investors to the Conservative Land Society and the National Assurance and Investment Association were placed in *MW* (5 November 1853, pp. 712–13), indicating that musicians were a target market.

[133] EllaC, MS 6 (account book), p. 248. The exact amount was £387 12s 6d. His additional investments of 1853 are noted, ibid. and on p. 4.

[134] Op. cit., pp. 248, 250.

[135] Ella noted £660 0s 6d in shares in August 1853 (op. cit., p. 248). (On p. 4 he arrived at a slightly different total of £657 14s – possibly calculated in April 1853.) In January 1854 Ella calculated (p. 249) that six months' interest on £587 12s 6d of shares had rendered him £22 8s; if we assume roughly the same amount was produced in the next six months, then the annual dividend was approximately 7 per cent.

[136] Diary, 10 and 15 March 1854 (EllaC, MS 123), and MS 6 (account book), p. 246. A best guess here is that it was family property inherited from his sister Ann. Ella had discussed the sale of the house with Lyttleton Bayley and put the wheels in motion during autumn 1853: see diary, 5, 16 and 25 November 1853 (EllaC, MS 122). In June 1855 he invested £1,000 through the Union Bank – presumably in bonds – to mature in July 1858 'by advice of M^r. Clack' (MS 6, p. 246).

[137] Ella made annotations against Kiallmark's name in his account book (EllaC, MS 6, p. 246) as follows: 'spent the money & [?]never bought the Shares', recording 'nix' against the Kiallmark investments and ending 'all lost' and 'a swindler & bankrupt'.

in a cement business that failed, and Ella had to write off the capital of his first investments.[138] Fortunately, by this stage Ella's financial situation was such that he was able to absorb the loss – around £600 – although he was certainly burned by the experience.[139] As yet, though, in the mid-1850s, all his investments were producing small dividends, which supplemented his professional earnings and encouraged him to invest further still. This he did, paying close attention to half-yearly returns and the relative merits of different types of investment, whether bonds, debentures or preference shares. He also learnt when to sell, and was becoming shrewder by the day.

From about 1854, in full knowledge of what he was 'worth', Ella paid his social status some serious attention. He was already well connected to the fashionable world and trying to live according to its rules. Next he attempted to bolster his social position by putting himself up for the Westminster Club – men only – in Albemarle Street, Piccadilly. The Westminster was a respectable club, if not the most distinguished in town, and eligibility for membership was not restricted by profession or business (as was the case in other clubs), which helped a musician gain admission. Having been elected a member on 2 January 1854, Ella made the building a favourite place for dining, talking and playing billiards.[140] Then, in summer 1856, he took new lodgings in Harley Street West (no. 20, ground floor). Only a few streets away from Welbeck Street, this was a considerably smarter address with a rateable value almost double that of his former dwelling.[141] The Beethoven Quartett Society had held rooms at no. 76 (now the home of the Réunion des Arts); the painter J. M. W. Turner had once lived at no. 64; and Charles Lyell, the geologist, had just moved into no. 73 – all before it became known purely as the locality for medical specialists. Straight away Ella spent money having two rooms refurbished as a music library and an office, and in doing so created further signifiers of his social importance. Years later this office was described by Alice Mangold Diehl, an erstwhile pianist (turned novelist) whose mama took her to play to Ella, as a 'business sitting-room, where an Erard grand was somewhat ostentatiously drawn

---

[138] The bankruptcy is listed in *The Times* (13 June 1860), 5. The business was in Puriton, Somerset.

[139] The loss is an estimate based on Ella's own calculations in his account book (EllaC, MS 6): the money invested with Kiallmark stood at £563 15s (p. 246) in 1854, and £603 15s (p. 251) in 1857; the latter amount included a bond worth £520, which Kiallmark had said would mature in 1862.

[140] On his election, see the diary, 2 January 1854 (EllaC, MS 123).

[141] In 1853 the gross estimated rental on his dwelling in Welbeck Street was £94, its rateable value £85; in 1858 no. 20 Harley Street West had a rental of £168, a rateable value of £150 (from the rate books in CWA). Other properties in Harley Street (e.g. no. 20 Harley Street East) held an even greater value.

up on one side'.[142] Recounting Ella's self-conscious demeanour, she noted he sat behind a desk to interview them, having kept them waiting 'as aspirants for the favour of important personages are'.[143]

Between times, Ella's self-esteem was further boosted by an invitation to deliver lectures on music at the London Institution, a literary-scientific society with a grand neoclassical building in Finsbury Circus, in the City of London (see Fig. 17, p. 300). It had been established in 1805 for the purposes of giving the east an equivalent to the Royal Institution (established 1799) in the west, its founding agenda emphasizing the interdependence between commerce and science, literature and the arts.[144] The Institution's secretary, recent Musical Union newcomer William Tite, made Ella the offer (networks were again paying off), and it was a welcome opening for him.[145] The City was not an area into which his tentacles had so far reached, Tite, Brassey and a few other recently made acquaintances notwithstanding. And although migration to the outer suburbs would eventually reconfigure the social geography of the City district, mid-century the neighbourhood around Finsbury Circus was still regarded as the City's fashionable quarter, full of wealthy middle-class types: businessmen, bankers, stockbrokers, doctors and solicitors. Many of them, including those who joined the London Institution, sought serious cultural activities in much the same way as Ella's West End fashionables did. Potentially it was the sort of audience Ella relished. He accepted the offer.

London Institution lectures embraced a range of mostly scientific topics (music was included by dint of its 'science'), and Ella joined a list of speakers that already included, in music, William Crotch, Samuel Wesley, Edward Taylor, H. J. Gauntlett, William Sterndale Bennett and Henry Bishop, and in other spheres Michael Faraday (chemistry) and Dionysius Lardner (natural science).[146] Ella's lectures – two

---

[142] *DiehlMM*, 118.

[143] The episode is also given, with complementary details, in her later *The True Story of my Life: an Autobiography* (London: John Lane, The Bodley Head, 1908), 108–9. The extent to which the novelist's pen is at work here is difficult to tell; but none of the information contradicts the earlier account, and her other characterizations of Ella are in step with those by other contemporaries.

[144] On the foundation of the organization, see Janet C. Cutler, 'The London Institution, 1805–1933' (PhD, University of Leicester, 1976), esp. 1–22.

[145] Tite visited Ella on 22 July to make the invitation (1854 diary, EllaC, MS 123).

[146] Later, scientific discourses were given by men such as Richard Owen the naturalist and Norman Lockyer the astronomer. A nearly comprehensive list of lecturers is provided by Cutler, 'The London Institution', Appendix 6. On Wesley as lecturer there, see Philip Olleson, *Samuel Wesley: the Man and his Music* (Woodbridge: Boydell Press, 2003), 97, 198; on Bennett, see William Sterndale Bennett, *Lectures on Musical Life*, ed. Nicholas Temperley with Yunchung Yang (Woodbridge:

series, one in the 1854–5 season on different styles of music, and a second in 1855–6 on melody, harmony and counterpoint – were evening events, illustrated with music examples performed by a group of musicians under the direction of Kiallmark, probably *père*.[147] Ella prepared with care, visiting the lecture theatre beforehand, reading drafts to friends, and so on, and was pleased with the reception his lectures received.[148] In what was by now characteristic fashion, he made much of the undertaking in his Musical Union literature and gloated in his diary after the lecture on melody and harmony that the room had been 'Crowded – & people told me it was the best Lecture I had ever given'.[149] To be sure, the engagement stood to fulfil several agendas – of widening the catchment for his Musical Winter Evenings; of furthering his programme for educating taste; of increasing his profile in the minds of people who mattered; and of building links with businessmen who might help realize his own plans for a Musical Union institute. It was also reasonably lucrative. Ella was paid £106 for six lectures, and although he had to recompense the musicians himself, the fee still represented more than Piatti or Vieuxtemps got for six appearances at the Musical Union.[150]

Further afield, Europe continued to hold attractions for Ella, particularly once the unrest of the late 1840s had died down. Paris was the focus for professional purposes, and he was there in 1851, 1852, 1854 and 1855, fraternizing among others with Berlioz (he was a witness at Berlioz's marriage to Marie Recio in November 1854), Meyerbeer, Kreutzer, Tamburini, Sax and the *luthier* Vuillaume (from

Boydell Press, 2006); on Bishop, see Ann Lindsay Royle, 'Sir Henry Rowley Bishop as Musician and Educator: a Reassessment of his Career and Achievements outside the Theatre' (PhD, University of Leeds, 2005), 236–78.

[147] Kiallmark's involvement in both series is indicated by the published programmes and a review of Ella's lectures in *RMU* (1855), 42–4.

[148] His preparations are noted through the diary from October 1855 (EllaC, MS 124), *passim*, but see esp. the entry for 1 December 1855: 'Ill. News speaks well of my Lecture' (a reference to a report in *ILN*, 1 December 1855, p. 643). Ella further quoted one of the morning papers reviewing the autumn series in *RMU* (1855), sup., 44: 'the patient attention of 500 persons for two hours listening to a lecture on music, speaks for itself'. Ella's lecturing style, like much of his writing, seems to have included a 'vast fund of interesting anecdotes which he has stored up during a long life of experience both as a theoretical literary and a practical musician'. He also apparently 'analysed and explained' fugues and canons 'by the aid of a diagram, in so clear and familiar a manner as to interest the least musical part of the audience'. (Ibid.) Texts of portions of these lectures were published in *MR* (1857), p. xiii (Haydn) and p. xix (harmony).

[149] Diary, 3 December 1855 (EllaC, MS 124).

[150] Diary, 21 May 1855 (EllaC, MS 124), indicates the fee. In a diary note for 18 December 1855 Ella states: 'for 3. Lectures – Paid Smithson for Chorus [£]12 10[s]'.

whom he had bought a copy of a Stradivarius violin in 1844), and taking in the Opéra and additional musical pleasures.[151] There was the added possibility that he might hear, or hear of, the latest local talent; and his French social networks would have kept him up to date with developments, something that gave him a distinct advantage back in London. Meanwhile, other destinations beckoned. Soon he was participating in that increasingly fashionable leisure activity, made viable by growing rail communications: the touring European holiday. 1852 saw him travel via Brussels to the Belgian resort of Spa, and on through such centres as Heidelberg, Stuttgart, Munich and Salzburg to Vienna; then back to Paris, stopping off at Prague, Dresden, Leipzig and Berlin. In 1854 he made for different scenery and visited, among other places, Strasbourg, Geneva, Basle and Baden-Baden, as well as spending time in Paris once more. Apart from the excitement of discovering new landscapes, peoples and customs – occasionally music and musicians too – these travels brought him once more into the orbit of his English social world, for he frequently crossed paths with London patrons and, to a lesser extent, professional associates. He made new acquaintances too. Names and events were carefully recorded in his diary, and from them we detect that he called, for example, on the Earl of Westmorland in Vienna, spent time with Meyerbeer in Spa and saw Chorley in Dresden and Leipzig (1852); he also met up with the Bayleys in Geneva and breakfasted with the Hon. Captain Devereux in Baden-Baden (1854).[152] Networking with wealthy types was a principal reason for Ella's success in maintaining his audiences; and there was new satisfaction to be had from the knowledge that he, John Ella, had been seen abroad too.

Even so, Ella's upward mobility and social confidence could not eliminate shortcomings in pedigree and breeding, and he kept his Leicester tradesman's origins well concealed. (In fact, he was beginning to exercise curiosity about the Yorkshire side of the family, and in time this would lead him to assert a publicly respectable identity.)[153] He was starting to see himself as belonging to the upper

---

[151] His presence at Berlioz's marriage is documented in his diary (EllaC, MS 124, entry for 19 October 1854) and in a letter to Hallé (*Life and Letters*, 249–50). The violin purchase is noted, in Ella's hand, against a letter from Vuillaume in one of his scrapbooks (EllaC, MS 81, p. 51).

[152] Diary, 24–5 August (Spa), 24 September (Vienna), 19 October (Dresden) and 21 October (Leipzig) 1852; 27–8 August (Geneva) and 15 September (Baden-Baden) 1854 (EllaC, MSS 121, 123). Ella's obituary of Meyerbeer in *RMU* described the time they spent together in Spa and referred to other musical luminaries in town, among them Fétis and Sax; see *RMU* (1864), sup., 3–4. A handbill for a concert in Spa, attended by Ella, Meyerbeer and Fétis, is preserved in EllaC, MS 80, p. 129.

[153] Diary, 22 October, 2 November and 9 December 1853, and 10 January 1854 (EllaC, MSS 122, 123).

ranks – remarking, with a touch of condescension, to his diary that the family of one Mr Toon, a solicitor, was 'a pleasant specimen of the good, middle class' and noting John Barker: 'a thoro' good <u>dilettante</u>[,] but like most of his Country-men who have lived long abroad he is returned to England with prejudices against the Class system of social life among Aristocrats & <u>Apes</u> of Aristocracy <u>parmi</u> <u>nous</u>'.[154] Yet whether others saw *him* as anything other than a parvenu is open to question. Thackeray, an acquaintance and Musical Union subscriber, wrote Ella into his novel *The Newcomes* (issued in parts, 1853–5) and used him and other respectable London musicians as referential detail to point up the culture-seeking middle-class Baines household in Regent's Park, where the young, eligible Clive Newcome is invited to meet Baines's daughters.[155] Fanciful though it may seem, the possibility that Thackeray, in this of all satires on upward mobility, was making a veiled jibe at Ella – the newcomer who successfully conceals his identity from other would-be newcomers – is not inconceivable, since there were many people around who made a point of remembering Ella's former days as a lowly pit-player or mocking his social affectations.[156]

In particular, tensions were rife and growing between Ella and certain members of the music profession for a host of intertwined social and professional reasons. In spring 1857 hostilities surfaced publicly in two places: Davison's *Musical World*, which carried a series of bruising editorials and correspondence columns on the subject of 'Mr. Ella', and the leading theatrical paper *The Era*, which had a reputa-tion for peddling gossip.[157] The attacks covered familiar ground – for instance, that Ella's puffery of his artists in his analytical programmes ahead of performance was

---

[154] Diary, 7 November and 1 January 1853 respectively (EllaC, MS 122).

[155] The passage is quoted at the head of this section, and comes from the edition of *The Newcomes* by Andrew Sanders (Oxford: Oxford University Press, 1995), 340.

[156] Their relationship was one of acquaintances rather than close friends. We know that Ella dined at Thackeray's in 1852 (diary, 4 April 1852; EllaC, MS 121), and that a letter from Thackeray (dated 9 April, year not given) was prized enough by Ella for him to frame it with the writer's photograph (EllaC, MS 47), but its tone and sub-stance suggest relative formality. There is no trace of Ella in *The Letters and Private Papers of William Makepeace Thackeray*, ed. Gordon N. Ray, 4 vols (London: Oxford University Press, 1945–6), or in the supplementary volumes published by Garland in 1994. Thackeray would have been aware of some of the squibs made at Ella's expense in the columns of *Punch* around this time: 'A Musical Snuggery' (vol.22, 1852, p. 54) and 'The Boys and the Lamps' (vol.26, 1854, p. 223).

[157] *MW* (21 March 1857), 184–6; (2 May 1857), 280–1; (23 May 1857), 326, 327; (30 May 1857), 345–6; and (4 July 1857), 427. On *The Era* and its tradition of gossip and litigation, see Jane W. Stedman, 'Theatre', *Victorian Periodicals and Victorian Soci-ety*, ed. J. Don Vann and Rosemary T. VanArsdel (Toronto: University of Toronto Press, 1994), 162–76, at 167–9.

inappropriate, vulgar and lacking in discrimination – and they did so with the predictability of those predisposed to repudiate overt forms of commercial promotion.[158] One writer claimed Ella was brainwashing a gullible and ignorant group of fashionables.[159] There was also much muttering about Ella's pushing of his own achievements, skills and intellect in print – something which, distasteful though it seemed, was closely tied into the business of promoting the Musical Union, and a sign of the times. Increasingly, self-puffery was becoming the only way to make one's mark in the commercial Victorian world, apparent in George Eliot's novel *Middlemarch*. Her Dr Lydgate explains:

> I must do as other men do, and think what will please the world and bring in money; look for a little opening in the London crowd, and push myself; set up in a watering place, or go to some southern town where there are plenty of idle English, and get myself puffed.[160]

To top it all, there was professional antagonism towards Ella's impertinence in taking issue in his concert programmes with what the critics had written about Musical Union performances. Davison, who hated this aspect of Ella's operation, jeered at Ella's status as 'a mere speculator ("*entrepreneur*" would be the word) […] he neither performs nor composes himself', doubtless seeing his own position as journalist and composer as markedly superior, and singularly failing to acknowledge the significance and necessity of the risk-taker and middleman for musical activities in a modernizing concert world.[161] Most potentially damaging was a personal attack on Ella from a musician named Howard Glover (1819–75), who wrote for the *Morning Post* and who had taken offence at Ella's *Musical Record* column on London music which, in defence of exploited foreign musicians, had made oblique criticisms of Glover's running of the 'Educational Concerts for the People' at St Martin's Hall.[162] Glover proceeded to try to set the record straight

[158] Similarly, complaints that Ella's promotion of the makers of the pianos used in Musical Union concerts was in poor taste (*MW*, 3 May 1856, pp. 280–1).

[159] *MW* (23 May 1857), 327. The correspondence is signed 'An English Musician'.

[160] Cited in Morgan, 'Puffery', 32.

[161] *MW* (23 May 1857), 329.

[162] *MR* (19 May 1857), p. xi. The article criticizes 'importuning beneficiaries and needy speculators' who take advantage of foreign artists; the passage in question reads: 'All he [the artist] gets in return is a flourish from some journalist *impresario* that Herr, Monsieur, Signor, or Madame, as the case may be, was honoured with a crowded and brilliant assemblage of fashion and aristocracy, though late in the season, and that the gifted artist fully realized the high opinion *we* entertained of his genius at the "Educational Concerts for the People", a series of mongrel entertainments approved by the press, disapproved by the professors, and *conducted*

and to expose Ella's 'mendacity', poor character and sycophancy in a long letter to the *Musical World* that Davison published in May 1857.[163] As a piece of writing it is breathtakingly vitriolic in tone; in it Ella is cast as a 'perfect blank' of a musician, an aristocratic 'flunkey' and a 'laughing-stock' among his friends.

The rights and wrongs of the accusations are difficult to untangle: suffice to say that neither party was factually correct in all its assertions, and that Glover's account of Ella's character was excessively partisan, almost burlesque. What matters most is what these journalistic kerfuffles and their possibly deliberate timing reveal about the pettiness, hidden agendas, and latent social tensions within the British music profession. Davison was a reluctant admirer of Ella's activities, and although there had been some softening in his attitude in the 1840s, the fifties had brought renewed disputes. Ella had declined to book Davison's pianist wife Arabella Goddard, then at the beginning of her career, after she requested more money than Ella thought she was worth; and there had been other private disagreements between the two men.[164] More significantly, Davison was in the orbit of the Garrick Club around the time that Ella put himself forward for membership: 20 May 1857.[165] Curiously, and perhaps not a touch coincidentally, the same week attacks on Ella appeared in the musical and theatrical press. The Garrick was the gentlemen's club where actors, writers and artists famously mingled with aristocracy (compare the Musical Union), and would have had strong appeal to Ella as

> by a newspaper reporter [my italics], who had nothing to lose, nobody to pay, and everything to gain.'

[163] *MW* (30 May 1857), 345–6.

[164] On Arabella's fee, see diary, 1 March 1854 (EllaC, MS 123): 'Mrs A. Goddard asks £ao–ao [£10 10s] to play at the M.W.E. I refuse to give more than £5–5–'. Ella later (? late 1860s) defended his decision (as acting on Davison's advice) in a letter to Davison (in the Arabella Goddard Collection, Her Majesty's Theatre, Ballarat, Australia). I am grateful to Therese Ellsworth for supplying me with a copy of this correspondence.

On the Ella–Davison animosity, see the misunderstanding alluded to in Ella's letter to Davison of June 1851 (BL, Add. MS 70921, f. 93). For his part, Ella wrote warmly of Davison's criticism – especially of Mendelssohn – in *RMU* into the mid-1850s, even referring positively to their relationship: 'We have lived on the best terms, closely allied in friendship together for many years, but like "brothers at the bar", although occasionally opposed to each other on professional questions, in matters of feeling, and affection for the art, we are mostly agreed' (*RMU*, 1854, p. 10).

[165] The 1857 diary (EllaC, MS 126) indicates that Ella put forward his nomination on 20 May. The candidates' book in the Garrick Club Archives, London, confirms this and the names of his proposer (Charles Dance) and seventeen seconders (who did not include Davison).

a useful networking arena: indeed, a handful of Garrickmen were already among Ella's audience.[166] Social kudos was attached, with only a few distinguished – and clearly respectable – London musicians having achieved membership, among them Sir George Smart, Michael Costa and Michael Balfe.[167] Davison himself seems to have been trying for election, for a second time: he had been blackballed on his first attempt in 1854.[168] In the end, Ella withdrew his nomination. Whether it was a result of the smear campaign, or a change of priorities, is unclear.[169] But some of the mud stuck, as an apocryphal anecdote, relayed in print years later, suggests. Its message further indicates that Ella's upward social mobility eventually became well known:

> When he [Ella] was nominated for membership in the Garrick Club his proposer described Ella in the candidates' book, according to the French custom as *rentier*. This was noticed by Albert Smith, who, being a man brusque and blunt, dashed his pen through the description, and wrote in the word "fiddler".[170]

[166] E.g. Lord Saltoun, Tom Taylor and Owen Jones (ibid.). Sir Andrew Barnard had been a founder member of the Garrick (Richard Hough, *The Ace of Clubs: a History of the Garrick* (London: André Deutsch, 1986), pp. 15–16).

[167] Michael Sanderson, in his *From Irving to Olivier: a Social History of the Acting Profession in England from 1880 to 1983* (London: Athlone, 1984), shows that even actors were a minority group; but musicians must have been an even smaller presence.

[168] The candidates' books and committee minutes in the Garrick Club archives show that Davison's first attempt at election (February–March 1854) was unsuccessful. Exactly when he was elected is unclear (the archives have no trace of his subsequent election), but he did become a member, because on 17 April 1858 he was ousted for non-payment of his fee. I am grateful to Marcus Risdell, archivist at the Garrick Club, for help in tracing the circumstances of this membership. A letter from Thackeray to Davison (in *DavisonFM*, pp. 223–4) suggests Davison stood for election around August 1856.

[169] The withdrawal is noted in the Garrick Club's candidates' book, but no date is given. Ella did not note this action in his diary.

[170] Published in *The Falcon*, i, ed. T. J. Wilkinson (Thirsk, 1889), 250, in an account drawn in part from R. V. Taylor's sketches of 'Yorkshire' musicians. The records in the Garrick Club archives show this story, recounted some forty years after the event, to have little veracity. In the candidates' book Ella gave his 'rank' as director of the Musical Union, not rentier; and there is no evidence of the record having been altered or annotated. Still, Smith probably knew something of Ella's origins; he was in Thackeray's circle, and had written the second of the *Punch* pieces satirizing Ella, as Ella discovered (diary, 13 July 1854, EllaC, MS 123: 'A. Smith confessed that he wrote The Article in Punch, on the Sheet Music, & "Sable Ella"').

Howard Glover was not in the Garrick, but he and Davison were members of the same clique, which may explain some of his predisposed antipathy towards Ella; as might an occasion earlier in 1857 when an established London critic (? Davison) was refused admission to the Musical Union.[171] To some extent the mud-slinging was part and parcel of journalistic life in the Victorian era, just as it was indicative of a music profession that operated in a competitive market-place. Equally, professional jealousies of the self-important manager who had once been no more than a jobbing newspaper reporter and player – effectively one of 'them' – but who had moved on to greater professional and social success, were a strong motivating factor. Scorning Ella as a parasitic middleman and non-practitioner came easily, particularly in times when commercialism was threatening to overturn the established, genteel ways of the musical world.

There were also, underneath the anti-Ella campaign, other, equally potent class tensions deriving from the British music profession's long-standing, uneasy relationship with the *beau monde*, and from incipient changes to the *status quo* as musicians like Ella (Sir George Smart was another) gained unprecedented social access to the upper ranks. Envy, resentment and disparagement of those who managed such social advancement were common; and hostility towards the aristocracy could be heightened morally by championing the rights of the lower orders – Glover's 'People', with whom most musicians probably felt a natural affinity – to 'good music'. Continental musicians, who were fêted by the aristocracy and found it easy to gain access to their social milieu, were also prone to be vilified by many of their British counterparts, though here the picture was further complicated by the fact that foreigners were perceived to be robbing British-born performers of work, and to be limiting the opportunities for native composers to get their music played. Indeed, these xenophobic tendencies may have been further inflected in the 1850s by the immediacy of the 'refugee question' and a general hostility towards exiles in public opinion.[172] Ella's set-up, with its nexus of high society, European artists and non-British music, was doomed to be castigated by many of his peers; and though he did not respond directly to Glover's and Davison's charges, Ella continued to decry the insularity of the British music lobby, including Davison, and the antipathy of the press towards eminent European musicians (among them Clara

---

[171] Letter from 'An English Musician', *MW* (23 May 1857), 327. Glover's chumminess with Davison is described in *DiehlMM*, 142. Again, for his part, Ella had been generally positive about Glover as a critic (*RMU*, 1856, p. 32) before the outburst about Glover's concert initiative.

[172] The dialogue may have been inflected by hostilities towards refugees, which came to a head in the 1850s in spite of Britain's liberal policies on asylum. See Porter, *The Refugee Question*.

Schumann and Anton Rubinstein), from the platform of his *Musical Record*.[173] In any case, public outspokenness on what he passionately believed in was coming naturally to Ella, helped along as much by growing confidence in his social and economic position as by the experience and wisdom of ageing: he was now in his mid-fifties. Taking the knocks was part of life, and all prominent figures, including Davison, had to deal with them. Thackeray put it well: 'literary men must make enemies as they make friends'.[174] To survive, one grew a thicker skin and looked to the future and new initiatives.

---

[173] See e.g. Ella's article 'Rubinstein', *MR* (30 June 1857), pp. xxv–xxvi, and his 'Foreign Artists and Native Cliques', *MR* (14 July 1857), p. xxix.

[174] *DavisonFM*, 224.

CHAPTER 5

New Spaces, 1858–68

FROM the late 1850s Ella's position in London life looked unassailable. The Musical Union went from strength to strength, Ella's profits increased and he was able to take fresh initiatives and develop his high-minded agendas in new arenas. In turn, his sphere of influence, social advancement and overt cosmopolitanism continued to grow, and soon he would boast an address in Piccadilly, friends in high places, a stake in national debates on music, and connections and a reputation across much of central Europe. Even the trenchant Viennese music critic Eduard Hanslick wrote admiringly of Ella's achievements, describing Musical Union concerts (which he witnessed in 1862) as belonging to 'the best and most fashionable' and having 'something of the Hellmesbergers' efforts about them' – a reference to the high-minded quartet concerts in Vienna led by Joseph Hellmesberger.[1] For although slightly mocking of the (English) audience's need for guidance on music and of Ella's sometimes overblown language and pompous manner, he appreciated the innovative merits of the programme notes and was impressed by such audiences' 'exemplary' attention and quiet.[2] Eventually, though, Ella encountered setbacks – personal and professional – as his life and promotions in the 1860s took a series of turns, some of which he could never have envisaged, and most of which have escaped historical narratives. Ella dealt with these new situations pragmatically, without losing sight of what mattered to him. In fact, from the outside, it probably looked like 'business as usual'.

---

[1] *HanslickA*, 509. When visiting London more than twenty years later Hanslick lamented the passing of the Musical Union, having found 'no chamber music sanctuary as brilliant or as stable as Ella's Musical Union used to be' ('Letter from London [1886]', *Hanslick's Music Criticisms*, trans. and ed. Henry Pleasants (New York: Dover Publications, 1988), pp. 246–74, at 261).

[2] *HanslickA*, 513. The Musical Union was depicted as an exemplar of good audience behaviour. In another passage Hanslick described Ella as a 'vain old man who […] buzzes around, seizes artists' hands, smiles at the ladies, and when necessary turns the pages at the piano and does whatever artistic duties are needed' (p. 509). Ella was also someone who had 'the impudence to praise Beethoven' in his programme notes (p. 513).

🎵 St James's Hall

*I shall never forget the delightful hours which I have spent at the
Musical Union Concerts held at St. James's Hall. The quartet players
occupied a raised platform in the centre of the room – the sound was
thus equally diffused. The Professor, alive at all points, in every way
personally conducted the programme. He moved about amongst
his assembled friends like one in his own family circle; the élite of
English musical society was to be found there, and Ella looked as
if he felt that he was the real musical father of them all – and so, in
fact, he was.*
                                                        ❧ *HaweisJE*

THE building of a new concert hall was an important event for any fast-growing
conurbation in the mid-Victorian period, as the histories of such centres as
Birmingham, Liverpool, Leeds, Bradford or Belfast clearly testify. Here the erection
of a public space for the performing arts became unabashedly associated with the
development of civic identity and pride, not to mention a touch of urban rivalry.[3]
In London, the picture was different. The growing, sprawling capital had no focal
point in its geography, no unifying municipal government before the establishment of the London County Council in 1888, no single urban identity and consequently no one hall 'for London'. Public buildings and concert venues were, rather,
dotted around Westminster, the City, the inner suburbs and (later) the outer ones,
and carried mainly localized significance. At the same time the West End was
widely regarded as the acme of metropolitan cultural activity, its leaders wanting
to be seen to lead the nation's music. So as new, large halls were erected in cities
around the country in the 1840s and 50s, usually funded through private finance
and providing up-to-the-minute accommodation, the fact that London still had
no adequate modern venue for the performance of large-scale music rankled considerably, particularly with concert promoters.[4] It had been cause enough for Ella
to comment in 1849: 'Really, when we find in almost every great town in England
a music hall, and in London nothing better than the murky, ill-contrived Exeter

---

[3] See Roy Johnston, '"Here will we sit": the Creation of the Ulster Hall', *MBC*,
215–32.

[4] The building of concert halls mid-century typically involved the creation of a local,
private shareholding company. The establishment of the Colston Hall in Bristol
(opened 1867) is one example of this (see H. E. Meller, *Leisure and the Changing City, 1870–1914*; London: Routledge & Kegan Paul, 1976, pp. 57, 220); there
are many others. Such private investment was usually encouraged by municipal
authorities, who could see the economic and social benefits to the community that
a concert hall might bring.

Hall, we blush for the citizens of this mighty metropolis'.[5] And in the first prospectus for the St James's Hall Company (1856), which was formed to build a modern performance venue for London, it appeared as a key reason for the initiative, Ella soon afterwards visiting St George's Hall in Liverpool and declaring it 'beautiful, classical, and spacious'.[6]

Ella had a vested interest in St James's Hall. He began as one of its founding shareholders, and went on to become a member of the steering committee of six, sitting alongside three music publishers, Frederick C. Leader, Frederick Beale and William Chappell (the last two now in business together as Cramer, Beale & Chappell), the conductor Julius Benedict and one George Smith;[7] all later became directors of the company.[8] A site had been acquired in the fashionable

5   *RMU* (1849), 8. Ella conceded that conditions at Exeter Hall improved in 1850, when alterations, including a raised roof, were effected (*RMU*, 1850, p. 34), but by 1853 he was back campaigning for a good venue for music (*RMU*, 1853, p. 38).

6   The prospectus, issued by August 1856, opined: 'While this acknowledged want has long since been supplied in Liverpool, Birmingham, and other Provincial Cities, the Metropolis remains singularly deficient in proper accommodation for such performances [large-scale, high-quality ones], possessing, in fact, no building well adapted to the purpose.' (Scrapbook, EllaC, MS 80, between pp. 2 and 3.) Ella's comments on the Liverpool hall are in his diary, 10 October 1856 (EllaC, MS 125).

7   The founding shareholders are listed in the company's memorandum of association dated 9 August 1856, which is preserved in PRO, BT 31/3/24. As well as Ella there was Charles Moreing (architect), Thomas Patey Chappell (music publisher, with a business in New Bond Street), Edward Land (professor of music), Frederick Patey Chappell (solicitor), William Chappell (music publisher, in business with Cramer and Beale) and Owen Jones (architect). Between them they had agreed to hold 400 shares (value £4,000). Ella had twenty-five (value £250); most of the others held fifty. The largest shareholder was Moreing (who had originally sold the land to the company); he took 150 shares, though he sold them on relatively quickly.

   Of these shareholders, only two – Ella and William Chappell – were part of the 'Provisional [i.e. steering] Committee' (its membership is given in the prospectus of 1856; see EllaC, MS 80, between pp. 2 and 3). All the committee men held shares, mostly fifty apiece, except for Benedict who, like Ella, held twenty-five (see the summary of the capital and shares at 20 August 1857; PRO, BT 31/3/24). In a later list of shareholders (1867; ibid.), George Smith is given as a china and glass dealer; his address in 1857 was 57 Conduit Street, Regent Street.

8   By November 1857 there were eight 'Directors' leading operations, the six from the committee plus Edward Land (musician) and George Metzler (music publisher): a 'body of practical men' according to a feature on the back cover of *RMU* (1857), which included an account of the hall published in the *Observer* (21 November 1857).

area of St James's tucked between no. 28 Piccadilly and the Quadrant (curved) stretch of Nash's Regent Street; Owen Jones, formerly superintendent of works for the Great Exhibition and also a founding shareholder, was appointed chief architect. The company, one of the new 'limited liability' types which sought to protect the public at large, next sought to raise the projected capital outlay of £40,000, through shares issued at £10 each.[9] The take-up was fair, the project attracting a host of small investors, including many London musicians and music traders. Even so, the company sought takers for larger investments in the form of debentures (long-term securities). Apparently, Thomas Brassey had £4,000 worth.[10]

Undoubtedly, social networks played an important role in shaping the company's officers and first swathe of investors.[11] For his part, Ella was well known to Beale and the Chappell family, and had possibly been instrumental in putting forward acquaintances from the Musical Union, perhaps inveigling Jones as architect, suggesting Mrs Grote's husband's firm as one of the company's bankers, or persuading Brassey and others to invest. It was surely a measure of Ella's desire to shape West End music that he was at the project's nerve-centre: and as the sole concert manager among the directors he would have brought a range of valuable experience to the initiative, even if his relatively small share-holding limited the influence he would ultimately wield. Indeed, in spite of his dislike of committee structures, he found there were opportunities to mould affairs.[12] His diaries show that he had a say in all sorts of matters, including establishing rates for room hire and the nature of the seating, and arguing against holding promenade concerts in

---

[9] The Joint Stock Companies Act was passed in 1856, at the height of the railway building boom. It restricted the financial liability of each investor to the amount invested, should the company fail.

[10] Noted in Ella's diary, 22 December 1856 (EllaC, MS 125). Ella appears to have had debentures worth £500 (according to his account book, EllaC, MS 6, p. 241 and *passim*). There is no promotion of debentures in the prospectus of August 1856.

[11] The officers were: Robert Addison, the company's auditor, a former partner in Cramer and Beale's publishing house; Thomas Patey Chappell, the second auditor, brother of William; and Frederick Patey Chappell, the solicitor, who was presumably related to Thomas Patey and William.

[12] His difficulties in operating as a committee man are indicated by an entry in his diary, 10 December 1857 (EllaC, MS 126), when following a row with the Chappells about the appointment of a hall keeper (they felt it premature; Ella thought otherwise) and other matters, he resolved to retire from the board of directors. This resolution was never followed through, suggesting that Ella realized, especially once he had decided to move the Musical Union into the hall, that it was better to have some voice in the company's affairs than none at all.

the hall; there is also evidence that he sought to influence Jones on the interior's design.[13]

By today's standards the hall went up in double-quick time, opening on schedule on 25 March 1858 with a grand inaugural concert.[14] The building was state-of-the-art and on an impressive scale.[15] There were four points of entrance and five exits: Jones's Piccadilly frontage (Fig. 12) was linked to the main hall by a long corridor, while the Regent Street entrance offered more immediate access to facilities. The main auditorium, elegantly and ornately decorated in hues of pale blue, yellow, white and red, was situated on the first floor, reached by three wide internal staircases with spacious landings. A balcony extended around three sides of the hall and was crowned by an upper, third-storey gallery opposite the plat- form end. At night the room was lit, not by central chandeliers, but by several stars of gaslight hung from its barrel-vaulted, panelled ceiling (Fig. 13). Better still, the ventilation was said to be the best of any hall in town. Underneath the main auditorium were two smaller rooms, one intended as a refreshment hall, the other for concerts or functions such as scientific meetings and private dinners, it having been a corollary aim of the company to provide '[h]alls of a smaller description in a locality easily accessible and convenient for the aristocracy'.[16] In time, the venue would be deemed old-fashioned, inadequate, draughty and a fire risk: for now, it seemed a modern, elegant dream.[17] Chorley, reporting on the opening choral

---

[13] See the entries for 31 October and 17 November (room hire rates), 10 December (promenade concerts) and 31 December 1857 (seating): EllaC, MS 126. An undated letter from Ella to Fétis (surely written during 1857; WangerméeF, 403–4) asked for one of Fétis's publications on acoustics on behalf of Jones. It also indicated that Ella had views about how to arrange the concert platform. He explained: 'I propose that the organ in St James' Hall be constructed, so as not to obtrude into the orchestra and divide the executants. Thus I propose to arrange the large tubes around each side, the orchestra with the manuels [sic] in the centre.' On this matter, his ideas did not come to pass.

[14] Noted in Ella's diary, 25 March 1858 (EllaC, MS 127).

[15] The physical description that follows is drawn from more detailed accounts in ILN (3 and 10 April 1858), 353, 369–70; Athenaeum (27 March 1858), 409; and Survey of London, 31: The Parish of St James Westminster, part 2: North of Piccadilly (London: Athlone Press; University of London, 1963), 59–62.

[16] Prospectus (EllaC, MS 80, between pp. 2 and 3).

[17] A series of modifications to the building took place over the years (described in Survey of London), including amplified restaurant facilities with ovens in situ – a real innovation. But complaints grew of kitchen odours wafting into the main hall; likewise of sounds from the smaller hall penetrating (most famously, from the Moore and Burgess Minstrels, who performed in the small concert room for more than twenty years). The seats too were eventually deemed uncomfortable, and by

12 Exterior of St James's Hall: Piccadilly entrance. Engraving from the *Illustrated London News*, 3 April 1858. Reproduced with permission of the Rare Book & Manuscript Library of the University of Illinois, Urbana-Champaign.

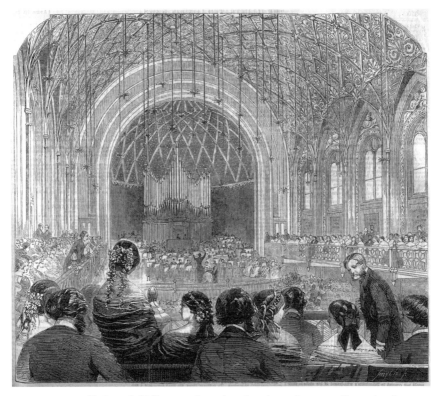

13 Interior of St James's Hall, set up for a choral-orchestral concert. Engraving from
the *Illustrated London News*, 10 April 1858. Reproduced with permission of the Rare
Book & Manuscript Library of the University of Illinois, Urbana-Champaign.

spectacle in his *Athenaeum* column, gave much of his attention to the décor and
colour scheme, remarking of the sound only that '[t]he ear has nothing to desire
in *St. James's Hall*'.[18] Ella, more circumspectly and pragmatically, noted in his
diary merely that, with just 430 people present, the acoustics were 'perfect in [the]
Balcony'.[19]

Ella decided to move the Musical Union out of Willis's Rooms into the new
hall in late December 1857. The relocation was necessary if Ella was to continue
to exploit the rising demand for his concerts, quite simply because his current
accommodation had begun to impose a considerable constraint on the enterprise.
As he put it: 'In Willis's Rooms, with our small *palco* in the centre, we have never

the 1890s there was a palpable need once more for a new, modern hall in the West
End.
[18] *Athenaeum* (27 March 1858), 409.
[19] Diary, 25 March 1858 (EllaC, MS 127).

been able to seat more than 550 persons', and although he admitted that far more bodies could be packed in 'irrespective of ease and comfort', to do so would have been unthinkable for a gathering of gentlefolk.[20] The new hall was much larger and more imposing than Willis's. Rectangular, with a semicircular apse for choir and organ at the west end, it measured 139 ft × 59 ft (the floor space was less: 95 ft × 57 ft), while its height, to the apex of the domed ceiling, was 60 ft.[21] All in all it was a hall for choral or orchestral music, so using it for chamber music raised many of the same issues that Ella had had to address at Willis's back in 1846. For even allowing for the drying effect on sound that bodies produce in a concert hall, and the possibility of giving performances in the round, there was still likely to be too much blurring reverberation for Ella's programmes of small-scale, intricate chamber music, where different instrumental lines and quicksilver changes in texture and effect needed to be heard.

Once again Ella did his best to make the space as intimate as possible. To reduce and dampen the acoustic space he curtained off the apse and the upper east gallery. He reintroduced the central podium, by now a sort of trademark, arranging the audience around it on the new, comfortable sofa benches, with the aim of achieving an equal and agreeable diffusion of sound (Fig. 14).[22] On paper it was an admirable plan. But after a pre-season try-out, attended by some 600, Ella felt compelled to admit to his diary: '[e]ffect good in some respects, less good in others'.[23] Even so, in his programme for the first matinée of 1858 he glossed the matter, advising listeners that the hall 'realises our most sanguine expectations of its acoustic properties', and citing Sir George Smart's reactions by way of endorsement.[24] Having listened from various spots in the hall, Smart had found them all satisfactory, including the 'upper end of the hall near the orchestra [area]', where he claimed to have 'heard every note of Mozart's "Adagio con Sordini"'.[25] In fact, fine adjustments were required, and Ella continued to assess the whereabouts of the best seats in the house – eventually concluding they were either to the right of the pianist and violinist, or in the front row of

[20] *RMU* (1857), 32. The quotation goes on to explain: 'Manchester Free Trade Hall, it is said, seats 4,000 of the *people*, but only 2,000 of the *gentry*.'

[21] Willis's reached only 30 ft.

[22] Ella likened the effect to waves emanating from the centre of a pond when a pebble is thrown in ('The Private Reception, April 8th', *RMU*, 1858, p. 7).

[23] Diary, 8 April 1858 (EllaC, MS 127).

[24] Ella's comments are in *RMU* (1858), 2. See also the letter from Smart to Ella, dated 10 April 1858, and published in 'The Private Reception, April 8th', *RMU* (1858), 7–8; in it Smart admitted his fears about the acoustic had been allayed.

[25] Ibid.

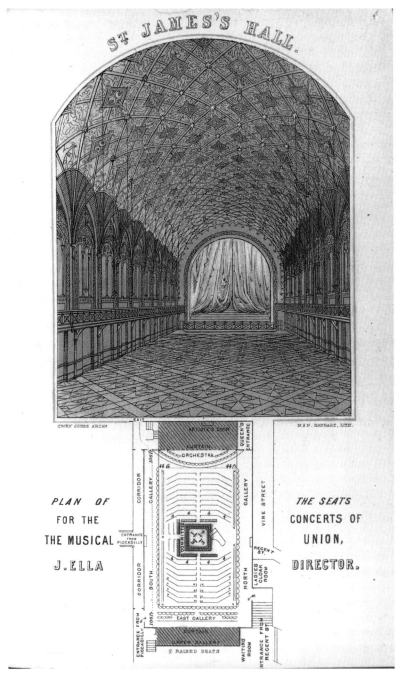

14 Interior of St James's Hall and seating plan for Musical Union concerts. Engravings published in the *Record of the Musical Union* (1858). © British Library Board. All Rights Reserved (P.P.1945.1). The committee members had reserved seats in the front row.

the north gallery and any part of the other galleries – and to contemplate other measures.[26] To judge from some press reporting of the first season at St James's, and Ella's public remarks to Musical Union audiences, not everyone was immediately convinced by the new locale.[27] But the dissent died down, and at the season's end the Musical Union committee officially approved St James's as the concerts' permanent base. The new venue's benefits were seen to outweigh its drawbacks.[28]

Ella's principal aim in moving to St James's – to increase his audiences – was realized spectacularly during that first year, which saw several appearances by Joachim and Rubinstein, including three concerts in which they played together. Rubinstein's presence was big news: his performances the previous season had seen to that, and his reputation as the most extraordinary of pianists already went before him. Memberships jumped by fifty. Single-ticket sales climbed once more, bringing in c.£500 across the series, and audiences apparently numbered around 800 on more than one occasion.[29] Chances to hear such artistry and musicianship were not to be missed – that point cannot be stressed enough, for this was happening long before international players could be heard in London night after

[26] *RMU* (1858), 21; sitting to the left or bass side of the pianist should be avoided at all costs. Ella also considered placing a canopy over the palco 'to disseminate the sound more laterally', and insisted that the piano lid should never be partially open, as this obscured the view of the pianist; it should, rather, be set either fully up or down. He recommended a closed lid for the 'delicate' music of the classical masters ('The Private Reception', *RMU*, 1858, p. 7).

[27] 'The new building has certainly the advantage of being able to hold a larger audience; but we are not satisfied as to its equal aptitude for "chamber" concerts' (*ILN*, 1858, p. 391). '[W]hatever difference of opinion may exist on the change of locality, no one, we believe, would exchange the convenience of St. James's Hall, for the discomfort experienced [at Rubinstein's performance in Willis's Rooms, 1857]' (Ella in *RMU*, 1858, p. 21).

[28] *RMU* (1858), 50. Ella defended the decision by suggesting that had the concerts remained at Willis's Rooms, the subscription would have had to have doubled and visitors disallowed. On previous occasions (*RMU*, 1858, p. 8 and *RMWE*, 1858, p. 20) he had outlined the shortcomings of Willis's. They included the inability to open windows because of the infiltration of street noise in the height of summer; inadequate seating, some people having to stand at Rubinstein's 1857 appearance; and the inconvenience to members of two societies meeting on the premises at the same time, in a building with only one entrance. All these matters were rectified at St James's Hall.

[29] Single-ticket sales are noted as reaching more than £530 in the account book (EllaC, MS 6), p. 47 (elsewhere calculable as being in the region of c.£482; op. cit., pp. 104–5). Ella's estimates of audience size can be found in *RMU* (1858): 780 people at the third matinée (p. 21), 800 at the fourth (p. 32).

night, all year round. The largest takings were for the concert on 25 May, in which (by all accounts, including Ella's) Joachim and 'Ruby' gave a stunning account of Beethoven's 'Kreutzer' sonata.[30]

Yet the best was still ahead. In the seven years that followed, the upward march of audience numbers continued, and the institution experienced a period of unprecedented glory involving a stream of great artists leading distinguished and memorable performances of classic chamber works, ever more listeners, continually rising profitability, and a growing renown for both the society's seriousness of purpose and Ella's unique achievements. The first season at St James's produced a record 480 subscribers (compared with 430 the previous year); by 1865 it had reached a high of 565.[31] Meanwhile, ticket sales were in good shape, and especially buoyant when eminent players were billed. In June 1859, 181 people paid to hear Clara Schumann and Joachim play Haydn, Beethoven and Mendelssohn.[32] Seemingly, the enterprise was undented by further attacks on Ella in the *Musical World* and by Davison's refusal to cover the concerts in that journal or *The Times* from 1858.[33]

Where were the audience recruits coming from? The network played a large part, membership still being regulated by the personal recommendation (in writing) of others already in the society, as in a latter-day tennis or golf club. In theory, only those with serious musical credentials as well as links to the 'community' were admitted, though whether anyone was ever turned down on technical

---

[30] According to the account book (EllaC, MS 6), p. 104, 246 single tickets were sold for this event. *ILN* (29 May 1858) wrote: 'Stimulated by each other they played with marvellous fire and brilliancy, giving a colouring to the music of which we had formed no conception. [...] This was one of the most splendid concerts ever given by the Musical Union.' The writer was possibly George Hogarth, who worked on the paper, 1845–70, or Charles Gruneisen, on whom Ella could always rely for positive comment.

[31] Account book (EllaC, MS 6), p. 47.

[32] Account book (EllaC, MS 6), p. 105 (6th concert).

[33] For anti-Ella coverage, see the editorial in *MW* (2 July 1859), 424–5, and correspondence and features in *MW* (2 July 1859), 430; (9 July 1859), 442; and (16 July 1859), 454; see also (4 October 1862), 627.
  The Times and *MW* ceased reviewing the concerts after a series of disagreements in print between Ella and Davison, mostly arising from the latter's critical account of one of Clara Schumann's performances, and from his knocking of Ella's promotion of Rubinstein. Davison's justification for the gesture is discussed in *DavisonFM*, 234. In fact, short reports of Ella's concerts returned to *MW* in 1864, quite possibly written by someone else on the paper. Davison continued to criticize Ella in discursive articles in this journal and elsewhere.

grounds is unclear, since the screening process was not formalized – something Davison lighted on in his press columns.[34] (On the other hand, Ella's club was not for the musically faint-hearted, so self-regulation was implicit.) Once enrolled, members were encouraged to buy one-off admissions for guests at the door, thus widening the social web further. Set against this, those getting in on tickets bought in advance from music shops were no longer necessarily linked into the membership network, though self-evidently such people would have needed the requisite wealth and leisure to participate in the first place. This aspect of Ella's administration, which aimed to attract a wider slice of aspirants to high culture, dated back to 1847, when Ella first advertised a limited number of tickets for sale at Cramer's and Ollivier's. Since then the number of vending outlets had increased to five, all in close proximity to Piccadilly (including Cramer, Chappell, and later Ashdown & Parry). Press advertising had widened, and the issue of tickets had ceased to be ostensibly sanctioned by Ella himself or limited in number, although names were carefully entered by Ella into a ticket book, after each concert, for two seasons at least.[35]

It was clear, too, that Ella's audiences were no longer exclusively from the West End. Some of the new recruits came from those newly built inner suburbs – Kensington, Clapham, Hampstead, Dulwich – into which wealthy families were moving. Others arrived from further out – Blackheath, Hendon, even the Home Counties – travelling up to town by train. It was indeed a sign of the times that in 1859 Ella had to try to ensure concerts began and ended promptly '[t]o suit the convenience of Members leaving town by the six o'clock train for their country residences'.[36] In fact, quietly and discreetly, an increasing middle-class element – albeit those from the upper layers, keen to identify with high society – seems to have been absorbed into the organization, as indicated by Ella's preparedness to advertise to potential ticket-purchasers in the *Daily Telegraph*, the new 1d broadsheet, from

[34] '[B]ut to obtain the *entrée* to the *matinées* of the "Musical Union," it is necessary either to procure tickets through the intervention of a member, or to acquire the privileges of membership; in which latter case the candidate for the right of buying a season-ticket must be nominated and formally introduced to Mr. Ella. As Mr. Ella graciously accepts all candidates who are duly presented to him, the process in question does not, as a rule, involve any serious difficulties. No certificates are required, no examination of any kind is imposed' (*MW*, 8 July 1865, p. 420; reprinted from the *Pall Mall Gazette*).

[35] A ticket book, indicating subscribers buying additional admissions on the door and the names of those who had bought tickets at a music shop, survives for the period 1859–60 (EllaC, MS 48). Payment of subscriptions was also more distanced, being now administered through the ticket outlets.

[36] *RMU* (1859), 17.

the early 1860s.[37] Meanwhile, the majority of listeners were increasingly women, the main consumers of music lessons: 72 per cent in 1860, a rise of some 12 per cent from ten years earlier. The womenfolk of piano manufacturer Henry Fowler Broadwood (1811–93), whose family were long-standing supporters of both the Musical Union and Ella's evening concerts, were typical of this musically informed and often quite critical following, if the diary of his daughter Bertha is anything to go by.[38]

Ella continued to hire, where possible, the best European instrumentalists, since it was star names above all else that drew in extra listeners. With the market growing, it largely depended on who was in London and available at the right time for Ella's season. Sometimes he had to settle for second best, which perhaps explains the once-only appearance of pianist Oscar de Cinna in the first concert of 1858 (playing Weber's piano sonata in D minor op. 49, he had neither the physical strength nor reputation to fill the hall with sound or visitors), and the presence of the violinist Herr Japha to lead Beethoven's quartet op. 18 no. 4 and Spohr's piano quintet op. 53 in 1863. (Bertha Broadwood described him as 'a new man of whom I thought no great things'.)[39] They were competent performers, but not top rank. Mostly, though, the Musical Union was host to the finest chamber music players, with Ella now almost always prepared to go the additional mile to secure a coveted booking, and paying more as needed, too.[40] Joachim and Rubinstein have already

---

37   This assertion about the middle-class audience is strengthened by the fact that the proportion of titled individuals in Ella's membership lists was declining while the total audience increased. In 1860 there were 137 bearers of titles, out of 640: some 21 per cent, compared with 119 out of 310 in 1848 (38 per cent) and 123 out of 523 in 1857 (24 per cent).

38   Bertha Broadwood's diaries (Broadwood Archive, Surrey History Centre, 2185/ BMB/5/13–15) for 1858–9 and 1863–4 show she, her sisters, other family members and friends attended Musical Union concerts. The Broadwoods had a town house in Bryanston Square and a country home in Lyne, Sussex. I am indebted to Dorothy DeVal for providing transcriptions of this material. The Broadwood family is carefully documented in David Wainwright, *Broadwood by Appointment: a History* (London: Quiller Press, 1982), 324–5.

39   Bertha Broadwood's diary, 26 May 1863.

40   A letter from Arthur Chappell to Ella, dated 7 April 1865 (EllaC, MS 156) indicates that Ella was keen to find a way to book Joachim for more than one concert per season. The costs of hiring stars, however, were considerable and mounting: Ella was forced, over time, to pay ever more for the top artists as their reputations and market values increased. Clara Schumann's fees were £26 5s for two concerts in 1859 (£13 2s 6d for each appearance), and £47 5s for three concerts in 1865 (£15 15s per concert). Joachim was paid £52 10s for five concerts (10 guineas per concert) in 1858, but received £126 for six performances (£21 per concert) in 1865.

been mentioned. Hallé and Piatti were an established presence too, offering continuity with previous years. Vieuxtemps, who had last appeared in 1854, was back for occasional seasons in the 1860s, and there were some celebrated, powerful performances by Clara Schumann, who returned in 1859 and 1865 to interpret Beethoven and Mendelssohn piano trios (always with Joachim and Piatti) and her late husband's glorious piano quintet op. 44. A 'solemn "priestess" of the art. Dressed in black, unsmiling and performing "serious" music' is how her modern biographer describes her[41] – she must have been the perfect Musical Union artist.

New sensations also arrived, among them the Polish-born, French-trained violinist Henri Wieniawski, who made his Musical Union début on 17 May 1859 leading quartets by Beethoven (op. 74) and Mozart (K387) and joining Rubinstein in a performance of Mendelssohn's op. 66 piano trio. His impact was immediate, the *Daily News* judging him to have 'few superiors' as a quartet player.[42] A fortnight later the Wieniawski–Rubinstein partnership was further interrogated via Beethoven's weighty 'Archduke' trio, already acknowledged as 'the grandest, chamber instrumental work ever produced'[43] and a piece reserved for the best interpreters. Thereafter Wieniawski became a frequent performer at Ella's concerts whenever he was in England. Another débutant was Leopold Auer, a pupil of Joachim, and later (like Wieniawski, whom he succeeded) professor of violin at the St Petersburg Conservatoire. He first led quartets for Ella in 1863 (Mozart's 'Dissonance', Haydn's 'Emperor', Beethoven's op. 18 no. 3 and Mendelssohn's op. 44 no. 1), and his playing pleased instantly. The *Daily News* felt his tone was 'similar to Joachim's in its rich and vocal quality', while the *Athenaeum* approved its lack of 'trembling' [vibrato] and praised his neat and 'very considerable' execution, tipping him as 'an excellent violinist beginning what we hope will be a long career'.[44] It was: he returned season after season.

But it was chamber-music pianists of calibre who were most coveted, and there were occasional appearances by up-and-coming keyboard players, including

Anton Rubinstein was most expensive of all: his £78 15s for five concerts (£15 15s per concert) in 1859 had increased to £130 for three concerts in 1867 (c.£43 per appearance). Information from the account book (EllaC, MS 6), pp. 45, 49, 53, 64, 69. The fees Ella paid to Joachim and Clara Schumann were slightly better than those offered to them by the Philharmonic around the same time (*EhrlichFP*, 129), though money would eventually become a sticking point there too.

[41] Nancy B. Reich, 'Schumann, Clara', *NGDM2*.

[42] *DN* (19 May 1859).

[43] *ILN* (4 June 1859), 539.

[44] *DN* (11 June 1863) and *Athenaeum* (13 June 1863), 785 [reprinted in *RMU* (1863), 28].

Edward Dannreuther, who partnered Auer in a movement from the 'Kreutzer' (1863; this work was fast becoming the test-piece for those who aspired to the heights of chamber music performance), Theodor Leschetizky, who gave Schumann's piano quintet with Joachim leading (1864), and Agnes Zimmermann, who played Schumann's Andante and Variations, op. 46, with Ernst Pauer (1864). In addition, pianists' interpretative skills as soloists were given an airing in the instrumental 'spot' at the end of each programme, where the solo repertoire choices were the artist's alone. The well-travelled Alfred Jaëll, pupil of Moscheles and famed for his Chopin (though not to everyone's taste – Bertha thought he 'murdered dreadfully' one of the waltzes),[45] was from 1862 the most often heard newcomer pianist, with a strong reputation in several quarters.[46] A less frequent, but fairly regular presence from 1860 was the Paris-based pianist Ernst Lübeck, a serious musician who favoured Beethoven's sonatas and introduced a handful of Bach preludes and fugues. Initially something of an unknown quantity (Bertha declared Lübeck's billing enough to keep the family away, for example)[47] and largely absent from the historical record, he was in fact a linchpin of the Armingaud-Jacquard quartet society in the French capital, and Berlioz rated him as a good player.[48] Though not in Rubinstein's class, both Jaëll and Lübeck had reasonably strong drawing power for the ticket-paying audience.

Handling the concert pamphlets from these years and marvelling at the seemingly seamless flow of fine artists who appeared for Ella, the twenty-first-century scholar can easily underestimate how much 'behind-the-scenes' activity went into making such magic happen. Yet as the Ella Collection shows, the 'fixing' of players and the negotiation of dates, fees, repertoire and other arrangements were becoming increasingly time-consuming affairs for Ella, who did everything singlehanded. It was an acknowledged fact that with transport networks opening up European travel, more and more big-name artists were embarking on punishing

---

[45] Bertha Broadwood's diary, 12 May 1863.

[46] The critic in *DN* (28 May 1862), probably the experienced George Hogarth, wrote with surprise after Jaëll's début in the Mendelssohn trio op. 66 that 'we have never heard that beautiful piece more exquisitely played – not even by Mendelssohn himself'. The *Orchestra* (27 May 1865), 132, later reckoned his 'beautiful touch and facile execution of the most difficult and brilliant music' had gained him 'wide renown on the Continent, since the retirement of Thalberg'.

[47] Bertha Broadwood's diary, 28 April 1863: 'We missed the Musical Union[;] we did not care much for only <u>Lübeck</u> was going to play.'

[48] On his reputation in France, see *FauquetS*, 151 and *passim*; Berlioz's remarks are in the thumbnail biography of Lübeck in *RMU* (1860), 1. We should note too that Ella paid him well (£15 15s per concert in 1863, substantially more than Hallé was getting: EllaC, MS 6, p. 61).

annual concert tours around Europe and even beyond. However, their spells in London were often limited, as were the number of available concert dates within Ella's short season, and bookings made at a distance could take months to sort out (self-evidently, there were no phones, faxes and emails to offer communication in an instant; telegraph was a recent innovation, to be used *in extremis*). If one wanted to secure top-flight performers, it was a good idea to get in early. Ella, ever forward looking, now typically began the processes in the autumn, with an initial letter of enquiry to a potential performer to see whether a trip to England was planned, thereafter employing diplomacy and persuasion as each case demanded. Alongside all this, and inevitably draining on time and ink, should be set the dozens of aspiring artists who wrote to Ella from abroad asking for an engagement, or who arrived on his doorstep with letters of introduction.[49] They were an indication of how far the Musical Union's reputation had travelled. All of them were dealt with cordially, Ella occasionally using his 'trials' – those extra matinées for testing new talent, sometimes new works – to assess the most promising. It was a busy life.

As far as repertoire was concerned during the early St James's Hall years, Ella insisted on a continuing exploration of the classical 'masters'. The one significant change was the admission of some of Schumann's chamber works: see Appendix II. Occurring largely at players' behests, it marked the start of a slow assimilation of Romantic ensemble music into the Musical Union's core stock. Schumann's piano quartet op. 47, which had been hurriedly abandoned by Ella fifteen years earlier, returned at Dannreuther's suggestion in 1863, and was subsequently demanded by Jaëll.[50] The piano quintet op. 44, initially championed by Clara Schumann (1859), was likewise taken up by Nikolay Rubinstein (Anton's brother, 1861), Jaëll (1862) and Leschetizky (1864); there were several repeat performances.[51] To his credit, and despite his private reluctance to embrace much modern chamber music, Ella had been gradually persuaded that these two works were worth persevering with, and had begun to develop some appreciation of them. Although they were becoming widely accepted and admired in Germany, pockets of antagonism remained

[49] Examples are preserved in albums of letters and photographs (EllaC, MSS 3 and 4). The diaries provide further illustration, noting for instance that 'M. Cramer, young Violinist from Amsterdam – wants to make his début' (diary, 19 March 1860; EllaC, MS 129), and recording Ella's verdict: 'Cramer 2–to–3 – à casa has talent but not any remarkable style' (diary, 20 March 1860).

[50] *RMU* (1863), 25; and (1865), 13.

[51] According to *RMU* (1864), 25, the two Schumann works were always 'the choice of one or other of our principal executants'. Clara Schumann repeated the quintet on her visit in 1865; Jaëll played it again in 1863, 1866, 1868, 1870, 1875 and 1877.

in Britain, as both Ella and Clara admitted.[52] Doing his best to advocate them to
audiences and perhaps in spite of his own instincts, he argued, for example, that
the quintet was a 'work so original, melodious, scholastic, and characteristic' that
it needed only to be heard 'efficiently performed, to be admired', as it was abroad
(the implication being that performance quality at the Musical Union would make
this possible), and he wrote his programme analysis in such a way as to point up
its technical qualities.[53] Putting the case for the première of Schumann's op. 105
violin sonata (given by Joachim and Jaëll) in 1864 was doubtless harder, and here
Ella stressed the proven difficulties of passing judgement on works after just one
hearing.[54] But genre and idiom came into the equation too, since the short, imaginative, end-of-concert piano solos by Schumann, Chopin, Liszt, Rubinstein and
others from the Romantic school required no such special pleading or explication,
and were evidently lapped up by Ella's listeners, especially when interpreted by a
leading pianist.[55]

   One of the less tangible, but significant, gains of the new performance setting
at St James's was its intensification of the sacral aspect of the concert experience.

[52] *RMU* (1865), 13: 'The pianoforte Quartet has yet to win its way to public favour
   in England.' In a letter to Ella dated 3 June 1865 (EllaC, ms 156), the British composer Cipriani Potter recounted how he had discussed with Clara the resistance
   to her late husband's music, and noted that 'she is perfectly aware of the prejudice
   existing'. One of the most strident opponents was the Mendelssohn-loving Chorley, who wrote at the time of Dannreuther's performance of the piano quartet that
   he would never 'become reconciled to the hardihood of ugliness which is therein
   paraded by way of originality' (*Athenaeum*, 20 June 1863, p. 817); and said of the
   quintet (Clara's performance): '[i]t is not music for us, nor can we consider its
   repetition here from time to time as a sign that a public is growing up to relish it'
   (*Athenaeum*, 29 April 1865, p. 594). In truth, not all critics or audiences seem to
   have been so opposed: after that same performance the *Orchestra*'s critic felt it was
   '[t]he *bonne bouche*' of a 'recherche [*sic*] banquet of classical music', and described
   Clara's warm reception by the listeners (*Orchestra*, 29 April 1865, p. 69), elsewhere
   alluding to the critical disputes about the quintet but insisting it was a masterpiece
   (*Orchestra*, 23 June 1866, pp. 195–6 [article headed 'Musical Society']).

[53] *RMU* (1862), 25. Ella had evidently admitted to Potter that his audiences did not
   naturally warm to Schumann's works, and that he had his own reservations ('I
   must give you great credit for introducing Schumann's music at your Matinées',
   Potter wrote in his letter to Ella cited above, 'since it is an annoyance to you, and
   you say your subscribers do not admire it'). Publicly in the *RMU*, however, Ella
   appeared something of an advocate for Schumann. For his more general views on
   the dearth of good-quality modern chamber music, see *RMU* (1863), 24.

[54] See the case made for the violin sonata in *RMU* (1864), 19.

[55] E.g. an encore was demanded after Hallé's rendition of Chopin's étude no. 3 in E♭
   (*MW*, 9 April 1864, p. 237).

With its vaulted, domed ceiling, arched windows and intricate sculpture, carvings and gildings, the main hall's interior was strongly suggestive of the architecture of the cathedral or temple, albeit with Moorish influence.[56] Once inside the building, the journey to the inner sanctum was conceived dramatically, via corridors (in the case of the Piccadilly entrance), staircases and landings.[57] On arrival, the 'worshipper' found the musical dimension reinforced by sculpted angels above the windows, holding scrolls bearing the names of Beethoven, Mozart, Haydn, Handel, Bach, Mendelssohn, Cherubini and others; and by the inscription of other composers 'sacred to memory', arranged in historical threesomes on panels underneath the windows.[58] On Musical Union afternoons the space was sanctified further by the positioning of the dais in the centre of the hall, covered with a 'bright crimson cloth' (Ella always having 'an eye to effect'), and by the disposition of the audience around it, with the intention that they focus in on the performance as if in communion at an altar.[59] In this analogy the artists become 'priests', blessed with the special capacity to transmit the composer's intentions to the listener. We can only guess at the nature and intensity of audience experiences, but the potential for both shared communion and private worship was clearly enhanced by the new setting.[60] At the same time, opportunities to engage viscerally or intellectually with the chamber music were fused in: concert-goers could identify at close range

[56] The Piccadilly entrance was deemed by *ILN* to embody 'unmistakable features of Alhambran architecture' (3 April 1858, p. 353), while the panelling of the grand hall ceiling was 'filled with peculiarly Alhambran enrichment in alto-relievo' (10 April 1858, p. 369). Chorley (*Athenaeum*, 27 March 1858, p. 409) thought the lights were suspended like 'the lamps in the mosques'.

[57] This exemplifies the broader point made by T. C. W. Blanning in his 'The Commercialization and Sacralization of European Culture in the Nineteenth Century', *The Oxford Illustrated History of Modern Europe*, ed. T. C. W. Blanning (Oxford: Oxford University Press, 1996), 131, that 'the sacral nature of a pilgrimage to the galleries [and theatres, he later suggests] was heightened by leading the visitor to the exhibits via carefully arranged steps, portico, hall, staircase, landing, and ante-chamber – in just the same way that subjects had once approached the throne-room. But now it was not the sovereign but Art which was the object to be venerated'.

[58] *RMU* (1858), 38.

[59] Recounted in *DiehlMM*, 116. The large organ, normally on view in orchestral and choral concerts, was obscured by the curtain during Musical Union meetings (see Fig. 14).

[60] However, according to Walter Willson Cobbett ('Musical Union', *CCSCM*), it was an admirable system 'from the acoustical point of view, but one which, I have been given to understand, tends to promote self-consciousness on the part of the artists'.

234 THE PURSUIT OF HIGH CULTURE

with the players' body language, or with the reactions of listeners sitting opposite them; they could participate in the more cerebral devotion that was encouraged by the programme notes and miniature scores; or they could flit between different modes of attention.

Whether the reading of programme notes during performance aided quasi-spiritual modes of 'communion' is debatable. As we have seen, Ella understood the limitations of their use as an aid to listening, always emphasizing the desirability of using programme notes ahead of and after performance: a means for home study or domestic devotion. In so doing he placed himself at the beginning of an honourable tradition of concert educators. George Grove, who produced a distinguished series of programme material for the Crystal Palace Saturday concerts, held similar views; so did the eminent music writer and pianist Donald F. Tovey.[61] The use of pocket scores, which Ella handed out to the most committed patrons before concerts,[62] was probably considered a superior means of connecting with the substance of the music during performance. Meanwhile, reverential silence was a *sine qua non*. On that Ella had always insisted, and would be remembered for it.[63] Thus, when the Musical Union was in residence, St James's Hall became the quintessential temple of high art. Indeed, high society's shared sense of duty to attend church regularly would arguably have made many in Ella's well-heeled audience at ease with the institution's rituals, which also allowed for intervals of pure sociability: we know that before and after performances the hall was abuzz with conversation and networking.

S T James's Hall was not solely associated with the Musical Union. With the passage of time, the venue became more closely linked to other concert series, including one significant institution, also for chamber music, with a rather different image: the Monday (later also Saturday) Popular Concerts. These concerts were established in 1859 under the direction of music publisher and instrument dealer

---

[61] Grove hoped listeners would read the notes before the concert or during the interval. Tovey sold his notes ahead of performances and structured the material around music examples, using only a minimum of connecting prose. These and related issues of listening and reading during concerts are explored in my 'Not Just "G.": Towards a History of the Programme Note', *GGMVC*, 115–42.

[62] *HaweisJE*, 1.

[63] Cobbett ('Musical Union') wrote: 'It was a sight for the gods when Ella rose from his gilded seat, held aloft his large, capable hands, and called for SILENCE in a stentorian voice. After this, no lord or lady present, however distinguished, dared to interrupt the music by fashionable or any other kind of chatter.' *HaweisJE* likewise suggested that '[a]ny attempt at talking or disturbance was promptly checked by the loud and authoritative "hush" of the Professor' (p. 1).

S. Arthur Chappell, brother of William and Thomas Patey Chappell (both substantial shareholders in the St James's Hall Company), and were initially designed to bring in desperately needed revenue to the hall during the quieter months of the year.[64] By 1862 they were running weekly between November and July, and eventually would become the talk of the town, and characterized by W. S. Gilbert in lines in *The Mikado* (1885), which sang of 'Bach, interwoven with Spohr and Beethoven, at classical Monday Pops'.[65] While Arthur Chappell was the public face of the institution, his brother Thomas (who ran the publishing house at 50 Bond Street) was almost certainly an influential force behind the scenes.[66]

There were distinct similarities between the two sets of concerts. The Pops were based around much the same serious instrumental repertoire that Ella was championing (Mozart, Beethoven, Mendelssohn and so on). Many artists played at both series – indeed, some of the string quartet line-ups were identical to the Musical Union's.[67] And analytical programme notes were provided for listeners, apparently at the suggestion of Davison, now something of a real foe, who became the Pops' official programme writer. Conversely, several differences were implicit, and striking too. Most notably, Chappell's enterprise was targeting a new clientele, one much larger, more casual and far more middling than the Musical Union's,

[64] There are several accounts of the early history of the Pops, with varying facts and emphases: see, *inter alia*, *A Story of Ten Hundred Concerts* (pamphlet, first published in a Pops programme, 4 April 1887) and Hermann Klein, *Musicians and Mummers* (London: Cassell, 1925), 117–23. The initial prospectus for St James's Hall grossly overestimated the rental revenue, assuming three performances a week for fifty-two weeks of the year – something unlikely given the still seasonal nature of London music.

[65] The scheduling of the concerts changed over time; but in the fourth season (1861–2) they were held weekly. The lines from *The Mikado* are taken from *The Savoy Operas: the Complete Gilbert and Sullivan Operas Originally Produced in the Years 1875–1896* (London: Papermac, 1983), 356. Another reference can be found in lines in *Patience* (op. cit., 196): 'Conceive me, if you can, An every-day young man: A commonplace type, With a stick and a pipe, And a half-bred black-and-tan [a Manchester terrier; a working-class ratting dog]; Who thinks suburban "hops"[,] More fun than "Monday Pops", Who's fond of his dinner, And doesn't get thinner, On bottled beer and chops.'

[66] The distinctive and joint activities of the various members of the Chappell family are difficult to untangle, and the personalities are sometimes muddled in the secondary sources. Modern histories of the Pops and the house of Chappell have yet to be written, their absence being compounded by a lack of business archives.

[67] Louis Ries (violin 2), Henry Webb (viola) and Piatti were a regular trio of lower strings at both sets of concerts in the early 1860s. On the Musical Union ensembles, see Appendix III.

and was the first serious attempt to bring high-class music into the realm of those to whom it had previously been denied. Performances were in the evenings, so working people could attend, and Chappell made a virtue of selling single tickets at prices ranging from five shillings to one shilling. (That said, from the 1864–5 season, affluent concert-goers were offered the opportunity to purchase an upfront subscription, reserving a particular sofa stall, on payment of £5 for the twenty concerts. Indeed, wealthy Londoners did attend Pops, an aspect that suggests a more socially diverse audience base than is usually assumed for this institution.)[68] In ethos, too, Pops performances were a little less austere than Ella's – songs were interspersed between the instrumental numbers in time-honoured fashion, and celebrated singers such as Sims Reeves and Charles Santley were billed; the programmes were longer, too. Added to this, Chappell made conventional use of the vast performance space, placing the players on the stage at the far end and packing the audience in rows in both the auditorium and all the balconies in an attempt to maximize the takings.[69] Given the interior architecture of St James's Hall and the nature of the music-making, it is quite likely these arrangements evoked at best an air of mass worship, an atmosphere that could never rival the distinctive aura of the consecrated inner sanctum that Ella had so carefully constructed for the Musical Union.[70] Still, it was, as Simon McVeigh has aptly commented, a 'timely identification of a business opportunity in bringing classical repertory to a wide audience eager for new cultural experiences'.[71]

What Ella thought about Chappell's developing venture is not recorded, but he almost certainly had mixed feelings about it. As a St James's Hall director and shareholder it was in his interest to see the venue flourish, and in a city where rehearsal opportunities were notoriously limited, there were gains to be had on both sides from the same group of musicians playing together and handling the

[68] Prices from *MW* (24 December 1864), 822. On high society attendance at the Pops, see Michael Musgrave, 'Leighton and Music', *Frederic Leighton: Antiquity, Renaissance, Modernity*, ed. Tim Barringer and Elizabeth Prettejohn (New Haven and London: Yale University Press, 1999), 295–314, at 298, and Paula Gillett, 'Ambivalent Friendships: Music-Lovers, Amateurs, and Professional Musicians in the Late Nineteenth Century', *MBC*, 321–40, at 324–5 and 340.

[69] A rare photograph of the St James's Hall interior, with audience formally arranged (1905; after the Pops' demise), is reproduced with the article 'St. James's Hall' in *Grove5* [plate 58].

[70] An engraving of a quartet playing at the Pops in *ILN* (2 March 1872, p. 201) suggests a few people were able to sit in 'orchestra' seats, behind the players, enjoying an intimacy akin to the Musical Union's. This layout is endorsed by a contemporary photograph in RAMm.

[71] *McVeighA*, 178.

same repertoire regularly. But quite likely too, Ella felt his position as London's chief chamber music promoter was being challenged by Chappell's initiative, especially when it became clear that the new enterprise was working well, that Arthur Chappell was becoming a force to be reckoned with in the world of London concert promotion, and that the Chappell family now wielded much influence in the running of the hall.[72] Not only was there potential for overlap and competition between the audiences for the Pops and Ella's concerts, but the Pops were soon stealing the limelight by putting on significantly more concerts than the eight Ella annually promoted in the same hall (around twenty-four events by the early 1860s). They were also operating over a longer season and reaching wider audiences. Already, by 1861, Chappell was taking the concerts on provincial tour,[73] and in 1865 he reconfigured the London series to include events on Saturday afternoons – the 'Saturday Pops' – presumably drawing in those middle-class working men who had a free half-day.[74]

It would have been widely accepted that Chappell's 'shilling' public would and could never gain access to Ella's concerts. But that did not mean that affluent, leisured supporters of the Musical Union might not investigate the sofa stalls at the Pops. (Nor, in fact, that there might be take-up from the Pops to the Union.) Ella's Broadwood women, for example, proved happy to attend both series.[75] In circumstances like these, was there not a danger some of Ella's people might switch

[72] Several family members were shareholders. By 1881 Thomas Patey, William and Samuel Arthur Chappell were serving as directors of the renamed St James' Hall Company, Limited: see the articles of association (1881) in PRO, BT31/2870/15837.

[73] *MW* (9 November 1861), 712: 'The programmes of these sixty-two concerts [so far given] (to which must be added eleven, held in Liverpool, Newcastle, Edinburgh, and Glasgow) have included […]'. By 1871 a fourth series of his London Monday Popular Concerts (with London artists) was being given in the Philharmonic Hall, Liverpool (programmes in BL).

[74] In time the potential audience on Saturday afternoons would expand to include many more of the white-collar middle classes. For background, see John Lowerson, *Sport and the English Middle Classes, 1870–1914* (Manchester and New York: Manchester University Press, 1993), 15–17.

[75] Pops attendance noted in Bertha Broadwood's diary, 13 April and 11 May 1863. The view of the two audiences as discrete class-based entities was promulgated by Davison in particular: the Pops being for the 'many', the Musical Union for the 'few'. Ella, in a vitriolic and public squabble with Davison over other matters in 1866, took him to task over this caricature, pointing out that on a night when royalty had attended the Pops, 'by far the greatest amount of money was paid for that entertainment by the "oiled and curled darlings of fame and fortune" [Davison's description of the Musical Union audience]' (*Orchestra*, 31 March 1866, p. 12). By the turn of the century, according to Paula Gillett ('Ambivalent Friendships', 340),

allegiance completely? Whether it was wariness of close competition, genuine lack of commitment to exploiting more middlebrow audiences, or both, that led Ella to cease his own out-of-season evening concerts (the 'Musical Union Soirées', successor to the Winter Evenings) in 1859 we shall probably never know. But he must have worried that the Pops were threatening the pre-eminence of his own institution, since although he occasionally went to them, he avoided mentioning them in his concert programmes and their literary supplements, even when his chosen subject was music in London, broadly conceived.[76] Meanwhile, Davison, never ceasing to adopt the stance of 'the people's champion' in his reviews of the Pops, persisted in caricaturing social contrasts between the two institutions in various newspapers, inevitably to Ella's detriment.[77] With the benefit of hindsight and knowledge of how the London concert market was to proliferate some thirty years later, fears that the extent of demand was finite and that audiences could not be 'shared' may seem unwarranted. But to Ella, unaware of what the future held, and cognizant of the difficulties of securing an adequate audience base, they seemed real enough, particularly in times of pressure for social change: the second Reform Bill, extending the franchise to respectable working men, would eventually become law in 1867.

In fact, in the short term it was less the loss of audience and more the loss of four special, long-serving artists that became the major issue for Ella, as in the space of two seasons (1866, 1867) Joachim and Hallé, then Clara Schumann and Piatti, ceased to play at Musical Union concerts, and began appearing at Chappell's Pops instead. Although Ella said little publicly about their secession, it was widely noticed, represented a significant break in continuity, and must have come as a severe blow, given that Hallé and Piatti were the rocks on which many of the Musical Union ensembles were built, and that all four players were among the biggest draws around for chamber music. As we have seen, the Musical Union had been enjoying unprecedented success with these players, including that record season of 1865. So why did they suddenly abandon Ella? The question is not easily answered, since the evidence connected with this episode is frustratingly slight, disparate and occasionally conflicting; but scrutiny of the documents, plus a little reading between the lines, leads one strongly to

---

some society people thought 'it was the "swagger" thing to go in parties to the Monday Popular concerts and line up for hours to sit in the shilling seats'.

[76] The one exception is a reference within the piece 'Music in London, 1865', *RMU* (1865), sup., 36, but this simply characterizes the institution with reference to 'popular songs sung by Sims Reeves, and popular pianoforte solos played by Miss Goddard (now Mrs. Davison)'.

[77] See e.g. a piece for the *Pall Mall Gazette*, reprinted in *MW* (8 July 1865), 420.

suspect the behind-the-scenes figure of Arthur Chappell as the source of the upheaval.[78]

By the mid-1860s Arthur Chappell was acting as a business agent for Joachim (Clara Schumann and Piatti followed), his operations foreshadowing the emergence of a stream of dedicated agents in the internationalizing market-place two or three decades later, and surely facilitating Joachim's working life in important ways.[79] This new activity gave the Chappells yet more power in the London concert world, and although initially willing to secure bookings for Joachim at the Musical Union, Arthur Chappell surely found his interests quickly conflicting with Ella's.[80] After all, it cannot have been coincidence that as soon as the Saturday Pops began to look profitable, Chappell's artists ceased to play for Ella. How matters unfolded is unclear, but it seems that Chappell either chose to restrict the availability to Ella of some of his star artists (by clauses in their Pops contracts, or by exorbitant fees demanded as their agent), or offered his principal players such lucrative terms that, for many of them, playing for Ella seemed decidedly small beer – not worth their continuing loyalty, particularly when performance opportunities were multiplying elsewhere.[81] For Chappell's business practices seemed to be getting him exclusive placement of some of his principal artists when it came

[78] The fact that archives for the Chappell business have not survived makes this a difficult area to interrogate. The evidence for the argument that follows has been pieced together from short references in Ella's diaries, 1866–7, and other documents in EllaC, initially led by remarks remembered in *GanzMM*; see n. 81 below.

[79] The earliest such agency was possibly run by George Dolby, whose business (established 1856) was close to Chappell's premises in New Bond Street; see Christopher Fifield, *Ibbs and Tillett: the Rise and Fall of a Musical Empire* (Aldershot: Ashgate, 2005), 2.

[80] A letter from Chappell to Ella dated 7 April 1865 (EllaC, MS 156) shows that Chappell was amenable to hiring out Joachim for a Musical Union concert on 9 May.

[81] *GanzMM*, 112–13, recounted the matter thus: 'When Arthur Chappell came on the scene and started the Saturday and Monday Popular Concerts he was anxious to get many of the artists who had been for so many years associated with Ella – and these all left Ella and accepted engagements with Chappell – Ella complained bitterly to me of their "ingratitude," as he called it. They were Madame Schumann, Madame Arabella Goddard, Joachim, and Charles Hallé – who, as Ella told me, had played sixty-six times for him. […] [T]hese artists were not allowed by their contracts to play for him any more'. Ganz (b. 1833), writing some fifty years after the event, mistakenly identifies Arabella Goddard (who never played for Ella), not Piatti, as moving over to Chappell; he also confuses the chronology, placing these events as coming towards the very end of the Musical Union's existence. The claim about the restrictive terms of Chappell's contracts remains uncorroborated.

to chamber music.[82] Chappell had the advantage, because his terms were far more generous than Ella's. Piatti apparently had a three-year contract with Chappell worth £800 per annum running from 1866 and guaranteeing at least twenty-four London Pops concerts, plus possible provincial tours and other engagements.[83] So when in 1867 calendar clashes suddenly looked inevitable, Piatti pulled out of Ella's concerts at short notice, saying: 'yesterday, he [Chappell] informed me that some engagements have been accepted for me in Paris during the month of April [...] I shall not be able to accept the same engagement [with the Musical Union] as last year'.[84] Unsurprisingly, bad feelings resulted and occasionally resurfaced.

Much remains unknown about Chappell's terms and conditions for the artists he represented.[85] But they were certainly emblematic of what would become the more aggressively business-like ways of running concerts, and against which Ella would eventually look old-fashioned. Ella's few recorded comments blame artists' disloyalty, rather than their agent's manœuvres, for the situation he found

[82] These artists were nevertheless allowed to play at London orchestral concerts – the Philharmonic Society's and at Crystal Palace, for example. But according to the evidence in the Philharmonic's archive in the BL (explored in *EhrlichFP*, 129), Chappell was, by 1868, dictating his artists' terms, and demanding fees considerably higher than those the Philharmonic had become accustomed to offering.

[83] The financial terms are according to Ella's pamphlet 'Signor Piatti' (EllaC, MS 81, between pp. 74 and 75; published by Ella in 1868 to justify his break with the cellist, which was inflamed by a row in a public restaurant). They work out at £35 per concert. Ella, by contrast, had been paying Piatti no more than £10 10s per appearance since 1860 (see account book, EllaC, MS 6, pp. 55, 57, 59, 61, 64).

[84] Letter from Piatti to Ella, dated 17 February 1867, printed in the pamphlet 'Signor Piatti'. Chappell's role in Piatti's secession from the Musical Union is corroborated by a spread of evidence, including scraps in the diaries (e.g. 15 May 1866: 'called on Piatti, é impiegato da Chappell' ['who is employed by Chappell']; EllaC, MS 135).

[85] Chappell remained business agent for Joachim and was soon representing Clara Schumann and Piatti (see *EhrlichFP*, 129, and miscellaneous Chappell correspondence in the BL: RPS/MS/338, ff. 117–125). Hallé's professional relationship with Chappell is less clear. Hallé became committed to the Pops, but I have found no evidence that he used Chappell as an agent for his own engagements. His break with Ella in 1866 (not his first: there was a disagreement 1858–9) may well have been of his own making. (Ella's diary, 30 March 1866, reads: 'C. H[.] refuses to play at M. U. 'cause I only offer him 2. instead of 4. matinées'; EllaC, MS 135.) I am grateful to Robert Beale for sharing his knowledge of Hallé's business affairs with me.

   Artists such as Wieniawski and Auer continued to play for both Ella and the Pops, which suggests they did not have restrictive terms in their contracts, and/or that they were prepared to insist on terms that enabled them to maintain their loyalty to Ella.

himself in; but there were several reasons why Ella would not have wished to take on the Chappell dynasty publicly, or admit that he could not match Chappell's fees.[86] Meanwhile, the significance of 1866–7 as a breaking point in Chappell's and Ella's relationship can be further deduced from the sudden, silent departure (most likely, removal) of Chappell & Co. (the firm headed by Thomas, and whence Arthur operated his agency work) in 1866 as one of the Union's official ticket sellers. Later, however, there seems to have been an informal agreement by Arthur Chappell no longer to schedule his London concerts in the same part of the season as the Musical Union – a change that was quietly brought in from 1867, suggesting a calming of relations between the two camps.[87]

In the face of all these difficulties, Ella continued to pursue a policy of excellence, bringing in cellists Grützmacher and Jacquard from abroad when Piatti announced his sudden withdrawal in February 1867, and insisting on more rehearsals for a new group of instrumentalists who were relatively unfamiliar with one another's playing.[88] He may have lost Joachim, but he could still call on three exceptional violinists, namely Vieuxtemps (1867), Wieniawski (1866, 1867) and Auer (1866, 1867, 1868), the last two of whom seemed to have grown as artists since their last appearances at the Union.[89] Hallé's absence, however, was not so easily compensated, 1866 seeing a procession of pianists, mixed in quality, in the weeks that Jaëll and Lübeck did not play.[90] These performers comprised the young, Paris-trained

---

[86] Blaming the artists is the tenor of the account in *GanzMM*, 113, and of Ella's footnote to Piatti's claim about Chappell committing him to work in Paris – 'I am told this is not true' (pamphlet, 'Signor Piatti'). Ella's continuing presence on the directorate of St James's Hall meant he had to work with the Chappell family.

[87] From spring 1867 the Pops season ended in the early spring (by April), removing potential conflict with Musical Union dates.

[88] Ella also claimed to have had to pay over the odds: see 'Signor Piatti', in which he states, 'I fortunately obtained the assistance of Grützmacher and Jacquard; but at a very considerable expense, to remunerate these artists for renouncing their engagements at Dresden and Paris'. This was an exaggeration: Grützmacher had received the same fee as Piatti, and Jacquard had been paid £12 10s per appearance – rates that paled against those paid to Wieniawski (£21) and Rubinstein (c.£43) the same season. See account book (EllaC, MS 6), p. 69. The need for the extra rehearsals is articulated in *RMU* (1867), 9.

[89] 'M. Leopold Auer's tone has marvellously improved since he was three years ago in London' (*Orchestra*, 14 April 1866, p. 42); 'M. Wieniawski returns with powers, if possible, immensely in advance of those he manifested in 1863' (*Orchestra*, 26 May 1866, p. 132).

[90] Hallé had also pulled out at short notice, causing problems for Ella, who was already contending with Clara Schumann's cancellation of her English tour for health reasons, and Lübeck's postponement of his. See the diary, 30 March 1866

Louis Diémer (a player of 'proficiency and promise' who performed in Beethoven's piano trio op. 70 no. 1), the Danish pupil of Von Bülow, Hartvigson (his playing of Schumann's piano trio op. 80 – hardly an easy choice for the London audience – was categorically 'not a success'), Mlle Gayrard Pacini (ex-Paris Conservatoire; she gave Hummel's piano quintet op. 87 with a 'crisp' touch), and Mlle Marie Trautmann, a *premier prix* winner in Paris (assisting Jaëll in Schumann's op. 46 piano duet – the début was 'eminently successful').[91] Thankfully for Ella there was the trump card of Anton Rubinstein, last heard in 1859, whose decision to tour Europe in 1867 and 1868 and agreement to play at the Musical Union must have seemed like a godsend, producing celebrated performances and healthy box-office: in 1867, 151 people paid to hear him perform his violin sonata with Vieuxtemps, and 236 came for the Director's Matinée, in which he also appeared.[92] So in the main Ella kept up appearances. However, the sudden cancellation of Vieuxtemps in 1868, which left Auer to lead the entire season's concerts, was obviously out of keeping with the Union's ethos of showcasing a range of lead players, and must have been noticed in some quarters.

As yet, a dip in subscriptions between 1865 and 1868 (a loss of possibly 100 names from the membership list, the biggest fall coming after the lacklustre 1866 season: see Appendix IV) was not a cause for alarm on Ella's part, especially since single-ticket sales had been especially buoyant in 1867.[93] But it is hard not

(Hallé) and 2 April 1866 (Lübeck; EllaC, MS 135), and the sequence of letters from Clara Schumann dated 19 January 1866, 5 March 1866 and 29 March 1866 (EllaC, MS 14/iii–v).

91   Remarks on Diémer, Pacini and Trautmann from the *Orchestra* (14 April 1866), 42; (12 May 1866), 102; and (26 May 1866), 132; and on Hartvigson from Ella's diary, 26 April 1866 (EllaC, MS 135). The *Orchestra* also noted Hartvigson's failure, the choice of the Schumann being 'too hazardous a work for so young a *debûtant*' (28 April 1866, p. 69).

92   Ticket sales for 25 June and 2 July 1867, noted in the account book (EllaC, MS 6), p. 112. The total number sold that season came to 728, up 283 on the previous year. Rubinstein's appearance at the 1868 Director's Matinée playing Mendelssohn's op. 66 trio and a clutch of piano pieces likewise drew in an extra 152 people (ibid.: tickets for 30 June), although his performance earlier in the season of Beethoven's 'Archduke', among other works, surprisingly attracted only 57 non-members (19 May).

93   The account book (EllaC, MS 6) does not record the number of subscribers after 1865 (for which it indicates 565). For totals from 1866 we have to rely on the published lists of members in *RMU*, which are inflated by the names of single-ticket purchasers. The loss of *c.*100 is a conservative conjecture calculated from the *RMU* totals for the seasons from 1865 (685) to 1868 (577), and acknowledging that single-ticket sales were high in 1867.

to suppose he was beginning to notice a downward trend. Moreover, the best artists were demanding higher fees, especially so since Chappell's encroachment of 1866; and Ella was having to pay them.[94] If nothing else, the situation needed monitoring.

❧ 18 Hanover Square

Government does nothing for music, <u>donc</u>, I will do something
Letter from Ella to Fétis, 19 October 1860; *WangerméeF*

TRANSPLANTING the Musical Union to St James's Hall was not the only matter on Ella's mind in early 1858. He was preparing for what turned out to be his last series of evening concerts, while contemplating the practicalities of a long-cherished plan: the establishment of a permanent institute for chamber music, funded initially through the Musical Union's audience networks.[95] As with all Ella's projects, this one was founded on his perception of a gap that needed to be filled and a situation that needed to be rectified, although in this instance there were two distinct aspects to the vacuum, one fully articulated by Ella, the other not.

The project's rationale, which Ella had explained several times before, was thus. What the West End of London lacked was a physical base (a building) for serious musical activities – not just concerts, but lectures, discussion, study, a library, reading room and so on. This absence of such premises, according to Ella's diagnosis, owed much to the general indifference towards music within government and cultured society at large (Musical Union members notwithstanding) and the consequent dearth of financial subsidy or patronage. Part of Ella's Musical Union campaign had always been to put music on an institutional par with the other arts and the sciences. He endorsed the 'right of a Handel to stand in the same line with a Raphael or a Titian, or a Mozart to rank with a Wren or an Inigo Jones' at the Royal Society, for example, and he bridled publicly against what he saw as the willingness of government and rich benefactors to fund fine art, but not music, his contacts with art institutions and painters bringing such contrasts

---

94 In 1867 Wieniawski was paid £21 per concert, compared with £15 10s the previous year. Calculations from the account book (EllaC, MS 6), pp. 66 and 69.

95 A notice about the institute, printed on the back cover of the 1856 *RMU* [BL set] and announcing that a council would soon be constituted and premises found in the new St James's Hall, would have been sent out to members early in 1857, so we can fairly assume the matter had taken on a new immediacy in Ella's mind.

into focus.[96] Ella had in mind for this new venture a cross between a London club (though this one would admit women) and a literary society, an institution that might develop the character of a serious salon in surroundings where 'the respectable members of the profession' could mingle with music-lovers, and visiting European performers could fraternize and perform.[97] It would also serve as a special site – another consecrated locality – for cerebral musical pleasure and edification.[98] At heart, it represented an extension of existing activities and agendas.

Linkage with the Musical Union was significant, since Ella was quietly hoping to include a permanent administrative base for his concerts. This was the other aspect of the unsatisfactory situation. For any concert enterprise, there were untold gains to be had from placing all resources – musical and secretarial – on one centrally located site. It was something the Philharmonic Society failed to achieve, though had had in its sights during its founding years. Ella, who like most musicians was used to working out of his lodgings (with all the difficulties that it entailed), must have yearned for dedicated accommodation for the Musical Union. And now it seemed a possibility, since an institute building could provide: offices to store and organize paperwork; space for keeping music, books and instruments; appropriate accommodation to receive visitors (whether 'customers' or 'suppliers'); rooms for auditions and practice; and a place to carry out his

[96] *RMU* (1851), 28. The words were the Marquis of Northampton's, President of the Royal Society, 1838–48. Ella was presumably thinking of the use of government money to found the National Gallery and to purchase private collections for it, or of government's injection of funding into the South Kensington Museum; on these projects, see Janet Minihan, *The Nationalization of Culture: the Development of State Subsidies to the Arts in Great Britain* (New York: New York University Press, 1977), 54–8, 121–6.

Ella had experience of the London art world and its patronage systems, being a regular attender of events at the Royal Academy and British Institution, and having social connections with the likes of Sir Charles and Lady Eastlake (President of the Royal Academy from 1850 and Director of the National Gallery, 1855) and the painter John Everett Millais. All were Musical Union members; the Millais family became good friends. A note in his diary, 30 July 1851 (EllaC, MS 120), indicates the close attention Ella paid to contrasts between the art and music worlds; 'saw C. Landseer who says that the R. Academy has received £1000 more than last last [*sic*] year!'

[97] The quotation is taken from a notice headed 'Musical Union Institute' on the back cover of *RMU* for 1850, a comprehensive exposition of what Ella thought this institution might comprise.

[98] An institution 'consecrated to the intellectuality of the musical art' was how Ella spelled out his vision. (Prospectus, dated Michaelmas 1860, for the Musical Union Institute.)

myriad writing, accounting and clerical tasks.[99] Not only that, but the possession of a good business address would increase the institution's 'visibility', suggest perpetuity and importance, and encourage newcomers into the audience fold.

We have already noted that there had been something of a stop-start element to Ella's plans. The kernel of the idea had been unveiled in 1849, when he had outlined a scheme for a privately funded music library that would rectify the lack in London of a reference collection of scores, educational tutors and literature on music which could be consulted freely and easily by the 'Musician of England'.[100] This was a personal hobby-horse that had its origins in his first acquaintance with the Paris Conservatoire library in the late 1820s. The British Museum's reading room still had fairly limited holdings of music, in spite of Antonio Panizzi's otherwise laudable attempts at collection building.[101] And public library provision of music, in the wake of the 1850 Public Libraries Act, was in embryo only; as one recent commentator has observed, 'it took well over 100 years before most public libraries provided music services that could satisfy even the basic needs of musicians and music lovers in the areas they served'.[102] In 1850 Ella had merged his library proposal with more elaborate plans for an entire institution called the Musical Union Institute, funded by annual subscription, giving small-scale concerts,

99 Very little of this agenda is stated in the early public statements of intent, but the idea of hiring out the rooms for rehearsals is noted on the back cover of *RMU* for 1850, and the use of the institute as a shop front for the Musical Union was put in place once the project began to be realized.

100 From a notice headed 'Musical Union Library' on the back cover of *RMU* for 1849. On the scope of the library it says: 'In futherance [*sic*] of the social and intellectual advantages of this organized Institution [i.e. Musical Union], I purpose [*sic*] to form a Library of Historical, Philosophical, and Theoretical works on Music; also of Practical Treatises and Methods for Voices and Instruments; complete scores of all great works, sacred and secular, of ancient and modern composers; critical essays, Journals, Reviews, and every species of musical publication in English, French, German, and Italian!' The article goes on to indicate that Ella saw the music libraries in the conservatoires of Paris, Brussels, Berlin and Vienna as models of open access and government support, though knew it would be foolish to try to rival the extent of their holdings.

101 See Philip John Weimerskirch, *Antonio Panizzi and the British Museum Library*, The 1981 AB Bookman's Yearbook (Clifton, NJ: Bookman's Weekly, 1982), 17–25, 101–7.

102 Malcolm Lewis, '"Shrouded in Mystery": the Development of Music Provision in Public Libraries in Great Britain, 1850–1950', *Music Librarianship in the United Kingdom: Fifty Years of the United Kingdom Branch of the International Association of Music Libraries, Archives and Documentation Centres*, ed. Richard Turbet (Aldershot: Ashgate, 2003), 17–56, at 17.

conversazioni and lectures as well as housing books and music and offering other facilities. He had obtained a few donations, including literature, an engraved portrait of Rossini, and even some money.[103] Yet not long afterwards (1853) the project had been mothballed, probably because the Réunion des Arts, the subscription club for concerts, trials and *conversazioni* which was now meeting at the former Beethoven Rooms in Harley Street, seemed to be fulfilling the same need.[104] The Réunion drew a membership of amateurs and professional musicians, and for a while had received Ella's support.[105] But as it began to look vulnerable (there was a crisis and a change of management in 1856), and the Musical Union's move into St James's Hall drew closer, signalling other fresh beginnings, Ella outlined his intention to move the institute project forward.

A formal announcement of the 'Musical Union Institute', to be established in the new hall, had been made on the back cover of the *Record of the Musical Union* for 1856 (distributed in early 1857). By April 1858 Ella was reminding concert-goers of his intention to house the institute and library in one of the smaller rooms at St James's Hall, the overarching mission being 'to extend the sphere of our action'.[106] In fact, this accommodation came to nothing. Although a considerable setback (having offices 'above the shop' would have been quite a coup), it did not deter him

[103] Notice headed 'Musical Union Institute' on the back cover of *RMU* for 1850. In addition, there was the possibility for revenue generation by hiring out the rooms for 'other [i.e. non-musical] purposes'. There was even mention of a fund to help poor but talented students gain access to important skills that would help them in their professional careers – studying languages and the science of music, for example.

[104] Suspension of Ella's institute plans is indicated by a rare committee resolution in *RMU* (1853), 12. The Réunion's initial aims are summarized in *MW* (17 May 1851), 315, and given in greater detail in a prospectus issued to advertise the relocation from rooms in Queen Anne Street to the Harley Street venue (printed in *RMWE*, 1853, pp. 15–16). As a venture, the Réunion was more broad-based than what Ella envisioned. As well as concerts and trials of new music, it provided *conversazioni* on literature and the arts, and exhibitions of painting and sculpture; there were also plans for lectures on the arts, and reading rooms, open 'daily from 10 a.m. to 10 p.m.' Whether reading rooms were ever in operation is unclear, although one paper noted that attendees could 'peruse (very few) choice and well-bound tomes' (*MW*, 29 March 1856, p. 204).

[105] At the society's heart was the concept of mutual exchange between professional and amateur musicians: see *MW* (5 March 1853), 152. Ella's participation is clear from his diary entries, but he is singled out in a review in *MW* (30 December 1854), 851, of a performance of Romberg's 'Toy' symphony: 'The subscribers seemed much amused with Romberg's juvenile symphony, and bestowed hearty approbation on Mr. Ella's energetic beating of the drum.'

[106] *RMU* (1858), 16.

from his goal.[107] Nor did the emergence – also in April 1858 – of yet another under-taking with aims strikingly similar to his own, including the provision of a library for its members. Rising from the ashes of the Musical Institute of London (defunct since 1853) and calling itself the Musical Society of London, this new organization included many of the members of the music profession who had been involved in the former Institute.[108] Ella refused to join (twice), giving it 'two years to die out'.[109] In fact, it kept going until 1867. The Réunion des Arts meanwhile seems to have fizzled out (in c.1859–60).

So Ella stepped up his campaign for donations, making amateurs rather than professionals the target audience. By 1860 his plans were becoming a real-ity. Sir George Clerk, long-standing supporter of Ella's projects, including the Musical Union, and a man publicly perceived to have musical interests (on the Earl of Westmorland's death he had been made chair of the Royal Academy of Music's management committee), agreed to act as a figure-head and advisor. A series of letters written by Ella that summer to apprise Clerk of progress illus-trates the depth of Clerk's interest in the scheme, as well as the cautious way in which Ella thought plans through.[110] Ella's burning concern was to drum up donations from 'old friends & patrons' (a short private circular was issued in July 1860, and Ella approached people individually), but he was also exercised about finding and furnishing premises and forming a small governing council.[111] For the accommodation, location was *the* vital consideration: it had to be in a

---

[107] The reasons for the St James's Hall idea being dropped are not noted in Ella's diary, but we may imagine that the other directors outvoted him on the proposal. Their principal responsibility to shareholders would have been to accrue maximum revenue from letting out the smaller rooms, and, under this rationale, burdening that space with permanent resources might have seemed unwise.

[108] All the members of the new Society had been associated with the Musical Institute of London. Charles Salaman was the principal mover. Aims were 'To promote social intercourse among its members and with musicians of this and other coun-tries; to form a musical library for the use of its members; to hold conversazioni, at which papers on musical subjects might be read, and subjects of musical interest might be discussed; to give orchestral, choral and chamber concerts, and occa-sionally lectures; to afford the opportunity of trying new compositions; to publish occasional papers, calculated to extend the theoretical and historical knowledge of music'. Cited in Alec Hyatt King, 'The Musical Institute of London and its Succes-sors', *MT*, 117 (1976), 221–3, at 222.

[109] Diary, 12 and 23 November 1858 (EllaC, MS 127).

[110] Manuscript letters in NAS, GD18/3946.

[111] Inventory and notes (?August 1860), and letter (28 July 1860) from Ella to Clerk (NAS, GD18/3946); copies of the July prospectus are held with these manuscripts.

convenient and socially acceptable part of town, and Ella eventually settled on leasing rooms on the first floor of a house in Hanover Square – no. 18, home also to Wessel & Co. (from 1860 trading as Ashdown & Parry), music sellers and publishers.[112] This elegant eighteenth-century square, sheltered behind Regent Street, was an appropriate choice, being not only the site of the celebrated Hanover Square Rooms – well known to musicians and concert-goers – but also the address of several learned societies and social clubs. The Oriental Club was next door.[113] The accommodation itself was rather tatty and required some outlay on refurbishment, Ella paying acute attention to detail, sensing the ambiance had to be just right. Even so, old habits died hard, and he economized where possible, with Clerk's encouragement – 'I am cautious & do not waste money, at starting', he told Sir George, cleaning and covering up the 'vulgar' rose-patterned wallpaper, for example, with pictures and prints.[114] As for the council, Ella hoped to entice a combination of 'practical Musical talent, & riches'.[115] With speed he approached a group of luminaries, most of whom agreed to take on these roles. Wealthy men with strong beliefs in the importance of music, these were public 'somebodies' and doers in their own right, and all were firm supporters of the Musical Union. One was the composer and church musician Rev. Sir F. A. G. Ouseley, Bt, a man with distinguished credentials both musical and ecclesiastical (professor of music at Oxford, precentor at Hereford Cathedral), and an ability to make things happen – he had founded St Michael's College, Tenbury in 1854.[116] He was complemented by another Anglican, the Rev. Edward Goddard, whom Ella felt would be a 'Capital Member of the Council [...] he has a fine library & is a member of the M.U. from 1845', and by John Leslie of Camden Hill, whose presence was justified because Ella wished 'to "socialize" the sister arts [...] [He] is a most accomplished Painter – amateur and [...] a constant visitor at the Mus: Union [...] a very popular and esteemed

---

[112] As early as 1853 Ella had been actively looking for appropriate accommodation, as is clear from his diary, 11 November 1853 (EllaC, MS 122): 'Was asked if Victoria St. w^d. do for my Institute – I think not. 'tis too far S. West'.

[113] The Oriental Club was an unnumbered building until 1867, when it became no. 18, and the Ashdown & Parry house was renumbered as no. 19 (parish rate books, CWA).

[114] Letter from Ella to Clerk, dated 28 July 1860 (NAS, GD18/3946); the Duke of Leinster, another trusted patron, also advised economy (letter to Clerk, 20 August 1868). Some people had suggested spending more lavishly.

[115] Letter from Ella to Clerk, dated 28 July 1860 (NAS, GD18/3946).

[116] Ouseley was on the committee of the Musical Union from 1852 and became its Vice-President in 1860. For more on Ouseley's life, see Nicholas Temperley's article in *NGDM2*.

dilettante'.[117] Also enlisted were representatives of new money: Thomas Brassey and William Tite, both of whom had been drawn to the Musical Union in the 1850s. They were named as 'trustees'. Tite was also honorary treasurer, a position to which he brought experience of not just banking but also the hazards of running a literary institution (it was Tite who was largely responsible for turning around the finances of the London Institution in Finsbury Circus; he was its secretary, 1829–67).[118] Ella was to be Director.

Meanwhile, financial donations, most between £5 and £20, were coming in from the extended network.[119] Privately Ella estimated that the gifts would produce a surplus, after initial expenses, of £1,000 (perhaps even £1,500 or more), which he intended to invest on the institution's behalf. Additionally, Musical Union members were invited to take out subscriptions to the Institute, Ella calculating this would raise 200 guineas per annum and cover most of the recurrent outgoings.[120] Expenditure would be kept low, Ella told Clerk, by not paying débutants or hiring expensive artists for trials.[121]

By the early autumn of 1860 Ella was ready to issue a detailed prospectus bearing the Musical Union 'logo' as guarantee of high culture, in the hope of drawing in more one-off donations and getting the number of subscribers up to 100. To 'defray all the outlay incident to the formation of the Institute' (including, presumably, the investment capital) Ella claimed to be aiming for £2,000 in donations in the first instance.[122] He also hinted at a second, heightened phase of activity

[117] Letters to Clerk dated 28 July and 14 September 1860 (NAS, GD18/3946). After his death, Goddard's large music collection was sold at Sotheby's, on 4 February 1878 (James B. Coover, *Private Music Collections: Catalogs and Cognate Literature*, Warren, MI: Harmonie Park Press, 2001, p. 150, entry 1055). From 1869 to 1871 and from 1874 to 1877 he served on the committee of the Musical Union. Irish-born John Leslie, who later became an MP and the first Baronet of Glaslough, is said to have been a skilled pre-Raphaelite painter. He too went on to serve on the Musical Union's committee, from 1875 until 1880.

[118] Tite's contribution to the London Institution is roundly described and assessed in Janet C. Cutler, 'The London Institution, 1805–1933' (PhD, University of Leicester, 1976), 188ff, while the circumstances surrounding his appointment as secretary are described there at p. 39.

[119] Ella deliberately stayed in London that summer 'so that I may reply to Donors'. Letter to Clerk, dated 20 August 1860 (NAS, GD18/3946).

[120] Extra income would be garnered from bank interest, special concerts, fees charged for lectures etc. Ella's thinking on revenue can be traced in the letter to Clerk dated 28 July (NAS, GD18/3946), and in the prospectus for the Musical Union Institute dated 'Michaelmas 1860' (copy bound in with *RMU*, 1860, in BL set).

[121] Letter to Clerk, dated 28 July 1860 (NAS, GD18/3946).

[122] Prospectus (Michaelmas 1860).

involving the development of the library collection, once the threshold of £5,000 had been reached.[123] The prospectus is filled with institutional rules and rhetoric, but gives a strong indication of the serious agendas and goals that Ella intended to pursue. There were six 'objects':

1. To provide Rooms for its [Musical Union Institute] Meetings.

2. To collect an extensive Library of Music and of Musical Science and Literature.

3. To provide instruments for the convenience of trials of new music.

4. To give receptions to foreign and native artists, Vocalists and Instrumentalists, and to afford them information in furtherance of their professional views.

5. To provide Lectures on the Art and Science of Music.

6. To publish a Journal, containing the transactions of the Society, useful information on the condition of the Art, and notices of artists in England and on the Continent.[124]

In addition, a programme of events to run between January and July 1861 was outlined, Ella counting on enough patrons being in town ahead of the high season to attend. The aim was to match the Cercle de l'Union Artistique, founded in Paris a few months earlier for the encouragement of chamber music and young artists, which was already (according to Ella) enjoying success.[125]

Looked at from his own practical viewpoint, the Musical Union Institute was poised to give coherence to many of the subsidiary activities that Ella had been developing over the past decade. These included: the Musical Union's trial concerts for aspirant European artists and new works; his lectures on music (he had

---

[123] Prospectus (Michaelmas 1860). Ella pledged to bequeath his personal library, instruments and money to the value of £2,000 once the money was raised.

[124] Prospectus (Michaelmas 1860). In *RMU* (1860), 30, 42, Ella intimated that he was keen to offer, through the Institute, a course of lessons on figured bass and musicianship to 'young amateurs', especially females.

[125] 'In addition to those numerous *réunions* in Paris [...] a Society is now being established, under the presidency of Prince Poniatowsky, including Auber, Rossini, Halevy [sic], and other eminent composers, on the committee, for the encouragement of the fine arts, with receptions for the *débûts* of musicians, trials of new music, and the union of artists and amateurs. This Society already numbers four hundred, paying 400 francs per annum, and is held in premises at a rental of 80,000 francs per annum!' (Prospectus, Michaelmas 1860). According to the entry in Joël-Marie Fauquet, *Dictionnaire de la musique en France au XIXᵉ siècle* (Paris: Fayard, 2003), the Cercle contributed most to the presentation of young talent such as Saint-Saëns, Bizet, Chabrier and Delibes.

been re-hired by the London Institution in 1858–9 and had given talks on instruments); chamber concerts for Musical Union 'types' during the winter months; the publication of a periodical on music; 'classes' for amateurs to practice vocal and instrumental music; and advice to amateurs on musical matters, whether purchasing pianos or recommending teachers.[126] As the Institute's Director he could justify a fee that would remunerate him for this work, and he would soon benefit from free accommodation in the Hanover Square premises.[127] On top of all this there was the almost immeasurable benefit to the Musical Union, and to his long-term ambitions for that society, of a dedicated administrative base, permanent address and 'shop-window' in the centre of town.

At the same time, the Institute project encapsulated many of Ella's larger goals, particularly his mission to elevate high art and to secure its meaningful reception. To these we can add his determination to make the case for music within metropolitan culture (something of a talking point now that 'Albertopolis' was coming into being in South Kensington). His broad wish was to establish a practical centre for musical culture in central London – most notably through the creation of a library – to address some of the lacunae in the city's musical resources. Indeed, the careful reader of 1860 might have spotted the first signs of this grandiose sub-text, that out of his small acorn a full tree might eventually develop, in ways similar to those that had seen the growth of art collections in the South Kensington (now Victoria & Albert) Museum:

> When I reflect upon the commencement of the British National Collection of Paintings, exhibited in a small, dingy-looking private dwelling in Pall Mall, and compare it with the valuable additions now collected at Charing Cross and Kensington Museum, partly bequests and gifts of rich and generous patrons, let me hope that this *nucleus* of the Musical Union Institute, by similar means, may expand into a national institution – that Music may be worthily recognised as an Art, and greater

---

[126] The last two of these activities were not listed as objectives of the Institute, but classes were announced in the prospectus, as was the provision of 'information […] in respect to musical instructors, the purchase of musical instruments, good editions of music and of musical literature' (Prospectus, Michaelmas 1860).

[127] How the financial arrangements worked is not entirely clear, but twice-yearly payments of *c*.£250 to Ella in 1861 (noted in the account book, EllaC, MS 55, p. 14) suggest this was his slice of the Institute's earnings. Reference to the Institute's 'paid custodian' in *RMU* (1865, sup., 19) may have been a reference to his role, though equally may have referred to the presence of servants, wages to whom were also paid.

facilities be afforded for its study as a Science, in this rich and powerful country.[128]

In a subsequent communication to Institute subscribers (January 1861) Ella inventoried the instrument collection housed at Hanover Square. It included old Italian violins: one Amati (worth £60), two Guarneri (£50 and £60) and a Stradivarius (£150) – their relative value being nothing compared with what they would come to be worth a century or more later. He also outlined the extent of the library that had been donated or bought: 500 books, several thousand pieces of music (presumably performance parts), a quantity of full scores, some rare autographs and so on, for members' use only.[129] Moreover he came clean about his ultimate agenda for the Institute. It was 'to solicit Government to provide ample accommodation for the library and property of this Institute, free of rent, in a central and convenient locality, to form a *nucleus* of a national library on a more extended scale, and to establish annually a course of instructive musical lectures' – ambitious, worthy plans for the long term, though his immediate aim was to keep donations coming.[130]

Ella had had the foresight to establish a mechanism to encourage donations. The Duke of Leinster, Lady Overstone (wife of Lord Overstone, the hugely wealthy and influential banker; both were Musical Union members), Mrs Morgan Clifford and the Archbishop of Canterbury (John Bird Sumner) were among the several Musical Union-ites who had been given membership discounts in return for

---

[128] Prospectus (Michaelmas 1860). Ella is referring to Marlborough House, Pall Mall, used from 1850 by the National Gallery (Charing Cross) as an overflow space for English paintings; it had been made available to, and developed by, Henry Cole for his Schools of Design between 1852 and 1857. See Anthony Burton, *Vision and Accident: the Story of the Victoria and Albert Museum* (London: V&A Publications, 1999), 26–40. The collection had reopened as the South Kensington Museum in June 1857. Interestingly, Ella's vision for improving the state of the arts came at the time when the South Kensington projects, under Cole's leadership and with the backing of the Society of Arts, were making significant headway.

[129] In 1860 he had purchased 'upwards of' 300 items from the sale of part of the music library of John Hullah, the pioneer of singing classes and eminent educator (as noted in the prospectus supplement, dated 1 January 1861, and bound in with *RMU* for 1860). Tite's account book (EllaC, MS 56, pp. 6–7), in Ella's hand, lists the items and shows the purchases to have been spread between vocal works – the bulk of them sacred, but there were also some opera scores – and books on music. Further building of the score collection of 'sacred and lyrical *chefs d'œuvre*' became an explicit aim of Ella's (see prospectus supplement, 1 January 1861), as did achieving complete sets of the best chamber music (whether in scores, parts, or both, he does not say).

[130] Prospectus supplement dated 1 January 1861.

making financial gifts to the Institute.[131] Some gave books, prints and instruments as well or instead. Anna-Maria Cornewall, for example, took out a subscription and let the Institute have full-score manuscript copies of eighteenth-century Italian operas, plus her late brother Charles's string quartets and Mozart piano concertos. Few of the financial donors, however, dug deep into their pockets. Tite and Brassey were the most generous, but they each gave only £100 – consider what they might have afforded – getting life memberships in exchange. And while Ella attracted a handful of donors from outside the social circle, the most generous of whom, Madame Erard, sent £50 from Paris and, later, one of the family's prestigious pianos (worth £180), the majority of the Institute's supporters were from 'within' the network, and there were no donations of a truly significant size.[132] Ella had made it a matter of unstated policy to restrict the membership to this group of amateurs until, as he privately explained to Fétis, 'I obtain money enough to complete my Library of all good and great books'.[133] Then and only then would he invite 'any professors [of music] to be a member'.[134] One imagines he hoped to avoid any sniping at the Institute's shortcomings from his professional peers, and reasoned that gifts were more likely to increase if social exclusivity was maintained. Besides, musicians were unlikely to make sizeable donations to the funds, and their participation might have put the Institute in direct competition with the Musical Society of London, which was also building a library.[135] But such gestures

[131] Donations brought benefits of reduced Institute subscription rates and life memberships to the givers. £5 entitled the donor to a half-price subscription; £20 produced one life membership and one free admission, while £100 guaranteed a life membership and three admissions.

[132] The piano was a personal gift to Ella, but he loaned it to the Institute (diary, 22 November 1860; EllaC, MS 129).

[133] Letter to Fétis, dated 19 October 1860 (*WangerméeF*, 452–3, at 452). He continued: 'I shall first collect all good editions of chamber music, then concert-partitions, lyrical and sacred'.

[134] Ibid. Ella went on to indicate that he would 'lend 1000 vols [of his own], all my instruments and autographs to the Institute and at my death[,] which I hope may not be soon, I propose to bequeathe all my library and instruments—selon le programme'.

[135] An inventory of this collection does not exist, but we know that the '[r]emaining library of the Musical Society' containing 'valuable and rare treatises and works on the history of music' was sold by Puttick & Simpson on 2 and 4 May 1868 (Coover, *Private Music Collections*, p. 272). Part of the library had been sold earlier, in 1862: A. Hyatt King, *Some British Collectors of Music, c.1660–1960* (Cambridge: Cambridge University Press, 1963), p. 55, describes this lot as comprising the collections formerly owned by the British musicians W. Horsley and J. W. Calcott – 'not a very exciting library, but [one that] showed a discriminating taste for Italian

of exclusion were equally likely to inflame old antagonisms, and could easily be interpreted as another example of Ella trying to align himself with high society.

In spite of Ella's initial optimism, to say nothing of his wealth of experience in gathering support for his initiatives – 'I am very sanguine about this Institute's vitality' he had told Clerk in summer 1860[136] – his greater expectations for the Institute were never realized. There was an inaugural concert and much speechifying on 5 February 1861. Piatti and Vieuxtemps were among those who played (the latter apparently for a reduced fee), and ninety people were present.[137] Further evening concerts ('receptions') with new artists and music, and a series of lectures or 'discourses' (written and given by Ella) were given during 1861, and a smaller flurry of activities took place in 1862.[138] The instrument collection and library appear to have been used by members, and the book and music holdings increased through donations and a few purchases.[139] Meanwhile, the council, in contrast to the committee of the Musical Union and in keeping with its trusteeship of others' money, seems to have been closely involved in institutional affairs, Ella checking speeches and meeting frequently with Clerk and Tite, and so on.[140] But by the end of 1862 Ella was admitting that not enough money had been raised to develop the Institute in the way he had hoped. The flow of donations, healthy in the beginning, had slowed. In January 1861 they totalled £793 2s 0d and by Michaelmas had reached £940 14s 0d; a year later (Michaelmas 1862) they had

cantatas of the early eighteenth century and for Italian theory of the age of Galilei and Eximeno'.

[136] Inventory and notes sent to Clerk, probably written August 1860 (NAS, GD18/3946).

[137] The event is described in the diary, 5 February 1861 (EllaC, MS 130), *RMU* (1861), 10, and in a report in *ILN* (9 February 1861), 121, which gives a summary of the speech Ella made, outlining his aims for the library among other things. The expenses for the receptions are noted in Ella's Institute account book (EllaC, MS 55), p. 11: for the session on 25 February, for example, Vieuxtemps was given a token 10s 6d – a far cry from his fee for a public performance at the Union concerts.

[138] A report of one of Ella's lectures is in *ILN* (23 February 1861), 165. Dates for the Institute's meetings can be traced in Ella's diaries.

[139] There is no evidence of rules for the use of library materials, or records of borrowing. However, notes in Ella's hand inside an ex-Musical Union Institute volume (Reicha's *Cours de composition musicale*), now housed in RCMl, suggest he sometimes allowed items to be taken away: 'Lent, August 21st, to Mr Kirkman by J Ella'. For a list of purchases and donations for 1860 and 1861 see EllaC, MS 56, pp. 6–7, 10–12. The chief acquisition was items from the sale of part of John Hullah's library; see n. 129.

[140] As per diary entries for [3] February, 13 February and [24] November 1861 (EllaC, MS 130).

grown by only £12 2s.[141] Money had been deposited in the bank, and there was enough revenue from annual subscriptions to keep the institution ticking over. But there were outgoings to be factored in too (rent, servants and so on), and simply not enough capital, as he told readers of the *Record of the Musical Union* in January 1863, to 'justify me in throwing open the rooms, and their contents, to the use of the musical world; or in making any further outlay of the donations in hand in the purchase of costly publications'.[142] Quite possibly Ella hoped this statement might stimulate donations, though whether it could ever produce the additional £4,000 he was aiming for, even he must have doubted. To boost affairs he put his own, considerable music library at the disposal of the Institute members – the items were housed on site, Ella having been 'in residence' since 1862.[143] The Institute's library probably needed a boost; its profile seems to have been a mixture of vocal scores of eighteenth-century operas and oratorios, many in manuscript – the sorts of items that had gone somewhat out of fashion and use by 1860, which probably made giving easy – plus parts to string quartets, quintets and so on. Among donations were choral works and theory books given (1861) by the music publisher Robert Cocks – hardly his bestsellers, but that is scarcely to be surprised at, since music publishers were hardly likely to be supportive of any initiatives that might steal revenue.[144]

Over the next three years, to judge from Ella's diary and the Institute's extant account books, activities became sporadic, and subscriber numbers, which had never reached Ella's self-imposed limit, declined sharply – presumably a case of cause and effect. Donations all but ceased. The organization was keeping going, but capital was declining annually.[145] How long could it continue? And what about the grand plan for the library? Such questions must have preyed on Ella's mind.

---

[141] Totals taken from the prospectus supplement of 1 January 1861 and Tite's Institute account book (EllaC, MS 56, p. 8). They are largely in line with the donations documented in Ella's Institute account book (EllaC, MS 55, pp. 2, 4, 6 and 12).

[142] Preface to *RMU* (1862), dated January 1863. In fact, Ella had been cautious about how much he spent on books and music: the Hullah sale items were the largest expense, totalling £44 7s in all (EllaC, MS 56, pp. 6–7).

[143] Prospectus (Michaelmas 1860). That Ella had always intended to merge his own library (a catalogue of which is preserved in EllaC, MS 54) with the Institute's is indicated by the announcement in *RMU* (1849); see also n. 134.

[144] Other sizeable donations included Italian opera manuscripts from the Dowager Countess of Westmorland and a selection of literature on music from Mrs Engebach of Campden Hill, Kensington. These gifts, along with Cocks's, are listed in Tite's Institute account book (EllaC, MS 56, pp. 10–12).

[145] As evinced by Ella's Institute account book (EllaC, MS 55), pp. 15–17. The balance, which had stood at £272 13s 6d in January 1862, had dropped to £188 2s 0d by

In summer 1865 Ella, Tite and Brassey took a decision regarding the library. The books and music were to be offered to the South Kensington Museum, along with a proposal from Ella to add his own library, instruments and the sum of £1,000 on his death.[146] The gesture followed a series of negotiations between Ella and Henry Cole, the driving force behind the South Kensington Museum, the sole secretary of the Department of Science and Art, a fellow ambassador for high culture and the shaping of public taste, someone already cognizant of the problems in the nation's music schools, and a serious music-lover who had recently (1864) become a follower of the Musical Union.[147] This revised plan still realized many of Ella's longer-term goals, and the adaptation was easily justified, since back in 1853 one patron had allegedly promised £1,000 once Ella's 'small beginnings were joined to that of the Prince Consort for a public Library [of the arts].[148] A letter to Cole, published for Musical Union members to see, made clear Ella's hopes that South Kensington would further the Institute's work, and bring into being the national music library and perhaps even the full-scale music institution he had envisioned. To strengthen the argument, the late Prince Albert was said (on the Earl of Westmorland's authority) to have harboured aspirations for the type of institute Ella had founded.[149] In the event, Cole gratefully accepted the gift on behalf of the museum's governors, and Ella put an upbeat interpretation on the arrangements

Michaelmas 1863. By 1864 it was down to £160. These pages also suggest that by 1862 Ella was paying rent to the Institute, rather than receiving a fee.

[146] Ella explained the decision in 'The Musical Union Institute', *RMU* (1865), sup., 19–20. (In the event, his final will did not include such a bequest.) There was a suggestion, too, that he would further add to the Institute's collection 'with the funds at my disposal'.

[147] He remained in the Union until 1880. Cole's professional career is discussed in Minihan, *The Nationalization of Culture*, 96–137, and Burton, *Vision and Accident*, *passim*. The latter indicates that Cole's agendas were geared more towards shaping working-class taste than Ella's were, although both shared a belief in the power of education to change attitudes towards high culture.

A more anecdotal account of Cole's strident public personality is uncovered in Elizabeth Bonython, *King Cole: a Picture Portrait of Sir Henry Cole, KCB, 1808–1882* (London: Victoria and Albert Museum, [1982]). On Cole's role in reforming music education, see David Wright, 'The South Kensington Music Schools and the Development of the British Conservatoire in the Late Nineteenth Century', *JRMA*, 130 (2005), 236–82.

[148] *RMU* (1865), sup., 19.

[149] Ibid. Westmorland seems to have acted as a conduit for communication with the prince until 1858; see Ella's diary, 19 November 1858 (EllaC, MS 127), which notes that he had received a 'letter from Lord W. declining to ask any more favors of Queen & Prince &c'.

in his programme literature. Yet there was no disguising the fact that the Musical Union Institute would now never be the cradle for Ella's grand schemes, and even Ella could not completely mask his disappointment that his initiative had had to be saved by another institution.

What is so striking about this episode is that, despite Ella's ability to attract audiences for Musical Union concerts (demonstrating that there was a section of high society prepared and eager to invest in a serious concert culture), when it came to establishing a broader programme of activities and worthy goals he was not able to obtain sufficient support. High-calibre performers – vital in marketing Musical Union concerts – were usually conspicuously absent from the Institute's performance events, which were far more low-key, and this is something that may have told against the project. But the fact was that a tradition of providing large amounts of financial support for musical activities – substantial 'private patronage' – did not seem to exist among London's wealthy classes. Nor could it be easily created. 'Where are the rich musical philanthropists, in this city of palaces and merchant princes?' Ella had asked rhetorically in 1851, his mind full of the private giving witnessed in the sphere of fine art.[150] In 1865, the answer was that those that *had* emerged had shown themselves not prepared to sink large sums into an institution for the general promotion of music within their own circles, let alone for the wider public. Nor were they prepared to help build musical infrastructure. And anyway, there was too much happening simultaneously, notably the (bigger) plans at South Kensington and an enquiry into the state of music education, to detract from Ella's scheme. In this respect his initial optimism about the Institute's future had been vastly misplaced.

Without doubt, there were always likely to be difficulties in persuading people to invest in an art form that was by its very nature intangible and temporal. Thus Ella's emphasis on the library as the cornerstone of the Institute was well construed, since scores and instruments were the physical artefacts from which the aural experience was conjured up, and they represented tangible evidence of investment. But clearly that was not enough. In truth, unwillingness to give financial support to projects for the nation was also experienced in the British art world, where, according to historian Dianne Sachko Macleod, 'élite patrons […] were comfortable in their time-honored roles of private connoisseurs, and saw no reason to extend themselves into other [i.e. public] arenas', which were deemed to be a government responsibility.[151] '[N]ational practice' had traditionally held that

---

[150] *RMU* (1851), 56.

[151] Dianne Sachko Macleod, *Art and the Victorian Middle Class: Money and the Making of Cultural Identity* (Cambridge: Cambridge University Press, 1996), 97.

'[art] patronage should be conducted on a private, not a public, level'.[152] On this last point there were glimmers of change, as government put public money into the South Kensington projects. All was of course relative, but both private and public patronage of art was much stronger than it was for music. So from Ella's perspective, as he had watched the South Kensington projects flower with money from government, art seemed to be doing well in terms of national support. '£17 000 voted for the [Brompton] <u>Boilers</u> [i.e. the South Kensington Museum]', he had grumbled to Clerk in summer 1860, '& no mention of Music, shows the temper of the H. of Commons'.[153]

Could things ever change? Ella had thought they could, and may well have considered gaining the ear of some music-loving members at Westminster as his initial challenge. He had drawn two MPs, Clerk himself (Tory) and Tite (Liberal), into the Institute's council, and on 12 July 1860 he had visited the Houses of Parliament, speaking to men known to him – Lord Hotham, George Bentinck, John Turner Hopwood (all Tories) and Edward Horsman (Liberal) – all of whom were associated with the Union.[154] There is no proof positive that he lobbied them about the cause of music, but that must have been a likely reason for his visit, which lay well outside his normal routines and coincided with the period during which the Select Committee for the South Kensington Museum was sitting. Yet the reality was that none of these parliamentarians had much sway over the thinking of Palmerston's government; only Bentinck was on the select committee. If Ella were to have stood a chance of influencing parliamentary policy on this or other matters, he would have had to have enlisted men with ministerial appointments to the Institute's cause. But nobody in high office had shown any inclination towards the sort of music-making that went on at the Musical Union. As a more practicable means for achieving his ultimate aim, networking with the South Kensington movers and shakers – notably Cole – must have seemed a better alternative, since their schemes were already in receipt of parliamentary aid.[155] What is more, as Ella knew, music was nudging towards a place on the South Kensington agenda: even

[152] Macleod, *Art*, 97, paraphrasing Minihan's discussion (*The Nationalization of Culture*) of the 1830s.

[153] Inventory and notes to Clerk, probably written August 1860 (NAS, GD18/3946). The Select Committee on the South Kensington Museum reported on 1 August 1860; the vote for £17,000 was carried on 18 August (*The Times*, 20 August 1860).

[154] Diary, 12 July 1860 (EllaC, MS 129). Lord Clarence Paget had arranged for Ella to be admitted to the building.

[155] The South Kensington land was purchased with profits from the Great Exhibition, but more money was needed to develop the site. The government contributed public money through the 1850s and 60s (Minihan, *The Nationalization of Culture*, 123–6).

before Albert's death in 1861 the prince had discussed with Cole the possibility of establishing a music hall, and by spring 1863 a site had been reserved for it.[156] (It would become the Royal Albert Hall, though Cole would eventually have to raise money for it privately.)

Cole's acceptance of the Institute's music library for the South Kensington Museum (whence it eventually went to the Royal College of Music library) was arguably the best outcome Ella could have achieved.[157] And, pragmatist that he was, Ella continued to look to the future if not posterity, suggesting he would continue to add to the collection (presumably spending the residual capital) until its relocation to Kensington occurred. In placing a distinguished music collection in the bosom of a national art library and gallery he may have hoped to force the issue of support for music, and to demonstrate the need to treat and fund music and art alike. Perhaps he felt personal glory might follow. If fine art could have the Sheepshanks Gallery, named after its donor, the merchant and art collector John Sheepshanks, why not the Ella Gallery for music? Meanwhile, until the transfer of the collection took place (in 1868), the Musical Union Institute's practical activities at Hanover Square continued on a modest basis, and Ella lived there as resident curator.[158] The arrangement made good sense from Ella's viewpoint; it enabled him to maintain a select West End address for himself, and the administrative base for the Musical Union.

Around the time this was happening, Ella championed another, interlinked cause for concern: the state of British conservatoire education and the consequent poor standards of proficiency in British-trained musicians. It was a question on which he (among others) had held forth, critically, for years.[159] He had become aware that fine art, with its nationwide Schools of Design, which came under the

[156] Bonython, *King Cole*, 56–7.

[157] In 1900 the music, which had probably always seemed something of a white elephant, was passed to RCMl, where it still resides. A copy of Ella's letter to the Museum, dated 7 August 1868, is preserved in EllaC, MS 163. It states that he sent 'some 200 Vols [of music and books] of all Sizes', a 'Portrait in oil of Rossini, painted 1826, busts of Handel, Mendelssohn, Beethoven & Paganini[,] & Her M. the Queen & the late Prince Consort (by Nobb)'. In fact, a printed list of bequests and donations to the Museum, 1851–1900, notes that the collection comprised '329 Volumes of Music, 6 Busts, 1 Oil painting (a portrait of Rossini)' [information kindly supplied by V&A Archives Department]. Ella's letter says that Tite made it a condition of the gift that 'the Music be placed Apart, & open to Public inspection'.

[158] E.g. in 1868 Ella revived the Institute soirées: see *RMU* (1868), 20, sup., 17, 25. Rubinstein played in all three, including on one occasion Schubert's piano trio in B♭ with Auer and Jacquard.

[159] E.g. *RMU* (1850), 18; and (1853), 9–10, 32.

government's Department of Science and Art and were managed (from 1853) by the indefatigable Cole, seemed again to be doing better than music, and he upped the pace of his campaigning in the 1860s as he grew into his now double role as Director of the Musical Union and its Institute, doubtless feeling that his position gave him a duty to speak out and a right to be listened to.[160] It was 'a national disgrace' that there was no publicly funded academy to educate talented young musicians for the profession (his own formative experiences weighing heavily, one imagines).[161] Why was there no conservatoire where gifted students from poor families could be placed on scholarships, where teaching would be executed to high, rigorous standards and through the employment and adequate reimbursement of a high-calibre professorial staff, and where standards of student attainment would match those found abroad? There were several effective models that could be seriously investigated, the state-funded conservatoires in Paris and Brussels usually topping the list of exemplars, with St Petersburg a new, impressive contender.

The timing of Ella's utterances is significant, since in the mid-1860s the matter was finally getting serious consideration as the Society for the Encouragement of Arts, Manufactures and Commerce, promoters of the Great Exhibition, established a committee of enquiry into the state of British music education (including the parlous condition of the Royal Academy of Music) compared with that found abroad. Cole, a member of that society, played a central role in the process, which ran from May 1865 until February 1866.[162] Sitting alongside Cole on the committee were others from the Musical Union circle: Sir George Clerk and Lord Gerald Fitzgerald. Several witnesses were called, among them Sir George Clerk and Henry Cole themselves, Charles Lucas (Academy principal), Michael Costa, Sir F. A. G. Ouseley, John Hullah and Henry Chorley; written evidence was taken too from a range of musicians, including military and cathedral men. Transcripts of the proceedings appeared in the press, with many of the views and observations expressed in line with Ella's own thinking. Like many interested observers and participants Ella hoped the enquiry would recommend that government adequately fund a national academy of music and place it at South Kensington (the central School of Design had moved into the South Kensington Museum along

---

[160] E.g. *RMU* (1859), sup., 22–3 [an account of Henry Chorley's proposal to the Society of Arts for a National Academy of Music, providing talented students with a good, cheap education]; (1860), 2; (1863), sup., 37–9 (esp. 39); (1865), sup., 9–10, 12, 17, 35, 36.

[161] *RMU* (1861), 2.

[162] Cole chaired most of the meetings. Ella's remarks in *RMU* (1865) coincided with the committee's sitting.

with the Department of Science and Art, and had become the National Art Training School in 1863). So he elaborated in Musical Union literature on what he felt needed to happen in this eventuality, including the appointment of an able chief administrator.[163] (Doubtless, too, he hoped the ex-Institute books and music in the South Kensington Museum would become the kernel of a conservatoire collection.) And he wrote at length of his favourable experiences of musical standards and educational opportunities abroad.[164] In sum, Ella aimed to contribute to the debate from the sidelines, to lobby those from the Musical Union involved in the enquiry, particularly Cole, whom he was seeing socially, and to appeal to those with tentacles into government.[165]

The committee reported in June 1866.[166] Its recommendations were well meaning: it emphasized the desirability of government providing adequate funding to establish and maintain a credible 'National Academy of Music' and provide free scholarships for gifted students; it believed some money could be found through public fund-raising; and it suggested the new institution should be developed from the Royal Academy of Music, which should take new premises in Kensington. But the document lacked persuasive strength and influence, and in the short term its suggestions were overlooked by government, Disraeli even choosing to axe the paltry £500 grant to the Academy in 1867.[167] Disappointed Ella may have been,

[163] See esp. *RMU* (1865), sup., 9–10. He may have envisaged himself as the 'experienced professor of independent means and moral influence' (p. 10), who would become the head of any new institution, though he equally may have hoped the role would go to Costa. If the former, this might explain why Ella was not called to give evidence to the committee, an apparent anomaly since he had so much first-hand experience of the best European musicians. He suggested the administrator should be someone 'on whose judgment reliance can be placed for the appointment of competent masters in each department. Such a man is to be found in London' (ibid.).

[164] E.g. the accounts of music in Paris and Italy in *RMU* (1865), sup., *passim*. He was also almost certainly responsible for the unsigned account of music in Florence ('Musical Institutes in Italy') in the *Orchestra* (30 September 1865), 6–7.

[165] As documented in Ella's diary, 1865–6. On 21 January 1865 (EllaC, MS 134) Ella first learned from Cole of the plans for the government enquiry while dining at Cole's house.

[166] *First Report of the Committee appointed to Inquire into and Report on the State of Musical Education, at Home and Abroad: together with the Evidence taken before, and Information collected by the Committee* (London: Bell & Daldy, [1867]). The report is dated 27 June 1866. The enquiry is well summarized and its significance trenchantly explored in *EhrlichMP*, 88–99.

[167] The grant had been allowed in 1864 by Gladstone, who reinstated it once back in office in 1868. See *EhrlichMP*, 87.

but he continued to campaign on this most crucial of issues, forever explaining to Musical Union readers the value and quality of European systems and underlining at every concert the link between the calibre of performer heard and the quality of his/her (European) education. In a few years' time, as the goal for a new academy came closer and Cole attempted to set up the National Training School for Music in Kensington Gore, Ella would enter the debate once more.

❧ 282 *Vauxhall Bridge Road*

Funeral & other Expenses have diminished my balance more than
usual   ∽ Letter from Ella to the Secretary of the
                                 Royal Society of Musicians, 25 March 1867

R IGHT now the scene switches to Ella's private world and a dimension of his life suppressed by earlier biographers. Throughout the 1860s Ella continued to keep his diary with daily regularity. More memorandum and appointment book than journal or log, its contents at this period are mostly specks of detail which, when pieced together, give a sense of the patterns of his professional life and the social networks he maintained. What they do not seem to yield are any insights into his inner thoughts or private domain. One Monday in July 1866, however, his guard is let down, and we discover something at once more personal and revealing.[168] Ella is summoned to a house in Vauxhall Bridge Road, which lay to the south-east of the new and bustling Victoria railway station, an area already becoming known as less than salubrious. On arrival he finds that a woman whom he calls 'MW' is 'no more!', having broken 'a blood vessel coughing at 16-15, & died immediately'.[169] He remains there all day, lamenting the passing of 'Beata Rosa–!', and returns home late that night, 'head paining me – hurt with grief until now I never felt'.[170] Who is this woman who can cause Ella to express such depths of grief? Why has she been invisible for so long? And why does it matter to a biography of a concert manager?

The answers to the first two of these questions are not easily come by, for much of the evidence is circumstantial, obscure and often conflicting. But we can start with what we know. 'MW', or Mary Webb as the diary later identifies her, was buried three days later in Brompton Cemetery in Fulham, the funeral being

---

[168] Diary, 16 July 1866 (EllaC, MS 135). The entry is marked as having special significance.

[169] Ibid.

[170] Ibid. The passages continues, somewhat ungrammatically and making only partial sense, as follows: 'adieu is so com è l'amore d'un angela' (farewell is so [? word missing], like the love of an angel).

organized and paid for by Ella.[171] The deceased was relatively young: her age at the time of death, depending on whether one believes the burial records or the death certificate (neither being infallible), was thirty or thirty-seven; Ella noted privately that she had died aged twenty-seven.[172] There were only four mourners, one of whom was the undertaker; as well as Ella, there was Miss Nellie (Ellen) Beech, who had been present at the death and registered it, and one Mrs Robinson, to whom we shall return. The grave in which Mary Webb was laid was later to become Ella's burial ground, but the commemorative obelisk that survives today bears no mention of her.[173] In the days after her death, Ella settled her affairs and organized the removal of furniture from 282 Vauxhall Bridge Road to 18 Hanover Square.[174]

In point of fact, the clues to Mary Webb's existence go back in the diaries at least ten years – although, deliberately veiled and abbreviated, they look completely insignificant to the unsuspicious eye. Looked at afresh, and cross-referenced with other primary documents, they reinforce the thought that this was someone whose life had meaning for Ella. He had been visiting her regularly – usually twice a week or more – since the mid-1850s, often for dinner or towards the end of busy days, after bachelor evenings at his club.[175] Out of season and away from London, whether in Scotland or in Europe, he would write to her frequently, also sending her letters to forward to bigwigs back home, and would visit her almost immediately upon his return. His account book confirms he gave her regular instalments of money. In fact he paid the rent on her lodgings, furnished them, paid other bills, and even hired a piano for her (perhaps giving her lessons).[176] From time to time the diaries hint that the woman he also sometimes referred to as 'Rose Webb' helped him out practically: sorting programmes, sewing and mending for him,

---

[171] The funeral took place on 19 July. Evidence that Ella paid for everything comes from the 1866 diary (EllaC, MS 135, *passim*), and his account book (EllaC, MS 6, pp. 155 and 125).

[172] Photograph album (EllaC, MS 1), p. 33. Thus born 14 April 1829, 1836 or 1839.

[173] Affirmed by burial records at Brompton Cemetery, Fulham (BR 45742 and 142600).

[174] See diary entries up to 18 August 1866 (EllaC, MS 135).

[175] The first appearance of 'MW' in the diary is in 1855 (EllaC, MS 124; entry for 14 November); whether Ella knew her before then is not clear. We know from parish rate books (in CWA) that by 1 April 1859 Mary Webb was installed in 282 Vauxhall Bridge Road (until 1865 it was numbered 10 Trellick Terrace); she is listed as the occupier until 1866.

[176] The hiring of the piano, an Erard, is noted in the diary, 18 November 1857 (EllaC, MS 126).

and so on.[177] He remembered her birthdays. She gave him a photo album 'to hold personal friends only' on one of his, though the picture of her that once adorned it is no longer there; all that remains are traces of a pencilled annotation, half-erased, indicating her tragic, early death, with the words 'Ella fui amata!'[178] Very occasionally she visited him; more often than not he went to her. What they categorically did not do was appear together in fashionable parts of town, and only rarely do they seem to have stepped out together elsewhere (and even then we sense the figure of 'Nellie' Beech as a chaperone).[179] She was never a member of the Musical Union, and he made no public reference to her.[180] In terms of Ella's professional and social life, she did not exist.

On the face of it, the likelihood is that Mary Webb was Ella's mistress, part of a secret life that he shared, albeit unknowingly, with such famous men as Charles Dickens, Wilkie Collins and Arthur Sullivan.[181] The neighbourhood around Victoria was shabby genteel at best, seedy and ridden with prostitution

[177] 'Rose' could have been an affectionate name, or a given forename (though it does not appear on her death certificate or in other formal documents; the parish rates and the cemetery records record her only as Mary). On her helping Ella practically, see the diary entries for 17 February 1860 (programmes) and 16 March 1860 (sewing): EllaC, MS 129.

[178] The gift of the album is noted in the diary, 19 December 1864 (EllaC, MS 133). The full inscription in the album (EllaC, MS 1, p. 33) reads: 'Rose Webb – Obitt 1866. July 16th aged 27.! – Ella fui amata! ['She was loved!' – or, allowing for a grammatical error, 'Ella was loved!']'. The forename 'Rose' appears to have been written over something else. The page once held another photograph, to judge from erased notes at the top of the page. It is impossible to tell whether one of two loose photographs of females preserved in the manuscript at this point is of Rose Webb. One picture is labelled 'Mrs. Haweis'. The other is of an unidentified, well-dressed female; it was taken by Fergus Brothers in Greenock.

[179] E.g. 'Crystal Palace by Chelsea bridge con MW + Nelly' (16 June 1858; EllaC, MS 127). Nelly [Nellie; Ellen] Beech [Beach] was clearly part of the secret – a friend, perhaps a relative, or even a housekeeper – and Ella stayed in contact with her in the weeks, months and years immediately following Mary's death. She lived in the vicinity: an address of 313 Vauxhall Bridge Road for E. Beach is noted in the back of Ella's 1866 diary (EllaC, MS 135).

[180] His reference to the funeral expenses in the communication to the Royal Society of Musicians cited at the head of this section made no mention of the deceased's identity.

[181] On Dickens, see Claire Tomalin, *The Invisible Woman: the Story of Nelly Ternan and Charles Dickens* (Harmondsworth: Penguin Books, 1991). On Collins, see William M. Clarke, *The Secret Life of Wilkie Collins* (Chicago: Ivan R. Dee, 1991). On Sullivan, see Arthur Jacobs, *Arthur Sullivan: a Victorian Musician*, 2nd edition (Aldershot: Scolar Press, 1992), esp. 161–2. There are also similarities with the

at worst, and always filled with the unknown faces of travellers: in sum, the perfect place to slide anonymously through nocturnal shadows.[182] Moreover, servicing a mistress was hardly an unusual aspect of male behaviour at this period, particularly in a society where bachelorhood by choice tended to be frowned upon; and we should hardly be surprised that the man who had eschewed marriage in the 1830s yet was clearly attracted to women should seek this less responsible form of physical and emotional satisfaction.[183] 'Vive les garçons say I for musicians', he had written in 1839, 'the burden of a rib would distract me!'[184]

As to Mary Webb's identity and persona, much remains mysterious, the historian's searches being hindered by her all-too-ordinary name, the absence of civil registration of births before 1837, and a lack of corroborative evidence on key points.[185] Perhaps, like the many affluent men whom the writer Henry Mayhew had observed frequenting the Pimlico area in 1852, Ella had simply sought out a discreet introduction to a 'quiet lady whose secrecy he [could] rely upon'.[186] Perhaps she had been a servant in a grand house of one of his many fashionable associates, and he had met her there, later installing her in this part of town. Or perhaps their association had other roots. Whatever the explanation, and whatever her family origins (these also remain unclear), there can be little doubt she inhabited a lowlier social world than did Ella. Her neighbours, according to the 1861 census, were mostly artisans, craftspeople and labourers; while what we know

double life of Arthur Munby, Victorian barrister and civil servant, on whom, see Derek Hudson, *Munby: Man of Two Worlds* (London: Abacus, 1974).

[182] According to Adam Stout, *Pimlico: Deep Well of Glee* (London: Westminster City Archives, 1997), 57, Pimlico became a nexus of brothels almost immediately Victoria station opened in October 1860. However, Isobel Watson, *Westminster and Pimlico Past: a Visual History* (London: Historical Publications, 1993), pp. 79–80, argues plausibly that there was nevertheless a second, genteel side of Pimlico, evidenced by the number of rentiers, artists, language and music teachers in residence. She suggests that the area most riddled with prostitution was around Lupus Street, roughly to the south of Vauxhall Bridge Road.

[183] On bachelorhood by choice, see John Tosh, *A Man's Place: Masculinity and the Middle-Class Home in Victorian England* (New Haven and London: Yale University Press, 1999), 173; on the use of prostitutes, see ibid., p. 130.

[184] Diary, 10 January 1839 (EllaC, MS 108).

[185] She is not to be confused, either, with the family of affluent John Webb, members of the Musical Union whose names crop up regularly in Ella's diaries. (For biography of these Webbs, see EllaC, MS 1, pp. 12–14.)

[186] Cited in Watson, *Westminster*, 79. Henry Mayhew, a journalist, was one of the first to write about the capital's poverty and social problems, in *London Labor and London Poor* (London, 1851–64).

of the rituals of her funeral – the absence of a full week of mourning, the presence of women at the burial, the 'luncheon' afterwards – further suggests the mores of a working-class milieu.[187] Whether she was by law a Miss or a Mrs is unclear,[188] but she had family connections in the Liverpool area and there was a young married relative, Martha Elizabeth Robinson [Robertson] (*née* Webb). Martha Elizabeth, known affectionately as Mollie or Molly, and who was supposedly Mary's daughter (though probably not, to judge from the way Ella refers to her and from other circumstantial evidence, his progeny), arrived from Manchester 'broken hearted' the day after Mary died.[189]

Adding to the enigma is the fact that in the years following 1856 Ella almost unfailingly noted against the inscription 'MW' the anniversary of a wedding day (13 or 14 November 1855) in his diary, suggesting an event of considerable personal significance, particularly as it was a day on which he saw her more often than not.[190] The principle of 'Occam's razor' would lead us to suspect this was a celebration of her marriage to Ella himself, but if so the union was clandestine and went formally unregistered, for no marriage certificate in their names has been found. An unregistered wedding is by no means impossible, even with the reforms to the

---

[187] On the social aspects of mourning, see Pat Jalland, *Death in the Victorian Family* (Oxford: Oxford University Press, 1996), 210–29, esp. 221 and 223.

[188] The death certificate reports that she was 'independent' and the daughter of one Isaac Webb, thus implying her status as spinster, though also setting up the possibility that she was Isaac's daughter-in-law. She appears in the rate books as 'Mrs.': this may have been a deliberate attempt to provide the cover of respectability, perhaps invoking widowhood.

[189] Diary, 17 July 1866 (EllaC, MS 135). Ella describes her as 'M^rs. Robinson (Molly, her [i.e. Mary's] child)' and goes on to explain that 'her husband, too, failed in business thru' Banks breaking' and then says 'Dear child – inconsolable'. She seems to have been married in Liverpool on 16 February 1863 to a Mr 'Robertson', according to Ella's diary entry for that day (EllaC, MS 132; here, confusingly, she is referred to also as 'MW'). No certificate of the marriage has been tracked down, so other aspects of the family relationships have not been verified. Perhaps the wedding was clandestine.

[190] See the diary, 14 November 1856, 11 November 1858, 13 November 1860, 13 November 1861, 13 November 1863 (EllaC, MSS 125, 127, 129, 130, 132). Some of the entries seem to have been made at a time other than that at which the main log of events was written. In the diary for 1855 (EllaC, MS 124) the entry for 14 November is marked off emphatically, as if to denote a special day, with some notes of appointments (not entirely clear, but connected with Drury Lane Theatre) and the line 'Slept chez Mr Raymond, – <u>M.W.</u>' Raymond's identity is unclear, though he and his wife are noted elsewhere as going to the Olympic Theatre with Ella; they lived at 80 Stanley Street, Pimlico, close to Lupus Street.

Marriage Act from 1753, which sought to outlaw such practices.[191] Indeed, if this was not the case, quite why he should have been so assiduous in remembering his mistress's marriage to another man, and why she would celebrate her anniversary with him, is not so easily explained. A less obvious scenario, but one that might go some way to explaining the wedding anniversary fixation, is that Mary Webb was Ella's (illegitimate) daughter from a liaison some years earlier when he was living among lowlier folk.[192] It would then follow that Mary's husband was dead or vanished; and that Mollie was the sixty-four-year-old Ella's grandchild. Save for one further scrap of evidence – a private letter written years after the event, where Ella refers to the woman who had died in July 1866 as the person he had intended to marry – this theory might obtain.[193] The best explanation of Mary's identity is that she was Ella's lover.

As regards Mollie, there is compelling evidence (discussed in Chapter 7) that she was Mary's niece, not her daughter, something which lines up with what we know of the two women's dates of birth.[194] Ella had been aware of Mollie since 1856, and he took her under his wing in the days following Mary's death, even changing his will in Mollie's interest a week later after some sort of revelation on her part, though revoking it the following day in favour of a cousin.[195] Thereafter

---

[191] For insights into the nineteenth-century legislation and continuities in clandestiny, see R. B. Outhwaite, *Clandestine Marriage in England, 1500–1850* (London and Rio Grande: Hambledon Press, 1995), pp. xxii–xxiii, 164–7.

[192] For instance, around the times 1829 or 1836, the possible years of birth according to the certification of her death and burial, when Ella was living in and around Soho.

[193] Letter from Ella to one Mr Lewis, dated 16 July 1880, discussing the pain of bereavement in connection with the recent death of their friend Tom Taylor: 'This <u>day</u> 14 years ago [*recte* 19 July], I buried a lady, to whom I should have been wedded very shortly after the date of her short illness, 1866, – ending with a broken blood vessel, in a fit of Coughin –' (RAMm, 2005.1317).

[194] The evidence is not watertight, but Mollie (Martha Elizabeth) was probably born either *c*.1841 or in 1845, which would make it virtually impossible that she was Mary's daughter.

[195] As we shall see, Mollie was pregnant by someone other than Mr Robinson, a Mr Finicane, whose name she subsequently took. The 'Disclosure of M^rs R^n.' (an announcement of the pregnancy? or that she was a niece, not a daughter?) and Ella's codicil conferring 'Rosa's Interests' to her took place on 23 July (1866 diary: EllaC, MS 135). Ella's overnight change of mind to leave everything to Edward Harley (diary, 24 July 1866; see also 26 July) was presumably related to these events, and certainly seems to have signalled a short-term cooling off of Ella's relationship with Mollie. Some of Mary's 'goods', hitherto placed 'in trust for M^rs. Robinson' at Taylor's Repository (diary, 18 July 1866), were to be sent to Hanover

Mollie remained in London, living in the Brompton area without male company as a 'Mrs Finicane', and Ella remained in touch with her, supporting her financially for several years. This was something he did always with discretion, keeping her existence – as he had Mary's – concealed from his fashionable entourage. One might indeed query why he would do all this if Mollie were not biologically linked to him, though it could have simply remained a way for him to keep Mary's memory alive.

Riveting as this sleuthing into Ella's invisible women may be on its own terms, the real question is why it should matter so much to our narratives. A first answer is that, regardless of whether 'MW' was Ella's common-law wife or his mistress (in the end, it does not matter which), her existence humanizes his character, explaining an otherwise puzzling 'lack' in his life and showing him to be indulging in patterns of behaviour that were typical for males of his time and position. She, moreover, gives us further insight into the duality of Ella's private and public worlds – for just as he kept his private views on modern, Romantic music well concealed, offering often diametrically opposed opinion in print from what he confessed to his diary, he was equally able to interleave an influential life in high society on the one hand with comings, goings and dealings in shabbier surroundings on the other. Such secrecy was par for the course in the lives of Victorian men who kept women; but it was also a measure of how far Ella had travelled from his days in Leicester that the successful London concert manager had no option but to keep Mary, whose social situation was lowly, hidden. Doubtless, his own social origins gave him strong points of connection with her and her niece. Maybe he felt more at home, deep down, in Vauxhall Bridge Road than he did in Hanover Square. But like his own family background, Mary Webb *et al.* were to be concealed from the world at large – and that is where the episode's greatest significance lies.

After all, apart from the setbacks with the Institute, 'John Ella Esq.' was by the early 1860s enjoying an enviable eminence in the world of London music and leading the life of a well-heeled metropolitan somebody. The Musical Union was achieving record audiences, its reputation for the best and most serious music-making looked immutable, and Ella was widely recognized as its clever and energetic architect. He was well adapted to the lifestyle of the fashionable gentleman, with an address in Piccadilly. His private finances, thanks to the concerts' success and his capital investments (and in spite of the troubles with his stockbroker),

Square, though Mollie was allowed use of some furniture (diary, 4 August 1866). He initially remained in contact with Nellie Beech more than Mollie, but in 1867 (to judge from the diary and information in the account book, EllaC, MS 6, p. 155) was loaning Mollie further items.

were in excellent health, and growing: in 1852 his share portfolio had amounted to some £660; by 1859 it had reached around £3,082, and by 1866 stood at a remarkable £4,909 18s 1d (indeed, his protestations to the Royal Society of Musicians, quoted at the head of this chapter, regarding his diminished funds need to be understood in this light).[196] And he was frequently found in the company of members of the Musical Union circle and their families, or with the cream of professional musicians, several of whom – Costa, Vieuxtemps and Piatti for example – became his good friends, and were much sought after in fashionable circles anyway.[197]

In fact, Ella's sense of his social status had taken a big step forward since he started exploring his genealogy in the early 1850s.[198] In 1858 the process was accelerated by enquiries from an antiquarian called William Grainge, whose preparation of a history of part of Yorkshire, *The Vale of Mowbray*, had uncovered a group of Ellas in the area in the seventeenth century, mostly 'yeomen and humble tillers of the soil'.[199] Grainge wanted to establish whether the (now) well-known John Ella was related to them. Indeed he was, and as such could be claimed as a famous son of the Vale of Mowbray.[200] Better still, though, there was evidence of a strong link with an old Saxon and East Yorkshire family of Ellas, of considerable wealth, and like many Victorian parvenus with pretensions to ancient gentility, Ella had probably relished providing him with his family's coat of arms, which he had copied at the Herald's Office. The Ellas had fallen on hard times after the English Civil War (in which they had fought for the royalists with 'loyalty and bravery'), but before

[196] As per Ella's account book (EllaC, MS 6), pp. 248 [1852], 242–3 [1859] and 228–9 [1866; excludes dormant capital of £1,300]. Slightly (but not significantly) different figures for 1866 are recorded on pp. 152–3 and 256–7.

[197] At this period he was often meeting with Tite and Brassey, visiting Sir George Clerk, Lord Gerald Fitzgerald and Lord Clarence Paget, or spending time *chez* the scientist Richard Owen, the artist John Everett Millais, or the dramatist and editor of *Punch* Tom Taylor (who had married Laura Barker, a vicar's daughter and talented amateur musician also known to Ella).

[198] Diary, 9 December 1853 and 10 January 1854 (EllaC, MSS 122 and 123).

[199] William Grainge, *The Vale of Mowbray: a Historical and Topographical Account of Thirsk and its Neighbourhood* (London: Simpkin, Marshall, 1859), 232. Five letters from Grainge to Ella, written between August and November 1858, are preserved in EllaC (MSS 88/ii and 156).

[200] Letter from Grainge to Ella, dated 16 August 1858, reads 'I should be right in including your name amongst the few distinguished men the "Vale of Mowbray" has produced in modern times' (EllaC, MS 156). Information linking the celebrated director of the Musical Union with his ancient forebears was published in Grainge's book.

that, as Grainge explained to him, Ella had been a gentleman, descended from a Saxon king, Æelle (or Æella).[201]

🎼 European centres

[W]et & dismal day – wish I was in Paris
〜 Ella's diary, 5 February 1867

O N 6 September 1866 Ella bade 'addio' to Nellie and Mollie and two days later set off on a long Continental tour.[202] There was nothing unusual in this: extended trips to Europe were part of the deep-seated cosmopolitanism Ella now represented, and he had been making them fairly regularly, once the London season had ended and his musical affairs had been completed, for the past decade and a half.[203] But whereas in the early 1850s he had simply been keeping generally abreast of European, mainly Parisian, musical life, his impetus during the late 1850s and 1860s became increasingly focused, his activities geared more directly to his professional needs. The Musical Union was now closely identified as a showcase for the best of European performers, and with the recent loss of Hallé and Joachim, Ella knew he had to keep it that way. There was no substitute for seeing, hearing and finding out what was going on *in situ*, and stays in the busiest musical centres, where the Musical Union's reputation was increasingly known, offered him unrivalled opportunities to scout for new talent, to network with old and new contacts, and to find out who was planning a London visit next season. There were also chances for touring, sight-seeing and socializing, and the possibility of gathering material to write about for publication at a later date; on this occasion, too, he probably held the additional hope of finding a neutral time and place to grieve his recent loss. Still, the main motivation was musical reconnaissance and 'busybodying' in the interests of his enterprise back home. Indeed, he increasingly took his office affairs with him, writing to those of his most coveted musicians who were elsewhere in Europe at the time, in the hope of securing those important bookings for the coming season.

Paris was a significant part of Ella's Continental experience, and many of his

---

[201] Grainge, *Vale of Mowbray*, 231–2. Letter of 26 October 1858 (EC, MS 88/ii): 'The extract you have obtained from the Herald[']s office [...] proves at once that the Ella of that day [1638] was a gentleman [...] and entitled to wear coat armour'. Other information on the family line is in Grainge's letter of 20 October 1858 (EllaC, MS 156).

[202] Diary, 6 September 1866 (EllaC, MS 135).

[203] Since 1858 there had been only two years – 1860 and 1861 – when he had stayed in England.

visits went no further. Yet at other times he journeyed on. He soaked up Baden-Baden in 1858, Brussels and several spa resorts in 1863, and parts of Italy in 1865 (a two-month stay, mostly in Florence, where he saw what was happening post-Unification), not to mention various staging posts in between. On the 1866 trip, which lasted until early February 1867, he travelled via Paris to Baden-Baden, on to Stuttgart, Salzburg and Vienna, where he spent November and December, taking in Pest before returning via Dresden and Berlin to the French capital (late December), and staying a full month in the city in which he felt most at home.[204]

Ella later described the 1866–7 tour as an Austro-German 'ramble' (a homage to Edward Holmes's *Ramble among the Musicians of Germany*, published in 1828),[205] and if longer-lasting and more geographically varied than most of the others he made during this decade, it was by no means untypical. For a start, it was a sociable experience. Ella was not, by nature, a solitary animal – nor could he afford to be in his line of business – and he delighted in embedding himself in foreign artistic circles, language by now rarely being a problem for him in such contexts.[206] Professional affairs segued easily as he looked up names already in his address book or worked out who were the best new performers around. In Baden-Baden, for instance, he called on Pauline Viardot and Clara Schumann, in Paris he saw Vieuxtemps and Lübeck (among others), and although he did not record it in his diary, surely they discussed travel plans and the possibility of playing at the Musical Union next season.[207] At a concert in Vienna he heard Madame Kolar ('a fine pianist […] nothing so good in England'), and shortly afterwards was advising her on the timing of a London début ('go first to Paris') and the possibilities of engagements with the Musical Union; while in Berlin he made a point of hearing

[204] The entire tour can be traced in the 1866 and 1867 diaries (EllaC, MSS 135 and 136).

[205] *RMU* (1867), 16.

[206] He was most at ease with French (at a dinner in Pest, for example, a group of twelve gathered, of which 'some spoke English – all French': see diary, 19 October 1866; EllaC, MS 135), though he seems to have had a less advanced facility with German, the diary for 9 October 1866 (EllaC, MS 135) noting his being 'amused without understanding much' at the Karlstheater, Vienna. His conversational and written German was, presumably, another matter.

[207] Diary, 14 and 17 September 1866 [Baden-Baden] and 10 and 26 January 1867 [Paris] (EllaC, MSS 135 and 136). As yet Clara had not withdrawn from Musical Union concerts, and Ella must have hoped that she would still come to London the following season (as indicated in her letter to Ella, dated 6 March 1866, in EllaC, MS 14/iv). In a letter from Ella to Clara, sent during the 1867 season (copy preserved in EllaC, MS 14/vi), Ella claimed she had promised to play at three concerts; she had obviously renegued on the deal made in Baden-Baden, joining 'those who have been forgetful of old associations'.

Liszt's pupil Carl Tausig play; and in Paris the young Alphonse Duvernoy.[208] On these occasions notes were usually made, particularly against the names of performers who seemed possibilities for the Musical Union should they undertake a London visit. Duvernoy was to be remembered as a 'good player', while the violinist Jules Armingaud was deemed to have played the introduction to the 'Kreutzer' sonata 'superbly'.[209] Pecking orders based on performance quality were mentally stored, this ability to sort out hierarchies of 'who played what well', giving Ella a strong advantage back in London. Of course, it was all predicated on keeping 'in the know', and Ella networked with a vengeance. In Salzburg he met the curator of the Mozarteum, Franz von Hilleprandt, in Pest the manager of the German Theatre and the composers Erkel and Volkmann.[210] In the Austrian capital he secured introductions to the critic Eduard Hanslick and the scholar Leopold von Sonnleitner.[211]

With the shortcomings of London's musical infrastructure at the forefront of his mind in 1866, Ella was also keen to learn as much as possible about the musical culture and repertoires of any newly encountered city. The acid test of any place was its performing standards and traditions, Ella lapping up as much live music as he could – his trip to Vienna, for example, adroitly timed to coincide with the onset of the local season.[212] Opera houses, training institutions, military bands, orchestral concerts, chamber music concerts, dances, Liedertafeln, church services – all came under Ella's aural and mental scrutiny as he filled his diary with epithets to jog the memory at a later date.[213] Among the several truly ear- and eye-opening musical experiences he encountered in Vienna was the performance of one of the Brahms sextets (works unknown in London) by Hellmesberger's party; a disciplined rehearsal of Beethoven's Fifth Symphony that produced 'nuance & expressive details more [?] complete than any I ever heard in London'; and 'some

---

[208] Diary, 18, 19 and 21 November 1866 [Vienna], 27 December 1866 [Berlin] and 15 January 1867 [Paris] (EllaC, MSS 135 and 136).

[209] Diary, 15 January 1867 [Duvernoy] and 30 January 1867 [Armingaud] (EllaC, MS 136).

[210] Diary, 26 and 30 September 1866 [Salzburg] and 18, 19, 20 October 1866 [Pest] (EllaC, MS 135).

[211] Traced through the diary entries for 10, 14, 17 and 18 November 1866 (EllaC, MS 135).

[212] As Ella noted later, in *RMU* (1867), 16, Holmes had visited Vienna when the city's music institutions were closed. While on his visit, Ella came across another Englishman, music journalist William Beatty Kingston (who wrote for *DT*). Kingston turned out to be equally eager to uncover local musical practices: see diary, 25 October 1866 onwards (EllaC, MS 135).

[213] 1866 diary, *passim* (EllaC, MS 135).

clever scoring of dance, and other music – Chopin, Mendelssohn' as he listened to Strauss's band in the Volksgarten.[214] On the whole, performance standards were to be wondered at, especially at the Vienna Conservatoire, although the quality of singing at the city's opera houses, and readings of Gounod's *Faust* in both Vienna and Pest, did not, Ella felt, match up to Costa's achievements back home.[215] As for new music, Wagner was offering big challenges. *Tannhäuser* in Baden-Baden 'did not please – nor me, nor public', there being 'too much noise & screaming',[216] although in Vienna six weeks later Ella found more in it he liked, including the soprano Louise Dustmann, '& should have regretted had I not seen this perform-ance'.[217] His impressions of *Lohengrin*, heard on Christmas Day in Berlin, were in a similar vein: Ella was intrigued by it though the audience was not, and he felt the work would not find favour in either France or England.[218] Meanwhile, he had seen Berlioz conduct *La damnation de Faust* in Vienna and witnessed the raptur-ous reception that the composer received, confiding in his diary that there were '6 recalls – poor B. was affected & I was overwhelmed with tears of sympathy – <u>grand score</u> this Faust'.[219]

Arguably the highest point of Ella's 1866 expedition to the city of the Viennese masters was his journey on All Saints' Day to Währing cemetery, on the city's outskirts, to lay a wreath at Beethoven's tomb.[220] It recalled memories of his first visit on a November day more than twenty years earlier (in 1845), when he had been profoundly and unexpectedly moved.[221] Then he had 'kissed the flag-stone

[214] Diary, 8 October 1866 [Brahms], 17 November 1866 [Beethoven] and 7 October 1866 [Strauss] (EllaC, MS 135). On the rehearsal and performance standards of the Beethoven, see also *RMU* (1867), 4. The first London performance of one of the Brahms sextets (op. 18) did not occur until 1867, at the Monday Popular Concerts, led by Joachim; see Michael Musgrave, 'Brahms and England', *Brahms 2: Biograph-ical, Documentary and Analytical Studies*, ed. Michael Musgrave (Cambridge: Cambridge University Press, 1987), 1–20, at 3–4.

[215] Diary, 13 October 1866 [Pest] and 7 and 8 November 1866 [Vienna] (EllaC, MS 135). Later recounted in *RMU* (1867), sup., 16.

[216] Diary, 19 September 1866 (EllaC, MS 135).

[217] Diary, 4 November 1866 (EllaC, MS 135).

[218] Diary, 25 December 1866 (EllaC, MS 135).

[219] Diary, 16 December 1866 (EllaC, MS 135).

[220] Diary, 1 November 1866 (EllaC, MS 135). He was accompanied by Kingston, who wrote it up for *DT*; Ella reprinted it as 'A Pilgrimage to the Tomb of Beethoven, 1866' in the front matter to *RMU* (1866).

[221] Ibid. Ella's account of his first (1845) journey to the tomb, and a transcription of the elegy, was published in *RMWE* (1852), 28 [as 'The Tombs of Schubert and Beethoven'] and reprinted as 'A Visit to the Tombs of Beethoven and Schubert' in

that covers his [Beethoven's] remains, and plucked a bunch of fern which grew at the base of the monument – a memento that I still preserve', before witnessing the spectacle of a silent procession to the grave of Schubert, which lay close by.[222] As it passed Beethoven's tomb the group had halted and paid its respects, thence proceeding to lay a wreath at Schubert's. Once outside the cemetery a four-part male chorus had sung a vocal elegy by Graun. Overwhelmed by the 'religious zeal of such spontaneous homage to departed genius', Ella had doubted whether any English musician who had not visited Germany could truly comprehend such events.[223] This had been a sacral experience writ large, and the passing of two decades had not lessened its impact, Ella writing after the 1866 visitation that '[w]ere I to live a thousand years I should never forget the emotion of this my third pilgrimage to the tomb of Beethoven', the intensity of the experience presumably sharpened by personal mourning for 'MW'.[224] In point of fact, the Austro-German region offered a range of openings for pilgrims seeking to connect with the lives of Mozart, Haydn, Beethoven and Schubert, and it is hardly to be wondered at that Ella, whose discipleship was so highly developed, now did so zealously. In Salzburg at the Mozarteum, for example, he inspected various 'relics of Mozart', artefacts connected with the young composer (note the religious vocabulary, significant in the light of contemporary references to Mozart as the divine Christ Child), and bought portraits and copies of manuscripts by Mozart.[225]

RMU (1852), 15; and (1865), sup., 15. Ella had visited a second time in October 1852, accompanied by Hellmesberger, and according to his diary (6 October 1852; EllaC, MS 121) he once more 'plucked some Fern to bring home'.

[222] 'Visit'. The Schubert procession was to commemorate the anniversary of his death.

[223] Ibid.

[224] 'Pilgrimage'.

[225] 'The Mozartium [sic], Salzburgh', RMU (1867), 8. Ella's acquisitions can be traced in his diary: e.g. entries for 1 October 1866 [Salzburg] and 21 November 1866 [Vienna] (EllaC, MS 135). For details of Mozart artefacts in the Ella Collection and elsewhere, and discussion of the significance of Ella's use of them, see Christina Bashford, 'Varieties of Childhood: John Ella and the Construction of a Victorian Mozart', Words about Mozart: Essays in Honour of Stanley Sadie, ed. Dorothea Link with Judith Nagley (Woodbridge: Boydell Press, 2005), 193–210.

Ella had begun collecting Mozartiana on his first visit to Vienna in 1845. Artefacts of Beethoven, notably autograph leaves from op. 121b (Opferlied; a gift from August Artaria) and a letter to Hofrat Karl Peters with a sketched canon, had been obtained on that earlier visit. Along with a lock of hair believed to be Beethoven's and items associated with Mozart, they passed after Ella's death to the Royal College of Organists, London (1914), where they were kept until being placed in 1981 for sale at Sotheby's (the lock of hair) or offered on loan to the BL (the autographs),

In Baden-Baden he obtained a viewing of Viardot's prized possession of the auto-graph manuscript of *Don Giovanni*, which she preserved in her house as if a holy object in a shrine.[226]

The Parisian finale to the 1866 tour ran a by now familiar course. There were convivial dinners at 'La Muette' (Madame Erard's grand house at Passy), evenings spent at the Italian opera house, the Opéra-Comique and even the Théâtre des Variétés (where he heard Offenbach's *La belle Hélène*), and Sunday afternoons at orchestral concerts at the Conservatoire.[227] Time was made for chamber music and for the round of social calls and talent spotting. Arriving in London on 4 Feb-ruary 1867, he declared his journey's end as looking 'dull, dreary, dismal, dirty, & wet & the antithesis of Paris'.[228] Eight months later, as the Exposition Universelle opened, he returned, eager to find out about the best in the latest musical instru-ment technology, in military bands and choral societies, and to capitalize on the heightened atmosphere and social mêlée that accompanied an event of this scale and significance. At this juncture, the identification of new, fine players was an even more pressing concern, now that Piatti and Clara had also flown the Musical Union nest; and Ella, who stayed more than four months, spent his time well.[229]

S TARTING around 1859, Ella began publishing lengthy accounts of his European experiences, particularly all things new and excellent, in the literature for Musical Union audiences. Much of what he had witnessed abroad underlined his developing arguments about cultural lacunae in Britain, and was excellent fodder for his campaign to persuade the British government to subsidize music, particularly in the sphere of education. As we have seen, Ella had been writ-ing occasionally about such matters since the early 1850s, but now extended essays appeared on music in Paris (1859, 1865, 1867–8), on the Continent in general (1863),

where the music and correspondence now resides as part of Music Loan 79. I am grateful to Stephen Roe of Sotheby's for information about the sale, which included autograph ephemera associated with performers and other composers that Ella had collected.

[226] For more on Viardot's construction of a temple to *Don Giovanni*, see Mark Everist, 'Enshrining Mozart: *Don Giovanni* and the Viardot Circle', *19CM*, 25 (2001–2), 165–89. Ella attempted without success to purchase the manuscript from her, according to *EllaMS1*, 179.

[227] Diary, 30 December 1866 and 1 February 1867 [Erard], 8 and 24 January 1867 [Italian opera], 17 January [Opéra-Comique], 23 January 1867 [Variétés] and 6 and 13 January 1867 [Conservatoire concerts] (EllaC, MSS 135 and 136).

[228] Diary, 4 February 1867 (EllaC, MS 136).

[229] The trip is documented in the diaries: see entries from 22 September 1867 to 14 January 1868 (EllaC, MSS 136 and 137).

and in Florence (in 1865); and there was a stream of shorter articles that made reference to other cities and national traditions, notably Vienna and Germany.[230] The material ranged wide, but there was one underlying message, which would be oft repeated in the historiography of music in nineteenth-century Britain: 'abroad' was better than 'home' when it came to music.

Should we believe him? The sceptic would say there is too rosy a glow around much of Ella's interpretation of foreign affairs; and common sense tells us that his impressions of Continental institutions were just that – an outsider's one-sided view, lacking the insights into the weaknesses and problems that any organizational system carried and of which indigenous musicians would have been acutely aware. Modern comparative studies are needed for a truly rounded assessment. That said, Ella had years of European musical experience behind him, had heard the very best players, and was a pretty shrewd judge of performance quality. He certainly did not distribute unstinting praise: he was willing to criticize foreign activities where he deemed it necessary and he was also prepared to vaunt what was good about Britain's rapidly changing musical life.[231] Yet much of what he said about Britain chimes with what is known of the *status quo* during the period, in particular the situation in London. For example, standards of orchestral performance were probably higher in the major European capitals, where detailed rehearsal and discipline were the norm. The Concerts du Conservatoire orchestra in Paris was the most accomplished of all, with its extraordinary unity of style and

---

[230] 'Music in Paris 1859', *RMU* (1859), pp. ix–xii; 'Sketch of Music in Paris 1865', *RMU* (1865), sup., 26–35; 'International Exposition, Paris, 1867', *RMU* (1867), sup., 9–15; 'Music on the Continent, 1863', *RMU* (1863), sup., 37–9; 'Sketch of Music in Florence 1865', *RMU* (1865), sup., 21–6.

On Vienna, see *inter alia*, 'A Visit to the Tombs of Beethoven and Schubert', *RMU* (1865), sup., 15; 'Chamber Music', *RMU* (1865), 22–3; 'A Pilgrimage to the Tomb of Beethoven, 1866', *RMU* (1866), preliminary pages; 'Lovely Styrian Land', *RMU* (1866), sup., 15; 'Music in Vienna, 1866', *RMU* (1867), 16; 'The Social Status of Musicians in Vienna', *RMU* (1867), 24; 'Philharmonic Society in Vienna, 1866–1867', *RMU* (1867), 28; 'Vienna and Paris Concerts', *RMU* (1867), sup., 15; 'The Musical Season of Vienna, Paris, and London, 1867–8', *RMU* (1868), sup., 4; 'Vienna Musical Conservatoire', *RMU* (1868), sup., 5; and 'Dance Music at Vienna', *RMU* (1868), sup., 24.

On Germany, see *RMU* (1861), 6; *RMU* (1865), sup., 2; 'Music in Leipzig', *RMU* (1865), sup., 7–8; and *RMU* (1867), 9.

[231] See e.g. his comments on the poor quality of performances at the opera in Vienna (*RMU*, 1867, sup., 16), or the weakness of contemporary Italian operas, Verdi notwithstanding (*RMU*, 1863, p. 38, and 1865, sup., 25). Likewise his pride in English choralism (*RMU*, 1861, p. 14), and the cheapness of much printed music (*RMU*, 1865, sup., 10).

homogeneous sound, but the Vienna Philharmonic Society and Leipzig Gewand-haus orchestras ran it a close second.[232] (In comparison, a heterogeneous style, the absence of adequate rehearsal and the infamous deputy system still dogged London orchestras.) Chamber music, too, was almost always, Ella remarked, per-formed with exemplary polish, with Paris, Pest, Vienna and Dresden outshining London, including (he admitted) the Musical Union.[233] Only in Italy, where musi-cal traditions had been focused almost exclusively on opera and the human voice up till now, did instrumental music-making have further to go. The new cham-ber music societies in Florence, the Società del Quartetto (established 1861) and the Società Sbolci (1863) were an encouraging development, Ella having advice to offer and sympathy for those who, like him, sought to develop a serious cul-ture for string quartet appreciation.[234] Meanwhile, military bands in Paris and Florence showed what standards could be achieved, and Ella was impressed that such groups were heard so frequently in public.[235]

A recurrent theme in Ella's travel writing was the issue of conservatoire edu-cation, and he repeatedly recounted examples of countries that subsidized the training of their young, promising musicians by providing educations either cheaply or free of charge (Belgium, Italy, France and Germany).[236] The contrast with the situation in Britain could not have been greater, and as we have seen, it was no coincidence that Ella wrote so prolifically on this topic at the time these issues were coming to public and government attention. In the same breath Ella applauded European subvention of theatres and orchestras, and he held up the Italian government as a model of a young and struggling administration that

---

[232] On the orchestral Concerts du Conservatoire, see 'Music in Paris 1859', p. x; 'Music on the Continent, 1863', 38–9; 'Sketch of Music in Paris 1865', 30–1; and 'Music in Paris 1867–8 – a Sketch', 12. On the Philharmonic orchestra in Vienna, see 'Phil-harmonic Society in Vienna, 1866–1867'; and *RMU* (1867), sup., 16; on the Leipzig Gewandhaus orchestra, see 'Music in Leipzig'.

[233] On the quality of Paris chamber music, see 'Music in Paris 1859', pp. xi–xii. In Vienna, Hellmesberger apparently held twenty rehearsals of his chamber group before a concert (*RMWE*, 1854, p. 28): compare the one or two practices for which Ella had to settle. See also *RMU* (1867), 1, and (1868), sup., 28.

[234] 'Sketch of Music in Florence 1865', 22–3.

[235] 'Sketch of Music in Paris', 33–4, and 'Sketch of Music in Florence', 24. French bands benefited from the training of their bandsmen at the Paris Conservatoire and from their use of Adolphe Sax's latest instruments, which helped produce homogeneous sound and good intonation.

[236] See e.g. 'Music on the Continent, 1863', 37–8; 'Sketch of Music in Florence', 21; 'Music in Paris 1859', p. x, and 'Sketch of Music in Paris', 27; and 'Vienna Conserva-toire – M. Krancevie', *RMU* (1867), sup., 1.

nevertheless attempted to siphon as much money as it could into the musical arts.[237]

Cultural attitudes to music and musicians abroad also drew Ella's attention: Paris had an exemplary salon culture and community of artists in spite of infighting among a few musicians, while its concert audiences were – Ella felt – more intelligent than their London counterparts, the listeners at Pasdeloup's Sunday afternoon concerts exhibiting a discrimination and critical judgement 'beyond belief among German and English sceptics'.[238] Italian opera audiences were deemed sober and attentive.[239] Austro-Germany's amateur music-making was nothing short of astonishing – a taste for 'good music' and performance abilities being found in every town and village and in all classes of society, thanks to a rigorous musical education for schoolchildren: in 1860 Ella claimed to have witnessed elementary pupils in Vienna being taught relatively advanced harmony (diminished sevenths).[240] Equally, Ella had always found that the *métier* of musician, whether in France, Austria or Germany, carried significantly higher status within society than it did at home.[241] Examples flowed: the French state honoured its musicians with awards and prizes from L'Institut de France, and gave its military bandmasters officer rank; J.-G. Kastner, historical writer and composer, received a full ceremonial funeral at his death in 1867; and in Vienna some musicians were assimilated into courtly circles.[242] How different from London, where the job of musician continued to lack professional standards and status.

That Ella's travel writing tended to circle around the same issues and observations was less about a lack of imagination on Ella's part and more an indication of his recognition that education and training, performance standards, music appreciation and the value a society places on cultural activities were interlocking concerns, in need of sustained attention in Britain. In principle, there was nothing new in what Ella was doing – many journalists before him from across Europe

[237] 'Sketch of Music in Florence', 21.

[238] Quotation from 'Sketch of Music in Paris 1865', 27. On salon culture, see 'Music in Paris, 1867–8 – a Sketch', 10–11; on concert audiences, see 'The French Opera in Paris, 1862', *RMU* (1862), preliminary pages; 'Music on the Continent, 1863', 39.

[239] 'Sketch of Music in Florence', 24.

[240] On the harmony teaching, see 'Practical Harmony', *RMU* (1860), 42. On Germany, see *RMU* (1861), 6, and, from the previous decade, *RMU* (1850), 10, 33; (1854), 20; (1858), 2.

[241] See e.g. 'The Social Status of Musicians in Vienna', and 'Social Status of Musicians in Paris', *RMU* (1867), 24, and sup., 12.

[242] 'Social Status of Musicians in Vienna'. Elsewhere Ella had queried the adage that Viennese musicians walked arm in arm with royalty ('A Musician in Vienna, 1845 & 1846', *RMWE*, 1852, p. 34).

had drawn similarly favourable pictures of music abroad, by way of trying to raise awareness of an issue they cared about back home. At the same time, Ella's desire to bring about change was indicative of something else at the heart of the Victorian psyche: the pursuit of progress, itself bound up with assertions of national pride. While Britain led the world in science and technology, the issue of funding and achievement in the arts (especially music) would remain an awkward embarrassment.

A T the close of the 1868 season Ella did not head off towards the Continent, but stayed in London to oversee the removal of the Musical Union Institute's library to South Kensington, and to vacate the Hanover Square premises, the lease on which was about to expire. The last three years had brought difficult times for him, many of them connected with loss: the death of 'MW'; the secession of four of his long-standing star players; his realization that the Institute's grand plans were not going to materialize in the way he had hoped; and his acceptance that its library was best placed elsewhere. There had been public quarrels too: first, a siding with the *Orchestra*, which was sued by the critic Desmond Ryan for libel over its questioning of his journalistic integrity; second, a series of spats with Davison, who had ridiculed, among other things, Ella's gift to South Kensington; and all manner of commotion after Ella issued a police summons against Piatti – once his good friend – for threatening him in public.[243] Ella, however, did not dwell on bad press, less still on failed outcomes. Experienced enabler that he had become, he cut his losses and regrouped.

[243] The libel affair around Ryan can be traced in reports in the *Orchestra* (10 February 1866), 309–11; (17 February 1866), 323–6 and 326–7; (24 February 1866), 339–40; and (3 March 1866), 359, 361–2.

Davison's ridiculing of Ella's gift, apparently printed in *MW*, supplemented his frequently scornful remarks about Ella, the Musical Union and the Musical Union Institute in that journal and elsewhere. One particularly nasty essay appeared in the *Pall Mall Gazette* and was reprinted in *MW* (8 July 1865), 420. Ella finally responded in the *Orchestra* ('The "Musical World"', 3 March 1866, pp. 363–4; and a letter to the editor, 10 March 1866, p. 375); the affair rumbled on in subsequent issues.

The dispute with Piatti (1868) heralded a rift between the two men. The police summons and hearing are recounted in the pamphlet 'Signor Piatti'. See also the account in the *Orchestra* (6 June 1868), 169.

CHAPTER 6

Adapting to Survive, 1868–79

Ella's home was to be in newly fashionable Belgravia – Victoria Square, site of some smart if modest town houses tucked away behind Grosvenor Place and Buckingham Palace Road with households of military men, civil servants and the like (Fig. 15).[1] He had searched hard for an acceptable location, Belgravia seeming sufficiently upmarket for a man of his position, and convenient for travel. Victoria station, gateway to many southern suburbs and the music at Crystal Palace, was a short walk away, and we may imagine there was the advantage to Ella of being able to relive memories of those nocturnal journeys to Vauxhall Bridge Road in nearby Pimlico. In Belgravia, as in much of London, well-to-do districts were buttressed by areas of poorer housing.

In August 1868 Ella moved into no. 9, having taken the lease for twenty-one years – a gesture that suggests he fully expected this would be his final dwelling place.[2] He was approaching his sixty-seventh birthday, and must have wondered how many more he would see. Men of artisan class born around 1800 were unlikely to live more than forty years, and he was now well in excess of this, thanks in part to an improved social and economic situation that had brought countless benefits to his health and well-being.[3] James Ella (b. 1804), seemingly the last of his brothers and sisters surviving in England and the one who had become the confectioner, had died in Birmingham in 1860;[4] and John Ella had already outlived several of his contemporaries from the musical world, as well as subscribers and patrons, many of them younger than him: among others, Henry Hill (d. 1856), Frederick Beale (d. 1863), Giacomo Meyerbeer (d. 1864),[5] Heinrich Ernst (d. 1865), the Earl

---

[1] As indicated by the 1871 census (CWA).

[2] 1868 diary (EllaC, MS 137), preliminary page [numbered 53]: 'Moved to 9 Victoria Square August 12th. all goods [to] house – Took lease for 21 years at £100 per annum'.

[3] Andrew Hinde, *England's Population: a History since the Domesday Survey* (London: Hodder Headline Group, 2003), 184, fig. 11.5; on the impact of occupation and social group on life expectancy, see Robert Woods, *The Demography of Victorian England and Wales* (Cambridge: Cambridge University Press, 2000), 203–46.

[4] Nothing is known of the death of Joseph Goddard Ella (b. 1806), who emigrated to America in the late 1830s. Likewise the death of Edmund Ella (b. 1817) is unclear.

[5] Meyerbeer's death caused Ella to pen a lengthy obituary and republish his analysis of *Les Huguenots* (first printed in *MW*, 1838) in *RMU* (1864), sup., 1–12, and shortly

15 View of Victoria Square, London, as photographed in 1960, looking at no. 6. Ella
lived at no. 9, three houses to the right. Reproduced by permission of Westminster
City Archives.

of Falmouth (d. 1852), Lord Saltoun (d. 1853), W. M. Thackeray (d. 1863) and Sir
George Clerk (d. 1867). Within a few years he would hear of the deaths of others:
Gioachino Rossini (1868), Hector Berlioz, Charles Lucas, Bernhard Molique (all
1869), and F.-J. Fétis (1871).

We should note too that around this time Ella briefly contemplated retirement. Three years back, he had intimated to Musical Union members that he was
tiring and might well step down as director after the twenty-fifth anniversary year
(1869).[6] And in December 1869 he was telling Fétis he had held hopes of being able
to 'retire, and live in Paris to end my life where music is not as in London, merely a
"métier".[7] This was by no means an impractical idea: he could have afforded a comfortable old age in his favourite city and, since the Musical Union was at something
of a cross-roads, having suffered undeniable setbacks with the departure of important artists, it might have been a good time to bow out. But it was not to be, Ella
explaining after a well-acclaimed season in 1869 that he was 'persuaded, however,

afterwards to issue it separately as the pamphlet *'Meyerbeer': Memoir and Personal
Recollections, with Analysis of 'Les Huguenots'* (London: Cramer, 1865).

[6] *RMU* (1865), sup., 17.

[7] Letter to Fétis, 10 December 1869 (*WangerméeF*, 588–9).

to remain in London and continue the direction of the Musical Union'.[8] Such an attempt to shift the responsibility for a decision onto others became characteristic as his final years went by, and presumably fed a strong psychological need within Ella to feel wanted. But he probably needed little persuasion to continue: this was a man who did not take naturally to a back seat in musical affairs, and whose energies, if occasionally flagging, were far from spent. In the decade that followed, Ella worked harder than ever, responding to the ongoing challenge of maintaining the quality and reputation of the Musical Union in the face of mounting difficulties and changing times.

✥ *Loss and continuity*

> *There is, in this leviathan city of wealth and intelligence, no lack of cheap entertainments, of singing and playing, of a mixed style of music; but in seeking to popularise music, the art is in danger of being vulgarised.* ✺ Ella, lecture at the London Institution; printed in *RMU* (1868)

THE vacating of 18 Hanover Square and the removal of the book and music collection to South Kensington symbolized more than the demise of the Musical Union Institute and its ambitious agendas. For Ella and his concert society it represented the loss of a business address in the heart of the music district, and the operating advantages and sense of institutional permanence that went with it. Ever optimistic, however, he retained some hope of being able to rebuild his 'shop front' in Victoria. 'Sent all my Institute Paper to be stamped with my address', he wrote in his diary in October 1868, organizing his new house to include use of the back drawing room as an office or 'studio' for interviewing and auditioning artists and conducting other professional affairs.[9] There was also the still not fully resolved issue of how to fill the

---

[8] Letter to Fétis. According to *RMU* (1869), sup., p. v: 'a very eminent musician, deploring the speculative tendency of concert givers advertising the wares of their shops, begs that I will not abandon the Musical Union'.

[9] Diary, 3 October 1868 (EllaC, MS 137). Several entries during August and September document the process of moving house, refurbishing the interior and settling in. The studio is fully described by Willert Beale, in 'A Morning Call on Mr. Ella', *Liverpool Journal* (18 February 1871; reprinted as preliminary pages to *EllaMS2*, 1–14, at 6–7): 'A delightful apartment is the studio; one of those back rooms in a snug bachelor's house in Belgravia, at the farther extremity of the entrance-hall. It is decorated with an exceptional display of portraits and glass frames containing autograph letters from eminent musicians. [...] Two sets of handsome oak bookshelves, with glazed panels, fill one side of the room, and are well stocked with

gap – or to rectify the impression of a gap – in Musical Union activities that had arisen since the departure of Ella's 'big four' players for Arthur Chappell's growing empire. Davison, it seems, delighted in suggesting that the old lustre had gone. Remarks in the *Saturday Review* of August 1868 (unsigned, but surely his, to judge from the tone of the whole review, which was coolly reprinted in the *Musical World* shortly afterwards) intimated that two appearances by Rubinstein and the leadership throughout the past season of Auer, admittedly not yet at the height of his powers, had not compensated for such a change-around:

> [W]e may state a fact that is notorious. The absence of Herr Joachim, Signor Piatti, Madame Schumann, Mr. Hallé, and other renowned artists has robbed the performances of the Musical Union of much of their *prestige*; and they are now, at the best, but second-rate exhibitions.[10]

Not everyone wrote in such blunt terms, and many critic-friends glossed over these matters,[11] but for Ella the challenge henceforth was to nix such impressions, and to rebuild the notion of a permanent state of excellence through a new group of alternating players, while not drawing too much attention to the loss of Joachim *et al.* How he did so over the next decade will be explored later in this chapter. For now we may simply observe that timing was on his side, the 1869 season giving him the opportunity to mount a self-conscious celebration of twenty-five years of the Musical Union, itself providing opportunities for looking back at the past in a positive light, and for revelling in the size and diversity of its roster of artists since 1845.[12] Ella called this season the 'Silberne Hochzeit' (Silver Wedding), a term drenched with suggestions of permanence, continuity and constancy. It was also eerily appropriate for a man both 'publicly wedded to one of the fascinating Muses' (as one

sacred and secular music. A small upright piano faces the door and a vivacious canary bird sits opposite its master, next [to] the fire-place. Books, newspapers, and manuscripts of every description lie scattered about in well arranged confusion.' Ella's use of the studio for interviewing musicians is indicated by his sketch of a visit from a young lady aspirant pianist and her pushy mama in 'A Lady's Midsummer Night's Dream', *RMU* (1877), 32.

[10] *Saturday Review* (15 August 1868), 229; reprinted in *MW* (12 September 1868), 631. Lübeck and Jaëll were the pianists at the other Musical Union concerts that season.

[11] Positive accounts in the *Queen*, the *Orchestra* and the *Yorkshire Orchestra* were reprinted in *RMU* (1868), sup., 1, 5, 9, 13, 17, 21 and 25.

[12] 'Combinations of Talent from the Year 1845 to 1869' were published in *RMU* (1869), preliminary pages.

contemporary commentator put it), and still privately grieving the loss of Mary Webb.[13]

In the event, the line-up of performers in 1869 differed only slightly from the previous season's. The great draw was Anton Rubinstein, whom Ella now counted among his close friends. Rubinstein appeared twice, essaying Beethoven's 'Kreutzer' sonata with Vieuxtemps, and Mendelssohn's op. 66 piano trio with Vieuxtemps and the cellist Ernest Demunck from Maurin's quartet party in Paris, on one occasion, and Beethoven's 'Appassionata' sonata on the other. The Russian had apparently come to England exclusively for these engagements – as yet an unusual action for a European performer, most of whom would take in as many concerts as possible to make a visit worth while.[14] Auer appeared again (he and Vieuxtemps led four concerts each); and three newcomers joined Jaëll on the roll-call of pianists: Carl Reinecke (pianist-composer, later director of the Leipzig Conservatoire); the young Madame Auspitz-Kolar (whom Ella had spotted in Vienna in 1866 and thought highly of); and Marie Trautmann (now Jaëll's wife). It was a good roster, and there were concerts of high quality and drawing power, the afternoons on which 'Ruby' appeared producing stunning ticket sales and breathless critical plaudits.[15] But as Ella monitored the relationship between pianists and takings in his account book, comparing the results season on season, he would have realized that the presence of the lion pianist was making all

---

[13] Beale, 'A Morning Call', 5. The idea and terminology of the 'Silberne Hochzeit' was, on Ella's admission, attributable to the Paris-based writer and critic Auguste de Gasperini, whom Ella had met in Stuttgart in 1866. Gasperini had said, publicly, of Ella: 'Although *célibataire*, M. Ella is *wedded* to his art, and I trust that I may live to see him celebrate the Silberne-hochzeit of his union'. Quoted in *RMU* (1869), sup., p. v.

   That Ella still clung to the idea of finding a wife is indicated by private remarks made to both Fétis ('Unhappily, Mrs Ella "non est inventus"', 10 December 1869; *WangerméeF*, 589) and Haweis ('unhappily Mrs E. non est inventus'; letter dated 17 December 1872, in UBCsc) in connection with his domestic situation.

[14] Ella claimed that Lübeck also made the journey to London expressly to play at the Musical Union, and had even refused a fee (RMU, 1869, dedication page). Rubinstein's gesture is further recorded in Ella's diary, 10 May 1869 (EllaC, MS 138): 'B[rie]f from Rubinstein, 5th May, [?]Gothenburg saying he would play no where else than at the M. Union'.

[15] According to the account book (EllaC, MS 6, p. 113), 132 and 272 tickets were sold for Rubinstein's concerts on 18 May and 1 June 1869 respectively; the previous three concerts, at which Reinecke and Jaëll had performed, produced no more than twenty each. For typical assessments of Rubinstein's playing and interpretative prowess, see the accounts from the *Queen* and *Bell's Messenger*, reprinted in *RMU* (1869), sup., pp. v–vi and xi.

the difference. In virtually all the other concerts, regardless of artist, the ticket receipts were lower than in previous years.[16] Was it sensible to expect Rubinstein to continue to come for future seasons, however strong the friendship? Ella must have known it was not. Indeed, in the medium term, the recruitment of artists with significant drawing power would become the big challenge.

The question of artists aside, one is struck how Musical Union concerts continued to place much the same emphasis on the 'sacralization' of high Austro-German art music, and on the creation of a special blend of the intimate, the religious and the cerebral. The works of Beethoven, 'the Master-mind in Chamber Music',[17] remained the anchor of the repertoire during these final years, and Ella paid repeated verbal homage to the 'immortal composer', as well as providing aural guidance to the listener on the individual items to be heard. Works by Mendelssohn, Haydn, Mozart and, now to an increased extent, Robert Schumann were the main supporting presence: see Appendix II. As we shall see, although there was greater willingness from Ella to include new fare, the society's reputation remained grounded on its austere programming and what one contemporary journal referred to as 'hard listening'.[18] Still, a glimpse at the Union's repertoire over its lifespan shows that what was played most often was not the toughest music available, but pieces with strong listener and performer appeal. Beethoven's and Mendelssohn's string quintets (works rarely played today) top the lists for the regular concerts, with works such as Schumann's piano quintet, Beethoven's and Mendelssohn's piano trios, Mozart's string quintet in G minor and Beethoven's classically wrought op. 74 quartet and the viscerally appealing op. 59 no. 3 following behind. Furthermore, the annual gala – the Grand Matinée, at which Ella typically drew his largest ticket-buying audiences and silently compromised higher artistic goals – became strongly associated with fixed repertoire. Since 1860 Beethoven's septet for winds and strings op. 20, one of the composer's genuinely popular pieces across the entire nineteenth century, and the differently coloured septet in D minor op. 74 by Hummel (for piano, winds and strings) had been the pillars of the matinée programme, under which a more variable group of smaller works, including songs, was placed. Ella continued this formula, which played strongly on notions of institutional tradition and continuity, right up to

---

[16] For example, the second matinée of the season brought seventeen visitors to hear Jaëll: in 1868 he had drawn thirty-seven; in 1867 it had been seventy-three. Of course, visitor sales were prone to volatility, but apart from Rubinstein's concerts, only the seventh matinée showed an increase – of a negligible six ticket sales.

[17] *RMU* (1870), 30.

[18] *MMR*, 6 (1876), 128.

1880.[19] It was designed to provide newcomers with an attractive introduction to small-scale ensemble music and the society's serious ideology, while delivering older hands some comfortable familiarity and a growing sense of societal ritual.

Other elements persisted. Throughout the 1870s the Musical Union's reputation for audience erudition and intelligent listening, particularly among its female members, remained second to none, and Ella continued to parade endorsements of the society and his directorship of it in the pages of the *Record*.[20] As regards clientele, there were, increasingly, issues to resolve about declining subscriptions and ticket sales – problems we shall examine soon. Still, in social profile the core membership remained much the same as in the early 1860s – people from (mostly minor) aristocratic families and an increased number from the leisured middle classes, individuals with a serious intention to increase their 'cultural capital'. Willert Beale, explaining the nature of this metropolitan enterprise to readers of the *Liverpool Journal* in 1871, described it thus:

> [L]et us pass a few minutes in St. James's Hall, and suppose the London season to be at its height. As we enter the spacious *salle*, you will observe that it is arranged very much after the fashion of a luxurious drawing-room. In the centre is a raised dais, surrounded by comfortable sofas and arm-chairs. Numbers of fashionably-dressed men and women are moving towards their respective places, indulging in lively conversation the while. They seem to be acquainted with each other, and to have been brought together by some impulse common to all. They form an indescribably intellectual-looking crowd, such as you might expect to meet at a scientific *conversazione*. They are all as elegantly attired as though they had come to attend a flower show. An air of refinement pervades the room.[21]

We may conjecture the 'names' Beale spotted: people who had lent support to the institution over several years, for example Richard ('Professor') Owen, Charles Landseer, members of the Legge family, Lord Gerald Fitzgerald, Mr and Mrs Tom Taylor, and Professor and Mrs George Busk, and more recent incomers such as the biologist and philosopher Herbert Spencer; Sir Charles Wheatstone, scientist and

---

[19] The exception was 1868, when Rubinstein played and the Hummel was substituted by Mendelssohn's C minor piano trio op. 66, a work that had become closely associated with him. It was 'purposely reserved for his farewell performance this day' (*RMU*, 1868, p. 31).

[20] See for example the page of favourable quotations printed in the preliminary pages to *RMU* (1873).

[21] Beale, 'A Morning Call', 1–2.

inventor of the English concertina; the recently knighted Michael Costa, and one Miss Glehn, almost certainly Mimi von Glehn, a fine amateur pianist and daughter of an immigrant merchant whose home in Sydenham was often alive with musical gatherings and a circle of eminent literary and musical figures, including George Grove.[22]

The committee provided further continuities. Although its personnel had changed over the years its character remained the same: men of influence, breeding and social-cum-intellectual status.[23] By 1869 it included the Rev. Edward Goddard, Lord Overstone, Lord O'Neill (an Irish clergyman, created 1st Baron O'Neill in 1868), the Earl of Rosse (an astronomer; the 4th earl), Sir Thomas Gladstone, Bt, elder brother of William and a businessman and one-time parliamentarian, and Sir Robert Gore Booth, Bt, Tory MP, who was committee chairman from 1869, succeeding Sir George Clerk. After the death of the Duke of Leinster in 1874, the presidency was taken by the Duke of Edinburgh, Victoria's second son, a keen amateur violinist and a prominent public supporter of music and the arts.[24] This position also functioned in the same, largely cosmetic, vein, providing the institution with its all-important badge of social-musical quality, integrity and (increasingly) history. On the concert management side, Ella's small-scale, autocratic method of operation likewise changed little.

In contrast, the Musical Union's sister institution, the Musical Union Institute, largely disappeared from view, in spite of Ella's initial intentions to keep some of its agendas alive. In summer 1868, for example, he was still hoping to find a venue for 'elementary discourses on Melody, Harmony, and Counterpoint' under its auspices, though this came to nothing.[25] One activity, however, did survive: annual parties for the children of members to celebrate the anniversary of Mozart's birth. Begun in 1865 under Institute auspices and stimulated by Ella's renewed interest in collecting Mozart memorabilia, these events comprised a series of imagined celebrations of the boy Mozart's birthday, and represented a continuation of Ella's avuncular enjoyment in putting on 'juvenile balls' for the children of his friends and acquaintances, which can be traced back at least to the

---

[22] See Valerie Langfield, 'The Family Von Glehn', *NBMS*, 3, ed. Peter Horton and Bennett Zon (Aldershot: Ashgate, 2003), 273–93; see also n. 140.

[23] Of the twelve committee men appointed in 1845, only the Hon. Major A. Legge and Hon. Lawrence Parsons remained.

[24] On Edinburgh as an enthusiastic, if not especially talented violinist, see John Van der Kiste and Bee Jordaan, *Dearest Affie … Alfred, Duke of Edinburgh, Queen Victoria's Second Son* (Gloucester: Alan Sutton, 1984), 28, 79, 100, 107, 169.

[25] *RMU* (1868), sup., 28.

1850s.[26] The parties, which (the diaries indicate) continued annually until 1875, seem to have been a whirl of children's games, romps, make-believe and music, reinforcing the notion of Mozart as the immortal child genius. They were a way for Ella to communicate Mozart's biography and extraordinary creativity to what he hoped would be the next generation of Musical Union subscribers by encouraging them to identify with and venerate the child composer *par excellence*. And they were equally part of the wider phenomenon of enshrining Mozart as the eternal, divine child, already manifest in other spheres of English musical life.[27]

The 1869 party took place at Tom Taylor's house in Clapham and was attended by a group of children from distinguished families in Ella's circle. There were a few invited adults, who helped the children prepare a little royalist entertainment, captured for posterity by a sketch, printed cast-list and synopsis which Ella chose to preserve. At the heart was Ella Riddle, a little girl who took the part of the Queen of the Romps. Parents and children played courtiers: Tom Taylor and his son Wycliffe and daughter Lucy; the sculptor Matthew Noble; John Everett Millais and his little Effie; and so on. Musicians Michael Costa and Luigi Arditi, who came along to help with the music, were also given roles. Ella cast himself as 'Amphytrion Union-Jack Ella'. Whether such divertissements were enacted every year, we do not know, but the 1869 tableau certainly placed Mozart in the upper-middle-class English social world, suggesting a natural alignment between Mozart and English aristocratic circles (evident, biographically, in the composer's visit to London in 1764–5), and implying ownership by English high society of one of the Viennese greats.

At the same time, these activities, and the apparent ease with which Ella identified with the upper social strata, were reflective of Ella's ongoing quest for acceptance in that world. In fact, by the 1870s Ella was a regular visitor at the country homes of the Paget family (Farnham and Anglesey), John Webb and his wife (Wrotham) and others, and consorted with them regularly in London at their invitation. The Pagets treated him with special warmth.[28] He doubtless wanted others to think he was fully accepted in such circles – as a letter to Haweis of October 1874 testifies:

---

[26] The parties in the 1850s were given in conjunction with his then friends the Kiallmarks.

[27] See Christina Bashford, 'Varieties of Childhood: John Ella and the Construction of a Victorian Mozart', *Words about Mozart: Essays in Honour of Stanley Sadie*, ed. Dorothea Link with Judith Nagley (Woodbridge: Boydell Press, 2005), 193–210.

[28] Lady Clarence Paget's 'Two Mazurkas for Pianoforte', published by Chappell & Co. (a copy of which is preserved in EllaC as MS 78/ii) is '[a]ffectionately inscribed to Professor Ella'.

I dined [with the Pagets:] Lord, Lady, Miss, & <u>two</u> beaux & we all went to see & were much amused with "<u>nos intimes</u>". In the stage box were Duke & Duchess of Wellington. Coming away, the Duchess (who owes me much, sending Costa to give her lessons &c &c &c) passed me without either a "<u>nod</u>, or <u>a wink</u>", Lady C. P. on my arm! – next day, I dined with the said party, (the duchess) & I ascertained that the Admiral [Lord Clarence Paget] and the Duke, were not bosom friends[.][29]

And yet, given Victorian society's hierarchical strictures, and a tendency for the upper classes and the musical world to mock aspirant emulators, it is hard to believe that Ella completely escaped ridicule, however much he seemed at one with parts of the *beau monde*.[30]

A further continuity in Ella's life after the move from Hanover Square can be found in his literary exploits. The Musical Union concert pamphlets had always been what Beale described as a 'curious medley of deep research, erudition and agreeable gossip',[31] and it was the anecdotal material, as opposed to the programme notes, that Ella now perceived as a rich source for a volume of reminiscences, a genre of writing then much indulged in by journalists in order to make a little money in old age. His *Musical Sketches, Abroad and at Home* was the result, a collection of miscellaneous short pieces and memoirs, many taken from Musical Union pamphlets; it was published in early 1869, an attempt to reach a wider audience.[32] A second edition (minor expansion only) followed in 1872, around which time, to judge from correspondence with Haweis, he was contemplating a companion volume, of 'more amusing chapters, by culling miscellaneously, jottings from my Diary'.[33]

[29] Letter to Haweis dated 29 October 1874 (in UBCsc).

[30] As per later reminiscences. According to *DiehlMM*, 116–17, '[t]o see him at his best was to see him […] seated airily conversing with some important dowager on the front bench, one of those ladies irreverently termed 'Ella's duchesses' by youthful members of the Union less socially important'. Likewise, *GanzMM*, 111: 'the honorary committee, mostly members of the aristocracy, sat in the front rows [at Musical Union concerts], in front of them being a kind of throne on which Ella sat, smiling to right and left of him at the distinguished people and applauding the performers. Truth to tell, they generally rather laughed at him, but he really did an immense amount of good by making classical music popular'.

[31] Beale, 'A Morning Call', 2.

[32] The volume was widely reviewed, mostly favourably. Some reviews were reprinted in the *RMU* (1869), sup., pp. ii–iv; see also p. v. Ella pasted reviews into his personal copy of the first edition: see EllaC, MS 85.

[33] Letter to Haweis dated 13 January 1873 (in UBCsc). See also the letters dated 8 August 1872 and 19 July 1873. It was possibly always Ella's intention to add material,

Meanwhile, the concert pamphlets remained important to Ella as a vehicle for propagating ideas. Much of his verbiage covered familiar ground, including, most prominently, the campaign to improve the quality of Britain's performance standards, musical education and infrastructures. On this, Ella's hopes were raised as news emerged (1873–4) of plans for a National Training School for Music in South Kensington: a new conservatoire for advanced musical study, offering a limited number of free, supported places and in line with the recommendations from the 1866 enquiry into music education. The school was inaugurated in 1876, with premises in Kensington Gore, opposite the Albert Hall, and was one of Henry Cole's pet projects; it was funded largely by private donation and public subscription. But hopes that this initiative might begin to remedy the general situation were short lived. The new school received only the tiniest of subventions (£500 per annum, like the Royal Academy of Music) and recruited less than a third of its target intake of students. Moreover, it began to fail in double-quick time – problems, both economic and managerial (it was ineptly led by Arthur Sullivan) were apparent by 1880 – showing Ella to have had considerable foresight on the matter, for even ahead of its opening he was arguing that more money needed to be found, and suggesting the appointment of the school's administrator would make the crucial difference between success and failure. Having 'the right man in the right place' was how he termed it, vividly recalling the consequences of inept leadership at the Academy in its early years.[34]

Ella continued to speak out on other heartfelt matters: his crusade for high art, and the accompanying diatribes against the rising tide of vulgar monster concerts and the culture of commercialization, was typical.[35] But arguably his most persistent hobby-horse now was the shortcomings of British music journalism. He had held forth in print on this theme for years, often with an intensity and directness that were characteristic of the rough and tumble of the press world. Predictably enough, practices on the Continent comprised the gold standard against which

since the first edition of *Sketches* was published as 'volume one'. In the event, an expanded third edition appeared (1878), rather than a second volume.

34 *RMU* (1875), 28. Ella also believed that amalgamation with the Academy – an idea much in the air at this time – would have been a good thing; on the suggestion of merger, see David Wright, 'Grove's Role in the Founding of the RCM', *GGMVC*, 224–5. On the history of the National Training School and Sullivan's leadership, see 'Grove's Role', 219–44, and the same author's 'The South Kensington Music Schools and the Development of the British Conservatoire in the Late Nineteenth Century', *JRMA*, 130 (2005), 236–82.

35 The remarks printed at the head of this section are indicative. See also his attack on 'the lowest grades of art, and the meretricious displays of vocal talent' in *RMU* (1875), 31.

everything at home was measured, then deemed inferior. He wrote with some truth, for the astonishing growth of both print and public performance in Britain since the 1830s had spawned a plethora of scribblers on music, of variable quality and knowledge. Chief among Ella's complaints – and here he echoed utterances by Berlioz and Fétis – was the singularly British practice of publishing anonymous criticism, which in Ella's view made it difficult for readers to evaluate the authority of an author, and to judge how much credence to give any published opinion. The contrary view, much discussed decades later as newspaper criticism eventually became attributed – that anonymity encouraged candour in the writer – passed him by, and he delighted in disclosing the identities of journalists in his columns for the Musical Union, all by way of claiming to improve the *status quo*.[36]

Behind Ella's campaign lurked a growing anxiety about the impact of any negative commentary on the Musical Union. Davison, Ella's chief detractor, and with whom he had by now had several bitter public interchanges, was the focus of much of his energy. While the once much-reviled Chorley had at last won Ella's social acceptance and public admiration as a critic (a situation that had possibly been helped along by their converging views on the shortcomings of British music education), Davison, who was enjoying a voice on the *Saturday Review* and the *Pall Mall Gazette* as well as in his other papers, remained the public opponent, his close association with, and promotion of, Chappell's Popular Concerts fuelling the fire. 'I am opposed by les frères Chappell, and the canaille [bastard] of the *Musical Press*, Davison' Ella told Fétis, privately, in 1869.[37] He surely blamed Davison for the wider impact of the lack of reviews of the Musical Union in those journals – what

[36] Ella's 'outing' of journalists and his views on anonymous journalism can be seen in *RMU* (1854), 9–11; (1856), 32; (1860), sup., 41; (1865), preliminary pages, sup., 4, 36; (1870), end pages; (1871), 12; and (1874), 16. Among others, Davison was named as the writer for *MW* and *The Times*, Chorley for the *Athenaeum*, Howard Glover for *MP*, George Hogarth for *ILN*, and Herbert Oakley for the *Guardian*. This was one of Ella's activities that particularly inflamed Davison.

[37] The cordial nature of Ella's dealings with Chorley at this period is strongly indicated by a letter from Chorley to Ella, dated 18 April 1868 (EllaC, MS 81, p. 67); Chorley retired from the *Athenaeum* in August 1868. Publicly Ella described Chorley in *RMU* (1865), sup., 36, as having 'done much for art', and in *RMU* (1871), 12, as standing apart from the generally poor quality of critic in England. He and George Hogarth were two of the 'ablest writers'.
   The remarks made to Fétis about Davison are in the letter of 10 December 1869 (*WangerméeF*, 589). A similar comment is found in a letter to Haweis of 28 May 1873 (in UBCsc): 'Davison & his foul set must be mortified with the success of Bulow?', a reference to Von Bülow's appearance at the Musical Union the day before.

amounted to 'almost universal silence by an influential portion of the daily press' for several seasons.[38]

It seems likely that Ella, in his heart of hearts, knew that Davison had good qualities as a critic of music, especially regarding the classical masters, having once been prepared to acknowledge this in public.[39] But issues of personality now took precedence, and Ella rarely passed up an opportunity to point out the foolhardiness of Davison's remarks about Rubinstein and his music back in 1857 and to diagnose such critical shortcomings as indicative of a xenophobia and parochialism all too prevalent among London music critics.[40] Many Musical Union artists had, in Ella's view, suffered from such bigotry and ignorance on more than one occasion, although in truth, far more had probably benefited from hacks who had taken Ella's promotional hype at face value and replicated it in their columns. Indeed, in entering the fray, Ella showed himself unable to rise above the pettiness of London journalism.

Most unconvincing as a viewpoint to modern eyes was Ella's repeated suggestion that English critics like Davison were wrong to write harshly of performers, Ella priding himself on having never penned anything that 'could give pain to any individual musician', and having not forgiven Davison for once making some

---

[38] First noted in 1865 in *RMU*, sup., 4. In a letter to Davison (Arabella Goddard Collection, Her Majesty's Theatre, Ballarat, Australia), which dates from the post-1866 period, Ella took his rival to task for ignoring the Musical Union in newspaper columns, while holding out an olive branch: 'I was in hopes you would [have] forgotten the past & continued friendly disposed towards [me].' I am grateful to Therese Ellsworth for supplying me with a photocopy of this letter.

[39] In *RMU* (1854), 10, he was prepared to cite a piece 'from the editor of the *Musical World*, a professor distinguished for his acumen, and passionate love of the art', drawing attention to his enthusiasm for Mendelssohn and praising the 'versatility of his powers in criticism and command of language'.

Davison's insightfulness about late Beethoven and his role in reforming the behaviour of concert-room and opera-house audiences are but two aspects of his critical personality that have been rehabilitated recently: see Christina Bashford, 'The Late Beethoven Quartets and the London Press, 1836–ca. 1850', *Musical Quarterly*, 84 (2000), 84–122, and Jennifer L. Hall-Witt, 'Representing the Audience in the Age of Reform: Critics and the Elite at the Italian Opera in London', *MBC*, 121–44.

[40] The Rubinstein episode was repeated in *RMU* (1872), 16, sup., p. v, and (1876), sup., 37. See also *RMU* (1873), sup., pp. i–ii: 'The *Times* critic, Mr. J. W. Davison, for once, is liberal and just towards a foreign pianist, and says that "*his execution is prodigious, and equally so is his memory*"'.

critical remarks about Clara Schumann's playing.[41] Such old-fashioned, genteel concern for artists' feelings, to say nothing of the implicit rejection of a journalism that made truly critical judgements of performers, seems more than a little disingenuous on Ella's part, since the (silent) sorting and selection of players in terms of their quality was the central tenet of Ella's operation, even if most of them were billed in superlative terms.[42] Moreover, it seems odd that Ella could not have accepted that, in an increasingly commercial concert world, judgements made publicly after performances would help audiences discriminate quality. His attitude here may have had much to do with shifting paradigms of performance criticism as a whole: a move away from a responsibility only to assess the music and the composer's message to one that included focus on the relative merits of the performer and his/her interpretation as well. But there was also at root, as Davison rightly spotted, a psychological inability on Ella's part to cope with any testing criticism of his achievements. The brilliant enabler had become somehow trapped by his own success, self-belief and vain-glory.

❧ *Revival and advocacy*

This Society was Founded in 1826, at the residence of the late Lord Saltoun, and is continued, during the Winter and Spring, in my Library, Victoria Square.—J.E.

ᗡ Società Lirica programme, 29 April 1876

We doubt whether any man has yet handled the Wagner question as practically (and this is what we want) as Professor Ella.

ᗡ Illustrated Review, cited in RMU (1873)

Nᴏᴛ everything Ella did after 1869 was related to the Musical Union or its Institute, but it was perhaps a symptom of increased caution born of age that his two new projects from the Victoria Square years were built on familiar ground. The first of these undertakings saw Ella revive the amateur club for private,

---

[41] Quotation from 'Rubinstein', *MR* (30 June 1857), pp. xxv–xxvi. Davison's treatment of Clara (and Rubinstein) still rankled in the 1870s: see e.g. *RMU* (1872), 16.

[42] Hanslick had remarked on this aspect, wryly, after his 1862 visit: 'The most famous artists therefore allow themselves to be engaged and the younger French and German talents consider themselves fortunate even without the fee to be allowed to play to this company. They get to play in an accredited location and moreover are introduced to the aristocratic and esteemed public in the programme as new talent. Thus every foreigner is of course "well known in Germany", also usually friend of Chopin's, favourite pupil of Mendelssohn's and so on.' (*HanslickA*, p. 509.)

unstaged performance of choral operatic extracts which had proved such a sterling way of enhancing his networks of serious-minded musical patrons earlier in his career. Although the musical climate around 1870 was one of growing amateur choral singing among all classes of society, particularly the lower orders, Ella kept his focus purely on London's upper social strata, drawing in West End types well versed in European opera and mostly from his existing social orbit.

The group, begun informally in late 1868 and launched as La Società Lirica in 1870, met regularly in Belgravia, initially *a casa* Ella, on Saturday afternoons from late autumn into the high season.[43] Later on, the meetings moved into the town houses of its members, people like Sir Robert Gore Booth (Buckingham Gate) and the Dowager Lady Antrobus (Grosvenor Square) who, as with most of the participants, were Musical Union followers.[44] The society was small – a choir of sixteen and a band of twelve, with members allowed to bring one guest to listen to final performances (though not to rehearsals) – and was a consciously private undertaking, organized through casual networks. Much 'supporting' activity – of trying out new arrangements and practising individual parts – took place outside of formal rehearsals and in an impromptu manner, as and when Ella was visiting members in the course of social life. Even so, Ella wisely levied a small subscription to cover outgoings, which included the hiring of soloists (typically inexpensive, middling singers, often on the verge of careers) and professional strength in the orchestra as needed. Choir members had fluency in Italian and French, the languages in which most works – including operas originally in German – were sung, though their technical musical skills, unlike their enthusiasms, were usually limited.[45] It was a decidedly amateur affair, in the best of senses.

The club's ethos centred around rediscovering notable numbers from serious, often neglected, operas: works such as Weber's *Oberon* and *Euryanthe*, Rossini's *Le siège de Corinthe* and *Moïse*, Spohr's *Jessonda*, *Faust* and *Zemire und Azor*, Méhul's

43 The foundation date is confirmed by a press cutting in EllaC, MS 9/xxiii. Ella's diaries from the end of 1868 onwards further indicate a series of informal amateur music practices of operatic excerpts on Saturdays, with people who became Società Lirica members: Lord Gerald Fitzgerald, Mrs Horace Twiss, Mrs Heather Bigg, John Belcher and so on (see e.g. entries for 13 February and 4 December 1869; EllaC, MS 138). The formalization of the society and the first season's activities can be traced through *RMU* (1870): 4, 8, 16, 20, 24, 29, and esp. sup., pp. i–iv and vi–vii.

44 A list of members for 1870, with some addresses, is preserved in the preliminary pages to the 1870 diary (EllaC, MS 139). They include Lord Gerald Fitzgerald, Mrs Bigg, Mrs Haden, Mrs Twiss and more than twenty other names, mostly from the West End, Kensington or Belgravia districts.

45 As admitted by Ella (*RMU*, 1870, p. 20, sup., p. vi).

Joseph, Hummel's *Mathilde de Guise* and Mozart's *La clemenza di Tito* and *Così fan tutte*.[46] Some of these, the vigilant reader will note, Ella had earlier promoted among the precursor amateur clubs or in private concerts, when those works were 'of the moment' on the London stage, or deemed worthy of introduction by Ella. But few were now in the repertoire. Rather, what was on offer in the early 1870s, whether at the Royal Italian Opera at Covent Garden or at Drury Lane (where Her Majesty's company was temporarily housed), was a sequence of post-Rossinian operas sung in Italian: typically works by Bellini (*La sonnambula*), Donizetti (*Lucia di Lammermoor, Linda di Chamounix, Lucrezia Borgia, La figlia del regimento*), Verdi (*Rigoletto, Il trovatore, La traviata*), Meyerbeer (*Les Huguenots, L'étoile du nord*), Gounod (*Faust*) and Flotow (*Martha*). Admittedly there were occasional performances of a small group of older works showing staying power and audience popularity, such as Rossini's *Semiramide*, Beethoven's *Fidelio* and Mozart's *Le nozze di Figaro* and *Don Giovanni*.[47] But revivals of the sort of opera that Ella now attempted to champion, such as Weber's *Der Freischütz*, were much rarer and, as the *Monthly Musical Record* put it in 1872, liable to be supported only by 'the lovers of good music, who […] form but a minority of the regular opera-frequenters'.[48]

Self-evidently, Ella's extracts had to be capable of being performed by the amateur forces at his disposal, leading him to select feasible numbers such as the introductory chorus in Act 1 of Weber's *Oberon* or the Turkish Hymn in Act 2 of Rossini's *Le siège de Corinthe*, and to abridge where necessary. The main emphasis was on discovering a group of sober stage works outside the theatrical repertoire, Ella being drawn in the first instance towards operas with serious subjects and historical or classical settings, whether biblical Egypt (Méhul's *Joseph* or Rossini's *Moïse*) or sixteenth-century Goa (Spohr's *Jessonda*), and thereafter towards numbers with distinguishing musical features: the introductory chorus to *Jessonda*, a dirge in canon at the octave, and the music for the nuptial ceremony in Rossini's *Guillaume Tell*, a fine piece of orchestration, for example.

Disentangling Ella's motivations for pursuing this quirky little opera club at a time when much of its repertoire was already available to the private sphere

[46] A picture of the amateurs' repertoire can be constructed from the reports in *RMU* (1870–8), from programmes for the Società Lirica, preserved in the Ella Collection (MS 9/xxiii, items 1–3; and MS 157), and cuttings pasted into Ella's diaries (e.g. 1874 diary, MS 143). The account of the 1870 season, in *RMU* (1870), sup., pp. ii–iv, gives a good flavour.

[47] Reconstructed from reports in *MMR* of the opera seasons for 1871 and 1872. For further information on the Royal Italian Opera repertoire, see Harold Rosenthal, *Two Centuries of Opera at Covent Garden* (London: Putnam, 1958), appendices.

[48] *MMR*, 2 (1872), 120. The remark was made in connection with the revival of *Der Freischütz* at Covent Garden.

through the medium of piano transcriptions and arrangements is tricky. To start with the obvious, opera was second only to chamber music as Ella's great and long-standing passion, and he had absorbed a vast repertoire, both in the Opera band in London and as a listener there and on the Continent. Nostalgia may have played a role. At a practical level, too, he had a rich stock of parts for numbers arranged from some sixty operas, left over from the Saltoun days, which could be exploited with ease and economy, and which may well have spurred him on. And with the demise of the Musical Union Institute, he had more time to play with. Typically, he claimed to have spotted an unfilled niche in the amateur market, for in spite of a wealth of singing societies in London dedicated to a variety of vocal genres, opera remained an untapped choral source for most, if not all, of them (he said).[49] While piano arrangements of operas might enable a partial, domestic re-enactment of moments experienced in the theatre in days gone by, and offer avenues for exploration of repertoire which amateurs would otherwise have not encountered, the reproduction of such works by piano alone must have left much to be desired, particularly in a culture that set great store by the art of singing. In addition, Ella's patrons were the sort of enthusiasts who embraced opera-going as a matter of course, and whose serious predispositions and amateur musicianship opened them to the possibility of taking on board a neglected vocal repertoire in this way, while heeding Ella's guidance and treating his musical judgements as sacrosanct. For his part, Ella was seeking to define a particular segment of neglected operatic music as quintessentially highbrow and to develop wider appreciation of it through participation and education. Indeed, although the Società Lirica had a less severe and sacral aura than the Musical Union, seriousness of purpose was implicit and full attendance was encouraged.[50]

It should be stressed that not all the operas were 'old' or outside the repertoire. There was a good amount of Meyerbeer (as there had been at Ella's Private Amateur Union in the 1850s), including excerpts from works still in performance at Covent Garden, notably *Le Prophète* and the much-loved *Huguenots*. There were also, from 1870, two works as yet unmounted on the English stage but familiar to Ella from his European travels, Wagner's *Tannhäuser* (premièred 1845) and *Lohengrin* (1850). Largely unknown quantities in England and somewhat controversial choices, these works were presented through a string of choruses, marches and

---

49 *RMU* (1872), preliminary pages: 'Vocal Societies abound in London for the practice of Oratorios, Cantatas, Madrigals, Glees, Part-songs, and even Ballads! – in short, for every species of sacred and secular music, except that of the Musical Drama, the most captivating and affecting, as it is the most difficult to sing and to accompany, without sensibility, passion, and intelligence.'

50 See e.g. *RMU* (1873), 16.

other excerpts, sung not in German, but in either French or English. That Ella was prepared to endorse Wagner in this way is quite striking, not to say unusual, since Ella rarely staked his own reputation on promoting controversial new music, particularly at such cost of time and effort. To bring it about, Ella took on hours of close work, arranging extracts and writing out parts, a task that added to his administrative burdens but indicated just how deep his commitment to the endeavour was.[51] In practice, the problems were legion. Wagner's music posed a real performance challenge, Ella deciding to simplify some of the harmony in the Pilgrims' Chorus from *Tannhäuser*, and complaining to Haweis that '£200 would not repay the labor & cost' of completing a set of choir and band parts for an excerpt from *Lohengrin*, since even with some professional stiffening all was unlikely to go smoothly 'owing to the impossibility of finding half a dozen good Professional Choristers [...] 20 rehearsals are required with such boobies'.[52] But there were other interlinked agendas for persevering with Wagner, as we shall shortly observe.

Ella continued to run the society until at least 1878.[53] The number of members remained small and there was no significant attempt to turn the organization into a money-making concern, although its public profile grew gradually. By the mid-1870s there were private performances before invited audiences, complete with printed programmes containing short informative notes (Fig. 16), a modicum of press advertising for members, and some reporting of events, as well as some other activities to be discussed below.[54] A corollary aim may well have been to maintain and extend his networks of patronage – an aspect central to the running of the

---

[51] Diary entries from the 1870s bear witness to the hard and time-consuming nature of the task, one that he persisted with regularly, even when a guest at country estates. In the 1830s he had employed a copyist; now he attempted the job single-handed.

[52] On *Tannhäuser*, see *RMU* (1875), 12. Ella's remarks on *Lohengrin* are in a letter to Haweis dated 19 July 1873 (in UBCsc).

[53] Possibly into 1879. There is no record of the society's meetings in *RMU* for that year, but Ella's diary for 1879, entry for Saturday 1 March (EllaC, MS 148), indicates 'Lyrics at 4/p.m.' and lists attendees.

[54] Press advertisements for new members, giving details of meetings as well as a rare report of a performance, are preserved in the preliminary pages to Ella's diaries, notably those for 1874, 1875 and 1876 (EllaC, MS 143, 144, 145). One advertisement (1875 diary) notes that Ella was also offering 'instruction gratis to young vocal students with good voices'. Audience attendance at meetings (typically called practices, not performances) was limited and by invitation or conferment of 'associate' status: as deduced from a printed programme for 2 June 1877 (EllaC, MS 157) and a press advertisement pasted into the front of the 1876 diary (EllaC, MS 145).

LA SOCIETA LIRICA, BELGRAVIA.

Last Programme of the Season,

1876-7,

SATURDAY, JUNE 2nd, AT FOUR O'CLOCK PRECISELY,

* No. 16, GROSVENOR CRESCENT, BELGRAVE SQUARE.

(THE RESIDENCE OF THE DOWAGER LADY ANTROBUS.)

SELECTIONS FROM

"OBERON," "LOHENGRIN," "EURYANTHE," AND "TANNHAUSER."

ARRANGED FOR A

CHAMBER CHOIR (16) AND BAND OF AMATEURS (12),

ASSISTED ON THIS DAY BY

MR. C. BECKETT, Tenor (of the Chapel Royal),

MISS DAY, Pianist, and MR LIDEL, Violoncellist.

FOUNDER AND DIRECTOR OF THE SOCIETY:

PROFESSOR ELLA,

9, Victoria Square, S.W.

This Amateur Society was first organized in 1826, at the residence of the late General Lord Saltoun, and is continued during the Winter and Spring, in my Library, Victoria Square.—(Vide last page.)—J. E.

16 Programme for a Società Lirica performance, 2 June 1877. Reproduced with kind permission of the Bodleian Library, Oxford. Short notes on the music are printed inside the pamphlet.

opera club up to the 1850s and one that took on increasing importance as the subscription base of the Musical Union started to look less secure.

In sum, the Società Lirica sits well with networking patterns established earlier in Ella's career, with his overarching agenda for promoting 'good music' in defiance of groundswells of popular taste all around, and with his belief that, as a recognized arbiter of taste and sacralizer of high art, he could have an impact. Meanwhile, there were signs of an ambitious secondary agenda: that the Società Lirica might be a prototype for the training of professional singers, since it was, as Ella repeatedly remarked, the lack of a national opera house that caused so little of this repertoire to be known and handed down, putting English-trained singers at a disadvantage compared with their European counterparts. Were he twenty years younger he would found such a singing school, Ella said in 1875.[55] The rhetoric came easily, but the enabler was ageing, and the big idea was destined to remain just that.

The second of Ella's 'new' projects was a public one. It began in 1871, a year after the inauguration of the Società Lirica, and involved a return to lecturing at the London Institution, possibly thanks to the intercession of William Tite, who had been a central supporter of the Musical Union Institute and was still a leading light in the City society.[56] Whether Ella had gradually realized that a forum for lectures was unlikely to come about through the Musical Union Institute, or whether his ideas for Institute lecturing were abandoned once the Finsbury Circus events became a permanent fixture for him, is not established; but at any rate the London Institution now became the main focus for this activity, offering Ella a large and relatively discrete public before which he could expound his ideas on the very best music. Apparently his audiences there regularly numbered between 700 and 800.[57] The lectures, which continued until 1876, also provided a good reason to sustain the Società Lirica.[58]

Although Ella had last lectured for the London Institution in 1858–9, his interest in the medium as an effective way of shaping the ideas of the literate classes

---

[55] *RMU* (1875), 28; see also (1873), sup., p. iii.

[56] According to Janet C. Cutler, 'The London Institution, 1805–1933' (PhD, University of Leicester, 1976), 190, Tite stayed on as vice-president after relinquishing the secretaryship in 1867.

[57] This was Ella's testimony (*RMU*, 1871, sup., p. iv). Later, he suggested the audience typically numbered 600 (*RMU*, 1875, p. 8).

[58] Lectures were planned for 1877 but cancelled on health grounds. Ella hoped to continue the following year but had to give up on the advice of his doctor (diary, 9 December 1877 and 18 January 1878; EllaC, mss 146 and 147); also noted in *RMU* (1878), 4.

17 View of the London Institution (where Ella lectured on music) in 1819. Engraving by Henry R. Cook. Reproduced with kind permission of the Guildhall Library, City of London.

had never been swayed, simply put on ice.[59] He had probably always harboured some hope of using public lectures to extend his sphere of influence beyond his West End networks. At least, that is one explanation for his approach to Hallé in 1856 about the possibility of setting up lectures in Manchester, where the cultured German immigrant community might have provided a receptive audience.[60] However, there was a limit to how far down through society Ella was prepared to go with his proselytizing, even though the lecture was such a sign of the times,

[59] These were lectures on instruments and instrumentation: see Cutler, 'London Institution', 351. Programmes for two lectures, in April and May 1859, are preserved in the Guildhall Library, London, bound in with others in a volume entitled 'Islington Literary and Scientific Society'. The gap in lecturing at the London Institution was possibly of Ella's choosing: in 1867 he had declined an invitation to give a lecture series there (diary, 5 February 1867; EllaC, MS 136).

[60] As indicated by Hallé's diary, 6 January 1856 (published in *Life and Letters of Sir Charles Hallé being an Autobiography (1819–1860) with Correspondence and Diaries*, ed. C. E. Hallé and Marie Hallé (London: Smith, Elder, 1896), p. 359). The project did not happen.

particularly prevalent as a means of social and moral improvement in working-class culture through mechanics' institutes, working men's clubs and the like. As Ella's writing shows, he despaired of the musical taste of the 'million' and hoped to see it changed, but he did not see himself as the man for that job.[61] His approach was, rather, top-down, and his target audience remained the educated classes – the City thus offering possibilities of expanding outwards.[62] Meanwhile, the London Institution's conferment of professorial status on Ella (March 1871) brought him increased authority and reputation as a pedagogue.[63]

Commencing in January 1871 Ella gave an annual series of evening lectures on music, covering a range of topics including: ballet and opera; Haydn, Mozart and Beethoven; melody, harmony and counterpoint; and the state of music education in Britain.[64] Choice neglected repertoire, including much opera, loomed large, Ella being well aware of the potential of the lecture podium for getting his convictions across. Some material, for instance his explorations of Wagner's *Tannhäuser* and *Lohengrin*, was prepared afresh, through there was also much recycling of material from the 1850s – an economy of means, without doubt, for lecture writing was yet another time-consuming activity.[65]

According to Ella's testimony and some press reports, his mode of address was one of scholarly knowledge lightly worn, a blend of instruction and anecdotal

---

[61] As in the passage cited at the head of this chapter, and within his lectures: see *RMU* (1875), sup., p. iii.

[62] There was also an attempt, at others' suggestion, to repeat some lectures in the West End; see *RMU* (1874), sup., p. vi. The Quebec Institute in Lower Seymour Street was the chosen venue, and Ella gave lectures on Haydn, Mozart and Beethoven on Saturday afternoons in April and May 1875, complete with choir and band. The size of audience was disappointing by Ella's standards; for fuller information, see *RMU* (1875), 4, 8, 12, sup., p. iii.

[63] The letter of appointment is preserved in EllaC, MS 156 (filed under 'London Institution').

[64] Documented in *RMU* as follows: Dramatic, Characteristic, and Descriptive Music (1871, sup., p. iv); Dramatic Music; Musical Education, Abroad and at Home (1872, sup., p. viii); Melody, Harmony, and Counterpoint (1873, p. 4); on various types of composition and instrumentation (1874, sup., pp. vii–viii); Haydn, Mozart, and Beethoven (1875, p. 16); Lyric Drama (1876, p. 16). Cutler, 'London Institution', lists lectures, including two scheduled for Ella in 1877 and 1878; but Ella's diaries indicate that he did neither because of ill health.

[65] A script for one of the 1874 lectures – 'On Rural, Rustic and Characteristic Music, Antient and Modern' (25 February 1874) – is preserved in EllaC, MSS 78/vii and viii, and shows the nature of revisions and emendations. It probably originated in the series for 1855. Other lectures (e.g. on melody, harmony and counterpoint) appear to have been repeated from the 1856 series.

diversion, in keeping with the ethos adopted by the London Institution in the later decades of the century.[66] Like the best of music lecturers, he insisted on his sessions being illustrated with live music examples, but rather than simply playing through passages at the piano, which Ella deemed an unsatisfactory means of reproducing orchestral sound and expression, he engaged performers to assist.[67] In the 1850s he had hired vocal soloists, a few members of the chorus from the Royal Italian Opera, and a pianist; in 1871 he still needed strong soloists and a competent keyboard player, but could now look to his amateur opera club for not only a choir but a mini-orchestra too.[68] This made effective use of resources, since the Società Lirica's singers and players were either already familiar with much of the repertoire Ella wanted to talk about, or in a good position to learn it. Unfortunately we do not know if the idea of the lectures had been mooted to Ella before he came to set up the opera society, or at what point the linkage of the two came together in his imagination. Nor can we tell if the music picked for the lectures was led by the choice of repertoire at the opera club, or vice versa. But clearly there was a close, strategically useful relationship between the activities.

Much remains unknown, too, about the content of Ella's 'discourses', although the 1872 lectures, which were published separately, give some insights.[69] They comprise four talks on dramatic music and one on the state of music education 'abroad and at home', which should be understood in the context of Ella's wider campaigning for government intervention in the conservatoire 'problem'.[70] Opinionated rhetoric, including lobbying on contemporary issues of wider importance, found its way into all of them; but in the main they treated their topics with seriousness and detail. Stylistically the lectures had much in common with Ella's programme notes for the Musical Union. Self-conscious erudition and antiquarianism, biographical anecdote and personal testimony all had their place, and there were

---

[66] Ella in *RMU* (1868), sup., 28; Cutler, 'London Institution', 129–30.

[67] *RMU* (1875), 20.

[68] Ella outlined the advantage of using the Società Lirica band in *RMU* (1874), sup., p. vi.

[69] *Lectures on Dramatic Music, and Musical Education Abroad and at Home* (London: Ridgway, 1872). The manuscript lecture surviving from 1874 (EllaC, MS 78/vii) provides further evidence of content, as do short extracts from other lectures published in *RMU*: (1873),16; (1874), sup., p. vi; (1875), 16, 20; (1876), 16; (1879), 28 [on Handel's *Harmonious Blacksmith*; from the lecture of 1855, not 1857]; (1880), 32 [on chamber music; from 1855].

[70] Part of a lecture on Spohr's *Jessonda*, which contained a call to arms for the new school of music in South Kensington to be properly resourced, was published in the *Orchestra* (February 1876), 201–2. It is quoted and discussed in Wright, 'Grove's Role', 226.

ambitious attempts at positioning each evening's chosen musical works within the broadest of canvases, Ella frequently making sweeping historical linkages between repertoires. However, the meat of Ella's classes was an exploration of a body of music, which was introduced, performed and explained in digestible chunks.

In the case of the lectures on opera, Ella set considerable store by elucidating – often with recourse to technical terminology – what made this music great, his central assertion being that opera, unlike sacred music, was poorly understood in England as compared with the rest of Europe.[71] All operas were presented through their storylines, Ella describing technical aspects sequentially within his summary of the unfolding drama and, whether consciously or not, playing on the centrality of theatre within English culture. Typically he would draw attention to examples of how the music articulated the dramatic or psychological action, as well as to intrinsically skilful techniques or beautiful effects within the score. This was all by way of explaining what made his chosen operas either music-dramatic *chefs-d'œuvre* or repositories of masterful composition, and was similar to the way in which he advocated and explicated the treasures of the chamber repertoire at the Musical Union. So while *Il barbiere di Siviglia* and *Guillaume Tell* were deemed the 'alpha and omega' of Rossini's creative genius, *Moïse* was said to contain 'pages of masterly writing' and some immortal moments; Cherubini's *Les deux journées* furnished 'a splendid illustration of his profound learning and deep imagination'; and the finales to the second acts of Wagner's *Lohengrin* and Meyerbeer's *Le Prophète* were masterpieces of dramatic expression and power respectively.[72] Not all the works that Ella earmarked for this mode of serious contemplation, whether within the confines of the Società Lirica or before a larger audience at the London Institution, became enshrined by later generations as exemplars of the genre. But for Ella, who was decidedly not hidebound by the need to judge operas only as artistic wholes, stretches of fine writing within a work were enough to bring it to others' attention. His approach to Wagner is telling in this respect. Able to empathize with the essence of Wagner's ideal of music drama, which he had first encountered on meeting the composer in Dresden in 1845, and able to recognize the importance of approaching the operas as complete theatrical experiences, Ella nevertheless explained the genius of *Tannhäuser* and *Lohengrin* purely through the composer's skill and imagination in harmony and orchestration in particular numbers.[73]

Yet even in these limited terms, Ella's advocacy of Wagner and his music, begun

---

[71] *Lectures*, 3: '[I]n no country are sacred works by the great composers better understood, and the *chefs d'œuvre* of lyrical drama *less so*, than in England.'

[72] *Lectures*, 23 [Rossini], 11 [Cherubini], 33 [Wagner], and 7 [Meyerbeer].

[73] *Lectures*, 17–18, 28–34.

at the Società Lirica in 1870 and under way at the London Institution by 1872, seems remarkable. It precedes not only the operas' first London stagings (*Tannhäuser* waited until 1875; *Lohengrin* until 1876; both were given in Italian) but also the foundation in 1872 of the London Wagner Society, which from 1873 gave concert performances of sections from a range of the music dramas, and prefigured the first upsurge in Wagnerism in Britain in the 1880s and 90s.[74] As an account of Ella's *Lohengrin* lecture in the *Musical Standard* (1872) put it: '[i]t is perhaps somewhat singular to find so old a professor of the art taking up with the modern Wagner – Wagner, the musical heretic, the so-called apostle of the music of the future', adding that it was Ella's unique cosmopolitanism and 'ripened judgment joined to a liberal mind' that made him open to such music.[75] From what we can tell, the Wagner Society's supporters – musicians of the calibre and enthusiasm of Edward Dannreuther (founder) and bigwigs such as Lord Lindsay (president) – stood apart from Ella's initiatives and their followings, suggesting distinctive groups and more than one seedbed for the championship of Wagner in 1870s London.[76]

To Ella's credit, he understood that wider public appreciation of Wagner's music, already perceived as difficult and controversial, would not happen overnight, and that the operas needed to be introduced carefully if horizons of expectation were to be changed. The *City Press* recognized the common sense behind what Ella was attempting:

> The comparatively few who believe in Wagner's music of the future have been trying to win over to their side the many who don't, and a great stir has been made over one or two performances given by the Wagner Society. Considering the opposition which, rightly or wrongly, has been offered to this composer's works, it might have been better had the society taken a leaf out of Professor Ella's book, and commenced operations by introducing a

[74] On the London Wagner Society, see *MMR*, 3 (1873), 38–9. It was preceded by a private group, the 'Working Men's Society' (founded 1867; Karl Klindworth was a significant figure), which played piano transcriptions of Wagner's works. For an overview of the performance and reception history of Wagner's music in Britain in the nineteenth century, see Anne Dzamba Sessa, *Richard Wagner and the English* (London: Associated University Presses, 1979).

[75] Reprinted in *RMU* (1872), sup., p. ii, and *Lectures*, 34.

[76] On the London Wagner Society, the Working Men's Society and Dannreuther's role in promoting Wagner, see Jeremy Dibble, 'Edward Dannreuther and the Orme Square Phenomenon', *MBC*, 275–98. On that circle in general, see Stewart Spencer, 'Wagner's Addresses in London', *Wagner*, 26/1 (2005), 33–51, esp. 44–51. I am grateful to Stewart Spencer for providing information on the constituency of the London Wagner Society.

few of the more melodious and attractive portions of Wagner's productions. Those who have heard Mr. Ella on this subject at the London Institution, and listened to the illustrations he then introduced, found no difficulty in enjoying them, but it is hardly to be expected that even a musical public will accept such peculiar novelties as the Wagner Society has been giving us without some previous training. In music, as in other matters, certain tastes have to be acquired, and it is too much to ask us to take them at a bound.[77]

As with the severities of chamber music, so with Wagnerian opera: newcomers to difficult music needed help and orientation, and Ella was there to provide them. But there were limits to how far this championship of Wagner by a man whose tastes had been fashioned in the first half of the century would and could go. While the visionary Dannreuther had begun exploring Karl Klindworth's piano transcriptions of the later music dramas, *Das Rheingold*, *Die Walküre*, *Tristan* and much of *Die Meistersinger*, within his private circle in 1868, and would continue the crusade publicly through the London Wagner Society's concert performances of excerpts from a wide range of works from 1873, Ella championed only those two earlier works – ones that are conventionally called 'operas' – that he had already seen and heard on the European stage.[78] Furthermore, Ella's understanding of the music had its bounds – he had struggled with much of it, and had none of Dannreuther's penetration of the theoretical dimension, nor any of the fervent determination or political agendas that came to be associated with Wagner discipleship in London.[79] Still, he heard Wagner's music in concert performance when he could, for Ella had learned over the years that one judged new music rashly at one's peril, having already substantially revised his opinion of Wagner's music since the mid-1850s.[80] And he was always keen to hear the works in the theatre. So in August 1876, at the age of seventy-three and at a time when interest in Wagner was definitely growing in London, he made the pilgrimage to Bayreuth – a supreme act of sacralization – for the first performances of the *Ring* cycle. Afterwards Ella confided to his diary

[77] *City Press* (15 March 1873).

[78] Dibble, 'Edward Dannreuther', 281–3.

[79] Dibble ('Edward Dannreuther', 283) describes Dannreuther's Wagner scholarship as 'the first serious theoretical assessment of Wagner's dramaturgical and musical ideas in English'.

[80] Ella attended London Wagner Society concerts in 1873 and 1874 (diary, 6 March and 9 May 1873; 23 January and 13 May 1874; EllaC, mss 142 and 143). He also witnessed the concert performance of *Lohengrin* at the New Philharmonic Society under the conductorship of Henry Wylde (diary, 11 June 1873), and wrote warmly of this attempt to make the music better known in *RMU* (1873), 28. Ella's initial opinions of Wagner's music can be found in *RMU* (1855), 33; and (1868), sup., 12.

the parts that pleased (notably the funeral march in *Götterdämmerung*) and those that bored (the 'scenas are tedious'), suggesting more than a little private ambivalence, though not any apparent gut reaction – positive or negative – to the music's decadent excesses, which became the subject of so much debate a few years later.[81] As Ella admitted to his Musical Union readers, he found too many stretches of 'dreary and monotonous declamation' in *Lohengrin* (he applauded the decision to truncate it for its London première), but felt they were handsomely compensated by the several discrete numbers and sections that he chose to promote.[82] Besides, he accepted that, in time and with hard work, enlightenment might follow: Wagner's music was worth persevering with.[83] Haweis explained: 'He never was a Wagnerite; he never pretended to like all that he heard; but he saluted the genius of the new master with a perfectly correct and infallible instinct.'[84] Meanwhile, Ella remained alive to the broader problems of winning public acceptance for Wagner's music in Britain – diagnosing the need for good actor-singers, adequate rehearsal time, and a comprehensible language of delivery, if progress were to be made.[85]

❦ *New artists, new music*

> *Papers full of sad news of war fields, & Paris revolution*
> [*W*]*rote to Baugniet, begging him to say if Brussels is safe –* <u>*on dit*</u>*,*
> *not.*   ❧ Ella's diary, 10 and 16 September 1870

> *Je m'empresse de Vous passer les morceaux que je vais jouer le 30*
> *juin* [...] *J'éspère que mon choix vous conviendra.*
>   ❧ Letter to Ella from Annette Essipoff, 25 June 1874

ELLA'S revitalized activities in opera promotion and education have necessarily remained apart from, and outpaced, the ongoing narrative of the Musical Union. In his own day Ella knew no such separation, and juggled

[81] Diary, 21 and 23 August 1876 (EllaC, MS 145).

[82] *RMU* (1875), 12.

[83] *RMU* (1868), sup., 12: quoting Socrates: '"What I understand [...] I find to be excellent; and, therefore, believe that to be of equal value which I cannot understand." Under shelter of this wisdom of the Athenian moralist and philosopher, I reserve my opinion of the merits of Wagner's declamatory treatment of the lyrical drama.' It is worth noting that Ella saw no conflict between admiring both Brahms and Wagner.

[84] *HaweisJE*, 3.

[85] *RMU* (1874), sup., pp. v–vi; (1875), 12. At Ella's lectures, as at the Società Lirica, the extracts from *Lohengrin* and *Tannhäuser* appear to have been sung in French and English respectively.

tasks accordingly; and, just as some Musical Union patrons subscribed to more than one of his enterprises, reaping social and musical benefits all the while, Ella's administrative work surely gained from the criss-crossing of his labours. We refocus now on the Musical Union, which continued to require his close attention, not least in the matter of replenishing the base of high-quality artists – an issue that in 1869 was still not resolved.

If it initially seems surprising that Ella did not travel to his much-loved Paris in the autumn of that year to renew his contacts and to seek out performers for the 1870 season, we should note there were pressing things to be done at home, and that he spent much time in London preparing music and supervising the fitting up of his studio at Victoria Square for the forthcoming opera club meetings. One imagines he reckoned adequate arrangements for the next Musical Union season could be made by correspondence. Perhaps so, but working thus in a rapidly expanding concert world was not easy. Difficulties concerning performers' availability were increasingly to be expected – artists' diaries were getting more packed, their schedules tighter, especially in the high season – and it was concert promoters like Chappell, not Ella, who were increasingly calling the shots. Old loyalties counted for a lot with Ella, so we can only imagine his dismay at learning in May 1870 that not only was Rubinstein not intending to come to England for the season, and thus could not play at the Union, but also that he had further resolved to end his 'career as – Virtuose'.[86] This decision would eventually be reversed – the Russian's immensely profitable tour of America was still to come – but Ella could not have known that, and to his credit he acted fast to secure the next best thing from St Petersburg: Theodor Leschetizky, who had proved a considerable draw, comparable to Clara Schumann, back in 1864. Leschetizky played in the last two concerts of the 1870 season to good acclaim, one newspaper endorsing him as 'truly a grand artist, endowed with sensibility and intelligence' after his performance of Rubinstein's op. 52 piano trio.[87] Meanwhile, Ella managed to achieve reasonable variety in his 'executants' for 1870, showcasing Auer and Jaëll, now stalwarts; Reinecke and Madame Auspitz-Kolar, two pianists recently tested at the Union; Agnes Zimmermann (back for the first time since 1864, in Schumann's piano quartet); and two new names: the eighteen-year-old Dutchman Jean De Graan, a Joachim pupil, as leader for four matinées; and Louis Lübeck, brother of the pianist, from Leipzig as the season's cellist. (Ernst Lübeck, as it turned out, had given his last performance for Ella. Suffering some form of mental instability from 1873, he died

[86] Diary, 13 May 1870 (EllaC, MS 139); see also the letter from Rubinstein to Ella of 10 April 1870 (MS 79, p. 1), in which Rubinstein makes clear his decision to end his playing career 'pour toujours'.

[87] *Bell's Messenger*, quoted in *RMU* (1870), 32.

in 1876.)[88] *Bell's Messenger* obligingly cooed that '[r]arely has any former season presented a more effective or brilliant combination of talent than Mr. Ella has this year brought together', and Ella inserted the notice in his annual *Record*.[89] But Ella would have known from experience that one good season did not guarantee permanent improvement, and that he must not take his eye off the ball if a cluster of the best players was to be retained, especially in the face of competition from Chappell. It seems likely a 'business' trip to Paris was in his mind.

Yet that was about to become an impracticality, the Franco-Prussian War taking hold in summer 1870. Ella followed news of events closely, concerned for his many friends and acquaintances there and about the ramifications the troubles might have for the Musical Union.[90] He watched, too, as refugee musicians – some familiar faces, others unknown – began arriving in London, especially during the Commune of spring 1871. Only a few were in time to be hired for the season's concerts, although many presented Ella with letters of introduction.[91] Of those he booked, the most notable was Camille Saint-Saëns, who lined up with Jaëll, Reinecke, Leschetizky and a Liszt pupil, Jacques Baur (also a refugee, who seems to have come with Madame Erard's recommendation), as Ella's pianists of 1871.[92] Two other performers, Jules Lasserre and L. van Waefelghem, became the season's cellist and viola player, bringing experience of quartet playing from Paris.[93]

---

[88] Lübeck's mental state is described in handwritten notes by Ella in a photograph album (EllaC, MS 1, p. 49). Taboos about mental illness may account in part for his name being absent from contemporary (and most later) biographical dictionaries, and yet we know that Berlioz admired him, that he had a strong reputation, especially in Paris, as a Beethoven interpreter, and that Ella paid him well.

[89] *RMU* (1870), sup., p. ix. The writer was possibly Rev. J. E. Cox, who is known to have attended concerts.

[90] As per the diary: news of events is reported in the entries for 8, 12, 16, 20, 25 August 1870 (EllaC, MS 139). In the last of these, Ella records having written to Baugniet and Lübeck, suggesting they seek asylum in London.

[91] In *RMU* (1871), 4, Ella claimed that between thirty and forty musicians had sought refuge in London. In *RMU* (1871), 32, he reckoned to have had letters of introduction from '23 Pianists, 14 Violinists, and 5 Violoncellists […] 2 Violists, 1 Flautist, several Vocalists, some Journalists, Composers, and two Impresarios'.

[92] On Baur, see *RMU* (1871), 1 and 4. Ella's diary, 5 April 1871 (EllaC, MS 140), reads 'Baur, from Paris, pupil of Liszt – is here. Erards speak of him as first rate artist.'

[93] Ella introduced these players as follows: Lasserre had a 'great reputation' in Paris as a soloist and performer of classical chamber music; Van Waefelghem, a Belgian, had 'obtained great distinctions on the Viola, both as soloist and as a member of the famed Schumann Quartet Party' (*RMU*, 1871, p. 4). For more on their profiles as chamber musicians, see *FauquetS, passim*. The men had played together in the Société Schumann (1869–70).

Similarly escaping the Continent was Sivori, an old hand, who led on three occasions.[94] Arguably the biggest advantage to Ella from the influx of Paris-based musicians, though, was bound up with networking and publicity, and he exploited opportunities shrewdly. Many of the incomers attended Musical Union concerts as guests, more than 100 free admissions being issued to exiled music-lovers and musicians across the eight concerts.[95] Ella also held social receptions for them.[96] It is hard to imagine there could have been a better way to spread the word about the Musical Union.

These actions, allied to Ella's resumption of talent-scouting in Europe in 1873 – in Vienna and Paris especially – and continued correspondence with contacts abroad, were doubtless a big factor in the remarkable consistency of high-calibre chamber music artists who appeared at his concerts from here on. Once more it was not a question of attracting dazzling performers, but of finding players of distinction with the 'sensibility and intelligence – to interpret satisfactorily the *chefs-d'œuvre*' of chamber music.[97] The facts speak for themselves. A new and stable quartet base emerged around the solid experience of cellist Lasserre, Van Waefelghem (viola) and Wiener (second violinist, from Prague – a 'well educated musician', to quote Ella),[98] with the Paris-Conservatoire-trained duo Benno Holländer and Otto Bernhardt occasionally substituting for them in the inner parts.[99] Above them sat a consistently superior class of first violin. Auer, playing better than ever, and the Italian violinist Guido Papini (from 1874) were the most frequent occupants

---

[94] The season's other leaders were Auer and Heermann; the latter was a chamber concert musician from Frankfurt, Brussels-trained: *RMU* (1871), 13.

[95] 'Music in London, 1871', *RMU* (1872), sup., p. v.

[96] *RMU* (1871), 25.

[97] *RMU* (1880), 16. See also *RMU* (1875), sup., 1, where Ella remarked that he preferred to hear artists for himself, rather than take someone simply on recommendation: 'From long experience and frequent disappointment, I have reason to trust only my own ears in order to judge correctly of the talent of musical executants.' The remarks were made in connection with the curtailment of visits abroad during and after the 'reign of terror, 1871'.

[98] *RMU* (1876), 1.

[99] According to Ella, Holländer had been associated with the violinist Guido Papini on the Continent and had won first prize at the Paris Conservatoire on the violin. He had also held an appointment at the King of Holland's court (*RMU*, 1876, p. 1). A biography of him appears in *Grove3*.

Ella published a small biography of Otto Bernhardt in *RMU* (1869), 5, which suggested he had first encountered the performer as a young protégé of Meyerbeer's in 1846, and that it was Meyerbeer who had been instrumental in getting him a place at the Paris Conservatoire. See also *RMU* (1871), 4.

of the leader's chair, each playing three or four times each season, and bringing more stability to the quartet line-up than hitherto (see Appendix III).[100] Papini had performed at the Società del Quartetto in Florence, Ella having heard him on his visit of 1865 and remarking that the then eighteen-year-old led quartets 'with spirit, feeling, and intelligence' and 'irreproachable' intonation; nine years later he was maturing well.[101] Complementing them were other distinguished chamber players from Paris. The celebrated Jean-Pierre Maurin, long-standing leader of the Société Maurin-Chevillard for the performance of Beethoven's late quartets, came in 1872 (even though in London he played nothing later than op. 59).[102] Vieux-temps was back in 1873, for four concerts; and Martin Pierre Marsick, the Joachim pupil whom Ella had recently heard in quartet concerts in Paris, played in 1878 and 1879.[103] Only Pablo Sarasate, trained and based in Paris, and essentially a solo-ist, was not to everyone's taste in this setting (1874).[104]

As always with Ella's concerts, variety was most notable in the roll-call of visiting pianists, who at this stage of the century were in more plentiful supply than violin-ists. Selection was important, and all the keyboard players Ella booked had much experience of, and sympathy for, serious chamber music. Jaëll made two or three appearances annually, up till 1879, always expanding his range of repertoire; and there were two new 'regulars', both from Paris and both favouring ensemble works with piano by Beethoven, Mendelssohn and Schumann: Alphonse Duvernoy, an adequate player regarded for his crisp, rhythmic precision (1872 onwards); and Madame Montigny-Rémaury, who arrived in 1875 with recommendations from just about anyone who mattered – Rubinstein, Vieuxtemps, Ambroise Thomas and Gounod – and who quickly lived up to expectations as an intelligent pianist.[105]

---

[100] On Auer's improvement, see Ella's diary, 6 June 1871 ('Auer is improved'; EllaC, MS 140) and *MMR*, 3 (1873), 93 ('Auer [...] has been playing more grandly than in any previous season').

[101] Remarks from the 1865 diary, quoted in *RMU* (1874), 1.

[102] *RMU* (1872), 4. On his Paris career, see *FauquetS*.

[103] *RMU* (1878), 1.

[104] *MMR*, 4 (1874), 105: 'it must be confessed that in the concerted pieces led by him one often missed the breadth of style of the German school, [...] it was in his solos that he created the greatest effect'. Actually, Ella had heard him play the Bruch concerto, and not chamber music, in Paris in 1873 (*RMU*, 1874, p. 17).

[105] Montigny-Rémaury was probably the better player. Although Ella promoted Duvernoy in superlative terms, he was forced to admit this pianist lacked '*l'eponge*, at the tips of his fingers' (*RMU*, 1875, p. 12), perhaps in response to criticism in *MMR* that Duvernoy lacked refinement and musical feeling (1873, p. 66; 1874, p. 89). In contrast, Montigny-Rémaury was held in particularly high regard, including by Von Bülow (*RMU*, 1878, p. 32); see also the article on her in *FétisBS*.

More occasional appearances by artists from a range of national schools added aura: Hans von Bülow (1873, 1878), a pianist with a prodigious technique and extraordinary memory powers, whose Beethoven interpretation was unrivalled and whose appearance at the Musical Union Ella had long coveted;[106] Annette Essipoff (Anna Esipova), a powerful player and Leschetizky student (whom she later married), said to be second only to Clara Schumann in the female ranks (1874, 1879);[107] Camille Saint-Saëns (1876, 1877), 'classical pianist of a high order', who had chosen Mozart's G minor piano quartet on his first visit in 1871;[108] and the Berlin-trained Xaver Scharwenka (1879), whose arresting playing of Beethoven's 'Appassionata' drew wide praise for its passion and intellectualism.[109] There was also one final, much cherished performance by Anton Rubinstein, now back on the concert platform (30 May 1876) playing the D major piano trio by Beethoven, op. 70 no. 1, and an extended group of solos: 'a great feast – not to be forgotten' (Ella).[110] There was also a flow of competent players who achieved lesser reputations: Alfonso Rendano, Oscar Beringer, Marie Krebs, among others. Although no significant patterns of pupil–teacher dynasties can be traced onto the Musical Union platform, the conservatoires at Paris and Leipzig were breeding grounds for many of Ella's performers.

It was to Ella's advantage that a slot at the Musical Union remained a coveted engagement for most European instrumentalists. The sheer pleasure of the musicianship and performance experience (the sacral atmosphere and Ella's intelligent audiences), not to mention the further work that might well ensue – either private engagements or public concerts elsewhere – were still enough to enable Ella to secure some enviable bookings. Indeed, with all his top-rank artists, especially those such as Leschetizky and Auer, whose loyalties he hoped to cultivate, Ella was the perfect blend of host and agent: meeting artists at the railway station, inviting them to his home for dinner, taking them to his club, to public concerts in London, and to soirées at his patrons' houses, organizing other engagements for

---

[106] Bülow had taken some persuading, Ella having hoped to book him as early as 1866 (*RMU*, 1866, p. 8); see also *RMU* (1874), 16, on his refusal in 1872. On Von Bülow's pianism and formidable memory, see *RMU* (1870), sup., p. iv; (1873), 11; sup., p. i.

[107] *RMU* (1875), 16. On Essipoff's début at the Musical Union (1874), which 'attracted the largest audience of the season', see *MMR*, 4 (1874), 105. See also the article on her in *FétisBS*.

[108] *MMR*, 1 (1871), 95. See also the account in *Bell's Messenger*, reprinted in *RMU* (1871), 28: 'The touch of M. Saint-Saëns is so delicate and elastic as to refute, so far, the old superstition that would separate the province of organists from the domain of pianists'.

[109] See the summary of press reviews in *RMU* (1879), 8; also *MMR*, 9 (1879), 94.

[110] Diary, 30 May 1876 (EllaC, MS 145). 796 people attended.

them in the private sphere, lending them money, and so on. Little wonder Haweis described him as having 'secured the hearty friendship of the numerous artists whom he engaged', Ella relishing both their company and the task of creating an artistic milieu for them in London.[111] Meanwhile, for those listeners who might have been equally drawn to competitor events such as the Pops, the chief advantage of the Musical Union afternoons remained their intimate, salonesque atmosphere.[112] Davison's son admitted as much in his biography of his father: 'Doubtless it was pleasanter to form part of the small and select audience that gathered round the players at the Musical Union than to be crushed in hot St. James's Hall to hear a string quartet diluted by space into thinness'.[113]

By the late 1860s Ella's taste in chamber music had hardened, and there seems little doubt he preferred the repertoire's classical bedrock to anything else. In the years that followed, the music of Beethoven, Mendelssohn, plus Mozart and Haydn (in that order), continued to dominate at Musical Union concerts in keeping with its founding ethos, although Schumann's music now shared the limelight (see Appendix II). Programming choices were always negotiated with artists, and over the years Ella had come to expect that performers, especially younger ones, would ask to play particular ensemble works, often contemporary ones.[114] As far as we can tell, he acquiesced if he felt the music was serious enough, which normally meant being persuaded it was appropriately clever in its construction. Experience had shown that, with effort on the part of players and audiences, new works might become assimilated, the piano quartet and quintet by Schumann, now fully accepted as much-loved repertoire, being the case in point. In fact, in the decade or so from 1868 the infiltration of new ensemble music at the Musical Union was keenly felt, as the core repertoire was augmented by a series of mostly one-off performances of modern or untried works, many of which the players argued for. In the main, Ella was willing to subjugate his gut feelings to the opinions of European

---

[111] *HaweisJE*, 3.

[112] Edward Speyer, in *My Life and Friends* (London: Cobden-Sanderson, 1937), 26, discriminated between the 'shilling' public at the Pops who sat in the 'orchestra' area, and the 'occupants of the stalls, mostly permanent subscribers, [who] represented art, science, politics and society. The "Pops" had become a social function.' He remembered 'as regular attendants the Brownings, George Eliot and G. H. Lewes, Lord Leighton, Lord Chief Justice Cockburn, white-haired Mrs. Moscheles, and many other distinguished personnages'.

[113] *DavisonFM*, 231–2.

[114] 'It often happens that the pianist makes it a condition, in his engagement, to play a particular composition' (*RMU*, 1871, sup. p. v). Here Ella was discussing the problems that arose when the work requested had already been played during the season.

musicians he admired, or to bow to wider critical acclaim abroad, quickly justify-
ing the inclusion of an unknown work on the back of its having been well received
in Paris, St Petersburg or Vienna.[115] Thus Jaëll, who had already insisted on much
of Schumann's major piano output, on Schubert's neglected B♭ piano trio op. 99
and on Brahms's op. 26 piano quartet, now introduced Raff's violin sonata in E
minor op. 73 (with Vieuxtemps, 1869), Schubert's 'Trout' quintet (1873), Brahms's
remaining two piano quartets (op. 25 in 1875; op. 60 in 1876) and Fauré's first violin
sonata (with Auer, 1877). Auer asked for Beethoven's op. 95 (1877), which was so
far unperformed at the Musical Union, and brought from Russia Tchaikovsky's
first quartet (1876). He also suggested Schubert's A minor string quartet op. 29
no. 1 (1872) and probably the string quintet in C major, still only slightly known
in London, the performance of which, with 'certain curtailments' to relieve its
'attenuated' form, he led in 1873.[116] A programme note by Ella, unaided by a score,
made a reasonable case for the quintet, though in his diary after the performance
he confided that the work 'bored me to death'.[117] We may imagine that Ella more
readily programmed the D minor string quartet 'Death and the Maiden', which,
along with the piano trios, was the Schubert work that held 'most favour with artists' and was being slowly assimilated into the Union's repertoire.[118] Yet Schubert's
music almost certainly still held problems for Ella, as it did for many of his English
contemporaries.

Composer-pianists usually wanted to play their own music. For many this
meant requesting one or two of their piano solos for the concert's coda. But those
who had ensemble works to their name would inevitably put them forward too,
as was the case with Reinecke, who gave his own piano quintet (op. 83, 1870),
piano quartet (op. 34, 1871) and piano trio (op. 38, 1872), and with Saint-Saëns,
who introduced his piano quartet (op. 41, 1876) and piano trio (op. 18, 1877). It
is virtually inconceivable that Ella would have objected. Other prophets of 'new'
ensemble music included Von Bülow, who gave Rheinberger's 'Brahmsian' piano
quartet in E♭ op. 38 in 1873; it was repeated in 1876 with Anna Mehlig at the keyboard. (Described by Ella as a 'valuable acquisition to the library of chamber

[115] As e.g. with Tchaikovsky's first quartet, which had 'long charmed the *dilettanti*
in Russia' and which Ella hoped would 'receive in this country the same favour
bestowed upon it in St. Petersburg and Moscow' (*RMU*, 1876, p. 34). Likewise:
'Auer assures us that in St. Petersburg the [string] Quartets of Schumann are in
great favour […] and two of the executants this day […] are members of a society
in Paris specially devoted to the study of Schumann's Chamber Music' (*RMU*, 1871,
p. 25).

[116] *RMU* (1873), 24.

[117] Diary, 17 June 1873 (EllaC, MS 142).

[118] *RMU* (1873), 2.

18 Photograph of Leopold Auer, with autograph inscription to Ella and a quotation of the opening bars of the Andante Cantabile from Tchaikovsky's String Quartet no. 1, 1876. Reproduced with kind permission of the Bodleian Library, Oxford.

music', the work went on to be frequently played in London for at least thirty years.)[119] He also performed Saint-Saëns's cello sonata op. 32 with Lasserre, to whom the work was dedicated, in 1878. Meanwhile, Raff's music was introduced by the German pianist Ernest Stoeger (the piano trio in G major op. 112, 1875) and by Lodovico Breitner, pupil of Rubinstein (the piano quintet in A minor op. 107, in 1877).[120]

The one new composition Ella was especially won over by was Rubinstein's op. 52 piano trio, which was first played by the composer in 1857. Leschetizky performed it twice (1870, 1871), to be followed by Jaëll (1875, 1878), Breitner (1877) and Madame Essipoff (1879). Doubtless aware that Rubinstein's skill as a composer had been much debated by London critics, Chorley and Davison in particular, Ella assured readers that the trio had 'become a standard work among first class pianists on the Continent', and admitted to having proposed it himself for performance (by Jaëll) in 1875.[121] The idea of programming Rubinstein's cello sonata was often Ella's too, to judge from at least one diary entry: Lasserre gave it five times, partnering the pianists Madame Essipoff, Charles-Wilfrid De Bériot (son of the violinist and Maria Malibran) and Madame Montigny-Rémaury.[122] Whether Ella's motivation was a heartfelt belief in the music or a shrewd exploitation of circumstance is not revealed. One guesses it was the latter. Rubinstein was someone Ella needed to cultivate, and besides, Ella knew the sonata was an audience favourite, repeating it occasionally 'by desire'.[123]

New repertoire required Ella to write maiden programme notes, and from these we can gauge how he was aiming to shape listeners' understanding of Romantic chamber works. Unsurprisingly, given Ella's frame of reference, the main elements he focused on were originality of themes, clever working-out, and command of established compositional forms and techniques. He also emphasized the interchange of material between the parts, effectively applying a classical filter to all he heard. He was ready to point up drama and passion in Raff, plaintive expressiveness in Tchaikovsky and poetry in Saint-Saëns, but such expressiveness was always

[119] See Alan Bartley, 'Chamber Music Concerts in Suburban London, 1895–1915: Aspects of Repertoire, Performance and Reception' (PhD, Oxford Brookes University, 2004), 223 (n. 23).

[120] On Stoeger, see *RMU* (1875), 1; on Breitner, see *RMU* (1875), 12; and (1876), 9.

[121] *RMU* (1871), 25; and (1875), 21. Chorley, for example, described Rubinstein's output as 'unequal' (*Athenaeum*, 22 June 1867, p. 829); Davison had been vituperative about the trio in 1857.

[122] Diary, 29 April 1878 (EllaC, MS 147) shows that Ella proposed to De Bériot that he play the cello sonata with Lasserre.

[123] *RMU* (1875), 13, indicates that the two movements of the sonata were programmed in accordance with the desire of some members.

implicitly subordinate to structure and technique, the ideal Romantic chamber music being Brahms's.[124] Unlike most modern works, which put 'subtlety of treatment' or 'contrast of *nuance*' before clearly audible form, Brahms's music was robust, 'replete with clever devices, and novel effects of combination'.[125] Not that Ella was able to articulate much about Brahms's technical ingenuity, though occasional hinting at the generation of thematic material in works by other composers does suggest he had at least a basic awareness of organicism.[126]

All in all, repertoire selection was a balancing act. Ella's loyal subscribers, especially the older ones, were probably happier with the familiar, while his new brand of artist was often keen to explore the growing repertoire. However, we should note that no performer ever objected to Ella's requests to play Mozart or Beethoven, such was those composers' increasing status as the pillars of the chamber repertoire.[127] The 1870s concerts reflected this mix of tastes and demands, Ella occasionally satisfying requests from the audience.[128] Indeed, remarkable as it may seem for someone wedded to classically wrought composition, in the mid-1870s Ella began, for the first time ever, to promote the Musical Union as a home for both the old and the new in chamber music, in a move that was partly paralleled by his willingness to persevere with Wagner in other spheres of his life. He would forewarn listeners that their initial reactions to modern or unfamiliar chamber works might be cool, and advocate they keep an open mind; he would provide programme notes and hints for appreciation; and he would make a new virtue of his concerts being a repository for neglected and modern music of quality, boasting in a retrospective account in 1879 to have 'endeavoured to introduce new works of merit, when favourable opportunities present themselves of their being efficiently performed', and adding that the 'concerted music of Rubinstein, Raff, Reinecke, Rheinberger, Silas, Lalo, Eckert, Saint-Saëns and Brahms, has not

---

[124] On Raff, see Ella's notes on the violin sonata (*RMU*, 1869, pp. 6–7); on Tchaikovsky, the guide to the first quartet (*RMU*, 1876, p. 34); and on Saint-Saëns, the notes to the piano quartet (*RMU*, 1876, pp. 34–5).

[125] These were Ella's sentiments about Brahms's piano quartets op. 25 and 60 (*RMU*, 1875, p. 18; and 1876, p. 23).

[126] E.g. in his programme notes for Reinecke's op. 34 and Saint-Saëns' op. 41 (*RMU*, 1871, pp. 6–7; and 1876, pp. 34–5).

[127] Ella's principles of programme building are described in *RMU*, 1871, sup., p. v.

[128] Sometimes he would respond to requests from subscribers to include a particular piece; see e.g. *RMU* (1876), 13. This could mean repeating a work within the season: in a letter to Haweis, dated 9 May 1874 (in UBCsc), Ella notes that he has been 'requested to repeat the Quintet, of Mendelssohn [op. 87], as some 30, or more, members were Absent chez la Reine'. The Director's Matinée gave a further opportunity to accede to patrons' requests; see *RMU* (1872), 29.

been neglected'.[129] Some of this change of heart was undoubtedly about survival in times when box office was looking problematic, and Ella as always played an opportunistic card. New music was what his star players wanted to perform, and he needed to keep them sweet. Also, performances of unusual repertoire were likely to be of 'great attraction' to fellow artists, and might even raise the Union's public profile.[130] The performance of the Tchaikovsky quartet, in a concert that unusually contained no classical work at all (Saint-Saëns' duet for two pianos and his piano quartet were the other main ensemble pieces), apparently drew 'more applications for free admissions' than any other of that season's concerts.[131] In any case, the frequent presence of more adventurous repertoire stood to give Ella an advantage in what – as we shall soon see – was an increasingly competitive market for audiences. While the Pops had stolen a march on the Musical Union in terms of the promotion and repeated performance of Schubert's and Schumann's chamber music (Hallé notably championing Schubert's piano sonatas), few of the contemporary works that Ella's players introduced were heard at the rival series for some years, and in certain respects there was more of a cutting edge to Ella's repertoire than to Chappell's at this period.[132] Even so, some critics felt Ella could have been more *outré* in his programming, a review of the Tchaikovsky concert in the *Monthly Musical Record* noting the astonishing warmth of the quartet's reception and suggesting that Ella was 'inclined to undervalue the appreciative powers of his audience in respect to new works, as well as to Herr Auer, at whose instigation it was introduced'.[133]

For all the emphasis on the modern, the Beethovenian ideal remained firmly intact and the balance of repertoire moved only slightly away from the classical heartland towards compositions by contemporary composers, albeit works with a conservative feel: see Appendix 11. There was a more modern edge to the 1870s programming than in the 1840s and 50s, but the newer works of Raff and Reinecke were effectively substituting for the once healthy quota of music by Spohr and Onslow that had fallen from favour by 1870. Thus Ella's public proclamations about welcoming new music reflected a fresh emphasis, rather than a significant change of direction, less still any meaningful weakening of the sacralization of the classical masters. Very few of the newly introduced compositions were performed more

[129] *RMU* (1879), 17.

[130] *RMU* (1876), 33.

[131] *RMU* (1876), 33.

[132] The Tchaikovsky quartet, the Fauré sonata and the Saint-Saëns works were given at the Musical Union before they were heard at Chappell's Pops. The Pops, however, introduced more Brahms than Ella did, probably due to Joachim's presence.

[133] *MMR*, 6 (1876), 129.

than once, Ella's concern seeming to be less about a vision for driving unknown works into the repertoire than about accommodating artists' wishes and drawing audiences. Jaëll twice more played Brahms's op. 26 piano quartet (1871, 1879) and Auer led reprises of Tchaikovsky's quartet (1877), but these were among the exceptions. Equally, much new music remained untouched: for example, the remainder of Brahms's published chamber output, including his string quartets and sextets, the first cello and violin sonatas, some of which were being aired at the Pops. (This even though Ella trumpeted Brahms as 'one of the new lights in the musical horizon of modern Germany', and seems to have privately admired his music.)[134]

Some Brahms, like much late Beethoven, would have demanded preparation time that was downright impractical, in spite of the fact that Musical Union performances were now boasting an increased amount and quality of rehearsal, and improvements in string ensemble. In 1872 Ella's quartet players put in a minimum of three rehearsals for each concert – one or two more than Ella had been used to getting, although still nowhere near the luxurious twenty that Hellmesberger had once told him were the norm for a Viennese concert.[135] He presented this fresh emphasis on practice as the performers' choice: Auer, Papini, Maurin, Van Waefelghem, Lasserre and other such chamber musicians being players who 'do not grudge time and patience at rehearsals', and ones who were effectively imposing Continental standards on their London music-making.[136] Given the busy-ness of the high season, which had always put rehearsal time at a premium with Ella's players, this was certainly unusual and out of keeping with past ways of operating, and since there is no evidence that Ella was paying for more rehearsal, we can only assume that necessity concentrated performers' minds. With so many of Ella's regular instrumentalists gone permanently to the Pops, including Piatti and Ries (an experienced second violin), and his new ones unused to playing together, extra practice was presumably the only way of maintaining standards, especially in unfamiliar repertoire that had to be got up from scratch. An experienced musician to lead rehearsal was an asset here, as Auer's familiarity with the Tchaikovsky

---

134   *RMU* (1871), 13. In June 1873, Ella's intention to programme Brahms's piano quintet in June 1873 was shelved in favour of the 'Kreutzer' sonata (*RMU*, 1873, pp. 21, 25). Ella's diary, 19 June 1873 (EllaC, MS 142), suggests that Jaëll had played some part in making Ella change his mind.

135   See e.g. *RMU* (1872), 9, and sup., p. vi; (1875), 5. The comments on Hellmesberger are in *RMWE* (1854), 28. In *RMU* (1874), 15, Ella noted the desirability of four rehearsals for each concert; in such circumstances, he said, he might have been tempted to give more of the 'late' quartets of Beethoven.

136   *RMU* (1875), 5.

quartet or Reinecke's role in preparing his own music apparently showed.[137] Ella was quick to proclaim that this improved preparation was producing a 'better matched' ensemble 'than any combination of talent I have hitherto obtained from among the cosmopolite republic of musicians in London', and he challenged audiences to listen closely for unanimity of string tone and playing style.[138] In a letter to Haweis (1874), he elaborated:

> The Trio [Beethoven, op. 70 no. 2] had four rehearsals & never was so well played – In short, with the Perfection of the <u>Beeth:</u> Quartet, Adagio & Presto – altogether, I do not remember so satisfactory a Seance. The <u>authoress Miss de Glehn</u> (of M[endelssohn]'s letters[,] a clever creature) sends me a Vol:- with enthusiastic <u>en</u>comium – saying she never heard <u>the</u> Quintet[139] so perfectly played – In the scherzando, how clear, supple P[apini]'s shake –
>
> Ries having no shake, used to wobble
>
> clumsily, en <u>imitation</u> – tho' not perfection – the <u>triad</u> [i.e. the upper strings] go well together & glad <u>you</u> Perceive the nice balance[.][140]

Whether all critics could hear the difference is debatable, but at least one paper claimed that 'thanks to care in rehearsing […] [there was] a finish and unity of style seldom attained'.[141] Still, this must have been a far cry from the standards that would be set by the touring quartets who represented the new breed of dedicated ensembles. These included the Bohemians, with Josef Suk as second violin, at the century's end, and the all-British Wessely Quartet, which was established in 1900 with Hans Wessely as leader and Lionel Tertis on viola, and which claimed to have had more than 100 rehearsals before giving its first concert in the Bechstein Hall.[142]

---

[137] On Auer, see *RMU* (1876), 34. On Reinecke, see *RMU* (1870), 5; and (1872), 3.

[138] 'Le violon du quatuor', *RMU* (1872), sup., p. vi.

[139] Op. 87. The Beethoven quartet mentioned was op. 18 no.3.

[140] Letter to Haweis dated 9 May 1874 (in UBCsc). Mary Emilie ('Mimi') von Glehn had recently produced an English translation of Mendelssohn documents edited by Ferdinand Hiller (*Mendelssohn: Letters and Recollections* (London: Macmillan, 1874)).

[141] *MMR*, 3 (1873), 108.

[142] On the Wessely Quartet, see W. S. Meadmore, 'British Performing Organizations', *CCSCM*; for further discussion of this issue, see Bartley, 'Chamber Music Concerts', 228.

🔊 *Problems and constraints*

[T]he expenses of the concerts now greatly exceed the amount of subscription. ⚬ *RMU* (1878)

APPEARANCES can be deceptive, as every historian knows. The introduction of new artists and music had done much to revitalize the artistic side of the Musical Union, and if one looked at the performance activity alone, one might imagine that all was well. It was not. Underlying problems of audience retention and finance emerged during the decade, and combined with the perennial problem of finding the right artists in an increasingly competitive market-place, and they preoccupied Ella season after season.

By the early 1870s a downturn in subscriptions was becoming evident.[143] There was also a drop-off in the all-important, volatile, single-ticket sales, in spite of Ella having enhanced his base of European artists, an action that had hitherto succeeded in drawing newcomers.[144] To be fair, some turnover of subscribers between seasons was a normal occurrence, and there had usually been enough new members to compensate for the seceders; but now, the trend was downwards. Ella was predictably quick to react, instituting a direct appeal to subscribers to nominate names (1871); discounted (even free) subscriptions for piano teachers who brought along pupils (1871); family tickets for individual matinées (1872); publicizing just what good 'value for money' a Musical Union subscription represented (1873 onwards); and, throughout, deliberately talking up the institution with such measures as listing the names of new members and approving publicly when lapsed ones returned to the flock.[145] For all that, the trend did not seem reversible. The general decline of the casual, ticket-buying audience was equally worrying. Admittedly this income source had always been volatile, but lately Jaëll, Leschetizky and others were proving unable to draw in the numbers they had attracted a few years back, and in spite of their playing newer

---

[143] Given an absence of precise information on subscription income for the 1870s, the downturn has had to be calculated from the printed membership lists, which show a fall from 576 in 1870 to 456 in 1873, declining further (419 in 1878) thereafter. Since the lists inflate the totals by including the names of prominent visitors, one may conjecture that the subscriber base was possibly as low as 350 by the mid-1870s.

[144] Ella's account book indicates that total ticket sales dropped from 656 in 1869 to 324 in 1870 and 317 in 1873, with a low point in between of 250 in 1872 (EllaC, MS 6, pp. 113–15).

[145] *RMU* (1871), 29; (1872), 32; (1873), 29; (1870), 32.

repertoire.[146] Even the Grand Matinée was suffering: whereas single admissions had totalled 151 in 1865, a figure that was fairly typical, by 1873 Ella could rake in takings from only sixty-eight.[147] Meanwhile, the season's outgoings were high – top artists' fees, which had been creeping up through the 1860s, often through the aegis of concert agents, added to the pressures on Ella's budget, and from now on he did his best to keep them in check.[148]

So what was going on? As Ella's published annual necrologies show, the first generation of Musical Union subscribers was dying off; others were leaving, and new members were not replacing them in adequate numbers, in spite of continued networking by Ella. Publicly he mused that among male aristocrats, in particular, there had been a lessening of interest in learning instruments, and playing and supporting chamber music since, say, the 1840s, when the likes of lords Saltoun, Westmorland and Falmouth took the lead in quartet playing and concert attendance.[149] This may have been so (studies of male aristocratic music-making in the late nineteenth century may yet corroborate the view), and certainly it provided Ella with a plausible explanation, but since the Union's principal constituency was female it is unlikely to have been a significant cause. More likely the roots of the difficulties lay elsewhere, since the Union was not the only concert institution facing such challenges.

In his study of the Philharmonic Society the historian Cyril Ehrlich suggested that the winds of change, which by the 1890s would become gales, were beginning to blow across London concert life in the 1870s, notably affecting the Philharmonic Society, whose management was looking tired and myopic.[150] More and more

[146] In the mid-1860s Jaëll had regularly drawn sixty or seventy ticket purchasers to a concert; in 1864 Leschetizky attracted eighty-six. By the early 1870s, however, Jaëll's numbers were down to about thirty for any one concert; in 1871 Leschetizky attracted forty-eight. (EllaC, MS 6, pp. 110–15.)

[147] EllaC, MS 6, pp. 111 and 115. The star pianist for the 1865 Grand Matinée had been Lübeck; in 1873 it was Leschetizky.

[148] Whereas Vieuxtemps had commanded c.£12 per concert in 1853, by 1867 he was getting almost £33. This was still less than the £130 that Ella paid Rubinstein for three appearances (over £43 a concert) in 1867; account book (EllaC, MS 6), p. 69. The general increase in fees was noted by Ella in *RMU* (1870), sup., p. vii: in 1847 the total fees for the season totalled £210; by 1867 they amounted to £530. Although accounts for the 1870s do not survive, occasional notes in Ella's diaries and letters suggest that from now on he kept a tight rein on fees. The great Sarasate, in 1874, was offered only 50 guineas for four concerts (letter of 17 March 1874, from Sarasate to Ella, in EllaC, MS 156).

[149] *RMU* (1875), 16.

[150] *EhrlichFP*, 112–31, esp. 124–5.

concerts were on offer across a longer, ever more competitive season, stretching almost all year round. Agents were beginning to develop international networks for artists, pushing up fees and sharpening business practices. And audiences for music, still growing in numbers and widening socially, were being offered ever more choice. Consequently they were becoming less keen to bind themselves to a commitment through old-fashioned subscription, preferring to pick and choose by taking tickets on an *ad hoc* basis. At the Philharmonic, the relationship between subscription and ticket income altered radically in favour of the latter during the decade.[151]

These incipient changes to concert culture were also expressed in terms of London's urban space, as venues of various shapes and sizes were added to the conurbation. In the West End, for example, there was St George's Hall in Langham Place (1867), a moderately large venue used for theatre and entertainments; the smaller Langham Hall, nearby in Great Portland Street; and the comfortable Steinway Hall in Wigmore Street (1875; later the Groatrian Hall), run by the piano firm, which would become a favourite place for chamber music before the Bechstein (now Wigmore) Hall moved onto the scene. South Kensington had the enormous redbrick Albert Hall (1871), financed by a combination of government grant and private investors purchasing seats or boxes.[152] Concerts in grand houses also flourished. Meanwhile, in the suburbs, where small vestry halls and the like were emerging a-plenty as badges of local identity and forums for sociality, there was another big building on the horizon: Alexandra Palace in northern Muswell Hill, rival to the Crystal Palace in Sydenham; it opened in 1873. The growth and spread of population, allied to advances in transportation such as the building of the Metropolitan, Circle and District underground railway lines which moved people around the central area with ease and speed, and the overground trains and trams which ushered people from and to the suburbs, formed the backdrop to these changes. Concert-going was now somewhat different from the 1840s, when carriages brought mainly West End residents a short distance to the Musical Union's door. And for someone like Ella, competition was sharper than ever.

The thicket of concert activity, however, remained April to early July – and even if the Pops were no longer buttressing Musical Union matinées, Ella was competing for audiences against ever more events. In public, he was unlikely to admit as much, preferring to put it more subtly: 'Alas! the few real lovers of music among opulent and aristocratic families have so many calls upon their

---

[151] *EhrlichFP*, 115.

[152] Ella attended the pomp and circumstance of its opening concert on 29 March, noting afterwards: 'I could not hear all' (1871 diary; EllaC, MS 140).

time … that the wonder is that they are able to attend so many places as they do'.[153] But the essence of the matter suggests a surfeit of supply and choice. The week of 19 May 1873, for instance, offered many high-profile performances in addition to a Musical Union matinée with Jaëll and Vieuxtemps. There were afternoon chamber concerts led by pianists Alexandre Billet (Tuesday) and Charles Hallé (Friday), a recital by Von Bülow (Thursday), a benefit for the singer Christine Nilsson (Wednesday), plus orchestral concerts and recitals at the Crystal Palace and a grand ballad concert at the Albert Hall, to name the more prominent. Added to these were musical events of novelty (Moore and Burgess Minstrels) and charity (an Amateur Orchestral Society concert in aid of a hospital), and a range of art exhibitions, lectures, and other entertainments.[154] From this, the inescapable conclusion is that not enough listeners were choosing Ella's select musical afternoons above other options. One serious possibility that might explain the drift away from the Musical Union is the ongoing private concerts of instrumental chamber music at the house of the painter Frederic Leighton in Holland Park Road from 1867, and his engagement (seemingly through Chappell) of Ella's lost players, Joachim, Piatti and Hallé in particular.[155] Perhaps it is coincidence, but this was the same year that Ella's subscription list, hitherto growing, began to dip.[156] Leighton was a supporter of both the Musical Union and Chappell's Pops. His annual spring parties, plus other less formal events through the year, spawned an atmosphere that would have passed as a description of the Musical Union: a mix of artists, writers, aristocracy, Members of Parliament and even journalists, all listening to serious music that included readings of Beethoven piano sonatas by Hallé, what became legendary performances by Joachim of Bach's D minor chaconne, and forays into Brahms's chamber music.[157] Were these and other private 'salons' in West End houses during the high season draining potential audiences away from Ella? Was this part of a wider retrenchment by the fashionable set in the light of an encroaching tide of public concerts for the middling and lower orders, perhaps paralleling what happened among

---

[153] *RMU* (1873), 32.

[154] Information from advertising columns in *DT* (19–24 May 1873).

[155] See Michael Musgrave, 'Leighton and Music', *Frederic Leighton: Antiquity, Renaissance, Modernity*, ed. Tim Barringer and Elizabeth Prettejohn (New Haven and London: Yale University Press, 1999), 295–314.

[156] Numbers (according to the membership lists) peaked at 669 in 1866. By 1873 they stood at 456. See Appendix IV.

[157] Musgrave, 'Leighton and Music', 299–304.

the London aristocracy during the 'rage for music' at the end of the eighteenth century?[158]

Whatever the reasons, in 1874 Ella decided to take action. With membership dropping, expenditure outstripping subscription income, the falling ticket revenue constituting 'the only surplus of the season', and Sarasate and Leschetizky making it known to Ella that they were compromising over their fees, it was crucial to reverse the decline.[159] In an attempt to stimulate demand, Ella cut ticket prices from half a guinea to 7s 6d; he also reduced expenditure on the gala concert by eliminating vocal music and the need to hire a singer or two. In print he claimed the price reduction had been made following the advice of certain members and the chair of the committee,[160] but the chances are that the man with the shop-keeping background had initiated the idea, and was using this endorsement as a way of allaying any fears of a loosening of exclusivity. Even so, 7s 6d tickets were still towards the expensive end of the market: many weekday afternoon concerts in the West End now offered a range of prices, right down to 2s 6d or 3s. Ella avoided any such sliding scale, nervous perhaps of widening the Musical Union's social sphere lest he should lose the upper-end of the audience: at Ella's prices, his concerts would always be, as one critic noted, 'confined to the "upper ten" and the middle classes'.[161]

Still, the result was that the downward trend in ticket income was halted, and some improvements noted – 550 tickets sold in 1874, compared with 317 in 1873, constituting an increase of c.£40 (c.22 per cent) in casual takings – enough for Ella to stop speculating this would be the Union's final season.[162] Furthermore, sales held up in 1875, and there was something of a mini-bonanza in 1876, with

---

[158] On the eighteenth-century context, see *McVeighCL*, 47. McVeigh observes an upsurge in private concerts accompanying the rapid growth of public concerts in the late 1770s and 1780s.

[159] Ella's remarks are in *RMU* (1874), sup., p. i. Sarasate's and Leschetizky's views are in letters to Ella dated 17 March 1874 and 4 May 1874 respectively (EllaC, MS 156). The latter pointed out that 'les conditions d'Ella et de la Philharmonique ne sont pas magnifiques'.

[160] *RMU* (1874), sup., p. i.

[161] Review of Rubinstein's concert (30 May 1876) in *The Queen*, reprinted in *RMU* (1876), 20.

[162] Data from the account book (EllaC, MS 6), p. 115. Mid-season, however, Ella had thought the price reduction was having little effect: 'The experiment of lowering the single tickets has not answered – The same sold last year at 10/6 as this at 7/6 –'. Letter from Ella to Mrs Radcliffe dated 8 June 1874, in the McCann Collection, Royal Academy of Music (item 2005.1314).

a season's total of 827.[163] This was mostly accounted for by the 478 people who rushed for seats to hear Rubinstein on 30 May 1876 – a summer afternoon's music that was greeted by truly heated enthusiasm, although even the subscription list seemed to be holding up that year.[164] Ella's willingness to follow artists' choices and admit some newer and novel repertoire may have helped too, at least in bringing in casual concert-goers who were eager to sample an unheard piece. The following year, however, ticket sales dropped again (down to 377), indicating once more that the institution could not be sustained by occasional appearances of one world-class star.[165] In 1878 Ella announced an increase in the ticket price for the Grand Matinée alone (back to a half-guinea), and at the season's end cut costs further by reducing to seven the number of concerts for the following season (1879).[166] The price rise was necessary, reflecting changes in the concert business during the Union's lifetime. For while a subscription list of 400 or so in the early 1850s might have produced healthy profit margins, in the late 1870s, with top artists' fees so much larger, it would not. Added to which, the revenue that ticket sales would have to have generated to compensate for this was of a magnitude completely unmet by Ella's concerts.[167]

In contrast, thanks to his canny exploitation of stocks and shares, and a life of thrift and careful accounting, Ella's private finances were healthy. At his death ten years later he would leave a personal estate of £6,663 1s 0d[168] – quite something for someone who in his youth had feared penury in old age. How different his life might have been had he stayed an orchestral musician: Henry Blagrove (died 1872) and Joseph Dando (died 1894) – two of the leading violinists of his generation, both of whom had attempted chamber music series – left effects of 'under

---

[163] Account book (EllaC, MS 6), loose endpaper showing ticket sales for 1875 and 1876.

[164] Account book (EllaC, MS 6), loose endpaper. In *RMU* (1876), 28, Ella noted there had been fewer secessions that season than ever before.

[165] Account book (EllaC, MS 6), front endpaper. Statistics for 1878–80 are not recorded, although visitor numbers are occasionally noted in Ella's diaries.

[166] *RMU* (1878), 21, and 'Musical Union Statistics, 1879', preliminary pages.

[167] At the Philharmonic the ratio of income from ticket sales to (declining) subscriptions rose from 22 per cent in 1868 to 68 per cent in 1878 (*EhrlichFP*, 115). Ella's ticket income actually fell during this same period: 728 tickets sold in 1867; 377 in 1877. Of course, vast differences in expenditure commitments meant that the orchestral society still did not break even, whereas Ella's enterprise, with so few players to pay, continued to stumble on.

[168] John Ella's will, proved 6 November 1888 (Principal Probate Registry, London). His estate did not include any land or property.

£450' and '£779 2s'.[169] Indeed, in 1869, when contemplating whether to wind up the Musical Union, Ella could breezily announce that '[i]n a pecuniary point of view, it is a matter of indifference to me whether this institution cease to exist or not'.[170] His financial livelihood no longer depended on the concerts – but that was assuming the Union did not start making a loss.

Had Ella been fifteen years younger, and not contemplating retirement, he might have done things differently once the downward trajectory emerged. Once – around 1860 – he had hoped to cultivate among his patrons 'young men who will see me <u>out</u> & chance be able to see the Union prosper after my death'.[171] But by the 1870s this idea seems to have faded. At least, that is a partial explanation for Ella's reluctance on the one hand adequately to train up an assistant and successor, even though he had known apprenticeship systems in Leicester; and, on the other, to seize the initiative and take steps to extend and exploit a different, bigger market.[172] He had shown no appetite for setting up a separate venture that was in head-to-head competition for the shilling audience supporting Chappell's Pops; his lack of success with the Musical Winter Evenings in the 1850s had probably been long remembered. In any case, his predilection for courting the world of wealth and fashion had been set in stone too early on for it to change now, and he was lately further constrained by his own *arrivisme*. That being so, one obvious opening that Ella curiously ceased to explore was the large and socially exclusive musical audience in the City, which (with a few notable exceptions) did not intersect with the Musical Union. If he could attract more than 700 people to his lectures on serious opera, why not mount a series of City Musical Union concerts on evenings following the Tuesday matinées, with the same artists repeating the previous day's programme? Such a measure would have avoided opening up the Union concerts at lower prices – which remained impossible to his way of thinking, given the high social ambiance and leisured clientele he had done so much to cultivate – and it would have allowed him to increase revenue through economy of means, and to offset the upwardly spiralling artists' costs.

Another option might have been to establish another enterprise for West

---

[169] See their wills in the Principal Probate Registry, London. Ella's diary (EllaC, MS 140) shows that he was involved in the administration of a relief fund for Blagrove in 1871.

[170] *RMU* (1869), sup., p. v.

[171] Suggested by a letter to C. H. Chichele Plowden in BL, Add. MS 37766, f. 13. The hope seems to have been that the committee men recruited for the Musical Union Institute would take over in time. The letter is dated 8 December 1854 by the BL, but internal evidence indicates a date of *c.*1860.

[172] See *McVeighA*, 169–70.

Enders based on more popular fare. Yet Ella's search for audiences would always be constrained by the Musical Union's uncompromising austerity and erudition, with which he was so identified. His vision for high culture, while occasionally and deftly moderated for economic reasons, was a strongly held and publicly stated belief system, and it is inconceivable to imagine that Ella would have vacated that position now. This was, after all, a man who had a few years back written that he 'would rather starve in defence of the glory of high art, than be enriched by the spoils of her degradation'.[173] If he toyed with the idea as times got harder, he quickly dismissed such possibilities. 'Tempted as I am, occasionally, to embark in some musical speculation of a popular character', he wrote in 1871, 'I am content to restrict my labours to that branch of music which appeals to the aesthetic few at the Musical Union.'[174] Similar constraints prevented a large-scale relocation to the world of contemporary chamber music, a move that would have been utterly out of keeping with Ella's tastes and the essential classical ethos of the Musical Union, not to mention at odds with the fundamental shape of the repertoire, and the sympathies of the core audience. Meanwhile, it was the concerts' very atmosphere, the golden, reverential silence of the audience, the serious devotion to the classical ideal, as well as personal loyalties to Ella, that continued to magnetize some of the very best players at less than their desired rates. Von Bülow was prepared to waive his fee in later years, an extraordinary bonus for Ella, given that this star could draw large numbers: in June 1878, 222 visitors arrived to hear him in the 'Archduke' trio and other works.[175] Writing to Ella at the end of the 1879 season, Von Bülow congratulated him on the fine behaviour of his concert public, adding that he liked 'so much all your arrangemen[t]s and feel so much more comfortable in playing at your Institution than anywhere else'.[176]

O NE further challenge for Ella from 1874 was his health. As age and diminish-ing vision caught up with him he claimed to want to ease his working life, presumably wondering how much longer he could continue with jobs in which reading, writing and stamina were a central part.[177] Letting go, however, was

---

[173] *RMU* (1865), sup., 18.

[174] *RMU* (1871), 30.

[175] The waiving of fees is noted in *RMU* (1878), 17, 24; and (1879), 21, 25. See also the diary, 5 June 1878 ('[Dinner] with Bulow, who will play 18th gratis'; EllaC, MS 147). Some of Ella's negotiations with Von Bülow were done through the agent N. Vert. The 222 visitors are recorded in Ella's diary, 18 June 1878.

[176] Letter from Von Bülow to Ella dated 15 July 1879 (EllaC, MS 156).

[177] *RMU* (1874), sup., p. i: 'I am anxious to lighten the burthens [*sic*] of my future life. […] I am warned not to abuse my remaining physical power'; and letter to Mrs

another matter. The extraordinary pace and bustle of his professional and social activities had not let up, and since the early 1870s he had placed further demands on himself with the Società Lirica and London Institution, while still giving the odd harmony lesson, advising patrons on the purchase of pianos, and so on. His expeditions to Paris had recommenced in 1873, continuing until 1878, with a more extended tour, taking in German cities and the Bayreuth pilgrimage, in 1876, and a ten-week sojourn in Paris in 1877. Admittedly he had reined in a few of his activities, and had turned a few offers down.[178] But on the whole he remained a busy man, bonded to his lifestyle.

Like most Victorians, aware of the proximity of death, he had always been anxious about his health, even though he had had little more to contend with than the simple, common ills. Yet the impact of ageing could not be evaded forever. Fatigue came more easily – 'dead tired' or equivalent was inscribed in his diary at the end of quite a few busy days.[179] More specifically, the 1876 tour was marred by a debilitating bout of sickness and what was diagnosed as rheumatism, and further coloured by a doctor in Baden-Baden advising against his intended journey to St Petersburg.[180] Lecturing at the London Institution in January 1877 was cancelled because of illness during the lead-up period.[181] For a man of remarkable energy who had 'hitherto the blessings of uninterrupted good health', this slowing down was not easily borne.[182]

Still, old age brought its compensations, especially in an era when maturity was respected, Ella gradually becoming established as a grand old man of London musical life.[183] Birthdays were regularly celebrated among his musical and

---

Gray, dated March 10 [1874] (BL, Add. MS 70844, f. 88): 'I am now 71, and anxious to retire – still, I hope to keep on with health'. In *RMU* (1875), 29; and (1877), 32, he notified audiences that he would continue for the following seasons, 'health permitting'.

[178] E.g. Ella had refused an invitation from Henry Cole in 1872 to take on the direction of concerts at South Kensington, pleading poor health. See the copy of Ella's letter to Cole in his diary (opposite the entry for 16 May 1872), which begins: 'I am suffering from overwork' (EllaC, MS 141). In 1874 he had declined repeating his London Institution lectures; *RMU* (1874), sup., p. i.

[179] E.g. diary, 3 July 1875 (EllaC, MS 144).

[180] Diary, 25 September 1876 (EllaC, MS 145): 'Vu D<u>r</u> <u>Evans</u> who told me not to go in Oct<u>r.</u> to Russia'.

[181] Diary, 9 December 1876 and 18 January 1877 (EllaC, MSS 145 and 146).

[182] Quotation from *RMU* (1874), sup., p. i.

[183] A biography of Ella in *The Falcon*, i, ed. T. J. Wilkinson (Thirsk, 1889), 249–50, dubbed Ella the 'father of the Royal Society of Musicians' – an epithet derived from his long-standing membership of this society for musicians' aid.

intellectual men-friends, with 'anniversary dinners', presents, letters from abroad, telegrams too (typically from Rubinstein, Auer and Papini) and speeches – all of which were written up for the press in true 'high society' fashion.[184] The guest list ('Menu-Intellectuel') for the 1878 celebration shows both the social flavour and the eminence of Ella's entourage: Haweis representing theology; the distinguished physicians Seymour Haden and William Bowman medicine; Richard Owen for 'science' and Millais for painting; the sculptor Thomas Thornycroft; the critic Gruneisen, who proposed the birthday toast and gave a formal tribute; Liberal MP and magistrate Arthur Otway for legislature, and barrister John Horatio Lloyd for law; Costa, Frederick Lablache and W. A. Barrett on behalf of music; the dramatist Tom Taylor; the architect John Belcher; Thomas Phillips (Union Bank) for finance; one A. H. Novelli for 'commerce (international)'; and Lord Clarence Paget for the Navy.[185] Meanwhile, a revised, expanded edition of the *Musical Sketches* was prepared for publication with the assistance of Belcher, amateur bass and now close friend and advisor.[186]

In late 1877 Ella became aware of eye trouble, and not long afterwards was advised by his oculist William Bowman to resign his lecturing at the London Institution permanently.[187] Bowman considered Ella was 'quite ½ blind!' in the left eye, and suspecting a cataract (wrongly, as it turned out), eventually recommended an operation.[188] The surgery took place in November 1878, Ella oblivious thanks to

[184] The diaries show these took place from his 70th birthday (19 December 1872) onwards. Accounts were published in *RMU* (1873), 4, and in the preliminary pages to *RMU* for 1875, 1876, 1878, 1879 and 1880.

[185] The guest list is reprinted in the preliminary pages to *RMU* for 1878; see also 'A Musical Union Réunion', *Orchestra* (January 1879), 181; reprinted ibid. Invitations survive in EllaC, MSS 35 and 79 (between pp. 16 and 17) for 1876 and 1879 respectively. MSS 57/xlvii and 35 offer further memorabilia for the parties of 1876 and 1877. Letters from Ella to Haweis, dated 17 December 1872 and 'Friday à minuit' [19 December 1873] (in UBCsc), also give a flavour of the events.

At the December 1879 gathering Thomas Thornycroft's son, W. Hamo Thornycroft, presented Ella with a bust of himself. For photographs of the bust, see EllaC, MSS 13, 57/liii and 66.

[186] *Musical Sketches, Abroad and at Home*, revised and edited by John Belcher (London: William Reeves, 1878). Belcher had written on architecture and on music (*Lectures on the History of Ecclesiastical Music*; London: Unwin, 1872).

[187] Diary, 2 February 1878 (EllaC, MS 147): 'vu Dr. Bowman, who advised me to desist lecturing, & wrote a note to show – the Ln. Institution.' Bowman was an eminent ophthalmic surgeon, with a large private practice; he was later awarded a baronetcy. See the article on him by D'A. Power, revised Emilie Savage-Smith, in *ODNB*.

[188] Quotation from Ella's diary, 21 January 1878 (EllaC, MS 147). The decline of Ella's sight, his attempts at using spectacles, and the operation can be traced here: see

the recently discovered benefits of chloroform anaesthesia.[189] But sight was not fully restored, and by the middle of the 1879 season Ella accepted further optical decline. With increasing weariness from running his 'one-man show', he became reconciled to winding up the Musical Union, informing his subscribers that '[w]ith increased age and failing sight, I am anxious to escape the labour, anxiety, and correspondence (above 1000 letters every season) involved in the direction of the Musical Union'.[190] Società Lirica meetings fell away around the same time, and Continental travel was not attempted. Meanwhile, the scrawly handwriting in his diary showed the increased signs of visual impairment.

Given the financial difficulties that Ella was experiencing with the Musical Union by this point, ending operations was a sensible move. The delegation of activities to a paid secretary was out of the question, because Ella's conception of concert management remained wholly autocratic. Even so, the decision was not taken lightly, or without personal apprehension, as shown by these private remarks of July 1879: 'If these Doctors agree that I must retire to save my one–right–eye – Alas! I must? If I do, says a friend[,] I'll sink – die of ennui.'[191] Moreover, his entrepreneurial spirit and urge to make a difference were still burning. Who but Ella would then have added, at the age of seventy-seven: 'I hope not – I would rather set up a R.[oyal] A.[cademy] of Music', bringing into play an idea he had mooted to Fétis a decade before, and reflecting his continuing interest in national education. (He was now an external examiner at the National Training School for Music.)[192]

> esp. entries for 18 February, 9 March, 29 May, 14 August, 14 October, 20 October and 23 November 1878 onwards.

[189] Diary, 25 November 1878 (EllaC, MS 147). After the operation (25 November) the diary was written for a short period by an amanuensis.

[190] *RMU* (1879), 21. The first intimation that the surgery had been unsuccessful was given in *RMU* (1879), 9.

[191] Letter to Mrs E. Roche dated 8 July 1879, in BL, Add. MS 46345, ff. 152r–153v (at ff. 152v–153r).

[192] Ibid. To Fétis, he had said: 'I am giving [*sic*] to end my career, by founding a school of harmony and musical instrumental acquirements' (letter dated 10 December 1869; *WangerméeF*, 589). The letter to Mrs Roche (see n. 191 above) was written two days before Ella acted as an external examiner for the recently founded, though foundering, National Training School for Music [NTSM], established under Sullivan's leadership in 1876. Ella's report, not requested by the school until February 1880 – itself an indictment of managerial sloppiness – was, like the other examiners', short, Ella noting that the institution was still young, that student achievement had been 'quite satisfactory' (in such circumstances), and advising the 'formation of a Library without delay' (Minutes of the NTSM Committee of Management, 16 February 1880, Appendix VI: RCMa, 001/1, p. 234). For all his diplomacy, Ella probably held private reservations about the new institution.

Presumably with the agreement of Bowman, whom he continued to consult, Ella decided on one further Musical Union season.[193]

The examiners for 1880 (a group chaired by Charles Hallé and including Michael Costa; Ella did not serve) harshly condemned standards, and Sullivan resigned in 1881. We know from Ella's diary (19 July 1880; EllaC, MS 149) that he saw their report at the school, noting that it was 'not very complimentary to Sullivan'. I am indebted to David Wright for providing information on Ella's role as an NTSM examiner and for helpful explanation of the institutional processes; for more on evolving standards of tuition and assessment at the NTSM, see his 'Grove's Role', 225–9.

[193] In his diary, 2 October 1879, Ella noted his 'sight failing more and more!'. On 12 November Bowman increased his spectacles prescription to give more strength to his right eye (EllaC, MS 148).

CHAPTER 7

Endings (1880–8) and Legacy

Ella commenced his swansong season in April 1880 with the intention of reprising 'the most admired works by the great masters' and showcasing some of the finest players who had appeared in recent years.[1] The concerts certainly exemplified the Musical Union's abiding essence. Quartets were led by Papini and Auer, with Wiener, Holländer and Lasserre as lower strings. Scharwenka, Joseph Wieniawski and Von Bülow were among the pianists. Repertoire included string works by Mozart (D major quintet and quartet K499), Haydn (quartets op. 71 no. 1 and op. 77 no. 2), Beethoven (the op. 29 string quintet, the third Razumovsky quartet and the newly introduced op. 95, which Ella announced as an 'especial favourite' of the amateurs in St Petersburg but privately admitted he found 'incomprehensible'), Mendelssohn (the B♭ quintet op. 87), and Schubert ('Death and the Maiden' quartet).[2] Music with piano comprised the three great trios by Beethoven (Von Bülow playing op. 70 no. 1 and op. 97 on a specially demanded Bechstein instrument), Mendelssohn's C minor trio (with Wieniawski), Schumann's piano quintet (Mme Montigny-Rémaury), and Hummel's septet op. 74 (Duvernoy, who played it at the Grand Matinée; this included the by now expected Beethoven septet). Von Bülow also performed Beethoven's solo sonata op. 31 no. 3, and Duvernoy and Auer gave two movements of the celebrated 'Kreutzer'. All were well-worn works at the Union's concerts, many were Ella's choices, and as such there was little room for the contemporaneity that Ella had accepted in recent years, a few solo instrumental pieces excepted.[3]

ᨀ *Closure*

It was a creation of other times, and cannot survive its founder
ᨑ *Orchestra* (April 1880)

Economically, it was time for Ella to pull out, the 1880 season seeing the smallest ever subscription list (380 published names, probably masking an actual total of significantly fewer) and diminished box-office at some performances.

---

[1] *RMU* (1880), 5.

[2] Ella's published remarks on op. 95 are in *RMU* (1880), 22. For private comment, see his diary, 22 June 1880 (EllaC, MS 149).

[3] E.g. Scharwenka's scherzo in G♭ for two pianos, Von Bülow's piano impromptu op. 27, and Popper's gavotte in D for solo cello.

Just twenty-eight single tickets were sold for the first matinée and forty-two at the second one, Ella noting to himself that the 'Circle [was] nearly empty!'[4] The presence of the magnificent Von Bülow at two concerts drew in 117 and 179 additional listeners respectively – a fair and profitable showing, especially since the pianist once more refused an 'honorarium'.[5] But that was an exception and heralded nothing significant. Besides, while Ella received letters from loyal subscribers who were sad to see the institution fade, and while the *Monthly Musical Record* declared it 'would be a sin to allow these delightful meetings to come to an end', more distanced observers possibly sensed that the Musical Union, with its unique and unilateral leadership, had had its day.[6]

   That would go some way to explain the veiled depiction of the Musical Union and Ella in one of George Bernard Shaw's early novels, *Love among the Artists*, written between May 1881 and January 1882, and published serially in 1887–8.[7] As literary scholar Phyllis Weliver has shown, in an episode set in St James's Hall in 1880, the Antient Orpheus Society, a 'venerable artistic institution' and 'the foremost musical society in Europe' (surely the Musical Union), is described as promoting Beethoven, favouring conservative programmes, and showing 'willful neglect' of English composers.[8] Present at one of its concerts is a character called 'the Professor' – undoubtedly Ella – who adores Beethoven and takes the matter of listening extremely seriously. Significantly, the society is facing extinction. Its audiences, clearly bourgeois-aristocratic and deliberately depicted against the backdrop of increasing mass entertainment, commercial enterprise and social unrest, are fearful of its demise. Of course, these correspondences have their limits: Shaw's construction of the Antient Orpheus (which was depicted as an orchestral, not chamber, society) is ultimately something of an amalgam, blending elements of the Philharmonic Society – also in financial difficulty around this time – and its committee mechanisms, and perhaps even the long-defunct Antient Concerts,

---

[4] Diary, 27 April 1880 (EllaC, MS 149).

[5] Diary, 11 and 25 May 1880 (EllaC, MS 149). Ella responded to Von Bülow's generosity with a gift of a silver cup costing £10 9s 6d (diary, 29 May 1880).

[6] Letters of regret from Ella's loyal followers are preserved in EllaC, MS 156 (from Beaufort, Smyth and others). The quotation is from *MMR*, 10 (1880), 71.

[7] This thesis is developed in Phyllis Weliver, *The Musical Crowd in English Fiction, 1840–1910: Class, Culture and Nation* (Basingstoke: Palgrave, 2006), 130–55. Her argument is wide-ranging, and discovers correspondences between the novel and a range of contemporary cultural phenomena, including the early manifestation of the English Musical Renaissance, Wagnerism and aestheticism, and the rise of a mass audience for music.

[8] George Bernard Shaw, *Love among the Artists* (Chicago: Herbert S. Stone, 1905), 165–8.

into an imagined institution.[9] But the symbolism of the conceit, coming from Shaw, who though not a Musical Union member was already writing a little music criticism on the London scene and must have known of the society's existence, is striking.[10] He had begun to demonstrate the beginnings of his socialist leanings and to comment on the affectations of high society.[11] And he would not be the first to link the Union's downfall with social change and the emergence of a mass culture for music.

At the final concert (29 June) Ella announced unexpectedly that the Musical Union would not wind up after all, but would continue next season under the direction of a 'highly esteemed professor', the cellist Lasserre, with an annual Grand Matinée for Ella's benefit.[12] As always when Ella announced a break with established practice or a new direction, he attributed the suggestion to one of his members – in this case 'an influential quarter'.[13] Given that there had been no period of handover or training for Lasserre, that Lasserre was unproven as an entrepreneur, and that the society was already experiencing financial difficulties, it was a tough assignment for the cellist. Many contemporaries probably wondered how effective the new leadership would be, and at least one critic queried the wisdom of such a change.[14]

Little is known of Lasserre or his decision to take on the institution. He ran the 1881 season in the Ella mould, with many of the same performers, the provision of analytical programme notes, and a continuation of Ella's programming ethos of the 1870s which had peppered the Musical Union's classic repertoire with more modern compositions. Wiener, Van Waefelghem and Lasserre were the foundation of the string quartet, the leading of which was shared between Auer and Paul Viardot, son of the great singer, though in many eyes a somewhat disappointing fiddler.[15] A changing roster of pianists resulted in one appearance

[9] Weliver, *Musical Crowd*, 139–41.

[10] It is not impossible that Shaw, who arrived in London in 1876, had occasionally attended Musical Union concerts.

[11] Notably in *The Irrational Knot* (1880); see Weliver, *Musical Crowd*, 133–4.

[12] *RMU* (1880), 25.

[13] Ibid.

[14] *MMR*, 10 (1880), 115 [quoted in the Introduction]; see also the prophetic remarks quoted at the head of this section.

[15] *MT*, 22 (1881), 302: 'A better first violin than M. Paul Viardot might and should have been obtained. This somewhat feeble though showy player has proved the weak point in an otherwise good quartet.' An unidentified press review of the 10 May concert, inserted in Ella's 1881 diary (EllaC, MS 150) opposite the entries for 2–5 January, reads: 'It is sometimes better to speak plainly, instead of using language to conceal thought. M. Paul Viardot, who has been put forward to lead the

each by Dannreuther and Rubinstein, and performances by three lesser artists, the eighteen-year-old Liszt pupil Alfred Reisenauer, the Leipzig-trained Theodore Ritter from Paris (another student of Liszt, he had played for Ella in 1860–1) and the Dutchman Carl Heymann, who had studied with Hiller in Cologne.[16] The music ranged from favourite string quartets by Haydn, Mozart, Beethoven and Mendelssohn to repertoire only occasionally heard at Musical Union concerts, for instance Schubert's C major quintet, Schumann's A minor quartet op. 41 no. 1 and Saint-Saëns' piano trio op. 18. New territory was also broached: Paul Viardot played Corelli's 'La Folia' variations, Lasserre and Dannreuther gave Parry's sonata for cello and piano in A major – almost certainly the pianist's choice, and a foray into British music that Ella would almost certainly never have initiated – and there were performances of two recently composed pieces by Rubinstein.[17] These were his violin sonata in B minor op. 98, written in 1876, which he played with Auer; and his string quartet in F minor op. 106 no. 2, dating from 1880 and dedicated to Ella, a work that was deemed to show both 'the customary good qualities and failings' that had come to be expected from the Russian.[18]

Meanwhile, Ella maintained a shadowy presence in the season's activities, even though he had formally signed over the Musical Union's direction to Lasserre in January 1881.[19] For, whether out of obligation (Ella had loaned him £100) or genuine desire for guidance, Lasserre continued to consult Ella and keep him abreast

Musical Union, as first violin, is not up to the mark. His great name was not won, and never would have been won, by himself. He plays the violin well, but not well enough for the Musical Union.' For his own part, Ella noted, after observing the violinist in rehearsal, that Viardot 'joue com[m]e un eleve' [plays like a student] (account of 24 April 1881, entered opposite the diary entries for 17–20 April).

[16] *RMU* (1881) gives biographical sketches of Reisenauer (p. 1), Ritter (p. 9) and Heymann (p. 17).

[17] In her analysis of *Love among the Artists*, Weliver further connects Lasserre's programming of Parry's sonata with the Antient Orpheus's turn towards British Music. The fictional society commissions a work entitled *Prometheus Unbound* from a composer called Owen Jack, a direct reference, she argues, to Parry's *Scenes from Shelley's Prometheus Unbound*, which was performed in Cambridge eight months before Shaw began work on the novel (Weliver, *Musical Crowd*, 140–1).

[18] *Athenaeum* (2 July 1881), 24. This was the quartet's première. The sonata had already been played at 'the Popular Concerts and elsewhere' (ibid.).

[19] Diary for 10 January 1881 ('Signed this day transfer of M.U. to Lasserre') and 25 January 1881 ('L. returned agreement stamped'; EllaC, MS 150). The idea of transferring the Union to Lasserre seems to have been discussed the previous autumn, when Ella hoped that Lasserre would run the society for at least three seasons; see diary, 30 October 1880 (EllaC, MS 149). From this and subsequent entries it appears that a Mme Cahagne acted as a business associate of Lasserre's.

of developments.[20] Ella also prepared the programme notes and liaised with sub-scribers and committee men. How the institution's finances worked under Lasserre is not known, and it is unclear whether the Grand Matinée receipts were given to Ella as he intended; if they were, it would have been almost impossible for the society to break even. However, Lasserre's selling of reserved seats for Rubinstein's appearance at the final matinée (a notable break with Musical Union practice) at a price of one guinea strongly suggests the balance sheet was uppermost in his mind.[21] In the meantime, Lasserre made no attempt to move the audience away from its 'exclusive circle of amateurs' towards 'the general music-loving public',[22] so in all likelihood the subscription list and audiences continued to diminish. Indeed, by spring 1882 the institution had foundered, Lasserre announcing that, 'in consequence of circumstances beyond control', the concert series would be cur-tailed.[23] Ella wrote in his diary simply: 'Notice of Musical Union deceased'.[24] This really was the end of an era, and a vindication of Ella's skill as an organizer. As the writer Henry C. Lunn aptly noted, events since Ella's retirement had shown 'how much the personality of the founder had to do with its [the Musical Union's] success'.[25] (One might even wonder if Ella had sanctioned the season, expecting failure, to underline his crucial role in the set-up.) At the same time, the episode demonstrates what limitations there now were to autocratic concert management, old style. The modernizing and highly competitive concert world that beckoned required more robust and formalized ways of managing this sort of enterprise.

In autumn 1880 another long-standing aspect of Ella's life came to a close. It was a private matter, linking back to his liaison with Mary Webb. She, it will be remembered, apparently had a younger relative named Martha Elizabeth ('Mollie', a.k.a. Mrs Robinson), who went to live in the Brompton area after Mary's

[20] The 1881 diary (EllaC, MS 150) shows the two men were in regular working contact. That the £100 was a loan (a financial transaction is noted on 11 January 1881) is spelled out later in the diaries: see the notes opposite the entry for 16 Decem-ber 1881 and the information recorded for 10 July 1882, when the loan was finally repaid (EllaC, MSS 150 and 151).

[21] Indicated by a review in the *Athenaeum* (2 July 1881), 24, and by an advertisement in *DT* (27 June 1881).

[22] *MT*, 22 (1881), 402 [essay by Henry C. Lunn].

[23] *MT*, 23 (1882), 278 [by Lunn].

[24] Diary, 12 April 1882 (EllaC, MS 151). Information noted against the entry for 16 December 1881 (EllaC, MS 150) suggests that Lasserre had left his domicile (124 Bond Street) penniless, and was asking for financial aid.

[25] *MT*, 23 (1882), 429.

death as one Mrs Finicane.[26] Ella had kept in contact for most of the intervening years and had done much to help her financially and materially, as he had done Mary.[27] His frequent journeys to Martha Elizabeth's were strongly reminiscent of patterns established in Mary's day (though the neighbourhood was smarter), and he even referred to her in his diary as 'MW'.[28] Martha Elizabeth, in return, seems to have helped out with administrative chores for the Musical Union, mended shirts, cooked for him, and provided him with hours of her company and emotional support, in much the same way Mary had. And while prepared to be seen with her occasionally in public, perhaps passing her off as a distant relative – in spite of himself, he once took her to the Christy's Minstrels show ('very silly, stupid

[26] Martha Elizabeth's changing identity, from Webb to Robinson and then to Finicane [Finucane; Finacane], is confirmed by addresses at the back of Ella's 1866 diary (EllaC, MS 135). A child (fathered by Finicane) was stillborn to her in December 1866, as Ella discovered while in Paris (diary, 31 December 1866).

Martha Elizabeth lived at 39 Hollywood Road (until 1872), 2 Milton Maude Villas, Maude Grove (1872–5), 2 Wharfedale Street (1875–9) and 42 Warwick Road (from 1879). She appears in the 1870 rate book for Hollywood Road as Elizabeth Finicane. In the 1871 census she is listed as 'Elizabeth Finucane', a 30-year-old lodging-housekeeper and widow, born in Nantwich, Cheshire (thus born c.1841, and in keeping with her known family connections in the Liverpool/Manchester area). Living with her is her younger 'sister' Alice Sutton (aged 15; born in Liverpool) and a domestic servant. (Archival documentation from the Kensington and Chelsea Local Studies Library, London.) Evidence of a marriage to Finicane has not been unearthed; she possibly styled herself as a widow for respectability. See also n. 30 below.

[27] Their relationship had had ups and downs in the years after Mary's death, and some 'late unhappy differences' between them had resulted in Ella once more withdrawing his loan of furniture and other items to her in the winter of 1867–8; see diary, 9, 20 and 30 December 1867 and 6 February, 17 May 1868 (EllaC, MSS 136–7).

A reconciliation in July 1869 ('after 6 years', possibly a reference to her 'marriage' to Robinson in February 1863) enlivened Ella and precipitated a change of his will in Martha Elizabeth's favour: this is my reading of shorthand in the diary, 2 July 1869 (EllaC, MS 138), and subsequent entries, esp. 8, 19, and 20 July. Around this time, or perhaps a few years later (to judge by the colour of the ink Ella was using), he changed a description of her in his account book (MS 6, p. 155) from 'the only daughter of the above [Mary Webb]' to 'the niece'. Whether this was a simple correction of information, or whether Ella was somehow covering his tracks regarding his relationship with Martha Elizabeth (and Mary Webb), is unclear.

The 1870s diaries show Ella providing sums of money, furniture, food etc. to Martha Elizabeth's household.

[28] He also refers to her as 'Mrs F' or 'Lizzie'. The presence of Alice Sutton as Martha Elizabeth's companion during this period is confirmed by several diary entries.

and childish') at St James's Hall[29] – he nevertheless kept her apart from his own
social circle. But in September 1880, following serious disagreements between
Ella and Martha Elizabeth, who was about to marry an American named Mitchell, the connection was severed once and for all.[30] Lawyers were involved as
Ella clawed back the money he had advanced her on a house in Warwick Road,
reclaimed his furniture and wrote Martha Elizabeth out of his will as well as his
life.[31]

As he adjusted to these changes to the pattern and substance of his existence,
Ella was also forced to accept that his sight was still declining.[32] Wary, for instance,
of venturing out in the dark or in London's infamously foggy weather, Ella felt
his world constricting – 'Alas! I shall never more <u>see</u> Rome – I fear, even, Paris',
he wrote to Haweis in December 1880, just before a second operation to treat

[29] Alice went too. Diary, 3 August 1870 (EllaC, MS 139).

[30] 'Violent scene […] parted foes' (diary, 21 September 1880; EllaC, MS 149). The
essence of the grisly events can be construed from the diary (entries from 12
September onwards), but the detail of the disagreements over Martha Elizabeth's
future is hazy: many entries are in shorthand, not all of which I have been able
to decipher. One possibility is that she had recently (1878) given birth to a child,
fathered by Ella, and that Ella, worried about Martha's impending marriage,
wanted to make the child a ward of court. This did not come about, and Ella was
left to 'weep to lose my B.' (shorthand in diary, 21 September 1880; EllaC, MS 149).
There are also faint suggestions that Ella had proposed to Martha Elizabeth more
than once, and had been refused.
   James Edgar Mitchell and Martha Elizabeth Webb were married by licence at a
church in Earl's Court on 30 July 1880. On the marriage certificate Martha's father
is given as 'Egerton Webb' (not the music critic Egerton Webbe, despite the Liverpool family connections), and she is described as a spinster, endorsing the suggestion that her marriages to Robinson and Finicane were clandestine. She is listed
as aged 35, implying a birth year of 1845 (her birthday, we know from Ella's earlier
diaries, was celebrated on 22 or 23 April). I have not found a record of her birth
as either Webb or Sutton for this date; however, a Martha Webb was born near
Nantwich on 8 October 1845, which broadly concurs with the information given
in n. 26 above.

[31] The estate was left to Ella's cousin Edward Harley of Loughborough. Ella signed
the will, which was the last he ever wrote, on 23 September 1880 (Principal
Probate Registry, London). Ella had kept in contact with the Harleys, and in
recent years had taken an interest in the education of a younger relative, Ella
Harley.

[32] The 1880 diary charts further eye trouble and consultations with Bowman: see
26 and 30 April, 2 August, 4 September, 11, 12, 24 and 26 November, 8, 9 and 15
December 1880. (EllaC, MS 149). Ella was also complaining of poor hearing: see 19
and 20 February, 2 December 1880.

the 'poor one fading – eye'.[33] The surgery, again in Bowman's hands, produced short-term improvements, but within months Ella's vision was worsening. He complained that he could not see to analyse Rubinstein's new sonata, and relied increasingly on Belcher's help in the preparation of the programmes.[34] Further operations were discussed but eventually judged futile, and by the end of 1881 Ella had resigned himself to a world of darkness, his lifelong diary habit reduced to a bland listing of appointments made and letters written, all in the hand of a servant acting as amanuensis.

Still, he had a comfortable old age, and was able to live easily on the interest from his investments. They totalled £6,950 in 1880, and were later (1881) supplemented by a nest-egg of £530, raised by some 200 subscribers to a formal Testimonial Fund under the presidency of the Earl of Dunmore.[35] And Ella spent his hours sociably. First-hand accounts of Ella's personality in his final years describe someone characteristically optimistic and bright, with mental faculties intact – someone determined to go on getting the most out of life as best he could.[36] There were visitors a-plenty from high-society and musical spheres, many of whom read aloud to him; occasionally he ventured out, guided by a chaperone. If he had his dark moments of reflection, he kept them well hidden.

Ella died on 2 October 1888, weeks away from his eighty-sixth birthday, and was buried in Brompton Cemetery three days later, in the same plot as Mary Webb. The death certificate recorded 'cerebral haemorrhage [i.e. stroke] and hemiplegia

---

[33] Letter to Haweis in an amanuensis's hand, dated 11 December 1880 (in UBCsc). The operation took place on 30 December 1880; see the diary for that day: 'no pain no fever' [amanuensis's hand] (EllaC, MS 149).

[34] 'Sonata of Ruby to analyse – cannot see' (diary, 22 June 1881; EllaC, MS 150). Within four months of the operation, Ella had become aware that his sight was still weakening. After a walk in Green Park, he wrote: 'fine day – the glare of sun, is very blinding, & I feel, becoming gradually more blind' (diary, 15 April 1881; EllaC, MS 150).

[35] A prospectus (dated October 1881) for the fund is preserved in one of the scrapbooks (EllaC, MS 81, between pp. 74 and 75). There was a twenty-three-strong committee of aristocrats and notable figures in artistic life, including (for music) Sir F. A. G. Ouseley, Bt, the recently knighted Sir Julius Benedict, Rev. J. E. Cox, Rev. H. R. Haweis and John Stainer; Sir Henry Cole and J. E. Millais were among the non-musicians. Ella's financial legacy at his death is documented in Chapter 6.

[36] Wrote Haweis (HaweisJE, 1–2): '[H]e is quite blind, but still hale and hearty, in his eighty-third year, and surrounded by a faithful and devoted circle of friends'. Letters written to Ella in the 1880s (EllaC, MS 156) testify to the strength of his circle and the warmth in which he was held, while correspondence of 1881, from Ella to Sterndale Bennett's son (preserved in the private collection of Barry Sterndale Bennett) demonstrates Ella's desire for sociability.

3 months', the latter being a type of palsy on one side of the body that often follows apoplexy, and which ties in roughly with the description, given by his friend T. L. Southgate, of Ella becoming paralysed three weeks before his death.[37] An obelisk was later erected above the grave, with dates of birth and death; the inscription ran 'In Memory of John Ella [...] Founder of the Musical Union London'.[38] His place of birth and Mary Webb's name were notably absent.

✿ *Posthumous reactions*

> *When the musical jealousies of our time have subsided, and the musical history of the nineteenth century comes to be written, the name of Professor Ella will be remembered with respect and sympathy.*   ✿ *HaweisJE*

IN the days and weeks following Ella's death a clutch of obituaries appeared. Duly respectful, though not always entirely accurate in matters of fact, they memorialized a warm human being as well as a cosmopolitan and well-connected *animateur*; and they commended Ella's achievements largely in terms of the Musical Union, its analytical programmes and the wide reputation for excellence and fashionability that the institution had enjoyed.[39] Some even suggested, oversimplistically, that the Musical Union had given rise to the Popular Concerts.[40] Carping at the personality of the man fell silent.

Ella's burial had been modest – 'in the presence of his sorrowing friends', as one obituarist put it[41] – and, though nobody said so, in stark contrast to the pomp and ceremonial that had accompanied the last rites of his near contemporary, the

---

[37] *MS* (6 October 1888), 215.

[38] The stone is now eroding badly.

[39] The most extensive obituary, by T. L. Southgate, appeared in *MS* (6 October 1888), 213–15, entitled 'John Ella'. See also *The Times* (4 October 1888); *MP* (5 October 1888); *MW* (6 October 1888), 781; *ILN* (13 October 1888), 440; and *MT*, 29 (1888), 665. Some of the tributes introduced errors or glossed points in ways that would eventually become unhelpful to the historical record.

[40] The idea was put forward in the *Times*, *MW* and *MT* obituaries, perhaps drawing on Haweis's observation (*HaweisJE*, p. 3) that '[t]he Monday Populars are, perhaps, the most striking fruit of Ella's labours. He created the taste, he sowed the seed.' Southgate's obituary claimed the Musical Union was 'the true parent of the Monday Popular Concerts', while the article on Ella by J. A. Fuller Maitland in *DNB* described the Pops as the 'successor' to the Union.

[41] Southgate, 'John Ella', 215. A notice of the burial in *MW* (13 October 1888), 796, noted among the mourners: 'Lord Clarence Paget, Messrs. G. A. Osborne, W. H. Cummings, E. H. Turpin, H. Lazarus, H. Goodban, J. Belcher, T. L. Southgate,

composer William Sterndale Bennett, at Westminster Abbey in 1875.[42] Bennett was one of several prominent men in London's musical world – including the conductor Michael Costa, the composer and organist of St Paul's Cathedral John Stainer, the lexicographer and first director of the Royal College of Music George Grove, and W. G. Cusins, one of the Queen's Musicians – who had been knighted during the previous twenty years, and the nature and place of Bennett's burial were a reflection of his national recognition. That Ella did not receive a knighthood seems symptomatic of the gulf that had developed between him and the groups that formed the British musical 'establishment'. He had never been rooted in the networks that might have produced the honour: a court appointment, which might well have been possible in the 1830s, had eluded him; and royal patronage of the Musical Union had never been particularly significant. Moreover, and in spite of his campaigning for improvements to London's musical infrastructure, he had long positioned himself apart from many of the institutions, such as the Royal Academy of Music, that promoted the interests of British music and musicians directly; and he had rarely intersected with the leading networks of church and cathedral organists. The Musical Association (later Royal Musical Association), founded in 1874 as a learned society for music, had been formed largely from such circles, but Ella had played no part in it, in spite of a lifetime spent cultivating a self-conscious seriousness.[43] A loner in business affairs, he had made his mark on musical life in a peculiar manner and through somewhat unorthodox routes; and his position in society remained equivocal, his lack of prowess as a soloist or conductor not helping his case for recognition. Some of Ella's supporters campaigned for a knighthood for him in 1887.[44] But an ideology was emerging as to which

Arthur Coleridge, Duncan Davison', and a 'number of ladies'. A preliminary service was held at St Peter's, Eaton Square.

[42] Ella had been in one of the many carriages in Bennett's funeral procession, as part of a deputation from the Royal Society of Musicians: see *MW* (13 February 1875), 107. He had once noted how the death of the military musician J.-G. Kastner had been marked in a similarly grand manner in France (*RMU*, 1867, sup., 12).

[43] Analysis of the social backgrounds of the members of the Musical Association is provided by Joanne Dibley in her 'The Musical Association as a Victorian Learned Society' (MA diss., Oxford Brookes University, 2004) [includes database]. The membership included several composers, organists, journalists and scientists with amateur musical interests.

[44] The evidence for this is found in press cuttings from the *Pall Mall Gazette* in the back of Ella's 1887 diary (EllaC, MS 155). An article 'The Musical Knights' lobbied for knighthoods for Ella, John Hullah and Henry Leslie, 'three musicians who have lifted music in England, educationally, technically, and socially, into its present proud position', and made the case for Ella largely on account of the Musical Union; a letter to the editor from John Belcher, in response to the essay, reminded

types in the musical world were worth honouring in Britain, and which were not. Facilitators and organizers were, it seems, mostly beyond the pale.

Posterity's view of Ella has changed over time. Ten to twenty years after his death, the modest and polite obituaries were replaced by personal reminiscences – ranging from the dewy-eyed to the trenchantly critical – and by franker appraisals, some written by men who had known him, and all inflected by the ideas of their times.[45] Some writers found reasons for the Musical Union's demise, not always with the insights and distance that history later brings. The crucial point here is that London music had, over the nineteenth century, become increasingly accessible to the middling and lower orders. By the 1890s the South Place Sunday chamber concerts in Finsbury and events sponsored by the People's Concert Society in the East End were bringing high art music to the working classes like never before; and amateur participation among the 'people', especially singing and brass banding, was one of Britain's most notable cultural achievements.[46] Simultaneously, general attitudes towards the ruling, landed élite were beginning to be transformed. The 1880s had been troubled years for the British aristocracy (the Third Reform Act of 1884 had made voting a right, not a privilege, for two out of three men; socialism was on the march), and although significant decline in power and prosperity would come only after World War I, their authority ebbed away gradually in the last two decades of the century, accompanied by a weakening of unquestioning public respect for their hierarchies. Little surprise, then, that the Musical Union, an institution that had even in its day become a caricature of aristocratic

> readers that Ella's contribution to musical culture went further, and claimed him as the inventor of the programme note and the person who had introduced almost every distinguished European performer to the British public.

45 On Ella the man, much ink was spilled by, among others, Alice Diehl (*DiehlMM*; *The True Story of my Life: an Autobiography* (London: John Lane, The Bodley Head, 1908)), Henry Davison (*DavisonFM*) and Wilhelm Ganz (*GanzMM*). See also the assessments of the institution in 'Some Pictures of the Past', *MT*, 35 (1894), 377–81, at 378–80; Joseph Bennett, 'Victorian Music, VIII: Chamber Music', *MT*, 38 (1897), 803–6, at 804–5; and Walter Willson Cobbett, 'Musical Union', *CCSCM*. Much of this material formed the basis of subsequent accounts of Ella's life and work.

46 On chamber music for the people, see Alan Bartley, 'Chamber Music Concerts in Suburban London, 1895–1915: Aspects of Repertoire, Performance and Reception' (PhD, Oxford Brookes University, 2004). On community music-making and the significant amount of art music performed by choirs and bands, see Dave Russell, *Popular Music in England, 1840–1914: a Social History*, 2nd edition (Manchester: Manchester University Press, 1997), part 3. On the broader context of intellectual pursuits among the working classes, see Jonathan Rose, *The Intellectual Life of the British Working Classes* (New Haven and London: Yale University Press, 2001).

association, should be viewed at the end of the century with a mixture of hostility and amusement, its death correlated to the diminishing of aristocratic authority (and by implication the upsurge in socialism) and the arrival of a mass culture for classical music. Or that Ella, whose social climbing and liaisons with the nobility had always been flagrantly displayed, was the source of contempt. Joseph Bennett, for one, mocked Ella and his 'Duchesses', and in 1897 depicted him as someone ruthless in his social ambitions, living in the 'cold shade of aristocracy' and hovering around the upper classes with 'ready smiles and a flexible back'.[47] Like a few others, Bennett was keen to play down the significance of Ella's achievements, dismissing his abilities as a performer – 'a somewhat indifferent violinist'.[48] Elsewhere we find the developing view of the entrepreneur (Ella) as someone engaged in a second-class, 'service' activity for music.[49] Nevertheless, most of Ella's detractors admitted that he had done remarkable work in his promotion of high culture and in his development of audience appreciation of chamber music, and that he had set examples and standards that other concert-givers and listeners had followed. Bennett chose to explain this broader achievement in terms of social emulation:

> [Ella's] crowning grace is, however, that, never mind by what means, he invested chamber music and its concerts with the glamour of the "hupper suckles [upper circles]." Englishmen so dearly love a lord, and are so ready to imitate him, that this may be considered a very important achievement indeed.[50]

Meanwhile, one account of Victorian chamber music, published three years earlier, had struck a note that would resonate for some time. It made much of the social, aristocratic dimension of the Musical Union, and did so by polarizing it against the (by implication) 'worthier' music for the people that was suggested by Chappell's and others' initiatives, and using the popularization of serious music among the middling and lower orders as the one-dimensional explanation of the Musical Union's extinction.[51]

[47] Bennett, 'Victorian Music', 804–5.

[48] Bennett, 'Victorian Music', 804. Ella is also referred to as 'an orchestral violinist of no particular mark' in 'Some Pictures'; this passage (p. 378) goes on to say that he 'had the wit to see that his true vocation was that of *entrepreneur*'.

[49] Edward Speyer, *My Life and Friends* (London: Cobden-Sanderson, 1937), 24–5 [anecdote about Lübeck refusing to allow Ella to sit at the artists' table in the Café-Royal].

[50] Bennett, 'Victorian Music', 805.

[51] 'The popularisation of music killed the Musical Union. For one thing, the "Pops" arose, and when the best performances could be heard for at most five shillings, it was not in the nature of things that a more costly rival, however select and however

Tropes like this one had their origins in the earlier newspaper columns of J. W. Davison, and unquestionably contained a grain of truth. The opening up of classical music to the masses was but one facet of the changes and growth in concert life that were creeping in around the time the Musical Union folded, and which would soon have required, had Ella remained in charge, a considerable reinvention of the institution and the establishment of new ways of drawing audiences, who were seemingly starting to 'shop elsewhere'. Still, any idea that demand among high society for serious music in intimate, socially exclusive surroundings had disappeared by the early 1880s holds little water, since the vitality of chamber music in private salons until well after the end of the century strongly suggests the contrary.[52] Perhaps what had changed was high society's willingness to be publicly associated with such a formal organization as the Musical Union, even as casual purchasers of tickets. Meanwhile, the persistent influence of a handful of Victorian sources on the Musical Union's historiography, the strength of the reaction against the British class system through much of the twentieth century, and the popularity of writing history 'from below', explains something of the enduring characterizations of Ella and his institution, and why as a subject it was doomed to neglect for decades.

❧ *Persona and achievements*

So what, from the perch of the early twenty-first century, does this biographer make of the man who was John Ella, and of his contribution to Victorian music and culture? His was, without doubt, an extraordinary working life, commencing among the jobbing musicians of Soho and ending in financial independence in Belgravia – a story of successful upward mobility at once typical of the aspirations of the Victorian lower-middle classes but rarely achieved by members of the music profession. Background and formative influences played their part, much of Ella's relentless quest for social advancement and respectability being typical of the provincial, artisan-class circumstances of his birth. (Indeed, as with his later contemporary Edward Elgar, born in Worcestershire to a piano tuner and music dealer, a tendency to conservative politics, establishment values, and

much glorified by aristocratic prestige, could continue to flourish' ('Some Pictures', 378, 380).

[52] Bennett ('Victorian Music', 805) wrote: 'After a fairly long and undoubtedly useful life, the Musical Union broke up and passed into limbo. Mr. Ella was getting old; music had become democratised, and the aristocracy less exclusive'. On the vitality of private music in high society at the end of the century, see *McVeighA*, 167; for a specific study, see Valerie Langfield, 'The Family von Glehn', *NBMS*, 3, ed. Peter Horton and Bennett Zon (Aldershot: Ashgate, 2003), 273–93.

obvious coveting of the visible signs of success may likewise be interlinked.)[53] More specifically, the years in Leicester gave him the head for business that would become intensely advantageous in the London musical market-place; and they almost certainly contributed to his acceptance of authority and his developing awareness of the openings that high society patronage could bring, not to mention the musical opportunities that Paris might offer an ambitious young fiddler. The seeds for turning a nobody into a somebody were sown early on.

Self-evidently, Ella got where he did largely because he aspired so strongly to self-betterment in material and non-material ways, and because he sought out imaginative methods for achieving his goals. He was both persistent and shrewd, and developed early on a yen for the most serious music and respect for high culture that henceforth characterized his professional aspirations. His patchwork musical-intellectual education – a classic story of opportunities seized, much of it outside the norms of the British musical 'system' – was highly formative, shaping Ella's unique set of skills and insights. But while this independence gave him an edge over his contemporaries, it left him lacking both professional qualifications and shared educational experiences with others of his generation. His assimilation into high society was similarly destined to remain less than absolute, even by the end of his life when he was enjoying a new level of social acceptance among certain families. This was partly because Ella's attitude towards the nobility had been grounded in his natal social class, around a type of discernible servility which, however much it was giving way in the mid-nineteenth century to more of an equality between musician and patron, would always mark him out. Ella could not help but play the courtier. He might advertise his familiarity with wealthy families, and indeed share in their social lives in ways that eighteenth-century musicians would never have done; but there is reason to think that part of the *beau monde* laughed at him, albeit affectionately. If factors like these made Ella an outsider in the communities he tried to assimilate into – a *parvenu* musically, intellectually and socially – they may also have helped him to connect with the dozens of Continental musicians in London who were so central to his professional activities and cosmopolitan outlook; he held special affection for Costa and Meyerbeer, both European Jews. Paradoxically, too, a sense of 'difference' (not to mention confidence gained from his myriad social connections) may have given him the strength to sustain his independent position. Meanwhile, the troubled and ambiguous relationship between British musicians on the one hand, and the closely aligned aristocracy and Continental performers with whom Ella increasingly

[53] This line of thought was developed by David Cannadine in 'Sir Edward Elgar as a Historical Personality', at 'Music in Britain: a Social History', seminar, Institute of Historical Research, University of London, 10 February 2003.

consorted on the other, left him an easy target for back-biting from members of his profession – a path that led inevitably to his becoming a controversial figure, though by no means universally loathed.

For while Ella was a driven man, he was also an enthusiastic and personable one, and had many friends. Haweis described him as '[a] good diner-out, a capital talker, a genial wit', adding that he 'always had a good story, a polished address, and an appropriate repartee'.[54] It is easy to suspect that his yarns were prone, as was his concert promotion, to more than a touch of exaggeration, self-importance and prolixity.[55] Like most people, he loved to gossip; and he relished being in the thick of musical affairs. Intermixed were a certain vanity and egotism, a persistent manner when trying to get what he wanted, an occasional outspokenness, and an ability to play the chameleon – qualities that could cut both ways when exploited professionally.

As a performer, Ella was good but not outstanding. Probably hampered by his unorthodox training, he was nevertheless competent enough to hold his own in the rank and file of a London orchestra, and was a sensitive chamber music companion.[56] His skill as a composer and arranger was on much the same level – workmanlike and well suited to the markets he aimed to exploit. These basic career elements – eventually discarded – gave him an inside knowledge of music and the musician's world, qualities that combined with his tradesman's background to make him a formidable 'enabler'.

Throughout his life the Continent was a constant source of inspiration for Ella. Early on he found models for strengthening the taste for chamber music in London in both Parisian salon culture and the ideas of Baillot and Fétis, his enshrinement of the Austro-German repertoire thus being strongly mediated by Franco-Belgian thinking. And increasingly his outlook became unabashedly cosmopolitan. Yet for all his Europhilia, he yearned to improve the status of music

---

54 *HaweisJE*, 3.

55 *DiehlMM*, 120: '[H]is stories-in-chief were of his own prowess. There was a certain tale of his capture of a salmon in Scotland, which lengthened by a few sentences each time of telling. There had been a time when, beginning with the serving of the fish [at dinner], it was well over by the appearance of the cheese. But the last time the writer had the honour of hearing it, it was barely half through – in fact, Ella had not begun to "play" the monster from his slippery perch among the rocks – when the ladies rose to leave the table.'

56 Henry Phillips (*Musical and Personal Recollections during Half a Century* (London: Charles J. Skeet, 1864), vol. 2, p. 2) remembered watching him in an orchestra: 'It is true you could not hear him; but his mode of bowing, his energy, and peculiar action, when arriving at any great or prominent passage, made the spectator at once put faith in his passion for music, and skill in its execution.'

at home; in his use of language he became practised at playing the patriotic card, appealing to feelings of cultural inferiority or superiority as the case required. Still, however much he might imply it was a sign of strength, not weakness, that the best from abroad be recognized and planted in native soil, or insist that the development of an intelligent listening public for chamber music was an indication of national progress (already challenging stereotypical European views of the British), his singular promotion of Continental players at the Musical Union and the corresponding absence of British works from concerts set him at odds with those who promoted native talent. Alice Diehl in 1897 remembered him as the 'avowed enemy of British art'.[57] If a touch unfair to Ella (he thought well of Sterndale Bennett's music, and felt Sullivan had promise as a serious dramatic composer), the tag nevertheless reflects the depth of feeling that the issue produced in Ella's lifetime.

Ella's significance to music history is as a concert entrepreneur more than anything else, regardless of what some music dictionaries once suggested.[58] His importance stems from his success both in shaping the taste of audiences and conditioning them to respectful, attentive behaviour when listening, and in sustaining a top-quality concert institution over thirty-six years. The fact that he also made a substantial commercial profit from his concert society in times when such an achievement was far from normal has been a principal theme in this book, and does not need relabouring here. What is worth emphasizing is that his modes of operation were symptomatic of someone working during a period of change. This is why in Ella we find an odd confluence of older and newer ways of running concerts. For example, much of the Musical Union apparatus as set up in 1845 – the use of a subscription system, the establishment of a committee of grandees ostensibly with artistic control, the reliance on a patronage network and personal contacts in creating an audience, the correlation of social élites with high-class music, and the interconnection between Ella's concerts and the rest of his professional activities – made it look much like an eighteenth-century initiative, not a million miles from the London concert world Haydn experienced. Several of these elements remained in place throughout the Musical Union's lifetime, most particularly the image and conduct of a select, private society and the 'cottage-industry' aspect of its administration, Ella carrying on an enormous correspondence with his members single-handedly. But newer, more business-oriented thinking arrived too, Ella taking financial control of the organization in 1846 and increasingly introducing practices that pointed to the future. These

---

[57] DiehlMM, 117.

[58] Entries on Ella in Grove5 and NGDM1 imply that his importance was as a violinist, conductor and critic.

included: the quest for the best chamber players; the sale of single tickets to 'out-
siders'; the monitoring of box-office receipts and an awareness of individual artists'
drawing power; the exploitation of press advertising and hype to draw a public
and enhance the notion of quality; the advertising of piano makers in concert
programmes; and the subtle tempering of artistic principles to attract or retain
audiences. Although this shrewd, commercial approach ruffled feathers occasionally, especially among the press, without it the Musical Union would never have
lasted.

Indeed, the need to blend the pursuit of high culture with commercial realities,
while downplaying any sense of aggressive exploitation of the market, was a sign
of the time, place, and social-economic world Ella was operating in. All the while,
the image of the exclusive club endured, the high-born committee becoming orna-
mental yet useful to Ella as a shield for introducing change, even if such a public
association with the old social order may have eventually undermined the Musical
Union's viability.

Other aspects of the Musical Union's success can be related to the confluence
of geography and time-period. When Ella set up the institution in 1845, the special concentration of Britain's serious-minded nobility and gentry in London
during the season made it the one place where sufficient demand for chamber
music from this tranche of society could be found. Put another way: had Ella
founded his Musical Union in Manchester, his audience profile would have
been quite different; had he attempted to build an institution on his London
model in an English market town it would have surely been unsustainable. As
the years went by, the growth of middle-class wealth in the expanding London
suburbs (including well-heeled women with time on their hands and a desire
for serious music, and a network of transport communications to bring them in
and out) gave Ella the opportunity to tap a bigger market while not overly dis-
turbing the institution's established social identity. Furthermore, the position of
the metropolis as a vibrant cultural centre where national debates on the arts
and sciences took place, where learned societies and professional bodies typically met, and where new museums and galleries were being founded, made it
the obvious centre of attraction for anyone seeking the blend of artistic nourishment that so many of Ella's supporters seem to have wanted. London's abun-
dant concert life was part of the cultural picture, since the sheer number of able
European musicians willing to try their luck in London each season, and the
capital's function as the first port of call for new arrivals and a central node for
travel, gave Ella a pool of top-class performers to draw on that was second to
none. As for the organization's declining profits in later years and its ultimate
demise under Jules Lasserre, here it was the incipient changes to the organization and supply of concerts, including competition from bigger players like

Chappell, and the ways in which metropolitan audiences, including high society, were now making their leisure choices, that were the likely main roots of the problem.[59] As we have seen, for the institution to have survived, Ella's old ways of operation required imaginative reinvention, not simple replication.

Be that as it may, by creating a lasting concert society with the best of players, and effectively institutionalizing salon culture and the 'sacralization' of the core chamber music repertoire, Ella consistently drew positive attention from the musical world, both in Britain and around Europe. Significantly, Ella was not just concerned with trumpeting high art: he wanted to communicate the aesthetic significance of his preferred repertoire, and to build a serious, lasting taste for chamber music, ideas that resonated with serious-minded people everywhere. He was the first in Europe to institutionalize the use of programme notes and silent listening, and did so on a sustained basis. His programme notes were emulated in various social settings by concert-givers in London and beyond: as far afield as Amsterdam.[60] Yet Ella was not the inventor of programme notes or of silent listening (nor was he a particularly insightful notewriter: his own contributions pale, for example, alongside those of George Grove, himself untrained in music); and it would be foolish to cast him as the sole agent of the upsurge in quiet, informed listening in Britain, which clearly owed much to broader cultural conditions. But he was an important catalyst for these trends. His concentrated programming, his continued insistence on appropriately reverential atmosphere and behaviour in the concert room, his supply of music-appreciation literature, and his entreaties to audiences to honour high art through intellectual-cum-spiritual engagement

---

[59] The extent to which 'unstable economic and social conditions' contributed to the end of the Musical Union, a line of argument developed in Weliver (*Musical Crowd*, 139 and ff.), is less clear. Weliver's analysis follows Shaw's politically charged construction of the Antient Orpheus Society as fearing for its future against the backdrop of political agitation in the 1880s. Quite possibly this was a contributory factor, some members of the Musical Union audience falling away and preferring private chamber salons or the Pops for fear of being publicly associated with an organization synonymous with social élitism. Yet Weliver (p. 140) admits that themes of social influence are not the most pervasive in the novel.

[60] E.g. a programme for a concert given by the pianist Mortier de Fontaine at the Odéon, ?Amsterdam, in January 1850 provided analytical notes with music examples in emulation of the Musical Union (copy preserved in EllaC, MS 80, between pp. 118 and 119). Also, when Charles Hallé began chamber concerts in Manchester, he asked Ella to provide him with programme notes: see Christina Bashford, 'Educating England: Networks of Programme-Note Provision in the Nineteenth Century', *Music in the British Provinces, 1690–1914*, ed. Rachel Cowgill and Peter Holman (Aldershot: Ashgate, forthcoming). According to Ella (*MR*, 1857, p. xviii), his notes were also borrowed for use in Dublin.

with it, went further than anyone else had done at that date, particularly with the London élite. The need to educate and reform upper-class behaviour in the concert room and opera house had been on the lips of many British critics, including Davison, in the 1830s and 40s, as shifting cultural codes and musical value systems came into play, though ideas and methods for achieving change were notoriously different.[61] Ella's unique ability to get the nobility to bow to his musical and social authority was impressive and distinctive, and placed his audiences in contradiction to the prevailing stereotype for upper-class listeners. Meanwhile, his proselytizing for high art reaped commendation, and within his own sphere of influence Ella increasingly commanded power and respect, so that by the end of his career he stood to shape serious musical taste in a significant slice of London society: not only within the Musical Union but outside it as well, through his published writings, lectures in the mercantile City district, and amateur opera club. In 1878 Ella claimed he had reached some 50,000 people, a total surely exaggerated but indicative nonetheless.[62]

❧ Broader cultural significance

ACROSS this book the narrative has switched between a close focus on Ella and a broader view of his institutions and their audiences. Now, then, is the time to consider the significance of the general aspects of the story for a history of music and culture in nineteenth-century Britain. Let us start with findings that run against the grain. One of the most striking revelations about the Musical Union is that its membership included a sizeable number of aristocrats who were eager and willing to sign up to the society's serious musical endeavours, and who demonstrated a desire to learn how to listen and an ability to do so. It is a finding that counters prevailing correlations between class and listening habits, and one that challenges the assumption made, both in Ella's day and ours, that the British nobility lacked musical sensibilities and sophistication, its culture construed as hopelessly bound up with pleasure and anti-intellectualism, and evinced by its celebrated long-standing interest in country sports.[63] This is not to suggest that the Victorian nobility has been wrongly characterized as to its musical-intellectual orientation – certainly, Ella's aristocrats were a small subsection of their number,

[61] Jennifer L. Hall-Witt, 'Representing the Audience in the Age of Reform: Critics and the Elite at the Italian Opera in London', *MBC*, 121–44.

[62] *EllaMS3*, 435.

[63] John Hullah, in his evidence to the parliamentary inquiry into music education in Britain (1865), complained of general musical ignorance among the upper classes, including women (*EhrlichMP*, 93).

and the exception not the rule – but it is to place a footnote against rigid stereo-typing of the group as a whole.

There is further pause for thought in Ella's audience, broadly construed – not just the Musical Union audience but the publics for all his concerts, his opera club and lectures. As a group that mixed minor aristocracy and gentry with the wealthy middle classes – increasingly as the decades elapsed – it nevertheless pulls against the prevailing idea that the audience for classical music in the nineteenth century was essentially a mass and middling one, and sounds an important note of cau-tion about easy class-based explanations of London concert history. More work is needed on the upper echelons of concert-goers before firm conclusions can be reached. What is clear, however, is that Ella's institutional settings provided *bona fide* sites for the intermingling of upper social groups and for the assimilation of 'new money' into high society. Willert Beale's account of the atmosphere at the Musical Union ahead of a concert, cited in a previous chapter, vividly describes how such occasions blended the social with the musical, calling up simultane-ous images of the scientific *conversazione* and the flower show.[64] Implicit in his cameo is the possibility that such people were also seeking the refuge of a socially exclusive milieu for their musical appreciation – and, given that these were times when even the opera house was losing its cachet as the principal meeting place for members of high society as the middle classes infiltrated it, such an idea cannot be disregarded. And yet caution is needed, since the Musical Union entourage had little room for the chattering, lightweight fashionables who were the more typical frequenters of the Italian Opera: with Ella's followers, a desire for social exclusivity emanated from a shared seriousness of musical purpose. Of course, a purely social or sociological analysis might still propose that they were using membership of the Musical Union to articulate their class and power, and nothing more. But this study insists that these were people whose hard-acquired intellectual enjoyment of music was a fundamental stay of life as well as a principal marker of social identity and difference. For if one point emerges above all others from studying the Victorians, it is that the experience of live classical music was intensely pre-cious and gave rise to an extraordinarily forceful 'desire' to consume it among all social groups. So while the Musical Union may have given its members a public and symbolic form of 'cultural capital' (the institution's profile in the press saw to that), it also provided a way for their musical aspirations and tastes to be privately and meaningfully legitimated and extended.

A further source of astonishment, then and now, comes from the discovery that so many women supported the Musical Union; consistently around 70 per

[64] Willert Beale, 'A Morning Call on Mr. Ella', *Liverpool Journal* (18 February 1871); reprinted in the preliminary pages to *EllaMS2*, 1–14, at 1–2.

cent of the audience was female. This finding counters another stereotype that the intellectual, scientific appreciation of music was an endeavour predominantly suited to men (albeit those from the music profession), and that music was a social, not cerebral, activity for women. 'Ladies following the music with scores in their hadns [i.e. hands] is a sight as much to be surprised at, as rarely to be found', wrote Onslow, approvingly, in 1846; while in 1872 a successor to Chorley on the *Athenaeum* suggested with similar wonder that '[t]he stranger [...] observes aged dowagers and young spinsters sitting round the inclosed circle with books in their hands, and if a glance can be obtained of their pages, it will be seen that the books are scores of the music to be executed'.[65] Of course, the power behind the Musical Union remained in the hands of one man, and the official hierarchy (or committee) was exclusively male, so claims about female involvement in the society must be tempered accordingly. But the army of 'Mrs Grotes' played an important part in sustaining the club, and this may have contributed to the development of wider, private networks for serious conversation and artistic pursuits among high-class women in the capital.

Meanwhile, we might speculate that Ella's promotion of the cerebral aspect of chamber music, and its reinforcement with the masculinity of science through the printed analytical programme note, had an importance for the Musical Union's leisured male constituency: that it was an attempt to counter prevailing cultural ambiguities and prejudices in 'respectable' British society about the manliness of playing or listening to chamber music, and to trigger change in attitudes and practice.[66] And not just attitudes related to class and gender. By giving the transitory concert experience the permanence of print, Ella may well have been seeking to raise music's stake in the national claim to be treated on a par with the plastic arts. This is quite possible, for if his rhetoric about the Musical Union is to be believed, Ella was concurrently fostering hopes of improving how serious music was treated

---

[65] The letter is printed in *MW* (23 May 1846), 245–6; the report is from the *Athenaeum* (20 April 1872), 504.

[66] The ambiguities around the manliness of being seen to play quartets seriously almost certainly extended to appreciating chamber music. Ella admitted in *RMU* that female aristocrats tended to have better appreciation of fine music than their male counterparts (1858, p. 54). He also expressed frustration with objections that cultivating the mind through music was not consistent with manliness, and sighed that it was largely women and the clergy who gave public support to the arts in England, including the Musical Union (1868, sup., 15). Such perceptions possibly shaped the later view that Victorian Britain did not have a serious chamber music culture, since upper-class quartet playing, where it existed, remained hidden from view, taking place in such locations as country houses, Oxbridge colleges, expatriate communities and garrisons.

and valued in Britain. Only by improving the musical taste and sensibilities of the guardians of cultural power would changes in the *status quo* come about. By showing such men what a 'quality' concert institution looked and sounded like, and by developing their understanding of why such serious music-making and appreciation were of profound importance to a civilized society, one might eventually bring about Continental-style courtly patronage or government support for music on a meaningful scale.

A SPECTS of the Musical Union's history also contribute to an understanding of broader trends and norms in cultural life. As an institution that fostered silent, close listening, the Musical Union was part of a larger historical shift wrought over more than a century (not only in Britain but in Europe too) during which audiences at musical events began quietening down, behaving with a new decorum typically associated with the bourgeoisie, and approaching the musical event in a more reverential and introspective manner. The causes of such a change are much debated, though are bound up with altering norms of social behaviour, with new ideas about art music's importance within culture, as well as with the forces of Romanticism. Ella's concert society was one among an initial cluster of such developments in listener attentiveness in Britain, although his matinées went much further in developing it, making the Musical Union at once typical and atypical.

Meanwhile, the successful uptake of Ella's programme note idea elsewhere was bound up with a peculiarly British, nineteenth-century type of listener appreciation that was in existence well before programme notes, repertoire guides and so on spread to other countries around the *fin de siècle*. It was a striking phenomenon, owed a good deal to Ella, and arguably shaped a distinctive and uniquely British type of structure-oriented, narrative (almost 'academic') listening in which audiences attempted to follow the linear sequence of thematic and tonal events during performance. Why this genre of music writing should have evolved so strongly in Britain is a large topic that cannot be adequately treated here, but several factors were involved, including: a market-driven concert infrastructure that encouraged competition between organizers; the emerging sacralization of culture; the centrality of reading, self-education and religious devotion to the Victorian way of life; and a way of writing about music that resonated with identifiable national traits of empiricism, rationalism, science and process, industry and progress.

Taken together, the literature and practices of Ella's Musical Union provide a rich example of sacralization at work in nineteenth-century Britain, and reveal a concrete contribution over thirty-seven years to a new reverence for music, to emerging protocols in the concert hall, to the definition of an accepted canon of

composers, and to the developing concept of classical instrumental chamber repertoire as the apex of musical thought and expression. Here the Victorian readiness
to accept the judgements of cultural authorities played an important part, complementing Ella's visionary and educative zeal. Without taking this argument to
the extreme position whereby nobody in Ella's audience had the wit to think for
him- or herself, or to question Ella's understanding of pieces of music, it seems not
unreasonable to suppose that in general terms Ella's concert publics took on board
his critical assessments of the repertoire, its hierarchies and interpreters, as well as
his exhortations to serious, silent worship. Two pieces of evidence may speak for
many here: firstly, Eduard Hanslick's observation of 1862: '[t]he attention and quiet
of the listeners is exemplary. They are supported by the reading of little booklets
which the ladies and gentlemen eagerly read through'; secondly, a personal letter
to Ella from Thomas Hare, barrister, written in 1880 to 'the man who first taught
me what really good music was'.[67]

The question remains as to how typical the Musical Union's sacralization of
music was in the British context. Certainly, it fitted with a wave of London chamber concerts (1830s onwards) that espoused high musical values, and it was by no
means the sole institution to sacralize chamber music. Future research may tell
us more. With hindsight, too, we can discern the Musical Union as one origin
of many of the values and ideologies surrounding classical music that we inherit
(and challenge) today, especially in the concert hall: its formal rituals, the wealthy
social profile of its audience, its fixed repertoire of masterworks from the past, and
its celebration of the composer's intentions as embodied in the musical text. Set
against this, some of its sacralizing practices, such as seating in the round with
the platform – or 'altar' – physically a central point, were somewhat unusual for
the time; faithfulness to the musical text in performance was understood more
loosely then than it is now; while the blending of the sacral with the intellectual
and, particularly, the social is a phenomenon only rarely recovered in modern
chamber music performances. Moreover, there is a little evidence that, for all

[67] *HanslickA*, 513. Hanslick's observations are general, but made in the context of
a discussion of the Musical Union and Ella's notes. He goes on to suggest that
Englishmen and women feel a need to have their opinions specified in this way:
'Just as someone going to the Rhine would not be without his Murray [travel guide],
so he will not completely enjoy Beethoven without a synoptical analysis' (ibid.).
Hare's letter, dated ?1 March 1880, is in EllaC, MS 156.

On Ella's judgements of his performers, see Alice Diehl, who estimated that:
'[w]ith the exception of a few recusants in the back-seats, Ella's auditors accepted
Ella's artists at Ella's valuation' (*DiehlMM*, 117). Only someone like Harriet Grote
seems to have been prepared to express her own and changing views on the merits
of Hallé's playing to Ella (letter, dated 3 July 1850, in EllaC, MS 81, p. 73).

Ella's insistence on silence, some murmurings of approval were the accepted response to a particular nicety of execution during performance, not unlike connoisseurs at a modern jazz evening, though almost unimaginable in a recital hall today.[68]

Whether the sacralization of music in nineteenth-century Britain had more or less in common with what went on in Europe cannot be adequately answered by one case-study; yet the findings *vis-à-vis* the Musical Union may turn out to be both typical of the British situation and, in some respects, distinctive within Europe. After all, however much Ella played on a dichotomy between an artistically worthy, élitist high culture and the vulgar, market-led popularization of the arts (an opposition much promulgated in Europe at the time), the fact remains that commercial imperatives underpinned the Musical Union, and were symptomatic of the centrality of the market-place in Victorian musical life. More than once Ella compromised his artistic goals to ensure economic survival. But he was careful to conceal the evidence of commercially led decision-making, and play up his vision of art for art's sake. In times when the accumulation of wealth was becoming ever more widespread in society, with Ella a classic exemplar, this looks like a classic Victorian denial. (On the other hand, markets for music were growing in Europe too, and such contradictions may well be found elsewhere. Comparative studies are needed.)

Meanwhile, with Britain generally regarded as never more religious than in the Victorian age, the sacralization of music may well have acted as a supplement to revealed religion for many people, while for others it constituted a substitute.[69] In addition, while sacralization may well have been directly tied up with nation-building and expressions of national identity in mainland Europe, particularly Germany,[70] for mid-nineteenth-century Britain the picture was arguably more nuanced, even contradictory: particularly for music, where artistic cosmopolitanism reigned and state support was largely lacking. With the Musical Union, national agendas were evoked by Ella from time to time and appeals made to patriotic pride, for ultimately Ella wanted to improve patronage for 'good' music. However, cosmopolitanism was central to his vision, and he celebrated the united endeavour arising from joining European music and artists with British audiences (which reflected well on musical sensibilities in Britain), rather than venerating British creativity. A 'réunion aux artistes

---

[68] *ILN* (27 June 1846), 419.

[69] See T. C. W. Blanning, 'The Commercialization and Sacralization of European Culture in the Nineteenth Century', *The Oxford Illustrated History of Modern Europe*, ed. T. C. W. Blanning (Oxford: Oxford University Press, 1996), 128–33.

[70] Blanning, 'Commercialization', 139–43.

distingués de toutes les nations' in the name of high musical art was how Ella repeatedly described the Musical Union in its early years. Coming from a man for whom chamber music had already been, and would continue to be, the conduit to many eminent social and cultural spheres at home and abroad, that slogan seems well chosen.

APPENDIX I

Sample Programmes for the Musical Union and Musical Winter Evenings

Information derived from *RMU* and *RMWE*.

1. Musical Union concerts

The Musical Union Matinées. 10th Season.
1854. Willis's Rooms.
No. 1. Tuesday, April 25th.

PROGRAMME

Haydn	*String Quartet in D major, Op. 71, No. 2**
Mendelssohn	*Piano Trio in D minor, Op. 49*
Beethoven	*String Quartet in E minor, Op. 59, No. 2*
Mendelssohn	Pianoforte Solos – 'Lieder ohne Wörte'

* *RMU* gives this as Quartet in D, No. 70.

The Musical Union Matinées. 19th Season.
1863. St James's Hall.
No. 3. Tuesday, May 12th.

PROGRAMME

Beethoven	*String Trio in C minor, Op. 9, No. 3*
Schumann	*Piano Quintet in E flat major, Op. 44*
Mendelssohn	*String Quintet in B flat major, Op. 87*
Pianoforte Solos	
Jaëll	*Chant du Matin*
Chopin	*Waltzes. C sharp minor, Op.64*
	A flat major, Op. 42

The Musical Union Matinées. 33rd Season.
1877. St James's Hall.
No. 5. Tuesday, June 12th.

PROGRAMME

Mendelssohn	*String Quartet in E minor, Op. 44, No. 2**
Schumann	*Piano Quintet in E flat major, Op. 44*
Tchaikovsky	*String Quartet in D major, Op.11* (Second time in England)

Pianoforte Solos

Chopin	*Polonaise in C sharp minor*
Jaëll	*Romance in A flat major*

* RMU gives this as Quartet No. 4.

2. *Musical Union Director's Matinées*

The Musical Union Matinées. The Grand Matinée. 13th Season.
1857. Willis's Rooms.
No. 7. Tuesday, June 30th.

PROGRAMME

Haydn	*String Quartet in F major, Op. 77, No. 2**
Beethoven	*Sonata in A minor, Op. 47* for Piano and Violin
Beethoven	*Adelaide, Op. 46*
Hummel	*Septet in D minor, Op. 74*
Rubinstein	Persian Melodies
	Zwölf Lieder, Op. 34, No. 9
	Zwölf Lieder, Op. 34, No. 11

Pianoforte Solos

Chopin	*Nocturne in B major, Op. 62*
Handel	*Harmonious Blacksmith*, Air and Variations
Bottesini	*Duet Concertante* for Violin and Double Bass

* RMU gives this as Quartet in F, No. 82.

The Musical Union Matinées. The Grand Matinée. 22nd Season.
1866. St James's Hall.
No. 8. Tuesday, July 3rd.

PROGRAMME

Mendelssohn	*Piano Trio in C minor, Op. 66*
Beethoven	*Septet in E flat major, Op. 20*
Benedict	*Scene and Air*, 'Richard Cœur de Lion'
Violoncello Solo	
Schubert	*Litanie*
Pianoforte Solos	
Lübeck	*Toccata, Op. 15*
	Berceuse in A flat (repeated by request of Members)
Beethoven	Allegro Vivace, Scherzo from *Piano Sonata in E flat major, Op. 31, No. 3** (repeated by request of Members)
Gounod	*Barcarolle*, 'Où voulez-vous aller'
Hummel	*Septet in D minor, Op. 74*
Pianoforte Solos	
Jaëll	*Impromptu*

* *RMU* gives this as 'Scherzo from Finale E flat; Op. 31'.

The Musical Union Matinées. The Grand Matinée. 29th Season.
1873. St James's Hall.
No. 8. Tuesday, July 1st.

PROGRAMME

Beethoven	*Septet in E flat major, Op. 20*
Hummel	*Romanza*, 'Mathilde de Guise'
Pianoforte Solos	
Duvernoy	*Barcarolle in A minor*
Scarlatti	*Piece No. 123*
Weber	Scherzo in A flat major, from *Sonata No. 2*
Mozart	*Aria*, 'Non più de fiori' (*Clemenza di Tito*)
Violin Solos	
Spohr	Adagio, from *Concerto No. 9*
Brahms	*Danse Hongroise* (arranged by Joachim)
Hummel	*Septet in D minor, Op. 74*

3. Musical Winter Evenings

Musical Winter Evenings. 2nd Season.
1852. Willis's Rooms.
No. 4. Thursday, March 11th.

PROGRAMME

First Act

Mozart	*String Quintet in C major**
(Anonymous)	*Song*, 'Meeting and Parting'
Beethoven	*Piano Sonata in C major, Op. 53* ('Waldstein')

Second Act

Spohr	*Double Quartet in E minor, Op. 87*
Loder	*Song*, 'I heard a brooklet gushing'
Mendelssohn	*Piano Trio in C minor, Op. 66*

Pianoforte Solos

Chopin	*Le Nocturne*
Heller	*La Chasse*

* K515.

Musical Winter Evenings. 3rd Season.
1854. Willis's Rooms.
No. 3. Thursday, March 23rd.

PROGRAMME

Haydn	*String Quartet in G major, Op. 76, No. 1**
Molique	*Piano Trio in B flat major, Op. 27*

An Interval of Ten Minutes

Mozart	*String Quintet No. 4 in D major*†
Mendelssohn	*Variations Concertantes, Op. 17* for Piano and Violoncello
	Tema Andante con moto

* *RMU* gives this as 'No. 76 (Pleyel ed.)'.
† K593.

Analysis of Repertoire at the Musical Union and Musical Winter Evenings

Musical Union, 1845–81:
Number of performances of ensemble repertoire (with piano sonatas)

	1845–9	1850–4	1855–9	1860–4	1865–9	1870–4	1875–9	1880	1881
Total concerts	42	49	42	44	40	40	39	7	7
Beethoven	48 (1)	56 (9)	45 (5)	47 (6)	40 (6)	35 (2)	31 (2)	9	5
Brahms					2	1	3	1	
Haydn	20	16	19	18	13	14	11	2	2
Hummel	4	3	6	7	6	5	5	1	1
Mendelssohn	13	33	25	23	24	14	23	3	2
Mozart	18	21	17	16	13	14	10	2	1
Onslow	11	6	1						
Rubinstein			3		3	5	9	1	3
Schubert		2		2	7	8	2	1	2
Schumann	1		2	8	11 (1)	11	14 (2)	2	2
Spohr	8	8	9	10	7	2			
Weber	2 (1)	1 (1)	1 (1)	4 (4)		5 (5)			
Others*	7	12	4	2	3	5	17	1	3

Note: Figures in parentheses indicate the number of piano sonatas included in the total. Analysis excludes all other solo piano repertoire; includes piano duets. Extra matinées are included in the analysis. Repertoire is as programmed.   *Sources: RMU* and EllaC.

* *'Other' composers:*
Figures in brackets indicate number of works by composer, if more than one.

1845–9	Sterndale Bennett; G. Hellmesberger; Maurer; Mayseder [3]; Osborne
1850–4	Alard; Bach; Bottesini; Eckert; Hiller; Maurer; Mayseder [2]; Mollenhauer; Tartini [3]; Verhulst
1855–9	Boccherini; Bottesini; Chopin; Molique
1860–4	Boccherini; Lalo
1865–9	Chopin; Raff; Thern
1870–4	Reinecke [3]; Rheinberger; Rust
1875–9	C.-W. De Bériot; Chopin [2]; Fauré; Raff [2]; Rheinberger; Saint-Saëns [5]; Tchaikovsky [5]
1880	Scharwenka
1881	Chopin; Parry; Saint-Saëns

Musical Winter Evenings and Musical Union Soirées, 1852–5, 1857–8:
Number of performances of ensemble repertoire (with piano sonatas)

	1852–5	1857–8
Beethoven	17 (5)	3
Haydn	6	2
Hummel	2	
Mendelssohn	11	3
Molique	5	1
Mozart	11	4
Onslow		1
Schubert	2	1
Schumann	1	1
Spohr	9	4
Others*	4	3

Note: See note to preceding table.   *Sources: RMWE* and *RMU.*

* 'Other' composers:

| 1852–5 | Kalliwoda; Moscheles; Pauer; Silas |
| 1857–8 | Mayseder; Silas; Weber |

Musical Union, 1845–81: Most frequently performed works
(excluding Director's Matinées)

Rank	Composer	Work	No. of performances
1	Mendelssohn	Quintet op. 87	23
2	Beethoven	Quintet op. 29	21
3	Schumann	Piano quintet op. 44	19
4	Mendelssohn	Piano trio op. 66	18
5	Beethoven	Piano trio op. 70/1	16
	Beethoven	Piano trio op. 97 'Archduke'	16
7	Mozart	Quintet in G minor [K516]	15
8	Beethoven	Quartet op. 59/3	14
	Beethoven	Quartet op. 74	14
	Mendelssohn	Quartet op. 12	14
	Mendelssohn	Quartet op. 44/2	14
	Schumann	Piano quartet op. 47	14
13	Beethoven	Piano trio op. 70/2	13
	Beethoven	Quartet op. 18/2	13
	Beethoven	Quartet op. 18/6	13
16	Haydn	Quartet op. 77/2	12
	Mendelssohn	Quartet op. 81 [fragments]	12
	Mendelssohn	Cello sonata op. 58	12
	Mozart	Quartet in C [K465]	12
	Mozart	Quartet in D [K575]	12

Note: Analysis includes extra matinées, and includes works performed in part as well as complete.

Musical Union, 1845–81: Most frequently performed works (including Director's Matinées)

Rank	Composer	Work	No. of performances
1	Beethoven	Septet op. 20	31
2	Hummel	Septet op. 74	25
3	Mendelssohn	Quintet op. 87	24
4	Beethoven	Quintet op. 29	22
5	Mendelssohn	Piano trio op. 66	21
6	Schumann	Piano quintet op. 44	19
7	Beethoven	Piano trio op. 97 'Archduke'	17
	Beethoven	Violin sonata op. 47 'Kreutzer'	17
9	Beethoven	Piano trio op. 70/1	16
	Mendelssohn	Quartet op. 12	16
11	Beethoven	Quartet op. 59/3	15
	Mozart	Quintet in G minor [K516]	15
13	Beethoven	Piano trio op. 70/2	14
	Beethoven	Quartet op. 18/6	14
	Beethoven	Quartet op. 74	14
	Mendelssohn	Quartet op. 44/2	14
	Mendelssohn	Cello sonata op. 58	14
	Schumann	Piano quartet op. 47	14
19	Beethoven	Quartet op. 18/2	13
	Haydn	Quartet op. 77/2	13
	Mendelssohn	Quartet op. 81 [fragments]	13
	Mozart	Quartet in D [K575]	13

Note: Analysis includes extra matinées, and includes works performed in part as well as complete.

Performers at the Musical Union and Musical Winter Evenings

Performers announced for concerts; information mainly from *RMU* and *RMWE*.

1. *Primary Performers at the Musical Union*

Primary performers are defined as: leaders of ensembles (vn I), the core players of a string quartet configuration (vn II, va, vc) and pianists. Secondary string players (e.g. 2nd viola players in string quintets) and occasional collaborating artists (wind players, singers, etc.) are not included in this list. Calculations exclude the Director's Matinées, thus normally a total of seven concerts. Numbers in parentheses indicate the number of performances given by that performer/group of performers in a season. Extra *matinées* are listed separately.

> Abbreviations: vn = violin; va = viola; vc = violoncello; pf = pianoforte; * = 1 shared performance as primary performers

Season	Leaders (vn I)	Other Strings (vn II, va, vc)	Pianists (pf)
1845	Sainton* (5); Deloffre* (2); H. Blagrove* (1); Sivori (1); Vieuxtemps (1)	Goffrie, Hill, Rousselot (3); Deloffre, Hill, Hausmann (1); Deloffre, Tolbecque, Rousselot (1); Nadaud, Hill, Rousselot (1)[†]; Sainton, Hill, Rousselot (1); Thirlwell, Hill, Hausmann*, Pilet* (vcs) – (1)	Mrs Anderson (1); Benedict (1); Kuhe (1); De Meyer (1); Osborne (1); Roeckel (1); Sterndale Bennett (1)
1846	Vieuxtemps (3); Sainton (2); Sivori (2); Deloffre (1)	Deloffre, Hill, Piatti (3); Deloffre, Hill, Hausmann (1); Deloffre, Hill, Kellerman (1); Deloffre, Hill, Lucas (1); Deloffre, Hill, Rousselot (1); Goffrie, Hill, Pilet (1)	Mme Belleville-Oury (1); Benedict (1); Osborne (1); Mme Pleyel (1); Sloper (1); Sterndale Bennett (1)
1847	Vieuxtemps (2); J. Hellmesberger* (2); Joachim* (2); Deloffre (1); Goffrie* (1); G. Hellmesberger* (1); Sainton* (1)	Deloffre, Hill, Piatti[‡] (3); Deloffre, Hill, Hausmann (1); Deloffre, Hill, Rousselot (1); Deloffre, (J. and G.) Hellmesberger, Piatti (1); Goffrie, Hill, Pilet (1)	Sloper (2); Benedict (1); Mme Dulcken (1); Schulhoff (1)

† Goffrie, Ella and Goodban also for Spohr double quartet.

‡ Thirlwell, R. Blagrove and Howell also for Spohr double quartet.

Season	Leaders (vn I)	Other Strings (vn II, va, vc)	Pianists (pf)
1848	Sainton (4); Deloffre (1); Hermann (1); Molique (1)	Deloffre, Hill, Piatti* (6), Pilet* (vcs) – (1); Goffrie, Hill, Piatti (1)	Hallé (3); Billet (1); Osborne (1); Roeckel (1); Sterndale Bennett (1)
1849	Ernst (3); Sainton (3); Alard (1)	Deloffre, Hill, Piatti (4); Deloffre, Tolbecque, Piatti (2); Deloffre, Hill, Cossmann (1)	Hallé (5); Goldschmidt (1); Sterndale Bennett (1)
1850	Ernst (3); Sainton (3); Alard (1)	Deloffre, Hill, Piatti (7)	Hallé (3); Heller (1); Miss Loder (1); Silas (1); Sterndale Bennett (1)
	Performers for 1 extra matinée: Sainton (1)	Deloffre, Hill, Piatti (1)	Hallé (1)
1851	Ernst (2); Sainton* (2); Laub (1); Sivori (1); Vieuxtemps (1); Deloffre* (1)	Deloffre, Hill, Piatti (4); Deloffre, Hill, Menter (1); Deloffre, Hill, Seligmann (1); Witt, Hill, Piatti† (1)	Hallé (5); Pauer (1); Sterndale Bennett (1)
	Performers for 4 extra matinées: Ernst (1); Laub (1); Sainton (1); Sivori (1)	Deloffre, Hill, Menter (1) Deloffre, Hill, Piatti (3)	Golinelli (1); Hallé (1); Pauer (1)
1852	Sivori* (3); Vieuxtemps* (3); Joachim (1); Laub (1)	Pollitzer, Oury, Piatti (3); Moralt, Oury, Piatti (3); Mellon, Oury, Piatti (1)	Hallé (3); Mlle Clauss (2); Pauer (1); Mme Pleyel (1)
	Performers for 2 extra matinées: Vieuxtemps (2)	Mellon, Oury, Piatti (1)	Mlle Clauss (1); Mme Pleyel (1)
1853	Vieuxtemps (6); Bazzini (1)	Goffrie, Hill, Piatti (4); Goffrie, H. Blagrove, Piatti (3)	Hallé (3); Mlle Clauss (2); Haberbier (1); Hiller (1)
	Performers for 2 extra matinées: Vieuxtemps (2)	Graf, Ries, Jacquard (1); Graf, Ries, Drechsler (1)	Napoleon (1); Mlle Graever (1); Mlle Staudach (1); Hiller (1)
1854	Ernst (5); Molique (1); Vieuxtemps (1)	Goffrie, Hill, Piatti (5); Ernst, Hill, Van Gelder (1); Goffrie, Hill, Van Gelder (1)	Mlle Clauss (3); Hallé (2); Napoleon (1); Sterndale Bennett (1)
	Performers for 2 extra matinées: Pollitzer (1); Bazzini (1)	De Smits, Ries, Paque (1); Deichmann, Ries, Van Gelder (1)	Silas (1); Mlle Moullin (1); Napoleon (1)

† Watson, Mellon and Pilet also for Spohr double quartet.

Season	Leaders (vn I)	Other Strings (vn II, va, vc)	Pianists (pf)
1855	Ernst (3); Sainton* (2); Cooper (1); Molique (1); Goffrie* (1)	Cooper, Hill, Piatti† (6); Carrodus, Hill, Piatti (1)	Hallé (5); Pauer (1); Mrs Robinson (1)
1856	Ernst (3); Sainton (2); Cooper (1); Sivori (1)	Cooper, Hill, Piatti (2); Cooper, Goffrie, Piatti (2); Carrodus, Hill, Franchomme (1); Carrodus, Hill, Paque (1); Cooper, Hill, Franchomme (1)	Hallé (4); Mme Schumann (3)
1857	Ernst (4); Sainton (2); H. Blagrove* (1); Molique* (1)	Goffrie, H. Blagrove, Piatti (5); Goffrie, H. Blagrove, Paque (1); Ries, Goffrie, Piatti‡ (1)	Hallé (3); Mme Schumann (2); Mlle Molique (1); A. Rubinstein (1)
	Performers for 1 extra matinée: Sivori (1)	Goffrie, H. Blagrove, Piatti (1)	A. Rubinstein (1)
1858	Joachim (4); Sainton* (2); Molique (1); H. Blagrove* (1)	Goffrie, H. Blagrove, Piatti (5); [H.] Blagrove, Piatti (1); Goffrie, R. Blagrove, Piatti§ (1)	A. Rubinstein* (4); Andreoli (1); De Cinna (1); Mme Szarvady (1); Pauer* (1)
	Performers for 1 extra matinée: Bott (1)	Goffrie, Ries, Di Dio (1)	Lemmens (1)
1859	Joachim (3); Sainton (2); Wieniawski (2)	Goffrie, H. Blagrove, Piatti (7)	A. Rubinstein (4); Mme Schumann (2); Mlle Suppus* (1); De Meyer* (1)
1860	Sainton* (3); Straus (2); Becker* (2); Carrodus* (1); Hill* (1)	Goffrie, R. Blagrove, Piatti⁵ (7);	Lübeck (3); Hallé (3); Ritter (1)
	Performers for 1 extra matinée: Straus (1)	Carrodus, R. Blagrove, Piatti (1)	Lübeck (1)
1861	Vieuxtemps (4); Wieniawski (2); Sainton (1)	Ries, R. Blagrove, Piatti (6); Ries, Webb, Piatti (1)	Hallé (2); N. Rubinstein (2); Boscovitch (1); Pauer (1); Ritter (1)
	Performers for 1 extra matinée: Straus (1)	Carrodus, R. Blagrove, Piatti (1)	Hallé (1)

† Carrodus, Webb and Paque also for Spohr double quartet.

‡ Pollitzer, R. Blagrove and Paque also for Spohr double quartet.

§ Ries, Webb and Paque also for Spohr double quartet.

⁵ Carrodus, Webb and Paque also for Spohr double quartet. Schreurs, Webb and Paque for a second performance of a double quartet this season.

Season	Leaders (vn I)	Other Strings (vn II, va, vc)	Pianists (pf)
1862	Joachim (5); Becker (1); Laub (1)	Ries, R. Blagrove, Piatti (7)	Hallé* (4); Jaëll (2); Heller* (1); N. Rubinstein (1)
	Performers for 1 extra matinée: Laub (1)	Ries, Webb, Davidoff (1)	Mlle Caussemille* (1); N. Rubinstein* (1)
1863	Auer (3); Vieuxtemps (2); Japha (1); Pollitzer* (1); Sainton* (1)	Ries, Webb, Piatti† (7)	Hallé (2); Jaëll (2); Lübeck (2); Dannreuther (1)
	Performers for 1 extra matinée: Carrodus (1)	Ries, Webb, Piatti (1)	Miss Schiller (1)
1864	Joachim (2); Wieniawski (2); Sivori (2); Sainton (1)	Ries, Webb, Davidoff (3); Ries, Webb, Jacquard (2); Ries, Webb, Paque (2)	Jaëll (3); Hallé (2); Leschetizky (1); Pauer* (1); Mlle Zimmermann* (1)
1865	Joachim (6); Lauterbach (1)	Ries, Webb, Piatti (7)	Mme Schumann (3); Hallé (2); Jaëll (2)
1866	Auer* (5); Wieniawski* (3)	Ries, Goffrie, Piatti‡ (7)	Jaëll* (3); Diémer (1); Hartvigson (1); Lübeck (1); Mlle Pacini (1); Mlle Trautmann* (1)
1867	Auer (4); Vieuxtemps (2); Wieniawski (1)	Ries, Goffrie, Grützmacher (3); Ries, Goffrie, Jacquard (3); Ries, Goffrie, Daubert (1)	Jaëll* (3); A. Rubinstein (2); Mme Jaëll* (1); Lübeck (1); Mlle Mehlig (1)
1868	Auer (7)	Ries, Goffrie, Jacquard (5); Ries, Goffrie, Grützmacher (2)	Lübeck (4); Jaëll* (2); Mme Jaëll* (1); A. Rubinstein (1)
1869	Vieuxtemps (4); Auer (3)	Ries, Bernhardt, Demunck (5); Ries, Bernhardt, Albert (1); Wiener, Bernhardt, Albert§ (1)	Mme Auspitz-Kolar (2); A. Rubinstein (2); Jaëll* (2); Mme Jaëll-Trautmann* (1); Reinecke (1)
1870	De Graan (4); Auer (3)	Ries, Bernhardt, L. Lübeck (7)	Mme Auspitz-Kolar (2); Delaborde (1); Jaëll (1); Leschetizky (1); Reinecke (1); Miss Zimmermann (1)

† Watson, Hann and Paque also for Spohr double quartet.

‡ Watson, Hann and Paque also for Spohr double quartet.

§ Zerbini, Hann and E. Vieuxtemps also for Spohr double quartet.

Season	Leaders (vn I)	Other Strings (vn II, va, vc)	Pianists (pf)
1871	Auer (3); Sivori (3); Heermann (1)	Bernhardt, Van Waefelghem, Lasserre (7)	Jaëll (2); Leschetizky (2); Baur (1); Reinecke (1); Saint-Saëns (1)
1872	Maurin (4); Auer (2); Heermann (1)	Wiener, Van Waefelghem, Lasserre (6); Wiener, Van Waefelghem, Daubert (1)	Jaëll (2); Rendano (2); Duvernoy (1); Logé (1); Reinecke (1)
1873	Vieuxtemps (4); Auer (3)	Wiener, Van Waefelghem, Lasserre (7)	Duvernoy (3); Jaëll (3); Von Bülow (1)
1874	Papini (4); Sarasate (3)	Wiener, Van Waefelghem, Lasserre (7)	Jaëll (3); Beringer (1); Duvernoy (1); Mme Essipoff (1); Mlle Krebs (1)
1875	Papini (7)	Wiener, Van Waefelghem, Lasserre (4); Wiener, Bernhardt, Lasserre (3)	Duvernoy (2); Jaëll (2); Mme Montigny-Rémaury (2); Stoeger (1)
1876	Papini (4); Auer (3)	Wiener, Holländer, Lasserre (5); Bernhardt, Holländer, Lasserre (2)	Jaëll* (2); Breitner (1); Duvernoy (1); Mlle Mehlig (1); A. Rubinstein (1); Saint-Saëns* (1); Stoeger (1)
1877	Papini (4); Auer (3)	Holländer, Van Waefelghem, Lasserre (7)	Jaëll (3); Breitner (2); Duvernoy (1); Saint-Saëns (1)
1878	Marsick (4); Papini (3)	Wiener, Holländer, Lasserre (6); Heimendahl, Holländer, Lasserre (1)	De Bériot (2); Jaëll (2); Mme Montigny-Rémaury (2); Von Bülow (1)
1879	Papini (3); Marsick (3)	Wiener, Holländer, Lasserre (6)	Mme Essipoff (2); Jaëll (2); Mme Montigny-Rémaury (1); Scharwenka (1)
1880	Papini (4); Auer (2)	Wiener, Holländer, Lasserre (6)	Mme Montigny-Rémaury* (2); Von Bülow (2); Beringer (1); Scharwenka* (1); J. Wieniawski (1)
1881	Viardot (4); Auer (2)	Wiener, Van Waefelghem, Lasserre (5); Van Waefelghem, Lasserre (1)	Heymann (2); Ritter (2); Dannreuther (1); Reisenauer (1)

2. Performers in the Musical Union's Annual Director's Matinées

Abbreviations: vn(s) = violin(s); va(s) = viola(s); vc(s) = violoncellos;
pf = pianoforte; db = double bass; fl = flute; ob = oboe; cl = clarinet;
bn = bassoon; hn = horn; acc = accompanist; harm = harmonium

1845
Sainton, Goffrie, Deloffre, Nadaud (vns);
Hill, Guynemer (vas);
Rousselot, Casolini (vcs);
De Meyer (pf);
Howell (db);
Lazarus (cl);
Baumann (bn);
Puzzi (hn);
Pišek (voice);
Benedict (acc)

1846
Sainton, Sivori, Vieuxtemps, Deloffre (vns);
Hill (va);
Piatti (vc);
Mme Pleyel (pf);
Pišek, Mlle di Mendi (voice);
Benedict (acc)

1847
Sainton, J. Hellmesberger, Joachim, Deloffre, G. Hellmesberger, Thirlwell (vns);
G. Hellmesberger, Hill (vas);
Piatti, Rousselot (vcs);
Mme Dulcken (pf);
Howell (db);
Ribas (fl);
Barret (ob);
Jarret (hn);
Pišek, Mlle di Mendi (voice)

1848
Hermann, Molique, Sainton, Deloffre (vns);
Hill, Mellon (vas);
Piatti (vc);
Hallé (pf);
Mlle di Mendi, Garcia (voice)
Benedict (acc)

1849
Sainton, Ernst, Joachim, Deloffre (vns);
Hill (va);
Piatti (vc);
De Fontaine (pf);
Bottesini (db);
Mlle Graumann (voice);
Hungarian Vocalists;
Wallace (acc)

1850
Sainton, Ernst, Deloffre, Goffrie, Watson (vns);
Hill, Mellon (vas);
Piatti, Pilet (vcs);
Hallé, Heller (pf);
Mlle Graumann, Stockhausen (voice);
Hungarian Vocalists (with small orchestra)
Eckert (acc)

1851
Sivori, Sainton, Ernst, Laub, Deloffre (vns);
Hill (va);
Piatti (vc);
Hallé, Pauer (pf);
Bottesini (db);
Reichart (voice);
Eckert (acc)

1852
Vieuxtemps, Pollitzer (vns);
Oury, Webb (vas);
Piatti (vc);
Mlle Clauss, Hallé (pf);
Bottesini (db);
Gardoni (voice)
Pilotti (acc)

1853
Vieuxtemps, Goffrie (vns);
H. Blagrove (va);
Piatti (vc);
Mlle Staudach, Blumenthal, Napoleon (pf);
Bottesini (db);
Wuille (cl);
Baumann (bn);
Harper (hn);
Lefort (voice);
Frelon (acc)

1854
Vieuxtemps, Goffrie (vns);
Hill (va);
Van Gelder (vc);
Hallé, Napoleon (pf);
Howell (db);
Remusat (fl);
Barret (ob);
Lazarus (cl);
Baumann (bn);
Harper (hn);
Lefort (voice);
Li Calsi (acc)

1855
Ernst, Cooper (vns);
Hill (va);
Piatti (vc);
Hallé (pf);
Bottesini (db);
Reichart (voice);
Fiori (acc)

1856
Sivori, Cooper (vns);
Goffrie (va);
Piatti (vc);
Mme Schumann,
Andreoli (pf);
Howell (db);
Lazarus (cl);
Baumann (bn);
Harper (hn);
Mme Viardot (voice)

1857
Sivori, Goffrie (vns);
H. Blagrove (va);
Piatti (vc);
Mme Schumann, Mlle
  Staudach (pf);
Bottesini (db);
R. S. Pratten (fl);
Barret (ob);
Harper (hn);
Von der Osten (voice)

1858
Joachim, Goffrie (vns);
H. and R. Blagrove (vas);
Piatti (vc);
A. Rubinstein (pf);
Mme Lemmens Sherrington,
  Santley (voice);
Ganz (acc)

1859
Wieniawski, Goffrie (vns);
H. and R. Blagrove (vas);
Piatti (vc);
A. Rubinstein (pf);
Mlle Artôt, Mlle Meyer
  (voice);
Silas (acc)

1860
Sainton, Goffrie (vns);
R. Blagrove (va);
Piatti (vc);
Hallé, Lübeck (pf);
Howell (db);
R. S. Pratten (fl);
Barret (ob);
Lazarus (cl);
Hausser (bn);
Harper (hn);
Mlle Artôt (voice);
Engel (harm);
Li Calsi (acc)

1861
Wieniawski (vn);
R. Blagrove (va);
Piatti (vc);
Hallé, Lübeck (pf);
Howell (db);
R. S. Pratten (fl);
Barret (ob);
Lazarus (cl);
Hausser (bn);
Harper (hn);
Sedie (voice);
Ganz (acc)

1862
Joachim, Ries (vns);
R. Blagrove (va);
Davidoff (vc);
N. Rubinstein, Jaëll (pf);
Gilardoni (db);
Svendsen (fl);
Lavigne (ob);
Pollard (cl);
Raspi (bn);
Paquis (hn);
Orpheus Glee Union

1863
Auer (vn);
Webb (va);
Piatti (vc);
Hallé, Lübeck (pf);
F. Pratten (db);
R.S. Pratten (fl);
Barret (ob);
Lazarus (cl);
Hausser (bn);
Harper (hn);
Mlle Artôt (voice);
Ganz (acc)

1864
Joachim, Ries (vns);
Webb (va);
Davidoff (vc);
Hallé (pf);
F. Pratten (db);
R.S. Pratten (fl);
Barret (ob);
Lazarus (cl);
Hutchins (bn);
Harper (hn);
Gardoni (voice)

1865
Straus, Ries (vns);
Webb, Hann (vas);
Piatti (vc);
Lübeck (pf);
Howell (db);
R.S. Pratten (fl);
Barret (ob);
Lazarus (cl);
Hutchins (bn);
Harper (hn);
Engel (harm);
Mlle Enequist, Hauser
  (voice);
Ganz (acc)

1866
Auer, Ries (vns);
Goffrie (va);
Piatti (vc);
Lübeck, Jaëll (pf);
Howell (db);
R.S. Pratten (fl);
Barret (ob);
Lazarus (cl);
Hutchins (bn);
Harper (hn);
Mme Parepa (voice);
Ganz (acc)

1867
Vieuxtemps, Ries (vns);
Goffrie (va);
Jacquard (vc);
A. Rubinstein (pf);
Howell (db);
R.S. Pratten (fl);
Barret (ob);
Lazarus (cl);
Hutchins (bn);
Harper (hn);
Lefort (voice);
Ganz (acc)

1868
Auer, Ries (vns);
Goffrie (va);
Jacquard (vc);
A. Rubinstein (pf);
Howell (db);
Lazarus (cl);
Hutchins (bn);
Paquis (hn);
Wallenreiter, Lefort (voice);
Ganz (acc)

1869
Auer, Ries (vns);
Bernhardt (va);
Demunck (vc);
Mme Auspitz-Kolar,
  Lübeck (pf);
Jakeway (db);
Svendsen (fl);
Lavigne (ob);
Tyler (cl);
Raspi (bn);
Paquis (hn);
Mlle Regan (voice);
Ganz (acc)

1870
Auer (vn);
Bernhardt (va);
L. Lübeck (vc);
Leschetizky (pf);
Jakeway (db);
Barret (ob);
Lazarus (cl);
Hutchins (bn);
Paquis (hn);
Lefort (voice);
Ganz (acc)

1871
Auer (vn);
Van Waefelghem (va);
Lasserre (vc);
Leschetizky (pf);
Jakeway (db);
Radcliffe (fl);
Barret (ob);
Lazarus (cl);
Hutchins (bn);
Paquis (hn);
Gardoni (voice);
Ganz (acc)

1872
Auer (vn);
Van Waefelghem (va);
Lasserre (vc);
Rendano, Duvernoy (pf);
Jakeway (db);
Radcliffe (fl);
Barret (ob);
Lazarus (cl);
Hutchins (bn);
Paquis (hn);
Lefort (voice);
Ganz (acc)

1873
Auer (vn);
Van Waefelghem (va);
Lasserre (vc);
Duvernoy (pf);
Jakeway (db);
Radcliffe (fl);
Barret (ob);
Lazarus (cl);
Hutchins (bn);
Paquis (hn);
Mrs Bradshawe-Mackay
  (voice);
Ganz (acc)

1874
Sarasate (vn);
Van Waefelghem (va);
Lasserre (vc);
Mme Essipoff (pf);
Jakeway (db);
Radcliffe (fl);
Barret (ob);
Lazarus (cl);
Hutchins (bn);
Paquis (hn);
Ganz (acc)

1875
Papini, Wiener (vns);
Bernhardt (va);
Lasserre (vc);
Mme Montigny-Rémaury,
  Duvernoy (pf);
Delamour (db);
Radcliffe (fl);
Du Brucq (ob);
Lazarus (cl);
Hutchins (bn);
Van Haute (hn)

1876
Auer (vn);
Holländer (va);
Lasserre (vc);
Jaëll (pf);
Jakeway (db);
Radcliffe (fl);
Du Brucq (ob);
Lazarus (cl);
Hutchins (bn);
Van Haute (hn);
Mlle Redeker (voice)

1877
Auer, Holländer (vns);
Van Waefelghem (va);
Lasserre (vc);
J. Wieniawski (pf);
Jakeway (db);
Radcliffe (fl);
Du Brucq (ob);
Lazarus (cl);
Hutchins (bn);
Van Haute (hn)

1878
Papini, Wiener (vns);
Holländer (va);
Lasserre (vc);
Mme Montigny-Rémaury
  (pf);
Jakeway (db);
Radcliffe (fl);
Du Brucq (ob);
Lazarus (cl);
Hutchins (bn);
Stennebruggen (hn)

1879
Papini, Wiener (vns);
Holländer (va);
Lasserre (vc);
Von Bülow (pf);
Jakeway (db);
Radcliffe (fl);
Du Brucq (ob);
Lazarus (cl);
Hutchins (bn);
Stennebruggen (hn)

1880
Auer, Wiener (vns);
Holländer (va);
Lasserre (vc);
Duvernoy (pf);
Jakeway (db);
Radcliffe (fl);
Du Brucq (ob);
Lazarus (cl);
Hutchins (bn);
Stennebruggen (hn)

1881
Auer, Wiener (vns);
Van Waefelghem (va);
Lasserre (vc);
A. Rubinstein (pf)

3. Performers at the Musical Winter Evenings/Musical Union Soirées

Arabic numbers in parentheses indicate the number of performances given by that performer/group of performers in a particular season.

Abbreviations: vn = violin; va = viola; vc = violoncello; pf = pianoforte;
db = double bass; fl = flute; ob = oboe; cl = clarinet; bn = bassoon;
hn = horn; acc = accompanist; * = 1 shared performance

Season	Leaders (vn I)	Other Strings (vn II, va, vc)	Pianists (pf)	Other Performers
1852 6 concerts	Leonard (2); Sainton (2); Molique* (2); Oury* (1)	Mellon, Hill, Piatti† (3); Mellon, Oury, Piatti (1); Schmidt, Hill, Piatti (1); Pollitzer, Oury, Demunck (1)	Pauer (3); Aguilar (1); Hallé (1); Silas (1)	Le Jeune (va II; 2); Webb (va II; 1); Bottesini (db; 1); E. Pratten (db; 1); Briccialdi (fl;1); Nicholson (ob; 1); Lazarus (cl; 2); Baumann (bn; 1); Harper (hn; 1); Mme Leonard di Mendi (voice; 2); Swift (voice; 2); Benson (voice; 1); Marras (voice; 1); Reichart (voice; 1); Mori (acc; 1); Vera (acc; 1)
1853 4 concerts	Molique (4)	Mellon, Goffrie, Piatti (4)	Hallé (2); Mlle Clauss (1); Pauer (1)	Webb (va II; 3); Mme Doria (voice; 2); Miss Dolby (voice; 1); Goldberg (acc; 1)
1854 5 concerts	Molique (3); Ernst (2)	Goffrie, Hill, Piatti (4); Pollitzer, Ries, Piatti (1)	Hallé (3); Mlle Graever (1); Klindworth (1)	The Brothers Holmes (vns; 1); Ries (va II; 1); Lazarus (cl; 1); Mme Amadel (voice; 1); Rummel (acc; 1)
1855 4 concerts	Ernst* (3); Molique* (2)	Goffrie, Hill, Piatti (4)	Pauer* (3); Sloper* (2)	Webb (va II; 1); Barret (ob; 1); Lazarus (cl; 1); Snelling (bn; 1); Harper (hn; 1)
1856	No evening concerts held.			
1857 3 concerts	Ernst (1); Molique (1); Sainton (1)	Goffrie, H. Blagrove, Piatti (3)	Derffel (1); Hallé (1); Pauer (1)	R. Blagrove (va II; 1); Paque (vc; 1); Chamber Choir, conducted by Land (1); Vocal Union (1)
1858 4 concerts	Sainton (3); Molique (1)	Goffrie, H. Blagrove, Paque (1); Goffrie, Schreurs, Paque (1); Goffrie, H. Blagrove, Piatti (1); Goffrie, Schreurs, Piatti (1)	Pauer* (3); Mlle Molique (1); Sloper* (1)	R. Blagrove (va II; 2); Paque (vc; 1); Papé (cl); Orpheus Glee Union (1); Quartet Glee Union (1); Vocal Union (1)

† Watson, Webb and H. Piatti also for Spohr double quartet.

Musical Union Audience Statistics

Year	Published audience lists*	Paying subscribers†	Year	Published audience lists*	Paying subscribers†
1845	195	146	1863	630	510
1846	331	275	1864	682	550
1847	350	257	1865	685	565
1848	310	200	1866	669	–
1849	306	200	1867	617	–
1850	347	274	1868	577	–
1851	365	300	1869	581	–
1852	413	342	1870	576	–
1853	493	385	1871	567	–
1854	476	386	1872	430	–
1855	523	369	1873	456	–
1856	507	423	1874	416	–
1857	525	430	1875	437	–
1858	551	480	1876	465	–
1859	590	510	1877	441	–
1860	640	555	1878	419	–
1861	649	550	1879	397	–
1862	646	530	1880	380	–

* Taken from the annual *RMU*; figures from 1847 include visitors as well as members.

† Taken from Ella's account book (EllaC, MS 6), p.47. No figures given after 1865.

Supplementary Notes on John Ella's Family

🎵 John Ella senior – *John Ella's paternal grandfather*

Baptized 1741 at Kir[k]by Knowle; died 1799, buried at All Saints' Church, Loughborough.

A farmer in Yorkshire, he took other work when he settled in Loughborough (1774). He is described by William Grainge (*The Vale of Mowbray: a Historical and Topographical Account of Thirsk and its Neighbourhood*; London: Simpkin, Marshall, 1859, p. 232) as a 'civil engineer'; this follows John Ella's description of him in EllaC, MS 88/vi, and concurs with evidence in records of canal surveying on the River Trent in the late eighteenth century (West Yorkshire Archive Service, Wakefield, C229/35/6/2). He also worked as a distributor for the *Leicester Journal* (see death notice, 23 Aug 1799).

Letters of administration, granted thirty years after his death to his daughter (he left no will), describe him as a 'Gentleman' and 'late of Loughborough' (LRO, PR/T/1829/51).

🎵 Richard Ella - *John Ella's father*

Born in 1769, probably in the Kir[k]by Knowle area of the North Riding. According to notes made by John Ella (EllaC, MS 88/vi), Richard's birthplace was Thirsk. Died 1822, buried at St Martin's Church, Leicester.

Moved to Loughborough while a child. Apprenticed to the baker William Woodcock in 1784, then to Henry King (1787) and later to John Young of Loughborough (*Register of the Freemen of Leicester*: ii: *1770–1930*, ed. Henry Hartopp; Leicester: Corporation of the City of Leicester, 1933, p. 466).

Married Kitty Goddard (born 1778; died 1838) on 16 Feb 1801 at St Margaret's Church, Leicester. Her parents, Joseph Goddard (see below) and Ann Bown [*sic*], had been married in the same church in 1774.

🎵 Joseph Goddard – *John Ella's maternal grandfather*

Baptized Kirby-Muxloe, Leicestershire, in 1751; died 1839.

Probably the Joseph Goddard with a carpentry business in Belgrave Gate, Leicester, who is listed in the extant rate book for St Margaret's parish (1801) and in trade directories from 1805. Also probably the same Joseph Goddard noted by Hartopp (*1770–1930*) as the master of a carpentry apprentice who completed his training in 1796. (This source also notes a Joseph Goddard, a woolcomber made free in 1768; presumably the same person listed in a 1784 Leicester Directory as a hosier in Belgrave Street, and in *A Copy of the Poll* [...] *Taken in the Borough of Leicester* [...] *1800* (Leicester: Ireland and Son, 1801) as a woolcomber in Belgrave Gate.)

❧ Michael Ella – *John Ella's great-uncle*
Brother of John Ella senior. Baptized 1732 at Kir[k]by Knowle; died 1799.

Moved to Leicestershire, *c*.1761. Title deeds for the purchase of land in Loughborough document Michael Ella as an innholder there in 1776 (Nottinghamshire Archives, DD/BK/1/232–4), an occupation he was still pursuing in 1786 according to the apprenticeship records of one of his sons (also a John), transcribed in Hartopp, *1770–1930*, 469. In A. Bernard Clarke's *Directory to the Inhabitants of Loughborough 1795–1848* (handlist, *c*.1934; in Loughborough Library, Local Studies Collection), he is noted as an innkeeper and freeholder in 1795, and in business with others as Ella, Douglas & Poynton (boat owners) from 1794; by 1799 this company had expanded to become Ella, Coleman, Douglas, Burbidge & Co., according to a clause in Michael Ella's will (LRO, PR/T/1799/62/1–2). Later manifestations of the family business are listed in local trade directories for Leicester and Loughborough into the 1830s.

❧ James Ella *&* William Fisher Ella – *John Ella's cousins*
James Ella (baptized 1768 at Kibworth, Leicestershire) was Michael Ella's eldest son, who married into the wealthy Fisher family. He died in 1834. James's son William Fisher Ella was baptized in 1801 (at Wymeswold, Leicestershire) and died in 1859.

According to Sidney Pell Potter, *A History of Wymeswold* (London: J. Miles, 1915), 10, William Fisher had purchased the Wymeswold estate and manorial rights in 1777; these passed into the Ella family on James Ella's marriage to Elizabeth Fisher in 1796. The family wealth included some 400 acres of land, part of which was sold off by the trustees of William Fisher Ella's will in 1872 (information from LRO, Ella family papers, MISC-1260).

Select Bibliography

1. *Principal manuscript and archival material*

John Ella Collection, Faculty of Music Library, University of Oxford [163 MSS including diaries and correspondence; handlist prepared by Christina Bashford and John Wagstaff, 1997, rev. 2005]

Leicester Record Office, MISC 1290, 1294 [Ella family papers]

Royal Society of Musicians, London, A322 [John Ella's membership application, correspondence and related papers]

2. *Additional correspondence*

Arabella Goddard Collection, Her Majesty's Theatre, Ballerat, Australia [with J. W. Davison]

British Library, London, MS 37766, ff. 12–13 [with C. H. Chichele Plowden]; Add MS 42575, ff. 246–7 [Mrs Owen]; Add MS 42578, f.68b [Richard Owen]; Add MS 46345, ff. 152–3 [Mrs E. Roche]; Add MS 70844, f.88 [Mrs Gray]; Add MS 70921, f.93 [J. W. Davison]; RPS/MS/343, ff. 149–156 [Philharmonic Society]

National Archives of Scotland, Edinburgh, GD18/3946 [with Sir George Clerk]

Royal Academy of Music, London, McCann Collection, MSS 2005.1311–1320 and 2005.107 [various correspondents]

University of British Columbia, Vancouver, Special Collections and University Archives [with H. R. Haweis]

François-Joseph Fétis: Correspondance. Comp. and ed. Robert Wangermée. Sprimont: Editions Mardaga, 2006 [with Fétis]

Hector Berlioz: Correspondance générale. Ed. Pierre Citron *et al.* 8 vols. Paris: Flammarion, 1972–2002 [with Berlioz; vols. 4–6]

Life and Letters of Sir Charles Hallé being an Autobiography (1819–1860) with Correspondence and Diaries. Ed. C. E. Hallé and Marie Hallé. London: Smith, Elder, 1896 [with Hallé]

3. *Print material authored by Ella*

Lectures on Dramatic Music, and Musical Education Abroad and at Home. London: Ridgway, 1872.

'Meyerbeer': *Memoir and Personal Recollections, with Analysis of 'Les Huguenots'.* London: Cramer, 1865.

The Musical Record (1857). [Copies consulted from BL; bound in with *Record of the Musical Union*]

Musical Sketches, Abroad and at Home. London: Ridgway, 1869; 2nd edition, 1869 [*recte* 1872]; 3rd edition, rev. and ed. John Belcher. London: William Reeves, 1878.

Record of the Musical Union (1845–81). [Differently paginated sets are in existence. The copies consulted for this study were in EllaC (for 1845–55), BL (1845–80) and RCMp (1881).]

Record of the Musical Winter Evenings (1852–5). [Copies consulted from EllaC and BL]

Unsigned contributions to the *Athenaeum, Court Journal, Morning Post* and *Musical World.*

4. *Extant musical compositions by Ella*

Amo te solo: a Favorite Italian Canzonetta as a Duett, for Two Soprano Voices, or Soprano and Tenore, with an Accompaniment for the Piano Forte or Guitar. London: F. T. Latour, [1828].

Quadrilles, as Duets, for two Performers on the Piano Forte. London: Lonsdale & Mills, [1830].

Victoria March, for Two Performers on the Piano Forte. London: R. Mills, [1838]; 3rd edition, Lonsdale [after 1869]. MS version, for piano with cello accompaniment, in British Library, London, Add MS 38488 A.

Souvenirs de Chipstead (Kent): Quadrilles and Waltzes ... for Two Performers on the Pianoforte with Accompaniments (ad lib). London: Mills, [1839].

A Duettino, for Flute, and Piano Forte. London: Wheatstone & Co., [1850].

5. *Other printed sources*

Anonymous. 'Some Pictures of the Past', *Musical Times*, 35 (1894), 377–81.

Bashford, Christina. 'Ella, John', *The New Grove Dictionary of Music and Musicians*, 2nd edition, 29 vols., ed. Stanley Sadie. London: Macmillan, 2001.

—— 'John Ella and the Making of the Musical Union', *Music and British Culture, 1785–1914: Essays in Honour of Cyril Ehrlich*, ed. Christina Bashford and Leanne Langley. Oxford: Oxford University Press, 2000, 193–214.

—— 'Learning to Listen: Audiences for Chamber Music in Early Victorian London', *Journal of Victorian Culture*, 4 (1999), 25–51.

—— 'More than Dedication?: Hector Berlioz and John Ella', *The Musical Voyager: Berlioz in Europe*, ed. David Charlton and Katharine Ellis. Frankfurt am Main: Peter Lang, 2007, 3–24.

—— 'Varieties of Childhood: John Ella and the Construction of a Victorian Mozart', *Words about Mozart: Essays in Honour of Stanley Sadie*, ed. Dorothea Link with Judith Nagley. Woodbridge: Boydell Press, 2005, 193–210.

Beale, Willert. 'A Morning Call on Mr. Ella', *Liverpool Journal* (18 Feb 1871); reprinted in John Ella. *Musical Sketches, Abroad and at Home*. 2nd edition. London: Ridgway, 1869 [*recte* 1872], preliminary pages 1–14.

Bennett, Joseph. 'Victorian Music, VIII: Chamber Music', *Musical Times*, 38 (1897), 803–6.

Cobbett, Walter Willson. 'Musical Union', *Cobbett's Cyclopedic Survey of Chamber Music*, 2 vols., comp. and ed. Walter Willson Cobbett. Oxford and London: Oxford University Press, 1929–30.

Davison, Henry, comp. *From Mendelssohn to Wagner: Being the Memoirs of J. W. Davison, Forty Years Music Critic of 'The Times'*. London: William Reeves, 1912.

Diehl, Alice M. *Musical Memories*. London: Richard Bentley & Son, 1897.

—— *The True Story of my Life: an Autobiography*. [London: n.p., 1859]; London: John Lane, The Bodley Head, 1908.

Fétis, F.-J. 'Ella, John', *Biographie universelle des musiciens*, 2nd edition, 8 vols., ed. F.-J. Fétis. Paris: Firmin Didot, 1866–8; sup., 2 vols., ed. Arthur Pougin, 1878–80.

Fuller Maitland, J. A. 'Ella, John'. *Dictionary of National Biography*, 66 vols., ed. Leslie Stephen and Sidney Lee. London: Smith, Elder, 1885–1901.

——, rev. John Warrack. 'Ella, John', *Oxford Dictionary of National Biography: From the Earliest Times to the Year 2000*, 60 vols., ed. H. C. G. Matthew and Brian Harrison. Oxford: Oxford University Press, 2004.

Ganz, A. W. *Berlioz in London*. London: Quality Press, 1950.

Ganz, Wilhelm. *Memories of a Musician: Reminiscences of Seventy Years of Musical Life*. London: John Murray, 1913.

Hanslick, Eduard. 'Briefe aus London [1862]', *Aus dem Concertsaal: Kritiken und Schilderungen aus den letzten 20 Jahren des Wiener Musiklebens, nebst einem Anhang: Musikalische Reisebriefe aus England, Frankreich und der Schweiz*. Vienna: Wilhelm Braumüller, 1870, 487–517.

Haweis, H. R. *John Ella: a Sketch from Life*. Pamphlet, London, 1885; first published in *Truth* (1 Nov 1883), 620–22.

Husk, W. H., *et al.* 'John Ella', *The New Grove Dictionary of Music and Musicians*, 20 vols., ed. Stanley Sadie. London: Macmillan, 1980.

——, rev. John Ravell. 'John Ella', *Grove's Dictionary of Music and Musicians*, 5th edition, 9 vols., ed. Eric Blom. London: Macmillan, 1954.

Klein, Herman. *Musicians and Mummers*. London: Cassell, 1925.

McVeigh, Simon. '"An Audience for High-Class Music": Concert Promoters and Entrepreneurs in Late-Nineteenth-Century London', *The Musician as Entrepreneur, 1700–1914: Managers, Charlatans, and Idealists*, ed. William Weber. Bloomington and Indianapolis: Indiana University Press, 2004, 162–82.

Phillips, Henry. *Musical and Personal Recollections during Half a Century*. London: Charles J. Skeat, 1864.

Ravell, John. 'John Ella, 1802–1888', *Music & Letters*, 34 (1953), 93–105.

Scholes, Percy A. *The Mirror of Music, 1844–1944: a Century of Musical Life in Britain as Reflected in the Pages of the Musical Times*. London: Novello, 1947.

Southgate, T. L. [Obituary of John Ella], *Musical Standard* (6 Oct 1888), 213–15.

Weber, William. *Music and the Middle Class: the Social Structure of Concert Life in London, Paris and Vienna*. London: Croom Helm, 1975.

Weliver, Phyllis. *The Musical Crowd in English Fiction, 1840–1910: Class, Culture and Nation*. Basingstoke: Palgrave, 2006.

Index

References to illustrations appear in italics.

Mortier de Fontaine, Henri, 166, 167 n.11, 349
 n.60, 369
Morton, Sarah, 16
Moscheles, Ignaz
 attends Musical Union, 154
 and Beethoven piano sonatas, 169
 chamber music, 362
 depicted in Thackeray novel, 199
 and Ella's réunions, 111, 112 n.234, 115 n.1
 Ella's view of his piano playing, 84
 his own chamber music concerts, 101, 137,
  169
 inspires Ella to play Beethoven, 105
 invites Ella to play chamber music, 41
 performer at Philharmonic Society, 40
 septet, op. 88, 104
 teacher of Alfred Jaëll, 230
 and William Horsley, 110
Moscheles, Mrs, 312 n.112
Moscow, 313 n.115
Möser, Carl, 101
Moullin, Mlle *pianist,* 365
Mozart, Wolfgang Amadeus
 celebrations of his birth, 287–8
 chamber music
  Ella's early experiences of, 27, 41
  in Musical Union repertoire, 115, 179, 187,
   285, 312, 316, 361–3
  in Musical Winter Evenings, 182, 188, 189
   n.77, 362
  in Philharmonic Society concerts, 102
  in Pops concerts, 235
 choral music, 159
 clarinet quintet, 187, 188, 189
 compared with Wren and Jones, 243
 controversy in *Musical World,* 86
 as divine child, 274, 288
 lectures on, 301
 manuscripts of, 126, 274–5
 music in the British Museum, 47
 music measured against Beethoven's, 86, 197
 music measured against Handel's, 86
 music measured against Rossini's, 86
 name depicted in St James's Hall interior, 233
 name depicted on Musical Union ticket, 121
 operas, 46 n.114
  La clemenza di Tito, 104, 295, 359
  Così fan tutte, 295
  Don Giovanni, 40, 59, 80, 82 n.95, 275, 295
  Le nozze di Figaro, 40, 295
  Die Zauberflöte, 40
 piano concertos, 253
  in D minor, 77

(Mozart, Wolfgang Amadeus, continued)
 piano quartets, 110 n.227
  in G minor, 167, 311
 sacred music, 41, 158 n.130
 sonatas, 17, 110 n.227
 string quartets, 28, 107, 108, 119, 131, 135, 141
  n.90, 335
  in A, K464, 197 n.103
  in B♭, K458, 187
  in B♭, K589, 187
  in C, 'Dissonance', K465, 131, 198, 229, 362
  in D, K499, 332
  in D, K575, 131, 145, 362, 363
  in D minor, K421, 108
  in G, K387, 131, 179 n.50, 197, 229
 string quintets, 104, 119, 141 n.90, 188
  in C, K515, 198, 360
  in D, K593, 108, 187, 332, 360
  in G minor, K516, 131, 196, 198, 285, 362, 363
 symphonies, 40
 vocal music, 201
 William Gardiner and, 28
Müller, August, 174 n.30
Munby, Arthur, 265 n.181
Munich, 209
Murray travel guides, 354 n.67
Musard, Philippe, 95
Musical Association, 341
Musical Institute of London, 180, 247
Musical Record, The, 191, 211, 215
Musical Society of London, 247, 253
Musical Standard, The, 304
Musical Times, The, 56
Musical Union
 analytical programmes [analyses]. *See under*
  'programme notes [analyses]' *below*
 archives, 9
 audience
  aristocratic image of, 146, 155, 289 n.30,
   342–3, 350–1; *see also under* 'profile' *below*
  attending Pops, 237
  behaviour, music appreciation and
   listening: assessed, 343, 347, 349–50, 353;
   and the concert environment, 135–7, 223–
   5, 233–4; Ella's strategy for, 137–41; Ella's
   vision/inspiration for, 120, 121, 137–8,
   143–4, 195; Hanslick's description of, 216,
   354; reputation for, 285, 286, 311, 343; role
   of programme notes in, 120, 138–9, 190–1,
   315; women and, 352; *see also under*
   'concert atmosphere and seating' *and*
   'programme notes [analyses]' *below*
  competition for, 322–3